W9-CYS-097

LABOUR, LAND AND CAPITAL IN GHANA

ROCHESTER STUDIES In
AFRICAN HISTORY and the DIASPORA

Toyin Falola, Senior Editor
The Frances Higginbotham Nalle Centennial Professor in History
University of Texas at Austin

(ISSN: 1092-5228)

*Power Relations in Nigeria: Ilorin
Slaves and Their Successors*
Ann O'Hear

Dilemmas of Democracy in Nigeria
Edited by Paul Beckett and
Crawford Young

*Science and Power in
Colonial Mauritius*
William Kelleher Storey

*Namibia's Post-Apartheid Regional
Institutions: The Founding Year*
Joshua Bernard Forrest

*A Saro Community in the Niger Delta,
1912–1984: The Potts-Johnsons of
Port Harcourt and Their Heirs*
Mac Dixon-Fyle

*Contested Power in Angola:
1840s to the Present*
Linda Heywood

*Nigerian Chiefs: Traditional Power in
Modern Politics, 1890s–1990s*
Olufemi Vaughan

*West Indians in West Africa, 1808–
1880: The African Diaspora in Reverse*
Nemata Blyden

*The United States and Decolonization
in West Africa, 1950–1960*
Ebere Nwaubani

Health, State, and Society in Kenya
George Oduor Ndege

Black Business and Economic Power
Edited by Alusine Jalloh and
Toyin Falola

Voices of the Poor in Africa
Elizabeth Isichei

*Colonial Rule and Crisis in Equatorial
Africa: Southern Gabon ca. 1850–1940*
Christopher J. Gray

*The Politics of Frenchness in Colonial
Algeria, 1930–1954*
Jonathan K. Gosnell

*Sources and Methods in African History:
Spoken, Written, Unearthed*
Edited by Toyin Falola and
Christian Jennings

*Sudan's Blood Memory: The Legacy of War,
Ethnicity, and Slavery in Early
South Sudan*
Stephanie Beswick

*Writing Ghana, Imagining Africa:
Nation and African Modernity*
Kwaku Larbi Korang

*Labour, Land and Capital in Ghana:
From Slavery to Free Labour in Asante,
1807–1956*
Gareth Austin

LABOUR, LAND AND CAPITAL IN GHANA

FROM SLAVERY TO FREE LABOUR IN ASANTE, 1807–1956

Gareth Austin

 UNIVERSITY OF ROCHESTER PRESS

First published 2005

University of Rochester Press
668 Mt. Hope Avenue, Rochester, NY 14620, USA
www.urpress.com
and of Boydell & Brewer Limited
PO Box 9, Woodbridge, Suffolk IP12 3DF, UK
www.boydellandbrewer.com

ISBN 1–58046–161–1

Library of Congress Cataloging-in-Publication Data

Austin, Gareth.
 Labour, land and capital in Ghana : from slavery to free labour in Asante, 1807–1956 / Gareth Austin.
  p. cm. – (Rochester studies in African history and the diaspora, ISSN 1092-5228 [v. 18])
 Includes bibliographical references and index.
 ISBN 1-58046-161-1 (hardcover : alk. paper)
 1. Ashanti (Kingdom)–Economic conditions–19th century. 2. Ashanti (Kingdom)–Economic conditions–20th century. 3. Land tenure–Ashanti (Kingdom)–History–19th century. 4. Land tenure–Ashanti (Kingdom)–History–20th century. 5. Labor–Ashanti (Kingdom)–History–19th century. 6. Labor–Ashanti (Kingdom)–History–20th century. I. Title. II. Series.
 HC1060.Z7A723 2004
 330.9667'018–dc22
                                    2004021237

A catalogue record for this title is available from the British Library.

This publication is printed on acid-free paper.
Printed in the United States of America.

To my father and mother, who first stimulated my passions
for Africa and history.

CONTENTS

Part I. Context and Concepts

Part II. Social Relations of Production and Trade, 1807–1896: Absent and Imperfect Factor Markets

Part III. Slavery as Hobson's Choice: An Analysis of the Interaction of Markets and Coercion in Asante's Era of 'Legitimate Commerce', 1807–1896

Part IV. The Decline of Coercion in the Factor Markets of Colonial Asante: Cocoa and the Ending of Slavery, Pawnship and Corvée, 1896–c.1950

Part V. Social Relations of Production and Trade, 1908–1956: Towards Integrated Factor Markets?

Part VI. Freedom and Forest Rent, 1908–1956

ILLUSTRATIONS

Maps

Plates

Figures

TABLES

PREFACE

This book has grown from a project to which I have devoted my primary research over the quarter-century since I first went to Ghana, as an undergraduate: a broad study of indigenous capitalism in Asante, and in southern Ghana in general, during the nineteenth and twentieth centuries. The early published result of the project was a series of essays ranging over political economy, production techniques and entrepreneurship, and the social organisation of production. This book, which I began to plan at the end of 1993, focusses on the latter. Accordingly, it supersedes only two, at most, of those earlier papers; while referring to the others for context.

For research funding I am extremely grateful to the UK Economic and Social Research Council, which financed my doctoral research at the University of Birmingham, and a post-doctoral fellowship at the Institute of Commonwealth Studies, University of London. I did shorter periods of research during breaks from teaching at the University of Birmingham (with a grant from the Centre of West African Studies' Travel Fund), at the University of Ghana, and then at the London School of Economics, which I joined in 1988. The LSE's Staff Research Fund enabled me to fill gaps and pursue leads from my earlier, generally longer periods of archival and oral research.

Publication of this book has been made possible by a grant from the bequest of the late Miss Isobel Thornley to the University of London; and by one from the Scouloudi Foundation in association with the Institute of Historical Research, University of London.

The British Museum graciously allowed the reproduction of two of the illustrations in this book. Three others are photographs, evidently taken by P. B. Redmayne in the 1930s. I have made every reasonable effort to identify the present copyright-holder, unsuccessfully. I hope that Mr. Redmayne would have been pleased to see his work reproduced so long afterwards. I thank the Royal Anthropological Institute for permission to quote from the Rattray Papers. Some of the material on pawning (though here revised, extended and integrated with broader themes) was previously published in my essay 'Human pawning in Asante, 1800–1950', published by Westview Press in Toyin Falola and Paul E. Lovejoy (eds), *Pawnship in Africa: Debt Bondage in Historical Perspective* (Boulder, 1994), and reprinted by Africa World Press in Lovejoy and Falola (eds), *Pawnship, Slavery, and Colonialism in Africa* (Trenton NJ and Asmara, 2003). A few sentences in later chapters here originally appeared in my 'The emergence of capitalist relations in South Asante cocoa-farming, c.1916–33', *Journal of African History* 28 (1987).

I am very grateful indeed to Malcolm McLeod for his generous help with the illustrations for this book. I learned much from the referees' reports on the manuscript. I also benefited from the assistance of the LSE's copyright advisor, Maria Bell. The maps were drawn by Mina Moshkeri at LSE, where my departmental colleague Tim Leunig gave me valuable advice on graphics. Aashish Velkar helped compile the index.

Many more individuals have helped me in my research than I can possibly thank here—and that is just the archivists and librarians, among whom I must mention specifically the staff of the national archives of Ghana, especially those who I got to know so well in Kumasi and Accra, and Paul Jenkins and Veit Arlt of the Basel Mission Archive. Mr. E. Adu Acheampong (formerly Chief Technical Officer, Cocoa Services Division, Ghana Cocoa Marketing Board) was always diplomatic, understanding, and good humoured in translating and generally assisting me in most of my early interviews. Francis Anin was excellent as my assistant in 1987. For further fieldwork assistance I am grateful also to A. K. Ageman, Yaw Sekyere Baah-Nuakoh, J. W. Owusu—and to my friends Sylvester Kwaku Annin and Yaw Owusu Darkwa, of whom more below.

For hospitality and other kindnesses in Kumasi I am very grateful to the late Mr. T. E. Kyei and to Mrs. Peggy Appiah. My friend Kwami Abradu, who I first met when he was a junior administrator in Bekwai, introduced me to many parts of Ghana. Above all I am grateful for the help, hospitality, friendship and wisdom of my many-time hosts in Bekwai, Mr. Sylvester Kwaku Annin and Sister Yaa and their children, and Mr. Yaw Owusu Darkwah. I am also highly appreciative of the staying power and intellectual and human qualities of my colleagues, academic and administrative, at the University of Ghana, when I had the privilege of teaching in the history department there, 1982–85.

I have acquired numerous scholarly debts during both my Ghanaian research generally, and in writing this book specifically. I am grateful to John Dunn, who focussed my West African research interests on Ghana, and to Paul Coby, whose initiative took both of us there to research our respective undergraduate dissertations for the University of Cambridge.

I still miss Marion Johnson (d. 1988)'s enthusiastic advocacy of her many theses about Ghanaian economic history. I have benefited in a variety of ways from the intersecting research communities in which I have been fortunate to participate, particularly the LSE Department of Economic History, the (U.K.) History and Economic Development Group, and the African history community in London and far beyond. Many of the arguments presented in the chapters that follow have been improved by feedback on presentations I have given over the last decade: in London at LSE and in both the economics and history departments at the School of Oriental and African Studies; at various of the annual meetings of the (U.S.) African Studies Association; and at conferences, workshops and seminars elsewhere in Britain and the United States, and in Canada, Germany, Ghana, Norway, South Africa and Switzerland. I am grateful to both the participants and the organizers. For generous advice on papers preparatory to this book I am particularly grateful to Kwame Arhin, Stanley Engerman, Larry (S. R.) Epstein, and Bill (W. P.) Kennedy. For generous advice more widely I thank Linda Sampson and Tracy Keefe, the keystones of my department over many years.

In its length—and, I hope, its depth—this book represents a personal act of persistence amid an academic environment which, alas especially in Britain, has seemed increasingly to discourage the kind of projects which require a long time, and which produce the kind of results which require substantial space for proper presentation and analysis. In this context I particularly thank Toyin Falola, without whom I very much doubt that this book would have been publishable in any form recognizable and acceptable to its author. I am also very appreciative of the patience of University of Rochester Press. I am more grateful than I can say to Tony Hopkins, for his persistent encouragement, support and advice, from when he supervised my doctoral dissertation to the present. I am highly appreciative of the encouragement, friendship and solidarity throughout the writing of this book, as well as constructive criticism on arguments presented here, which I have received from fellow historians of Ghana, and of western Africa generally: particularly Rod Alence, Amos Anyimadu, Jean Allman, William Gervase Clarence-Smith, Jan-Georg Deutsch, Andreas Eckert, Paul Lovejoy, Susan Martin, Paul Nugent, Richard Rathbone, Richard Roberts and Larry Yarak. Tom McCaskie has helped to remind me why we do all this during marathon phone conversations – almost invariably at his expense! He also generously helped with proof-reading. I am also extremely grateful to Ivor Wilks, for his learning and generous encouragement. I was never his student, but in a broader sense all of us who study Asante history are his students.

I am immensely grateful to my teachers at school as well as at university, and to my own students, from whom I have learned much over the years. During the decade in which I was writing this book, however, my biggest debt has been to my family. The love, humour, sanity and strength of my wife, Pip, permitted and helped me 'to keep on keeping on'. It has been marvellous to have the experience of growing older with our three children, Becca (who accompanied me on a research trip to Ghana in 2000), Lily (whose suggestions contributed to the design of the dust jacket), and Madeleine (who, like this book, has taken a decade to reach her present length).

Gareth Austin
London, July 2004

NOTE ON NAMES

The Akan are the cultural group to which the Asante belong, defined by common possession of the Akan or Twi language. Other Akan populations were and are to be found to the west and east of Asante, and especially to the south, where Fante, Akyem and other southern Akan states or chieftaincies occupied the bulk of the territory between Asante and the sea.

There is no standard practice in the spelling of place names in Asante, nor of deceased people. In this book I have followed a principle suggested to me by Professor Adu Boahen, of spelling place names in their 'Twi' form, except for a few places which are much better known within as well as outside Ghana by the spellings which appear on the road signs: Kumasi rather than Kumase, Obuasi rather than Obuase, Bekwai rather than Bekwae. Implementation of the principle is inevitably a matter of judgment, and here as in other aspects of name-spelling, there is no perfect solution. 'Ghana' is used for convenience to refer not only to the post-colonial state but also to the corresponding precolonial and colonial territories. The latter comprised the Gold Coast Colony, Ashanti, the Northern Territories and, after the First World War, British Mandated Togoland (see Map 2). 'Asante' is used in preference to 'Ashanti' except where the latter formed part of an official title, such as Chief Commissioner of Ashanti. The names of individuals are spelt in the usual Asante-Twi way (Kwame rather than Kwami, for example) except when they are spelt otherwise in the original sources. There is an exception to the exception: where the sources themselves are inconsistent, or when they offer a spelling that is clearly a bizarre foreign rendering, which sometimes happens in the early nineteenth-century European accounts.

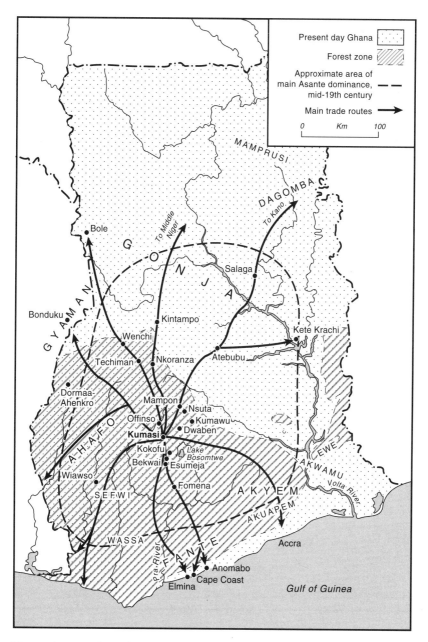

Map 1. Asante in the mid-nineteenth century.

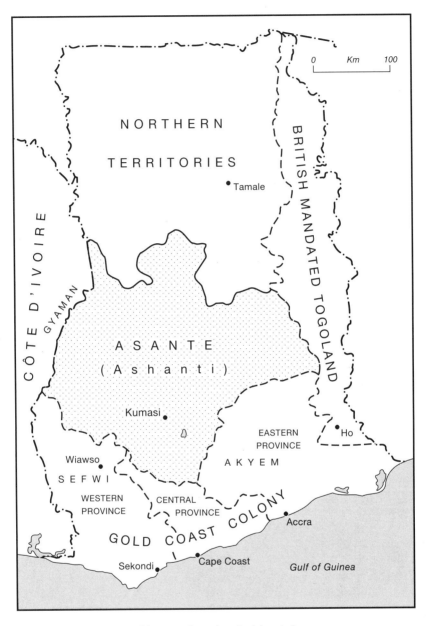

Map 2. Asante and its neighbours in the early colonial period.

Map 3. Colonial Asante.

NOTE ON THE MAPS

The maps were drawn by Mina Moshkeri, Head Cartographer, London School of Economics. Map 1 was informed by maps in Ivor Wilks, *Asante in the Nineteenth Century: the Structure and Evolution of a Political Order* (Cambridge, 1975, 2nd edn with new preamble, 1989), 11; M. D. McLeod, *The Asante* (London, 1981) and T. C. McCaskie, *State and Society in Pre-Colonial Asante* (Cambridge, 1995), 32. The administrative boundaries in Map 3 are based on R. B. Bening, 'Evolution of the administrative boundaries of Ashanti, 1896–1951', *Journal of African Studies* 5 (1978), 123–50. The map represents the district boundaries as of 1925, with the addition of the boundary between Amansie/Bekwai and Adanse/Obuasi, as it stood in 1937. The division of Asante between Western and Eastern provinces was short-lived, 1921–33. The main difference between the colonial Western Province and the post-colonial Brong-Ahafo Region is that the latter also includes the northern swathe (comprising mostly savanna) of the former Eastern Province.

1

INTRODUCTION

This book examines the changing relationships through which resources were mobilised for production during the development of an agricultural export economy. The process entailed a transformation in the breadth and intensity of land use: a transition from a sparsely-populated rural economy within which cultivable land was allowed generous fallow time or was not cultivated at all, to a steadily more populous, much more commercial agriculture in which little tillable space escaped cultivation altogether, in which rotation cycles had become ever shorter, and much land was under permanent cropping. This trajectory is characteristic of the modern economic history of tropical Africa. It has involved opportunities for prosperity but entailed the depletion of natural resources and, because land varies greatly in its economic potential, conflicts over access to the most valuable lands, and thereby over the appropriation of their fruits. The book describes and analyses a West African history of property rights and markets—of ownership and control—in what economists call the factors of production: labour, land and capital. A major concern here is to explore the broader implications of this story, for African and comparative historiography and for social science theory.

In history the specifics of place and period are usually critical. This is a study of the Asante forest zone: which was the heartland of the eighteenth-nineteenth century kingdom of Asante, before forming most of the British colony of Ashanti, which in turn became the Ashanti and Brong-Ahafo regions of the Republic of Ghana. Asante is of inescapable importance in Ghanaian history. The kingdom was one of the major polities of precolonial West Africa, its imperial reach at one time or another grasping tribute from most parts of what is now Ghana. Subsequently Asante became a major

1

(from 1943–44, the biggest) contributor to Ghana's status, from 1911 to the late 1970s, as the world's largest producer of cocoa beans. If Asante is central to Ghanaian history, Asante history has to be understood in the context of Ghanaian history more generally: specifically, of Asante's relations with neighbours to both south and north. It was through the southern forest-zone that Asante participated in the import-export trade with the Atlantic economy. It was from the north, from the savanna, that Asantes imported labour—slaves in the nineteenth century, free migrant labourers in the twentieth—crucial in the exploitation of Asante's natural resources.

1807–1956 may be seen as a distinct period in two respects, which make it appropriate as the chronological frame for this book. First, it was distinguished by relatively favourable economic and political conditions for indigenous as well as, during colonial rule, foreign private enterprise. This gives a basic coherence to the era, despite the succession of major changes over this critical century and a half: from the ending of the Atlantic slave trade, through the cash-crop 'take-off' and British rule, to the struggle over the terms of decolonization in the 1950s. Second, this choice of period allows us to follow the Asante control of the 'Ghanaian' forest zone from a near-monopoly of the whole zone, achieved in 1807, through a series of enforced retreats, including the British occupation in 1896, to what may be regarded as a defining dilution of what had been the Asante monopoly of the income from the Asante forests themselves, in 1956. The grounds for this periodization will be elaborated later in this chapter.

In Sub-Saharan Africa generally, and perhaps especially in those countries whose colonial experience did not include significant alienation of land to European settlers or planters, the growth of agricultural exporting was marked by a combination of the emergence of 'capitalist' institutions, notably wage labour, and the persistence, in modified and perhaps even novel forms, of 'precapitalist' ones such as family and cooperative labour. The issue of how this combination should be interpreted is central to the debate about the causes of the region's relative poverty, and the prospects of overcoming it. Specifically, historical investigation of the social forms through which productive resources were put to work should explain the origins and dynamics of this characteristic institutional mix, and examine its consequences for economic efficiency, welfare and inequality. As this book attempts to show, Asante can provide a generally well-documented example of such a pattern of agrarian development. This is thanks to the primary sources available on Asante history, which appear to be richer than those for almost anywhere else south of the Sahara.

The general theme of the causes and consequences of changes and continuities in property rights and markets in factors of production surely has to be central to the writing of African economic history and to any empirically-grounded theory of the political economy of economic development. One might have expected that detailed studies of specific historical cases over the long term would have been written during the heyday of marxist influence in African studies in the 1970s and early 1980s. But, as it turned out, the historical research on social relations of production concentrated largely—though very fruitfully—on the history of one factor, labour: especially the previously neglected story of internal slavery and its eventual abolition, and the emergence of wage relations.[1] One might also have expected that the growing influence of rational-choice political economy in African studies in the 1980s and 1990s, with its theory of the evolution of property rights, would have inspired thematically broad and chronologically extended studies of African experience. But, again, such work has been focussed on the history of a single factor: this time land, and largely for the twentieth century only.[2] Yet across a wide range of theoretical schools it would be agreed that the history of any one factor, and of the social forms in which it was employed and transacted, can be understood only in its interactions with those of the others. This book is intended to help fill this gap.

Addressing an under-explored theme is important in itself, but in this case it is also a means to contribute to a further end: to redress the relative neglect of Asante and of Sub-Saharan economic history generally. The immediate context of this observation is that while Asante has a rightly-celebrated historiography, it has been more voluminous on political and social than on economic history and has mostly reflected rather than transcended the traditional precolonial/colonial division of academic labour. It also neglected the colonial period, on which the secondary literature is the slimmer yet the primary data are the thicker. However, three recent books have added much to our knowledge of that era while one of them, T. C. McCaskie's remarkable micro-history of a village on the outskirts of Kumasi, follows its subject from the 1840s to c.1950. These books are written explicitly in the genre of social history, though with significant economic dimensions.[3] The present study tries to broaden the bridge between precolonial and colonial historiographies, and to give systematic treatment to key aspects of the economic history of the colonial period, as well as of the precolonial nineteenth century. Except for Kwame Arhin's slim though valuable monograph on traders, it is the first book specifically devoted to Asante economic history.[4]

The broader context is the relative neglect, over the last two decades, of the economic history of Sub-Saharan Africa, within both African studies and comparative economic history. Research in African economic history made great progress in the 1960s and 1970s.[5] While some excellent work has been done in the area since then, the most popular research agendas among historians of Africa in the 1980s and since have concerned issues of culture and identity. This 'cultural turn' has produced some extremely important work, notably on Asante.[6] But the volume of new research in economic history has been comparatively modest.[7] Where material phenomena continued to be studied they now tended to be treated in cultural rather than economic perspective. For instance, what colonial officials thought about labour attracted more attention than the actual workings of labour markets.[8]

It is striking that research interest in Africa's economic past should have waned during a period when publications on Africa's current economic affairs proliferated.[9] The latter trend was partly a response to a widespread anxiety, inside and outside the continent, about the performance of African economies. A perverse imbalance has emerged: while issues of sustenance and accumulation weigh so heavily upon the present, the further marginalisation of Africa's economies has been accompanied by the marginalisation of their histories. This study is intended to contribute to an overdue revival of economic history, not just within African historiography, but within African studies generally.

While African economic history was being relatively neglected by historians and economists of Africa, it is hardly surprising that Africa's economic history—other than its external slave trades—has tended to occupy negligible space in the emerging literature on 'global history'.[10] Yet Africa's economic history is potentially as relevant as that of, for example, preindustrial Europe for the empirical exploration of the kind of concepts with which a plausible theory of the political economy of long-term development, and the obstacles to it, might be constructed.[11] One aim of this book is to contribute to precisely such exploration.

Besides the importance of property and markets in factors of production, and the need to give greater priority to research on Africa's economic past than has recently been the case, there is a further general reason why a study of the kind attempted here should be valuable and indeed timely. While many historians have looked away from economic issues, there have been major theoretical developments in economics and, relatedly, in political science. These developments offer challenges for those of us researching African economic history to which we have only begun to respond.

Meanwhile historians, anthropologists and economists of Africa have made major advances in developing rich new literatures on environmental and on gender history. The challenge here to economic historians is to integrate the insights of these studies into their own work. The next section outlines these developments in the theoretical and historical literatures. Three further sections complete this chapter, respectively defining some key concepts, describing the sources used, and outlining the chapters that follow.

A. Recent Theoretical and Historiographical Developments and African Economic History: Institutions, Gender, and Environment

Earlier generations of economic historians of Africa found productive inspiration in ideas drawn, variously, from classical and neoclassical economics and from marxist theories of historical change and marxist-inspired 'history from below'. These approaches have by no means exhausted their usefulness: history, including economic history, is not a 'paradigm' subject in which a new conceptual framework totally displaces its predecessor.[12] But the recent trends in complementary literatures have much for economic historians of Africa to consider. This section will introduce the relevant ideas from economics and rational-choice political science, and those from the Africanist literatures on gender and on the environment. As the discussion proceeds I will relate both to the evolution of the economic historiography of West Africa.

The trends in rational-choice theory can be seen as addressing the two basic limitations of traditional neoclassical economics as a source of insight into historical processes. That is, its inability (in contrast to marxism) to offer explanations for the existence and effects of the institutions within which economic activity takes place (such as property rights, firms, households and markets themselves), and its old concentration on models of perfect competition. Both limitations have been tackled vigorously in recent decades.

Attempts to make institutions part of what economizing logic can explain have been made in a wide-ranging body of work in economics, political science and related disciplines. Such studies have proliferated since 1960, when perhaps the key founding text was published, and have diversified beyond the boundaries associated with the original collective label of 'New Institutional Economics'.[13] If this is a 'school', it is one which encompasses internal disagreements on many issues. It is referred to below, interchangeably, as 'new institutionalism' or 'rational-choice political economy'. In this literature the term 'institutions' is defined broadly as rules, comprising both laws and informal conventions. This usage will be followed throughout the present study. The defining common features are the attempt to make the institutional context endogenous (an object of explanation) and to do so by extending the logic of neoclassical economics. Thus 'new institutionalists' have sought to use the calculus of optimising individualism to unpack the collectivities surrounding and overlapping economic behaviour. Such work has challenged the traditional tendency, in both neoclassical economics and marxism, to treat the household as a unit for economic analysis. Instead the emphasis has shifted to modeling the potentially divergent material interests of different members of the household.[14] This theme is pursued in the empirical analysis offered in later chapters. More immediately, Chapter 2 includes a brief exposition of the new institutionalist theory (or set of related models) of most general relevance to the subject of this book: the theory of induced institutional innovation.

Africanists were unexcited by the early manifestations of new institutionalism, which perhaps seemed to offer an overly determinist, excessively optimistic, and in some cases ideologically driven model of how institutions got better and better. But in the 1980s new institutionalism arrived in African studies through the more subtle and non-dogmatic pen of Robert Bates, much of whose work explored the causes, not of economic progress as such but, rather, of why inefficiencies persisted.[15] In the 1990s the first monographs appeared offering 'new institutionalist' accounts of change over several decades in specific African societies.[16] These valuable works succeeded in illustrating the potential of the approach, but their analyses were constrained by relatively slight use of the available archival sources. It is also fair to say that they were very much 'applications' of the theory that inspired them. What is now needed are more open-ended explorations of the value of the theory in relation to a more extensive body of primary sources.

New institutionalism could be said to deal with imperfect competition because it starts from the observation that real markets are rarely 'frictionless'. Experience departs from perfect competition in ways which new institutionalists try to understand in terms of problems of cooperation. Specifically, the incentives to individual actors may differ from those which would produce the most 'socially efficient' outcome. In much work by new institutionalists and by many economists who would not accept the label, such problems are related to imperfect information. Information may be unavailable or costly to one or all partners to a contract. Much recent work on less-developed economies has considered such issues. The label 'new development economics' was applied early to this trend.[17] By whatever name, this literature has now reached the stage of being digested into advanced textbooks.[18] Yet, so far, it has not received the systematic and critical attention it merits from historians of Africa.

To illustrate the potential benefits to such historians of drawing on these trends in economics it is useful to relate them to perhaps the most fundamental achievement of the existing economic historiography of Africa, especially of West Africa. Back in the 1950s and early 1960s, the era of political decolonisation when research in this field took off, there was an orthodoxy that Africans' economic behaviour, before and even during and since colonial rule, was generally not 'economically rational'. Accordingly, it was supposed, resources were not allocated according to the logic of scarcity that underlies market economics. This assumption was influential within 'modernization theory' and received its most subtle formulations in the substantivism of Karl Polanyi and his students, who applied it specifically to the history of West Africa as well as to other regions of the world.[19] But the historical research of the 1960s and early 1970s, extended later by careful and detailed critiques of specific substantivist propositions, demolished such models as accounts of historical West African economies.[20] More positively, the economic historiography of West Africa tends to emphasize the rationality, agency and enterprise of indigenous economic actors, both before the colonial occupation and within the constraints of colonial economies.[21]

The debunking of substantivism in the West African context parallels trends in the economic historiography of other regions of the world. The general debate has moved on, in that it is now widely recognized that the substantivists overestimated the degree to which economic phenomena are 'embedded' in their cultural and social contexts in 'precapitalist' societies; while, conversely, understating the extent to which economic activity is so embedded in 'capitalist' ones. The 'problem of embeddedness' is a broad historical one, which simple 'traditional/modern' or 'precapitalist/capitalist' dichotomies are inadequate to frame.[22]

This leaves a problem of where to go from here. Market forces may have existed in precolonial and colonial West Africa, but no-one assumes that markets were always present or, where present, perfect. The 'new development economics' may help us to explore this side of West Africa's economic experience more fully than was done when attention focussed on the issue of African economic rationality. New institutionalism may help us explain the institutional settings of West African economic activity. Along with other theoretical approaches,[23] it may also help us make more sense of the problem of embeddedness. This is partly because, like marxism (but unencumbered by the labour theory of value, though not always free of its own burden of market idealism), it directs attention to the structures conditioning individual economic behaviour, which may make as much or more difference to outcomes as individual mental calculus.

We noted above that one virtue of new institutionalism is that it facilitates recognition by economists of the need to disaggregate the household: to recognize that the interests of its members may not be identical. This complements insights from recent historical research on gender issues in the history of Sub-Saharan Africa. Particularly illuminating work has been done in Asante history, especially by Jean Allman and Victoria Tashjian, who have succeeded both in revealing new evidence about the gender dimension of Asante history, and in interweaving it with the general history of the society.[24] The present study pursues the question of how and how far access to productive resources was structured on gender lines, and with what effects on efficiency and on the distribution of income, and how and how far this changed over the long period under discussion.

Environmental history is another growth area of the literature[25] which offers insights for economic history, not least for students of property rights. Let us set this in the context of a long-established tool in economic history: the factor ratio. That is, the scarcity/abundance of labour, land and capital in relation to each other, given the technologies in use at the time concerned. Work on tropical Africa generally, and on West Africa specifically, has made productive use of this concept. A. G. Hopkins, in particular, argued that West Africa should be seen as 'labour-scarce' in the precolonial and colonial periods, and used this observation to help explain both the use of coerced labour in precolonial and colonial times and Africans' choice of technique in agriculture.[26] Development economists have also considered the implications of the characteristic resource endowments of 'land-abundant' tropical regions.[27] It can be crucial, however, to consider how much, and how importantly, the composition of each factor varies in the historical context concerned. Quality and fungibility can matter. From this perspective a promising tool of analysis is François Ruf's concept of 'forest rent', which will be defined and extended below.

Finally in this section, a methodological affirmation. The approach to theory taken in this book is deliberately eclectic. Generalizing claims and explanations are considered as tools for analysing history and are themselves critically evaluated in the light of the evidence.

B. Key Concepts: Forest Rent, Economic Rent, Property and Markets

This section introduces certain terms crucial to the analysis offered in this volume. 'Market' is used here in perhaps its most demanding sense (formulated by Augustin Cournot in 1897): a 'region' in which the prices of the same commodities tend to be equalised through competition.[28] This implies that an isolated transaction between a buyer and a seller does not constitute a market because price-equalization through competition cannot take place. It is conceivable that a broadly shared degree of relative scarcity of a particular commodity could evoke similar responses in a number of socially-isolated individual transactions; but this would not be through competition.[29] Again, Cournot's definition would not apply in full to a discriminating monopolist (or monopsonist), that is, one who used his dominant position to impose different prices on different buyers (sellers). Historically it is relevant to grade markets according to the extent to which prices are determined by competition. Under monopoly or monopsony competition influences prices, albeit one-sidedly. This represents the minimum level of competition that can be accommodated within the definition of market used here. 'Fragmented' markets are defined as 'not unified, even in the absence of [government] controls, so that different participants face different prices for similar goods and services'.[30]

The term 'property rights' is used in this book in the broad sense of entitlements to use resources in permitted ways. This definition, from the 'New Institutional Economics', amounts to a generalization of the old anthropological concept that in 'precapitalist' societies property in land or people comprised not unconditional ownership but rather a 'bundle of rights', each component of which is restricted (or, in 'new institutionalist' terminology, 'attenuated'), while the bundle is divided ('partitioned') between different owners.[31]

'Factor markets' are defined here as markets in which the commodities are property rights in factors of production. These may include, for instance, the purchase of people's time for a specific productive purpose, as in wage labour. They may also include slave trading: the purchase of people themselves for a wider—though, under the rules of the society, still not unrestricted—range of purposes, providing these include the provision of goods and services.

'Economic rent' is the surplus of income over opportunity cost.[32] That is, the difference between the return actually obtained for the supply of a resource and the minimum return necessary to elicit the supply of the resource in its current use.[33] Under perfect market conditions all factors would receive their marginal product,[34] so the actual return would equal the opportunity cost and therefore no rent would exist. Rents arise from departures from such conditions. Specifically, they arise if the supply of the resource in question is less than perfectly responsive (elastic with respect to) to price changes. Thus if labourers' earnings exceeded the minimum necessary to induce them to provide their services, the surplus could be described as rent. In sum, economic rent is a surplus above what could be obtained in a perfectly competitive market.

The concept of economic rent is useful for identifying who—if anyone—was 'exploiting' who and how. The term derives from classical political economy and has been adopted in some of the recent rational-choice work which will be discussed in the next chapter. In that literature rents usually figure as the incentives and rewards for individuals or groups to act in ways that are damaging for economic growth and general social welfare. But as a source of wealth beyond that achieved through market competition, rents may be a key source of savings, which may be chan-nelled in productive as well as unproductive directions. In principle, rents may also be the incentive and reward for constructive innovation, as with technological advances which give the pioneers temporary monopolies.[35] It is arguable that much of economic history, for worse and for better, turns on economic rent rather than profit.[36] We will see in the chapters that follow that factor markets in Asante have often been highly imperfect, rendering them potentially major sources of economic rents.

Ruf's 'forest rent' is an idea from an economist that is timely for his-torians of Africa. Recently there has been much high-quality research on a variety of aspects of the history of human interactions with the physical environment. Yet the ecological equivalent of the task of 'gendering' his-tory largely remains to be tackled: the environmental dimension tends to be added to historians' traditional questions, without usually changing the answers to the longer-established ones. 'Forest rent' is the kind of idea that can link environmental and 'mainstream' history. In this case it can be used to disaggregate the economic category of 'land' in a way that, I will argue, helps make sense of the history of property rights in land and labour in Asante.

Ruf has argued that experience with cocoa to date, worldwide, shows that it has always been more profitable to plant the crop on land freshly-cleared from primary or mature secondary forest than to re-plant it on old cocoa farms. Cocoa booms have been and continue to be based on the capturing of 'forest rent', the non-renewable reserve of soil fertility and related 'agronomic benefits provided by the forest'. Specifically, he defines the term as the difference in the cost of producing a given quantity of cocoa by planting 'after forest clearance' as against 'replanting on fallow land or after felling of the first plantation', the difference being a function of diminution in these 'agronomic benefits'.[37] Ruf thus coined the term specifically regarding cocoa production. Here I extend it to denote the market value of all the non-renewable productive assets provided by the Asante forest zone, including spontaneously-planted kola, rubber and 'timber'. In this historical context, one could even add known gold deposits, which in this immediate vicinity were, so far, confined to the forest zone, albeit fortuitously. As with cocoa, 'broad' forest rent is defined as a supply-side saving, a lower cost of production. The difference is that whereas with cocoa the saving is in the cost of first-planting compared to re-planting, with kola, rubber and timber in the period under review, the saving derived from using trees that were wild or 'semi-cultivated' (cleared around, for access) rather than planted at all. What should be noted is that, whether 'narrow' or 'broad', forest rent reflects the depletable nature of natural resources. It provided the basis of Asante's competitiveness in international commodity markets: for wild rubber, for example, before the onset of plantation rubber from southeast Asia, and then for cocoa.

There is another dimension to be considered. Throughout the period, in what is now Ghana and its neighbourhood, the most commercially valuable natural resources were located only in the forest zone. On top of the forest rent as such, there was thus a potential economic rent to be obtained from controlling this location and denying it to others—from obtaining a local monopoly. Economic historians have become increasingly aware that the particular demographic and ecological endowment of an economy can be extremely important as influences on its characteristic technologies and institutions, in the short and even in the very long term.[38] The notion of forest rent, in itself and considered also as a basis for economic rent, may complement and modify the factor ratio framework. Thereby it may help us to incorporate the particularities of the Asante economy's geographical and historical location into the analysis in a systematic rather than *ad hoc* fashion. In the period under discussion Asante was not simply part of a relatively land-abundant region of the tropics; it was in a specific ecological niche, a forest environment of a particular kind which faced its inhabitants with corresponding opportunities and constraints. The concept of forest rent can help us to express and examine the implications of the impermanence of these opportunities, founded as they were on the contestable control of non-renewable resources.

C. Scope and Sources of this Study

This section delineates and explains the institutional, chronological and spatial limits of the case-study undertaken in this book, in the process introducing Asante in more detail, and goes on to introduce the secondary and, at greater length, the primary sources.

Rural Asante, 1807–1956

The institutional setting is that of the *Asanteman*: the Asante state, as an independent entity and then under British overrule. This context gives the history examined here much of its unity, as opposed to being an assemblage of studies of politically separate districts. The kingdom was created at the start of the eighteenth century as a union of several small states. The population of these states shared with most of their forest-zone neighbours the practice of matrilineal descent and (with their own variations) the Akan or Twi language. Under the leadership of the Oyoko dynasty in Kumasi, however, the Asanteman was to surpass its original peers in size and might, creating a far-flung empire of provinces and tributary states. For much of the eighteenth century the sale and re-sale of captives constituted probably the largest source of government revenue and foreign exchange. As Western demand for slaves fell during the early nineteenth century, Asante increased its exports of gold and a semi-cultivated forest product, kola nuts. The last quarter of the nineteenth century saw two British invasions and, in between, a civil war (1883–8) and the beginning of a boom in the tapping of wild rubber. The imposition of British rule by the second invasion—which was unopposed—in 1896, was followed four years later by an unsuccessful revolt, mainly by Kumasis. Following its suppression, Asante chiefs and private farmers turned to establishing cocoa farms. Transport improvements helped make it profitable, for the first time, for Asantes to produce a fully cultivated, and therefore relatively resource-intensive, export crop. During the period of internal self-government that preceded Ghanaian independence in 1957, Asante became the centre of an intense struggle over the political economy of the new state. The Asante-based National Liberation Movement (NLM) campaigned for a federal constitution and low taxation of cocoa producers, in order to keep the bulk of the income from Asante exports within Asante, and with more of it in private hands than was beginning to be the case under the economic and political strategy followed by the Ghanaian government in Accra.

The period 1807–1956 may be characterised as one in which the indigenous private sector, from small producers and petty traders to rich masters, enjoyed relative freedom to make money. 1807, the year in which Britain, then the biggest slave-trading nation, banned its subjects from buying and selling slaves, marked the effective beginning of the closure of the Atlantic slave market.[39] The Atlantic slave trade had underpinned the domination of the Asante economy by the state, in the sense of the ruler and his chiefs. By contrast, I have argued elsewhere that a broad mass of commoners shared—unequally—in the acquisition of wealth through the production and trade of marketable goods between 1807 and 1896.[40] This clearly continued during the colonial period. I have also argued that when this widespread participation in the extra-subsistence economy was threatened by an over-taxing indigenous ruler or by a cartel of European merchants, it was defended by organized movements of export-suppliers (most of the latter being relatively small-scale) in alliance with chiefs.[41] Conversely, the choice of 1956 as the closing date for this study refers to the electoral defeat of the Asante federalist movement by Kwame Nkrumah's Convention People's Party. This secured the political conditions for the consolidation of the centralising tendencies of the Ghanaian state and, most importantly, for the policies of state-led economic development pursued in post-colonial Ghana until the adoption of 'Structural Adjustment' in 1983.[42]

1807 also saw Asante forces extend the kingdom's dominion down to the coast, making Asante hegemony over the 'Ghanaian' forest zone very close to complete. From 1826 onwards, an intermittent series of military reverses and rebellions cost Kumasi control over the territories beyond what became colonial Ashanti. Colonial rule entailed the possibility that the Asantes might lose their monopoly of the forest rent from Asante itself. We will see later that, as it transpired, this happened only marginally as far as agriculture was concerned, though more so for gold and timber. But the 1956 defeat of the campaign for a federal constitution for independent Ghana was a defining moment in this context too. For it meant that the tax share in the Asante forest rent could be spent anywhere in Ghana—and in many of the years that followed, much of it was.

The geographical framework of the study is rural Asante. This focus enables us to concentrate on the institutions surrounding the main activities of the Asante economy. It should be noted that 'rural' embraces more than agriculture. Gold production by 'traditional' methods of mining and winning was as rural an activity as harvesting kola nuts or tapping rubber trees. But though rural-based economic activities were dominant in the Asante economy, and overwhelmingly so as far as indigenous enterprise was concerned, they were not co-extensive with it. This study follows rural-based activities into the towns, for instance in the case of the marketing of agricultural produce, but it does not deal with specifically urban activities except in so far as they interacted with rural ones. Thus the Kumasi service sector and the large-scale mining by European companies during the colonial period, centred on the towns of Obuasi and Konongo, are part of the background rather than the foreground of discussion here.

Secondary Sources

Asante has inspired one of the richest ethnographic and historical literatures on any part of Africa. The most important research conducted during the colonial period was ethnographic, pioneered in the 1920s by R. S. Rattray, the official (but independently-minded) colonial government anthropologist.[43] He sought to give an account of what he regarded as the authentic Asante society, freed from the distortions of 'exotic influences' such as colonial rule and cocoa growing.[44] His interpretations emphasized the functional efficiency of Asante institutions, and downplayed the exploitative and conflictual aspects of some of them, notably slavery and human pawning. His work remains invaluable, not least because of its detail and the duration of his field experience. The anthropological and sociological work during the later colonial period, most notably by Meyer Fortes and K. A. Busia, was also broadly within the functionalist tradition.[45] One of its themes is particularly relevant to the present study, namely Busia's argument that a trend was underway in the 1940s and 1950s towards greater economic individualism, for example in the appropriation and transmission of farms.[46] Research on Asante history and society since Ghanaian independence has, above all, examined the history of the pre-colonial kingdom. The pioneer was Ivor Wilks, perhaps the fundamental achievement of whose early work was to show that the Asante state was precisely that, rather than the matrilineage writ large, as Rattray had urged.[47] Over the last thirty years studies have appeared from many hands on a variety of issues relevant to particular topics addressed in this book. These will be cited and discussed, as appropriate, in the chapters below.

Primary Sources

The rate of output of source material on the social relations of production and trade within Asante became more voluminous with time during 1807–1956, though this does not apply to every year or even every decade compared to the one before. There were also improvements in quality. During the early nineteenth century there was a drastic increase in the amount of data directly collected by Europeans from observation and enquiry within Asante, as opposed to information and speculation available on the coast. In the later part of that century and in the colonial period as a whole the rate of production of recorded statements by Asante, and also by foreign, participants in the Asante economy tended gradually to rise. During the colonial period there was an uneven but large growth in the volume, variety and reliability of quantitative data. This culminated in a big (yet relatively neglected) sample survey of the budgets of cocoa-farming households throughout Asante which, conveniently given the closing date of the period under study, was carried out by the government in 1956–57.[48] Because it asked a variety of questions pertinent to the present study, it is drawn upon in several chapters below.

For this reason it is appropriate to outline the scope and form of that particular survey here. It excluded what it defined as 'urban areas', namely Kumasi and the two mining towns.[49] It was conducted in two stages. The first was an enumeration of what was intended to be all the 'families' in a very nearly random[50] selection of 240 out of 940 potential survey districts throughout Asante. 'Family' was treated as a synonym for 'household', which was 'somewhat loosely defined as a group of persons living and feeding together'. The authors averred that 'there was no practical difficulty in dividing the occupants of each house into groups on this basis'.[51] In this book 'household' will be preferred when this definition is used, because in Akan usage the English word 'family' is usually applied to the *abusua*, matrilineage or matrilineal segment, as distinct from the conjugal unit. The survey covered 36,852 households.[52] The second stage was a detailed budget survey of a stratified sample comprising 1,620 families. This narrower sample was drawn exclusively from households whose members included at least one owner of bearing cocoa trees.[53] At this stage the authors were obliged to admit, implicitly, that despite the proclaimed absence of 'practical difficulty', their conception of a 'family', or indeed a 'household', was an over-simplification of Asante social reality. For the budget study they decided to exclude just over 30 per cent of cocoa-producing 'households', which were too complicated to be dealt with 'efficiently': because they were too large (over 15 people), too interconnected financially with 'other' households, or were 'abnormal' in structure (meaning, typically, that they were without an adult female). Most of the exclusions related to the first two of these categories, both of which would commonly have reflected polygamous marriages. 'Excessive cash transactions were to be expected mainly . . . where the husband and his wife or wives were living in separate houses, thus forming different household units according to the definition adopted in the survey.'[54] In most of the contexts in which this extremely rich survey is cited in the chapters that follow, its narrow conception of domestic arrangements is unlikely to have affected the conclusions in question. But the reader needs to bear in mind the potential risk from such over-simplification: a hazard of which some more recent users of survey methods seem to have been completely oblivious.[55] The enumeration was carried out from mid-May to end-July 1956. The budget recording was done through the six months of the main cocoa marketing season, September 1956 to March 1957.[56]

At all times there were great differences in the quantity and form of sources on specific institutions, notably because of differences between categories of source in the extent and nature of their concern with those institutions. For instance, as we will see, elderly Asante informants (together with the Fortes papers and an Asante autobiography) have made it clear that the sources of agricultural labour during the colonial period included cooperative work (*nnɔboa*) parties, but I have found no references to this in colonial documents. In contrast, the rules and legacy of the Asante form of slavery have made it rude to try, and perhaps impossible, to obtain information from Asante informants about specific cases of slavery, as distinct from the general features of the institution—whereas many individual cases are documented in colonial court and administrative records. Further discussion of source problems on particular issues is best deferred to the appropriate contexts in the chapters below.

In my general search for sources I sought variety. This study draws on colonial administrative and legal records, and papers preserved by former colonial officials; on my own interviews, conducted primarily as part of a case-study of the Amansie district, south of Kumasi, with farmers, retired cocoa buyers and public officials; on publicly-available collections of other scholars' fieldnotes from Rattray onwards, including Fortes's papers from the Ashanti Social Survey of 1945–6;[57] on archives of European missionary societies, banks and cocoa-buying companies; and on contemporary publications, official and unofficial.

The single most useful source was the Ashanti Region Office of the national archives of Ghana,[58] situated in Kumasi. Its administrative and court records are even richer for the student of social and economic institutions than the collections of papers, mostly generated at higher levels of the colonial hierarchy, held in Accra and London. The assets of the Kumasi repository include documented statements from contemporary Asantes, albeit in the limited—but pertinent—form of petitions to the colonial government, statements in court and letters from chiefs to British officials. Despite the wealth of the literature on many aspects of Asante history, this is the first book to make extensive use of this archive, in the sense that previous ones have referred to just one (known until recently as the 'D' or 'ADM' series) of the various series in which its administrative records were originally listed, and to its higher-level court records.[59]

However, while I hope that this study will underline both the range and quality of the sources available on its subject, it by no means exhausts them. In almost every major category of source, there is more material to be found. Important parts of it are not as yet publicly available, and some have apparently been mislaid.[60] There is also scope for improving our understanding of the significance of key texts through the production of critical editions.[61] But the main constraint on my own search for and use of sources has been a shortage of time available for the task. In this practical respect, as well as in a general epistemological sense, the analysis that follows can only be provisional.

D. Outline and Organization

Outline of the Story

The pattern the sources reveal[62] has several threads. Of these the central one, I shall argue, is that of what, for the moment, can be called extra-familial labour. During the nineteenth century slavery and pawnage were the main sources of such labour, and were used on an increasing scale. During the colonial period there was a fundamental decline in labour coercion, a transition greatly facilitated by the income which Asante farmers derived from their rapid adoption of cocoa cultivation. This was followed by a growth of wage labour. But this turned out, in mid-century, to be an importantly different sort of watershed from that envisaged in narratives of modernization and proletarianization. The labourers, recruited largely from savanna areas to the north of the cocoa belt, used their freedom precisely to bargain with potential employers. They gradually secured better terms and insisted on changing the nature of the contract from simple wage labour to a form of managerial share-cropping. Thus the ambiguity of the notion of 'free' labour—free from ownership of the means of production, or simply free from coercion—is illustrated by the Asante experience.

Crucially, this labour story has itself to be explained in the context of the demand for, and control of, land. More precisely, it has to be understood in terms not of natural resources in aggregate but of the specific kinds of forest land which contained the most valuable natural resources in Ghana: gold ore and soils suitable for cocoa production. The rents, 'forest' and 'economic', which Asante chiefs and farmers derived from their control of such lands made possible the importation of labour, whether coerced or voluntary.

Again, the changing pattern of land use facilitated a transformation in capital formation: planting cocoa trees became the major form of investment. The assets so created became the usual form of collateral when substantial loans were made. The dynamics and welfare implications of the informal credit market became the subject of major controversy, which has continued to the present. For colonial Asante we find examples where market imperfections permitted the extraction of rents, in both short-term credit on forthcoming crops and long-term credit on farms themselves. Yet it is argued here that the Akan system of pledging farms—the direct successor to pawnage—was far from being simply a means of exploiting the borrower. By eliminating the lender's risk from default, it facilitated a competitive market in loans for farm-owners from fellow farmers: contrary to the usual image of 'Third World' agrarian relations.

Finally, all three factors, and the forms in which they were appropriated and applied, have to be considered in relation to the household as well as the market; and with reference not just to labour in general, but particularly in relation to the gender division of both work and access to resources. The development of an agricultural export economy involved, as we shall see, continuing conflicts along gender lines and marked differences, for instance in the rates at which females and males were able to become free from slavery and pawning; and in the terms on which they were able to secure shares in the productive assets of the cocoa economy.

Organization of the Discussion

The substantive chapters are organized in six groups of three. Part I expands on the conceptual framework and the historical contexts. Chapter 2 offers an introduction to the debate about the development of capitalist relations in Africa, and to the theory of induced institutional innovation. Chapter 3 gives an overview of the evolution of Asante natural resources, economy and polity over the period. Chapter 4 outlines the changing relationship between outputs and factor inputs.

Parts II and III examine a major era (1807–96) whose dominant characteristic, from the perspective of factor markets, was the use of coercion (physical and social) in the acquisition of extra-familial labour and long-term loans. The purpose of Part II is to develop a description of the pattern of property rights and markets in the period: successive chapters (5–7) discuss land tenure, labour institutions, and capital and credit arrangements. Part III analyses the causes and consequences of that pattern. Chapter 8 examines the economics and political economy of slavery and pawning, testing the standard rational-choice economic explanation for slavery against the Asante evidence. Chapter 9 examines the gender and kinship dimensions of the social relations of production. Chapter 10 pursues the implications for individual careers, welfare and conflict.

Part IV is the hinge upon which the story turns. It examines a double transition, and considers the causal relationships—if any—between the two processes: the decline of slavery and pawning, and the growth of cash-crop farming. Chapter 11 asks why the British administration took 12 years to implement its international commitment to prohibit slavery and pawning. Chapter 12 traces the survival and decline of the various forms of coerced labour. Chapter 13 examines causation, and provides a test of the induced institutional innovation hypothesis.

Parts V and VI consider factor markets in an era (1908–56) in which coercion was decreasingly available as a means of obtaining workers and collateral. Part V establishes a description of property rights and markets in factors of production for the period concerned—with a chapter (14–16) on each factor of production. Part VI analyses the causes and implications of the pressures for change in land tenure as cocoa cultivation was extended (Chapter 17), the spread of lending on cocoa crops and farms (Chapter 18), and, of most far-reaching importance, the history of free labour contracts over the 1910s–50s (Chapter 19).

Finally, Chapter 20 summarizes the findings and comments on their significance for rational-choice theories and for the history of capitalism, agrarian change and economic development in Africa.

PART I

Context and Concepts

Chapter 2 offers a brief exposition of two sets of ideas that generate issues and hypotheses which will be drawn upon in subsequent chapters: the debate about the historical development of capitalist institutions south of the Sahara, and the evolutionary theory of property rights and of rent-seeking. Chapter 3 sets out the general economic, ecological and political contexts for the chapters that follow. It offers the first overview of the history of Asante economic resources and activities over the extended period covered by this book. Chapter 4 examines the relationships between output and factor inputs (the production function) over the period. The analysis suggests that we need to revise existing understandings of choice of technique in West African economic history: for the precolonial period, for the transition to cash-cropping, and for the established cash-crop economy of the middle and later colonial period.

2

THEORIES AND DEBATES:

SOME TOOLS FOR THINKING ABOUT THE HISTORY OF PROPERTY AND MARKETS IN ASANTE AND BEYOND

The first chapter introduced the conceptual framework of this study, defining key terms and identifying general theoretical and historiographical reference-points. Some readers will be content to proceed directly to Chapter 3. Others, however, will find a brief elaboration of certain aspects of the conceptual framework necessary, either for an introductory (if necessarily compressed) exposition or to clarify definitions.

Two particular sets of ideas have fed the debate on the history of property and markets in factors of production in Africa and elsewhere. The general controversy about the dynamics of, and constraints upon, economic development in African history turns to a great extent on the extent and significance of the evolution of markets and private property rights in factors of production. This discussion is surveyed in Section A. The specific theory of institutional change offered by the rational-choice school is expanded upon in Section B: the induced innovation or evolutionary theory of property rights and, conversely, of rent-seeking. In line with the eclectic and open-ended approach to theory declared in Chapter 1, the emphasis in both sections is on setting up questions and hypotheses for the empirical investigation which follows.

A. Marxist, Dependency and Agrarian-Populist Perspectives on the Development of Capitalist Institutions in Africa

The mix of market and non-market relations in the social organization of production in Africa has stimulated controversy over how far market institutions have 'emerged' and proliferated; whether their spread is finished; whether they have raised and can promote economic efficiency and with what implications for equity; and how far their spread has been driven by external or internal forces. Within this debate it is useful to distinguish four basic positions as points of reference in the chapters to come. These are the contrasting marxist and dependency views; and the 'static' and 'dynamic' versions of the agrarian populist position.

There is a widely-recognised parallel between the new institutionalist notion that technological or demographic change may create disequilibrium within the property rights system, inducing changes to such rights, and Marx's view that new 'relations of production' appear—albeit by revolution rather than evolution—when change in the 'material productive forces' brings them into 'conflict with the existing relations of production or—this merely expresses the same thing in legal terms—with the property relations within the framework of which they have operated hitherto'.[1] However, marxists have seen this model of endogenous change in property rights as less relevant as an account of the origins of capitalism in Africa than what might be called Marx's exogenous model, in which capitalism was brought to precapitalist societies by the imperialism of the most advanced capitalist ones. From this perspective the emergence of market institutions in the region is evidence that its long-term trajectory is indeed towards a high level of economic development. Thus for John Sender and Sheila Smith the fact that, as of the mid-1980s, wage labour was vastly more common than it had been at the start of colonial rule was much more significant than the fact that it still accounted for a considerably smaller proportion of the workforce of African countries than of Western ones.[2]

From a dependency theory perspective the order of significance is reversed: the reproduction of apparently archaic relations of production is seen as the major cause of Africa's continued poverty.[3] Dependency theorists argue that the region's transition to capitalism is already over: having amounted merely to the integration of precapitalist institutions into a 'peripheral' form of capitalism capable of generating only small advances in productivity, and most of whose surplus is exported to advanced capitalist economies or, if spent locally, is consumed rather than invested.[4]

Since the 1960s the main argument in the marxist and dependency literature on the causes of the coexistence of 'precapitalist' and 'capitalist' relations of production in Africa has been about whether it constituted an unequal 'articulation' of the two, under which the former subsidised the latter. For example, most hired labourers in colonial Africa were not landless proletarians but male seasonal migrants, who, while working for much of the year for wages, nevertheless retained rights of access to land in their home areas. Their families used these rights to support the migrants when they were sick, unemployed or too old to work, and also to rear the next generation of labourers. The result, according to the 'articulation' argument, was that employers did not have to pay the full supply cost of their labour. Rather, they offered just enough pocket money to persuade young men to accept employment while their households supported them.[5] Similarly, merchants were able to pay lower prices for cash-crops to the extent that much of the cost of production was absorbed by a non-market institution, the farming household, which might provide the land and much of the labour and capital.[6] This line of thought has been extended to rural women who, it has been argued, supplied goods and services to the market either without direct remuneration, for instance when wives helped on husbands' cocoa farms, or in return for sums too low to compensate for the subsistence cost of daily reproducing their labour.[7] Other radical historians have argued, however, that the 'articulation' thesis exaggerates the licence for social manipulation enjoyed by capitalists. In southern Africa, for example, the migrant labour system originated, if it did not remain, as a compromise between the demands of employers on one hand and of the labourers and the elders of their rural communities on the other: labourers and their headmen initially exerted considerable control over the terms on which labour was sold.[8] This revisionist literature epitomizes a major current in marxist historiography generally: the emphasis upon class struggle rather than market prices, state power, or the interests of the ruling class in isolation, as the principal determinant of institutional outcomes.[9] The issue of who benefits from migrant labour will be examined for our West African case in Chapter 19.

'Agrarian populism' is a convenient label for views of partly subsistence-oriented rural economies that emphasize the resilience of their institutions and strategies in the face of supposedly modernizing forces from outside. Populist positions on agrarian history, in contrast to marxist or rational choice perspectives, are not necessarily linked to a more general theory and have been put forward from a variety of premises. In the present context we should distinguish sharply between 'static' and 'dynamic' variants.

By the former I mean the traditional belief that African institutions are precisely traditional; originally and abidingly so, in the sense of being hostile to market forces and individualizing economic activity and social identities. This idea seemed commonsense in the heyday of modernization theory and of substantivism. But, as noted in Chapter 1, it has been overtaken by subsequent historical research. West African societies may have resisted particular forms of capitalism and of incorporation in the world economic system, but the notion of a general refusal to respond 'rationally' to relative scarcities is discredited. Thus in the case of land tenure, for instance, by the mid-1990s a critic could observe that 'the conventional wisdom' is that 'indigenous land rights, under the impulse of market forces, are capable of significant autonomous evolution in a beneficial (efficiency-enhancing) direction'—providing the state facilitated rather than obstructed.[10]

The efficiency and initiative of West African farmers in responding to both resource constraints and market opportunities are central to the work of the 'agrarian populist' writer most relevant to Asante agrarian history, though she might not accept the label. Polly Hill's famous study of the pioneers of Ghanaian cocoa-farming, in what is now the Eastern Region of the country, stressed their entrepreneurial qualities and also the capacity of their existing institutions to accommodate the rapid, large-scale adoption of an exotic and permanent crop. She argued that land sales were no innovation of the era of cocoa and colonialism, and that the same was true specifically of the institutions through which migrant farmers cooperated to purchase land.[11] Similarly, Hill disputes any assumption that widespread agricultural indebtedness was new, or that it led to a further concentration of ownership in what was already, as she notes, a highly unequal society.[12] The resilience of their farming households is seen as being founded not simply in resistance to unwelcome changes, but in a dynamic adaptability of both institutions and techniques, which has enabled them to seize market opportunities as well as to cope with a variety of dangers.

Just as the efficiency and distributional significance of migrant labour can provide a key test of conflicting marxist and dependency arguments, a good test of the merits or otherwise of the agrarian populist position, especially its dynamic version, is provided by the issue of the efficiency and distributional significance of sharecropping. The characteristic form of share contract in Ghanaian cocoa farming has been valuably examined by A. F. Robertson, who vigorously disputes any claims that it is either anachronistic or transitional, and insists rather that it is enduring and that this staying power is grounded in efficiency.[13]

Finally, a central proposition in the literature on Asante, and on Ghana and West Africa generally, is that the state was broadly a restraint on the development of capitalism: specifically, that it resisted the development of individual property rights and the emergence of an indigenous capital-owning class. For the precolonial Asanteman, a long series of varied studies by Wilks, Arhin, McCaskie and others has emphasized the dominance of the nineteenth-century state over the exchange economy and over the acquisition of people and lands generally. These scholars have gone on to explore the conflicts between the central government, merchants and provincial chiefs over the distribution of wealth, and the ideologies dealing with its accumulation.[14] Recently, as indicated earlier, I have questioned the extent of state domination of wealth accumulation in the nineteenth century, and offered a revised view of the conflict surrounding it.[15] Historians of Asante, particularly Arhin, have argued that colonial rule removed at least the fiscal barriers to making and keeping private fortunes.[16] On the other hand, the literature on colonial West Africa generally has tended to emphasize the social conservatism of British policy, anxious to restrain rather than promote the operation of market forces. An interesting contribution, made with particular reference to Ghanaian cocoa farming, has come from G. B. Kay and Anne Phillips, who combine a dependency-theory view of the colonial state as actively opposing the development of African capitalists, with a marxist emphasis upon class struggle, in the form of what they see as the emergence of a strong local capitalist class challenging the dominance of foreign capitalists.[17] Further, M. P. Cowen and R. W. Shenton have argued that the failure of British banks to supply credit to West African farmers was not for any lack of enthusiasm on the part of the bankers but, rather, was the result of a colonial government policy of resisting the development of private property rights in land, including the right to mortgage it.[18] This and the other issues mentioned in this section will be pursued in later chapters, where the debate on the emergence of agrarian capitalism in Africa is examined, for one major case, in what I would insist is an essential perspective: that of the changing relative scarcities of labour, land and capital. New institutionalism has a specific theory, or even a pair of theories, to offer on this.

B. The Evolutionary (Rational-Choice) Theory of Property Rights

New institutionalists' theorizing uses as a baseline the idealized model of a world in which resources are allocated through perfect competition. They recognise that in human experience such conditions are rarely met but analyse these realities as deviations from the model. There are many models of such deviation, but for present purposes we can distinguish two basic stories, one optimistic, one pessimistic with respect to the growth of the economy as a whole. In the optimistic account institutional inefficiencies (deviations from perfect competition) arise as an unintended byproduct of such processes as population growth and technological innovation. These inefficiencies impose costs on some individuals or sets of individuals, creating a demand from them for reform. This happy story is known as the theory of induced institutional innovation. In this book it will also be referred to by the more specific label of the evolutionary theory of property rights. In the pessimistic story individuals act, in isolation or in combination, to maintain or create deviations from perfect competition which, though costly to others and to the economy as a whole, create gains for themselves. This sad story is the theory of rent-seeking. It will be noticed that both accounts share the same assumption about human behaviour: that people act to maximize their individual net incomes. Let me spell out these ideas in a little detail.[19]

In new institutionalist terms a property rights system is 'socially efficient' to the extent that it creates incentives to individuals to use resources in ways consistent with the interests of society as a whole. A property rights regime achieves this insofar as it 'internalises' benefits and costs, that is, ensures that those who gain from using a resource in a particular way incur a corresponding share of the costs. By definition, this eliminates 'externalities' (costs and benefits to others, i.e. to non-contracting parties) and thus removes the opportunities for 'free riding': enjoying the benefits of a resource without sharing correspondingly in the costs. In this context the most important attribute of property rights is 'exclusivity', the power to deny others the same use of the resource concerned, because this internalises at least some of the gains and losses from the activity. For example, cultivation simultaneously derives gain from soil fertility and depletes it. If one tiller has sole rights of cultivation he or she receives the full benefit of using the soil, *and* also has the full incentive to ensure that its fertility is restored. Besides creating exclusivity, property rights also reduce 'transactions costs', the costs of making and enforcing contracts (which themselves may achieve exclusivity). Many transactions costs arise from divergence of interests between 'principals' (such as landlords, lenders, slaveowners and employers) and 'agents' (such as—respectively—tenants, borrowers, slaves and employees). At least in a world of imperfect and unequally distributed ('asymmetric') information, such divergence produces incentives for one party to take unilateral advantage of the other either before the contract has been made ('adverse selection') or after it ('moral hazard'). But establishing property rights is itself costly. Thus it is only efficient to create or refine property rights if the net gains are positive.

According to the theory the mechanism of induced institutional change is set in motion by an exogenous change which alters the relative scarcity of factors of production: as with a fall in population that makes land relatively more abundant and labour relatively less so (we can omit capital to simplify this hypothetical case). The shift in physical ratios is reflected in a shift in relative factor prices—at least implicitly. In our example the most efficient combination of land and labour for producing a unit will now involve more land and less labour than before. This implies a shift in the 'social efficiency price' of each factor: this price being defined as the highest return that could have been obtained from that unit if used for another activity or by someone else for the same kind of activity.[20] In our example the social efficiency price of land would fall while that of labour rose. We can equate the social efficiency price with the 'social rate of return' on a resource: the return that would be obtained if the resource is combined with complementary resources in the proportions that precisely reflect their relative scarcities. In a perfect market the social efficiency prices would be explicitly translated into the amounts paid for the hire of the respective factors. For illustration let us assume that labourers receive wages and that much of the land is operated by tenants. If the change in social efficiency prices is indeed accommodated by the existing property rights regime there will be (in terms of the theory) no pressure for change in those rights. But if, for instance, wages and land rents are fixed (or are simply less than perfectly elastic) then an individual labourer will receive a wage which is less than his or her now raised social efficiency price: it is less than his marginal value product (the value of the output added by the addition of his labour) would be if his labour was combined with complementary resources in proportions reflecting the physical relative scarcities.[21] Conversely, tenants will be paying more for land than its social efficiency price. The overall result is that the private rate of return—the incentives to economic agents, be they individuals, households, firms and even the state—does not correspond to the social rate of return. The theory predicts that this will lead to a relatively inefficient combination of resources: total factor productivity (output divided by the sum of inputs) will be lower than it could be if the institutions were otherwise arranged. This implies waste: output may be lower and input higher than they need be.

But would anybody notice? If they did, would the incentives to them as individuals to exert themselves in the cause of reform be sufficient to overcome the temptation to free ride? The theory envisages that some individuals would gain personally from closing the gap between private and social returns. This implies that it is not merely a discrepancy but a disequilibrium: a situation in which individuals have incentives to alter their behaviour. Enterprises (individual or otherwise) would gain from higher total factor productivity. Continuing with the example, labourers would gain if their wages reflected their true scarcity. Tenants and land buyers would gain if the price of land was allowed to fall to reflect its now-greater abundance. Existing landowners would lose. When an existing property rights regime does not adjust to changed factor scarcities the owners of the now more abundant factor will receive marginal revenue greater than its social efficiency price. This surplus is an economic rent, as defined in Chapter 1: the supply inelasticity from which it arises being the non-adjustment of the property rights system to the changed supply situation. In our example the economic rent is paid by tenants to landlords and, implicitly, by wage earners to employers.

According to the theory of rent-seeking, rational individuals or sets of individuals faced with a chance to acquire or keep an economic rent will endeavour to do so.[22] For instance, 'socially efficient' changes may be blocked, rather than undertaken, by the state if they would reduce tax revenue or reduce the incomes of influential private groups.[23] Such 'opportunistic' behaviour helps to account for cases in which socially inefficient property rights persist or may even be deliberately created.[24] Thus from the same assumptions about human motivation we obtain precisely opposite scenarios. The problem then is to explain which interest will prevail.

A related issue is how to interpret institutions whose general features may be understood, with equal logic, as implying either the extraction of rent or a socially-efficient adaptation to particular circumstances. The key example in the context explored in this book is 'interlinked' or, better, 'interlocked' transactions, where a contract in one market is simultaneously a contract in another. This concept has been much discussed in development economics, primarily with reference to sharecropping deals in South Asian agriculture.[25] In these a principal, acting simultaneously as landlord and employer, makes an arrangement with an agent who is both tenant and worker.[26] For Asante history the notion of interlocking is pertinent for understanding not only sharecropping but also the pawning of humans and then—more questionably, as we shall see in Chapter 18—the pledging of cocoa farms. In pawning and pledging, productive assets were transferred to the creditor for the duration of the debt, not simply in response to default. Thus the pawning contract set the price of capital (or consumption credit) but also included a price for the labour of the pawn. The pledging agreement could be seen as setting the price of working capital as well as putting a price upon land use rights and upon fixed capital (the cocoa trees). In this study we will consider the historical evidence about such institutions in Asante. The neoclassical intuition would be that interlocking contributes to efficient resource-allocation by overcoming the gaps in the markets and very high transactions costs that would otherwise exist.[27] For instance, without interlocking most would-be borrowers would have suffered in that they would have been unable to get loans at all, because of the high administrative cost to creditors of running small accounts and the high risk of default on both interest and principal. In contrast, radical critics see interlocking as extracting flows of income and transfers of assets on terms which reflected highly imperfect market conditions: economic rents. Their argument is that an insistent popular need for credit to finance basic consumption gives moneylenders an inelastic demand for the scarce resource of liquidity. They exploit this to transfer the risk of default from themselves to the debtors. The interlocking of markets permits the extraction of surplus through the acquisition of productive assets under an agreement made under duress, at prices which consequently undervalue the assets.[28]

Returning to the general problem of explaining whether socially-efficient or inefficient interests will prevail, various propositions have been put forward within the rational-choice literature. Douglass North noted that present choices may be constrained by past ones ('path dependence').[29] Mancur Olson maintained that small groups tend to be more effective than large ones in achieving collective goods because their individual members have less incentive to free ride.[30] Bates, with reference to twentieth-century Africa, has argued that large numbers of small producers are in a structurally weak position compared to small numbers of large producers.[31] There are empirical difficulties with these interesting arguments[32] and there is clearly more to the political dimension of institutional choice than can be usefully encompassed by the new institutionalist vocabulary introduced above. More is involved than costs, information problems and interest groups (and their coalitions), important as all these are.[33] It seems important to broaden the understanding of the state within the rational-choice tradition and, more specifically, to explore how far the negotiation and conflicts surrounding institutional choice can be illuminated by models of strategic behaviour.[34]

Thus rational-choice political economists recognise that a purely economic explanation of institutional change will be incomplete; and have posited various ways of finishing the job. So far the latter efforts have succeeded in making the analysis more nuanced, but not much more determinate. The more subtle the theory has become, the more it seems to multiply contingency rather than to clarify causation. But perhaps this reflects historical reality; on a modest scale this book will provide a test of this.

A further query is, methodologically, of an opposite kind: whether the rational-choice approach wastes information (is 'reductionist'). The anthropologist Pauline Peters argues that a purely instrumental explanation of institutions is precisely reductionist.[35] Certainly the logic of the theory of rent-seeking seems self-defeating if it is intended as a sufficient account of the state.[36] Whether the same objection is convincing when applied to micro institutions will be considered for Asante in subsequent chapters.

It should be emphasized that the risk of reductionism entailed in the rational-choice approach arises from one of its virtues: that it seeks determinate explanations. 'Rational' choice per se merely means choosing one's preferred alternative, whatever that happens to be: the general definition is purely formal, implying nothing about the content of the preferences. But when qualified or restricted to mean specifically the maximisation of net income, the very narrowness of this restricted sense avoids the risk of tautology[37] and offers the ambition of 'explaining much by little'.[38] This advantage can be surrendered when the conception is broadened to allow for 'constrained optimization'. When a farmer, for example, is assumed to balance income maximization with risk minimization and possibly other goals, there is a danger that anything that he or she does short of suicide is taken to confirm the preconception. Thus there may again be, paradoxically, a trade-off between sophistication and explanatory power. The need to escape such a trap will be borne in mind in the empirical analysis here.

Despite these cautions, the evolutionary theory of property rights provides a valuable framework, expressing important hypotheses on how property rights affect economic activity; how they change, and why efficient changes may not occur. It contrasts intriguingly with the theoretical approach that market economists have traditionally adopted to analyse the cash-crop expansion of early colonial West Africa: the 'vent for surplus' model(s).[39] In these models growth of output occurs while total factor productivity remains unchanged. That is, the contention of these authors is that the great expansion of output was achieved within the same production function, simply by putting to work previously unused land and labour. If so, there would be no pressure for property rights to change unless and until the early growth of export agriculture was succeeded by a phase in which some farmers specialized in export production.

In later chapters it will be argued that the evolutionary institutionalism introduced in this section is useful in analysing the history under investigation; but that, as with the more persuasive of the notions surveyed in the section before, by itself it is insufficient.

3

ASANTE, 1807-1956:

THE STATE, OUTPUT AND RESOURCES

This chapter delineates the changing political, economic and ecological settings in which resources were put to work over the period. Section A outlines the political institutions and policies within which Asantes pursued their livelihoods. It describes the structure of government and assesses what the states (precolonial and colonial) claimed to do and what they lacked the power to do. Section B surveys the output of goods and services, from which the demand for factors of production derived. It summarizes the varieties and approximate scale of subsistence and extra-subsistence economic activity. Section C describes the stocks of labour, land and capital. Finally, Section D draws together the implications of the previous sections for markets and property rights in productive resources. The primary purpose of the chapter is to provide a foundation for the analysis developed in subsequent chapters. But the discussion is also intended to contribute directly to the literature: on various specific points, and in the sense that the overview of economic activity and resources presented here is the first to be offered for the colonial era in Asante, let alone for our period as a whole.[1]

A. Government: Structure, Pretensions, Limitations

This section begins with a description of the structure of government, vertical (the hierarchy) and horizontal (the metropolis and the provinces), and of the major conflicts and changes over the period. I then outline the demands and claims made by the nineteenth-century kingdom and by the colonial regime on the population, especially fiscal. Following this, I emphasize a theme that is often overlooked, especially in precolonial contexts: the role of the state as a facilitator of economic activity. Finally in this section, we note the limits of state control: especially the inter-related constraints of limited resources and of potential or actual opposition from among the population.

The Structure and Location of Political Power

The Akan term for a polity of any size, whether independent or incorporated in a larger entity, was (and is) *oman*. For convenience I will reserve the word 'state' for the macro polities: the *Asanteman* (Asante as a political whole) and the colonial and Ghanaian states. Component *aman* will be referred to as 'chiefdoms' or 'chieftaincies', reflecting the convention in Ghanaian English that their heads are known as 'chiefs'. The elementary level of political organization in precolonial Asante, and in the chiefdoms as they operated under colonial overrule, was the matrilineage (*abusua*, pl. *mmusua*). It was through membership of an *abusua* that free (non-slave) Asantes were integrated into the polity. The matrilineage head (*abusua opanyin*) owed allegiance to a sub-chief: an *asafohene*, 'captain', or an *ɔbirɛmpɔn* (pl. *abirɛmpɔn* or *abonsamfoɔ*), 'chief'. If he lived in a village he would also be under a headman (*odekuro*), who was addressed as *nana*, 'chief', but was appointed by the head chief rather than chosen by his own elders, and lacked the main symbol of chieftaincy, a ceremonial stool. Head chiefs were of two kinds: provincial and Kumasi-based. This distinction requires elaboration.

The major provincial chiefs, the *amanhene* (sg. *omanhene*), were those whose chiefdoms (the *amantoɔ*) had joined with Kumasi, under the leadership of the latter, in creating the Asante state: Mampon, Nsuta, Dwaben, Kokofu and Bekwai. During the eighteenth and early nineteenth centuries, however, they were obliged increasingly to share the limelight with the Asantehene's metropolitan subordinates. The leadership of the Asantehene in the territorial expansion of the period enabled the central government to secure the largest share of the conquered lands and revenues, and to strengthen central authority, political and judicial, over the *amantoɔ*.[2] The original Kumasi sub-chiefdoms were rewarded with additional lands and subjects. Furthermore, several Asantehenes used their powers of patronage to create new stools, thereby consolidating the ruler's own control over government.[3] These offices were also endowed by their royal patrons with grants of land and subjects. By no means all the grants were the fruits of empire. Many communities within the *amantoɔ* were sequestrated by the Asantehene's courts, in punishment for rebellion or other offences, real or alleged, and redistributed to loyal or favoured servants, who on some occasions were among the *amanhene* but more often held one of the stools created by the ruler.[4]

Partly because of the conquests and redistributions of communities and lands, boundaries of allegiance and ownership were distant from being geographically coherent. Kumasi chiefs had villages far from the capital, often intermixed with villages serving provincial head chiefs. The spatial pattern was more of a network than a set of contiguous frontiers.[5] Moreover, as will be explained later, in the nineteenth-century economy there was little need to define stool boundaries with precision. The combination of these facts helped to create the conditions for a proliferation of disputes over land and rent when cocoa cultivation was adopted.

The reallocation of communities by the central authorities was a source of long-term conflict, as *amanhene* sought to recover villages and lands that had once belonged to them. Meanwhile within those Akan-populated areas which, though outside the *amantoɔ*, had been subjected to full administrative incorporation in the Asante state once they had been conquered,[6] there was a powerful tendency towards secessionism. This applied, most notably, to the southern district of Adanse and to the western district of Ahafo. Both varieties of centrifugalism were liable to be challenged, however, by other local chiefs or interests who allied themselves with Kumasi.[7] Decentralist or secessionist initiatives would emerge when the Kumasi government was weak, as it was after military defeat in 1874 (when the British burned the capital), and, especially, during the civil war of 1883–88. The peace settlement which enabled Asantehene Agyeman Prempeh I to begin his reign was obtained at the price of the restoration to provincial chiefs of many communities and their associated lands.[8]

In 1896 the British stopped short of formal annexation but imposed a skeleton administration under a Resident. After defeating a major uprising in 1900, primarily by Kumasis,[9] Britain formally annexed Asante with effect from 1 January 1902 (at the same date the British territories to the south, which since 1874 had been the Gold Coast Colony and the Protectorate,[10] were merged formally under the name of the former). The 'Ashanti' administration was headed by a Chief Commissioner answerable to the Governor of the Gold Coast Colony.

The British at first tried to capitalise on provincial sentiment by exiling the Asantehene, in 1896, and by declaring the abolition of the Kumasi chiefs' authority and property rights outside the Kumasi district itself. Meanwhile they elevated a number of provincial sub-chiefs to the rank of *omanhene*.[11] But such drastic intervention from outside proved difficult to maintain. In the face of continued local conflicts and complaints, the colonial regime gradually came to the view that it would be politically and administratively easier to govern through the Asantehene than it had proved to be by bypassing him. First Agyeman Prempe was restored as 'Kumasihene' in 1924. Then in 1935 the governor of the Gold Coast announced the 'restoration of the Ashanti Confederacy'. It was headed by a Council of Chiefs under Agyeman Prempe's successor, Osei Agyeman Prempeh II, who was now recognised by the colonial administration as Asantehene. The confederacy included all the chiefdoms which regarded themselves as Asante, plus, from the west, those Bron chiefdoms which opted in, including Wenchi. Also restored was the formal political and territorial authority of the major Kumasi sub-chiefs (now termed the 'clan chiefs') over their old domains outside Kumasi district (including Ahafo). Correspondingly the various *amanhene* created by the British were demoted to sub-chiefs each under a Kumasi chief.[12] The tide of centripetalism was to be turned after Ghanaian independence, it may be noted, when Nkrumah followed his victory over the NLM by honouring his promise to his anti-Asantehene supporters by creating a new region of Brong-Ahafo, separate from the Ashanti Region.[13]

Within colonial Asante the executive initially acted as the judiciary: the only British courts were the commissioners' courts, with limited appeal to the Supreme Court of the Gold Coast and to the West African Court of Appeal. Barristers and solicitors were not permitted to represent clients in courts within Asante from 1906 until 1933[14] and thereafter only in British courts. Most cases were brought, initially at least, before chiefs' courts (now named Native Tribunals).[15] Thus it was only late in the period, and then only in part, that the courts were separated from the executive.

Government Demands and Claims

We have seen that, before 1874, the central government of Asante demonstrated the capacity to intervene in property rights in the sense of restructuring and redistributing the ownership or sovereignty over lands and subjects. It also demanded heavy death duties and rents on the use of some natural resources.[16] Besides these it obtained revenue from a variety of sources, some of which were also tapped by chiefs: war booty; tributes paid by defeated or otherwise subordinated rulers; taxes on the income of the Asante population at the point at which it was earned, such as market tolls and gold-mining rents, plus a range of occasional levies which, for at least part of the country, sometime in the later nineteenth century, were apparently consolidated into an annual poll tax; court fees and fines; the occasional labour services of all subjects (in war or public work); and the regular labour of the chiefs' servants, the *gyaasefoɔ*, who farmed, traded, escorted and in other ways served them.[17] The political culture favoured the self-acquisition of wealth, providing it contributed to stool revenues, ultimately if not necessarily immediately.[18]

Taken together these exactions within Asante and outside helped to justify the government's contemporary reputation as an unusually power-ful state by nineteenth-century West African standards, not only militar-ily but also in the ability of government to control the lives of its own people. That impression was cultivated by the Asante government itself, not least amongst its own subjects, as has been vividly documented by McCaskie.[19] Asantehene Mensa Bonsu put it this way to a visiting mis-sionary in 1876: 'It is a tradition among us that Ashantis are made to know they are subjects, altogether under the power of their King'.[20] This was done most vividly through a cult of funerary killings to honour deceased notables by providing them with subordinate companions whose presence would enable them to maintain their own social rank in the afterlife.[21] Convicted criminals and northern slaves were particularly liable to be selected for oblation but some free Asante, some of whom were described as volunteers, also died.

These oblations illustrate a general point, which has been urged and detailed by McCaskie: the mental universe of both government and people was far from secular.[22] The attitudes and likely responses of ances-tors, witches and shrines had to be taken into account by any actor calcu-lating the probable outcome of a possible action.[23] In principle the use of productive resources, and the exercise, creation and alienation of property rights over them, might be affected by the threat of sanctions from such sources or by the degree to which the values those sanctions enforced had been internalized by the actors.[24] As far as economic life is concerned, religion determined the day of rest from farming, as it did in monotheis-tic societies of the period. Though some sources specify the day as Thursday,[25] T. E. Bowdich, who stayed in Asante in 1817, stated that the day varied from family to family,[26] presumably reflecting the decentralised character of Asante religion. Fear of witchcraft might increase costs: for the colonial period there is evidence of cocoa farmers paying for protection against possible witchcraft from matrikin jealous of their success.[27] The cost of such insurance, however, clearly was not sufficient to deter the huge investment booms, in the form of cocoa-planting, which (as we shall see) occurred near the beginning and again at the very end of the colonial era in Asante.

In general, threats of what in secular terms would be considered 'supernatural' sanctions, and appeals to related values, were exercised at all levels of social and political seniority. Chieftaincy was a sacred office because chiefs were intermediaries between their living subjects and the royal ancestors.[28] Above all, as the Asantehene emphasized annually through his *Odwira* festival (a 'feast of the dead', as Busia described it), the central government had a comparative advantage in this arena too.[29]

The colonial regime announced itself to many of the villages of Asante by requisitioning labour, through the chiefs, especially to carry loads before the railway was completed. Punishment levies of labour were imposed after the 1900 rising on subjects of those chiefs who had participated in Yaa Asantewaa's rising.[30] After this early phase, however, colonial appropriations were paid in cash. The central government did not impose a direct tax.[31] Rather, its main source of revenue was import duties, enabling the regime to limit both political risk and collection costs. As in the Gold Coast Colony, and in southern Nigeria, this reliance on customs duties instead of direct taxation—the latter being usual practice elsewhere in the European empires in Africa—was made possible by the fact that agricultural exports, and therefore import-purchasing power, were exceptionally high compared to most other colonies. The opportunity to grow cocoa, and farmers' response to it, was decisive here.

The costs of the state in the colonial period included those of the maintenance and operation of chieftaincy, under the system of 'indirect rule'. The chiefs' sources of revenue included the fees and fines charged by their courts, royalties paid by any European or other firms with timber or mining rights on chieftaincy lands, and rent paid by non-subjects with bearing cocoa farms on those lands. In addition, chiefs occasionally levied per capita taxes on their own subjects (with a higher rate for men than for women, evidently reflecting perceived income differentials). As we will see, these levies were often prompted by heavy legal costs arising from disputes over boundaries with neighbouring chieftaincies in response to the new value that cocoa gave to the land.

By the end of the colonial period a fundamental fiscal innovation had occurred, though it was not initially intended as such. The government inserted itself between the cocoa producers and local buyers, on the one hand, and the world cocoa market, on the other, by declaring a statutory state monopoly of cocoa exporting. Introduced as a wartime expedient in 1939, this arrangement was reconstituted in 1947 as a permanent fixture in the shape of the Gold Coast (later Ghana) Cocoa Marketing Board.[32]

The export monopoly gave the state unprecedented capacity to raise revenue from the cocoa growers, simply by keeping a large part of the proceeds it received for the crop on the world market, minus the costs of exportation. This institutional innovation began a trend in the political economy of Ghana, for the substitution of administrative and political mechanisms, including patronage, for the market as the major channels through which resources were allocated and fortunes pursued.

The State as Facilitator of Economic Activity

The precolonial kingdom performed several roles which, whether intentionally or incidentally, had the effect of facilitating trade and extra-subsistence production by both private and state enterprise. It enforced a currency zone with a single, general-purpose, currency. While cowries were used in the northern transit markets, within Asante itself gold dust (*sika futuro*) was, in the words of the Methodist missionary Thomas Birch Freeman, 'the only medium of purchase or exchange for the wants of life'.[33] Brodie Cruickshank, a long-resident merchant and administrator on the Gold Coast, noted that 'In Ashantee it is forbidden to sell or pass [cowries] . . . at all, under very severe penalties'. He argued that the use of gold dust as a medium of exchange on the Gold Coast had hindered the expansion of the economy because 'its supply was so limited, and so little diffused'.[34] Whether he was right or not, there seems to be no evidence of this problem occurring in Asante. The main reason for this was probably that the government ensured a constant flow of new currency, offsetting that which left the economy in payment for imports. By law all nuggets of gold above a certain size, on their discovery, had to be sent to the Asantehene's treasury.[35] There they were reduced to gold dust, part of this product being returned to the miner and his chief. The scale and significance of this was highlighted by the Frenchman Marie-Joseph Bonnat, in a journal he drafted while captive in Asante, 1869–74:

> If it [gold] arrives in Europe in dust form, it is because this dust is the currency [*la monnaie courante*] of the country and the nuggets are pulverised to facilitate transactions. In Kumasi only [*seulement*] there are more than a hundred workers solely occupied in this work which I have often examined close up.[36]

Moreover in Asante, at least, it seems that the inflexibility of gold as a medium of exchange was eased because very low-value commodities—traded for that reason exclusively by women, as we shall see in Chapter 6—were bartered. The state also reduced transport costs by obliging villagers who lived along major routes to repair the damage from wear, rain and encroaching vegetation.[37]

The nineteenth-century state also sought to restrain abuses of power by its own servants. In 1817 Bowdich witnessed the promulgation of a law under which government officials on their travels had to ' "offer a fair price" ' when they wanted food, and if the offer was refused, to ' "then demand one meal" ' only before proceeding.[38] This, he commented, 'was particularly consolatory and beneficial' to slaves sent to farm in the remote areas. He wrote that 'the greater part' of the portion of their produce that they would otherwise have kept for themselves (having fulfilled their obligation to their masters), 'had been pilfered in common with the poorer class of Ashantees, (nominally but not virtually free), under various pretences, either in their distant plantations or on the arrival at the markets, by the public servants of the King and the Chiefs'.[39] Bowdich may well have exaggerated the scale of such appropriations, but the law he described should have strengthened the property rights even of slaves.

Above all, it was the military power of the late-precolonial state, especially before the 1874 defeat, and the policy of its government which secured for Asantes the 'broad forest rent' from their lands and reinforced it by the exploitation of locational advantage: possession of the geographically-dominant position in the transit trade. To be precise, in terms of natural resources the eighteenth-century conquests delivered for Asante a local monopoly of kola nuts and a near-monopoly of gold. These were defended with relative success until 1874.[40] In contrast, outsiders—specifically seasonal migrants from Akyem—were to participate as principals in the extraction of wild rubber in Ahafo, probably in the late 1880s and certainly in the 1890s. This was made possible by the fact that by the end of the civil war in 1888 Kumasi had lost control over Ahafo, hence the Akyem were able to enter and negotiate with local chiefs.[41] Meanwhile, as will be detailed later in this chapter, for over thirty years before 1874 a national monopoly of the transit trade (preventing Hausa traders from the north and Fante traders from the south from dealing directly with each other) was a further source of economic rent.[42] The government used its control over transit routes to deny savanna polities the opportunity to import European weaponry: with highly select exceptions the re-export of guns and gunpowder to the north was prohibited,[43] reinforcing the Asante advantage in relation to its savanna neighbours.

Let us now consider the record of the colonial regime in these same respects. It, too, enforced a general–purpose currency, and in this case a more 'diffusive' one. The fact that the precolonial currency had been gold dust had the fortuitous virtue, in this context, that its de-monetization did not necessarily reduce its exchange value: in contrast to the asset losses suffered by holders of precolonial currencies in most other parts of West Africa.[44] On transport, the colonial government was responsible for the introduction of mechanization, in the form of the railway, which was built and operated by the state.[45] The construction of motor roads was in some cases by the initiative of chiefs and villagers.[46] But the administration was also generally keen to promote the building and upkeep of roads, at least within Asante (roads which fed the railways were preferred to roads which, by matching their routes to the coast, competed with them: thereby aggravating the government's financial burden, as the railways were state-owned).[47] 'Talking hypercritically', wrote Chief Commissioner F. C. Fuller of the early roads made in the colonial period, 'the want of bridges, easy gradients, and lack of ballast, render these Roads of little value for vehicular traffic as yet; but they open up the Country in a wonderful manner and spell moral as well as material progress.'[48] Expenditure on roads, and education and agricultural research, reached new heights after 1945, when 'development' became politically imperative.[49]

On the abuse of power by government servants, it is interesting to note that the new regime faced repeated complaints of looting of food-stuffs and other items by the 'Hausa' troops in the colonial army. Like its indigenous predecessor, the colonial government had to try to impose discipline on its agents. In its first two decades at least, government carriers and soldiers emulated the precolonial officials in giving rise to accusations of abusing their position to make private seizures of foodstuffs.[50]

Finally, colonial policies had mixed implications for Asante economic rents. The indigenous monopoly of the transit trade was ended. European mining and timber companies obtained long-term leases. Much less well-known is the fact that the colonial regime permitted European agricultural interests to acquire land, for rubber and cocoa plantations. Such plantations were indeed established in the southern district of Adanse.[51] But the language of colonial officialdom generally supported Asante ownership of Asante soil. The policy was certainly to discourage sale of land to Africans from outside Asante. These points will be documented and developed further in later chapters. It can be said that in general British policy tended to maintain or even reinforce the control by Asantes, as distinct from other Africans, of the broad forest rent.

The Limits of State Power: Resources and Resistance

Having described the structure of government, and outlined its pretensions, let us now consider the limits of state power. Emmanuel Akyeampong and Pashington Obeng have argued that, despite the ruler's claims, in Asante belief supernatural power 'was available to all'.[52] More prosaically, in most of the nineteenth century the kingdom had no standing army, nor even a monopoly over conscription. When required, forces (including already recruited, but not mobilised, troops) were summoned by the Asantehene, from his Kumasi subordinates and through the relatively autonomous *amanhene*.[53] Partly because of this, partly as a result, the Asantehene's control over the population was subject to important constraints.

One was the risk of revolt, local or general. This was facilitated by the ubiquity of firearms, for—McCaskie has argued—possession of a gun was considered a right, duty and hallmark of free manhood.[54] Revolts were usually by tributary states or provincial chiefs, but in 1883 Asantehene Mensa Bonsu was deposed by a popular uprising.[55] Ironically, he had recently created a standing regiment of riflemen, recruited from outsiders (northerners, mostly slaves).[56] Evidently this innovation—presumably intended for use against Britain—failed to ensure his security at home.[57]

A second constraint (applying to chiefs as well as to the Asantehene) was the combination of low population density and a forest environment. The details of this and its implications for the production function will be discussed later. An implication for institutional choice was that to demarcate territory (as the colonial administration was to find with chiefdom boundaries), let alone to survey individual farms, in this high-forest setting was expensive.[58] Further, any attempt to make farmers' access to land conditional on large payments would have required great resources to attempt and even then been administratively, militarily and politically difficult to achieve. It was surely a reflection (in part self-reinforcing) of the weakness of the central government's day-to-day presence in the provinces that the state had only a vague sense of its own territorial extent. For as Wilks has shown, the rulers of the *Asanteman* considered their frontiers to lie a notional twenty-one days' travelling distance from the capital, in all directions; to the south, ten would have been more accurate.[59]

A third constraint was the availability of neighbouring powers as a source of possible refuge, support and inspiration to Asante dissidents.

This was particularly important after 1874, when the British prohibition of slavery in the Gold Coast Colony and Protectorate meant that runaway slaves could seek refuge over Asante's southern border. Meanwhile Asante political exiles gathered in British territory and argued that their own country needed institutional reform—perhaps enforced by British annexation—to bring Asante into line with the Gold Coast: for example, the abolition of death duties, which they claimed were an infringement of private property rights and a deterrent to enterprise.[60]

The colonial government, too, operated under powerful constraints. The most pressing was usually lack of resources, for the administration of Asante suffered the general colonial commitment to financial self-sufficiency.[61] The transition from fiscal minimalism to a doctrine of active 'colonial development' was not much manifest in expenditure in Asante until the late 1940s. As will be shown below in relation to the enforcement of the law on slavery and pawning, the British administration was extremely short of manpower, especially in the early years. Though the 'thin white line' was gradually thickened, both with more commissioners and more agricultural officers and other technical specialists,[62] the implementation of laws and policies always had to be done to a great extent through Asante personnel. This meant very largely the chiefs and their officials, until 1951–52 when elected local and district councils took over some of the chiefs' functions.[63]

In two important ways the chiefs were unlikely to be fully obedient substitutes for a more expensive, direct-rule, colonial administration. First, the government lacked the means to monitor chiefs' behavior to ensure that they enforced colonial rules even when they were against chiefs' own interests and/or convictions. For example, as we will see in Part Four, chiefs were hardly conspicuous in the enforcement of the prohibition of slavery after 1908. Second, in the long term the effectiveness of chiefs as an instrument of colonial rule depended, paradoxically, on their enjoying a degree of autonomy from it. They could only retain support from their subjects if they earned their respect as defenders of their interests. This tension can be seen in the chiefs' support for the cocoa hold-ups in Asante between 1927 and 1938, when farmers and brokers refused to sell cocoa beans to European firms. In 1927 and 1930 the colonial authorities forced chiefs to abandon threats to punish holdup-breakers. But in 1937–38, faced with a much more widespread holdup movement, they seem to have felt that it would be politically unwise to force the chiefs into more than nominal respect for the colonial law against restraint of trade.[64]

The capacity of chiefs to enforce established rules was undermined by the spread of Christianity, which weakened the ideological dominance of chiefs, as to some extent custodians of indigenous religion. Initially at least, it seemed to provide a delinquent's charter for citizens wanting to avoid *corvée* and other obligations to the chief.[65] In principle it also weakened the claims of ancestors as a constraint upon the alienation of land. Against these challenges to the old mental order was a tendency towards syncretism, accepting elements of Christianity and preserving or adapting elements of indigenous belief: worshipping God and acknowledging the ancestors' continued membership in the family and polity, fearing the devil but also the witch.[66]

During the colonial period perhaps the major problem for Asante suppliers was foreign competition: in the form of intensified competition with indigenous artisanal products and the presence of European import-export agents. On the other hand there was not only no direct taxation but also very little compulsory appropriation of land for foreign use. This relative freedom to accumulate enjoyed by the private sector during the late precolonial and colonial periods was defended, when it came under specific threat, by the formation of organised coalitions of export-producing commoners, poor and rich alike, which also attracted or compelled support from some chiefs. To elaborate an observation made above, the decisive element in the coalition of forces which overthrew Asantehene Mensa Bonsu in 1883 was a broad mass of commoners. They seem to have been motivated by outrage at the imposition of uncustomarily high taxes and fines upon their extra-subsistence activities, such as gold mining.[67] When, during 1927–38, farmers and brokers in Asante participated in the cocoa 'hold-ups', they did so in protest against successive produce-buying cartels formed by European firms in those years.[68] Finally, during the decolonization era the NLM drew much support from chiefs and cocoa farmers in its opposition to Nkrumah's internal-rule administration in Accra. The formation of the NLM was provoked by the government's refusal, in 1954, to pass on a recent rise in the world price of cocoa. The Movement argued for a federal constitution and low taxation of cocoa producers, so as to keep the bulk of the income from Asante exports within Asante, and with more of it in private hands than was beginning to be the case under the economic and political strategy followed by the Ghanaian government in Accra.[69]

Alliances between commoners and chiefs proved to be the most efficient method for Asante suppliers, most of them small-scale, to dispute the terms of their relations with produce-buying monopolies and governments, enabling them to make powerful challenges. However, the three challenges noted in the last paragraph were of successively diminishing effectiveness. Finally, as noted in Chapter 1, Nkrumah's defeat of the NLM in 1956 should be seen as making possible a new period in Ghana's political economy, one beyond the scope of this book: the era, lasting until 1983, of intensified policies of state-led economic development.[70]

B. Output: Varieties and Scale

Let us first define the distinction between 'subsistence' and 'extra-subsistence' economic activities. A nutritional definition of 'subsistence' would be almost impossible to apply to the available data, and even in principle would be less often relevant to the operations of households and palaces than one based on the uses to which the producers put their output. In this book 'subsistence' refers to the production of goods or services for consumption within the immediate social unit (from a conjugal family to a chief's household) in which they were produced. 'Extra-subsistence' means trading and the production of goods for consumption outside the producing unit.

The pattern of export demand shifted fundamentally during the first three decades of the nineteenth century:[71] with the closing of the Atlantic slave market to Asante suppliers, and, in response, a revival of gold exports to pay for European goods and the beginning of a great rise in kola nut exports to the savanna. Timothy Garrard estimates that the annual average output of the Akan goldfields as a whole rose from 27,000 ounces in the second half of the eighteenth century to 35,000 in the first half of the nineteenth.[72] Asante's dominance of these goldfields was diminished by the loss of its tributary states south of the Pra river following defeat by the British, Fante and Ga at the battle of Katamanso in 1826. But the Asante share was still 'over half, perhaps three-quarters'.[73] In mid-century, according to Cruickshank, 'The principal supply of gold' for export from the Gold Coast 'is received from the Ashantee traders'.[74]

The kola exports went primarily to the Sokoto Caliphate, the vast Islamic state created by the 1804 jihad and centred in what is now north-central and north-west Nigeria, with its commercial capital at Kano.[75] Lovejoy estimated the number of kola traders operating between Salaga—apparently designated by the Asantehene as the market place within which Asante and Savanna merchants should conduct their business[76]—and Kano in the 1820s and early 1830s as at least one to two thousand a year, probably 'much higher', with an equal number of transport animals.

Further, he quoted an 1857 report which implied that about 6,000 donkey loads, approximately 270 tonnes, reached the Niger crossing each dry season on one of the two main routes to the Caliphate and beyond.[77] LaTorre estimated that the value of Asante's kola exports to Hausaland rose 'at least ten times' during the nineteenth century.[78] Asante purchases from Hausa traders included slaves, some of whom were probably among those re-exported to the Fante states.

The trade in slaves and other commodities to the coastal states was long-established but was stimulated in the 1830s. This was partly because of a peace treaty of 'Peace and Free Commerce' between Asante and Britain (signed in 1831), and partly because that decade saw Gold Coast palm oil exports beginning to take off. Cruickshank stated that 'immense numbers' of slaves of savanna origin 'are being annually imported' by Fantes from Asante middlemen.[79] Fante merchants imported European goods and sold some of them on to Asante traders.[80] The Asante government gave Asante traders, state and private, a monopoly of the transit trade between the coast and the savanna markets. Hausa and the other northern merchants were excluded from Asante by c.1840 almost until 1874.[81] By the time of the major war with Britain in 1873–74, Asante could be said to have made a successful commercial adaptation to the loss of the Atlantic slave market.[82]

Much of the demand for extra-subsistence goods and services was internal. There is evidence of a considerable volume of production for local markets, as well as of the re-selling of imported goods. Iron was imported, from savanna producers as well as from Europe, as was cotton cloth; but iron-working, spinning and weaving were major activities in Asante itself. Other active handicrafts were gold-smithing, carpentry (including the making of stools), pottery, basket-weaving and bead making. It is important to note that all these activities served popular demand, through the market, as well as meeting elite requirements (in some cases by command).[83] It is also necessary to emphasize that food production was not confined to subsistence. Forest products such as edible snails, bush meat, palm nuts and palm wine, plus fish from Lake Bosomtwe, were sold in market-places.[84] So were foodcrops and cooked food: in the daily markets in Kumasi (two of them at the time of Bowdich's stay in 1817) and in smaller markets elsewhere.[85]

The military defeat of 1874 and its immediate consequences removed the political foundations of part of the commercial success. The British consolidation of authority over the Gold Coast Protectorate and the quickly-following legislation against slavery within it reduced Asante's export or re-export trade in slaves to Fanteland to a trickle. The humbling of the Asante kingdom inspired a wave of secessions by the remaining tributaries.

These included Gyaman, a major gold producer; and the entrepôt of Salaga. The Asante government's ability to enforce a national monopoly of the coast-savanna transit trade was shaken, though the British intention of compelling Kumasi to permit free trade through its territories was pursued too intermittently to be successful. This issue remained unresolved until the 1896 invasion.[86]

By 1884 a new export trade had begun, this time to the coast. Having started in south Asante,[87] it spread widely in western Asante once the civil war was over.[88] The Asante rubber trade seems to have been initiated by rubber traders from the Gold Coast, but Asante producers and traders responded to this new export market, thereby intensifying the country's links with the Atlantic economy. Rubber output continued to grow in the early years of colonial rule, but after surpassing 1,300 tonnes in 1906 and again in 1907 it fluctuated sharply around a downward trend.[89] Despite government encouragement, rubber was not profitable as a fully culti-vated[90] crop in Asante, certainly not by comparison with cocoa. The respective trends in the output of these two pure export crops are illustrated in Figure 3.1. Once the natural supply of rubber trees approached exhaus-tion, the Asante rubber industry was doomed, save for a brief revival in the Second World War because of military demand.[91]

Kola remained profitable, as a semi-cultivated crop, well into the cocoa era. Farmers even planted it in the 1920s, though apparently only on a relatively small scale.[92] This buoyancy was partly because kola 'has this advantage over the cocoa industry that it is unaffected by the changes and

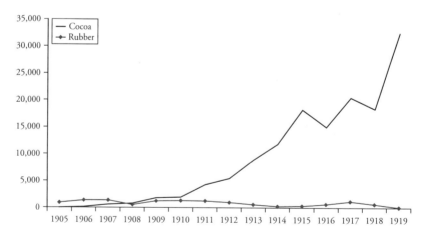

Figure 3.1. Asante agricultural exports, 1905–19 (tonnes).

chances of the European market'.[93] That was an exaggeration as purchasing power in northern Nigeria was affected by, for example, the demand for groundnuts in Europe, but kola did offer a degree of insurance to those Asantes who continued to harvest kola while adopting cocoa. When cocoa prices were low during the latter part of the First World War, for instance, increased attention was given to kola.[94] Because kola left Asante by donkey and, from the 1920s at least, by lorry to the north as well as by rail and steamer to the south, the figures for total Asante kola exports had to be estimates, such as the 6,000 tonnes estimated by the government for 1923–24.[95] At the end of the decade the Department of Agriculture made its most serious attempt at accuracy. Using a combination of census methods and road-gate checks the Department put total exports from Asante at 5,200 tonnes in 1929–30.[96] The officials believed exports were now rising, partly stimulated by merchants adopting lorry transport and partly because migrant labourers working on Asante cocoa farms were buying nuts to carry and sell during their homeward journey north. Even so, there is some oral evidence that kola production declined in the southern district of Amansie when cocoa-farming emerged as an alternative.[97] The same was reported for the Gold Coast Colony in 1930.[98] It seems that Asante kola production became more concentrated in the areas in which the spontaneously-grown trees were densest. Within western Asante, 'In the centres where indigenous Cola is common there is generally over-production, and a supply of selected nuts can be reaped to furnish any small increase in demand', reported a survey officer in 1929.[99] Conversely, even during or just after a cocoa hold-up, in January 1931, the District Commissioner of Bekwai visited two villages in the south of Amansie 'situated in a kola bearing area' but found that 'no sales take place'.[100]

Cocoa was brought to Asante in the late 1890s. Widespread planting of cocoa trees began only after the 1900 revolt, and cocoa beans were first noted in the official trade statistics in 1906.[101] It is necessary to observe that in Asante cocoa was exclusively an export crop, so that figures for export can be treated as sales figures, and—in most years—as equivalent to figures for marketed output.[102] It is also important to remember that, being a tree-crop, investment in cocoa has a several-year lag between planting and fruition, and a further period before maximum output is reached. Plotting the expansion of output year by year is made difficult because of gaps in the evidence. For certain years figures appear to be lacking altogether. Furthermore, we know that by the 1920s some cocoa left Asante by lorry. So for those years afterwards for which we have only railings data the total output is unknown. The first column of Table 3.1 summarizes those annual figures which seem to be comprehensive, or close enough not to affect the issues addressed in this book.

It is possible, however, to outline the expansion of production.[103] Annual railings of cocoa beans easily exceeded 1,000 tonnes in 1909, and passed 10,000 tonnes in 1914, 20,000 tonnes in 1917 and 30,000 tonnes in 1919. The original cocoa 'take-off' in Asante, which was concentrated in eastern and southern districts such as Amansie, may be said to have ended when the early period of generally high real producer prices ended in 1916. But planting resumed after the war, both in the now-established cocoa districts and further west. In the 1920s in all these areas where cocoa-planting was proceeding, population grew faster than in Kumasi or in the districts bordering the savanna—reflecting net immigration.[104] In the mid-1930s railings totalled 92,000 tonnes in two crop years in succession, demonstrating the growth in the area under cultivation to c.1929. Further expansion of capacity was slowed but not eliminated by the relatively low real producer prices that prevailed during most of the world depression of the 1930s and by even lower ones paid to West African producers during the Second World War. Asante's contribution to the aggregate output of colonial Ghana was becoming increasingly important for negative as well as positive reasons. Swollen shoot disease and soil exhaustion were reducing output from the Eastern Province of the Gold Coast Colony, the original centre of cocoa growing. Meanwhile the making of new cocoa farms and the extension of old ones had been prohibited by the Ashanti Confederacy Council of Chiefs, in 1938, from fear that food production was being neglected. With the removal of the ban in 1946 and higher prices after the war, railings reached 127,000 tonnes in 1948–49; though this figure was not exceeded until 1956–57, when the total was over 136,000 tonnes. Again, population growth was particularly fast in the districts where new cocoa planting was greatest.[105] The all-time Asante record for annual cocoa output is 312,000 tonnes (again including Brong-Ahafo) in 1964–65, the record year for Ghanaian output as a whole (557,000 tonnes).

Let us put these numbers and dates in perspective. At the level of Ghanaian cocoa-farming as whole two great waves of planting may be distinguished: the take-off, during which the most intense planting was in approximately the twenty years to 1916; and the 1950s. The take-off in (eastern and southern) Asante may be regarded as part of the earlier planting boom (to be precise, part of its middle and latter years). Western Asante especially, but also eastern and southern Asante, played leading parts in the later planting boom. Asante as a whole became the largest cocoa-producing region in Ghana in 1943–44. In 1947–48, and then from 1954–55 onwards, Asante contributed more than half of the aggregate output of Ghana—which was consistently the biggest producer of cocoa in the world from 1911 to the late 1970s. So this was an enormous cash-cropping achievement, from an area with a total population of just over 400,000 in 1921, and just over four times that in 1960.

The most precise evidence on the extent to which cocoa dominated rural economic life comes from the first stage of the 1956–57 survey, which included households in which no-one was engaged in cocoa farming. Of 36,251 Asante adult males, 47.8 per cent (17,341) described their occupation as cocoa-farmers or cocoa-and-food farmers. A further 212 were identified simply as 'farmers', and 721 as agricultural labourers,[106] most of whom probably worked on cocoa farms. Thus, in rural Asante by the end of the colonial period about half of the indigenous adult male population was directly engaged in cocoa cultivation; and the proportion was much higher among the non-Asantes, who comprised most of the hired labour force (of whom more in Chapters 16 and 19). Most of the other men recorded in the survey (retailers, builders, wood and metal workers, clerks) would have obtained their incomes largely out of expenditures made by cocoa farmers, labourers and brokers. Male cocoa income, spent or redistributed (by husbands giving 'chop money' to wives, for example), was clearly a major source of female incomes. But the survey also found that 47.66 per cent (25,148 of 52,760) of Asante adult females were cocoa or cocoa-and-food farmers. 12,047 were apparently food-only farmers, while 468 were simply 'farmers' and 27 were agricultural labourers.[107]

The demand for non-agricultural artifacts undoubtedly expanded after the introduction of cocoa with the enlargement of purchasing power that resulted from the expansion of agricultural exports. Alas we lack sufficiently comprehensive information to offer general estimates of the real value of cocoa incomes. Fortunately, a proxy—limited but useful—is available, because it is possible to express the value of cocoa incomes in terms of their capacity to buy imported textiles. Kay and Hymer used the colonial government's export and import returns to calculate indices for nominal cocoa prices and for the prices of 'Clothing, leather and textiles'. The cocoa prices concerned are Accra rather than Kumasi prices. If data exist which would enable the construction of an index of Kumasi prices for the whole period, they have yet to be found. For present purposes, Accra prices, though not ideal, are very helpful because it seems clear that 'up-country' prices varied roughly in line with coast prices.[108] A textiles index is highly relevant because much more cocoa-farm income appears to have been spent on imported clothing and cloth than on any other single category of purchases. 'Clothing, leather and textiles' figured heavily in the import statistics for Ghana as a whole, being the largest item during the years 1924–30 and 1944–53. For the rest of the cocoa-exporting part of the colonial era in Asante, 'Food, drinks and tobacco' was the largest item of imports into Ghana. This includes the period of the Asante cocoa-farming families' survey, 1956–57.[109] Yet the survey found that, during the six months of the main cocoa season, the cocoa-farming families spent nearly two and a half times as much on clothing—predominantly imported though, as we will see, not exclusively so—as on 'Imported food' and 'Drink and tobacco' (mostly imported, but some of the drinks were local) combined.[110] Thus for rural Asante, particularly with reference to the purchasing-power of cocoa income, textile prices are the most pertinent. Table 3.1 includes a column which presents the ratios of the cocoa and textiles price indices for the respective periods concerned. It is, in effect, a partial measure of how the cocoa-producing community's barter terms of trade moved during the colonial period. The

Table 3.1. Asante cocoa exports and purchasing power, 1905 to 1956–57

Period	Mean tons per year	Cocoa/textile price indices	Textile-purchasing power of cocoa income
1906–1909	811	1.83	9.54
1910–1914	6,349	1.72	74.63
1915–1919	20,563	1.13	144.16
1932–3–1936–7	82,200	0.49	282.11
1937–8–1941–2	84,360	0.3	171.32
1942–3–1946–7	83,200	0.22	126.61
1947–8–1951–2	113,660	0.84	643.41
1952–3–1956–7	116,980	1.55	1,202.23

Note: The figures are 5-year averages except for the first period which is 4 years. The export data to 1919 are for tons railed from Asante stations; the 1932+ figures are for purchases in Asante.[1] The gap in between is for years where such figures as I have been able to obtain are for railings only; which is insufficient as, during this period, a significant proportion of cocoa left Asante by road. The third column is calculated from two price indices, respectively for cocoa and for 'Clothing, leather and textiles', constructed by Kay and Hymer (in each case, 1953 = 100).[2] The final column was obtained by converting the Asante cocoa tonnage figures into index number form (1916 = 100) and multiplying by the price index ratios in the column before.
[1] Source for tonnage to 1919: *ARAs* for the years concerned. Source for tonnage for 1932–3 to 1937–8: Department of Agriculture, 'Cocoa Crop Prospect Reports' (found, e.g., in NAGK Bekwai File 66, item 304) and Gold Coast Colony, *Report on the Department of Agriculture for the Two Years 1937–39* (Government Printer, Accra, 1939), 2. Source for tonnage for later years (which also confirms the 1932–3 to 1937–8 data): Merril J. Bateman, 'An econometric analysis of Ghanaian cocoa supply', in R.A. Kotey, C. Okali and B.E. Rourke (eds), *Economics of Cocoa Production and Marketing* (Legon, 1974), 315.
[2] Kay with Hymer, *Political Economy of Colonialism in Ghana*, tables 21c and 20b.

final column expresses the changing purchasing power of Asante cocoa income, in terms of imported textiles.

Where indigenous craft products faced competition from factory-made imports such competition intensified in the colonial period, most obviously because mechanized transport reduced the cost of imports. Thus the colonial administration reported home in 1910 that 'The younger generation is fast adopting European clothes instead of native cloths'.[111] Yet indigenous weaving—though not spinning—survived. This calls for detailed historical research, but it appears that Asante weavers adjusted by adopting imported yarn and specializing in the higher-quality cloths, especially those with the most cultural significance. The administration noted in 1908 that 'The Ashanti are expert weavers. They obtain imported yarn and weave a variety of characteristic cloths of astonishing durability.'[112] The 1956–57 survey found 411 weavers among its sample of Asante men, plus 793 otherwise engaged in 'textile and leather product making', together making 3.32 per cent of the sample. Even more of the Asante women (1,363, or 2.6 per cent) were textile and leather producers[113] (presumably including tailors). Meanwhile indigenous goldsmiths and blacksmiths continued to work in Asante.[114] Thus, though the transition to a 'monocultural' economy went far, the term always remained relative. Indeed, the cocoa trade and the incomes derived from it were the basis of the growth of motor transport, which in turn required a new craft industry to maintain the vehicles. The 1956–57 survey found 183 metal machinists and fitters.[115] In 1959, in Ghana as a whole, over 8,000 workers were employed in vehicle repair.[116]

Among long-established Asante products, besides craft manufactures, we have seen that kola continued to be produced and exported in the cocoa era. Indigenous gold mining had been in decline in the late nineteenth century, partly because of producers switching to rubber collection.[117] This reallocation of labour away from the gold pits was decisively reinforced when cocoa was adopted. The reasons for the demise of indigenous gold production will be elaborated below. Gold mining rapidly became the preserve of European companies hoping to assemble sufficient capital to apply European deep-mining methods to suitable concentrations of ore. As it turned out, from many would-be European gold producers in Asante, only the pioneer survived and indeed went on to prosper on a large scale: Ashanti Goldfields Corporation at Obuasi, with Konongo Gold Mines a distant follower. To judge from their royalty payments, Ashanti Goldfields' output, 1897–1947, totalled over £35 million.[118]

Western firms also dominated the export of timber, without sustaining a monopoly of it. The timber business, though established fairly early in the colonial period, became a significant supplement to cocoa on the Asante export menu only after the Second World War. By then logging enterprises were established in, for example, Asante-Akyem, Amansie and Sekyere districts.[119] Logging required a relatively large stock of capital. This is probably why the industry began and, to beyond the end of our period, remained largely in expatriate hands. In what became the prime timber district, Ahafo, the first documented logging concession was registered in 1947 by an expatriate firm, Glikstens, while the first saw-mill was opened the following year by another, the Mim Timber Company.[120] By c.1958–59 the latter employed several hundred artisans and unskilled labourers.[121] In Adanse 'very extensive [timber] operations' were being undertaken by 1952 by another expatriate enterprise, R. T. Briscoe (East Asiatic Company).[122] From c.1948, in Ghana as a whole, there was a spurt in the number of indigenous entrepreneurs involved in the timber industry. But by the end of the colonial period their share of export shipments was still only a few per cent.[123] In Asante some had already been operating, for instance (albeit on a small scale and temporarily) within the Konongo Gold Mines concession during the mid-1940s.[124] A few successful indigenous timber contractors had emerged, above all B. N. Kufuor's Bibiani Logging and Lumber, which began in the 1940s with a concession from Kufuor's father, the chief of Nkawie in Kumasi district. But in Ahafo in 1956 there was as yet only one African contractor, P. A. Yeboah. The man who was to become, by the 1970s, the wealthiest Ahafo entrepreneur, W. K. Ennin, had only just (in 1955) borrowed the sum with which he was to enter the logging business. It is significant that the amount (£4,000) was enormous by the standards of most Asante cocoa-farmers, and that it was secured on an urban property (his house in Kumasi).[125] In short, timber had begun to offer comparatively wealthy Asante the opportunity to become much richer. But the colonial era ended with the rural economy overwhelmingly agricultural, especially for its indigenous inhabitants.

It is clear that the colonial era saw a major expansion in the aggregate consumption of food crops. This reflected the growth in the numbers of both seasonal and permanent residents, plus higher purchasing power for some. Kumasi itself became an ever larger magnet for marketed foodstuffs.[126] In the smaller cocoa-marketing towns, too, a sizeable demand emerged by the 1920s from northern labourers resident during the cocoa marketing season.[127] Part of the demand for foodcrops within Asante was met by suppliers from outside the Asante forest zone: thus from areas where cocoa farming was not an option and foodcrops might be the most profitable crop. Perhaps the major example was the development of rice production in the Ejura district, the closest savanna area to the Asante capital—'mainly by immigrants from the Northern Territories', at least at first.[128] Rice was also grown around Kumasi itself, often by Mende immigrants presumably drawing on their knowledge from Sierra Leone.[129] Much of the enlarged foodcrop supply in the first third of the century was actually grown on young cocoa farms: plantains and cocoyam being planted partly to provide shade for the immature cocoa plants. The same applied during the second wave of cocoa-planting, in the 1950s.[130] The marketing of food occupied much labour, especially around and in Kumasi. The colonial annual report for 1920, relatively early in the expansion of the city, commented that 'a large proportion of the female population in the Coomassie district must be engaged in the daily transport of foodstuffs.'[131] We will return to this aspect of the gender division of labour later.

To summarize this section so far, the fundamental change in the pattern of demand over 1807–1956 as a whole was the emergence of a massive external demand for produce grown in Asante. The enlargement of kola exports during the nineteenth century, and the rubber episode in the late years of that century, were in response to a significant growth in external demand for semi-cultivated produce which was a precursor of the demand for a fully-cultivated crop, cocoa, from the beginning of the following century. This qualitative and quantitative change in final demand was, in turn, undoubtedly the major source of change in the derived demand for factors of production. To the expansion of exports we must add substantial growth in the quantity of foodstuffs sold in Asante: most of which was supplied by production from within Asante.

It is important to note that there is no unambiguous evidence of farming families giving up the production of their own starch staples and vegetables, even when the supply of land for food cropping became tight in older cocoa areas in the 1940s. The nearest to such evidence comes from the data on occupations in the 1956–57 survey of cocoa-farming families. Among the 22,835 men and 40,487 women who were categorised as cocoa and/or food farmers, 9.0 per cent of the men and 4.9 per cent of the women were recorded simply as 'cocoa farmers'.[132] Even given that these apparent 'specialists' represented only small minorities of the farmers, the most plausible interpretation is *not* that they grew no foodcrops at all. Consider the gender dimension. The absolute numbers of Asantes listed as purely 'cocoa farmers' are 1,916 men and 1,917 women.[133] It is hard to believe that nearly 2,000 women farmers could have been growing only cocoa. For we will see in detail in later chapters that the rest of the evidence, much of it very specific, is that the great majority of cocoa farmers (in the sense of farmowners; but the same applies to the great majority of cocoa farm-managers) were male. The most reasonable interpretation of the enumerators' category 'cocoa farmers' is that it meant cocoa-tree owners who grew foodcrops only for their own consumption, or who marketed food surpluses so small that they or the enumerators did not consider this activity worth mentioning when defining their occupation.

Overall, we may assume that this 'subsistence' or own-account output of foodcrops expanded during the post-1918 era as a whole, approximately in proportion to the increase of population. It is difficult to establish whether there was a net increase or decrease in non-agricultural production, as some lines expanded but others shrank. What stands out is the huge increase in extra-subsistence agricultural production, primarily though not exclusively for export, both in aggregate and per head.

C. The Stocks of Labour, Land and Capital: Quantities and Characteristics

Labour: Population Density and Immigration

In a primarily agricultural society the most fundamental determinant of labour supply was the ratio of population to cultivable land. For economic and other reasons, population growth was much valued in the precolonial Akan states. Securing high fertility was 'a major preoccupation'.[134]

Wilks and Ray Kea have argued that the emergence of the Akan states from the fifteenth to the seventeenth centuries was underpinned by the winning of gold, its exchange for slaves sold by both the Juula from the savanna and the Portuguese at the coast, and the application of those slaves to the clearing of forest.[135] This could be considered a self-reinforcing investment in population growth, as well as specifically in slaves.

Following the creation of the Asanteman, the eighteenth-century wars of conquest brought Asante not only much additional territory but also many tens of thousands of captive men, women and children. A high proportion of these, especially of the able-bodied males, were sold into the Atlantic slave trade.[136] But it seems clear that many were resettled within Asante, to swell the numbers of the chiefs' servants, and to add to the numbers of their subjects in general.[137] For example, according to a statement in 1930 by the *odekuro* of the village of Yapessa, south of the lake, he and his subjects were the descendants of Techiman people captured during its conquest by Asantehene Opoku Ware [in 1722–23], who were resettled under the Krontihene of Kokofu.[138] The practice continued when opportunities permitted in the wars of the nineteenth century.[139]

Population figures are non-existent for the beginning of the period but for the end are not only extant but generally plausible. The precolonial government did not conduct censuses, and the estimates ventured by scholars have had to be based on contemporary European estimates of Asante's military strength. In his 1975 book Wilks examined contemporary estimates of the number of 'men able to bear arms' and tentatively concluded that 'metropolitan' Asante—roughly similar to Asante as defined in the present study—had a population of 725,000 in 1817, which proceeded to fall calamitously: to 558,000 in 1863, 250,000 in 1901, and 208,000 in 1911, before recovering to 292,000 in 1921.[140] Marion Johnson criticized Wilks's numbers for 1817 and 1863 as far too high, and she also doubted that there had been much of a decline between these dates. Using contemporary estimates of the number of 'armed men' she proposed a figure for total population in 1863 'of the order of 160,000'.[141] The first colonial 'census' of Asante, in 1901, was a misnomer as it was conducted by estimation rather than counting.[142] What the census report observed of a broader geographical area generally would have applied to Asante: short-staffed commissioners in charge of wide districts 'have been compelled to accept the returns of the Local Chief, or of illiterate Policeman for the scattered villages under their control'.[143] Indeed, commissioners' estimates would have been especially unreliable in the aftermath of the 1900 rising, when they had very small resources themselves while the chiefs and people would have had an incentive to minimize the recorded numbers for fear that, for example, the figures would be used as the basis of requisitions of forced labour. In that context no more could be expected 'than an intelligent guess.'[144] The first real census was held in 1911, but the Chief Commissioner of Ashanti reported that it was 'generally admitted' that it understated the population by at least 20–25 per cent.[145] Conversely, the census officers believed that the growth of population indicated by the returns for 1921 and 1931 was exaggerated by a progressive increase in the comprehensiveness of the counts, as administrative resources increased and as people became less fearful that the data would be used to their detriment, for example, to facilitate the introduction of direct taxation.[146] The Chief Commissioner warned that the recorded rise between 1911 and 1921 'is not necessarily a natural one'.[147] Even the 1948 census may have missed some of the population;[148] while the 1960 one may actually have over-counted.[149]

Table 3.2. Census returns of the population of Asante, 1901–61

Year	Population	Population density (per square mile)	Average annual increase (%)
1901	345,891[1]	14.2	
1911	288,037	11.8	−1.67
1921	406,640	16.7	4.12
1931	578,702	23.7	4.23
1948	818,944	33.6	2.44
1960	1,697,050	68.7	8.93

[1] 'Includes an estimate of 10,240 for Kintampo, then administered with the Northern Territories' (de Graft-Johnson, 'The population of Ghana 1946–1967', facing p. 6). Source: J.C. de Graft-Johnson, 'The population of Ghana 1946–1967', *Transactions of the Historical Society of Ghana* 10 (1969), table facing p. 6.

What can we make of these numbers? There is little dispute that the nineteenth-century figures are very unreliable. We can have little confidence in the accuracy of the data for men who were armed or capable of bearing arms; we are uncertain about the precise geographical areas to which they related; and we can only guess the ratio between the 'military' figure and the size of the general population. On circumstantial grounds it seems highly unlikely that population fell between 1817 and 1863. As Wilks conceded, 'The period was, for the most part, one of peace and material advancement, and no unusually virulent or widespread outbreaks of plagues or the like are known to have occurred during it'.[150] In this context it is reasonable to dismiss the notion of a drastic decline before 1863: as Wilks himself came close to doing in his reply to Johnson.[151] On the other hand, the notion of a catastrophic decline in the late nineteenth century, from mortality and especially from mass exile, is supported by abundant evidence. Specifically, casualties from disease and enemy action were heavy in the campaigns of 1869–73 against the Ewes east of the Volta, the Fantes on the coast and the British. Almost certainly larger still was the exodus of several major chiefs and many thousands of their followers after defeat in the civil war of 1884–88. Dwabens, Adanses, Kokofus, Dadiases, Manso Nkwantas, Denyases and Mampons were amongst those who left Asante territory *en masse*.[152]

Following the British occupation of Asante, and the consolidation of colonial rule after the 1900 uprising, most of the exiles returned.[153] There was also considerable net immigration of non-Asantes, especially to Kumasi, in connection with the expansion of commerce.[154] Thus, the apparent fall in population between 1901 and 1911 is contrary to most of the circumstantial evidence.[155] The 1911 colonial report on Asante was surely right to imply that the 1901 figure had been inflated: 'The imagination of the Native peoples the Forest with Spirits and the imagination of the Officer peoples it with men, but experience tends to dispel the fears or hopes of either'.[156] In 1918 the world influenza pandemic cost 9,000 lives in Asante, according to a government estimate;[157] and this appears to have been an understatement.[158] After that there is no dispute that, while successively more comprehensive census enumerations may overstate the rise, the Asante population grew steadily through a combination of natural increase and net immigration.[159] Working backwards, it seems reasonable to accept the census figures from 1921 onwards as fairly accurate, though probably still undercounting until 1960. We can assume that the real figure for 1911 was higher than the recorded one, meaning that there were probably between 300,000 and 350,000 people within the colonial borders of Asante; and, more riskily, that the real number for 1860 would have been similar to that for 1817, and probably quite close to the 1911 level.

From the 1920s onwards, and especially in the 1950s, Asante had the fastest population growth in Ghana. Asante's average annual increase of 8.93 per cent for 1948–60 compares with 2.00 per cent for the North and 5.56 per cent for the South.[160] This can reasonably be seen as a response to (as well as a reinforcing cause of) the fact that during this period the Asante economy was also outpacing not only the northern savanna region but also the Gold Coast Colony. The latter had less room for further exploitation of its natural resources and, as implied above, bore the brunt of swollen shoot disease.

The Asante economy was able to draw upon an external labour reserve, to the north in the savanna. The presence of northern workers is reflected in all these figures.[161] In the nineteenth century the savanna was the major source of slaves, who became part of the permanent population and have therefore been included in the discussion above. During the colonial period, however, following the prohibition of slavery and pawning the labour force was supplemented with seasonal immigrant labourers, also mostly from the savanna. A high proportion of these came from neighbouring French colonies.[162]

The post-influenza and especially post-1945 combination of natural increase and immigration, temporary or permanent, multiplied the population without making it abundant. Asante with its colonial boundaries comprised about 63,500 square kilometres (24,500 square miles).[163] Thus a population of 325,000, as perhaps in 1911, would have meant 5 to the square kilometre (13 to the square mile), while according to the censuses there were more than 7.7 per square kilometre by 1931 and nearly 27 by 1960 (per square mile, 20 and 70 respectively). If we exclude Kumasiand the mining towns of Obuasi and Konongo we arrive at an average population density per square kilometre for rural Asante (including the market towns) of 11.2 in 1948 and 22 in 1960 (respectively, 29 and 57 per square mile).[164] The rural population was rising but, as will be shown below, even at the end of the colonial period its density was not enough to make land availability a constraint on expanding output except in certain areas which were not only relatively highly populated but which were also distinguished by having had particularly large areas planted with cocoa trees.

In discussing the supply of labour we must consider its quality as well as its quantity. Institutional influences on this, such as whether labourers were free or coerced, will be discussed in later chapters. Here it is important to note that quality was somewhat constrained by pathogens, notably endemic parasites. For economic activity the greatest health problem was almost certainly malaria, because of the recurrent bouts to which its victims were subjected as well as the death toll it inflicted.[165]

Land: Rain, Forest and Gold

Throughout the period annual rainfall was usually heavy. It was commented in the mid-1970s that Lake Bosomtwe had 'risen continuously' since the early nineteenth century.[166] In the mid-twentieth century rainfall in the Asante forest zone averaged 150–190 centimetres a year, with relatively low average variation between years.[167] This provided the natural conditions for the moist-semi deciduous variety of 'high' or 'closed' forest.[168] A companion of the British invasion force of 1896 gave the following description of the vegetation surrounding the route from Cape Coast to Kumasi shortly after crossing the River Pra and entering Asante by the central-southern district of Adanse:

> The exuberance of the vegetation is almost incredible, and the track each side was walled in by a tangled mass of leaves, branches, creepers, and tree trunks, while the gigantic cotton trees towered far above the other giants of the forest. The earth itself is covered with a thick layer of fallen leaves, out of which spring masses of ferns, moss and creepers; above these are shrubs, and luxuriant undergrowth, while long sinuous stems and adnascent creepers twine and interlace with the branches above, festooning the path in a hundred different curves till an unbroken network is formed, over which the branches of higher trees intermingle and form a perfect leafy canopy.[169]

This 'exuberance of the vegetation' requires qualification: the quotation refers to the roadside, 'where the undergrowth revels in the light'.[170] But the interior of the forest was almost as hard to negotiate. A colonial forestry officer, after many years experience of the 'Gold Coast forest' (in which he specifically included Asante), gave the following description:

> The traveller who tries to make his way through constantly finds his path barred by massive lianes and by great trees whose crowns of thick foliage are so densely interlaced as almost to shut out the rays of the tropical sun overhead. He cannot walk upright for any distance but must be constantly creeping or bending with eyes directed downwards to note the running surface roots which lie like snares in readiness to trip him. It is like an immense, almost impenetrable, vault supported by gigantic pillars and spreading a mysterious shade; lianes like enormous cables stretch from tree to tree and bind the crowns firmly into an inseparable canopy. But he does not see this vault, nor the trees, nor the great lianes and flowers, for the leaves of innumerable little lianes and creepers form a thick curtain which lines the wall of bushes and shrubs. He proceeds between two compact walls of verdure and sees only low branches and enormous fallen trunks over which he scrambles with difficulty. Occasionally a flower, some lily or ground orchid, brightens the gloom.[171]

The size of the trees meant that clearing the land for cultivation was costly. In the absence of capital-intensive technology full clearance within a short time was extremely labour-intensive.[172] The burden could be lightened somewhat by the application of time and fire. After making initial inroads with the axe, the farmer could leave the late-dry season atmosphere to dry out the exposed vegetation, which could then be cleared with the help of fire.[173] Joseph Dupuis, who visited Kumasi from Cape Coast in 1820, describes this technique for Asante, though emphasizing that much more cutting was required than in the coastal scrubland (where he also observed it), and that drying took longer.[174]

The fertility, superficially so abundant, was precarious. The forest ochrosols, the most widespread and fertile category of soils in Asante, are 'easily tilled' and 'relatively well-drained', partly through the numerous streams. But most of their nutrients are concentrated within the humus topsoil which comprises only the top 30–40 centimetres. Hence fertility is easily depleted if the soil is exposed directly to rain, wind and sun.[175] In this environment sustainable agriculture required that farmers protect the soil where possible, for example by maintaining or creating foliage cover.[176] Fertility is also rapidly depleted by cultivation. The potential for using animal dung as fertilizer was greatly restricted by the endemic presence of sleeping sickness (trypanosomiasis) in the West African forest zone. Hence farmers practiced land rotation with long fallows. A visiting Wesleyan missionary, W. Terry Coppin, was evidently describing this when he wrote in his journal in 1884: 'the people every year clear a fresh place to cultivate believing that last year's soil has lost all its nourishment'.[177] A 5–10 year fallow is necessary for the regrowth of thicket and perhaps of early secondary forest, while ten to twenty years are required for the appearance of full secondary forest. The later is necessary for full restoration of fertility in the long term.[178] William Allan suggested that in this environment the 'critical population density' (the maximum population supportable from a given area with given technology) 'for the old subsistence agriculture was between 85 and 130 people per square mile' (33–50 per square kilometre), probably approaching 'the higher figure'.[179]

There is no doubt that the Asante forest zone as a whole was well within this limit during the nineteenth century, as the preceding discussion of population estimates indicates.

Even Wilks's improbably high total for 'metropolitan' Asante in 1817 implies an average of only 30 people per square kilometre (78 per square mile).[180] The density of population and cultivation was above average in the central areas of Asante, those within the *amantoɔ*. During the nineteenth century foreign visitors travelling towards Kumasi from the coast were repeatedly struck by the contrast between the outlying district of Adanse and the more central Amansie area, wherein lay two *oman* capitals, Bekwai and Kokofu. On entering Amansie, wrote Bowdich, 'the plantations became more frequent and extensive, and numerous paths branching off from where we travelled, shewed that the country was thickly inhabited . . .'[181] T. B. Freeman made similar observations from a journey taken in 1843.[182] By 1881 Adanse was in temporary secession from Asante when the British official Captain Lonsdale left it for 'Ashanti' itself:

> No sooner has one entered Ashanti and passed through one or two of the numerous small villages which dot the road than one is aware of having reached a new country. A system of some kind impresses itself upon the senses.[183]

Such impressions were reinforced as Kumasi was approached. Bowdich's companion W. Hutton wrote of the final section of the route, between Amansie and the capital, that 'the country [was] more open and better

Plate 3.1. A path through the Akan forest. This is a British photograph, possibly taken near Wenchi, probably from the late nineteenth century or the very beginning of the twentieth. Source: Foreign and Commonwealth Office Library, London. An earlier reproduction appeared in McLeod, *The Asante*, 21, and I thank Malcolm McLeod for generous help with and advice on this photograph.

cultivated'.[184] It was a similar story on other sides of Kumasi. For example, in 1844 the Wesleyan missionary George Chapman found the Kumasi-Dwaben route 'well inhabited', the scale of farming indicating that 'other and populous villages are near'.[185]

Indeed, if there was anywhere in Asante where land was scarce enough for fallow periods to be shortened to below the level required for full restoration of fertility we may assume that it was in the vicinity of Kumasi, probably within a day or half-day's journey—on foot and laden—of the capital's markets. Wilks has argued that in the nineteenth century fallow periods in the hinterland of Kumasi and the largest provincial towns were ten years or less.[186] Yet even this suggestion of a modest intensification of rotation cycles may be exaggerated. Johnson modelled land use around Kumasi in 1907, by when most of the exiles had returned. She postulated that each settlement marked on the Gold Coast survey maps of that year was surrounded by farmland, of which at any one time part would be cultivated and the rest in various stages of fallow. She assumed that, for example, a settlement of 100–500 inhabitants would require as farmland all the land within a half-mile (0.8 kilometre) radius. The map Johnson produced on these premises shows a substantial proportion of the forest left outside the rotation altogether, implying that land use was not intensive even around Kumasi.[187] We may conclude that, certainly in general and probably almost everywhere, land for cultivation was abundant in the strict sense that the marginal product of land must have been zero. To summarize, from what is known of the soils, crop repertoire and farming techniques, fallows were long enough for full restoration of soil fertility. There thus existed a big reserve of soil fertility, available for utilization when a sufficiently attractive market for crops became available.

The Asante forests offered a variety of resources valuable for use by the immediate exploiter and also with commercial potential. Though many of the gold deposits lay too deep to be accessible with pre-mechanical technology some of this wealth was retrievable via mining with simple tools; gold was also found in rivers and on the earth after rain.[188] Hunting was practised by specialists, though even by the early nineteenth century big animals were fairly rare. Ivory, for example, was mostly obtained from trade with savanna areas, especially the kingdom of Kong, northwest of Asante.[189] The collection of large edible snails was a popular wet-season activity,[190] while some men went south to the Fante areas to search for them,[191] evidently to make money.[191]

Kola and rubber trees grew wild within the Asante forests but to exploit them commercially it was necessary to 'semi-cultivate': in the sense of clearing the surrounding bush, primarily to enable the collector or tapper to gain easy assess.[192] Johnson went so far as to maintain that there was some deliberate planting of kola trees, at least by the 1880s, in Dwaben, east of Kumasi.[193] The nearest to evidence for this that, with the help of the Basel Mission archivists, I have been able to find is the following passage in a letter from a missionary, Mohr, in 1881:

> The high road after a tiring six hours' walk led us to some Asokore plantations. . . . In this region you find the Asokore Kola-nut trees that because of their quality are especially appreciated at the big Salaga and Bontoku market. They are carefully tended. Nya-mfa, the place where we stayed overnight, is located in such a Kola-nut forest.[194]

This is clear evidence for 'semi-cultivation' as opposed to simple 'collection' of wild produce. But it does not show 'cultivation', given that this term presumes deliberate planting. The kola trees are in a 'forest', and are not described as on the 'plantations'. For Asante as a whole the relationship between demand and naturally-available supply was such that kola-nut producers did not need to plant the trees: 'tending' was enough.[195] Wild rubber trees were evidently less numerous than their kola counterparts, and were frequently felled by the collectors. After the colonial takeover the government promoted the deliberate planting of rubber trees, especially in the 1900s, but met with little positive response.[196] The return on the labour involved evidently seemed unattractive to the farmers compared to that on planting a new, exotic plant: cocoa. It was the availability of this outlandish crop, and the prices foreigners were willing to pay for it, which provided the incentive that encouraged Asantes to put a significant part of their forests under permanent cultivation.

The spread of cocoa cultivation was itself patterned to some extent by local variations in soil fertility. Poorer soils would have slowed the accumulation of profits by the pioneer cocoa farmers, thereby delaying and reducing their reinvestments in new farms. For example, this accounts, in large part, for the fact that the Amansie district, centred commercially on the railway station at Bekwai, became a much more intensive producer than its southern neighbour Adanse, which was closer to the coast and traversed by the same railway.[197]

As a permanent crop, cocoa broke the pattern of ecologically sustainable cultivation characteristic of precolonial Asante, under which soil fertility was restored by long fallowing. In Asante the colonial period saw a combination of Asante cocoa-farmers and brokers, European merchants and the colonial and transitional governments, together capturing much of Asante's 'forest rent'. Over the decades the cocoa trees evidently decreased the fertility of the soil.[198]

By mid-century cocoa was also reducing the availability of land for food farming in Asante. We have noted that Asante and other Ghanaian cocoa farmers used food crops, specifically plantain and cocoyam, to shade immature cocoa plants. For this reason cocoa- and food-farming have often been seen as complementary. But this complementarity is reversed once the cocoa trees are sufficiently mature to form a shade canopy, depriving shorter plants of light. For the 1940s there is evidence that in Amansie district, at least, fallows were being shortened and for the first time cassava (manioc) was being widely adopted locally, both in the diet and on the farm. In the early 1870s Bonnat observed of the (free) Asantes 'They do not cultivate cassava for they despise it', though slaves grew it 'in abundance' 'in the woods'.[199] The late T. E. Kyei recalled of his Agogo childhood in the 1910s that 'cassava . . . was not an important or popular item of food in those days. It was grown mainly to feed pigs.'[200] In the 1940s in Amansie cassava was chosen, apparently as a substitute for the traditional staple, plantain, because the former would grow well on the marginal-quality land that was increasingly all that was left over for the extension of any sort of cultivation in this comparatively long-established cocoa district[201] in which fallow periods on the remaining foodcrop land were 'becoming too short for rejuvenation'.[202] McCaskie reports that it was grown in a similar default role on the outskirts of Kumasi in the early twentieth century: on relatively infertile land in the most densely populated part of Asante.[203] This is evidence of decreasing availability of land, at least in localities where population was relatively dense and cocoa cultivation widely established. Already, the combined effect of the spread of cocoa and food-crop cultivation had been to replace much of the forest by a mixture of farms and secondary bush.[204] Thus there were signs that the end of the era of land-extensive cultivation was in sight in some of the older cocoa-growing areas of southern and eastern Asante; despite the further extension of the area under cocoa (evidently on to more marginal land) that was to occur even in those districts in the 1950s. In western Asante (especially the forest areas of what is now Brong-Ahafo Region), however, the 'land frontier' remained open—in a natural sense though, as we will see, not always in an institutional one.

Transport was overwhelmingly land-based: none of the rivers in the Asante forest zone were navigable on more than a very small scale. Endemic trypanasomiasis meant that haulage had to be by human porterage until the introduction of engine power. The heaviness of the rains meant that the trade routes required regular, labour-intensive maintenance to prevent the forest from reclaiming the space: even before the columns of porters of the precolonial era were replaced by lorries whose axle-loads did much to rut the roads.

Finally in this section we must focus again on rain. If the level of rainfall conditioned the economic potential of the land, its seasonal distribution segmented the supplies of labour and farm income. The Asante forest zone has two wet seasons, a major one from about March to early July, a lesser one roughly in September and October.[205] Throughout the period discussed in this book, demand for labour in agriculture (food and cocoa-growing alike) peaked during the planting, that is wet, seasons. Conversely, farm income flowed in during the harvests, which for cocoa and for the majority of food output meant the dry seasons. For cocoa, specifically, the main crop was ready for harvest during the first three months of the main dry season, from November. In this it displaced or replaced the major non-food farming occupations of the nineteenth-century economy, with the partial exception of kola nut collection.[206] All these occupations took place largely in the dry season: kola and rubber production, long-distance trade, gold mining and handicrafts. There were directly climatic reasons for this: for example, the wet season flooded gold pits and hindered travel. But given the biological priority of food production, and the intensity of the demand for food-farm labour in the planting season, it was the dry season in any case which offered the main opportunities for other pursuits.[207] We will see below that these seasonal patterns influenced the markets for labour and credit, though to degrees and in forms which altered over the period.

Capital: Working and 'Fixed'

Capital, defined as man-made assets that yield a flow of income (in kind or otherwise) over time, links past economic activity with present and future.[208] The length of time involved can have implications for the nature of property rights in particular assets and for how they are transferred. That is, the social relations surrounding an asset which is effectively immobile and which yields income over thirty to fifty years (such as a cocoa tree)[209] are likely to differ from those surrounding one which is instantly moveable and is capable of yielding returns within months (such as a stock of trade goods)—as we will see in later chapters. It is conventional to distinguish between fixed capital and variable (or 'working') capital. Such a distinction can only be relative to the period with which the observer is concerned. Ultimately no capital asset is truly 'fixed', in the sense of permanent: machines and trees age and decay. But in view of the

importance of the annual cycle of seasons in Asante economic life throughout this period, it is useful to distinguish between assets which offered
returns within a year of their creation (which is how we will define 'working capital') and assets which offered returns only after more than a year
('fixed capital').

In the nineteenth century the fixed capital directly involved in production comprised gold pits, handlooms and a variety of simple tools for
farming (principally the cutlass and hoe)[210] and mining (notably a 'narrow
shovel' or 'soil-chisel').[211] It should be noted that the pits dug by miners
in one year could be reused, if there was any ore remaining, once they had
dried out after the intervening rainy season. Most relatively deep pits were
vertical shafts.[212] However a mine established near Manso Nkwanta to the
southwest of Kumasi, apparently in the late nineteenth century, had a
tunnel (measuring about 2.15 by 2.75 metres) that followed the reef
75–90 metres into the hillside. The roof was 'supported by timbers along
its whole length'.[213] Trypanosomiasis prevented the keeping of the kinds
of animals useful in production or haulage. Transport infrastructure comprised the networks of local paths which connected to what Wilks has
called the 'great roads'.[214]

The early colonial period saw a transformation in the quality and
quantity of fixed capital. Railway lines were opened to Kumasi from
Sekondi in 1903, and from Accra in 1923. The European gold mines at
Obuasi and Konongo, themselves major items of fixed-capital formation,
were probably the prime intended beneficiaries of the particular routes
adopted by the railway builders,[215] but both railways provided actual and
prospective cocoa farmers with cheaper access to their markets. Motor
roads had a similar effect over a broader area from the 1910s onwards, when
the motor lorry became a practical proposition.[216] By mid-1924 Asante
had over 1100 kilometres of 'motor and motorable' roads.[217] Already by
1914, and more so by the early 1920s, Asantes were running small fleets
of commercial lorries in competition with Europeans and Levantines.[218]
That competition was highly effective, driving the price of haulage down
and many competitors out of business. The colonial administration's
report for 1927–28 observed that 'A large European motor transport company ceased operating in Ashanti and many of the larger Syrian lorry owners are disposing of their fleets presumably due to the fact that they are
unable to compete with the ever-increasing African owner-driver. . . . The
general opinion amongst firms interested in transport is that cost of
haulage has now reached its possible minimum'.[219] Meanwhile, and crucially, a massive process of indigenous capital formation was taking place

at the initiative of tens of thousands of farmers. The adoption of cocoa transformed the composition of Asante's economic assets. Cocoa trees offered decades of annual income flows to those prepared to wait years for the first pod.

Annual crops may be regarded as capital goods in two phases of their cycle and over the cycle as a whole. The first phase is between harvest and planting: when a portion of the old crop is retained to plant in the next planting season ('seed corn'). The second is from planting until harvesting: the growing plants meet the definition of capital goods in that they are man-made, in the sense of having been deliberately planted, and they offer a future return. The process of weeding around naturally-planted kola and rubber trees was also an investment in the next harvest. We should note, though, that in a property rights perspective both planting an annual crop and clearing around a wild tree constituted longer-term investments in that the labour established a claim to the repeat use of the plot or tree. Finally, over the whole period between one harvest and the next, food-stuffs need to be stored to feed the population until more food is available. This 'subsistence fund' may be regarded, in part, as an investment in future labour.

Working capital was important for production and trade because the final consumer did not generally pay for the product when production began nor even at the point, in time and space, where it was completed. Between that point and payment by the final user often stretched physical distance—the need to transport the produce—and certainly time during which whoever provided the labour, in production and transport, needed to consume food and other items. These costs were equally real whether absorbed implicitly, as by a sole producer, or made explicit through payments such as money wages. We will see later that there was a major seasonal element in the demand for working capital; though the nature of this altered over the period. For the cocoa era it is abundantly documented that producers tended to obtain credit outside the harvest season.[220] Besides being the period when supply was most available from cocoa-buyers seeking to secure forthcoming produce, this was also the time when they had no income coming in, and therefore most desired outside finance. For the nineteenth century we lack direct evidence but circumstantially it is very likely that there was a similar peak in producers' demands for credit (though supply was much more constrained). This would have been towards the end of the rainy season, shortly before the main foodcrop harvest and soon before the resumption (probably after the harvest) of specifically cash-earning activities.

D. Implications: Shifting Contexts of the Evolution of Factor Markets, 1896–1956

From the preceding sections we may derive several key observations which will help frame the subsequent examination of factor markets and related property rights.

The proposition, from vent-for-surplus theory, that even so dramatic an expansion of production as the rise of cocoa-farming early in the colonial period can be accounted for by the deployment of a leisure reserve inherited from the precolonial era, is put in doubt by the evidence that extra-subsistence output was much larger in the pre-cocoa era than can comfortably be reconciled with any meaningful notion of such a reserve. Indeed, throughout the period discussed in this book indigenous labour was supplemented by widespread use of labour obtained from the savanna: though the method of such recruitment changed fundamentally with the transition from slave to wage relations.

The problem of explaining how extra-familial labour was obtained in this era of the development of an agricultural export economy is made harder by the physical abundance of land. Unless there were significant net economies of scale in production (an issue to be examined in the next chapter) and in the absence of a dispossessed local population, employers' ability to attract labourers would depend on their possession of some critical resource that potential labourers lacked. With all the forms of production mentioned above new entrants would lack some skills that experienced practitioners had acquired: but in none of the main cases—gold, kola, rubber and cocoa—was this potential employer's advantage more than very temporary.

On the other hand, throughout the period savanna dwellers to the north of Asante lacked independent access to the most economically valuable kinds of land. Northern Ghana and Burkina Faso, to use their present names, were short of known exploitable auriferous terrain and, being outside the forest zone, they lacked kola, rubber and cocoa trees, whether wild or cultivated. Whereas micro-level differences in land quality within Asante may not have mattered much in this context, land quality made a big difference at a macro level.

This natural-resource advantage enjoyed by Asantes may be seen as a form of economic rent. That is, the opportunity to exploit wild kola or rubber trees or gold deposits created a rent equal to the difference between the value of this output and the value of the foodcrop or other output that could have been derived from the land. Similarly—to this extent—the adoption of cocoa by Asante farmers hugely increased the economic rent on cultivable land in Asante, in that there was a great difference between the income they could get from using land to grow cocoa and from using land exclusively for food farming. Economic rents arise from inelasticity in supply, and the supply of these natural assets was fixed.

It was also the subject, in the precolonial period and to some extent also in the colonial, of a political monopoly in that it was impracticable (and in the nineteenth century probably dangerous) for a northerner to seek permission to work these natural resources as an independent producer, rather than as an agent, free or otherwise, of an Asante principal. The military strength of the kingdom secured a regional monopoly or near-monopoly of certain natural assets. Colonial overrule maintained Asante possession of Asante lands. Under both regimes Asantes possessed a resource of 'broad forest rent' that their savanna neighbours lacked.

In principle the opportunity to gain a share of this rent might attract labour from less endowed neighbouring regions. But this would only be so if the rent was large enough to be divided with mutual net profit between an employer and an employee. Thus its mere existence did not mean that it was automatically enough to form the basis for free wage contracts. In this respect there was a major difference between the key nineteenth-century and twentieth-century exports. We have noted that cocoa was much more lucrative than the commodities that it replaced (again contrary to vent-for-surplus models) or, in the case of kola, far surpassed it in volume and value of output. The value of the 'rent' from ownership of cocoa land varied with the producer price, but it is clear that it was usually much higher than that on the possession of rubber or kola trees or—with indigenous mining techniques—gold-bearing land. How this difference affected the way in which labour was obtained will be examined in later chapters.

Finally, the use of land became much more intense over the period: by the mid-twentieth century there were the beginnings of land scarcity in certain localities. How the land tenure system responded, and generally how it interacted with forms of labour and borrowing, will also be explored below.

4

THE CHANGING RELATIONSHIP BETWEEN INPUTS AND OUTPUT, 1807–1956

Having considered the changing stocks of the individual factors we can now examine how they were combined. Let us therefore consider the relationship between output and the inputs of the various kinds of resources: the production function (or rather functions, as they changed over the period). Understanding this is necessary for any analysis of factor markets. The chapter is intended to do much more than summarize existing knowledge. Rather, it puts forward several major propositions about production functions in Asante—ideas which are relevant as hypotheses, arguably, for other settings not only in Ghana but in West, and indeed sub-Saharan Africa more generally.[1]

Section A suggests that is necessary to modify the accepted view in the economic historiography of West Africa that precolonial economies were labour-scarce. Section B observes that the case of Asante cocoa contradicts the vent-for-surplus interpretations of the cash crop revolution in the region. Section C shows that the farmers' characteristic land-extensive methods of growing cocoa made economic sense throughout the colonial period. Section D offers a general statement of the production functions over 1807–1956. In this context it argues that we need to reconsider (and for the colonial period at least, to abandon) the proposition, put forward in notable studies from economists, that in their choice of techniques Asante and other Ghanaian cocoa-farmers essentially substituted labour for capital. Section E considers the evidence about the relationship, if any, between scale of production and efficiency. Section F reflects on the implications.

A. Production Functions and Choice of Technique: Labour Scarcity and Seasonal Abundance in the Nineteenth Century

Arguably the production function is the most basic area of neglect in recent studies of the precolonial economic history of Africa. The most incisive publications appeared in 1973. A. G. Hopkins emphasised the importance of labour scarcity and environmental constraints in explaining choice of techniques, especially in agriculture.[2] Philip Curtin identified the low opportunity cost of labour during the agricultural slack season as the condition that permitted the existence of gold-mining in Bambuk, an area now mostly in (southwest) Mali.[3] Subsequent work has greatly extended our knowledge, not least for Asante, but the logic of the various insights has by no means been tested to its limits. Indeed, Curtin himself cautiously avoided generalizing from gold-mining to other non-agricultural activities or from Bambuk to wider geographical areas. He also avoided contrasting the abundance of labour in what was, by default, the mining season with its scarcity in the rest of the year. Or perhaps in Bambuk labour was not particularly scarce in the main agricultural seasons because this area was, rather unusually in Sub-Saharan Africa, characterised by a 'small amount of tillable land'.[4] The latter condition certainly did not apply in Asante which, as we have seen, was relatively land-abundant. In this fundamental respect it fits Hopkins's general picture of precolonial economies in West Africa. In this section we consider exactly in what sense 'land abundance' and 'labour scarcity' are accurate characterizations of the Asante economy of 1807–96. It is argued that the economy was indeed land-abundant in most practical senses, and that it was labour-scarce in agriculture. But two important qualifications are offered. The stock of fixed capital was larger, and its importance greater (if only in the short term), than has been recognised in the literature. Further, even with the abundance of cultivable land, labour was relatively abundant during the agricultural slack season, which mattered for choice of technique.

The nineteenth-century economy of Asante was land-abundant in the economic sense that the expansion of output was constrained by the availability or cost of other factors rather than land. Capital was scarce; but its supply was largely determined by the level of inputs of labour, using simple tools (in some cases, with considerable skill). This should be qualified with respect to time. Because gold pits and handlooms were relatively enduring, their supply in any one year was largely dependent on how many existed at the end of the previous year. Apart from the making of new looms or the digging of new pits, the stock was little affected by the allocation of labour within the current year. In farming capital formation took a different, yet partly related, form. Crucially, the production of even annual crops was facilitated by past investment of labour in clearing the forest. A study of the weight of vegetation in mature (40–50 years old) secondary forest of this kind in Ghana reported an average of 146 tonnes per acre oven-dried, implying a moist weight of about 300 tonnes. In contrast, after 20 years of fallow, secondary forest would weigh about 100 tonnes.[5] Thus a *dadaso*, a farm cleared and cultivated in a previous year,[6] was a capital asset, the economic effect of which was to increase the returns on the labour now expended on replanting and weeding it during the current year. Again, keeping paths clear of obstructive vegetation was cheaper than clearing high forest to make the paths in the first place. The same applied to weeding around semi-cultivated trees. Hence an important distinction is required. Over the span of a year or less the quantity of output was a function of the amounts of both current labour inputs and of the level of fixed capital. Thus the short-term production function, it should be emphasized, was a two-factor one.

The longer-term production function, however, was a single-factor one. For, as the stock of fixed capital comprised the net accumulation of past labour inputs specifically directed to the creation of capital goods, over any term longer than a year the quantity of output was overwhelmingly a function only of the level of labour inputs (using simple tools). Thus, with the prevailing technology, Asante fitted a widespread pattern in precolonial West Africa: of being labour-scarce in that it was the quantity and cost of available labour which was the main determinant of the level of output.[7] This implies that the most efficient allocation of resources would use as little labour as possible in relation to the supply of land. Under the prevailing environment and technical constraints, restoration of soil fertility required long fallow periods. But the rotation, even once every 15–20 years, allowed for some economy on labour. Thus Asante farming methods were land-extensive and labour-saving.

The linked ideas of land-abundance and labour-scarcity needs are not sufficient, however, as an account of the precolonial production function; not even when elaborated to take account of the need for a long plot-rotation cycle in farming. While land was abundant in the sense that there was more of it than the population could work, it was not accessible to productive use for a considerable part of the year. Planting had necessarily to be done during the rains; weeding was necessarily a rainy-season chore because that was when the weeds grew; and the crops had to be harvested when they were ready, early in the dry seasons. In defining the 'agricultural year' we should also include the last few weeks of the major dry season, during which land was cleared in preparation for cultivation. Doing this work then, rather than spreading it throughout the dry season, was economical in that after months of drought fire could be used as an instrument of clearance. The rest of the calendar year comprised the heart of the dry season: the three to four months between harvesting and land preparation (November–February). The implication of this is that 'land' as a factor of production ceases to be homogenous if it is viewed as a flow rather than a stock. That is, if land is redefined as access to natural resources over time. Specifically, the utilization of this resource was restricted by the climate, in that with the available crop repertoire there was very little of productive value that it was possible to do on the farms for much of the dry season.

This in turn implies that, while output during the agricultural off-season was still very largely a function of labour inputs alone, the opportunity cost of labour was much less than in the rest of the year.[8] Given that the transport constraints meant that the Asante population had very largely to feed itself if it was to survive, in a physiological sense agricultural-season labour was inescapable while off-season work was discretionary.

The low opportunity cost of dry-season labour facilitated the supply response to demand for extra-subsistence goods (and reduced the incentive for capital-intensive technological innovations). Conversely, the level of extra-subsistence production was a function mainly of how the agricultural dry season was used. The income received from this output was largely what made effective the Asante demand for labour through the market, whether for slaves in the nineteenth century or free workers in the twentieth.

This explains a contrast, which has gone surprisingly unremarked in the historiography of Asante and of West Africa generally, between the choice of techniques in agriculture and in extra-subsistence activities undertaken during the dry season especially (in some cases by default) in the agricultural off-season.[9] In contrast to agriculture, these other activities were pursued in ways which must be recognised as labour-intense. In the case of the use of head-porterage for transporting goods, there was no available alternative. More significant is the case of weaving, where it is hard to see any technical obstacle to using relatively broad looms rather than the narrow looms characteristic of Sub-Saharan Africa generally and of West Africa particularly. Plate 4.1 illustrates the narrowness of the strips in which cloth was woven in nineteenth-century Asante.

Plate 4.1. Nineteenth-century Asante cloth in British Museum.[10]
Reproduced by permission of the British Museum (© Copyright The British Museum).
An earlier reproduction appeared in McLeod, *The Asante*, 152.

As of the 1970s 'traditional' Asante looms produced woven strips of
7.5–10 centimetres, which matches Bowdich's observation from his 1817
visit that 'the web is never more than four inches [10 cm] broad'.[11] With
a broader loom, output per weaver must have been substantially higher.

The preference for the narrow loom may be ascribed in part to an aesthetic preference for its product, and partly to its very low capital cost. These considerations account for the survival and relative prosperity of specialist weavers through and beyond the colonial era.[12] But in the nineteenth century it was facilitated also by the fact that the opportunity cost of labour during the season in which most weaving was done was much lower than it was during the agricultural year. Similarly, it was only because it was a dry-season activity that a European observer (as if in anticipation of Curtin on Bambuk) could remark of Asante gold-mining in the 1890s that 'The native's work costs him nothing; consequently, where all is profit, he can afford to work very poor rock such as Europeans could not touch'.[13] Labour was scarce and, accordingly, was saved where it was possible to do so during the busy seasons in agriculture; whereas in the agricultural slack season labour was abundant and was freely expended.

B. The Transition to Cocoa as a Rise in Productivity: The Inapplicability of 'Vent-For-Surplus' Models to the Explanation of the Asante 'Cash-Crop Revolution'

Though vent-for-surplus theories[14] have been relatively unfashionable since the 1970s they have yet to be systematically refuted and an alternative analysis put in their place in the economic historiography of West Africa. This is not the book to attempt these tasks in detail. But it is necessary to outline the evidence and to try to draw the appropriate conclusions on the matter, as a basis for the arguments developed in subsequent chapters.

Partly because of the labouriousness of the techniques in use, the Asante labour-force seems to have been occupied through the dry season: with many of the activities described earlier, notably mining, artisanal production, kola and rubber production and export-import trading and carriage. This renders implausible a starting assumption of the vent-for-surplus model, that there was a leisure reserve which could later be drawn upon for cocoa production.[15]

The nineteenth-century changes in the composition and scale of output can be said to have altered the general input/output ratio of the economy, but the effects were very largely quantitative rather than qualitative, and relatively modest at that. The post-1807 rise in the production of kola nuts, and the later take-off of rubber production, meant an increase in the production of semi-cultivated items. Compared to kola production in the eighteenth century the nineteenth century evidently saw a rise in total factor productivity in value terms, but there is no reason to believe that there was a change in the factor proportions involved. By contrast, the coming of cocoa was a change both ubiquitous and profound for the Asante forest zone.

Mechanized transport contributed greatly to the fulfilment of the exotic crop's potential as a means of raising returns on land and labour in Asante. The adoption rate was partly a function of local cocoa prices: that is, of access to market which was in turn a function of distance from the railway or motor road. Though local farmers had begun to plant cocoa even before the Sekondi-Kumasi line was built, the railway's impact on producer prices was surely critical to the rapidity and extent of the initial spread of cocoa cultivation in the south and centre of Asante.[16] Cocoa had been planted in western Asante by c.1910, at least in the Tano Valley and around Takyimentia.[17] Yet the spread of cocoa west of the Kumasi district was, relatively, rather gradual over the next third of a century. By the 1946–47 and 1947–48 crop years the share of 'Western Ashanti' (the future Brong-Ahafo Region) in combined 'Asante' (Brong-Ahafo plus the future Ashanti Region) cocoa sales averaged 34.5 per cent. For 1955–56 and 1956–57, on the other hand, the figure had risen to 42.1 per cent.[18] This lag is partly attributable to the absence of a railway and to the relatively slow expansion of the motor-road network in this more lightly-populated region of Asante.

The scale on which cocoa was adopted in Asante entailed a major demand for labour. There is a misconception in some of the literature that 'Cocoa does not need large labour inputs'.[19] This assumption made more plausible the claim by advocates of vent-for-surplus theory that the cocoa 'revolution' had been based simply on the activation of previously idle labour. I have examined elsewhere, in detail, the evidence on labour inputs in one of the major cocoa-growing districts, Amansie. It appears that by 1914–15, for example, as the 'take-off' phase of local cocoa planting approached its close, cocoa farms would have required at least a third, perhaps well over half, of the working year of the equivalent of the entire male labour force.[20] Consistent with this, and exactly contrary to vent-for-surplus theory, there is considerable evidence of labour being reallocated to cocoa farming from existing (extra-subsistence) activities such as gold mining.[21]

What the adoption of cocoa cultivation in the colonial period entailed was not, as protagonists of vent-for-surplus models thought, a cure for what they believed was demand deficiency, merely permitting and/or stimulating an expansion of output within the same production function. Rather, it involved a new production function, with a higher level of output for each possible level of inputs. This was partly a function of world demand, and of the introduction of mechanized transport which greatly increased producer shares of the world price. But underlying the profitability of cocoa over existing exportable products in the Asante repertoire were ecological or agronomic characteristics with economic consequences. Cocoa enabled Asante producers to make full use of their soils: to capture the forest rent. It also enabled them to make even more use of a given level of labour supply over the year, because the harvesting of cocoa was a major task performed over much of the dry season. Cocoa greatly increased the economic rent on Asante forest land and offered much higher returns to labour than the established export activities, including indigenous gold mining.[22] Cocoa trees represented a vast new stock of fixed capital which greatly increased the returns on land and labour. As this implies, the new production function was not only higher than its predecessor, it combined factors in different proportions. This will be explored in the next two sections.

C. The Implications of Cocoa for Farmers' Choice of Techniques: Extensive or Intensive?

The task of analysing the production function in cocoa farming is complicated by a major controversy that ran throughout the colonial period, and which to some extent continues today, over whether intensive or extensive methods are optimal in Ghanaian conditions. The government agricultural specialists advocated, and the European planters practised, techniques of cocoa farming that were intensive in the sense of involving a high ratio of labour and capital to land. In contrast the African farmers generally adopted land-extensive techniques, economising on the input of cooperating factors per unit area.

The colonial Department of Agriculture propounded a series of recommendations about cocoa production.[23] These were united by an insistence that the farmer's aim should be to maximize and sustain output from a relatively limited area under cocoa. Thus the department vigorously criticised farmers' propensity to establish additional farms, often many kilometres from their original ones, rather than concentrating their efforts on the latter. Officials also advocated that individual cocoa trees should be spaced relatively far apart. They believed that this helped to maximise yield per unit area. Again, they urged farmers to treat disease and pest attacks as intensively as they could. The intensive approach to pests and diseases involved primarily the removal of diseased pods, pruning of trees, frequent and thorough harvesting, and burning or burying the husks of pods. Finally, they emphasized the importance of fermenting the beans thoroughly before presenting them for sale.

Farmers' practices were generally very different. Asante cultivators, like many of their counterparts further south, tended to establish a series of cocoa farms at increasing distances from their home village.[24] They planted the trees very close together.[25] Though pruning and other sanitation measures were not unknown on their farms, they were much more infrequent than the Department recommended. How often they went round their trees harvesting whichever pods had ripened varied with the price they could obtain for the product. When faced with falling yields, whether because of soil degradation or because of infection or infestation, they tended to replant elsewhere rather than to put more labour and capital into trying to restore yields on existing farms. Let us elaborate on this propensity to move and plant again.

In the mid-1940s Fortes recorded in his fieldnotes his findings from a visit to Kwotei, a village about 8 kilometres southeast of Kumasi.

> Most of the men are cocoa farmers in Ahafo, in & around Bechem. According to Opanin Safo, they first went to Ahafo in 1928, when the cocoa in the vicinity of the village began to fail. Safo said this was due to soil deficiencies[.] Farms producing 200 loads are now yielding only 1/10th of that. Most of the villagers have very big farms in Ahafo.[26]

In one sense this continued the long-established technique of land rotation as a response to the tendency for yields to decline in response to continued cultivation. The difference with cocoa was that, as a 'permanent' crop bearing for thirty years or more, it could barely be rotated in any cycle short enough to be relevant to an individual working life. But if fallowing was not available to revive the land under cocoa, the farmers could respond to deteriorating yields by establishing new farms on fresh forest land.

Perhaps most indicative of the land-extensiveness of farmers' methods was what W. S. D. Tudhope, the Director of Agriculture, described in 1919 as 'The universal native practice' in dealing with farm sanitation problems.[27] Specifically, it was directed against capsid infestation. An account of it was offered in 1948 by Kojo Dunkwoh of Kumasi, who was probably himself a cocoa farmer. He called it the 'Weeds Overgrown' method:

> When a cocoa-farm is partly attacked by 'Akate' [capsid], the farmer leaves that portion infected uncleared; left to wild plants, weeds, and climbing stems to overgrow that portion for three years good. The farmer will inspect period by period, and in due course, he will find that . . . the infected area had entirely changed, and had become fresh and flourishing trees with fine dark and long leaves appear [*sic*]. The farmer would then engage labourers . . . to clear out the wild weeds and plants; he will find that, that method had proved successful: the trees turned out to be new, and healthy.[28]

Though this profound difference between the land-extensiveness of African farmers' practices and the intensive approach urged by the government's agricultural experts (and applied by the few European plantations) proved to be enduring, we should recall that in the early colonial period in Asante the question of how best to grow cocoa in West Africa was relatively new to all concerned. It is reasonable to postulate that African farmers sought to place cocoa within the 'mental model'[29] of their long-established land-extensive approaches. They evidently redrew the model to accommodate a permanent crop and the need to plant successively further from home. But the arrival of cocoa did not mean that land had ceased to be relatively abundant. On the contrary, its basic advantage in the Asante (and West African) context was that its physical characteristics made it particularly efficient as a tool with which farmers could exploit that abundance (could tap the 'forest rent'). So it is hardly surprising that African farmers continued to favour extensive methods. It is equally unsurprising that British officials and planters expected intensive techniques to prove the more efficient. The very fact that the country they worked in was a British colony would have seemed inconceivable without there being a gulf in productivity between the economies of Britain and, in this case, Asante. British economic success had been based on technological advances which, in agriculture as well as in manufacturing, were far more capital intensive than were 'traditional' African methods. The early colonial period was hardly one in which most British residents would expect to have technical or economic lessons to learn from Africans. Meanwhile European agricultural officers and planters could draw on knowledge about cultivation techniques in South America and the West Indies, but had as yet very limited experience of the crop in West African conditions.

Over the decades parts of the Department of Agriculture's advice proved to be wrong in its own terms. Wide spacing is no longer considered to be conducive to high yields per unit area, especially with the Amelonado variety of cocoa[30] which was the only one in use on Ghanaian farms before 1950. The intensive approach to farm hygiene failed on the European plantations and by the early 1930s its rationale was undermined by the findings of research conducted in Ghana and Nigeria by the colonial agricultural departments themselves.[31] Already in 1916 Governor Clifford had observed that, despite the recommendations of their department, agricultural officers 'very generally admit that recovery usually results' from the weeds-overgrown method of dealing with capsid.[32]

For the rest the Department's recommendations were correct if returns on land and quality of produce were the priorities, as it assumed. But they were inappropriate in terms of the resource endowment, and the relative factor costs, that faced the farmers and to which the farmers' very different choice of techniques appears to have been a response. With fresh land available it made sense to use it when the yields on an existing farm fell, whether because of fertility or hygiene problems. The 'weeds overgrown' policy saved labour and, to some extent, capital. Close planting fitted a general pattern of using land where possible rather than labour and capital. This may seem paradoxical, so let us consider close planting in more detail.

It had the disadvantage, given that its logic was to save labour (and/or thereby working capital), that weeding young plants was more labourious where they were tightly packed rather than arranged in wide rows.[33] This problem was aggravated by the fact that they tended to be arranged irregularly, having been sown fairly randomly apparently in order to save time in that process. The pay-off came later. Narrow spacing meant the early formation of a shade canopy, thus removing the need to weed thereafter.

Further, in terms of yield, close spacing is particularly superior to wide spacing in the early years of bearing.[34] This early return on investment of labour and capital would be particularly valuable in an economy in which these were the scarce factors. Again, dense planting appears to have been well adapted to the specific ecology of the Ghanaian forest zone. In 1943 a specialist report observed: 'One hears criticisms sometimes of the closeness of the planting, but this seems to be rather an appreciation of the low fertility of the soil, the closer planting being generally more apparent on the poorer classes of soil'.[35]

Farmers' performance over the colonial period demonstrates clearly that their methods produced better economic results than those advocated by the Department and practised by the European planters. At a macro level, Ghana's success in rapidly achieving, increasing and sustaining the position of the world's largest producer of cocoa suggests that the farmers cannot have been far wrong. At a micro level, as I have shown elsewhere, the commercial failure of the British planters in competition with African farmers in Asante and elsewhere in Ghana is precisely attributable to the planters' use of intensive techniques inappropriate to the prevailing set of relative scarcities.[36] Thus we may conclude that the farmers' initial approach, based on their knowledge and prior experience of the economic and physical environment, turned out to be close to optimal for the adoption of cocoa.

But what about learning from experience and responding to change? The behaviour of Asante farmers shows that they did not simply or dogmatically follow a preconceived set of practices, in which case their success could be regarded as a fortunate gamble. Though close spacing of trees became their standard practice, some farmers had experimented with wider spacings. In Amoafo in Amansie the first cocoa trees were deliberately spaced at wide intervals because planting materials were initially scarce.[37] Later, government agricultural instructors reported some success in persuading farmers to space more widely (for example, at 15 foot [4.57 metre] intervals 'instead of the present system of planting about' 8 feet [2.44 metres] apart).[38] Such reports came from Kumasi district in 1908 and Asante-Akyem in 1912.[39] Besides this willingness to experiment with tree spacing, farmers demonstrated a pattern of pragmatic optimizing in the case of preparation of beans for market: they were willing to put in the labour and capital required to ferment beans well, but only when the cocoa-buyers gave higher prices for better quality beans.[40]

What evidence is there of learning, either 'by doing' or from research, among the European interests involved? There are distinctions to be made. Government administrators tended to be relatively open-minded. The statement from Governor Clifford quoted above was in the context of rejecting a proposal from government agriculturalists that the cultivators who did not follow the Department's prescription for farm hygiene should be fined. Again, whereas the Department of Agriculture fretted that Ghanaian cocoa was the 'vin ordinaire' of the world cocoa market, an administrator observed: 'There has been a very strong demand hitherto for the local quality, and as there is room in the wine industry both for vin ordinaire and vintage claret, there seems to be room in the cocoa industry for different qualities of cocoa'.[41] In 1936, however, the Ashanti Confederacy Council of Chiefs gave chiefs' courts power to fine or imprison farmers who presented for sale 'any cocoa which is not thoroughly dry.'[42] Meanwhile the planters and the agriculture department stuck firmly to the intensive approach. Being occupationally focussed on agriculture they may have found it particularly hard to compromise their sense that this approach embodied what they thought of as the characteristically European virtues of discipline, tidiness and energy. The rigidity of this attitude proved fatal for the profitability of the European plantations in Asante and elsewhere in Ghana.[43] The government agriculturalists could maintain the same outlook for longer because they did not have to make money to survive. The department appeared content to run a model plantation on the same intensive lines at what, commercially, would have been a fatal loss.[44] Research findings from colleagues gradually undermined some of its specific initial recommendations, as we have seen. But the general direction of government research on techniques of cocoa cultivation was to find more effective ways of being intensive in West African conditions: to be right next time, as it were.

This scientific effort was stepped up after the emergence of a new and extremely serious threat to the health of cocoa farms. A new cocoa disease, to be known as swollen shoot, appeared in the Eastern Province of the Gold Coast Colony in the 1930s. In 1940 the government botanist, A. F. Posnette, identified its cause as a virus.[45] There seemed to be no practical alternative to the removal of all trees that might possibly have the pathogen. This 'cutting out' policy was particularly unwelcome to farmers because the trees to be destroyed included those which, though diseased, were still bearing pods; plus other trees which as yet showed no sign of infection. For the purpose of this book we do not need to explore the political economy of the controversy that ensued, for the disease had relatively little impact on cocoa output in Asante. Yet the controversy about how to treat it was significant for farmers in Asante as well as elsewhere in that, for the first time, government agricultural science made a major contribution to best-practice in cocoa farming in Ghana. It was, moreover, a discovery that went against the grain of farmers' preconceptions. Having described the rationale for the 'weeds overgrown' method (in the passage quoted earlier), Kojo Dukwoh went on to claim that the method would work for swollen shoot too, which he identified with *akate*,[46] the farmers' name for capsid infestation. But this time the farmers did not know best.

From 1944 government scientists, based at the new Cocoa Research Institute at Tafo in the Eastern Province of the Gold Coast Colony, proceeded with a range of trials designed to offset the damage which swollen shoot was doing to Ghana's cocoa supply capacity. Breeding experiments eventually resulted in a succession of earlier-maturing, higher yielding varieties of cocoa.[47] In 1956 the Ministry of Agriculture made chemical pesticides available to some indigenous cocoa-farmers for the first time at prices that made them seem worth using.[48] Fertilizers were to follow. This combination of innovations,[49] taken as a package, raised the possibility of a fundamentally new production function for cocoa in West Africa. Compared to the production function within which farmers were used to working, the share of capital and (net) labour in total factor inputs would be higher and that of land, lower.

For the present analysis three cautionary observations should be made. The first is that, simply, the new inputs only began to be available at the very end of our period and their initial impact (including on the proportions in which farmers combined factors) was so modest that they can largely be ignored when we seek to explain the property rights regime in factors of production, and the related markets, as they existed to the end of the period. Amelonado continued to account for the overwhelming majority of new plantings through the 1950s,[50] presumably because most farmers could obtain it at no cash cost from their own or their close relatives' existing farms. The 1956–57 crop year—the year of the household survey—was the first in which chemical pesticides were used on a significant scale. Even so it was a fraction of the level at which they were to be used over the following several years. They may have added between one and two per cent to the total 1956–57 crop, though it may well have been less.[51] On the other hand, the new inputs are relevant to assessments of possible subsequent trends.

Second, the economic and ecological superiority of the new inputs and techniques over the established ones remained very questionable even after 1956–57. D. Leston's examination of the evidence concluded that while routine insecticide use had raised yields in the short term—though not in all the Asante field trials—the longer-term benefits were doubtful, especially because the insecticides killed the ants who were the capsids' natural predators.[52] Meanwhile fertilizers could raise yields, but research in southwestern Nigeria concluded that their use was profitable only if producer prices were relatively high.[53]

Finally, how useful was it to raise yields per unit area while land remained relatively abundant? Insecticide and fertilizer use seemed to be profitable for farmers only when the producer price was relatively high and/or when the inputs were subsidized. In short, the technical advances of the 1950s may be seen as significant primarily as a step towards a more intensive approach to cultivation that would (perhaps after further technical progress) eventually become appropriate—in the sense of optimal under the prevailing set of scarcities—as land became scarce in the forest zone.

D. A General Statement of the Cocoa Production Function in Colonial-Period Asante

So let us now try to define the relationship between the various factor inputs and the output of cocoa during the colonial period. That is, before the post-war innovations raised the possibility of a change of production function. The definition we seek is a general one, because that is what is needed for the chapters that follow. Moreover, quantitative precision is probably not a serious possibility. Two contributory propositions are clear: that land remained relatively (though decreasingly) abundant to the end of the period; and that the ratio of capital to other factors rose with cocoa planting. What is more contentious is the relationship between capital and labour.

Land remained abundant in relation to labour and capital through-out the period. After a detailed survey of six villages in Ahafo from 1956 onwards the economist F. R. Bray reported, in early 1959, that it was still the case that 'in much of the country the area of land that he ['the farmer'] may work is not yet the limiting factor of production. . . . The farmer will try to clear as large an area as possible.'[54] Accordingly, as long as it remained relatively cheap to start tapping the forest rent elsewhere, there was no point in investing scarce labour and capital in trying to revive yields on existing farms (perhaps by importing chemical fertilizer). Thus land-extensiveness remained the optimal way of combining factors in farming to and even beyond the end of the colonial period. That is, it made sense to bring more land into cultivation, rather than to invest the scarce factors in extracting higher yields from the existing cultivated area.

The introduction and spread of cocoa farming, together with mechanized transport, raised the ratio of capital to land and labour. There was a qualitative change in the source of capital formation in that, while manual labour was indispensable in the laying of railways and the creation and maintenance of motor roads, the provision of transport infrastructure was no longer essentially a function of labour inputs. A lot of what it embodied was now technology rather than unskilled labour. Capital had been substituted for labour on a large scale, for reasons exogenous to Asante, though head-loading continued to be important at local level. In agriculture the arrival of cocoa meant that, in any period short of several years, output was limited by the existing stock of trees: present productive capacity was largely a function of past inputs into planting. In that sense the contribution of fixed capital to output was greatly increased.

Bray took the view that, given that it was not land, 'the limiting factor is capital and it is this factor that the farmer tries to economise'.[55] In a valuable dissertation completed in 1984 Francis Teal agreed, maintaining that 'the traditional production process in planting has as its economic objects substituting labour for capital, dense planting rather than insecticides and using labour and land intensively relative to capital inputs.'[56] In an abstract sense capital is likely to be the scarcest resource, almost by definition, in a poor economy. But fixed capital differs from unskilled labour in that it is not necessarily fungible and malleable. Historically, dense planting was not a substitute for insecticides: the latter were not a practical possibility for Asante farmers until the 1950s. In general terms the available technology did not embody sufficient capital (as opposed to capital embodying unskilled or semi-skilled labour, as with cocoa trees), or capital in the specific forms required, to make capital the decisive scarce factor.

We can be more precise about the role of fixed capital in cocoa production. Overwhelmingly the main form of fixed capital was the cocoa trees themselves. Their maturation period varied considerably. Since 1945, at least, the conventionally accepted figure for the time taken for Amelonado cocoa to begin to bear has been seven years. But it is clear, from the leading contemporary authorities and from oral testimony from elderly farmers, that during the early decades of Ghanaian cocoa-growing yields generally began earlier. If there was a change, it may have reflected the use of relatively marginal soils in some later plantings. But in 1931, for example, A. W. Cardinall stated that 'The trees usually bear fruit in their 4th or 5th year, when a considerable yield may be expected.'[57] The creation of this form of capital was again, as R. Szereszewski remarked, the ('tool-aided') 'capitalisation of current local labour'.[58] So over terms longer than about six years the one-factor production function still applied: productive capacity was mainly a function of the quantity of labour inputs, providing they were competently directed.

The available quantitative evidence shows that labour was overwhelmingly the main component of cocoa-farmers' costs in the colonial period.[59] Not surprisingly, therefore, they sought to save labour whenever it was possible and useful to do so. The planting of food crops on young cocoa farms to shade the immature cocoa plants saved labour on weeding. Far from saving capital at the expense of labour, as Teal implied, we have noted that close planting saved labour in the medium term because the early creation of a shade canopy cut short the task of weeding. Again, the 'weeds overgrown' method saved labour and any capital goods that might have been involved. Heap fermentation saved on fixed capital goods in the form of wooden boxes. But it also, and probably mainly, economized on labour. In short, we have seen that there was a clear pattern of saving labour in cocoa production wherever possible.

Let us draw the elements in this discussion together. The relatively abundant resource was land. Accordingly farmers sought to maximise the ratio between it and the scarce cooperating factors. In principle, capital was even scarcer than labour. But the possibility of substituting labour for fixed capital did not occur in key tasks until at least the 1950s, when spraying could be used in place of dense planting. Even then it was questionable whether this would achieve a net saving of capital, rather than a shift towards general intensification of land use, because of the cost of spray and of the equipment needed to deliver it. In principle again, the cost of labour could be ascribed to working capital. For besides wages or a share of the crop the employer was often expected to provide clothing, accommodation and food. Alternatively, in the case of food crops, the farmer might provide regular labourers (on annual or sharecrop contracts) with subsistence plots on which they could grow some of their own. This was land which the farmer had obtained virtually free for, as we will see, where rent was paid it was on cocoa trees, not on land used for subsistence-food production.[60] In this latter case, therefore, the farmer substituted land for capital to help meet the cost of labour. We can agree with Bray that farmers economized on labour because they lacked the means to hire more of it.[61] But note that, to the extent that this was so, it did not imply the substitution of labour for capital. On the contrary, the quantity of labour inputs was constrained by the availability of capital. Furthermore, labour inputs were not simply a function of the investment of working capital. Recruiting labour was a problem for farmers, as were the terms on which labour was obtained. But once recruited it was largely self-financing. The conclusion is that labour, like capital, remained scarce in itself to the end of the period with which this book is concerned.

E. Economics of Scale and the Pattern of Demand for Factors of Production

It remains to consider the possibility that returns to scale varied with scale of production. This matters because whether the scale of production influences the cost of producing a single unit may have important implications for the demand for productive resources. Economic advantages of scale may exist in two forms. There may be an entry threshold, a level of resources below which it is impossible to produce or trade the item(s) in question. There may also be increasing returns to scale, where unit costs fall as the enterprise's output rises. Such an effect is entailed where there is a fixed entry threshold, but such a threshold is far from the only possible source of increasing returns. Conversely, diseconomies may exist, giving small producers a competitive edge over large. Common empirical observation suggests that these are most likely to result from institutional rather than technical constraints: where supervision is costly, for example. If scale made a big difference to unit production costs we would expect it to affect the demand for inputs, with implications for markets and perhaps property rights in factors of production. If big farmers were more efficient than small, for instance, it is likely that resources would be bid away from the latter to the former. If the scale advantage was substantial, individuals might find it paid to abandon working for themselves or for a member of their family, and instead become a hired employee on a big farm. One implication of this for property and markets would be that coerced labour would be unnecessary for the existence of large units of production.

Identifying entry thresholds is relatively straightforward in the sense that even a single case of a small supplier existing and surviving against potential or actual competition from larger ones would demonstrate that small-scale production was technically possible and commercially sustainable. Documenting the presence or otherwise of increasing or decreasing returns to scale is much harder. Where quantification is impossible it is necessary to make inferences from the technical and physical characteristics of the production process. It is relevant also to look at the scale on which suppliers actually operated, but this has to be done carefully to avoid circular arguments of the form 'most farmers were small therefore there were no significant economic advantages of scale; there were no significant economies of scale, thus most farmers were small'.

In 1973 Hopkins argued that the 'modern' period in the economic history of West Africa was characterized by scale neutrality in production and trade, and that this era opened, not with European invasion, but with the early-nineteenth century transition in the Atlantic export trade from slaves to palm oil and groundnuts.[62] Subsequent research has, on the whole, provided support for the view that technical scale-neutrality applied in production. On the other hand, there has been controversy about whether economic advantages of scale really disappeared, or rather persisted strongly into the era of 'legitimate' commerce.[63]

Consideration of the Asante evidence suggests that the notion that bigger was more efficient needs to be applied selectively even in trade. In transport the basic unit in the nineteenth century was the head load. In the colonial period foot transport was gradually though incompletely displaced by mechanized methods, but it was still possible for an individual trader to hire space on a lorry or train, most obviously by carrying her own load to the vehicle. In this context it is clear that in terms of labour and capital requirements (working capital to acquire and hold the stock of trade goods and to maintain the labour force) there was no entry threshold to exclude even individual traders working alone, and it is unlikely that returns increased significantly with scale.

Where scale economies surely did exist was in the process of transacting itself. It would have been cheaper for an import-export merchant to deal face-to-face with a relatively small number of people. Hence intermediation was a crucial role: bulking export produce and breaking bulk with foreign commodities. Middlemen could compete with each other for access to export-import merchants: for custom and, especially in the cocoa era, for credit. A large intermediary had an advantage over a small one because he had more supply and/or demand to offer the import-export merchant, and because credit given to him would be cheaper to administer and probably better secured than if the same sum was divided among a number of small traders. Thus it is plausible that increasing returns existed, not in the lower part of the scale of trading operations, but when a trader expanded his or her operations beyond a certain size. This proposition, based on the descriptions of the processes, is consistent with the distribution of trade that we observe throughout the period. The pattern was one of very widespread participation in trade combined with the presence of a small minority of large traders, epitomizing the possibility of making substantial fortunes through exceptionally successful trade. In precolonial Adanse, 'In every town, trading provided the source of revenue for the inhabitants. If one did not trade he [*sic*] was forever poor'; but certain individuals, such as Kwaku Akore of Dompoase, made fortunes from trade sufficient to earn celebrity and official recognition within the chiefdom.[64] In the colonial era entry into cocoa broking was extremely widespread, but this apparently extreme competition did not prevent some people from becoming large-scale operators.[65] Meanwhile the market places were thronged with 'petty traders', but some food-sellers ran large-scale operations.[66]

Turning to the various forms of production in the nineteenth century, the fact that commoners participated extensively in producing gold, kola and rubber indicates that there were no significant entry barriers. The nature of the collection process in gold and kola suggests that while a producer with much labour could produce far more than a lone individual, there is no reason to expect that the unit cost would have been lower. Requirements and advantages of scale appear to have been, respectively, absent and negligible if they existed at all.[67] The case of gold is complicated by the variety of ways in which it was possible to produce it. There has been controversy over the relative efficiency of the methods open to small-scale, commoner producers—panning and the main one, shallow-pit excavation—compared to the method that, presumably, was in practice possible only for stool labour forces: deep mining.[68] In the absence of figures it is difficult to settle the issue definitively. But without a capital-intensive technology that would raise returns to labour it is hard to see why digging deeper should necessarily have been a more efficient use of scarce labour than panning or shallow digging. On the contrary, deep mining required breaking through hard rock, and greater problems of darkness and enhanced risk of flooding. It is therefore not simply because of labour supply constraints that the major study of gold mining in the Akan region, by Raymond Dumett, emphasizes that deep mining was 'the *exception* and not the rule' (his emphasis).[69] For all three exports ownership of production was widely if unevenly distributed.[70] Research is particularly lacking regarding production of goods produced mainly for local markets or domestic use. But it seems highly likely, from the physical processes involved, that scale advantages were also minimal or absent in, for example, snail collection or narrow-loom hand-weaving.

In cocoa cultivation, in West Africa and beyond, expert opinion seems agreed that small farmers were at least as efficient as large.[71] In this context, Figure 4.1 must give pause for thought, because it is at least consistent with the opposite view, that larger farms were able to obtain higher unit output than smaller ones. Let us look more closely.

The graph displays figures for returns to labour on bearing cocoa farms calculated from the findings of the 1956–57 survey of cocoa-growing households in Asante.[72] To be precise, these are returns to the potential labour force, if we were to assume that all adults present could have worked on the cocoa farms. Looking at the top curve, the return on hired labour appears to be higher on the very smallest category of farm than on the next. But that reflects the fact that on very small farms most of the work was done by the farmer and perhaps his or her spouse and children, which makes the apparent productivity of any hired workers on such farms look more impressive than it really was. But the general shape of the hired labour curve, and the uniform trend shown by the curves for more inclusive

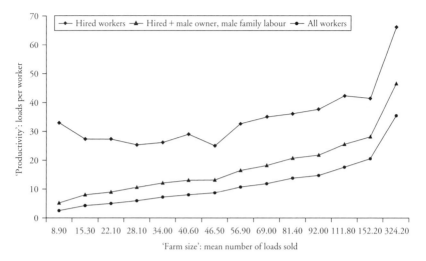

Figure 4.1. Labour 'Productivity' and 'Farm' size: Labour inputs and farmowners' output on bearing cocoa farms in Asante, 1956–57.[73] 1 'load' = 60 pounds (27.2 kilograms).

categories of labour, is clear: the output/labourer ratio increased with scale. There are three major possible explanations for this outcome.

The first hypothesis would be that there really were technical advantages of scale in cocoa production. This, however, seems unlikely in that we lack a strong explanation for how this can have been the case. The tasks involved in harvesting and fermenting cocoa beans, for example, do not appear to be the kind that would offer economies of scale. There was a striking absence of expensive indivisible capital goods: no ploughs or machinery, nothing more costly than cutlasses and fermenting trays. In this respect the alterations to the production function of Ghanaian cocoa in the 1950s, with a new variety plus widespread access to insecticide, appear to have made little or no difference. In 1966 Tony Killick observed that 'The existence of economies of scale in cocoa farming is not . . . well documented'.[74] The bulk of the evidence, and the circumstantial reasoning, favours the view that in physical terms cocoa reproduced an established characteristic of Asante rural production: constant returns to scale.

A second hypothesis would shift the focus from technique to institutions. There is an elegant argument in the comparative literature, formulated by Amartya Sen and others, that in relatively poor agrarian societies there is often an inverse relationship between farm size and returns to land and capital.[75] In this view such relationships are the result of imperfections in the factor markets, the result of which is that small and large farmers face different sets of factor prices. Land and capital are cheap for large producers but very expensive for small ones, while with labour it is the other way around. The small producer, with only a little land and unable to acquire expensive equipment, may as well put in as many hours as he can manage, even when the returns for the extra hours were meagre. Taking all farms together, the result would be that returns to land and capital were higher on small farms than on large; while the opposite would be true of returns on labour. This model, too, is compatible with Figure 4.1. Indeed Teal, using much smaller samples, has suggested that it applies in Ghanaian cocoa farming generally.[76]

Unfortunately we cannot test the matter directly because the labour data in the 1956–57 survey are not matched by corresponding figures for the relationship between output and the scale of inputs of capital and of land. But it seems unlikely that the hypothesis applies, because in two fundamental ways the circumstances were very different from those its authors had in mind. First, land was generally available, easily and often freely, to small as well as large farmers. Second, there were no 'lumpy' capital goods such as ploughs with ox teams which would have induced large producers to invest capital in ways which would increase the returns on labour. There was thus no reason for small farmers to substitute labour for land, and no effective way for them to substitute labour for capital.

Dissatisfied with these two hypotheses, let me offer a third. This links the life cycle of cocoa, as a tree crop, to what we know about the trends in cocoa production, and indeed in demography, at the time the survey was made. The proposition is that the relationship depicted in the charts is not the result of scale economies in production, nor of dualistic factor markets, but rather reflects differences between farmers in the maturity of their cocoa trees. That is, the farmers with the higher outputs tended to have relatively little immature cocoa, hence their labour forces look highly productive because they were working mostly on bearing farms. Conversely, the farmers producing less were doing so, generally, not because their farms were smaller, or would be smaller by the time their expansion was complete, but because the bulk of their trees were still immature. So their labour forces look less productive, not because they were working less efficiently but because a higher proportion of their efforts were going into making and weeding farms that had yet to come into bearing (or at least into full bearing). This hypothesis, like the other two, fits the chart. Unlike them, it is not contradicted by strong counter-arguments. Positively, it matches the specifics of a period in which both current output and future capacity were rising fast. The crop year 1956–57 saw Asante output up for the fourth year in succession, at a new record of 135,000 tonnes, while in 1964–65 it peaked at over 312,000 tonnes.[77] Meanwhile, of 17,911 households enumerated in the survey as owning cocoa, 38.2 per cent had only bearing trees; 22.1 per cent had only new, non-bearing, trees; while 39.7 per cent had both.[78] Significantly, the households who possessed only young cocoa were smaller on average, at 5.2 people, than those with mature cocoa (7.12 for those with only mature cocoa, 7.77 for those with both young and bearing trees).[79] In the context of the rapid population growth described in Chapter 3, this suggests that many new households had recently created their first cocoa farms. The immature cocoa, it seems, tended to be owned by younger households. That their current output was correspondingly smaller does not mean that their use of labour was less efficient. Thus the proposition that there were no economies of scale in cocoa production appears—after all—to hold for Asante, even at the very end of the colonial period.

It is important to add that there is no evidence of significant net diseconomies of scale, apart perhaps from supervision costs, either in nineteenth-century production or in cocoa cultivation.[80] So cocoa is a case where the neoclassical assumption of constant returns to scale actually seems to apply! This helps to explain the distribution of ownership of output throughout the period: always very unequal, but without any clear tendency towards concentration.

In the period from the end of the Atlantic slave trade to the internal strife of the 1880s a sizeable private sector emerged in the production and trading of marketables.[81] I have suggested elsewhere that this sector is best understood as consisting of a relatively small number of producers and traders rich enough to be reckoned among the *asikafoɔ*, the wealthy, of Asante society plus a mass of small-scale suppliers.[82] In other words, the distribution of income and wealth was wide but very unequal. For the twentieth century there is overwhelming evidence that the distribution of income among cocoa farmers was very unequal. This is apparent from every cross-sectional survey that has ever been done, and from other sources besides. But it has yet to be demonstrated that this represented cumulative differentiation rather than simply persistent inequality.[83]

F. Implications

Throughout the period the volume of output was determined primarily by the level of labour inputs. In a predominantly agricultural society land is literally the fundamental factor of production; but in this case, as often in Sub-Saharan history, labour was the most important. The control of labour was critical economically, socially and politically: in the struggles of families and individuals to do more than survive, to achieve social recognition and personal satisfaction; in the ambitions of chiefs to enhance the wealth, power and fame of themselves and their stools. Even so, had the vent-for-surplus theory applied there would have been relatively little for students of the labour market to explain, because even the dramatic rise of cocoa-farming would have been accounted for by the deployment of a leisure reserve. But we saw in Chapter 3 that extra-subsistence output was much larger in the pre-cocoa era than would be expected had there been significant under-use of labour. The present chapter has taken the issue a stage further by noting that cocoa output was to require more labour inputs than the theory can comfortably accommodate. Despite consistent efforts by farmers to economize its use in agriculture, often against the advice of the colonial Department of Agriculture, the potential workforce seems to have been fully engaged throughout the century and a half under review.

I have also emphasized, however, three important complications to the main story of labour scarcity and engagement. One is the disparity that existed in the nineteenth century between the extremely high opportunity cost of labour in the rains, where physical survival could depend on the timely performance of tasks, and the relatively low opportunity cost of dry season work: a gap that was essentially closed in the colonial period by the adoption of cocoa cultivation. The second is the accumulation, absolutely and relatively, of fixed capital in the economy: especially with the coming of cocoa and mechanized transport. Therefore in the short term, which meant several years in the case of cocoa farming, output was a function not only of current labour inputs but also of the existing capital stock. Finally, throughout the period, there was the need for working capital, perhaps on credit, to cover the time between the performance of labour and the receipt of its reward.

This chapter has argued that scale advantages were absent in production, both before and during the cocoa era. This makes it harder to explain how extra-familial labour was obtained. Despite the physical abundance of land shown in Chapter 3, economies of scale could have made wage employment pay for both parties, because larger producers could offer others the chance to earn more by accepting employment than the potential labourers could make by working for themselves. Without scale economies there was no reason for potential labourers to take employment unless they were denied access to land by institutional means.

PART II

Social Relations of Production and Trade, 1807–1896: Absent and Imperfect Factor Markets

The ultimate purpose of this part is to offer a systematic description of the institutions within which users of labour, land and capital obtained these resources, from the beginning of the end of the Atlantic slave trade to the imposition of colonial rule. But in a contentious and, in certain respects, under-researched subject a description can be established only through analysis. The discussion will focus on the extent to which, and the forms in which, markets operated. In the process we will reconsider critically the significance of certain concepts in the literature on the nineteenth century, such as sharecropping and cooperative work groups. More generally, we need to assess how far the ending of the Atlantic slave trade and the growth of the kola and rubber trades strengthened the commercial element in the social relations of production and trade. I will begin with the rules of ownership and control, formal and informal, over the most abundant factor, land, and proceed to discuss those that applied to the scarce resources of labour, capital and credit.

We will see that the Asante state enforced private property rights, notably those of slave-owners and creditors. Property rights create incentive structures, but they also distribute power, giving rights over resources to some and denying them to others. Underpinning the extensive extra-subsistence activity of the Asante economy, as we have seen already, was the state's military and political actions, which secured for Asantes the lion's share of the more valuable natural resources of the neighbourhood.

5

LAND TENURE, 1807–1896

There is a little-remarked dichotomy in the literature on precolonial or 'traditional' land tenure in Asante.[1] The colonial-era ethnography of Rattray and Busia maintained that before colonial rule alienation of land, though legally conceivable, had been rare in the case of mortgage and 'unknown' in the case of sale.[2] This would not surprise an economic historian. In market terms the surplus of the potential commodity could be seen as sufficient reason for the lack of exchange, without necessarily following Rattray and Busia in emphasizing religious constraints.[3] The postcolonial historiography, however, has shown that actually a lot of land alienation went on in the eighteenth and nineteenth centuries.[4] But while Rattray greatly understated the frequency and scale of precolonial land alienation, in his later work he identified a crucial distinction within the Asante conception of land tenure which allows us to reconcile the buying or selling of land with the absence of the conditions of scarcity of cultivation rights which would normally be necessary to account for the existence of a market.

This pivotal distinction was between the land itself and its use or occupation. A logical consequence of this was that property in crops, trees and buildings was regarded as separate from property in the land on which they stood.[5] Ownership was legally superior to use-right, in that it was the landowning stool (chieftaincy) which had the right to allocate use-rights. While holders of use-rights or property standing on the land were entitled to mortgage or sell their holdings, this required the formal consent of the landowner. Use-rights were always conditional upon continued recognition of the landowner as precisely that. The landowner had reversionary rights if the user abandoned his or her property on the land or died without an heir.[6] Otherwise, the maxim *afuo mu yɛ deɛ, asase yɛ ɔhene deɛ* applied: ' "the farm is my property, the land is the king's" ', in Wilks's succinct rendition. Rattray glossed it: ' "The farm (meaning really the produce), or the right to make use of the farm, is mine, but the land, i.e. the soil, is the Chief's" '.[7] Let us consider property in the land itself (Section A) before discussing use-rights and property on the land (Section B). The concluding section will summarize, and put this discussion of land rights within Asante in the context of regional political economy.

A. Property in the Land Itself: A Pseudo-Market

Ownership of the land itself has often been described as corporate, vested in a stool or lineage. It was considered to be exercised by the chief or lineage head on behalf of the present, past and future members of the ɔman or *abusua*. Therefore the interests of future as well as present members of the polity and family were supposed to be taken into account whenever alienation of the land was considered, and the permission of the ancestors had to be given.[8] Hence, alienation was regarded as a last resort. It could take the form of pledging (*awowasi*)[9] or sale (*tramma*). Even after a sale the former owners could ask purchasers to let them buy the land back, paying the original sum plus a premium. Rattray opined that 'Without much doubt public opinion and the influence of a chief would generally result in the request being granted'.[10]

Last resort or no, during the eighteenth and nineteenth centuries there were many instances of the ownership of stool lands being transferred for money, or in settlement of monetary obligations.[11] This was part of the redistribution of land and subjects, largely orchestrated by the central government, noted in Chapter 3. A very high proportion of these transactions seem to have originated in the Asantehene's authority to impose fines on chiefs, often to the extent of extortion.[12] Contrary to Rattray's view, whatever custom or 'public opinion' said, it was highly unlikely that most of the alienations would have been reversed but for the unprecedentedly weak military and political position of the central government at the end of the civil war in 1888.[13] With a gun not far from its head the new government made restorations—without compensation.

According to Wilks, during the nineteenth century court fines also induced land sales at lineage level. Swinging fines on individuals created debts for which their lineages were responsible. Those lineages with land near Kumasi, and to a lesser extent other towns, could and in many cases did solve their need for cash by selling land to 'wealthy functionaries and entrepreneurs in the towns'.[14] Unless all these purchasers had been given stools of some sort, the implication is that—despite Rattray's insistence that 'individual ownership in land was literally unknown'[15]—an individual without a stool could acquire land, through purchase or in settlement of a debt. The land would belong to the individual during his or her lifetime. It only became corporate property if the purchaser was a chief, or became one, or when he died.[16] Chiefs were not considered to have individual property.[17] Commoners were entitled to a life-interest in wealth they acquired for themselves, but upon their death, after deduction of inheritance tax, it became lineage property.[18]

We should note explicitly that there existed superior and inferior levels of ownership of the land itself. This is not to be confused with caretaking or tenancy, where a subordinate stool or village headman was assigned the control of land on behalf of the landowner. What we may call inferior ownership meant that a lineage owned its land subject to continued performance of its members' obligations as subjects, and acknowledgment of the ultimate and reversionary claim of the village headman or stool which had originally granted it the land. Where the land-granting stool had been obliged to sell the land the inferior owner presumably had to recognise the claims of the new superior owner. Land-owning stools extended 'generous encouragement' to non-subjects ('strangers' in the Akan sense) to settle on their lands.[19] At nominal cost—'a small offering of rum to the spirits' of the landowners' ancestors—they would be given land which they could pass on to their heirs, again provided that they and their heirs continued to recognise the reversionary title of the granting chief, and rendered him the payments and services, including military service, expected of subjects.[20] Rattray believed that with the creation of the Asante state the Asantehene came to exercise superior ownership over all lands in Asante, even those of the *amantuo*: whose rights over their respective lands had originally been as complete as the Asantehene's over the Kumasi lands.[21] Busia strongly denied that the Asantehene had acquired such rights.[22] It seems most plausible that the Asantehene's influence over the distribution of land within the *aman* was not based on superior ownership[23] but rather on the capacity of his court to inflict fines that induced mortgages or sales of land and subjects. More generally, LaTorre noted that mere political superordinancy did not in itself give a stool control over land sales by its subordinate stools. In a 1924 court case the Asantehene's *okyeame* ('linguist' or spokesman) Kwasi Nuama ruled that [in customary law] the fact that one of the Asantehene's Kumasi sub-chiefs, the Adontenhene, was the political superior of certain smaller chiefs, did not entitle him to a voice in their land sales.[24]

In the context of a surplus of cultivable land, property in land as such had little value for production and trade. The economic return on ownership was fiscal rather than directly commercial: in the form of the token payments described above plus certain rents on the exploitation of gold and other natural wealth on the lands. We have already seen the example of gold nuggets (beyond a certain size) being required to be sent to the Asantehene's treasury, which would return part of the value, in gold dust, to be divided between the local chief and the finder.[25] Economically, the general point was made, albeit with some exaggeration, by K. Y. Daaku's informants in Adanse in 1969: 'In the old days, the whole land lay empty . . . The land was just there . . . if a chief owned land . . . it only meant in effect that he had a larger supply of venison and nothing more . . . land was not very valuable in the old days'.[26]

The relative abundance of land gave immigrants wanting to settle considerable bargaining power. In this context we must conclude that the reason why rights of ownership of land as such were sought after was primarily political, and to a lesser extent fiscal. If this was a market, it was not in land as a factor of production—except to the limited extent that it was about rights over access to minerals, wild animals and commercially valuable trees—but rather in sovereignty over subjects and ownership of land as such. The 'market' in such property was subject to such heavy political manipulation that it is misleading to call it a market at all.[27]

B. Land Use Rights and Property on the Land

By contrast, land use rights were of immense economic significance: which is by no means to say that they all had commercial value. The pattern of these rights reflected the variety of the productive resources that Asante lands offered, encompassing means to keep body and soul together and also means to make a fortune, together with the capacity of the state to extract a share of such value.

Chiefdoms tended to restrict access to wealth-producing resources such as gold deposits and kola trees, and/or to charge rent for exploiting them. Whereas usually subjects or citizens of that chiefdom (*ɔmani*) were free to start looking for kola or rubber trees, or for gold, non-citizens (*ɔman-frani*) had to obtain permission.[28] Some stools had a policy of refusing it.[29] More commonly, strangers had to pay a large share of their earnings to the landowning stool, usually one third or two thirds.[30] In some places subjects too had to pay,[31] though often at a slightly lower rate such as (in the case of rubber in western Asante) one half as opposed to the non-subjects' rate of two-thirds.[32] In Agogo (assuming that what was true in the 1910s also applied in the nineteenth century, which in this case seems likely) both subjects and non-subjects were free to collect snails, but had to pay a share to the stool.[33]

In Asante generally, it seems that any subject of the landowning stool, or any stranger with permission from the chief, could claim a kola tree simply by clearing the bush around it.[34] In most parts of Asante the same probably applied also to rubber trees that had been similarly 'planted by nature', though an informant in Manso Nkwanta denied this.[35] In Asiwa, near Lake Bosomtwe, I was told that clearing land around a rubber tree did indeed establish ownership of it.[36]

Hopkins has suggested that the decline of the Atlantic slave trade, and especially the growth of 'legitimate' commerce, led to greater commercialisation of land.[37] For Asante, however, there is no indication that new kinds or levels of royalties or rents were imposed on land or its natural products in response to the growth of export production of gold, kola nuts and rubber during the century.[38] The most likely explanation is that the additional demand could be met by weeding around and harvesting naturally-planted trees, without having to devote extensive—or perhaps any—acreages to planting cash-crops.[39]

In a sense the rent charged by landowners, for the exploitation of commercially-valuable minerals and trees found naturally on their lands, was a form of sharecrop tenure.[40] To judge from Rattray's account, it was possible in law for this principle to be applied also to farming. He described what he took to be a leasehold system under which 'the grantee held land from the grantor in return for a fixed annual payment in the form of a proportion of the produce derived from the soil'.[41]

However, in most of Asante at least, cultivation rights were virtually a free good. Land-owning stools offered the right to grow food, literally *didi asaseso*, 'to eat on the soil',[42] without charging anything that could be described as rent, to both subjects and non-subjects, providing that they performed the duties of subjects. Given this, a farmer had the right to continued use of any plot which he or she, or his or her matrilineal ancestors, had cleared from the bush.[43] This applied to lineages establishing farming rights on stool land, and to the individual establishing rights on land belonging to his or her lineage.[44] In general, in food farming as with clearing around kola trees, the investment of personal labour created a sort of private property. As C. K. Meek observed in a broad West African context, 'as in the case of land, so with trees, labour creates rights'.[45]

If access to land for food farming acquired a market value anywhere, it must have been within marketing range of Kumasi and the other towns of central Asante. Wilks and McCaskie have made tantalizingly brief statements that sharecropping emerged around Kumasi, and (according to Wilks) the likes of Mampon and Bekwai, by the early nineteenth century. Publically available evidence for this is as yet elusive.[46] But Wilks is explicit that he sees this case of sharecropping as 'a form of landlord tenure'.[47] They see the growth of sharecropping as partly a response to a growth of urban demand for food during the eighteenth and early nineteenth centuries. Given that most foodstuffs would deteriorate rapidly in a tropical preindustrial environment, and, more decisively, that transport depended on headloading and that 'laden carriers would seldom travel more than ten miles [16 kilometres] a day in the forest',[48] this market could be supplied only from farmland within a narrow radius. Both authors emphasize what they see as an intensification of farming, for example a shortening of fallows.[49] Yet, as was shown in Chapter 3, it is doubtful that land was scarce for the purpose of cultivation, even around Kumasi, until the cocoa era. If a factor market in cultivation rights emerged, it seems much more likely that the newly valuable resource was not soil fertility as such but the profitable location which made it possible for producers to get significant wealth from growing food, just as they might already do from mining gold. Alternatively or additionally, this apparent development of sharecropping in food production may have been a form not of tenancy but rather of labour. This possibility will be discussed in the next chapter.

C. Conclusion

To summarise, sharecrop rents were levied in some of the cases of extraction of commercially valuable natural resources from stool lands. It seems that this may also have been true of land devoted to commercial food farming around the larger centers of population. Elsewhere, any charges for cultivation rights were of only nominal economic value. They were simply acknowledgments of the landowners' superior claims. Thus, while the demand for land as a political and fiscal asset led to a politically-determined pseudo-market in ownership of the land itself, over most of Asante the right to cultivate land was essentially a free good. This distinction was expressed in the legal separation of ownership of land itself from ownership of its products. I would prefer to say that a factor market in land was 'absent' rather than 'missing', because in the economics literature the latter adjective tends to carry the connotation that, if market forces were only allowed to operate, such a market would exist. In this case, by contrast, land as a productive resource was not scarce and only artificial means could have created a market in access to it. The growth of export demand for semi-cultivated products during the nineteenth century was not enough to change this.

Finally, we should put this account of 'internal' land tenure in the context of the regional distribution of natural resources. To recall points made in Chapter 3, the gold dust and semi-cultivated produce that dominated Asante's nineteenth-century export menu were fruits of the forest zone, secured by the military power of the Asante state to the exclusion of the inhabitants of the savanna.

6

THE MOBILIZATION OF LABOUR, 1807–1896

Contrary to the conceited assumption that the social organization of our industrial societies is uniquely complex, it is arguable that the social organization of labour in—for example—nineteenth-century Asante was more complicated still. This is epitomized by the difficulty of separating familial from extra-familial sources of labour, or non-market from market ones. Slaves originated outside the family, indeed usually from outside the society, but over successive generations their descendants were treated increasingly as junior kin. Pawns were extra-familial workers to the master who received them; but in serving as pawns these individuals were usually fulfilling an obligation to their own matrikin, and the contract under which they laboured was fundamentally one between matrilineages (this will be detailed in Chapter 7). Again, the institutions of slavery and pawning had major non-market features; yet there was a market in slaves and even in pawns.

It seems clear that at any given moment throughout the period the majority of able-bodied people were working for themselves or in conjugal or kin-based units. To reflect this fundamental point the various forms of such labour will be discussed in the first section, which will also consider other forms of labour based on (at least proximately) non-market relationships: including subjects' work for chiefs. Yet it was the kinds of labour that could be recruited through a market that offered the main opportunities to principals (individuals, household heads, chiefs) to achieve economic and demographic expansion. For this reason, as well as because of the comparative density of the available evidence, I will go on to devote more space to slave and pawn labour.

A. Self and Social Obligation

Let us consider in turn self and family labour, which was organized to a great extent on gender lines, and then cooperative labour groups and *corvée*. The most immediate source of labour was oneself. Even slaves could work for themselves if they had time left over from the owner's requirements. Slaves, children, wives and husbands all had a measure of economic autonomy: in particular, the right to keep the fruits of their independent labours.[1] But children, pawns and slaves had first to fulfill their obligations to their masters, mistresses and parents. More strikingly, there were crucial differences even between free spouses in the amount of time each had available for independent work, and in the economic significance of that work. Let us begin by considering the division of labour in food farming.

Wives and husbands both contributed to foodcrop production. In that sense nineteenth-century Asante is an example of how the term 'female farming system' can over-simplify when applied as a generalisation to hoe-based farming south of the Sahara.[2] Indeed, Allman and Tashjian put their emphasis strongly on 'mutual assistance' between spouses.[3] It is crucial to disaggregate by task and therefore by season. Rattray was told that men and women were jointly responsible for clearing land and making food farms (yams, plantain and 'corn' [maize] were specifically mentioned).[4] Other sources, however, reveal differences. Men 'clear the forest', noted Coppin in 1884.[5] Reported oral testimonies from old people in the late twentieth century are definite that land-clearance, at least in the sense of removing trees, was specifically considered men's work in the nineteenth century,[6] as well as since. Women may well have done lighter clearing, while the subsequent tasks, from planting to harvesting, were women's work,[7] with the qualification that men might contribute to harvesting because of its urgency.[8] Thus men's contributions were considered essential at the start of the process, and might be important at the end. Overall, though, it was Coppin's view that women did 'the greater part of the farming'.[9]

That women spent (and were socially obliged to spend) much more time on food-cropping than men did is supported by the results of the following simple quantitative exercise. We do not have direct evidence on the time devoted to particular tasks in this period. But Wilks made a valuable set of estimates, inevitably based on more recent observations, about the labour required for a family of 'about five' to grow enough staple foods to feed itself given roughly the same kinds of tools, soils and climate that prevailed in Asante in the preceding few centuries.[10] Wilks envisaged that farming was largely done by males.[11] But if we relate the conclusions reached in the preceding paragraph to Wilks's data on the labour requirements of individual tasks we find a different picture. In Wilks's simulation land clearance took less than 10 per cent of the total labour inputs of a three-year crop cycle: 38 'man-days' out of 399. If we assume that men were also responsible for fencing the field (there is no direct evidence of this, but it seems likely on analogy with house-building, which was men's work),[12] the male contribution totals 88 days: less than 30 per year. Even allowing that men may have done some of the harvesting too (which is assumed to total 26 'man-days' over three years), the implication is that women averaged over a hundred 'man-days' of food-farm labour per year.

The other tasks for which women were responsible were primarily domestic: caring for children, cleaning ('sweeping' and 'polishing floors'), 'going for firewood, drawing water',[13] and preparing food. Rattray was told that cooking was joint men's and women's work, but any impression of parity must be dismissed. Even the most arduous task in Akan cooking was 'generally performed by females', to judge from Freeman's observations at Fomena in Adanse.[14] This was the making of fufu by pounding starch-rich vegetables 'with a large wooden pestle in a mortar. These mills are to be heard going in almost every house, during certain hours of the day'. One person would be 'using the pestle, and the other keeping the food in a lump, by plying it with her hands, that the pestle may act more effectually'.[15] In contrast, men's tasks outside food-farming, apart from the above-mentioned house building, were specifically or potentially money-making ones: long-distance trading, gold panning and mining, kola and rubber collecting, weaving, metal working, woodcarving, umbrella making, hunting and trapping animals, and palm wine tapping.[16]

The implication is that women's primary obligations concerned daily reproduction in the broadest sense; whereas, except at peak labour periods in the agricultural year, men were expected to devote their economic energies to extra-subsistence activity: specifically, to the acquisition of wealth. This distinction was explicit in official ideology. At his annual *Odwira* festival the Asantehene would speak the following words: 'Life to this my Ashanti people, Women who cultivate the farms, when they do so, grant the food comes forth in abundance.'[17] The Queen Mother of 'B-' in her *adae* ceremony completed the statement of the proper economic roles of men and women: 'May the women bear children and men gain riches'.[18]

This is not to say that women (slave or free) were completely excluded from extra-subsistence, thereby potentially self-enriching, activity. It is likely that in this period, as towards the end of the eighteenth century, exceptional women entered and succeeded in predominantly male activities such as long-distance trade.[19] But women's opportunities generally were severely constrained, especially by shortage of labour: lack of time of their own, and lack of assistance in this area from their husbands.

As a result, they tended to dominate or even monopolize those extra-subsistence pursuits which could most easily be combined with their prior domestic obligations, notably spinning (which was specifically considered women's work),[20] and production for, and trading in, local markets. Kokofu women bought fish at Lake Bosomtwe and retailed it in Kumasi.[21] 'Selling garden eggs' was considered women's work as apparently (the passage is not entirely clear) was selling other foodstuffs: plantains, palm nuts and beans.[22] At least in part, such local market activity could indeed be a means of fulfilling those domestic obligations, contributing to the sustenance of the family as well as to higher real incomes. For example, women traded food-stuffs grown in Kokofu at the market about 6 kilometres away in Ahuren. With the money they received they bought meat to cook at home.[23]

The extra-subsistence activities followed by many women tended to be the less lucrative among these occupations: whether because they were a default choice, or because of abundant supply—many women being willing to enter them. Take pottery, for instance:

> It is stated that in ancient times pots were invariably bartered in exchange for food, and that they were never sold for gold dust or whatever was the currency of the time. This caused their manufacture to lie in the hands of the women folk . . . 'as it was not worth the while of the men to make them.'[24]

There is a qualification to this, but one that reinforces the general point. One of Rattray's informants distinguished between 'plain pottery', which was women's work, and more elaborate pottery, which was men's.[25] Only men were allowed to make pots in human or animal forms.[26]

When women participated for their own gain in the more lucrative activities, such as kola collection, they did so on a smaller scale than men—which is not surprising given that they had much less time available for the purpose. Men cleared around kola trees, and thereby acquired ownership of them. Whether partly because of this, or purely because of their time constraint, in the Kintampo area (at least) women harvested the first and third kola crops, which were minor, while men harvested the second crop, which was known as the *abiribara* or plentiful one: 'For then the work was more profitable'.[27]

Women and men gave some help in each other's work. The question of whether—or rather when—help from one spouse to another created a claim to ownership needs to be considered carefully. According to Rattray, 'Any outside assistance from the husband or her children, especially if the rough clearing of the farm and heavy tree-felling had to be done by them would make . . . [the] crops her husband's'. He wrote this in the context of 'A woman might own crops, especially ground-nuts [peanuts], which it was a woman's especial work to cultivate'.[28] In practice—though not necessarily without dispute—if a woman planted and tended a crop herself, it seems that she was accepted as its owner.[29] Thus husbands had the responsibility to clear land on which their wives would grow plantain and other staples. The men did not thereby acquire ownership of the crops. Conversely, wives helped in cash-earning tasks such as washing what the miners had dug up for gold[30] and, less often, long-distance trading. But in these it was generally men who took the roles, which apparently entitled the performer to the prime share of the fruits of the joint labour: going underground,[31] or leading and defending the trading expedition.[32] One of Rattray's informants, appar-ently in Mampon, told him that wives used to accompany husbands to trade in the north and at the coast, 'but all the profits she makes are the husband's'.[33]

Besides help from spouses, married adults could expect contribu-tions of labour from their children, including unmarried adults. Despite the importance of the extended family in other aspects of Asante life, the basic work unit was the conjugal family.[34] In a matrilineal society girls would have helped their mothers whether the labour unit was conjugal or lineage-based. What was significant in this context, therefore, was that boys generally worked for their fathers rather than their mothers' broth-ers.[35] This explains why (in Rattray's example above), when a woman's children—in this context, presumably sons—cleared land for her to plant, the crop became their father's property. In such a case their efforts counted as an extension of his own. Similarly, according to Arhin, 'prospective grooms organized collective self-help (*nnɔboa*) groups of age-mates for work on the farms of prospective fathers-in-law and mothers-in-law, and not on the farms of mother's brothers'.[36]

For the colonial period there are a number of elders' testimonies—oral, and in one remarkable case, written—to the widespread use of the *nnɔboa* system in the form of exchange of labour between neighbours, in rotation, to tackle tasks too large to be handled in the time available by the conjugal family alone.[37] It is easy simply to assume that this was a traditional institution. Yet, having surveyed the literature for Africa generally, Ken Swindell has pointed out that 'Co-operative labour may be a relatively recent phenomenon, or at least one which became more widespread and important after the decline of domestic slavery and the development of new cropping systems'.[38] Thus it may have been a response to an increase in demand for, and a reduction in alternative sources of supply of, farm labour. Further, Peter Geschiere has analysed the emergence of working groups among Maka farmers in southeastern Cameroon. This was a response to the labour demands of their adoption of cocoa (and later coffee) cultivation, especially from the 1950s. He emphasizes that wage labour was 'not unfamiliar' to the Maka, and that, conversely, 'The Maka working groups were certainly not "traditional": although they exhibited some traits also present in older forms of organization, they were based on new ideas of collaboration . . .'[39] I have found only one piece of evidence of neighbourly labour exchange in nineteenth-century Asante specifically. This is another report by Arhin, based on oral testimony from Ahafo in the mid-1960s, that in the pre-cocoa era 'to harvest and split large collections of kola pods, the village had recourse to village *nnɔboa*'.[40] However, the term is in Rev. J. G. Christaller's *Dictionary of the Asante and Fante Language* of 1881, where it is given the general definition of 'co-operation in farming work' without reference to any characteristic form of such cooperation.[41] Further evidence specific to Asante may yet be found. In any case a paucity of references to *nnɔboa* in nineteenth-century written sources does not necessarily mean that it did not exist as an institution (rather than perhaps as an attribute of any joint farmwork) during the period concerned, any more than does the silence in the colonial records about *nnɔboa* in the twentieth century.[42]

Single example though it is, Arhin's description of kola-harvesting by *nnɔboa* provides a specific social form to the general notion mentioned by Christaller. From this it seems likely that the rotating exchange of labour between neighbours or fellow-villagers was a recognized institution in nineteenth-century Asante; but it also seems probable, following Swindell's argument, that recourse to it was relatively infrequent because of the availability of slaves and pawns within households. A possible variation is that masters lent their slaves' services to each other in rotation. This was to happen during the cocoa era except that it involved wage-employees rather than slaves.[43] It is to be hoped that these hypotheses will be tested by further research. It must be acknowledged that prospects are not particularly bright. Oral sources, which help for the colonial period, are unlikely to be reliable on a matter which does not enter formal oral tradition and for a period now too distant to be within the memory of anyone still alive. In such a context it is all too easy for replies to be generated in what one might call the suppository imperative tense ('it must have been'): that is, to be mere backward projections, consciously or otherwise, of later practices or present preconceptions about the past.[44]

Chiefs enjoyed a form of *corvée*: the right to summon work parties of their subjects. According to Rattray 'agricultural' services '(*afum adwunmayo*) were rendered, by the lesser important persons, every man and woman would work on the chief's farm a few days each year'.[45] Similar parties could be used, for example, to construct a building or maintain paths. The early Wesleyan Methodist school chapels in Bekwai and in neighbouring Denyase were built by order of the chief, apparently by his subjects generally,[46] though it is possible that it was just by his own servants. To expand an observation introduced in Chapter 3, the inhabitants of villages alongside the 'Great Roads' were responsible for their upkeep. They could be fined for each 'nuisance' on the road; on the other hand, they might be paid if the demands on their labour were especially great.[47] Travellers were expected to help, by joining any group they came across clearing the way; alternatively, part of the traveller's 'Cloth was torn off as toll'.[48] In at least some areas chiefs used *corvée* in mining. It was recalled in an Adanse village that (in the nineteenth century at least) the chief 'could . . . summon the people to dig up gold for him'.[49] Dumett has emphasized the importance of *corvée* in gold-mining in the Akan states generally.[50]

The forms of labour described so far were all based upon social obligation to the user. By their nature the size of such labour units could only be comparatively small, in the case of the conjugal family, or temporary, as with the *corvée* and, insofar as it operated in this period, *nnɔboa*. Principals wanting labour on a larger scale needed to resort to some sort of market. The rest of this section will consider the evidence about whether hired labour existed and then examine in detail the use of slaves, while human pawns will be discussed in Chapter 7 in the context of credit.

B. Absence of Free Hired Labour

Rattray was 'convinced' that in Asante 'the idea of work of any kind being remunerated by a fixed wage was . . . unknown', and that Asante Twi had no words to express it until 'a Fanti term was borrowed later'.[51] He did not define his periods with any precision. In 1881 two Asante princes resident on the coast hired porters for long-distance trade.[52] The only indications that wage labour may have existed within Asante itself before 1896 also relate to long-distance porterage. Circumstantially, if wage labour developed while slavery and pawning were flourishing one would expect it to be in this sector, because its labour requirements were both large, given that headloading was very labour-intensive, and temporary, which meant that it could be cheaper to use contract wage labourers than to acquire permanent unfree ones. From the Dutch records René Baesjou noted an instance, in 1859, when a merchant from Elmina called Eminsang, trading in Kumasi, hired porters from a Kumasi chief to bring him textiles from the 'English' port of Anomabu. When the party reached Kumasi, Eminsang claimed that part of his order was missing, and accordingly 'refused to pay the porters' wages'.[53] It is not clear how the wages were supposed to be divided between the porters and their master, as they presumably were. But what seems almost certain is that the chief supplied porters from among his own servants, for a commission if not for the whole wage bill. If so, this was not free labour but, rather, a secondary market in the services of the slaves or other servants of the master concerned. We do know that free commoners carried loads for state traders in the Salaga trade before 1874. But this was in return, not for wages, but for the right to share the state's privileges of exemption from road tolls and first use of this market when the trading season began: they carried trade goods of their own on top of the state's load of 2,000 nuts.[54] They are best described as traders paying a labour charge for entry to a closed market.

As part of his pioneering work on Asante long-distance trade, Arhin reported that in the late nineteenth century rubber brokers operating in Ahafo (and in neighbouring Sefwi and Gyaman, which were—at least formally—British and French territory respectively) 'employed' indebted men, mostly from Akyem rather than Asante, 'to produce rubber which they shared with their employer'.[55] If so, this would be the closest the precolonial Asante economy came to the employment of free wage labour, and the only case of voluntary sharecrop labour (as opposed to sharecrop tenancy) in Asante before the cocoa era. The sole source that Arhin cites for this is a report by H. M. Hull, a British commissioner, on his tour in Sefwi. Though Hull was writing sixteen months into the colonial period, he made it clear that this large-scale seasonal migration from Akim was a regular rather than a novel event,[56] implying that it must have begun before 1896, probably several years before. But on re-reading the document, I can find no evidence that producers were 'employed' (in the sense of hired) at all. Arhin may have been misled by the fact that Hull used the ambiguous word 'workers'. In the context, he seems to have done so in order to distinguish producers from 'traders'. Certainly he does not indicate that they were employees:

> it is quite an ordinary occurrence to find Akim towns where all the able-bodied men are absent in this pursuit. Arrived at the site selected, they hire a stretch of land for usually about 5 months. When the time is up they take their produce to the Coast, sell it, buy goods and return to sell these and get more rubber.[57]

Further, while Hull did indeed indicate that the seasonal migrants had debts to pay, the context in which he did so raises an alternative possibility. He writes that 'I have been pretty well all over Akim' and proceeds to assert that Akyem (Akim) 'people' [men?] 'are not energetic, . . . prefer sitting to standing, and doing nothing to work, although they are keen as petty traders and of course collect large quantities of the Kola nut which abounds in their forests.' He notes that 'Gathering rubber is fairly hard work'. It was in this context that he went on to say that 'The Akims . . . are great gamblers and are cursed with rapacious Chiefs, so . . . are continually contracting heavy debts which occasionally must be worked off.'[58] The construction and content of Hull's paragraph invite the suspicion that he could not imagine Akyem men devoting themselves to months of sustained labour many days' walk from home if they had a choice. But can what he admitted was merely an 'occasional' need really account for a regular seasonal migration, moreover one in which it is quite normal to find Akyem towns from which '*all* the able-bodied men' (my emphasis) are so engaged? An explanation which fits much more comfortably with the evidence is that this general migration was a response to a general opportunity to make money, enabling some to get richer as well as permitting others to pay their debtors. We will consider the significance of this seasonal immigration by Akyem tappers in the next chapter. Meanwhile, in the absence of evidence of debt-propelled sharecroppers, we can conclude that the evidence for the existence of any form of hired labour by free people in the precolonial Asante economy is almost non-existent.[59]

C. Sources of Slaves

In contrast, it is clear that slavery was a critical part of the nineteenth-century Asante economy. In 1906, in a petition against the abolition of slavery, the omanhene and elders of Adanse stated that 'every town in this

Ashanti consist[s] of three heads . . . I. The real town born, II. Captives and marrying born from other places, and III. slave borns'.[60] In this sub-section we will see that slaves were occasionally produced from amongst the 'real town born'; but that captives were the major source of first-generation slaves; and that those who reached Asante via purchase or as tribute from the original captors originated mostly from savanna societies to the north.

Rattray described how a free-born Asante could become a slave, an *akoa pa* or *akoa tororo* (a subject . . . in real servitude)'. This could be either through capture in a civil war, or through sale by his or her kinsmen. The latter could arise either out of exasperation, where an *abusua* member repeatedly got himself, and by extension his lineage, into debt; or out of desperation, when financial exigency drove the family to sell a member, who might be 'perfectly innocent' of creating the debt.[61]

In 1908 Nana Osei Mampon, the occupant of one of the major Kumasi stools, Bantama, commented on the intention of one of his captives to return home, taking her children with her: 'If Adjua Badu's people the Wassaws be allowed to take her and [her] children away, it will instigate all other captives mostly forming the Ashanti towns, to leave for their native lands, and this place will be lessened in population'.[62] By 'captives' both he and the Adanse elders quoted earlier presumably meant not only people seized by Asante armies but also those purchased from external captors, and those sent to the Asantehene as part of the tribute from subjugated foreign states. Those taken directly by Asante forces included other Akans, such as (according to the Bantamahene) Adjua Badu.

Most of the captives sent in tribute, and probably all those obtained from trade, came from the savanna to the north.[63] First-generation northern slaves, the *nnɔnkɔfoɔ* (singular, *ɔdɔnkɔ*), were conspicuous in Asante society both visually and linguistically. On their faces they had the ritual scars which were then characteristic of people from their area of origin.[64] They tended to speak little or very imperfect Twi, as Basel missionaries observed on both sides of Asante's southern border.[65] In both respects they are an exception to a classic problem with European eyewitness accounts of slavery in Africa, namely that Europeans often had difficulty distinguishing slaves from other junior ranks of society. However, there was no such means of distinguishing their children, nor Akan slaves, from free Akan. Because of this contrast it is likely that our sources understate the importance of Akan slaves, absolutely and relatively. But there are firm indications from Asante sources as well as foreign observers that the *nnɔnkɔfoɔ* were far more numerous.[66]

The one large quantitative source on the origins of slaves in Asante derives from 1837–42, when the Dutch had an army recruitment station in Kumasi buying captives for military service (after formal manumission) in what is now Indonesia. Asantehene Kwaku Dua Panin had contracted to supply 1,000 slaves within a year but in the event produced only 235 over five years.[67] However, the Dutch obtained 1,170 additional slaves from individual Asantes. The head of the station, Jacob Huydecoper, an Elmina man of mixed African-Dutch descent, recorded the birthplaces and names of most of these additional 'recruits'. Joseph LaTorre has provided a study of this material.[68] There is no reason to think that the origins of these men purchased by the Dutch differed significantly from those of men bought at the same time by Asantes. If the distribution of the geographical origins of female slaves in these years was the same as that of male slaves—which seems probable—then we can assume that the pattern found in the Huydecoper data apply to both genders. LaTorre reports that he was able to identify the geographical/ethnic origins of 605 individuals. Only one was Asante. There were three other Akans, all Brons; and only one Ewe. The majority of those identified, 59.2 per cent (358), were Mossi and 7.9 per cent (48) Gurma, both from what is now Burkina Faso. More than a fifth (23.5 per cent: 142) were from what is now northern Ghana, among which the largest contingents were Dagomba (10.7 per cent: 65) and 'Grunshi' (6 per cent: 36). The latter is a traditional label for members of a variety of politically decentralised societies in northwestern Ghana and across what is now the Burkina Faso border.

I have three comments to add to LaTorre's analysis. First, it seems geographically, politically and economically likely that most of 46 of the remaining 53 identified individuals were brought to Salaga by Hausa caravans from the Sokoto Caliphate.[69] Second, the geographical sources of new slaves varied greatly according to whether and, if so, who Asante was fighting in a particular period. In certain other years of the nineteenth century Ewes or southern Akans would have been likely to figure among any large set of captives. In 1817, for example, after many years of Asante campaigns on the coast, Bowdich's companion Hutchinson found himself petitioned by Fante slaves ('commonly very old, and of the female sex') wanting to return to the coast from whence they had been taken by Asante armies.[70] Again, the 1869 invasion of Eweland furnished Asante with large numbers of captives.[71] Third, LaTorre remarked that the Dutch data conflict with a 'general impression' given by other sources, namely, 'that the "Grunshi" were the prime source of Asante slaves'.[72] The proposition that 'Grunshi' were the most numerous among the captives fits, for example, a somewhat later (mid-1850s) claim that the great majority of slaves imported into Asante were non-Muslims captured and sold by Muslims.[73] Again, according to Johnson

'Most of the slaves passing through Salaga were described as "Grunshi"'. Her sources mostly related to the period during which Salaga was closed to Asante traders, after 1874. But her observation is relevant because many of the slaves would have reached Asante indirectly, mainly via the markets at Kintampo and Atebubu.[74] The crucial point is that the main source of slaves imported by Asante in the nineteenth century was the savanna societies to its north, on both sides of what is now the Ghana/Burkina Faso frontier. In 1970 the geographer Kwasi Boaten observed that 'The many domestic slaves [*sic*] found in practically all the Asante homes attest to the extent and popularity of the slave trade with the north'.[75]

D. Institutions of Incorporation: The Family and the Chief's Household

Over successive generations people of slave descent faced diminishing degrees of subordination. Let us now examine the institutional means by which captives were socially and spatially absorbed into the Asante economy. The first generation of colonial administrators of Asante emphasized that even *nnɔnkɔfoɔ* had been integrated promptly into their masters' families. In the words of C. H. Armitage, Commissioner for the Southern District of Ashanti, 'These natives on entering their "master's" house immediately become one of the family and usually adopt the family name. They work in the interests of the family and share in it's [*sic*] success and prosperity'.[76] Bowdich referred to 'the middling orders' as slave-owners.[77] Despite the secrecy that continues to inhibit the identification of individuals of slave descent, it seems that most commoner matrilineages owned some slaves by the time the slave trade was ended in the later 1890s.[78]

An *ɔdɔnkɔ* could marry a free Asante. Such unions much more commonly involved slave women rather than men. Bowdich noted in 1817 that 'very few of the slaves' had wives.[79] A favoured slave could be an exception, as in the case of 'old Ageana', an official who became known to the Basel missionaries imprisoned by the Asantes in 1869: 'Himself a slave of Adu Bofo, [commander of the Asante army] he, in his turn, owned numerous slaves, and a great collection of wives.'[80] Rattray thought it possible that the only male slaves allowed to marry were the Asante ones.[81] Decades later, Wilks was told by Asante informants that '"in the old days"' . . . 'a male slave might often become the third, fourth or even fifth husband of a (by then elderly) free woman'.[82] It is possible to document rare exceptions: of slave men marrying young free women. The Fortes papers from the Ashanti

Social Survey include an account of the story of a male 'slave bought from one of the traders during the Wassaw War' and settled at the village of Akyina in Kumasi district. His 'masters' were so pleased with his work 'that they decided to marry a girl for him', the girl evidently being a 'free' Asante subject.[83] This slave-groom, as a Wassa, was himself Akan.

More remarkably, the Basel Mission records contain a case, indeed far removed from the Asantehene's court, of an Asante woman marrying an ɔdɔnkɔ.[84] This evidently took place in south Asante, probably in the 1880s or early 1890s. Kwadwo Donko, 'a slave from his boyhood' married 'a certain woman of the same village where he lived [who] offered herself to him'. The woman (who is not named in the source) had herself been pawned as 'a small girl'. Donko, who had become 'a fetishman by profession', had to redeem her from her master, to which end (according to his own testimony, apparently) he had to borrow at high interest. In the mid-nineteenth century Cruickshank had reported for a neighbouring Akan society, the Fante, that it was thought 'derogatory for the daughters of the land to intermarry' with foreign slaves.[85] Perhaps this case is the exception to Rattray's rule that 'proves' Cruickshank's, in the sense that the indigenous Asante subject was herself not free at the time she sought marriage and may well have regarded herself as, unfortunately, an unlikely choice for a more socially eligible suitor. The fact that the place where they were living—to which her master had taken her—was 'remote' could have reinforced her predicament. We can only speculate about whether the social circumstances of the marriage contributed to its tragic ending. Though 'they lived together for a considerable length of time' he eventually murdered her. For this he was executed in 1906.[86] The possibly significant point for our purposes is that, according (presumably) to his own account, what led him to murder was not only that her behaviour had become 'disobedient, peevish & always quarrelsome', and then adulterous, and that she appropriated the food crops he had grown, but the fact that the headmen, elders and the villagers as a whole sided with her entirely. Eventually, 'as nobody of the village cares [*sic*] to speak in his favour concerning the matter, & the behaviour of the wife [was] still unbearable, the husband at last got very annoyed & made up his mind to put an end to the case by murdering the wife'. If his story is true, was the total lack of sympathy he received from the free population entirely because of his individual behaviour or was it partly because he was a foreign-born slave with the temerity to marry a young Asante woman?

In terms of matrilineal principle any children from such a union would have been free[87] and full members of their mother's *abusua*. The children of a slave mother and a free father would found a cadet branch of the father's lineage, whose unorthodox relationship to the matrilineal system would be concealed by a powerful legal prohibition on revealing anyone's social origins.[88] A rare glimpse of this practice, via its legacy, was offered in 1945–46. Then the Ashanti Social Survey asked 592 married women in the town of Agogo in Asante-Akyem to which matriclans they and their husbands belonged. In an exogamous system, as this was, one would expect that all spouses would be from different clans. In fact nearly eight per cent (46) of the women

> stated that their husbands were of the same clans as themselves. A check of the information suggested that some of them had given wrong information, but the majority were women of slave descent or belonging to attached lineages not of the authentic line of descent of their husband's lineages. Several such attached lineages are found at Agogo, associated especially with the two largest and politically most powerful lineages . . . The rule of clan exogamy is thus still strictly observed. . . .[89]

During the reign of Asantehene Mensa Bonsu (1874–83) the Omanhene of Kokofu, Osei Yaw, was destooled by the elders 'for being fond of disclosing the origin of his subjects (i.e. reproaching them with their slave ancestry)'.[90] An *ɔdɔnkɔ* was a legal person, able to swear an oath [and thereby bring a case] and recognised as a competent witness. A slave could also own property, including another slave, and (at least residually) might inherit from the master.[91]

The family was not the only institutional framework for the incorporation of foreign slaves and their descendants into Asante society. Low concentrations of slaves could be absorbed in this way. But large concentrations, such as were acquired by major chiefs, needed to be organized and controlled within a larger social unit. Chiefs dealt with this problem primarily through the institution of the royal household, the *gyaase*. Large numbers of new slaves seem to have been sent to join its members, the *gyaasefoɔ*.[92] As Rattray reported for the chiefdom of Kumawu, slaves 'were given land and their descendants formed whole villages'.[93] We may assume that by the end of the eighteenth century, and indeed well before, the majority of *gyaasefoɔ* were not *nnɔnkɔfoɔ* but rather were descended from them, in whole or in part. Rattray noted for Kumawu that the villages of slaves and their descendants 'could be sold *en bloc*, when the inhabitants became the subjects of the purchaser'.[94]

The *gyaasefoɔ* constituted a stool labour force who not only fulfilled domestic and ceremonial duties but also discharged the state's direct involvement in production and trade. Rattray stated 'there is little doubt that the *Gyasefo* were in olden times recruited from the slave class'.[95] The chief and elders of Adanse implied as much when they complained, in 1906, that if slavery was abolished 'what could the Kings, Chiefs and Headmen' do, for 'all our drums, blowing horns swords [sword-carrying], elephant tails Basket carrying and farming works are done by these' [*sic*].[96] In Kumawu 'Slaves purchased at Salaga become hammock-carriers, or if females, floor-polishers or washerwomen'.[97] The domestic role of slaves and their descendants within chiefs' establishments is exemplified in remarks made by the queen mother of Agogo in an interview in 1946. She said her house-maids 'were descendants of slaves and hostages taken in the Ashanti wars. The custom, [*sic*] has been, for each slave to send a daughter to serve the Queen Mother'.[98] The *gyaase* was formally sub-divided into groups responsible for specific functions in the chiefdom, from cooks to executioners. The hornblowers were also the stool's traders, the *batafoɔ*. The *gyaasefoɔ* contributed directly to the stool's supply of marketable commodities. In Kumawu, for example, whereas the chief claimed only a portion of war captives and kola nuts obtained by his other subjects (one third in the case of kola, for instance), his were all the captives taken and kola collected by the *gyaasefoɔ*.[99] One of the prime functions of the *gyaasefoɔ*, as a later Gyaasehene of Bekwai testified, was to farm for the palace.[100] It was presumably as a result of their efforts that Bowdich could write that 'The chiefs are fed bountifully by the labours of their slaves'.[101] The missionary Coppin, keeping a diary of his journey to Kumasi in 1884, described the village of Adumasa (a few miles from the capital) as having 'about 50 people the slaves of a chief in Afeyiasi [Feyase] which we passed through a little while before. They work the plantations.'[102]

A feature of the social—and spatial—absorption of large con-centrations of slaves, and also of their economic deployment, was the dispatch of newly-imported slaves 'to create plantations in the more remote and stubborn tracts'.[103] Bowdich was referring specifically to the years following British withdrawal from the Atlantic slave trade in 1808, but a Basel missionary and his party came across what appears to be evidence of the continuation of this practice much later. Travelling in Asante-Akyem during 1884, the group 'marched from Kumawu to Agogo in one day, passing only small hamlets, and hunters' houses. In the second part of the march apparently most of the inhabitants of such settlements turned out not to be able to speak twi [*sic*], being "donkos" [*nnɔnkɔfoɔ*]'.[104]

It may useful to suggest that there may be a link between the establishment of slave settlements and Wilks and McCaskie's account of sharecroppers, comprising both slaves and free subjects, producing food for urban markets. In view of the present lack of published evidence on this it may be suggested that in the case of the slaves sharecropping was a labour rather than, as Wilks suggests, a tenancy arrangement. Sharecropping is plausible as a device by which slaveowners could organize their workforces to produce food for the market despite supervision problems.[105] We may assume that masters sought to maximize the crop produced for them by the slaves. This entailed motivating the slave, whether partly by carrot or entirely by stick, to maximize his or her output; and securing as large as possible a proportion of the crop above what was necessary for the slave's own consumption. The problem was that close supervision of farm production would have been difficult in what was still a fairly lightly-populated region. In this context it may have been enlightened self-interest for slaveowners to allow slaves to keep what Wilks suggests was 'a nominal third (*abusa*) of the produce'.[106] Bowdich's observation, quoted above, that newly arrived captives were sent to farm the more distant and difficult lands, concluded that 'their labour was first to produce a proportionate supply to the household of their Chief, and afterwards an existence for themselves'.[107] This may have meant a formal share of the harvest. Masters would thereby have put a ceiling on their exploitation of the slaves and given the latter an incentive to maximise their output.[108] By making that ceiling high the owners retained the lion's share of the surplus. In practice, given the difficulties of preventing slaves from concealing part of their harvest, it is likely that slaves managed to get more than that in total. In short, a sharecropping arrangement may have been a compromise between the slaveowners' desire to get as much out of their slaves as possible, and the slaves' capacity deliberately to limit their labour inputs as well as to conceal part of their output. Where sharecropping slaves were settled near urban markets they would produce foodcrops; further afield their 'surplus' would presumably be in a commodity such as gold or kola (especially as most of the kola trees were relatively distant from Kumasi).[109] It is interesting to note that Bowdich implied that even slaves, along with the free poor, needed to sell produce on the market in order to secure 'an existence for themselves', having first supplied their chief's household. When describing their vulnerability to being plundered by state officials, in the context of the 1817 proclamation of a ban on such abuses, he stated that the pilfering took place 'either in their distant plantations or *on their arrival at the markets*' (my emphasis).[110]

E. Supply and Demand for Slaves

In the aftermath of British withdrawal from slave-buying the inflow of captives appears, not surprisingly, to have exceeded Asante's internal demand. When Bowdich visited in 1817 he heard that few slaves were being bought. As a result, 'so full were the markets of the interior', prices were extremely low.[111] In the early 1820s the government sought to reduce the numbers of slaves it received in tribute and replace them with other forms of wealth. Yet this policy was not—perhaps could not be—sustained. Asante's requirements for human tribute stabilized at relatively high levels. Part of this was because of the tributaries' resistance or inability to switch to alternatives: those provinces which could pay in gold or livestock were already doing so.[112] But part of it is attributable to rising demand for slaves within Asante. Despite the availability of tribute and direct capture (war or raiding) as sources of supply,[113] in the middle decades of the century Asantes appear to have been very active as purchasers of captives. Huydecoper reported that he was in competition with substantial demand from inside Asante. This, according to LaTorre's study of his correspondence, obliged him 'to be conciliatory with those who offered slaves to him, for fear that they would sell their slaves elsewhere if not satisfied with his terms.'[114] His successor, H. S. Pel, observed of the Asantes in 1842 that ' "the greatest part of their slaves are purchased in various markets in the interior" '.[115] Relying apparently on other sources, the author of an early secondary-source description of Asante published a similar statement in 1857. For all the war prisoners they took themselves, wrote Rev. J. Leighton Wilson, 'much the greater proportion' of slaves owned by Asantes were 'sold' to them after capture in 'the interior'.[116] To judge from the fragmentary figures available, which are collected in an appendix to this chapter, slave prices in Asante revived from c.1820 to c.1840. Part of this is attributable to re-export demand mainly from the Fante states, fuelled by the take-off of palm oil exports there. The Dutch recruitment-buying mission also contributed, temporarily and modestly. But the price revival is also further evidence of increased market demand for slaves within Asante.

With the available technology, as we saw in chapter 4, both gold and kola production were highly labour-intensive. Much of this work was done by free people operating within the conjugal family unit, by pawned Asantes, by *corvée* labour for chiefs, by slaves imported before 1807, and by descendants of such slaves.[117] But it is a reasonable assumption that the growth of net imports of slaves contributed to the expansion of gold and kola output from about the 1820s to about the late 1860s. That is to say, much of the increased labour was supplied by slaves who were retained within Asante when previously they would have been re-exported.

A general feature of the period between the British invasions, 1874–96, was an apparent increase in the numbers of slaves running away from their masters, combined with the continued and, in the early 1890s, intensified import of northern slaves. Some slaves fled Asante for the Gold Coast to take advantage of the British emancipation ordinance.[118] It may have been partly to reduce the incentive to escape that the Asante government announced in 1876 that in future funerary killings should be restricted to convicted murderers. That the risk of oblation was an effective motive for escape is consistent with a remarkable source. This is a potted autobiography by a man baptised in the Gold Coast by the Basel Mission as Mose (Moses), who had earlier been an ɔdɔnkɔ in Asante under the name Musa Dagarti.[119] He fled from slavery, apparently before 1876, shortly after his owner had threatened that ' "As soon as a human sacrifice comes again, I will exchange you (for a slave condemned to death)." ' His master unwisely sent him to buy salt outside Asante, to the south in Akyem. He was presumably escorted, as part of a larger expedition, but he managed to stay there rather than return to Asante.[120] However, it seems clear that both before and after 1876 most slaves remained with their masters.

The import of new nnɔnkɔfoɔ continued, despite the reduction in tributes consequent upon the diminution of Asante's empire. Indeed, the flow appears to have increased in the early 1890s, when the northern slave markets were flooded with supply from the Almani Samori Ture. Though it was as late as 1895 that Samori Ture's forces established themselves in the northern hinterland of Asante,[121] informants place such emphasis upon him as a source of Asante slave imports[122] that one must assume that for several years beforehand people captured by his army had been reaching markets attended by Asante slave-buyers.

Though outpaced by supply it is very likely that the demand had also risen after the civil war, as Asantes sought to offset war casualties, and the victorious chiefs tried to populate the lands abandoned by the many of their enemies who had taken refuge in British territory. These chiefs found at least a partial solution outside the market. War captives were resettled in their captors' lands, in continuation at an intra-Asante level of the long-established policy towards people captured in Asante's external wars. For example, Kokofus captured by Dormaa forces were settled on Dormaa lands at the village of Kwameasua, and they (or at least their descendants) were treated as Dormaa subjects.[123]

There was also great demand for captives from private entrepreneurs engaged, in particular, in the kola business or the booming rubber trade. This had to be met largely through the market. A detailed example is provided by an archival record of statements made by about twenty Asante and Fante rubber traders and producers from British territory who were operating in the forests of eastern Côte d'Ivoire in 1897. The documentation is the result of their misfortune; their having been dispossessed during a local conflict which became a diplomatic incident between Britain and France.[124] They included Kwamin (Kwame) Diaba, from Adubease in Adanse, who based his rubber business in the Dormaa area, apparently on what became French territory. The local chief allowed him land on which he established 'a village and farms'. Besides his wife and children he claimed that he had had 'about 40 servants' there.[125] Arhin notes that 'servants' was a euphemism for slaves in the context of the British prohibition of slavery on the Gold Coast[126] and, one may add, of fear among Asante owners that this would be extended to Asante. From fieldwork in 1970 Arhin learned of a trader from Dormaa itself who was said to have had about 170 slaves 'during the Samori wars'.[127] As Arhin has commented, the fortunes of individual markets—Atebubu, Kete Krachi, Kintampo and Wenchi—'waxed and waned with the supply of slaves', waning finally when British forces drove Samori Ture's caravans away.[128]

It is important to emphasize that the nineteenth-century trade in slaves operated widely within Asante society and deeply within the forest heartland of the country. An aspect of this is that physical marketplaces for slaves were far from being confined to the frontiers of the state. On the contrary, there was a wholesale trade in slaves supplying local markets. Informants in Adubease in the 1960s stated that slaves had been sold in the old market there.[129] LaTorre reported from fieldwork in 1975 that 'in southern Asante, Ankase is remembered as a place where one could go to buy slaves, if the trip to Salaga was considered too far'.[130] The reference to Salaga implies that this was before 1874, since it was then that Salaga broke loose of Asante dominance. At some point during the next seven years the Asante government created a replacement major kola market at Kintampo.[131] In northeastern Asante 'Slaves were sold at Asokore', in what was evidently a regular market.[132]

Finally, in this section, it should be made explicit that the market in slaves was precisely that. The most comprehensive tabulation so far of recorded observations of slave prices during the period is presented as an appendix to this chapter. It demonstrates vividly that prices were differentiated according to the age and other characteristics of the slaves, and varied over time. The evidence does not establish a clear long-term trend.[133] But it shows movements in prices paid by Asante buyers, within Asante and in the savanna markets from whence came Asante's main supplies, which can be readily attributed to specific shifts in the balance between supply and demand. For example, prices were very low in the two periods of well-documented over-supply: the immediate aftermath of the collapse of British demand for slaves, and the Samorian episode of the earlier 1890s (though in 1895–96 prices may have risen at the prospect of colonial invasion leading to suppression of future opportunities to buy slaves).[134] Conversely, in the early 1840s, when competition for slaves was more intense and supplies less abundant, prices were much higher. To come to Cournot's classic definition of a market, it also seems clear that the 'law of one price' operated.[135] While prices fluctuated over time and varied at any one time between slaves with different attributes, at any given time there appears to have been a going rate for slaves perceived as having similar characteristics, as was exemplified by Huydecoper's lack of room for manoeuvre. In this context it is significant that (as noted earlier) state traders enjoyed the privilege of first access to the Salaga market when the trading season began, to enable them to take advantage of the probable early-season peak in kola prices. This 'imperfection' is most plausibly seen not as compromising the market nature of the kola-slave trade, but rather as a rent-seeking response to the very fact that it was a genuine market, in which competition created a price-equalizing tendency.

F. Slavery and the Labour Force

Despite the assimilative dynamic of the Asante institution of slavery, the latter term was no misnomer. Not only were slaves frequently (even usually, at least in the 1840s and 1890s) acquired by purchase, they could also be resold (or sold for the first time, if acquired other than by purchase). This was not a mere hypothetical possibility. Though Huydecoper believed slaveowners were very reluctant to re-sell, precisely such re-sales (motivated by the need to pay court fees or fines) were the 'best' source of the 1,070 slaves that he bought from private sources (i.e. other than from the Asantehene).[136] Musa Dagarti's testimony confirms that re-sale was an option in the minds of slaveowners.[137] Conversely, slaves' rights could be highly contingent. Owners were not allowed to appropriate possessions that slaves acquired for themselves but, according to Rattray, 'An Ashanti proverb sums up the situation . . . thus: "A slave may eat to repletion while his master remains hungry, but what the slave has is, after all, only wind in his stomach"'.[138] Slavery in Asante had specific characteristics; but there is no reason to dispute the applicability of the general definition of slavery as ownership of one person by another.

Very large numbers of people of slave or slave-descent were available for work. Maier has suggested 6,500 as a rough approximation of the average number of new slaves imported per year, including Akans.[139] Her calculation represents only captives given in tribute or taken by Asante forces themselves, and thus presumably should be regarded as applying to the era of empire before 1874. If we follow Pel and Wilson (quoted above), the estimate for the total of newly imported slaves should be more than doubled for the 1840s and 1850s, once slaves bought in the markets are included.[140] Rather than offer even more speculative numbers for other years, let us draw the implication that matters for the present discussion. Every year the numbers of first-generation slave labourers was diminished by death, injury and illness. Accordingly it is impossible to make a serious quantification of the cumulative effect of slave imports on the size of the labour force in Asante. For what it is worth, the Basel missionary Kühne was reported by a British journalist as saying in 1874, after his four years as a prisoner of the Asante state, that '"the population appears to consist in about equal parts of Ashantees and slaves"'.[141] This seems remarkably high, not least given the risk that such a ratio could pose to the security of masters and the state. What is clear, and crucial when discussing the labour market, is that at any one time masters as a whole relied on slaves forcibly imported within the last year or two for several per cent of their labour forces.

Overall, gender and the conjugal family provided the major lines on which the non-market labour force of nineteenth-century Asante was organized. Meanwhile the labour market was exclusively in slaves and pawns. Quantitatively, by far the biggest change in the Asante labour market between 1807 and 1896 seems to have been a major expansion in the net importation of slaves: by chiefs and commoners alike. Pawns were another major source of labour, and pawning was a significant component of the labour market. Pawns worked in farming,[142] trading,[143] gold mining and kola harvesting.[144] But pawnship was also a credit institution and we will consider it under that heading.

G. Conclusion

Non-market mechanisms, especially coercive ones, were widespread and important in the supply of labour—and we will see in the next chapter that this was also true of the other scarce factor, capital. The economic distinction between subsistence or, broadly, reproductive activities and extra-subsistence, potentially enriching ones was to a large extent institutionalized on gender lines by a division of labour which concentrated responsibility for the former in female hands while giving men the obligation and opportunity to focus their energies on the latter.

The chapter has also considered the sparse evidence about co-operative work groups and sharecropping in agriculture, and suggested that both should be seen in the context of the widespread use of slave labour. That is, such work groups were probably rare because of the widespread availability of slaves and pawns, while share terms were used to overcome information-asymmetry problems by giving slaves a positive incentive to work in the absence of effective supervision. During the early nineteenth century the combination of the closing of the Atlantic export market for slaves and the expansion of export demand for kola nuts led to a reorientation of the export sector of the economy from the re-export of captives to production of exportable goods within the country. This in turn seems to have led to a major increase in the permanent importation of slaves. The importance of slavery within the economy was undiminished by the time of the British occupation. On the contrary, the flow of imports had recently intensified. By contrast we have seen that the apparent evidence of an emergence, before the colonial takeover, of a modest amount of free labour in rubber tapping and perhaps porterage turns out to be a mirage.

APPENDIX

NINETEENTH-CENTURY SLAVE PRICES

The following table offers the most comprehensive assembly so far of the quantitative observations on slave prices within Asante, and in the markets just north of the forest zone in which Asantes purchased slaves. For most of the century this primarily meant Salaga. But in 1874 Asante permanently lost control of the town and Asante traders were excluded from its market. During the remaining 22 years before the colonial occupation Asantes instead bought slaves in Kintampo or Atebubu. Even for these years, though, Salaga prices are a pertinent guide to the prices paid by Asante buyers because the same Hausa caravans would visit both Salaga and the markets still attended by Asante traders, to buy kola from them as well as sell them slaves.[1]

The table was inspired by earlier ones constructed by Joseph LaTorre and Emmanuel Terray.[2] I began by checking, as far as I could, those of their figures that fall within the scope of this study; and supplemented them with such further observations as I was able to obtain.[3] In interpreting the numbers it is important to bear in mind the nature of the individual observations. It will be seen that the captives concerned spanned different ages, both sexes, and were not always sold in open market places. So the context of each observation is indicated in the table.

I have followed LaTorre in converting the values given in the original sources into the standard Asante gold weights, using the same conversion rates. This method has two advantages. First, the Asante gold weight system was the way in which Asantes themselves calculated prices within their economy. Second, the value of gold was relatively stable against European currencies over the period, and also over space. In contrast, the value of the obvious alternative currency, cowrie shells, varied greatly with distance from the coast and depreciated during the nineteenth century.[4] At Salaga the cowrie lost more than half its 1820 value by the 1870s.[5] However, a rate of 1,000 cowries to the British shilling and German mark then endured until after 1889, the date of the final cowrie-denominated report of slave prices at Salaga.[6] I have omitted one set of cowrie prices for slaves at Salaga, because they are undated—but they fall within the range of prices in the table.[7]

The most widely available commodity measure is the price of kola nuts. In several instances the table gives kola values for slaves. This helps us towards a sense of the real, as opposed to nominal, price of slaves. But it should be cautioned that kola prices varied drastically according to season: 'A load of kola costs, according to the time of year[,] 6–20 shillings'.[8] The unit in which kola nuts were measured was the head 'load' (which Bowdich, quoted below, calls a 'basket'). This comprised 2,000–2,500 nuts, weighing—according to a colonial survey—about 80 lbs (nearly 40 kg).[9]

The values in the table are given both in British pounds (£1 = 20 shillings and, first, in *agyiratwefa*. The latter was an Asante unit of gold by weight. In European sources it was known as the *ackie*, a form used for brevity below. The *ackie* was about 1.95 grams or 1/16 of a troy ounce (which is 31.2 grams, compared to 4.4 grams for the standard ounce or *mithqal*). It is useful to relate the *ackie* to a larger unit which is mentioned elsewhere in this book and in one of the notes below: the *peredwan*, which was about 70.4 grams, 2.25 troy ounces or 16 standard ounces or *mithqals*.[10] On this basis 1 *peredwan* equalled 36.1 *ackies*, which is perhaps the best metric. In practice the conversion rate seems to have varied somewhat. Bowdich reported from 1817 that there were 40 *ackies* to the *peredwan*, with 36 ackies being equivalent to the slightly smaller *benna*.[11] From the early 1870s Ramseyer and Kühne implied that the *peredwan* was 34.7 *ackies*, or possibly 27.4.[12]

The *peredwan* was 'conventionally valued at £8 sterling in the nineteenth century'.[13] According to Bowdich the [troy] ounce was valued at £4 sterling in Asante in 1817, implying (given his statement that 1 *peredwan* = 40 *ackies*) £10 per *peredwan*. Ramseyer and Kühne reported eight pounds two shillings (decimal £8.10) to the *peredwan*.[14] From several observations LaTorre derives the generalisation that before 1843 1 *peredwan* = £9.05, or 1 *ackie* = 5 British shillings (£0.25).[15] The latter actually implies £9.025 to the *peredwan*. To avoid this ambiguity, the relevant figures in the table below (those within the years 1820–43) are calculated directly in *ackies*. For the rest of the century LaTorre has £8.15 to the *peredwan*, or 4 shillings 6 old pence (£0.225) to the *ackie*.[16] The latter means 4,500 cowries to the *ackie* for those later-nineteenth century prices which were quoted in cowries.

Some of the late nineteenth-century prices, mentioned in German or Swiss-German sources, were given in marks. This was presumably the German reichsmark, created in 1872. Its value was fixed against gold until 1914. It was thus also fixed against other gold standard currencies: including sterling, at 20.429 marks to the British pound, very nearly 1 mark to 1 British shilling.

To summarize the conversion rates used in the table below (except where a different rate is indicated in the source itself): 1 *ackie* = 1/36 *peredwan* = £0.25 to 1843, £0.225 after 1843 = 4.957 marks (1872 onwards) = 4,500 cowries (Salaga only, in the later nineteenth century). As a precaution against conversion errors the prices in the units used in the original source are given (in brackets after the *ackie* price) wherever I have been able to do so.

Table 6.1. Nineteenth-century slave prices in Asante and the northern markets

Year	Northern markets	Asante	Source
1817	A1.2 (2,000 cowries or 1 'basket' [termed a 'load' of kola nuts]): 'the greatest price given; so full were the markets of the interior' (Bowdich, *Mission*, 333).[17] No A or £ equivalent given.	A12.8; £3.20 (0.8 ounces) per man: rate at which the royal treasurer commuted into 20 slaves a debt owed to the Asantehene in gold (Bowdich, *Mission*, 296).	Bowdich
1823		A6–7; £1.50 ('about' 30 British shillings) [6.77 *ackies*] in Kumasi	*Royal Gold Coast Gazette*
1836		A24–32; £6–8[18]	LaTorre (MK 4005).
1837–42		A34; £8.50 [presumably for an able-bodied man]: 'paid by the Dutch recruiter in Kumasi, 1837–42'. This seems to have been a premium rate.[19]	LaTorre (NBKG 519).
pre-1867[20]		A45; £9.79 (200 marks)[21] for a boy of 11+, sold to an Asante official by a Muslim northerner. Source states the sale was within Asante; given the pre-1874 date, was it in fact in Salaga?[22]	'Mose'
1867–74		A18 (£4) apparently paid for Wassa female bought in Kumasi as a young girl[23]	NAGK D905

Year			Source
1871		A34; £7.75 (£7 15/-): valuation of a man slave presented by Asantehene	Ramseyer and Kühne (A)
1872		A22; £4.95 (22 dollars):[24] a 'steady man' (an Ewe captive), bought by Ramseyer and Kühne themselves while in captivity in Kumasi	Ramseyer and Kühne (B)
pre-1874	A8–15.55; £1.80–3.50 (36,000–70,000 cowries) at Salaga Equivalent of 3–5.8 loads of kola		Ramseyer and Kühne (C)
pre-1874	<A8; 2–3 loads of kola		Brackenbury
pre-1874	A2.22–3.33; £0.50–0.75 (10–15/-) for a man at Salaga	A32; £7.20 (2 ounces of gold). The source gives the price also as 36 dollars, which might imply A36.[25]	D. Asante
pre-1874	A5–11.1; £1.125–2.50[26] (4 ½–5 loads {*apakan*} of kola, i.e. 9–10,000 nuts) for a man at Salaga A7.77–15.55; £1.75–3.50[27] (14,000 kola nuts, i.e. 7 loads) for a woman at Salaga		Rattray
1877	A4.5 minimum, A6.75–9 average (£1 minimum, £1/10/- to £2 average), and slave exchanged for 'an Arabian cloak' at Salaga		Opoku (Jenkins)
	A4.35–17.40; £0.98–3.92 (20–80 marks: 'highest' 60–80 marks; 'but one can also see 20–30 marks. I saw one [slave] sold for 27 marks, another for 40. A third was exchanged for an Arab robe')		Opoku (Johnson) (same visit, different text)
1884	A8.9–A13.3 (£2–£3) 'average price of a strong		Kirby

	and healthy slave' in Kintampo	
1887	A26.7; £6 (120,000 cowries) for a 'full-grown man' or 'grown up girl'	Firminger
	A22.2; £5 (100,000 cowries) for a boy of 15	
	A15.5; £3.50 (70,000 cowries) for a child, boy or girl	
	These are 'average' prices at Salaga.	
1888	A30.4; £6.85 ('about 140' marks) for a man; 'nearly the same' for a 'female slave', in Salaga	Von Francois
	A15.2; £3.43 ('about 70' marks) 10-year old for a girl in Salaga	
1889	A6.7; £1.50 (30,000 cowries; 30 shillings): valuation 'by my followers' of each of two 'tall muscular fellows' to be sold in 'a market not far from Bontúku'	R.A. Freeman (book)
	A4.4–11.1; £1–2.50 (20,000–50,000 cowries, 'well-grown boys and young women being most in demand') at Salaga	R.A. Freeman (article)
1889	A17.4–26.1; £3.92–5.87 (80–120 marks) for 'a grown slave' at Salaga	Wolf
1892	A13.3–31.1 (£3–7) at Salaga[28]	Ferguson
1894	A17.4–26.1; £3.92–5.87 (80–120 marks) 'depending on his age and build' in Salaga. This was what a slave 'would fetch' in the past; not necessarily current price.	Klose

1895–6[29]	A62.2 (£14)[30] for girl in 'Wuratara' in what is now Côte d'Ivoire		ARG 1/2/30/1/8
1897–8	£2.50–4.00 in Salaga (purchased by Gonja locals)		PRO CO879/ 52: dd. 1 Jan. 1898
late 19th century		A11.1–17.8 (£2.50–4.00) at Asokore for a woman	Fortes papers 8.39
late 19th century		A0.1–32.0; £0.02–7.20[31] (between *kokoa* and *benaa*) at Edubiase. [The lower price should probably not be taken literally; informant perhaps quoting it rhetorically, to emphasise that prices could be very low]	Daaku
late 19th century	A7–21; £1.575–4.725	A18; £4.05	LaTorre (fieldwork)
late 19th century	A11–27; £2.475–6.075 A13–16; £2.925–3.60 A13–22; £2.925–4.95 A13–33; £2.925–7.42		LaTorre (UNESCO Gonja)

Key: 'A' means the gold *agyiratwefa* or *ackie*, unit of Asante gold dust currency.

Key to Sources

ARG 1/2/30/1/8	'Respecting "Slave Dealing" Recently Occurred at Sefwhi' (Ashanti M.P. 619/08): esp. statement by Yah Gimini, Obuasi, 11 Nov. 1905, encl. in G.W. Clotworthy Soden to CCA, 11 Nov. 1908.
D. Asante	Jenkins' *Abstracts*, 79–80: David Asante's report on his journey to Salaga in 1877.
Bowdich	Bowdich, *Mission*, 296, 332–33.
Brackenbury	H. Brackenbury, *The Ashanti War*, Vol. II (Edinburgh, 1874), 352.
Daaku	Daaku, *Oral Traditions of Adanse*, 45.
Ferguson	G.E. Ferguson to Governor, Accra, 9 Dec. 1892, p. 53, in Johnson , *Salaga Papers* (original in PRO Colonial Office African [West] Confidential Print, 448).
Firminger	R.E. Firminger to Undersecretary of State for Colonies, London, 30 April 1889, reprinted in Johnson, *Salaga Papers*, I (original encl. in NAGA ADM 1/88, Secretary of State to Griffith, 28 June 1889).
Fortes papers 8.39	Notebook entitled 'Asokore Bima II', recording testimony of Kwasi Frompong [*sic*], n.d. but c.1946.
R.A. Freeman (book)	Richard Austin Freeman, *Travels and Life in Ashanti and Jaman* (London, 1967: 1st edn. 1898), 320.
R.A. Freeman (article)	R.A. Freeman, 'The interior of the Gold Coast', *Macmillan's Magazine* LXXX: 476 (1899), 113.

Johnson	Johnson, 'Cowrie currencies', 345.
Kirby	Captain Brandon Kirby, 'A journey to the interior of Ashanti', *Proceedings of the Royal Geographical Society* 6 (1884), 450.
Klose	H. Klose, *Togo unter Deutscher Flagge: Reisebilder und Betrachtungen* (Berlin, 1899), extract transl. by Marion Johnson, in Johnson (ed.), *Salaga Papers*, I, p. SAL/17/11.
LaTorre (fieldwork)	LaTorre, 'Wealth Surpasses', 440–41, citing an interview by himself with Amoafohene Akuoko III, Kumasi, 18 Sept. 1975.
LaTorre (MK 501)	LaTorre, 'Wealth Surpasses', 440, citing Algemeeen Rijksarchief, The Hague, Netherlands (ARA) Ministerie van Koloniën (MK) 501, Roelofsen to Daendels, Accra, 15 August 1817.
LaTorre (MK 4005)	LaTorre, 'Wealth Surpasses', 440, citing ARA MK 4005: Koomm. Lans to Min. of Colonies, Elmina, 9 Jan. 1836 (no. 6A/Geheim).
LaTorre (NKBG 519)	LaTorre, 'Wealth Surpasses', 440, citing ARA Nederlandse Bezittingen ter Kuste van Guinea (NBKG) 519: Gamper to Governor van der Eb, Accra, 2 Oct. 1840.
LaTorre (UNESCO Gonja)	LaTorre, 'Wealth Surpasses, 440–41, citing *UNESCO Research Project on Oral Traditions, No. 1, Gonja*, ed. K. Y. Daaku (Institute of African Studies, University of Ghana, Legon, 1969).
NAGK D905	'Complaining of His Captive Woman Taken to Wassaw by Certain Men Without his Knowledge'.
PRO CO/879/52	'Report on Gonga Country' by C.H. Armitage, Asst-Inspector Gold Coast Constabulary, Pembi, 1 Jan. 1898.
Opoku (Jenkins)	Jenkins' *Abstracts*, 85: Theo. Opoku's report on his journey to Salaga in 1877. Jenkins's abstract is of an original English text by Opoku.
Opoku (Johnson)	Opoku, 'An African Pastor's Peaching Journey Through the Lands of the Upper Volta', transl. by Marion Johnson, in Johnson (ed.), *Salaga Papers*, Vol. 1, p. SAL/8/6. The original article was published in German in *Evangelisches Missions—Magazin* (Basel, 1885), having itself being translated from Twi by Christaller and Muller.
Rattray	Rattray, *Ashanti Law*, 36, 110.
Royal Gold Coast Gazette	*Royal Gold Coast Gazette* no. 34, 9 Aug. 1823.
'Mose'	Maier-Weaver, D., (translator), 'Autobiographical Reminiscences of an Asante Slave, "Mose"', a translation of an article by Wilhelm Rottmann in the Basel Mission periodical *Der Evangelische Heidenbote* (1892), *Asante Seminar* 3 (Northwestern University: Evanston, 1975), 19.
Ramseyer and Kühne (A)	Friedrich August Ramseyer and Johannes Kühne, *Four Years in Ashantee* (London, 1875), 125.
Ramseyer and Kühne (B)	Ramseyer and Kühne, *Four Years in Ashantee*, 168.
Ramseyer and Kühne (C)	Ramseyer and Kühne, *Four Years in Ashantee*, 2nd German edn, 290, extract transl. by Marion Johnson, in Johnson, *Salaga Papers*, I, p. SAL/32/1.
Von Francois	C. Von Francois in *Mitteilungen aus den deutschen schutzgebieten* (Berlin, 1888), transl. by Marion Johnson, in Johnson (ed.), *Salaga Papers*, I, p. SAL/18/1.
Wolf	L. Wolf in *Mitteilungen aus den deutschen schutzgebieten* (Berlin, 1888), transl. by Marion Johnson, in Johnson (ed.), *Salaga Papers*, I, p. SAL/12/1.

7

CAPITAL AND CREDIT, 1807–1896

In the nineteenth century the Akan language distinguished between money as such (*sika*) and capital. The main word for capital was *dwetiri*, defined in Christaller's 1881 Akan dictionary as 'a capital or stock of money to begin trade with; a fund employed in business or any undertaking'.[1] *Sika-tan* meant 'capital, principal (capital), stock.'[2] J. H. Nketia has noted that *tan* meant fruitful, so that *sika-tan* meant invested sum[3]—a route which conveys the economist's understanding of capital very precisely. It is possible that Christaller, in compiling what was the first Twi dictionary, himself stretched the meanings of words to try to convey unfamiliar concepts.[4] But his rendering of these terms appears to have been consistent with the usage of survivors from the nineteenth century interviewed by native speakers in the mid-twentieth.[5] A case will be presented shortly in which *dwetiri* was used in the 1940s by an elder recalling his own experience in the late nineteenth century. It will be evident from this example that 'any undertaking' could include a marriage as well as a business. But then it may well be said that in this context marriage was, among other things, business.

This chapter discusses the means of raising funds for productive investment, that is, for generating future returns. Three categories of source were available: the investor's own savings, equity participation by others, and loans. As we shall see, the market's direct role was confined to providing a large proportion of the latter. In an economy in which consumption and production were conducted within overlapping social units there was also a large overlap between loans to finance production and loans to finance consumption. Maintaining the household labour force could be an investment. Accordingly, the discussion of credit here will range over credit generally, rather than confining itself to such as can be

135

identified purely or largely as a form of or substitute for capital. The substantive discussion is organised in two sections. Section A considers advances, retained profits, and equity participation as sources of funds, and discusses the payment of interest (*mfɛntom*, defined by Christaller as 'interest, usury'; while the narrower term *nsi-ho*, 'additional sum required in repayment of a loan', specifically implied a rate of 50 per cent or less).[6] Section B describes the means open to lenders to ensure repayment. It discusses recourse to chiefs and priests, and to the seizure of hostages, before concentrating on the dominant institution in loan finance in nineteenth-century Asante: pawnship.

A. Sources and Cost of Funds

Foreign sources of capital and credit were negligible before colonial rule. Let us discuss them with appropriate brevity before devoting the rest of the section to domestic sources. European suppliers of credit and capital began to be sought and began to seek openings in Asante in the period between the British invasions, 1874–96. The post-1874 regime of Asantehene Mensa Bonsu, and especially the post-civil war regime of Asantehene Agyeman Prempe, tried to reconstruct and further develop the Asante economy as the basis of a modernized Asante state. Therefore the government was willing to give favourable terms to European private entrepreneurs who would provide investment and management for specific projects, including mining and railways, without subverting the authority of the independent Asante government. None of these central government concessions really got off the ground, at least partly because of opposition by the British government.[7] Meanwhile the Bekwaihene gave a mining concession at Obuasi first to a group of Fantes, and then, in 1895, agreed to transfer it to a British entrepreneur, E. A. Cade. Fearing that this would undermine Asante sovereignty, Asantehene Agyeman Prempe forced the Bekwaihene to repudiate the deal[8] (which under British rule was to materialise into the Ashanti Goldfields Corporation).

African entrepreneurs from British territory were involved in the Asante rubber trade from, and perhaps especially at, the start.[9] At least some of these brokers gave advances.[10] According to testimony in Manso Nkwanta in 1980 the brokers themselves received advances from European merchants at the coast.[11] The chronology is a little vague and it is possible that European credit reached Asante producers only after the colonial takeover of Asante; but it is plausible that it preceded it.

It seems that advances were also within the repertoire of Asante credit suppliers. Before the cocoa era in Ahafo, loans of 'a few months only' were 'made against repayment in snails or animal products'.[12] Some of the rubber brokers were Asante themselves and there is no indication that they were an exception to the tendency for brokers in general to offer advances ('advances are made in money to be repaid in rubber', noted Hull).[13]

For indigenous would-be investors generally the most obvious source of finance, for example for a trading expedition, was retained profits. The process of raising and investing capital was a normal part of becoming an economic and social adult, and then of continuing to live up to the social ideal of self-enrichment through hard work. A detailed example at the level of an individual career, that of one Kofi Pusuo, will be presented in Chapter 10.

It seems likely that equity participation within the conjugal or matrilineal family also occurred, in that relatives unable to make the arduous journey themselves might help meet the cost of trade goods and incidental expenses, in return for a share of the profits. The best-evidenced link between family wealth and working capital, however, was through inheritance. A standard method by which a father could launch a son's career as a social and economic adult without contravening the restrictions of matrilineal inheritance was to give him the capital to undertake a trade expedition. It was hoped that the profits would enable the son to fund future ventures, and sooner or later enable him thereby to acquire a wife or wives and slaves.[14] Meanwhile relatives might help each other through rotating loans. According to oral testimony from Techimentia (now in Brong-Ahafo) there was a system whereby members of a matrilineage would donate money from kola sales to one member who would go and buy four to six slaves with it. Next year they would do the same for another member. ' "As a result" ' some *mmusua* had twenty or more slaves.[15]

At the level of the Asante court, at least according to the hostile *Royal Gold Coast Gazette* published by the British at Cape Coast in 1823, loans were also provided to enable colleagues to obtain slaves. The difference was that this lending was not for the purchase of slaves to enlarge the purchaser's own labour force, but rather was an interest-bearing commercial loan to finance a slave raid, made in the name of the Asantehene's honour but intended to declare a profit.[16]

Regular cooperation beyond both the matrilineal and conjugal family units seems to have been difficult. There is no evidence that formal rotating saving and credit clubs, such as the *esusu* which had been pioneered in southwestern Nigeria, existed in Asante during the period.[17] A possible explanation, suggested by Robin Law to account for the similar (apparent) absence of such institutions in the kingdom of Dahomey, is that the centralizing monarchy preempted or opposed private cooperative institutions, which it may have seen as compromising its unlimited power.[18] This is plausible for Asante, if we distinguish cooperative groups from smaller-scale (in terms of the number of principals involved) forms of indigenous private enterprise, of which the regime seems to have been relatively tolerant. Loans were available outside the overlapping family circles, either at interest or, very self-consciously, interest-free through the benevolence of patrons.

The time-value of money was appreciated in nineteenth-century Asante. In 1817 Bowdich found the interest rate to be '33⅓ per cent for every forty days, which is accompanied after the first period by a dash of liquor'.[19] LaTorre argues that interest rates declined somewhat as the century went on. The evidence is thin but, as he notes, such a trend would be consistent with the evidence of a general accumulation of wealth over the period.[20] Hull reported that on rubber advances, as of early 1897, 'the lender gets 2 or 300 per cent for his money'.[21] This rate was not described as annual—though it would presumably work out at a formidable annual rate. This may have reflected local monopolies, rather than the general scarcity of liquidity, for Hull also maintained that brokers and chiefs collaborated to fine migrant rubber producers in order to make the latter desperate to raise cash on the spot instead of carrying their own rubber to the coast to get the maximum price. Far from home, an Akyem rubber tapper in Sefwi, Wenchi or Ahafo would lack contacts from whom he could borrow on less penal terms. But it should be noted that this was in a particular institutional context: Kumasi's control over the areas in question had for some years been non-existent (Ahafo and Sefwi), or restored but indirect (Wenchi).[22] In the absence of a centralized state the judicial process was left to local power structures which predatory traders managed to manipulate or usurp.[23]

Within the Asante kingdom itself it was clear that, as an Asante proverb put it, 'money does not go out to earn its livelihood and come back empty-handed'.[24] Or if it did, there was trouble. In 1823 the Nsutahene Yaw Sekyere led an Asante army against Krepe (Ewe), east of the Volta River. The venture was financed on credit which the commander raised himself in the expectation of returning with substantial loot. But he failed to achieve quick success and tarried in the field, as McCaskie remarked, 'throughout the rainy season, a notoriously difficult period for military operations, in direct defiance of a royal order to disengage', to postpone

Plate 7.1. Carved wooden umbrella top 'representing a saying about the snake which, even though it could not fly, finally caught the hornbill which owed it money' (McLeod, *The Asante*, 170, where an earlier photograph of the artifact appears).

Reproduced by permission of the British Museum, London (© Copyright The British Museum).

the reckoning with his creditors.[25] From Adanse there is evidence of interest-bearing loans being raised to finance trading expeditions to the coast. Such a loan was known as *kotobroni*, 'to buy from the white man'.[26] Appreciation of the value of loans, however, could be expressed by saving clients from the need to seek interest-bearing loans. In Adanse one rich man, Kwaku Akowuah, is said to have became famous for lending money 'without charging interest';[27] or perhaps he could be said to have earned social or political interest. In 1817 Bowdich found the Asantehene himself providing loans to start his protégés on a commercial road to private fortune.[28]

B. Enforcement and Security: Chiefs, 'Panyarring' and Especially Pawnship

In the first instance a credit contract was a private matter between the individuals and lineages involved. If a would-be borrower could not get a loan on the basis of bilateral trust between himself and a potential lender, he or she could seek a surety, that is, 'a man of some influence or standing, who guarantees that the loan shall be paid within a certain time'.[29] In the event of non-payment the creditor could turn to the state. Rattray described how a frustrated creditor

> . . . would go to his Chief (*gwane toa ohene*, lit. "flee and join with the Chief"). The latter would send his *fotuosani* (treasurer) with the creditor and demand the money. If the debtor still refused to pay, the Chief would give his treasurer authority to swear the *meho tame* oath, i.e. to say that unless the debt was settled, then "he hated the Chief". The money would be paid forthwith; the creditor would thank the Chief, giving a present for the *ahenkwa* ("palace" attendants).[30]

Alternatively the creditor 'might swear an oath upon the debtor to pay the debt—not to himself—*but to the Chief*' (Rattray's emphasis). If not paid immediately, the sum due would be doubled. The creditor might be given a share of it by the chief.[31] It appears that regular moneylenders would pay to receive accelerated access to the chief's enforcement authority. According to one of Rattray's informants:

> Certain rich men used to receive authority from the Chief to use his 'oath' to swear that a debtor must pay them, i.e. the creditors. These as it were money-lenders would receive white calico from the Chief, which they tied

on the small bundles of gold-dust which they lent out. Such men would pay the Chief perhaps £100 [i.e. 12–12 ½ *peredwan*] for the privilege.'[32]

Resort to state authority could go to the very top. According to Bowdich, 'The law allows a debtor' not only to obtain interest, but to use 'the King's weights' in measuring the gold dust due as principal. As the King's weights 'are one third heavier than the current weights of the country', this added a further 33.3 per cent of interest. But to make use of this procedure the creditor needed either to be 'esteemed enough by Apokoo the treasurer', or 'to bribe him' or engage 'to share the profit with him.'[33]

As an alternative to the state, a creditor could attend a shrine, calling upon the ɔbosom (god) to kill the debtor if he did not settle immediately. Payment would be made to the priest of the god who had been invoked, who was entitled to keep a percentage.[34]

Thus creditors had no lack of higher authority to call upon in pursuit of their claims. On the other hand, traditionally they might take the law into their own hands, in a practice known on the Gold Coast as *panyarring*. As Bowdich explained, 'When the patience of the creditor is exhausted, he seizes the debtor, or even any of his family, as slaves, and they can only be redeemed by the payment'.[35] Panyarring was said to have been prohibited by Asantehene Kwaku Dua Panin some two decades later, in c.1838.[36] This is what one might expect from a centralizing authority, impatient with disorder and willing to accept fees for enforcing repayments itself. If the ban was effective, it must have broken down—at the latest—following the violent overthrow of Asantehene Mensa Bonsu in March 1883. It would be no surprise if such a period saw a breakdown of peaceful relations between creditors and debtors when the parties were in different parts of the country, and liable soon to find themselves at war with each other. Individual calculations, precautionary or opportunistic, could easily become entangled in the political conflicts. In January 1884 it was reported to London that:

> Mr. Kirby stated that during his stay in Ashanti some temporary disturbances had brought to his knowledge the fact that messages had been sent out by the interpreters to some of the neighbouring villages in connexion with the stopping of a system of panyarring which was being carried on by the villages against the Coomassie people, who it would appear were refusing to pay to the villages the debts which were owing to them. . . .[37]

Later the same year a Basel missionary obtained the release of a man from Kwahu, in the Gold Coast Protectorate. He had been seized and imprisoned in the Asante-Akyem village of Adomfe because he was indebted to one of the villagers.[38] In view of the political circumstances it seems likely that Asante-Akyem villagers, like those around the capital, were responding to weakened central authority by reviving or intensifying the use of panyarring as a means of debt enforcement. Probably they had little choice if they wanted their money. In November 1885, the Cape Coast newspaper *The Western Echo* commented on the 'dullness of trade' with and within Asante, and diagnosed the cause as follows:

> From all sources (Ashanti) we learn that there is no prospect of trade reviving till the government take[s] the bull by the horns and set[s] the various contending parties at peace by establishing some settled form of government. Panyarring prevails to so great an extent that those who have the means to engage in traffic fear to invest their money in trade. . . .[39]

This confirms the impression that panyarring had indeed been rare before the breakdown of central government of the mid-1880s; as it seems to have been again by the early 1890s (to judge, admittedly, from absence of evidence), following the revival of central authority after the civil war.

In the Akan language the word *awowa* (plural *nwowa*) usually meant a pawn, a security given by a debtor to a creditor, to be returned upon repayment of the debt. The same word is better translated as 'mortgage' if the security remained in the hands of the borrower, as Rattray believed was so when land was the *awowa*. In that case the produce of the land was treated as interest and, in some instances, also as repayment of principal. Foreclosure meant converting the mortgage into a sale (*tramma*).[40] This may have been 'a last resource', as Rattray believed,[41] but we have noted above that there are many documented cases of this happening. Many of these cases clearly involved stool lands, but Rattray described how lineages might mortgage land. Matrilineages were responsible for debts incurred by any of their members. So it is not surprising that lineage property might be pawned. As we saw earlier, this could include land. Otherwise an *awowa* might be an object such as cloth or jewellery; or it could be a person— that is, a set of rights in a person.[42]

The pawning (*awowasi*) of people was usually a deal between matrilineages whereby the head of one *abusua* pawned one or more of its members to the other *abusua*. The authority of the matrilineage over its members is epitomized by the fact that if a husband was unable or unwilling to give his inlaws a loan that they required, or to pawn himself or his junior matrikin to raise the money, the inlaws had the right to make his wife divorce him so that they could pawn her. A husband who agreed to lend to his inlaws could take his wife or children in pawn because, by definition, his children did not belong to his matrilineage. The principle was illustrated by a Kumasi chief who stated that 'I pledged my sisters and nieces to their husbands who gave me money to pay the . . . £86.3/- to Nana Prempeh', to cover a fine and pacification fee.[43] The timing is, unfortunately, uncertain. It may have been during the last seven years of Asante independence, between Asanthene Agyeman Prempe's election in 1888 and his abduction by the British in January 1896. But it may also have followed his return from exile in 1924, as 'Kumasihene': for, as we will see in chapter 12, wife-pawning was still effectively legal in the late 1920s. Returning to the rules, a father who was unable or unwilling to provide his inlaws with a loan they required had no right to prevent them from pawning his children to others, nor was he expected to try to dissuade them.[44] It was said that a mother and her matrikin might let her husband pawn their children,[45] though some of the evidence for this is weak.[46]

Such an arrangement would amount to an *abusua* lending one or more of their members to an inlaw, so that he could borrow cash. However, I have found only two cases of paternal pawning. One or, probably, both occurred after the colonial takeover; but the new regime had taken no relevant action by the time these pawnings were made. One was apparently in the late 1890s when a Kumasi chief, the Ankobeahene (head of internal security) Yao Cheiu, pawned nine people at the town of Odumase. One of these was his own son.[47] The other was in 1907, when a Wenchi girl was pawned by her father, Yao Moshi, to an Asante woman.[48] People could also pawn themselves.[49] There is at least one recorded case of this happening, in which two brothers pawned themselves, apparently soon after the beginning of colonial rule.[50] This too is best seen in the context of matriliny, rather than as a deal between individuals. An individual might incur the need for a loan, but the *abusua* was ultimately responsible for the debts of its members. The individual might take or be given the role of pawn. If later he ran back to his kin, evidently they would be responsible for sending a replacement pawn or clearing the debt. However, pawning did not always involve the ultimate responsibility of the *abusua*. Chiefs could pawn any of their subjects (*nkoa*, sg. *akoa*),[51] and masters could pawn slaves, as by definition these had no kin in Akan society.[52] For the same reason masters could pawn their children by slave wives or concubines.[53]

The archives reveal cases where pawns were repawned by the initial creditor. This seems to have been accepted practice provided that the original debtor had first been given the opportunity to redeem the pawn and thus rescue the creditor from his or her own liquidity crisis. At least, this is what may have happened with a woman called Atta who was pawned by Kwasi Gyane, chief of Bare (22 kilometres northwest of Kumasi), probably before the British sack of Kumasi in 1874. The creditor, Chief Kyereme of M'bang, himself 'got into debt' and asked her chief and family to redeem her. But they were still 'short of money to pay the amount', so they 'asked' Kyereme to repawn her until they could afford to redeem her. According to her son, this is what Kyereme did, pawning her to Atipimoa (or Elipima), banished niece of the omanhene of Mampon, who was staying in M'bang. However, when her son later tried to redeem her, the Mampon royals maintained that Atipimoa had purchased her and her children outright.[54] The case of the two self-pawned brothers mentioned above provides a contrasting example of repawning. They had pawned themselves for £18 to a man named Piprah. But in 1905 one of them, Kwame Obenneh, complained to the district commissioner when he learned that Piprah had repawned his brother for £12, yet had not reduced the amount he claimed from Obenneh to a corresponding £6 (in fact he 'is claiming another £13/15/- from me').[55]

Debt was timeless, so if the pawn died the borrower had either to clear the debt or provide a new pawn. As the Adansehene and his elders put it in 1906, before the institution was effectively prohibited, pawning 'is not done only on account of a new debt, but family debt as well'.[56] The year before, the chief commissioner of Ashanti had observed that 'at present the offspring [if the original pawn was female; if male, probably a sister's child] would become the pawn on the death of the parent unless redeemed'.[57] If the debtor died his *abusua* were responsible for the debt, and had the right to redeem the pawn.

According to Rattray no monetary interest was paid on loans secured by human pawns, unless the pawn ran away or died without being replaced: the services of the pawn constituted the interest.[58] This was the situation in a case described to him by one of the parties in 1925.[59] However, this was far from always so, as is shown by the case of the above-mentioned Musa Dagarti. His master pawned him for 80 'marks' at about the beginning of the Asante invasion of Eweland in 1869. Probably only a few years later 'he redeemed me again for double that sum'.[60] Thus, despite the scarcity of data specifically for the precolonial period, we can say definitely that payment of monetary interest in addition to the pawn's services was at least not unknown.

Further evidence of money interest being paid comes from the colonial records for the years just before the prohibition of pawning. When

Ankobeahene Yaw Cheiu pawned those nine people at Odumase before the 1900 revolt, it was agreed that interest would be paid at redemption of £1/10/- per *peredwan*[61] borrowed, or 18.4 per cent. At least, this was what the creditors said in 1907 when they asked that the pawns be redeemed.[62] During or shortly before January 1903 in southern Asante a man, Kwasi Mpong, pawned a woman, Yaa Penim, for a loan of £16 at £4 interest.[63] Again, in December 1903 the British commissioner transmitted a request from the Adansehene that one of his subjects, a man named Kwesi Fiu, be allowed to redeem from a Bekwai subject, Kofi Esidu, 'a woman, Abina Antu with her two children' in return for payment of the principal plus interest of 25 per cent.[64] Similarly, in a 1904 case in the same area £3 was demanded on a loan of £11/15/-, or 25.5 per cent.[65] Comparatively far away, at Nkoranza, on the northeastern borders of 'metropolitan' Asante,[66] the acting district commissioner discussed pawning with local chiefs in 1906. He reported that the 'Custom here' was for interest of 25 per cent to be claimed upon the redemption of the debt.[67]

Where cash interest was charged this did not necessarily contradict the notion that the pawn's services themselves constituted interest. For interest rates on loans secured with pawns tended to be less than on other loans, secured on personal guarantees or promissory notes. The Yaa Penim case was heard just over a year after the opening of the district commissioner's court for Southern Ashanti. Of the first ten cases in which the rate of interest on loans was recorded in the Civil Record Book (spread over the period 29 September 1904 to 23 September 1905), Yaa Penim's was the only one which involved pawning. In two instances the interest rate was lower, but in both the loan was agreed for only a limited period: 20 per cent for a one month loan, 4 per cent for an 8-day loan. The remaining seven cases resembled Penim's in involving a loan for an indefinite period, with a flat rate of interest to be paid when the principal was returned. But in all these the rate was higher: in five it was 50 per cent, in one 53 per cent, and in one 33.3 per cent.[68] It should be emphasized that flat rates such as these might amount to a much smaller annual rate, according to how long the debt remained outstanding. However, the district commissioner, G. W. Clotworthy Soden, though himself opposed to proposals to prohibit pawning, evidently believed that high annual interest rates existed also on loans secured with pawns. He suggested that colonial courts should only enforce payment of interest up to a maximum of 5–10 per cent, on the grounds that 'This would act as a deterrent against the speculative gamble of lending money at high rates of interest on "Pawns"'.[69] In the case of Musa Dagarti, as we have seen, a flat rate of 100 per cent was paid. We lack sufficient data to make a safe generalisation, but it is at least consistent with the fragmentary evidence provided earlier about nineteenth-century inter-est rates in general to suggest that interest rates were higher during the period considered in this chapter than they were to be even in the early colonial period—even for borrowers in the 'informal' sector.

According to a relatively experienced colonial administrator, Armitage, in 1905, 'very frequently the result' of pawning 'is the marriage of the pawn to one of the daughters of the creditor's house'.[70] From other sources, how-ever, it is clear that, as with slave-free marriages, it was usually the husband who was the free person, and the proprietor, in such 'mixed' unions. We can distinguish two forms of pawn-marriage in Asante society: pawning before and after the marriage.

Early in the colonial period the missionary Edmond Perregaux described the betrothal of girls, sometimes even before they were born, to become pawn-brides of the family's creditors. He quoted the word *tisika* as the name of this institution.[71] There is no indication that the practice was new. In 1927 Rattray reported that 'In Ashanti there was an idiom indicating a particular form of marriage, where in addition to paying the parents the customary "bride price" or "head money", the man had, beforehand as a condition to the union, paid some debt (called *tiri 'ka*) incurred either by the woman he wished to marry or by her family. The idiom in such a case was, *to 'yere*, lit. "to buy a wife" '.[72] Rattray's choice of tense indicates that the expression predated the colonial period. Indeed, he went on to imply that the use of the term—though not the practice—had declined during the colonial period: it had fallen into disuse because it embarrassed 'the semi-educated African'. He also noted that where a husband divorced his wife because of 'her misconduct', 'should he have "bought his wife", i.e. paid a debt for the parents conditional upon his receiving her as his wife, he can claim repayment of this amount'.[73]

Pawning could also strengthen the husband's property rights within a marriage. We have seen that the wife's matrilineage could ask her hus-band for a loan. Indeed, according to Rattray an *abusua* deciding whom to pawn would give 'priority of selection' to married women among their members, that is, the married sisters or nieces of the lineage head.[74] Such a request might be made, according to Fortes, at any time during the mar-riage, 'the security being the wife's fidelity'. This type of loan was called *tiri sika*, literally 'head money'.[75] Our most detailed information about *tiri sika* comes from Fortes's unpublished papers from the Ashanti Social Survey of 1945–46. In this research Fortes and his colleagues found that *tiri sika* had been paid in some of the oldest respondents' first marriages, which would have been before c.1905.[76] Again, there is no indication that this was an innovation,[77] rather than a practice continued from the previous century. Lending to a wife's *abusua* considerably strengthened the position of the husband within the marriage. As Fortes noted, ' "head money" exploits the wife's lineage bonds' to reinforce her marital loyalty.[78] One might suspect, though, that it was hard for the husband to insist upon repayment of the debt. But certainly the status of creditor reinforced his economic position within the marriage. It gave him the right to half of any property his wife or child might acquire (this also applied to a father who accepted his child in pawn).[79] Otherwise, self-acquired property belonged solely to its acquirer until his or her death. After that, in principle, it would go to the deceased's *abusua*.[80] Also, a husband who took his wife in pawn was able to insist that she lived in his home.[81] Rattray implied that a husband who took his existing wife in pawn might also say (implicitly, like a man who acquired a new wife in pawn) *ma to me ye*, that he had 'bought' her.[82] By advancing a loan the husband would '*fa ne ye' si babi* (put his wife by his side), i.e. . . . ensure his having a hold over her'. The 'hold' Rattray describes is overwhelmingly economic.[83]

Let us consider such evidence as there is about the evolution of the quantity of pawning, and of the amounts lent on pawns, during the period. This will lead us to the question of in what sense, if any, there was a market in pawns; and if there was, exactly what was the resource that was being traded. It will be argued in Chapter 10 that pawning probably increased during 1807–96 as a whole. There seems to have been a surge of pawning, for different reasons, during the political troubles of the 1870s and 1880s. In late 1873 a special war tax was levied to meet the cost of the Asante invasion of the coast. According to the detained missionaries Friedrich August Ramseyer and Johannes Kühne, 'There were many upright, quiet men who had wished for peace and free trade, who lost half their families by the war, and were afterwards obliged to sell the other half to pay for it'.[84] It seems a safe assumption that Asantehene Mensa Bonsu's heavy taxes and fines led to a further round of state-induced pawning, and that the same happened during the civil war as the parties strove to raise large sums from their subjects. Bekwai alone was said to have spent 3,500 *peredwan*s (strictly, £28,525).[85] In 1982 an elderly informant said that his own father and mother had been pawned by the Bekwaihene to the chief of Elmina in exchange for guns and ammunition to fight the Adanses[86] during the Asante civil war of the mid-1880s.

It is reasonable to take the size of the loan on a pawn as a measure of the exchange value of the pawn to the holder. If the loan was never redeemed, it would in effect represent the cost of purchasing rights to the labour of the pawn for his or her life and to the labour of a replacement. The small number of cases and the very approximate dating of the majority of them prevents precision about trends. The earliest period for which I have information on even a handful of cases is the mid-nineteenth century, broadly defined, from perhaps as early as the 1820s until the outbreak of the revolt against Asantehene Mensa Bonsu in 1883. In these cases the sum was half a *peredwan* (then 17 *ackies*), except for a case during Mensa Bonsu's reign (1874–83), in which the sum was described later as 30 shillings,[87] then implying 6.67 *ackies*.[88] An 1884 pawning was for either half or a full *peredwan*.[89] Kwadwo Donko's future wife had been pawned for '£8',[90] i.e. one *peredwan*. We noted earlier that the year is unspecified in the source but was apparently in the 1880s or early 1890s. In c.1898 a pawn was redeemed for £7.75. The payment may also have represented head-money, for the (pawn-?) marriage between redeemer and ex(?)-pawn that followed.[91] Taken together, these instances point to a very tentative conclusion, that the unit size of loans rose (in gold terms) during the last years of Asante independence, possibly from the outbreak of civil strife with the uprising against Asantehene Mensa Bonsu in 1883. It is relevant to add that the first definite instance of pawning we have from after the British occupation of 1896 shows a still higher monetary value put on pawns. Specifically, the nine people pawned by Ankobeahene Yao Cheiu apparently in the late 1890s were handed over for two *peredwan*s apiece.[92] As will be detailed in Chapter 12, the evidence suggests that the size of loans per pawn rose further after c.1900.

Let us compare and relate the market for pawns to that for slaves. The evidence is fragmentary, but it appears that for most of the nineteenth century the exchange value of slaves and pawns was of the same order. The indications are that slaves were cheaper than pawns in the 1810s–20s, which is what might be expected from the glutted slave market that followed British withdrawal from the Atlantic slave trade: but the evidence for this period is extremely thin. In roughly the middle half of the century slaves gained in relative as well as nominal value, reaching a level about twice that of pawns. In the last dozen years of the nineteenth century the price of slaves seems to have fluctuated greatly but, on the whole, fell considerably; while the sums lent on pawns rose.

This conclusion must necessarily be cautious, in view of the data problems. For what it is worth, it can readily be attributed to a combination of the circumstances. One was an expanded supply of captives: during the Asante civil war and above all from the Samorian glut of prisoners in the mid-1890s. The other, conversely, was the British prohibition of Asante's slave trade in 1896, which probably strengthened the perception in Asante that the colonial abolition of slave holding in the Gold Coast in 1874 would be extended to Asante sooner or later. In the Gold Coast pawning increased after 1874, was only made a felony in 1892, and even that act was not followed by vigorous enforcement.[93] Thus the British actions in Asante in 1896 presumably made pawns much more attractive as a comparatively secure form of coerced labour.

That the size of individual loans on pawns should rise in apparent response to increased demand for pawns suggests that there was indeed a market in pawns. This is consistent with our other information about the practice, if we take it as a whole. Admittedly, some lenders were under social pressure to accept particular pawns, and conversely part of the value of a pawn to his or her master was presumably prestige derived from being seen to be willing and financially able to fulfill this social obligation. But pawns could be repawned, as we have seen, and by no means all lenders were under any social obligation to lend. Though the act of giving and taking a pawn was literally a face-to-face transaction, between parties whose relations with each other were often not simply economic, it is clear that it was also a market exchange. For the value of loans seems to have been much the same at any one time, while changing over time in response to shifts in the balance between supply and demand. Thus price equalization was at work. In this defining sense, there was a market in human pawns.

That the increased demand for pawns should represent, seemingly, attempts to substitute pawns for slaves is evidence that the market in pawns was to a large extent a market for their labour. This conclusion is also supported by the evidence about the economically important uses to which pawn labour was put. It is therefore reasonable to say that for the lenders the pawn market was, not exclusively but primarily, a labour market. For the borrowers it was a market for loans, which could be used for consumption or for capital. In the context of economic activities based on family labour there can be much overlap between the two.

But the slave and pawn markets also differed in basic respects. Slaves were mostly imported, and as a result were often purchased from foreign merchants. They also tended to be brought to market—literally to a market-place—in relatively large concentrations. By contrast, pawning deals were usually transacted between principals and their lineages within Asante and often within the same village. They almost always involved single-figure numbers of pawns, usually ones or twos. A sign of the differences between the two markets is revealed by a comparison of the monetary units in which slave and pawn 'values' are quoted in the sources. The price of slaves tended to be quoted in relatively small units, as Table 6.1 showed, permitting flexible price responses to changing relations between supply and demand. It was not so with pawning. The amounts lent on pawns were usually quoted in relatively large units. Of the 25 single or multiple pawnings for which I have information, stretching from about the second quarter of the nineteenth century to 1930, in no less than 18 or probably 19 cases the sum loaned, or the sum to be repaid, was a multiple of either the Asante half-*peredwan* unit, the *asuanu* (conventionally £4) or of £10[94] (the sums were, or were the equivalent of, £4, £8, £10, £12, £16, £20 or £32).[95] Regarding individual pawns, 30 or 31 were pawned for one of these sums[96] and only 11 for other amounts.[97] This data set includes six pre-1896 pawns (five cases). All but one of the people were pawned for either half a *peredwan* or, in one case, possibly a full *peredwan*.[98] Thus, while the sums involved were not fixed, the very high proportion of what seem to be standard units suggests that the precise amount lent was often rounded to the nearest such unit. This may have been at least partly a matter of convenience in these face-to-face transactions. It suggests the possibility that there was a customary element in the monetary valuations of pawns. Yet the exchange value of pawns was clearly not fixed: shifts in the balance of supply and demand may have been muffled by an element of customary rounding of prices, but they were not stifled by them.

C. Conclusion

Overall, it may be said that there was a capital market in nineteenth-century Asante, in the fundamental sense that those who had savings could find profitable ways of investing them, while those producers or traders who needed cash could find it too. The price (the interest rate) was at least plausibly the product of genuine competition. However, this market was severely limited by the absence of financial intermediaries, and therefore of a genuine 'credit multiplier': lenders could only lend their own money. Even so, this factor market in capital, together with its counterpart(s) in labour, was crucial to the extra-subsistence activity of the economy. At microeconomic level the expansion of output was largely a function of the acquisition of extra-familial labour, of which pawns were a major source, while the socially-widespread activity of long-distance trade was financed partly from interest-bearing loans.

Again as with labour, so with capital, it may be said that while there were markets for the scarce factors, they were highly imperfect. There were high transaction costs and no financial intermediaries while opportunities for equity finance were limited to partnerships based on personal trust or family ties. The markets for credit and labour were interlocked through the system of human pawning, which—as we will see in Part Three—may be understood as both a response to and a reinforcing cause of the imperfection of both markets. More generally, the central feature of the factor markets of nineteenth-century Asante was the interaction between coercion and market forces. We will now examine the causal relations involved.

PART III

Slavery as Hobson's Choice: An Analysis of the Interaction of Markets and Coercion in Asante's Era of 'Legitimate Commerce', 1807–1896

This part investigates the causes and consequences of the role of slavery and other forms of property in people in the nineteenth-century Asante economy. Chapter 8 examines the standard economic explanation of slavery against qualitative and quantitative evidence for Asante. It argues that such property claims, founded on coercion, reduced the supply price of labour and thereby made possible a much higher level of economic activity than would have been possible otherwise. Important as they were, we have seen that slavery, pawning and corvée were not the only sets of extra-economic relations to structure economic activity. The significance of the gender division of labour, and the primacy of the conjugal family unit over the otherwise socially-pervasive matrilineage, are discussed in Chapter 9. The opportunities that the pattern of property rights and markets in factors of production offered for individual careers of accumulation are explored in Chapter 10. It goes on to consider the implications for the welfare of the various parties involved, and issues of consent and resistance. In this context we ask whether, or how far, slavery and pawnship were instruments of social integration, underpinned by paternalistic ideologies, as well as means of extracting economic rent.

8

FACTOR MARKETS WITHOUT FREE LABOUR:

THE NIEBOER HYPOTHESIS AND ASANTE SLAVERY AND PAWNSHIP, 1307–1896

We have seen that slavery, slave trading and pawning were widespread in nineteenth-century Asante society and provided major inputs into the whole range of directly productive activities. This chapter analyses the causes, nature and results of this pattern of interaction between coercion and market forces in the acquisition and use of resources. Besides tackling a crucial aspect of the particular history of Asante social relations of production, this discussion is intended as a case-study in a wide-ranging controversy on which general positions have been strongly stated but which have been remarkably short on systematic empirical investigation. It includes the first attempt to quantify the cost of slave compared to free labour within a precolonial African society. From this analysis I will propose a simple model of the impact of coercion on labour markets in a land-surplus economy.

The classic economic interpretation of slavery, which we may call for generic convenience the 'Nieboer hypothesis', explains the existence of widespread slavery as a profit-maximizing response to a scarcity of labour in relation to land, in economies in which capital, however desirable, was not essential for subsistence (as it might be in pastoral societies).[1] The most influential restatements of this tradition, both succinct, were published over a quarter of a century ago. Evsey Domar's 1970 paper[2] was widely discussed by students of serfdom and slavery in Europe and the

Americas. For the West African context the Nieboer hypothesis received its classic formulation in five pages by Tony Hopkins in 1973.[3] Hopkins argued that land was abundant in relation to labour, and that in response, though 'there was a factor market in land . . . it was very limited' because 'land was not scarce enough to acquire a market value'.[4] Because of the easy access to land, potential labourers were physically and occupationally mobile and so enjoyed a strong bargaining position in relation to would-be employers. Hence the latter chose slavery in preference to wage labour, which, Hopkins insisted, was a genuine alternative: 'the use of slave rather than wage labour was a matter of deliberate choice on the part of African employers'.[5]

Since the early 1970s there has been a vast amount of research on the history of slavery within Africa;[6] yet systematic tests of the Nieboer hypothesis in relation to particular cases of slavery in the continent remain very rare.[7] So far as I am aware, this study is the first to attempt a quantification—admittedly crude—of the costs of slave compared to free labour in an African case. Maybe the critics have been satisfied with the various *a priori* grounds which have been offered for dismissing the hypothesis, contentions which will be discussed below. Perhaps more sympathetic scholars have considered the issue sufficiently explored. A particular barrier (but should it not be a stimulus?) to further exploration is the model's notorious indeterminancy. Nieboer, Domar and Hopkins all agreed, in effect, that an economy in which expansion of output is constrained only by the cost of labour is not sufficient for the existence of slavery 'as an industrial system'.[8]

This chapter considers the evidence for nineteenth-century Asante. This period is a particularly apposite one to consider in relation to the hypothesis, for Nieboer further posited that commerce was a supplementary stimulus to the growth of slavery: because extra-subsistence production increased the demand for labour, notably beyond the level where the 'drudgery' could be performed solely by ['free'] women.[9] We saw in Chapter 3 that in Asante, as in West Africa generally, the era from the beginning of the end of the Atlantic slave trade to the colonial partition was marked by uneven but major growth in extra-subsistence production. Asante shared in the expansion of both the regional trade, centred on the Sokoto Caliphate, and the Atlantic commodity trades. Research over the last twenty years has shown that, as the model would predict, the period also saw a great increase in slave-ownership within West Africa. This literature has also documented evidence that slaves were widely engaged in production for the market.[10] We saw in Chapter 6, again, that all this applies to Asante specifically.

The argument developed in this chapter is that the hypothesis that slavery was a profit-maximizing response to land abundance and labour scarcity is justified in this case; but that the sense in which it was a 'choice' needs to be clarified, for in economic terms it was Hobson's choice; while the concept of economic rent based on monopoly of natural resources and of locational advantage may provide *one* of the tools needed in the general search for a more determinate account of the political economy of slavery in African and even world history. The discussion is organized as follows. We need first to ask whether the prevailing factor ratio and production function fit the Nieboer prediction. This question is addressed in Section A, which goes on to highlight an important political economy aspect of resource allocation between Asante and the areas from which it imported captives. Section B considers, in relation to this case, the two standard objections to the hypothesis in the West Africanist literature. Section C compares the cost of free and slave labour, and explores the implications of this for the economic significance of coercion in post-1807 Asante. Section D presents a simple model to summarize the implications of the domestic part of the argument. Section E explores the corresponding issues for human pawnship.

A. Natural-Resource Abundance and Nineteenth-Century Asante

This short section is intended simply to focus points documented in chapter 4. I argued there that the land abundance/labour scarcity model is overly aggregative as a description of nineteenth-century Asante. First, it overlooks the fact that the supply of capital, in its various forms, was an important determinant of short-term output. Second, the homogeneity of land as a factor of production disappears when the supply of this resource is considered not as a stock but as a flow. But I also argued that, while both these points matter greatly in the context of choice of technique, they are not crucial to the issue of labour scarcity over the comparatively long timespan relevant for a decision on whether to acquire a slave. Over periods longer than a few months, in agriculture, or perhaps a couple of years in craft and mining production, output was a function very largely of inputs of labour. It was the level of labour inputs that determined the area of land cleared for food crops, the provision of capital goods in weaving and mining, and whether enough seed was planted for the following year. In this perspective even for activities undertaken during the agricultural off-season, when the opportunity cost of labour was low, it was still the level of labour inputs that principally decided the volume of (in this case non-agricultural) output. The crucial point here is that the forest heartland of Asante was very lightly populated relative to the carrying capacity of the land. We may conclude that, certainly in general and probably virtually everywhere, land for cultivation was abundant—unless the supply was constrained artificially, by political intervention—in the strict sense that its marginal product must have been zero. This in turn implies that the marginal product of labour must have been very close to its average product, as in Domar's formulation.[11]

Earlier chapters argued that in the absence of economies of scale in production potential employers were constrained by a lack of means by which they could profitably afford to pay workers more than the latter could make by working for themselves. But we also saw that, as free subjects of the Asante kingdom, they shared a collective natural-resource advantage over one set of potential workers: those from the savanna societies to the north. Their enjoyment of the 'broad forest rent'[12] was secured by the might of the Asante state, and reinforced by the exploitation of locational advantage: possession of the strategic position in the transit trade, through the forest, between the coast and the savanna, which the government used not only to give Asante traders a national monopoly but also to obstruct savanna polities from acquiring European weaponry. This did not mean that Asante did most of its own slave-catching: as we have seen, it could buy (or demand as tribute) slaves from the more powerful savanna states, which they in turn had obtained often from acephalous societies. The economic rent which Asante obtained by institutionalizing its natural-resource advantage was particularly significant for slavery: as will become apparent once we have considered the options available to Asante's rulers.

B. Objections to the Nieboer-Hopkins Approach: Politics and Culture Left Out?

Hopkins's analysis has provoked criticism over the years from marxist, substantivist and other directions: notably on the grounds that, in effect, it is either too determinist or not determinist enough. The former objection is that the hypothesis takes relative scarcities as given, and thus overlooks the possibility that the more powerful historical actors had a choice between slavery and free labour: specifically, it fails to allow the possibility that private appropriation of land could turn natural abundance into artificial scarcity. As Stephen Hymer had already remarked of the notion of land surplus: 'land, even when it is plentiful, can be made scarce if certain groups gain the power of excluding others from its use'.[13] It has also been observed of the Nieboer hypothesis generally that a ruling class in a labour-scarce, land-abundant economy might have further options for achieving income redistribution in its favour besides slavery: a landowners' or employers' cartel, or regressive taxation imposed on the free peasantry.[14]

The other objection is that the actors had no choice; for cultural reasons. Jack Goody, for example, maintained—contrary to Hopkins—that the question of a '*choice* between wage labour and slavery, as practical alternatives' did not arise. In Goody's view Hopkins's 'argument from economic principles appears to neglect the location of slavery in a social system'.[15] John Thornton has put forward a related view: that the reason why slaves were the characteristic 'form of private, revenue-producing property' in Atlantic Africa, whereas land fulfilled the same function in Europe, lay in 'divergence' between the two regions' legal systems.[16] Thornton's implicit assumption is that cultural difference is a sufficient explanation: that an alternative property system, such as one in which labour-time rather than persons were sold, was simply not conceivable whatever its economic implications.

Let us consider both sets of objections in relation to nineteenth-century Asante. A cartel of labour-users would seem impracticable because of the very large numbers of such potential principals dispersed over a wide area in which communications were restricted by the high forest and the disease-dictated reliance on head loading.[17] It is slightly easier to conceive of access to land being restricted: of the physical abundance of land being turned into institutional scarcity, turning most of the population into landless labourers. Indeed we have seen that the Asante courts manipulated the ownership of rights of sovereignty and political control over land: by imposing fines on individual chiefs obliging some of them to mortgage these rights.[18] Stanley Engerman has suggested, however, that 'often the success of political interventions will itself depend upon the land-labor ratio, influencing the ability to control the population'.[19] In nineteenth-century Asante, to create an artificial scarcity of land as a factor of production would have required far more detailed administration and enforcement than the state could afford. Moreover a relatively generous exercise of the stools' ultimate control over land was fundamental to the chiefs' enjoyment of support or at least acquiescence from their subjects. More prosaically, we noted earlier that the high-forest environment was a source of heavy transactions costs when it came to territorial demarcation.[20] It is therefore no surprise that (as described in Chapter 5), while the ownership of the land itself was vested in chiefdoms, cultivation rights—access to land as a factor of production—were, institutionally as well as physically, virtually free in most of the country at least. Strangers, and sometimes subjects, had to hand over a share of gold or other winnings from the non-renewable endowment of the lands: but such resources were themselves limited.

Arguably, the one really practicable alternative to slavery would have been the tribute option: making a free peasantry pay tax. But such a tax or internal tributary system without slavery would have been economically sub-optimal for both the ruling class and the peasantry. The Asante state did indeed get much of its revenue from the mass of free households, for example by taking a share of gold output.[21] However, as we also saw in Chapter 6, free commoner households and individuals themselves became major importers of slaves. As a result the size of those households' extra-subsistence output, and therefore their fiscal potential, was to a large extent a function of their resources of slaves and pawns.[22]

In broad rational-choice terms it makes sense to suggest that the most efficient system of exploitation from the viewpoint of the rulers of Asante was based on the importation of slaves. This is because the gains could be shared—unequally—across the 'host' society. Government and free subjects would have a joint interest in maintaining in servitude a group who would remain a minority of the population. For the governing elite this was much less difficult than it would have been to try to dispossess the mass of the population. Ultimately, the chiefs had nothing to gain from seeking to overturn the natural factor ratios that they could not achieve more easily by using their power of coercion, not to make the abundant factor scarce, but to make the scarce factor—selectively—cheaper. In terms of self-interest it benefitted chiefs and free subjects to join together in the exploitation of outsiders, paid for to a great extent by the economic rent derived from monopoly control of particularly valuable natural resources.

It seems likely, though at this stage of knowledge it can only be a very plausible assumption, that Asante's contemporary reputation as an intensive importer and user of slaves was justified. 'Slavery prevails here [in Asante], as it does in most parts of Western Africa, but on a larger scale.'[23] If indeed the scale of slaveholding, and the importance of slaves' contribution to output, were relatively high in Asante compared to most other polities in the region, it is reasonable to suggest that this was a function of Asante's advantage in economic rent.

Hopkins's insistence on the notion of choice was, at least in part, intended to highlight his rejection of any assumption that wage-labour was culturally unthinkable in precolonial West Africa. In the Asante case it is very plausible (on the account in Chapter 6) that the idea was not much 'thought' before the twentieth century, yet it would be wrong to infer from this absence the presence of a solid cultural template preventing any practice that did not fit into familiar slots. We have the 1881 instance of expatriate Asante princes readily becoming employers of wage labour,[24] and we will see later that Asante youths showed themselves similarly willing to accept casual wage employment when it became an economic option early in the colonial period.[25] Thus Hopkins's emphasis on cultural flexibility is vindicated in this case. But, as we will see in the next section, there was a decisive barrier to wage labour in nineteenth-century Asante. This barrier was not cultural but material.

Applying the Nieboer hypothesis entails a further pair of assumptions about Asante politics and culture respectively: that the distribution of coercive power was sufficiently unequal to make slavery physically possible, and that slavery was ideologically acceptable to those holding the coercive power. It is evident that this was the case: slaves were held, slavery was a legally-enforceable status, and there is no evidence of pressure for abolition from free members of the society. As in most other slave-holding societies in world history, as a form of exploitation slavery was directed mostly outwards, in that (as we have seen) most of the slaves were foreigners, especially *nnɔnkɔfoɔ* (singular, *ɔdɔnkɔ*) people from the northern savanna. Furthermore, again as in other slave-holding communities, the specific category of foreigners from whom most slaves were obtained tended to be seen as alien and inferior. McCaskie comments that is 'abundantly clear from reported speech and traditions, [that] the term [*ɔdɔnkɔ*] suggested a brute animality to the Asante, and connoted a non-human status.'[26] This needs to be balanced by the recollection that Asante men were happy to marry northern women and to count any offspring as their own. It is necessary to avoid the anachronistic assumption that the act of enslavement was in all eras felt by its perpetrators as an enormity. But it is reasonable to suppose that in nineteenth-century Asante society it was culturally, and therefore psychically, harder to envisage and treat fellow Akan, especially Asante, as slaves than it was with northerners, 'othered' as *nnɔnkɔfoɔ*. Meanwhile, this time in common with most other African slave-holding societies but in sharp contrast to New World slavery, a process of partial assimilation of the descendants of slaves reduced the risk of creating a hereditary slave caste.[27] These characteristics can be said to have reduced the psychic, political and military costs and risks in holding slaves.

C. A Comparison of the Cost of Free and Slave Labour: Slavery as Hobson's Choice

A key implication of the Nieboer hypothesis is that the supply cost of slave labour must have been much below that of wage labour. This section attempts to test this proposition as far as the evidence permits.

A direct comparison of the two kinds of labour in the same period seems to be impossible: precisely because slaves and wage labourers barely overlapped chronologically in the service of Asante masters/employers. It should be noted that this observation is itself evidence that free labour was not a real alternative to slaves as a source of regular labour while slavery was legal (and before the economic conditions conducive to it were changed by the adoption of cocoa cultivation, as we will see in Chapter 13).

But it is possible to develop a quantitative perspective from an oblique angle. First, European prospectors working in major Akan gold-producing areas around 1900 obtained an average yield of a shilling's worth of gold (range 10d.–1s.2d) per day.[28] Having compared this with other recorded returns, Garrard concluded that it 'is probably reasonable to take' this range as 'the average daily earnings of an Akan gold-winner up to the end of the nineteenth century'.[29] Broadly consistent with this is a statement (not cited by Garrard) in the colonial administrative report on Asante for 1898 that, while Asante men had largely abandoned 'gold washing' in favour of the wild rubber industry, 'Gold washing is now carried on mostly by the women and children, who can make on average 9d. to 1s. a day'.[30] On the basis of these observations we can assume that, around the turn of the century, the opportunity cost for a free able-bodied man in Asante of working for wages rather than working for himself in the dry season would have averaged at least a shilling a day. In 1911–13, when wage labour was beginning on Asante cocoa farms, the prevailing wage rate for (male) unskilled labour seems to have been between 1s. and 1s. 3d., of which the latter could include a 3d. subsistence allowance.[31] The cost of living for labourers does not seem to have changed much c.1898–c.1913, though this issue requires further research. So far price indices have been calculated only for various categories of imported goods, and from 1900. The most relevant of these, 'clothing, leather and textiles' showed a rise from 9 in 1900 to 10 in 1913.[32]

What stands out is that there was a gross difference in cost between wage and slave labour. Indigenous gold production was concentrated largely in about three months of the dry season.[33] If we make the relatively conservative assumption that labourers did the equivalent of 20 days' work a month for three months a year, average gold-season receipts at 1s. a day would average a total of £3 a head. Garrard assumed 75 days 'at the most' in three months,[34] which would imply average earnings of £3.75 from a relatively intensive season. The appendix to Chapter 6 assembled the available evidence on the prices of slaves within nineteenth-century Asante and in the markets from which, directly or indirectly, slaves were imported into Asante. The table in the next page expresses those prices in terms of the number of days of gold mining required to pay for a slave.

Thus in most of the years for which we have price observations, it seems that an able-bodied male or female slave cost the equivalent of one to three seasons' gold-mining, sometimes less, by a single miner.

Where slave prices were expressed in headloads of kola nuts, the implication is similar. Table 6.1 gives the following such prices: in the admittedly flooded markets of 1817, 1 load (Bowdich's 'basket'); in the years immediately preceding 1874, 3.58 loads (calculated from figures provided by Ramseyer and Kühne) or 2–3 (Brackenbury), or 4.5–5 for a man and 7 for a woman (according to Rattray's informant). According to Lovejoy, 'producers needed the harvest from only a few trees to obtain a load of 2,000 nuts. Individuals often accumulated as many as 10 loads.'[35] Ramseyer and Kühne commented that 'an Ashanti . . . can easily collect at home' enough nuts to 'enable him to buy a slave in Salaga.'[36] Terray has likewise found that slaves were very cheap calculated in relation to the prices of oxen, salt and guns from various observations at Salaga in the last quarter of the nineteenth century.[37]

To be sure, the intending purchaser would often have to use some of his (as it usually was) earnings from gold or kola production to pay for items other than slaves—though, importantly, little would normally go on food. For a young man working mainly for himself it could take a few years before he could afford a slave, as an example to be given in Chapter 10 shows. But someone able to concentrate the earnings of more than one miner or kola collector, such as a household head and/or an existing slave or pawn holder, could acquire slaves more frequently. Even if slaves could not be induced to work as hard as free people (a risky assumption),[38] they could be expected to pay for themselves within a very few years if they did not run away.

Rattray was told by an authoritative informant that, before 1874, higher prices were paid for female than for male slaves in Salaga. But in

Table 8.1. Days of gold mining required to obtain the price of a slave in nineteenth-century Asante

Year	Mining 'effort-price' of slave (days)	Comment/Source
1823	30	In Kumasi (*Royal Gold Coast Gazette*)
1836	120–160	Kumasi (or coast?) (LaTorre [MK 4005])
1837–42	170	Man. Paid by Dutch recruiter in Kumasi (LaTorre [NBKG 519])
pre-1867	195.8	Boy of 11+, sold in Asante(?) ('Mose')
1867–74	80	Young Wasa girl, in Kumasi (NAGK)
1871	155	Man, Kumasi (Ramseyer and Kühne [A])
1872	99	Man bought in Kumasi by Ramseyer and Kühne (Ramseyer and Kühne [B])
pre-1874	36–70	(Ramseyer and Kühne [C])
pre-1874	<36	In northern markets (Brackenbury)
pre-1874	10–15	Man, Salaga
	144	In Asante (D. Asante)
pre-1874	22.5–50	Man, Salaga
	35–70	Woman, Salaga (Rattray)
1877	30–40	Average, Salaga (Opoku [Jenkins])
	19.6–78.4	Range, Salaga Opoku ([Johnson])
1884	40–60	Average for 'strong and healthy slave', Kintampo (Kirby)
1887	120	Adult male or female, Salaga
	70	Boy or girl, Salaga (Firminger)
1888	137	Man, Salaga
	68.6	10-year old girl (Von Francois)
1889	30	'tall muscular' man, market near Bontuku
	20–50	Range, Salaga (R.A. Freeman)
1889	78.4–118	'grown slave', Salaga (Wolf)
1892	60–140	Salaga (Ferguson)
1894	78.4–117.4	Past, not necessarily present price range, 'depending on his age and build', Salaga (Klose)
1895–96	140	Wuratura, girl (ARG)
1897–98	50–80	Salaga (PRO)
Late 19th century	50–80	Woman at Asokore, Asante. (Fortes)
Late 19th century	negligible-144	At Edubiase, Asante (Daaku)
Late 19th century	31.5–94.5	Salaga
	81	In Asante (LaTorre [fieldwork])
Late 19th century	49.5–121.5, 58.5–72, 58.5–99, 58.4–148.4	Salaga (LaTorre [UNESCO Gonja])

Calculated from Table 6.1 assuming receipts from gold mining averaged 1 shilling per day. See Appendix to Chapter 6 for details of sources.

1887 a visitor to the same market reported that the prices for males and females were the same, being differentiated according to age rather than gender.[39] Though the price differential was not permanent, it confirms that the sums paid for females included an element reflecting their value as potential wives and as potential mothers of free men's heirs: a point developed in the next chapter. What matters here is that the fact that prices for females were raised by their roles outside direct production reinforces the conclusion that the price of slave *labour* power was very low compared to the price necessary to hire free labour.

Evidence about what happened in the early colonial period, when the end of slavery was first anticipated and then gradually realised, confirms that there was/had been a decisive disparity between the costs of slave and free labour. In 1925 Rattray was informed by village elders in Wam (south of Berekum in western Asante) that 'We have now stopped [gold] mining because it only pays when you have slaves'.[40] In a general economic and social survey in 1931, the Chief Census Officer stated that the shafts made by traditional mining methods 'are now no longer worked, as with the disappearance of slave labour the results would not possibly be sufficient to cover the expense.'[41] Earlier, at the very beginning of the colonial occupation, a British traveller opined that 'On the abolition of domestic slavery the kola industry in Ashanti will tend to die out'.[42] His prediction proved too pessimistic, but his implicit assumption that kola producers would not be able to afford to hire regular wage labour seems to have been justified. In the mid-1930s, for example, 'In the principal kola areas in Ashanti it is in most cases the owner himself who picks and prepares the nuts for sale but occasionally he may let his trees to another who will do this work for one half of the crop.'[43] An overview of the economic significance of slavery was provided by the chief and elders of Adanse in 1906. In a petition for continued government toleration of slavery and pawning they observed that, as Asante chiefs and headmen, they depended on the labour of slaves and the descendants of slaves 'as we have no money like Europeans to hire men to do necessaries for us'.[44]

The implication of the evidence considered in this section is that—until cocoa cultivation was adopted early in the colonial period—compulsion was a necessary condition of labour being cheap enough for there to be a labour market at all. Without coercion the reservation price of labour consistently exceeded the maximum wage rate which potential employers could have afforded. Amid such physical and institutionalized abundance of land there was too little occupational specialization to generate a market for goods sufficiently remunerative to make it profitable for a producer to employ a labourer on any terms that it would be profitable for the labourer to accept. It took force to reduce the labour-supply cost enough to make it possible for the supply and demand curves to intersect. Thus Domar's proposition applies: 'the wage of a hired man . . . will have to be at least equal to what he can make on his own farm; if he receives that much, no surplus (rent) will be left for his employer.'[45]

D. A Simple Model of the Impact of Coercion in the Labour Market of a Land-Surplus Economy

To summarize the implications of the argument so far, Figure 8.1 presents a simple model to illustrate the argument presented here about the market for *nnɔnkɔfɔ* in nineteenth-century Asante. The horizontal axis depicts the quantity of people available for purchase or long-term wage labour at a given time. The vertical axis depicts the price of labour. In the case of slaves, this meant the purchase price of 'average' captives, plus the net present value of the expected supervision costs (they can be assumed to have provisioned themselves) over the expected working lifetime of the slave. Note that where the slave was to have been engaged in sharecropping, the 'supervision' costs include the value of the fraction of output thereby conceded to the slave, as an incentive for staying and working for the master. In the case of hired labourers, the price means the net present value of the wages of a free labourer over a period equivalent to the expected working lifetime of the slave: wages equal to, or rather, greater than what a free labourer could make on his or her own farm. The demand curve (D) represents the schedule of the sums which users of labour were prepared to offer to acquire and maintain different quantities of extra-familial labour. Three supply curves are shown. S^v illustrates the amounts of wage labour that might be forthcoming if the price was high enough. Because of the virtually universal access to land and the absence of economies of scale, it never is: at no point does S^v intersect the demand curve. S^c represents the quantities of captives available for purchase at each price level. The element of coercion makes it possible, in this model, for the market to clear. We know that in the last few years before colonial rule the impact of Samori Toure's flow of captives would have been to shift the supply schedule of coerced labour downwards, a situation represented by the line S^t, implying a new market-clearing point combining a lower price and a larger quantity of coerced labour.

It is important to reiterate that this model relates to the domestic political economy of Asante. The discussion will be extended in the concluding

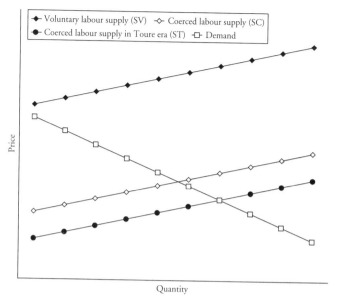

Figure 8.1. A model of the market for captives in 19th century Asante: Coerced clearance.

section to take account of the geo-economic and political contrast between Asante and its northern hinterland, from whence came most of the imported captives.

E. Debt Bondage in the Context of Coercion in the Labour and Credit Markets

Can pawning, too, be usefully analysed in relation to land abundance? Specifically, can we extend to pawning the argument that coercion was an indispensable element in the efforts of chiefs, household heads and young men to obtain productive resources—in this case, capital or labour—additional to those they already possessed? The same factor ratio and production function apply: beyond the short term land was, physically, relatively abundant. Thus, not only was labour scarce in relation to land but cultivation rights had no enduring economic value and were therefore worthless as collateral and as sources of interest. Logically, the same queries arise with pawning as with slavery: about whether the rulers did not enjoy alternatives to these forms of coercive rent-appropriation; or on the other hand, whether there were any cultural alternatives to them. In principle land could have been made artificially scarce. For the reasons given in the context of slavery, however, it is very hard to see how it would have been in the net interest of the rulers to do so; and it may well have been beyond their practical capability. Culturally, though, alternatives were clearly feasible. The fact that the same word was used for human and other pawns may be taken as a strong indication that there was no cultural obstacle to, for example, lending on land or farms rather than on humans. Indeed, we saw in Chapter 5 that there were instances of political rights over land being pawned or mortgaged in the nineteenth century. Moreover, we will note in Part Four that the pledging of farms was to be adopted in the twentieth century using the same term as for human pawning (*awowasi*).

Before pursuing the issue further it is useful to remind ourselves explicitly that, unlike slave buying, human pawning was a deal in two factor markets at once: those for labour (the pawn) and capital (the loan). It is thus an example of interlocked factor markets. But, whereas that concept[46] has generally been invoked in relation to contracts that were proximately free from physical and social coercion, a feature of this case is that human pawning was underpinned by the practice or implicit threat of coercion. Let us now examine the evidence about nineteenth-century human pawning in relation to the proposition that coercion was necessary for both the capital and labour markets to exist.

In the 1906 petition quoted earlier, the chief and elders of Adanse stated that 'we Ashantis take pawning as a mortgage of a house if any one get [into] debt and *as he has no house or land to mortgage*, then he is oblige[d] to give himself to someone who could pay till he repays it' (my emphasis).[47] Again, as a colonial official observed, even when the spread of letter-writers and colonial courts made promissory notes available, 'many families in reduced circumstances are not possessed of sufficient property to make it worth the while of prospective lenders to risk their money upon a mere note of hand'. No pawn, no loan.[48] Where, exceptionally, a large loan was given in such circumstances the rate of interest may be expected to have included a risk premium, and thus to be particularly high. We lack the evidence to test this, but the following case is suggestive. It may be recalled that Kwadwo Donko, whose marriage history we reviewed in Chapter 6, required £8 to redeem his future wife from pawnage, probably in the 1880s or early 1890s. As Donko

> . . . was poor & [a] stranger, & even a slave, [he] could not therefore manage to pay the said sum of money from his own pocket, but was obliged to

borrow. He got £4 from a friend & the rest £4 from another person & have (*sic*) of course to pay it back with high interest to the money owners. After all, the whole sum amounted to £17 Sterling. He did work very hard before he could pay back the whole amount.[49]

How this flat rate of 112.25 per cent worked out in annual terms we do not know, and therefore we cannot be sure that a risk premium was involved. But the case is consistent with that possibility, especially as far as the '£4 from another person' was concerned. We might expect that the overall rate would have been reduced by the fact that the other half of the loan came from a friend, who might not only be sympathetic but could presumably assess the risk relatively accurately. Neoclassicists tend to argue that interlocked factor markets work to the mutual benefit of both principals in the transaction[50] (moreover, the British official quoted earlier insisted that 'few "pawns" enter into their obligations unwillingly').[51] We will return to the issue of exploitation in Chapter 10.

Let us now build on our earlier discussion of the cost of slaves compared to free labour. Until the late 1890s pawns offered labour that was very cheap compared to the value of free labour. They cost the equivalent of an average gold-miner's earnings from one and a half seasons' labour. By the end of the 1890s, with the value of new pawns rising sharply while the supply of new slaves was constricted by the newly-imposed colonial state, a pawn was worth about five mining-seasons' output.

Thus the conclusion of our discussion of slavery, that coercion was necessary for any labour market to exist, is sustained for pawn labour too. In the case of pawning physical force, while ultimately a possibility, was combined with the moral pressure of family obligation. If pawning was a response to market forces in the sense that it was a response to relative scarcities, it was—like slave trading—a highly 'imperfect' market, grounded in the political control of elders, especially male elders, over both male and female juniors, or that of masters over slaves.

F. Conclusion

This chapter has examined the evidence about slavery in nineteenth-century Asante in relation to the West African and global debate over how far the existence of slavery can be explained as a profit-maximizing response to labour shortage in land-surplus economies (the Nieboer hypothesis). The last section extended the analysis to include pawnship. The argument is that the hypothesis, as far as it goes, applies strongly to this case as far as the *internal* political economy of Asante was concerned. The analysis included a crude but informative quantification of the cost comparison between slave and free labour: a basic exercise which appears not to have been attempted before for a West African economy. The findings reveal that the cost difference was a gross one. This result, plus other evidence, point to the conclusion that, while wage labour was genuinely an alternative possibility in cultural terms, it was *not* feasible economically. This fits Domar's version of the hypothesis. For the labour market to clear would have required widespread coercion. Such coercion was indeed applied, in the form of enslavement and pawning.

The main limitation of the Nieboer hypothesis is its political indeterminacy. On this the argument here began from the empirical assumption that Asante was rather unusual in its region, even in that now notorious period, in the scale of its slave imports. What made this possible was that the kingdom secured, not a proportionate share of a common property resource (as in the model sketched above), but rather a local monopoly over especially valuable natural resources. In this period the commercial value of the natural assets specific to the forest zone was apparently not high enough to persuade savanna-dwellers to offer their labour services to those who controlled these assets (even had prospective migrant workers not had reason to fear enslavement). On the other hand, the rent from control of these assets may be seen as making a decisive contribution to the financing of the persistent and socially-widespread importation of slaves. Thus the Nieboer hypothesis is inadequate once the analysis is extended beyond the borders of the slave-importing economy to include the areas from which the captives came. It is argued here that an emphasis on the supply inelasticity of natural resources, partly as a result of military and political intervention, is important if we are to develop a more nuanced understanding of the political economy of slavery in different areas and sub-periods of pre-colonial West African history. This perspective may also contribute to the general task of making the political determinants of the existence and scale of slavery in history genuinely endogenous.

We have examined why there were markets in certain factors but not in all, and why those markets took the coercive form that they did. We now turn to the non-market mechanisms which were also involved in putting factors to work, and to the non-factor aspects of the markets in labour and capital.

9

GENDER AND KINSHIP ASPECTS OF THE SOCIAL RELATIONS OF PRODUCTION, 1807–1896

The most basic part of the social organization of labour in the nineteenth century was the respective roles of the free members of the same household: this was 'basic' in that it applied whether or not they had slaves or pawns in addition. Accordingly, Section A considers the consequences for investment and the accumulation of wealth of the particular division of labour between free spouses that characterized nineteenth-century Asante, and asks why the conjugal family was the basic unit of work in this otherwise predominantly matrilineal setting. Section B examines how slavery and pawning related to men's strategies within the family structures of nineteenth-century Asante society. It discusses the gender dimension of the Asante demand for slaves and pawns and explores the implications of this for the relative importance of the productive and, in a broad sense, the reproductive uses of slaves and pawns.

A. Gender and Kinship in the Allocation of Household Labour

The discussion here focuses on two key aspects of the ways in which productive resources were channelled by 'household' institutions: a characteristic division of labour between the sexes, and the paradox, pointed out by Arhin, that 'in spite of their matrilineal inheritance system, the Ashanti basic unit of labour in mining, trading and farming has always been the conjugal family'.[1]

We have seen that women were expected to give priority to the activities that enabled the household to survive and reproduce itself, physically and socially. Men, though making certain important contributions to food farming (especially clearing the land), were responsible for the bulk of the extra-subsistence economic activities.[2]

The diary of one European visitor to Asante indicates that this division of labour was harmful to the physical well-being of women as opposed, by implication, to men. Having entered Asante for the first time, from the coast, and reached the small town of Dompoase, Coppin recorded his impression that in Adanse:

> A strong, healthy middle aged looking woman is a rarity. This is explained in 2 ways. The girls are married very early, & by reason of the hard life they are subjected to they age very quickly after they have borne 2 or 3 children.[3]

He added that 'these oppressed women go early to the grave.'[4] By the 'hard life' of women he specified their part in the division of labour: doing 'the greater part of the farming' on top of 'their domestic duties'.[5] Coppin's account of the effects of women's work on their health is not as yet confirmed by other sources, however, and we should be cautious about accepting the impressions of a single source, not medically qualified, on such a complex relationship.

But we can be clear about the implication of the division of labour for the accumulation of wealth: it was the men who had most of the opportunities to acquire money, and by extension ' "gain riches" '.[6] Thus, because labour input was considered to give title of ownership, the central mechanism of inequality within the conjugal family was not direct appropriation of the products of labour. The matrilineal system actually entailed the separation of husbands' and wives' possessions. Rather, it was a particular division of labour that reserved to men the lion's share of chances for self-enrichment. Thus, unlike in 'Yorubaland',[7] the post-Atlantic slave trade growth of market production by commoners[8] did not entail greater opportunities for women traders and producers specifically.

A further implication is that wives could be very important in husbands' economic strategies. A British officer, Major C. Barter, wrote in 1896 that 'The husband . . . can make over his wife to another man; and so great is the value of women for work, that the husband seldom has any difficulty in getting a wife off his hands, provided she be young and strong.'[9] While Barter clearly over-simplified the divorce procedure, his remarks confirm the importance of wives to husbands' calculations about labour recruitment.

Arhin used the term 'conjugal mode of production' to denote an 'independent production, but not consumption, unit' comprising 'a husband, as master and organiser, wife, adolescent children, pawns, and slaves, if any'.[10] We have qualified this by noting that in some cases, at least, there seems to have been a matrilineal contribution to farm labour, in the person of a nephew or niece. We have also clarified it, by insisting that this does not mean that tasks were anything like equally shared. But why was the conjugal unit the frame within which family labour and its rewards was organized, rather than the matrilineal segment? After all, it appears that the conjugal family was not the usual unit of consumption. A husband usually ate with his male matrikin rather than with his wife or wives and children.[11]

Arhin put forward an illuminating answer for the case of gold mining. Private (commoner) gold miners needed secrecy, because they might want to keep the larger nuggets instead of abiding by the law under which such finds were to be surrendered to the state to be pulverized and taxed. A miner would prefer to work with his own children rather than his sister's children precisely because the latter were his heirs: 'for that reason, they might betray an uncle who kept nuggets'.[12] The chance of finding a particularly big nugget gave a special sharpness to the issue of trust among miners. But liability to taxation or rent applied also in other extra-subsistence activities. This consideration, though, was not relevant to most food-crop production. Accordingly, Arhin's idea can usefully be supplemented with a more general explanation. In this context, it is arguable that the interests of principal and agent were more closely aligned if the latter was the former's son rather than his sister's son. The nephew was heir by right, unconditionally. The son could hope to get decisive help from his father, but only providing he worked for him faithfully and well.

Jack Goody hypothesized that the transmission of property from parents to children is associated with 'advanced agriculture' and therefore with a large surplus above what the producer can consume, whereas inheritance by brothers and nephews is associated with more backward agriculture, yielding only small surpluses at best.[13] In short, the more valuable the legacy, the more tightly it is kept within the conjugal family.

Goody's characterization of Sub-Saharan economies is too simple, as far as Asante was concerned. While it is true that Asante agriculture did not produce a big surplus until the adoption of cocoa (nor was there the demand for one), the economy as a whole generated substantial 'surplus' in terms of exchange value: in the form of its extra-subsistence products which, directly and indirectly, yielded *sika*, money. This may help to explain why Asante society was in a position intermediate—schematically, if not necessarily historically—between the two points that Goody postulated. Inheritance was formally and firmly matrilineal, but with the major qualification that fathers could help sons during their lifetimes. We will return to this at the end of the chapter.

B. The Gender Dimension of Slavery and Pawning

This section asks how the gender composition of the populations of masters, slaves and pawns, respectively, together with gender differentials in the market value of slaves and pawns, affected the practice of slavery and pawning. We also consider what our findings suggest about the motives and mechanisms behind the recruitment of slaves and pawns. In particular it may help us evaluate the relative importance of the 'reproductive' roles (biological and social) of pawns compared to their roles in production and trade. Let us first consider the gender composition of the owners of slaves and holders of pawns; then discuss the uses to which slaves and pawns were put; before examining the evidence about sex ratios and market values of the slaves and pawns themselves.

We know that some women were specifically the owners or mistresses of slaves and pawns, who served them as maids within the palace or home and in farming. Yet it is clear that the overwhelming majority of both slaves and pawns had male masters, even if the labour services of many of the slaves and pawns may at times have been made available to free women. Rattray was clear that a 'woman might own her own slaves, purchased with her own "money"'.[14] But while specific instances of male owners abound in the individual cases I have found in the archives, specific instances of female owners of slaves or holders of pawns are rare, though not non-existent. An example of a female slave-owner was Yaa Bosuo, whose maid, Akosua Krah, was purchased in the north as a girl, probably in about the early 1880s, and brought to the village of Wioso apparently to join the Kumasi *gyaasefoɔ*, where she lived with her mistress.[15] We saw an instance of a woman pawn-taker in Chapter 7—Atipimoa, 'Princess of Mampon'—and there are other known instances of women receiving—and also giving—pawns.[16]

A necessary explanation for the male preponderance among holders of slaves and pawns is the particular division of labour between free spouses under which, as we have seen, men enjoyed the lion's share of the purchasing and lending power. This, in turn, gave them most of the opportunities for buying slaves and taking pawns. But this is unlikely to be a sufficient explanation. For slaves and pawns offered specific advantages to men in a polygamous and matrilineal society. These advantages, which will be discussed shortly, would have constituted an extra incentive to men to use their gold to acquire slaves and pawns: specifically female ones.

Both male and female slaves, and pawns, were available for subsistence and extra-subsistence production. Adding more slaves or pawns of either sex within the social framework of either a *gyaase* or a conjugal family increased the labour force; while their gender, whichever it was, was unlikely to make that labour force less flexible. Women as well as men could farm or head-load; and while it was men who went underground, women did much of the other work in gold acquisition and processing.[17] But given that most of the tasks performed by slaves and pawns were ones in which output was partly a function of physical strength, while requiring relatively little skill, one might expect that male labourers would, in general, be preferred by prospective masters.

The uses of slaves and pawns in social and demographic reproduction were much more tightly 'gendered'. Had Asante women been allowed more than one husband this might have been different: but it is beyond the scope of a study of factors of production to seek to explain why this counterfactual was just that. Historically, compared to marriage with free women, slavery and pawning offered free Asante men opportunities to acquire more wives and children, at lower cost, and/or additional property rights over wives and children. Polygamy is not a sufficient explanation of this. Also crucial was the fact that the matrilineal system restricted fathers' rights over their children. The details are important: let us consider pawning and slavery separately.

We saw in Chapter 7 that for male creditors pawning could be a source of new wives—and thus of new children[18]—and a means of greater control over existing wives and children. Moreover, if a male creditor was not married to his female pawn, he had the right to treat her as his concubine, and to give her in marriage, generally to a nephew of his. Neither action cancelled the debt.[19]

For free Asante men, slaves had even greater advantages than pawns in the context of marriage, child-rearing and inheritance. For marriage to a slave offered the only way by which a man in a matrilineal Akan society could formally circumvent the limitations which matriliny imposed on fathers' rights in relation to their children. Terray put it precisely: for a free man a boy born by a slave wife was 'at once a son and a nephew'.[20] One of Rattray's informants in the Mampon area apparently remarked 'You will really like your slave wife the better[?] because she cannot go to her abusua and call her children and your own [to follow her away from your home]'.[21] Rattray himself wrote that a man's children by a wife who was his own slave woman 'were the only children over whom he had any real authority'.[22] It should be noted, however, that slavery itself could limit the paternal rights of free men. If the wife was the slave of another man, the children belonged to her master not her husband.[23] Slavery extended the paternal rights of free men only where the father was himself the slaveowner.

Slaves themselves, in practice, rarely enjoyed paternal rights. We observed in Chapter 6 that few male slaves seem to have had the chance to marry even a fellow slave. It should be remembered that, given polygamy, this would not necessarily have much reduced the contribution of slaves to the long-term growth of the population of Asante.

One would expect that the market value of property rights in male and female slaves would reflect not only their productive and reproductive uses but also the security of the property rights. The issue did not arise with pawning; in that the pawn's *abusua* had to provide a replacement if the original pawn died or fled. No such guarantee existed for slaves. At state level slaves could be a security problem, as we will see in the next chapter. More relevant to individual slave-buyers' decisions, however, was the risk that a slave might run away. As we saw earlier, escapes were a real problem for Asante slaveowners, especially after 1874. It is possible that Asante authorities and people believed that female slaves were much less likely than male slaves to rebel or escape. If so, this presumably reduced the price they were willing to pay for male as opposed to female slaves. But we have no direct evidence on this.

Analysis of the gender composition of slaves and pawns can add to the evidence adduced in earlier chapters about the importance of labour among the reasons why slaves and pawns were valued. If slaves and pawns were valued by their masters solely for (largely manual) labour we would expect that the majority of both would be males in their late teens and twenties. If supply constraints prevented this, the pattern of demand would be reflected in a high price premium for male slaves compared to female ones, and in larger loans being given per male pawn than per female pawn. If, in contrast, slaves and pawns were valued solely for 'reproductive' purposes (in the broad sense used here) by those who bought and lent on them, respectively, we would expect the overwhelming majority (perhaps all) of both to be females in their late teens and twenties. Again, if this was prevented by supply inelasticities, the pattern of demand would be revealed by much higher market values being placed on females than males.

According to an early secondary source, in the mid-nineteenth century, 'To supply the demand for women in Ashanti the surrounding country must be greatly drained of its female population'. The author implied that such was not the case for its male population.[24] LaTorre cites an interview in Amoafo, near Bekwai, for testimony that the tendency was for female slaves imported from the north to be retained, whereas males were more likely to be exported to the coast.[25] Oral evidence from Adanse confirms that slaves permanently imported into Asante were mostly female.[26] The government's annual report on Ashanti for 1898 implied that it had freed a total of 25 boys and girls from slave traders since either the invasion or since the Basel Mission opened 'a small slave home', evidently during 1898, to which 'we have been able to send all the children taken from slave dealers'.[27] Twenty-five women were also 'sent' there.[28] It is possible, admittedly, that some men too were freed from slave caravans but were recruited into the colonial army or police rather than being sent to the missionaries' 'slave home'. Even so, on balance it is reasonable to accept that the majority of first-generation slaves in Asante were female. It is clear, however, from numerous sources—some of which have been cited above in other contexts—that first-generation male slaves were common too.

The Basel missionary Kühne, on his release from Asante captivity in 1874, was reported to have remarked that ' "the woman' slave 'is rather the more valuable . . . to her master, being both a better worker and useful in other ways, and therefore when slaves are given for sacrifice the men are more often handed over" '.[29] We have seen evidence that higher prices were paid for female than for male slaves before 1874, but not by 1887.[30] That there was a differential at one period but not later suggests that the supply of female slaves may have risen, whether in response to the price signal or, literally, by accident of war. On the argument formulated above, the fact that female slaves were at a premium at one time is conclusive evidence that the demand for slaves was by no means purely for directly-productive labour. On the other hand, the search for such labour was an important component of the demand for slaves: otherwise there would have been probably no demand for male captives at all, let alone a later period of equal prices.

It is hard to get an overview of the gender ratio among pawns. The procedure followed here is to arrange all the cases of pawning for which I had sufficient information to identify the gender of specific pawns in the sequence in which the pawnings took place.[31] A 'case' is defined as a distinct pawning transaction, involving one or more pawns, whether or not the transaction later surfaced in our sources in isolation or together with other cases, related or otherwise.[32] The exact order is uncertain, but the following statements seem to be reliable on the information available so far. I have come across eleven such from the nineteenth century, of which anything from one to three are from after the colonial occupation of 1896. They yield a total of ten pawns identifiable as male[33] plus ten pawns, two of whom may have been pawned twice, identifiable as female.[34] Of these, the latest three cases involved five male and five female pawns (one of the latter possibly pawned twice, which would make six pawnings of females).[35] The sample is very small but it suggests, provisionally, that in the nineteenth century male pawns were about as common as female ones. The statement by Armitage in 1905, when he was a District Commissioner with several years experience in Asante, that pawns are 'usually' male[36] seems to have been at best out of date (as we will see in Part Four). But it was not the absurdity that one might think after reading Rattray's description of the order of preference among pawn-giving *mmusua*. This begins with the heads' married sisters and nieces and continues with unmarried sisters and nieces before coming to nephews and brothers.[37] Conversely, Rattray may have been right that matrilineages preferred to pawn female members. If this handful of known cases is representative the most plausible inference is that creditors considered the combined reproductive uses of pawns as less important than their services in production and trade. On 'price', my only evidence for the nineteenth century relates to a simultaneous pawning 'before the 1900 war began', probably after the 1896 occupation, in which the sums loaned on each person were the same.[38]

Taken together, the limited evidence points to the tentative conclusion that there was little difference between the number, and the market value, of male and female pawns in the precolonial nineteenth century. On the argument above, this indicates that creditors valued pawns both for their reproductive uses (otherwise male pawns were likely to have been either more common or to have secured larger loans, or both) and for their directly productive ones (otherwise male pawns would have been non-existent or at least much less valuable than female ones). If Rattray was right, there was a supply-side preference for pawning females. He may have overstated the willingness of cash-scarce matrilineages to pawn female members. By doing so they weakened the lineage's own call upon the varied output of the girls and women concerned.[39] But to the extent that he was correct, this supply-side bias would have been reinforced—given that the majority of slaves were female—by the fact that slaves were the main available alternative to free matrikin as potential pawns. But the fragmentary evidence is that such a bias was not reflected in the outcome, either in terms of relative numbers of male and female slaves or (though this is especially tentative) in their market valuation. If it existed, the preference for supplying females must have been met by a strong demand-side preference for receiving males in pawn. This in turn suggests that, whereas slaves were valued relatively equally for their reproductive and productive uses, pawns were valued largely for their labour. The latter conclusion fits the observation, made in Chapter 7, about the implication of the apparent increase in demand for pawns from 1896, in response to the colonial suppression of the supply of new captives.

A likely explanation for this difference between the source of demand for pawns and that for slaves is to be found in the security of the specific property rights involved. Pawns could be redeemed at any time at the initiative of the debtor. In contrast, a master had relatively secure legal control over his slave as long as they both lived. Thus buying female slaves as concubines or wives was a more secure investment than lending on pawns *for these purposes*. The possibility of early redemption was much less of a disadvantage in directly productive activities. Whereas a redeemed pawn-mother was likely to take her children with her when she left,[40] the value of a servant's labour in farming or mining or trading during a given year would not be made less valuable to the master if he or she was redeemed the following year. Hence the preference for females as opposed to males as pawns was likely to be less than the preference for females rather than males as slaves.

This section has shown that the 'reproductive' uses of slaves and pawns mattered as well as the directly 'economic' uses. The importance of these social (and long-term economic) roles has been examined partly by considering the market valuations of slaves and pawns. We have also seen that the labour uses of both kinds of 'unfree' dependent also mattered greatly to the masters. It might be thought that the fact that slaves turn out to have been valued perhaps as much or even more for their social and demographic potential as for their labour compromises the argument put forward in the last chapter. On reflection, surely, the contrary is true. The gap between the supply price of free and slave labour was wide as it was; but without the premium contributed by the 'reproductive' value of slaves, it would have been still wider. In other words, slave labour as such really was vastly cheaper than regular free labour could have been at the same time: to such an extent that the latter was—as yet—not an economic possibility.

Conversely, the Asante case makes it necessary to question the widely-accepted generalization that the majority of pawns in Africa were female.[41] Overall, the section has shown that both the demand and supply sides of slavery, and of pawning, had gender aspects with important consequences. Relating this to the other major concern of this chapter, the fact that slaves and pawns were held widely in Asante society, with the chiefs having considerable concentrations of the former, raises a difficulty with Goody's thesis about African inheritance. For it demonstrates that relatively low levels of agricultural surpluses did not necessarily mean an absence of substantial wealth.

10

EXPLOITATION AND WELFARE:

CLASS AND 'SOCIAL EFFICIENCY' IMPLICATIONS OF THE PROPERTY RIGHTS REGIME, 1807–1896

This chapter explores the implications of the pattern of rights and markets in productive resources for the economic and demographic strategies of individuals—differentiated as they were by rank. Slavery and pawning, as the major means of acquiring extra-familial resources, were crucial to the prospects of demographic and economic accumulation by commoners, and were important also for the wealth of chiefs. Section A relates commoners' and chiefs' acquisition and use of slaves and pawns to their respective patterns of demographic and economic accumulation. Section B reviews the evidence about the degrees and forms of accommodation, resistance and conflict involved in the social relations of production, and reflects on the implications for the evolution of the economy.

A. Imperfect Markets and Unequal Masters

Those factor markets which existed were highly 'imperfect' not only in the sense that they were based partly on coercion, but also in that some of the participants had extra-economic rights which gave them powerful privileges compared to ordinary free commoners ('free' in the sense of being neither slaves nor pawns). Thus while the acquisition of more labour was the generic key to expansion, alike for a commoner household or for a major chief, the distribution of specific social categories of labour, such as free wives, pawns and slaves, not to mention the right to *corvée*, was very unequal even among the free male population. This section examines and compares the options for, and constraints upon, the acquisition of productive resources that faced free commoners and chiefs respectively, and illustrates the paths of accumulation that some of them followed.

Commoners

We saw in Chapter 5 that access to cultivable land was not a problem for free subjects of an Asante chieftaincy, while access to gold or other valuable resources found in the forest was also easy enough, providing the required portion of the proceeds was paid to the stool. For working capital, sons could ask their maternal uncles and especially their fathers; while daughters could presumably ask mothers. As will be evident by now, fathers were much more likely to be able to oblige on a scale sufficient to enable the child to start an independent career. We have seen that it was normal for fathers to help sons in this way; though, as will be further illustrated below, a father might respond to a particular request by telling his son to make the most of what he already had. Credit might be obtained without collateral, especially if a relative or patron was willing to act as surety. For most people, however, to get a large loan it was necessary to provide a pawn. If the borrower himself or herself became the pawn, the chances of being able to accumulate significant wealth in the long term must have been small. To use pawning as a means to acquire working capital for economic expansion it was essential to have dependents available to pawn.

In this capital- and labour-scarce economy the 'critical path' to accumulation, on however modest or however grand a scale, lay through successive acquisitions of dependents: as potential means to obtain loans and, above all, as sources of labour. This economic climb was simultaneously a social climb: the assets required were the same, as will be elaborated later. The major social categories of such human resources were pawns, slaves and free spouses which, as it was men who had the main opportunities for self-enrichment, usually meant wives.

By default, the opportunity to acquire labour by lending on pawns was more important within the commoners' repertoire of instruments of self-enrichment than it was within that of chiefs.[1] For commoners lacked direct access to two of the sources of new slaves: prisoners taken by the Asante army and captives sent in tribute to Kumasi. But they could obtain pawns easily enough if they had the money. Hence commoners seeking labour might look first to the acquisition of pawns rather than slaves. Again, it is a reasonable assumption that pawning was of greater relative importance to those acquiring unfree labour on a small scale than to those acquiring it on a large scale. We noted in Part Two that whereas slavery was an effective means of mobilizing relatively large concentrations of labour (though it was not always so used), pawning was probably usually dispersed. Masters might capture or buy slaves in multitudes, stoolholders might pawn or sell the political control of villages amongst themselves, but debtors usually (though not always) approached creditors offering pawns in ones and twos. In so far as the increase in kola nut exports (in the early nineteenth century) and the advent of the rubber trade (during the last quarter of the century) gave new opportunities to smaller producers, pawnship was a major means by which they could take advantage of them. Based on fieldwork in the early 1960s in the Bechem-Techimentia area, Arhin emphasized the importance of pawn labour there in 'collecting, carrying and selling kola nuts' in the Asante northern trade in the last quarter of the nineteenth century.[2]

Commoners with cash could also exploit the indebtedness created by fines imposed in the chiefs' courts. Early in the colonial period in Gyaman, once a tributary state of the Asante kingdom, there was said to be an unholy alliance of chiefs wielding their power to fine and rich men using their lending power, the two parties conniving to extract pawns from hapless travellers.[3] In Asante too commoners with money to lend took advantage of the opportunities created by litigation in order to obtain pawns.[4] It was a general characteristic of the Asante political economy that both chiefs and commoners readily exploited the interaction of coercion and the market to accumulate wealth.

In addition, commoners might hope to derive indirect benefit from chiefs' privileged access to captives via patronage or private sale. Negotiating with the British in 1896 the Omanhene of Bekwai indicated as much: 'The King [omanhene] had a number of young slave girls that he was now going to give to his young men as wives'.[5] Much more importantly, to judge from the weight of evidence, commoners were free to use the other means of recruiting slaves, namely buying them in the market. Indeed, as we saw in Chapter 6, commoner ownership of slaves seems to have been very widespread. This may well have been primarily a nineteenth-century phenomenon. Until 1807 at least it had been easy for the state to sell any slaves surplus to chiefs' requirements into the lucrative Atlantic trade, rather than to private Asante purchasers.[6] During the next few decades the latter option largely dried up and, as we have seen, the price of slaves fell at first and then only partly recovered,[7] making it less lucrative to re-export slaves and cheaper for Asante purchasers to acquire them. There is much evidence of individuals and matrilineages buying slaves in the 'transit markets' where Asante forest-dwellers traded with savanna merchants. Given that slaves were being widely purchased, it is likely that a high proportion of them were bought by commoners as chiefs had the monopoly of the other sources, tribute and warfare. Besides lower prices, these purchases appear to have reflected—and reinforced— substantial net accumulation of wealth among commoners in the 1807–96 era as a whole.[8]

Obtaining pawns could lead to the acquisition of slaves, and slave-ownership (whether or not preceded or accompanied by pawn-taking) could enable a young man to acquire the means to marry. Again using his oral sources, Arhin stated for the Bechem-Techimentia area during 'the twilight of the Ashanti kingdom' that 'the use of pawns in the kola trade was the quickest way towards the acquisition of slaves. Enterprising men invested in pawns, expanded their trade in kola, and thereby acquired more slaves, who made an even greater contribution for the owner.'[9] A rare account of the career path of an individual commoner before the colonial occupation is to be found among a set of autobiographical 'marriage histories' collected by the Ashanti Social Survey in the mid-1940s. In recalling his youth, Kofi Pusuo was clearly referring to the late pre-colonial period before the new British administration made the importation of new slaves from the north illegal and increasingly hazardous.

> When I reached the age of Puberty, I expressed to my father the need to get married. My father put the matter before my family and when they asked me of my Capital 'Dwetiri' I told them I had £8. My father told me that was too small a capital to marry with. He then instructed me to trade in Kola and travel to the North to buy a slave with my own money before he would allow me to marry any girl I chose. I consented to fathers words bought a male slave . . . Once again father asked of the value of my wealth and I told him I had one slave 5 cover cloths and £5. He said that it was still insufficient to secure me a wife and therefore gave me a year more to work strenuously to increase my Capital before I married. By the end of the year I had increased my wealth with extra £10 and 10 cover cloths. He praised me for my inde- fatigable efforts and later laid hold on a girl and presented her to me as a wife. He performed all the marriage rites and ceremonies on behalf of the girl for me and gave me extra present in the form of money to marry the girl. 'ɔbɔɔ fotoɔ maa me' ['You established a foundation for me'].
>
> Two years afterwards I was able to buy 2 other slaves . . .[10]

In passing, let us note that the fact that bridewealth evidently much exceeded the price of a slave further reinforces the conclusion, reached in Chapter 8, that slavery greatly reduced the cost of obtaining labour.

On marriage, Bowdich observed in 1817 that 'Though polygamy is tolerated to such an excess amongst the higher orders . . . Most of the lower order of freemen have but one wife . . .'[11] For reasons noted above it is likely that as the century went on higher proportions of commoners acquired sufficient wealth to marry and even marry again; and if it was difficult or expensive to obtain an Asante wife, an imported captive might provide an alternative. Further, we have noted that commoners who made fortunes tended to be given public honours and offices. The privileges accompanying their titles would include entitlement to elevated compensation fees from anyone committing adultery with one of their wives.[12]

Finally, a comment on the specific significance of slavery compared to other means of acquiring additional labour. Those commoners who increased their wealth relative to the population as a whole evidently tended to expand their households through pawning and marrying, as often as they could afford. In this context, however, and despite their lack of privileged access to supplies of captives, slavery had three crucial features. First, whereas the acquisition of a wife or a pawn required that there be a willing or needy partner (in the form of a matrilineage as much as an individual) ready to make the deal, an Asante with the necessary money could probably rely on being able to obtain a slave when he wanted one from the market. Second, slave-buying was the form of investment in people which gave the investor the greatest control over the dependent person. Third, short of waiting for the next indigenous generation to mature, the import of captives was the only way in which commoner households as a whole (or indeed Asante principals generally) could expand their labour forces significantly rather than simply redistributing them.

Chiefs

Chiefs had privileged powers over both land and labour. Control over the allocation of cultivable land was not yet of much significance for the accumulation of wealth. Chiefs' rights over other natural resources gave them a rental income: when they allowed other principals to dig gold or tap rubber, for example. But in terms of the mobilization of productive resources, their most meaningful advantages in this period were their privileged rights over labour. Besides being able to call upon the occasional services of their subjects through *corvée*, they had the regular services of their slaves and, to a lesser extent, those of the descendants of previous generations of slaves. Chiefs (of all kinds) also enjoyed major advantages in access to new captives. Besides their monopolies of war (and raiding) and tribute as sources of *nnɔnkɔfoɔ*, they even had a head start in the import trade in captives. For state traders had the privileges of freedom from road tolls and the right of annual first access to the markets where slaves were offered for sale to Asantes. Admittedly—and significantly—this privilege was shared with their free porters, as noted above.[13] But in most years a group of the latter would have had to combine their receipts in order to afford a slave from the proceeds of the kola they carried on top of the chief's loads. In 1817 a single 'basket' of kola nuts could furnish the price of a slave: but after that prices were much higher.[14] In respect of pawns they had no particular privileges, beyond the fact that their judicial power gave them opportunities to induce a supply of pawns which commoners lacked: court fines and fees bred debts and therefore offers of pawns.[15] Chiefs and their senior officials also often had sufficient cash to provide the loans to meet the financial exigencies that their courts had created.[16]

The acquisition of slaves and pawns, respectively and collectively, offered different possibilities for chiefs than for commoners, and—relatedly—for large-scale than for small-scale users of labour. Despite scale-neutrality in production it is possible to draw a qualitative distinction between, on the one hand, the addition of a few slaves to a workforce that otherwise comprised members of the principal's conjugal and perhaps matrilineal family, and on the other, the use of slaves on a large scale and in concentrated form. This is one way of formulating the distinction between domestic and chiefly slavery.

It is reasonable to assume that the period during which chiefs had their highest share of all slaves in Asante was the 'long century' of, generally, Asante imperial expansion and military success from 1701 until 1807 and, to a lesser extent, until the 1831 treaty with Britain. For in this era, precisely because of the frequent military success, fighting and tribute were presumably the main sources of slaves imported into Asante.[17] Conversely, in this period commoners would have been most dependent on pawning (and marrying additional free wives) rather than slavery for additional labour. Describing his visit of 1817, Bowdich referred to:

> . . . those slaves, who, to prevent famine and insurrection, had been selected (from that fettered multitude which could no longer be driven off to the coast directly they arrived at the capital), to create plantations in the more remote and stubborn tracts[18]

Thus it seems that chiefs' slave-holding increased when its opportunity cost was reduced by the closing of the Atlantic slave market.[19] It is likely that slave ownership by the political elite at least continued unabated until 1873. Indeed, it may well have increased, as tribute, war and (if necessary) purchase replenished the stock of first-generation recruits to the *gyaasefɔɔ*. But this would have been an increase in absolute terms only, because it seems clear that the chiefs' share of slave acquisitions became much less monopolistic after 1807. For, as we have seen, the 1807–96 era saw widespread importation of captives by commoners.

Chiefs were able—and were expected—to have multiple wives. In Asante adultery was conceived as an offence against property rights: the theft of a husband's rights by another man. If the offended husband was a commoner this was considered a private matter (*efiɛsem*) and the legal damages were relatively modest. A 'poor man' would receive 75 per cent of the marriage payment (bridewealth) he had paid (one and a half *ackies* compared to two), plus a pot of wine, on Bowdich's evidence.[20] But the cuckolding of a chief was considered an offence against the state (*oman akyiwadee*) and he would receive ten times the bridewealth he had paid (ten *peredwan* compared to one).[21] Thus marriage payments could yield handsome returns in adultery fees: but, as Allman has emphasized, only for chiefs.[22] Some of them seem to have responded to the incentive that the law created to encourage 'unfaithfulness' among their wives in order to increase their incomes.[23]

Like commoners, chiefs could accumulate. People seeking high office were enjoined to do so, as Bowdich remarked in a much-quoted passage:

> It is a frequent practice of the King's, to consign sums of gold to the care of rising captains, without requiring them from them for two or three years, at the end of which time he expects the captain not only to restore the principal, but to prove that he has acquired sufficient of his own, from the use of it, to support the greater dignity the King would confer on him. If he has not, his talent is thought too mean for further elevation. Should he have no good traders amongst his dependents, (for if he has there is no difficulty) usury and worse resources are countenanced, and thought more creditable than a failure, ascribed to want of talent rather than to a regard of principle.[24]

Unlike commoners, chiefs had the privilege of being allowed to sacrifice their slaves on appropriate occasions. Freeman 'ascertained from an Ashantee . . . that the common people are *not at* liberty to sacrifice their slaves for the dead without the consent of the king, and the king seldom gives them that liberty.'[25] Paradoxical though it may be in strictly secular terms, the destruction of labour-power entailed in such killing was as much a part—albeit part of the finale—of a successful career as the acquisition of wives and slaves was during a chief-entrepreneur's lifetime. It was considered essential that a notable should be able to maintain his or her status in the afterlife. As in this life, the instrument of such status, and a measure of it, was the number of subordinates who accompanied the personage.[26]

From the perspective of a mourner who offered some of his or her own slaves as oblates, again, there is not necessarily a paradox about the 'voluntary' destruction of valuable workers. Such an act was intended, precisely, to cost something: in the broader sense of the English word, to be a sacrifice indeed. The leading mourners could not be seen—and would not want—to be 'cheap' themselves, as they would be if they stinted in honouring the dead. The son of a major Kumasi chief took his own life because he could not afford slaves for killing in his father's honor.[27] Moreover, those killed were understood to be joining the revered ancestor as servants: thus their services were not being wasted, only transferred. Besides the selfless imperative to do right by the deceased, for some heirs there may also have been the self-interested consideration that the good-will of the dead was of material importance to the continued well-being of those who survived.

It was possible to have condemned criminals put to death rather than slaves. Indeed, Wilks has pointed out that in the late 1840s, at least, it was possible to buy slaves in Kumasi 'solely for slaughter at "customs"'. The vendor must have been the state, and it is a reasonable assumption that the slaves concerned were *nkyere* (sg., *akyere*)—those already under sentence of death for crimes of whatever sort[28] or perhaps for being 'troublesome or useless' to their master.[29] Generally, it seems that a hard-working ɔdɔnkɔ was at much less risk than an *akyere*.[30] That the state would not allow most subjects to sacrifice slaves even if they wanted to do so, and that it allowed condemned criminals to be sold for funerals, can be seen as circumstantial evidence of a policy of trying to limit the slaughter of productive, obedient slaves. Kühne's reported statement (quoted above) about masters retaining female rather than male slaves was couched in similar terms. It is interesting to note that there are tentative indications that the incidence of slaves being killed at funerals in the first half of the nineteenth century varied inversely with the price of slaves.[31] If so, this would suggest that when working slaves became particularly valuable in economic terms, some owners at least became less willing to select them for funerary killing. To imagine that slave owners would give up only slaves who were in some sense surplus to their own current requirements would be to fail to allow that they took their beliefs seriously. But the evidence suggests that such beliefs were tempered with a degree of present-centred time preference or even secular pragmatism.

Conclusion: Unequal Masters and Socially Differentiated Sources of Labour

Commoners depended for extra-familial labour essentially on a (highly imperfect) market, on buying and lending, whereas chiefs might obtain it through the non-market means of tribute, capture or *corvée*. A major proposition put forward in this section is that pawns were more important for commoners and for the heavily overlapping category of smaller users of labour than they were for chiefs and the heavily overlapping category of larger users of labour. For all categories of masters of dependent labour, though, the availability of imported captives was crucial in that it eased the constraint imposed on their collective search for labour by the (at any given time) fixed size of the indigenous population. This included raising the number of potential pawns, in that borrowers occasionally resorted to pawning slaves.[32]

B. Welfare, Productivity, Exploitation and Resistance

This aim of this section is to synthesize and pursue the implications of the foregoing for the issues of accumulation, exploitation and 'social efficiency'. From both marxist and 'new institutionalist' perspectives the history of property and markets in the factors of production in the Asante kingdom would appear to involve much extraction of surplus or economic rent. The recipients were men, masters of slaves and pawns, and chiefs; the losers were commoner women, pawns and above all slaves. But there are other sides to the issue.

As a preliminary, it is important to note that some state interventions in property rights can be seen as examples of pareto-optimal intervention. In Agogo—the evidence is from the 1910s but it is hard to see why it should have been an innovation—the chief set the start and finish of the snail-gathering and bat-hunting seasons. No-one was allowed to engage in either activity except during the periods when the chief specifically authorized it. In the case of snails, at least, this was apparently to ensure that the stock of snails could replenish itself through unmolested egg-laying.[33] Thus we see the state—or this chieftaincy—acting not as a self-interested exploiter of subjects but as an impartial referee, limiting competition to ensure that all had something to hunt in the future.

More directly relevant is the observation that African forms of slavery and debt bondage have also been seen as comparatively benign. Most notably, the functionalist position, strongly urged by Igor Kopytoff and Suzanne Miers, is that African slave systems were essentially social rather than economic institutions, designed not to exploit labour but to absorb strangers. The assimilative character of such systems is seen as proof of this.[34] In Norman Klein's view, 'Domestic servitude was . . . a legitimizing doorway into Akan matriliny', though he emphasized that this did not apply to 'state slavery'.[35] Again, from the perspective of 'history from below' one might ask whether the exploited were able to offer resistance,[36] and whether such resistance or the threat of it led masters to make the institution less oppressive.[37] This final section first presents the claims and evidence for seeing slavery and pawnship in Asante as relatively mild forms of subordination. We then consider the other side of the story, and go on to discuss the issue of resistance. In concluding we reflect on the implications of these institutions for the economy as a whole.

Slavery and Pawning as Mechanisms of Social Integration

Consistent with the functionalist tradition, Rattray interpreted the Asante pawnship system, *awowasi*, primarily in terms of kinship. Indeed, much of the practice and even more of the ideology of pawning was consistent with matrilineal ideology. Thus the right of chiefs to pawn subjects who were not also their kin was justified or rationalized by analogy between the chief's position and that of a lineage head.[38] The context of kinship obligations does much to explain why, although slaves could be pawned, both borrowers and lenders apparently preferred to pawn their kinsfolk rather than slaves.[39] One of Rattray's informants told him that a slave was more likely to run away from the creditor than was a member of one's *abusua*, who would feel a family obligation to stay until the family could repay the debt.[40] The general principle of mutual responsibility extended to the obligations of men toward their wives and children, or rather, toward the in-laws. It was 'considered disgraceful' for a man to refuse to accept his wife or child in pawn.[41] More widely still, it was considered the duty of those who could afford a loan to assist impecunious kin by accepting pawns. An Asante saying ran '*okaniba na ode ka*, "the good citizen is he who assumes debts" '.[42] In 1908 the chief and elders of the town of Manso Nkwanta, petitioning the colonial government against proposals to prohibit pawning, insisted that the institution was essential to the welfare of the poor. Abolition, they predicted, would mean that:

> . . . for instance a poor man may contract debts and he will go after a richman for a loan, he will simply tell him to bring a man to secure, the poor man will tell the richman, that I get no one to secure me, the richman will refuse to give him such loan and tell him to [go a]way, and by that will induce the poor man to do himself some harm, if such things occurs [*sic*] in our districts it . . . will ruin us to the last.[43]

There were accepted constraints on the treatment of pawns by masters. Rattray was told in 1925 that 'If the master treats the pawns badly, the pawn can tell his *abusua* that they must redeem him in say a year or he will run away. If he runs away his *abusua* [are] not responsible so long as he does not run back to them'.[44] Rattray noted that the creditor had to pay for the search,[45] and could not claim his money for at least a year.[46] Should the pawn commit suicide, 'the creditor became responsible for all the funeral expenses, and the debt was also cancelled'.[47]

The first generation of colonial administrators of Asante, opposing pressure from their superiors for abolitionist actions, offered descriptions of slavery which anticipated the functionalist position.[48] According to Armitage, 'These natives on entering their "master's" house immediately become one of the family and usually adopt the family name. They work in the interests of the family and share in it's [*sic*] success and prosperity.' Again, 'The Chief wife of Kofi Yami, the "Head Linguist" of Bekwai is a "slave", but he leaves her in sole charge of the house and property when he is absent, and she is free to go where she likes.'[49] Rattray emphasized the slave's status as a legal person and a potential property-owner who 'ultimately might become heir to his master'[50] (though the latter seems unlikely in practice, given the prior claims of both matrikin and children). Owners seem also to have been expected to contribute to the funeral expenses of slaves, cheap as slave funerals usually were.[51] There is a case of this from the village of Dominase, in Amansie, in 1931. An owner, Kwesi Kyei, was unhappy at having to borrow £10 for the funeral of the sister of a male slave in apparent fulfilment of this obligation: his dissatisfaction evidently arising because the latter was at that very time asserting his freedom (while the district commissioner had refused to permit the owner to receive head-money in compensation).[52] That this contribution was seen as an obligation suggests that it was not an innovation, a concession of the era of emancipation. Finally, in the words of Bowdich, 'The good treatment of slaves is in some degree provided for, by the liberty they have of dashing or transferring themselves to any freeman; whom they enjoin to make them his property by invoking his death if he does not.'[53] The new master was obliged to recompense the old.[54]

For people of slave descent the Asante form of slavery was assimilative to a degree, a practice founded legally on the prohibition against revealing another person's social origins.[55] Wilks considered that 'within a generation or two' people of slave descent were accepted as ordinary citizens or subjects.[56] LaTorre, citing a wider range of sources, concluded that 'two generations seems a reasonable estimate'.[57] The point is that, under the rules in force in the nineteenth century, owners' property rights in slaves were gradually attenuated over the generations but never formally abolished. Conversely, even today, people of slave descent, at one level because of their social origin as kinless outsiders, have no customary right to occupy a stool.[58] Presumably this might not apply to descendants of a slave man and a free woman, who would be full members of the latter's *abusua*, but evidently (given the rarity of such unions) such descendants were rare. Gradual and incomplete though the process of assimilation is, it has been to a large extent a reality over the last century,[59] albeit helped by the decline of first-generation slavery in the colonial period. Even in the nineteenth century, some exceptional former slaves and descendants of slaves performed—and were allowed to perform—feats of social mobility. Some became regents—not holders—of long-established matrilineal stools, while others occupied state offices, rewarded by the grant of 'service stools' created by the Asantehene.[60] In the words of a later Asantehene, the *Gyaasehene* Opoku Frefre (d.1826) ' "had no family. He was a slave. But Opoku Frefre became very rich and he did many services for the Asanthene . . ." ' as general and as his major administrator. One of his sons became *Saanahene* (treasurer) to an Asantehene. Another was Adu Bofo, the general who led the invasion of Ewe territory in 1869.[61]

Finally in this sub-section let us return to pawning. If the functionalist view of *awowasi* was that its rules and practice was shaped by the pervasive matrilineal ideology and organization of Akan society, an oral tradition noted in the Fortes Papers points to another angle. This tradition purports to explain how and why the society adopted matrilineal inheritance. Abu, a long-ago chief of Adanse, 'wanted to mortgage his son', but his wife 'entirely refused'. So 'he begged his sister, Asɔ, who sacrificed one of her sons' to this end. In due course Abu 'rewarded his sister and her son' by changing the 'custom that sons should inherit their fathers', ruling that in the future sister's sons should inherit their uncles. 'This is the custom still followed by the Akan people', noted Fortes's informant. He added that 'We do not know whether this story is true or not.'[62] Besides showing that human pawning was at least believed to be a very long-standing practice in Asante, the tradition suggests that the direction of causality in the relationship between pawning and matrilineal kinship was not simply from the latter to the former.

Slavery and Pawning as Instruments of Exploitation

We have seen that there were consensual elements in Asante pawnship and assimilative elements in Asante slavery. However, this does not contradict the proposition that these institutions enabled principals to acquire labour beyond the limits of a free domestic labour-force composed very largely of their own individual efforts plus the services provided by free members of their conjugal family. Chapter 8 showed that coercion was indispensable if additional regular labour was to be secured at a cost which most Asante principals could profitably bear. By this token, big economic rents were extracted from slaves and pawns.

However the debtors and pawns fared, and while recognising that social obligation was often a motive for rich men to accept pawns, it is clear that lending money and taking pawns, not to mention acquiring *nnɔnkɔfoɔ*, were (or in the case of pawning were also) mechanisms of further self-enrichment. Asante was a polity that honoured (as well as taxed) self-enrichment, notably with the award of titles and even authority.[63] In this society wealth was defined in ways to which pawnship was particularly pertinent. The Asante notion of wealth was closely linked to that of hierarchy, and the goods that were most valued were those that could display rank[64] and, sumptuary laws permitting, contribute towards upward social mobility. Gold was 'the most evident measure of a citizen's wealth',[65] and pawns and slaves could contribute to its acquisition directly through labour in trade and mining, and indirectly through performing agricultural and domestic tasks that freed other labour for the task of getting more *sika* (gold, money). Furthermore, in an economy in which labour was scarce in relation to land, wealth and power could also be measured by the acquisition of dependent people.[66]

A distinction should be made here between the implications of the social origins of pawns and slaves, respectively, for the pattern of accumulation and inequality within Asante. Whereas most slaves were foreign, the majority of pawns were born in Asante, and we have seen that the majority appear to have been recruited apparently from the 'free' subjects of the Asantehene. In this respect pawning had distinct implications for social inequality within Asante. In so far as pawning operated as a social insurance mechanism it may have helped poorer matrilineages survive. But in so far as it enabled richer lines to get richer, and richer individuals to advance their careers, it may have been a source of cumulative inequality. This is particularly so because, as radical critics of interlocked factor markets observe, such deals often make it harder for the borrower to clear the debt.[67] With pawning, the debtor lost the services of the pawn, to that extent reducing his chances of being able to repay the loan.

The low status of slaves, and their physical vulnerability within the laws of the state, will be clear from the discussions above. The status of pawns was not as low as that of slaves, but that is about as much as can be said for it. In Rattray's fieldnotes the statement appears that 'No disgrace attaches to [a] person who is [an] *awowa* in Ashanti'.[68] Yet this is hardly consistent with a statement by Rattray's own informant K. Sapon (formerly head of the Mampon stool traders), that his pawned niece's creditor-husband 'dare not call her *awowa*'.[69]

Whether the pawns themselves were willing or unwilling, it is hard to see them as beneficiaries of this interlocked factor market. As individuals, they were not necessarily party to the pawning decision, and their interests were likely to be subordinate to those of the elders on either side. After all, in the Asante ideology of pawning equivalence was defined in terms not of individual but of family property. Thus when an *abusua* needed a loan the person offered as a pawn did not need to be the person who had incurred the debt.[70] Indeed, by the nature of the institution, the pawns were poor (otherwise they could have redeemed themselves) and dependent on elders or masters.[71] An example of pawning virtually perpetuating itself is that of the woman Atta who was mentioned above as being pawned twice during the late nineteenth century. The Mampon royal family claimed that her second 'pawning' was actually outright sale to themselves, of herself and her children, though this was much disputed by her son. Either way, she gave birth to a boy and a girl each of whom was later pawned separately. The girl herself mothered a daughter who was pawned.[72] Generally, if a pawn's *abusua* fell into deeper debt, the pawn might find herself or himself sold out of the matrilineage altogether, as a slave.[73] This fate was also an ultimate sanction open to an *abusua* against a member who repeatedly got them into debt.[74] As for imported slaves, if one was sold, she or he reached the very bottom of the Asante social ladder, forced to do the hardest and dirtiest jobs.[75]

Part of the exploitative potential of pawning was illustrated by a case early in the colonial period, before pawning was prohibited. One evening, apparently in 1904, one Yaw Donkor entered the small town of Abodom, in Amansie, accompanied by 'my small daughter'. Evidently a stranger to the place, he asked a group of bystanders the way to the latrine. When Donkor returned, one of them accused him of having 'done wrong because I bid him good evening before going to [the] latrine'. Given that Donkor would have greeted the locals before asking them directions, it is plausible that he was technically in breach of the taboo against addressing anyone on one's way to the latrine. His accuser persisted, and both parties were brought before the chief of Abodom who fined Donkor £11/15/-. 'I had no money . . . so they[?] told me to borrow the money & put my daughter in pawn which I had to do, with Linguist [chief's spokesman] Kofi Interesu, who said that the interest would be £3'. Donkor complained to the District Commissioner, who reduced his debt to £4.[76]

Resistance and Opposition to Slavery and Pawning

Resistance may be collective or individual. In the case of slavery in nineteenth-century Asante evidence of the former—more precisely, of the possibility of it—comes from the second decade of the century while specific cases of the latter are known from later decades. This is explicable as follows. The possibility of widespread disorder by slaves, and perhaps even a revolt, seemed most real when the state found itself with the problem of absorbing very large numbers of newly-imported captives, during the closing of the Atlantic slave market. By the 1840s the closure was complete, as far as Asante was concerned, but an internal answer had been found to the question of how to respond to the continuing availability of new slaves. Meanwhile, however, Asante had lost military control over the coastal region. This made it less difficult for slaves to escape from Asante and seek emancipation in the territory under British control. This became even more so after the 1873–74 war with the consolidation of British authority in the Gold Coast Protectorate followed by the abolition of slavery as a legal status within it.

The above-mentioned Opoku Frefre, 'the treasurer and chief favourite' of Asantehene Osei Bonsu,[77] emphasised to the Bowdich mission in 1817 that slaves retained in Asante (as opposed to being sold into the Atlantic slave trade) were liable to revolt.[78] Bowdich maintained that the law which was proclaimed in his presence against pilfering by state officials, thereby strengthening the property rights of slaves and other poor people, would not have happened without the political influence of some of the slaves themselves.

> This law protected them effectually; but, probably, had not that body, whose whispered remonstrances induced it, been made more formidable by the incorporation of a part of that surplus of foreign slaves the abolition had created, so arbitrary a government would never have accorded it.[79]

By 'incorporation' of some slaves Bowdich evidently meant that some had been given positions at the Asantehene's court. In the next paragraph he wrote that:

> The foreign slaves will naturally find advocates in those of their brethren, which are not a few, who from talent, devotedness, or policy have become confidential favorites [*sic*] of the Kings and Chiefs, who reckon on them as a protection against any sudden gust of sedition amongst their impatient subjects.[80]

Consistently with all this, Norman Klein has interpreted the dispersal of the un-exportable slaves around rural Asante as a strategy for diffusing the threat of such a revolt.[81] A degree of caution is in order. In their dealings with Bowdich's mission, the main aim of Asantehene Osei Bonsu's government seems to have been to try to persuade the British government to reverse its ban on slave buying by British subjects, or at least to allow ships from other countries to continue to buy. This was the context of Opoku Frefre's discourse quoted above. It was also, literally, the Asantehene's last word to Bowdich, contained in a message sent after him when he had set off from Kumasi back to the coast.[82] It is possible that the Asantehene's chief official stressed the risk of a slave revolt in the hope that the British would fear that an uprising would have a political outcome, such as anarchy, which they might regard as worse than having a powerful inland neighbour for themselves and their allies on the coast. As for the dispersal of slaves, we have seen that there is a sufficient economic explanation for it: to put them to most use, as producers of kola and gold. It is important to note that, contrary to Klein, there is no evidence that the policy—more precisely, the spontaneous practice of numerous slave owners —was new in 1817.

Yet the notion that the state sought consciously to avoid a slave revolt or other widespread difficulties in controlling slaves cannot be dismissed. It is possible that the Asantehene was being straightforward rather than disingenuous to the British representatives. His relations with Britain had not been so good as to exclude the possibility that the British might have welcomed the disruption or even collapse of his regime. Again, the fact that the law was proclaimed in Bowdich's presence may have been a foreign relations exercise; but this would not mean that the law itself was not real. The likelihood is reinforced by the fact that, as Bowdich and his colleagues found from uncomfortable personal experience, even in Kumasi itself the poor were by no means under the constant control of the authorities.

> The insolence of the lower orders here becomes insufferable, they proceeded even to pelting us with stones; after every effort on our part to conciliate them by the exhibition of the telescope and other novelties.[!] As may be expected in a military government, they are beyond the King's control, out of the field. He declared however, that he would behead any man I would point out to him. . . .[83]

To judge from this, the government had reason to try to ensure that those at the bottom of the social hierarchy were not needlessly provoked.

Perhaps it succeeded. There is no evidence for later years of a similar level of concern by the rulers about how to control the slave population as a whole, nor was there a slave revolt. The grievances of slaves do not figure in the documented motives for the rising against Asantehene Mensa Bonsu in 1883.[84]

The absence of a slave revolt is perhaps not surprising. It would have been extremely difficult for slaves by themselves to come together in numbers large enough to make much impact on the forces of the state. Meanwhile, the descendants of slaves, at least, had a status that gave them some stake within their local communities: especially as they were typically born of free fathers as well as slave mothers. In contrast, for an individual or a small group of slaves to try to escape was feasible, though dangerous and difficult given that their chances of getting to their own distant homes were usually remote indeed. We saw earlier that Musa Dagarti took refuge in the Gold Coast after his master had threatened his life, by saying that he would exchange him for a prisoner condemned to be killed at a funerary rite.[85] Some earlier (pre-1874) runaways gave essentially the same reason for their actions. In these cases, though, they needed to persuade the British not to submit to the Asante government's demands that they be returned.[86] This imperative may have led them to dramatise their plight, as for them to plead simply that they were fleeing captivity might well have been insufficient, given that slavery was not yet illegal in the Gold Coast.

There are at least three recorded cases of pawns running away from their masters, apparently back home (albeit, these occurred after the colonial occupation—but while pawning remained legal).[87] As the sources on pawnship, more than on slavery, have been dominated by chiefs and others who had no reason to oppose the institution, it is perhaps not surprising that there is not more evidence of resentment against pawnship as such. Moreover, writing in the 1920s, Rattray implied that the social ideal of pawning had been abused in the latter years before the colonial occupation,[88] in which case any opposition to pawning recorded in the early colonial records might have been relatively new. But, as indicated earlier, Rattray's historical vision was coloured by a tendency to assume that there had once been an 'authentic', ideal Asante social and cultural order: an assumption which has been undermined by the historical research which has been done since he wrote.[89] In 1909 the fact that the chief of Konkoma, on Lake Bosumtwi, had pawned some people (presumably his subjects) was given by his elders and his head chief as one of several grounds for deposing him.[90] But the charge was made within a year of the colonial prohibition of pawning in Asante, and thus may have been the result of tactical opportunism by his opponents rather than of resentment on their part against pawning as such. However, it is plausible—though unverifiable—that resentment in Asante against pawning (perhaps similar to that against panyarring,[91] the practice of kidnapping to force payment of a debt) was as old as pawning itself.

Given that pawns were mostly Asante themselves, and that the parties to pawnings were Asante matrilineages, it is perhaps not surprising that the accepted practices limited the extent to which pawns could be maltreated. But it is arguable, as we have already seen, that even foreign slaves, by their potential or actual resistance, obtained some mitigation of the institution which confined them. Terray has hypothesized that the assimilative aspect of Akan slavery—and by implication of African slavery in general—was a function of the limits of state coercive capacity.[92] These limits were very real, as was emphasized in Chapter 3. Particularly, in view of the abundance of land—and of forest at that—in relation to population, Terray's reasoning is highly plausible for the Asante case at least. As we have seen, while an owner could threaten an overtly recalcitrant slave with fatal punishment, such a threat could itself prompt an escape attempt, which might succeed. In any case, effective day to day supervision of slaves was very difficult, inconvenient and costly in an economy in which much agriculture and peacetime trading were performed in small groups or singly. In this setting it made sense to offer slaves the prospect of gradual amelioration, at least for their children and grandchildren. More immediately, as was suggested in Chapter 6, it made sense for owners to allow slaves to keep a share of their output.

Slavery and Pawning: Some Implications for Productivity, Markets and Welfare

It follows from the analysis in Chapter 8 that, by reducing the supply price of labour and facilitating credit, slavery and pawning made possible a much higher level of extra-subsistence economic activity than would otherwise have been the case. This was achieved at high transactions costs for the slave-owners and for the Asante state, not to mention the costs borne by the slaves and pawns themselves.

We have seen that even slaves, as well as pawns, were not without rights in Asante society. In particular, the Asante form of slavery shared the common African characteristic of gradual (if in this case incomplete) assimilation of people of slave descent. In that respect the functionalist approach is descriptively correct. But to conclude from this that these institutions were 'social' and not, or not also, 'economic' is to miss a crucial point. If slavery as an economic system was an attempt to overcome a very strong bargaining position enjoyed by uncoerced labour, it is not surprising that, as Nieboer commented from a comparative perspective, a 'strange compound of severity and indulgence . . . has . . . often been observed among slave-owners'.[93] This is especially so in the case of a slave-owning population whose ability to coerce was distinctly limited: the coercive power of the state, though spectacular on the battlefield, was rather weak in terms of ability to discipline labour over the forested expanse of its territory.

This has implications for the productivity of slaves. Evidence presented in Chapter 8 indicated that the purchase price of a slave varied between the equivalent of one and three average mining seasons' output of gold by a single miner. If slaves would deliver for their masters the full extra-subsistence output that the master might produce for him or herself, the implication would be that the investment of acquiring a slave would pay for itself within one to three years (and that is ignoring slaves' contributions outside extra-subsistence production). This is roughly in line with published observations from other parts of nineteenth-century West Africa.[94] Some slaves, working alongside free family members or under the eye of a more senior servant in a chief's village, may well have delivered income to their masters at rates similar to that of free workers. But those slaves who worked more autonomously are unlikely to have done so; hence the logic of giving them sharecrop terms.[95] On such terms, even if their productivity may have matched those of free individuals (the threat of occasional punishment perhaps offsetting the disincentive of the fact that they got only part of what they produced), the master's share would have been worth significantly less than what he could make for him or herself. Let us now focus specifically on the implications of slavery and pawning for markets and for welfare.

On slavery a major irony should be underlined. While the assimilative tendency of Asante slavery may be viewed as evidence of the social rather than economic character of the institution, it had the effect of continually reproducing the market demand for slaves. The same applied to the funerary cult, in that it provided a motive—a rational and powerful one given the prevailing system of belief—for new imports of captives.

Though pawnship often entailed heavy costs for the human pawns themselves, two aspects of this institution could be seen as relatively efficient in their historical context. First, the fact that debt was timeless, the absence of a statute of limitations,[96] looks alien to modern Western conceptions and might be assumed to hamper the efficient operation of market forces. Yet in a setting of low life expectancy and in a period of relatively high personal insecurity, the fact that the matrilineage took responsibility for a member's debt greatly reduced the lender's risk. It thereby made it easier for members to get loans, and probably reduced their cost too. Second, in terms of 'social efficiency' pawning was an example of that historically rare phenomenon, a 'pareto' improvement (one which made no-one worse off) on an alternative institution. Pawning greatly reduced the risk and transactions costs imposed on the lender, but also often on the borrower, by panyarring, which (as we have observed) was apparently banned in Asante in mid-century.[97] Kidnapping was replaced by a contract, which internalized the process of hostage-taking, employing the social pressure of the hostage's kin to induce loyalty and extract labour services.

For the Asante government the curtailing and eventual ending of the Atlantic slave trade created a major economic problem, of replacing what had been the major source of import-purchasing power. It also created, by 1817, a security problem because of the large numbers of initially surplus captives. But already the economy had begun to adapt, reviving or expanding the output of alternative exports. In resource terms what made this elasticity of supply possible was, above all, gradually increased application of slave labour. In that sense, the closing of the maritime export market for slaves provided its own solution to the task of adjustment in the Asante economy. Over the 1807–96 period as a whole, the accumulation of slaves—and pawns and additional wives—was the core of the careers of accumulation undertaken by commoners as well as chiefs. Theoretically, the availability of labour at below any conceivable free-market reservation price could have discouraged Asante entrepreneurs, private or state, from seeking a higher production function, perhaps through finding a more lucrative commodity to produce or adopting better equipment for producing an existing commodity. It is far from clear, however, that such a solution was available in these particular decades: unless it was related to the construction of railways, which the Asante kingdom began to seek before the colonial occupation.[98] However, despite the destruction and disruption of the civil war of the 1880s the Asante economy had no shortage of small entrepreneurs with the resources—especially of dependent labour—required to take advantage of an exotic but potentially profitable export crop, cocoa, when it became available to them at the very start of the colonial period. It will be clear from Chapter 9 that this prior accumulation, not simply of (usually modest) amounts of money but especially of labour resources, had a very pronounced gender dimension. Those with the 'accumulation' cards in their hand at the start of the cocoa era were mostly men.

PART IV

The Decline of Coercion in the Factor Markets of Colonial Asante: Cocoa and the Ending of Slavery, Pawnship and Corvée, 1896–c.1950

Having argued that in the nineteenth century labour and capital markets depended for their existence upon coercion, in the social form of various categories of property rights over people, in the next three chapters I examine the transition to a situation in which factor markets could and did operate largely through economic imperatives and incentives. The ending of slavery and pawning occurred under colonial rule and during the growth of export agriculture. In this the Asante experience—much neglected in the literature[1]—has many parallels with other parts of West Africa and beyond. This part has three aims, each significant for the general and comparative discussion of the end of property rights in people. First, by means of an unusually full analysis of the motivation of colonial policy (Chapter 11), it attempts to sharpen our understanding of why prohibition was long delayed. The term 'prohibition' is used advisedly: as will be seen, the measures taken against slavery and pawning (as distinct from slave trading) had none of the terminal efficacy connoted by 'abolition'. Accordingly, the second aim is to unravel some of the many strands of the decline of slavery and pawning 'on the ground' and to relate them to the trajectories of the other coercive institutions of labour mobilization (Chapter 12). The third aim is to examine the historical relationship(s), if any, between coerced labour and the development of the cash-crop economy (Chapter 13). The contribution of 'unfree' labour to the cocoa 'revolution' in colonial Asante turns out to have been major. Conversely, the ending of property rights in people is discussed as a test of the 'induced innovation' hypothesis. While the hypothesis fails as an explanation for the eventual colonial prohibition of slavery and pawning, it does illuminate the gradual decline of these institutions in practice. The argument here is that market forces made a crucial contribution to both the realization and the social unevenness of the emancipation.

11

WHY WAS PROHIBITION SO LONG DELAYED?

THE NATURE AND MOTIVES OF THE GRADUALISM OF THE BRITISH 'MEN ON THE SPOT'

For students of the relationship between rhetoric and action the most striking fact about colonial policy on slavery in West Africa is that the administrations in the various colonies mostly took years before implementing the commitments of their respective empires to end slavery and human pawning within their borders—on the face of it, bearing out the scepticism of dependency theory about imperialism as a promoter of 'modern' capitalist relations of production.[1] When British forces occupied Asante in January 1896 slave-owning had already been illegal in the British colonies in the West Indies and South Africa since 1834. In India and the Gold Coast the legal status of slavery (slavery as an enforceable property-right) had been abolished in 1870 and 1874 respectively. Yet it was not until June 1908 that slavery was prohibited in Asante.

The reasons most commonly advanced for the gaps between international and parliamentary commitments, on one hand, and policy in West Africa, on the other, are that officials believed that abolition would disrupt the colonial economies and create, simultaneously, rootless proletariats and angry and enfeebled indigenous political elites. This would undermine order and the system of 'indirect rule', and promote criminality and political dissent or rebellion, thus putting greater strain on colonial resources.[2] This chapter uses the detailed documentation in the national archives in Kumasi to analyse the colonial decision-making process as a test of the existing general explanations for colonial caution about the emancipation of slaves and pawns. The last section of the chapter describes the continued government support for *corvée*, long after 1908.

A. Emancipation Delayed, 1896–1908: The Problem of Interpreting Motive

The anti-slavery cause was invoked by British officials as a justification for the colonial occupation. Slave trading and 'human sacrifice' were forbidden by the British as soon as they took control in January 1896. But British 'respect' for 'the habits and customs of the country' (except for human sacrifice and slave dealing), proclaimed in treaties with various chiefdoms that year,[3] meant colonial acquiescence in the continuation of slave-holding and even pawn-creation. In 1905 Chief Commissioner F. C. (later Sir Francis) Fuller declared in an internal memorandum that 'It has been the consistent policy of the Government to recognise domestic slavery and "pawning" '.[4] Admittedly, the Gold Coast Colony's criminal code was officially applied to Asante in 1902, including the prohibition of the giving and taking of pawns.[5] But in 1907 Fuller stated that 'the Criminal Law against pawning has never been enforced in Ashanti', and 'it has been the rule for the Courts to recognise "pawns" as security for debts'.[6] It is clear that for the first decade of the colonial occupation of Asante the British administration made no effort to abolish slavery and debt bondage. There were even instances of British courts returning runaway slaves to their owners.[7] For example, in 1898 the British Cantonment Magistrate's court in Kumasi returned three Asante slaves to their owner after they 'attempted to return to their ancestral home'.[8] British toleration of slavery and human pawning reflected the conviction of the colonial government's 'men on the spot' that these institutions should be allowed simply to wither as economic and legal changes made alternative forms of labour and borrowing increasingly available.

From 1904, however, the local administration was subjected to pressure from their superiors in Accra and London who initially suggested, and increasingly insisted, that slavery and pawning be made effectively illegal. The local officials sought to still the strengthening wind of change by offering a series of proposals for moderate reforms.[9] Finally, the governor in Accra lost patience and personally dictated the wording of the ban to the administration in Asante. Thus, in effect from 22 June 1908, were slavery and human pawning prohibited. The measure was essentially against coercion: it was not illegal for someone to work voluntarily for another as security for a debt or in return for nothing but his keep.[10] Indeed, it was not until December 1930 that slavery as a property right in Asante was directly abolished in law, by the Re-Affirmation of the Abolition of Slavery Ordinance (Ashanti), which declared that 'slavery in any form whatsoever is unlawful and that the legal status of slavery does not exist'.[11] This, however, merely made fully explicit what was already administrative and court practice since the 1908 reform. In 1910 Fuller, as Chief Commissioner, which at that time meant that he was not only the head of the administration but also presided over the highest court in Asante, wrote to a Basel missionary that 'The law no longer recognises the status of slavery—ex-slaves are, therefore, at perfect liberty to leave their Masters'. Likewise 'the status of "Pawns" is no longer recognised by Law and . . . there exists no *legal* obligation on the part of pawns to redeem themselves or their children' (his emphasis).[12] The annual colonial report on Asante for 1908 declared simply (and without referring to the preceding controversy): 'Slavery and pawning have been abolished'.[13] The practice was more compromising, especially on pawnship. Fuller's letter noted that 'private negotiations with a view to redemption are allowed and even encouraged'.[14] Indeed, even after 1928 pawn-marriages seem to have continued to escape legal prohibition.

The administrative records of the colonial government provide an excellent source for the analysis of the motivation of policy on the issue of abolition. This does not mean that they make it easy to reach conclusions. On the contrary, the very wealth of the documentation should be a warning against premature certainties. This may be illustrated by two letters written to his superiors by Captain C. H. Armitage, a district commissioner and, during several months in 1907–8 while Fuller was on leave, acting chief commissioner. Armitage was a consistent opponent of legal measures against slavery and pawning. But the arguments he used to justify this position were less consistent. In September 1907 he expressed himself 'much impressed' with a memorandum by F. D. Lugard on slavery in northern Nigeria, in which the author 'fully appreciated the dangers of flooding the country with freed slaves, who, without money or relatives, would prove a menace to the community'.[15] Yet less than five months later, having been instructed to get on with emancipation, Armitage as acting chief commissioner included in his draft instructions to commissioners a provision which might as well have been designed to ensure precisely that freed slaves would become a propertyless 'flood' washing around the country:

> Should 'Slaves' appeal to you and demand their 'freedom' you should, while granting it, point out that they must at once leave the District in which

they have been residing, and that they cannot lay claim to any plantations, lands or other property which may have been granted to them by their Masters while they were in a state of 'servitude'.[16]

When the Governor criticised this clause Armitage defended himself on the ground that, while he noted Lugard's point,

> Another question however presents itself in Ashanti. If released 'Slaves' are to be allowed to remain in the Districts where their former masters reside to flaunt their freedom before the Ashantis, a constant and ever-increasing source of friction will be set up which will assuredly lead to trouble in the future. I regarded the instructions that released "slaves" should leave the District as an "Act of State", and of common justice to the Ashantis, who receive no compensation for their released "Slaves", as did the whiteman.[17]

Armitage was second only to Fuller in his prominence in the efforts of political officers in Asante to avert legal emancipation, and he seems to have been a major influence on the chief commissioner. In response to an attack on the policy of tolerating slavery and pawning, by the veteran Basel missionary Ramseyer in 1904, Fuller based his reply on a long quotation from a memorandum by Armitage.[18]

Armitage's apparent inconsistency is interesting methodologically because it illustrates the complexity of the problem of interpreting motives. It may be that actually he was consistent, genuinely worried that a proletariat might be created but even more concerned to ensure that the well-being of the former slaveowners was protected. It may be that his draft instruction was a desperate bluff tried in the hope of provoking his superiors into watering down their anti-slavery policy. Or, again, it may be that it was his original invocation of Lugard that was the tactical ploy, providing a case which he hoped would be more persuasive in Accra and London than his own arguments would be. Internal government documents, being originally confidential,[19] are a better source on government motives than are official public statements, which were necessarily made with an eye on the abolitionist pressure exerted by missionaries and humanitarian lobby groups, and mediated through a Colonial Office in London which was anxious to avoid being seen as soft on slaveowning. But even within the government this was a highly contentious issue on which submissions up the hierarchy were likely to be 'political', in the sense that a less senior official, such as Armitage, might use arguments calculated to persuade his superiors of the wisdom of a policy which he himself favoured for different reasons. Given such difficulties of interpretation it is not surprising that the internal correspondence provides elements which, taken in isolation, could be used to support any of a variety of political and economic explanations of the policies of the British administration in Asante. There is, however, one common theme that unites the arguments put forward for gradualist policies by various commissioners at various times between 1904 and 1908. This is a wish to preserve the interests of the Asante slave- and pawn-holders as far as possible.

This can be partly accounted for by fear that to alienate them would risk another rising. The belief that widespread, probably armed, opposition in Asante could be provoked by an announcement that slaves and pawns were to be freed preceded the 1896 invasion itself. Governor William Maxwell warned London that 'Native opinion here [on the Gold Coast] seems to be that while there is comparatively little objection to the establishment of a British Resident in Kumasi, universal fear is entertained that the establishment of British protection will result in the manumission of slaves. This I believe to be the main difficulty' in negotiations with the Asantehene. Maxwell added that 'it would be useful to me to be favoured with Your Lordship's instructions on the subject of slavery as it exists now in Ashanti and its possible modification when there is a British Residency' there.[20] Joseph Chamberlain, Secretary of State for the Colonies, proceeded with the utmost caution.[21] He did not reply directly on this point but instructed the Governor to inform the Asantehene that the British Resident to be imposed upon Kumasi would enforce the Asante obligations under the 1874 Anglo-Asante peace treaty, which included the abolition of 'human sacrifices', but 'will not otherwise interfere with the administration or institutions of the country'.[22] Maxwell did exactly this in his letter to the Asantehene, and instructed his subordinates who were to deliver it not to 'allude to the subject [of slavery] unless directly questioned.'[23] In the event, as we have seen, the invaders did make one institutional interference almost as soon as they arrived: prohibiting slave trading. One of the demands of the 1900 rising was 'Permission to buy and sell slaves as in the old time'.[24] Governor F. M. Hodgson's emphasis upon discontent over this issue as a major reason for the rising, though suspect insofar as it provided him with a convenient explanation for his failure to prevent the revolt, is thus highly plausible.

It was therefore consistent, and realistic, for administrators to expect that an emancipation decree would provoke enormous discontent, at least from chiefs, family heads and wealthy commoners: the people best placed to organise any further popular willingness to resist British rule, whether by war or otherwise. In August 1905 Fuller stated that action against slavery 'would be strenuously opposed at present'.[25] Four months later he 'reluctantly' recommended 'that the whole question' of government measures against slavery and pawning 'be deferred for the present', partly in view of 'the unsettled times, owing to the recent disturbances among several of the tribes'.[26] In December 1906 the Commissioner of the Southern District of Ashanti, Clotworthy Soden, wrote that he had 'taken every opportunity to sound the principal Chiefs and Headmen' about the measures proposed by the Governor, 'which—wherever I mentioned them—were received with consternation, and opposition and I fear they would have to be backed by force to insist on them being carried out'.[27] The following year Fuller reiterated that 'any drastic measures with regard to Domestic Slavery . . . would have to be imposed—may be by force'.[28] Finally, in May 1908, Armitage, who had himself been a key figure in British military operations in 1900, and in which he had been wounded,[29] appealed against the governor's rejection of his draft executive instructions:

> I am convinced that the Ashantis are daily becoming more amenable, and I dread the introduction of any measure which might cause a wave of discontent to sweep over the country, and retard the rapidly increasing prosperity of Ashanti.[30]

Besides fearing the possibility of resistance led by chiefs, the colonial administration in Asante was anxious to do nothing that would unnecessarily weaken the capacity of the chiefs to control and administer their subjects on behalf of the colonial state. In a different context, in July 1908, the Colonial Secretary, in Accra, noted that 'If the chiefs are to be efficient factors, they must have the means to support their dignity'.[31] Officials in Asante believed that slavery and pawning were a vital part of these means. Clotworthy Soden argued as follows, in the December 1906 letter quoted above:

> I am therefore inclined to urge strongly, that the very foundation of the power and importance, and I might almost say wealth of the Chiefs and Headmen, which at present is their domestic servants, and 'Pawns', should be removed very gradually as we find that we have substituted an equivalent, and given them the means of maintaining their position in spite of any restrictions we may place upon the out-of-date means by which they maintain their position at present—such as the educating of them up to agricultural, industrial, and commercial pursuits, and above all to a knowledge of the value of their land, which would eventually make the Chiefs and

Headmen wealthy enough to substitute paid servants, and labourers for their domestic slaves, and 'Pawns' of today. . . .[32]

As well as putting forward these pragmatic arguments the prominent 'gradualists' within the colonial administration in Asante also defended the established hierarchy of Asante society on grounds of social welfare. Fuller claimed that 'no unwilling slaves [*sic*] can be said to remain in Ashanti'[33] as slaves had only to cross into the Gold Coast Colony to be free.[34] Armitage maintained similarly that colonial rule had relieved slaves of the worst aspects of their status, notably 'the possibility of being sacrificed on the death of their masters',[35] so it was now anachronistic 'to call persons slaves in Ashanti'.[36] Again, he urged that 'few "pawns" enter into their obligations unwillingly', and that human pawning reduced the 'far from uncommon practice among Ashantis' of committing 'suicide to avoid liabilities'.[37] In Clotworthy Soden's view:

> The so called slaves in Ashanti are well fed, housed and clothed and in a word have everything they want at present to make them happy, and I think that is more than can be said of the 'sweated labourers' employed in connection with manufactories in civilised Europe, who have to struggle on in starvation and necessity of every kind for an existence.[38]

Howard Temperley has argued that 'the attack on slavery can be seen as an attempt by a dominant metropolitan ideology to impose its values on the societies of the economic periphery'.[39] In this case, clearly, the local representatives of the British empire consciously and persistently resisted the attempt. Some of them evidently admired aspects of the Asante social order and were passionately convinced that to undermine the property regime that sustained it would be unjust. More generally, they perceived strong reasons of political and fiscal expediency for stopping the abolition bandwagon from rolling over the Asante institutions of slavery and pawnship. Finally, in their correspondence there is no trace of Adam Smith's notion that free labour was more efficient than slave labour, a belief maintained—often, and increasingly, with misgivings—by abolitionists in nineteenth-century Britain.[40] Not only did they see slave-owners as pure losers from abolition, they also thought that such a measure might 'retard the rapidly increasing prosperity of Ashanti' as a whole. While Armitage may have meant simply that economic life might be disrupted by a 'wave of discontent', it is significant that neither he nor his colleagues seem to have even entertained the idea that free labour might be good for 'prosperity' in the long term. The commissioners' opposition to radical reform raises questions in relation to the theory of induced innovation. Was the local colonial administration obstructing a socially-efficient response to changing economic circumstances as the adoption of cocoa progressively altered relative factor scarcities? Or, when higher authority eventually imposed new rules, could it be that the latter bore no relation to an economic context still largely unchanged from the precolonial nineteenth century in which, as was argued in Chapter 8, the Nieboer hypothesis essentially applied? We will consider these questions in Chapter 13.

B. The Longevity of Government Support for Corvée

Another form of coerced labour was not, as yet, even in question: the chiefs' right to summon subjects to work for the stool. The colonial government itself exploited this device for its own purposes in its early years. Following the unopposed occupation in 1896 the British required the chiefs not only (as under the independent Asante kingdom) to ensure that the roads passing through their territories were in good order, but also 'to supply continually in rotation large numbers of carriers'.[41] In the words of the annual report for 1897:

> In the event of the Resident's orders with regard to the clearing of Roads, and the supply of carriers, etc., not being complied with fines have been inflicted. A threat of sending a force of Hausas [troops] to occupy their villages has always had the desired effect, the fines being immediately paid, the roads cleaned, and the number of carriers requisitioned for supplied.[42]

After the suppression of the 1900 revolt additional quotas of 'Punishment Labour' were imposed on those chieftaincies which had participated in the rising. These seem to have been served over the following two to three years.[43]

While the colonial administration fairly soon ceased to require such labour for carrying loads, 'communal labour' became a major source of the unskilled labour in the construction of motorable roads. The term may have been a euphemism, but there is no doubt that many communities wanted roads and many of their members were willing to contribute labour to get them.[44] The colonial regime, however, retained the statutory power to require *corvée* for road maintenance (government road construction being done by free labourers). This was essentially the same method that the Asante monarchy had used for the same purpose, except that the scale of the task had been greatly increased.[45] Meanwhile, as will be detailed in Chapter 13, early in the twentieth century the chiefs had used *corvée* to establish cocoa farms.

In May 1931 Britain ratified the international Forced Labour Convention of 1930 which pledged signatories 'to *suppress* the use of *forced* or *compulsory* labour in all its forms within the *shortest possible period*' (emphasis in the original).[46] The speed of metropolitan legislation was not matched by the 'men on the spot' in Accra and Kumasi. It was only in July 1935 that the Labour (Ashanti) Ordinance and corresponding legislation for the rest of Ghana was enacted. Though its stated purpose was 'to give effect' to the Convention, it preserved forced labour for both the chief and the colonial administration by taking advantage of temporary exemptions in the convention where the task concerned was urgent, beneficial to the community, and voluntary labour was unavailable.[47] It did, however, restrict forced labour to men of 18–45 years, and stipulated that in any community no more than a quarter of the residents in this category 'may be taken at one time for forced labour'.[48] The British administration's motive for maintaining *corvée* seems to have been basically fiscal economy. The main use of forced labour envisaged under the Ordinance, both at the administration's or at the chiefs' behest, was clearly for road maintenance. Governor A. R. Slater noted in 1930 that to pay labourers at 'ordinary market rates' would be much more expensive.[49] Therefore it would have required higher revenue—perhaps entailing the introduction of direct taxation—or else the abandonment of part of the road network, and thence of some cocoa farms.[50]

When political decolonization in Ghana began, with the establishment of a joint British-Ghanaian government in 1951, the new CPP minister for health and labour, K. A. Gbedemah, actually proposed the introduction of compulsory registration and direction of labour, fearing that otherwise there would not be enough labour for the large-scale development projects envisaged by the government. The Colonial Office and the International Labour Office advised that this would be in breach of the Forced Labour Convention,[51] and evidently the scheme did not proceed.

C. Conclusion

The British record on slavery, pawnship and *corvée* in Asante shows a consistent feature: the officials 'on the spot', in colonial Ghana (in the latter case) or in Asante specifically (concerning slavery and pawning) argued against abolition, while the pressure for it came from above and outside. The fiscal logic of preserving—and making use of—*corvée* was expressed unmistakably enough. The internal correspondence on slavery and pawning, as the British administrators of Asante sought to avert the implementation of the imperial commitment to abolition in 'their' patch of the empire, is more complicated, therefore illustrating the need for care in searching for motive amid the tactical expedients used in policy arguments within the colonial hierarchy. But it is clear that these officials were very anxious to preserve the interests of slave- and pawn-holders, partly so as not to provoke anger and perhaps even another rebellion; and partly because they recognized the importance of slaves and pawns to the wealth and status of the chiefs, on whom the colonial regime relied for effective government and social control at village and town level. In a specific form, the analysis here thus supports the existing general interpretation of the usually slow implementation of colonial commitments against slavery and pawning. As the next two chapters will show, in Asante the interests of chiefs and other masters were protected fairly effectively, primarily because slavery, pawning and *corvée* lasted long enough to equip the beneficiaries of these institutions to adjust to new circumstances.

12

THE DECLINE OF COERCED LABOUR AND PROPERTY IN PERSONS IN PRACTICE:

CHANGE FROM ABOVE AND FROM BELOW IN COLONIAL ASANTE, 1896–1950

Even when slavery and human pawning were banned, they were far from extinguished. This chapter considers how far and how fast slavery and pawning declined in practice, following the early suppression of the slave trade (and thus of imports of new captives) and of panyarring, the practice of seizing hostages to enforce repayment of outstanding debts. The evidence indicates that emancipation owed much to the initiative of slaves themselves, and their kin. It also shows that slavery and pawning lasted long enough to be important sources of labour in early Asante cocoa-farming. The same applies to the Asante form of *corvée*, in which subjects were expected to give labour service to the chief. We will see that emancipation was very uneven in social terms: the timing varied according to the age and, especially, the gender of the slave or pawn. The destiny of slaves or former slaves was also crucially shaped by whether they had originally been taken from outside the Akan world.

Before considering what happened with each of these institutions, it is appropriate to comment on the notorious source problems involved in trying to track the destinies of actual and former slaves and pawns in Africa. For Asante at least, the difficulties are less than has sometimes been supposed. To be sure, the customary secrecy about people's origins is far from dead, and it seems inconceivable that any sample survey could obtain respondents' full and frank answers to the kind of questions necessary to establish whether, for instance, the average income of people descended from slaves has caught up with that of the rest of the Asante population. Yet the secrecy has weakened somewhat,[1] and my experience is that in any case informants are quite likely to be willing to talk about institutional trends, presumably as long as they are not expected to name individuals.[2] Moreover, until recently signs of people having entered Asante society as *nnɔnkɔfoɔ* were apparent in the facial markings borne by first-generation former slaves—all now deceased—and in the marriages that occasionally took place within what were otherwise exogamous lineages.[3] Further indications may be seen in the continued performance of certain ritual services, in the kind of name traditionally given to a child of slave descent,[4] and where someone receives an otherwise surprisingly inexpensive burial.[5] 'Accusations'—this is how they were intended and regarded—of slave ancestry were and are made when candidates contest for a stool, or in quarrels between members of the 'legitimate' and cadet lines of a lineage.[6]

Besides remarks by individual informants (which are not always usable in print) and the general impressions of informed observers—primarily meaning scholars who are themselves Asante—the historian of emancipation has three particularly valuable sources. These are the papers of the Ashanti Social Survey of 1945–46, held in Cambridge; the Basel Mission Ghana Archive, held in Basel; and the colonial records held in the national archives in Kumasi, especially court record books and administrative correspondence.[7] The Ashanti Social Survey papers include scattered data on the remnants of slave-owner relations but also a systematic survey of individual marriage histories which offers much material on wife-pawning after 'abolition'. Even before the colonial occupation of Asante the Basel Mission highlighted the issue of freeing slaves in a journal it produced for its supporters (from 1894) entitled *Der Sclavenfreund* ('The Slave's Friend'). The mission remained much involved with the matter over the next several years. As priests and catechists established themselves in various parts of Asante they had to contend with the practice and legacy of slavery and pawning in their congregations and host communities. This is documented in their reports to Basel, though patchily so because, as Paul Jenkins observed in the case of a particular local church, African catechists tended to be more reticent than European missionaries about mentioning the presence of former slaves in their congregations.[8] As we will see, N. V. Asare in Kumasi was a notable exception.

Further information comes from government archives. In particular, as Richard Roberts and Suzanne Miers have noted, while the multitude of 'private negotiations between parties that were settled without litigation went unrecorded', court records 'are extraordinarily revealing' of the issues and attitudes[9]—generally, of the variables—involved in the ending of slavery and pawning. Moreover, trials were often associated with executive deliberation, leaving documentation in administrative records. The discussion that follows explores rather than exhausts the Basel and court materials. We will consider, in turn, what happened with *corvée*, panyarring, slave trading, slavery, and pawning.

A. Corvée: For the Colonial Government, for Public Purposes, and for the Chiefs

The administration tackled its own initial requirements for unskilled labour primarily by taking advantage of the chiefs' right to demand labour services from their subjects. This was applied to such tasks as carrying military and other government stores as well as keeping the roads clear. For instance, 'something like 8,000 loads' were carried by this means 'from Kumasi to the Hinterland' during 1898.[10] Afterwards the chiefs received payment according to the number of workers they had supplied. How much of the payment was passed on to the workers is unclear. The opportunity cost to the workers and their families must have been high when labour demands were continuous throughout the year, as the government stated they were in 1897,[11] thus including the planting season.

In one apparently exceptional case the cost in food was direct. In 1911–12, during the building of the main north road from Kumasi, the amanhene of Mampon and Nsuta were each required by the local acting district commissioner (the future official anthropologist R. S. Rattray) to provide 50–70 loads of food per day for eight months. This was to feed the 1,000–1,500 members of the construction gangs when they moved out of the forest and into the adjoining, sparsely-populated, savanna. The nearest savanna chieftaincies were called on for smaller supplies. In recognition 'Mampon received a present of £20' and the others were rewarded, in apparent proportion to their contributions, on the same scale.[12]

The British use of forced labour was heaviest in the first few years of the colonial occupation. In his report for 1898 the British Resident, Captain D. Stewart, admitted that 'there is a good deal of discontent at the constant orders for carriers'.[13] One of the demands of Yaa Asantewaa's rebels in 1900 was 'To be free from demands for carriers'.[14] In the aftermath of the revolt a high proportion of the demands took the form of the unpaid 'penalty' service imposed on chieftaincies who had participated in the revolt.[15] The government gradually found the system unnecessary as mechanized transport became available with the opening of the railway to Kumasi in 1903 and, from c.1914, the introduction of motor lorries.

Motor roads brought big increases in the prices offered to producers for their crops, most importantly cocoa. As a result, coercion was hardly required for the collective labour of villages to be provided in road building, under the authority of their chiefs. Indeed, there were cases of villagers constructing roads at their own or their chief's initiative for no payment. According to the commissioner of the Western Province, now Brong-Ahafo Region, in 1924, ' "The trouble in this Province is not to get the people to construct motor roads, but to hold them back from construction on their own; on lines which are badly graded and require too much earth work and bridging" '.[16] At that time the government's Public Works Department was responsible for the maintenance of only 27 per cent of the 'motor and motorable' roads of Asante as a whole. Responsibility for the maintenance of the remaining 841 kilometres lay with the 'political officers', that is, the district and provincial commissioners. Whereas the PWD could rely on hired labour, the commissioners had to operate mainly through the chiefs and their subjects. Similarly, 'almost all the work in connection with the construction of the ["Political Officers"] roads (except the concrete bridges and culverts) was done by the Chiefs and people under the direction of Political Officers'.[17]

Despite the acknowledged social benefits of roads, the distribution of the burden of roadwork could be contentious. In 1926 the chief of Moma in Sunyani district complained that 'the Road Work at Brosankro is troubling my people to avoid of working in their cocoa farms' (*sic*). Presumably as a result, 'all my youngmen and Elders['] cocoa is spoiling . . .'[18] A note of scepticism should be entered: this was in mid-December, a time for harvesting cocoa rather than planting or weeding, and in general few farmers in Ahafo had big cocoa harvests as early as 1926.[19] From the surrounding correspondence in the file it seems likely that the problem was not so much the opportunity cost of roadwork but which chief's subjects would have to do it. Either way it seems reasonable to assume that, overall, had roadwork not been compulsory considerably less of it would have been done: both because of conflicts over which community was responsible and because of free-riding by opportunistic individuals.

According to the chief commissioner in 1917, 'In Ashanti all weeding and clearing of Roads is female work'.[20] He would have known, as a result both of the official preoccupation with road maintenance and his frequent travels on Asante roads. This was not part of the nineteenth-century division of labour. The most likely explanation is that men withdrew from this form of *corvée* in order to concentrate on their cocoa farms—the making of which was overwhelmingly male-dominated during the 'take-off'. Fortuitously, by the time forced labour was restricted by law to men in 1935,[21] the rate of new planting was slowing in the face of generally lower cocoa prices.

Whether the use of *corvée* to create cocoa farms for the chief was as readily accepted is unclear: especially as this practice started while the colonial government was still imposing its highly unpopular requisitions of labour for headloading. Moreover, the work involved would have to be done at the same season as subjects could have been making farms for themselves (and the land-clearing phase, in particular, was one which—given the clear, established gender division of labour on this aspect[22]—male subjects would have been expected to carry out on the stool farms, just as on their private farms). Farms made by *corvée*, however, were officially considered to be the property of the stool rather than of the chief as an individual. It should be noted that the evidence of farms being made using this institution relates mainly to the 'take-off' phase of Asante cocoa planting (to 1916).

In 1940 the acting district commissioner of Bekwai (Amansie) stated that 'many of the chiefs in this District have exacted forced labour'. This was particularly for maintenance of the 'small feeder roads on which bush villages transport their Cocoa to the main roads maintained by Government' and for weeding public space ('clearing of the sanitary area round the Head-quarter town'). The chiefs made each able-bodied male 'of the community . . . responsible for a small stretch' of road. When 'the road is needed for Cocoa traffic', 'every person' had 'to put his part of the road in order by a certain date'. Anyone who failed to do so would be charged in a chief's court with 'failing to obey the lawful order of a Native Authority'. In the case of weeding, people [able-bodied men] in one 'division' (chieftaincy) had to contribute 'one day every 80 days'.[23] For male cocoa-farmers the opportunity cost would have been lessened by the low cocoa prices of the war years and perhaps also by the Ashanti Confederacy Council's 1939–46 ban on making new cocoa farms. Forced labour through the chiefs seems to have continued in this district even after the war, to judge from correspondence from 1946.[24] There is no reason to think that Amansie was exceptional in this respect.

B. Panyarring and Slave Trading

Allegations of panyarring were vigorously investigated by the colonial authorities, to judge from two cases in south Asante in 1903. In one the omanhene of Akyem Swedru, in the Gold Coast Colony, complained that a woman called Akua Nimo and her two children had 'been detained at Brofu Edru' in Adanse by a local man, Kwasi Adusei, 'as sureties for a debt' which he claimed was owed him by Akua Nimo's uncle.[25] The district commissioner, Major W. B. Davidson-Houston, reported to the chief commissioner that he had interviewed Akua Nimo and discovered that 'She is a Dadiasi woman, and married to a Kokofu man, who is at present in Ahafo—She is not detained by Kwasi Adusai at Brofu Edru, but has returned with her two children to her native town'.[26] In the other case a man named Yaw Dufuorh complained that his wife, Ablah Kwablah, had been seized by a Bekwai subject, Kobina Abuadji, 'for a debt' that Dufuorh 'owed him'. Davidson-Houston ordered the omanhene to send Abuadji and Dufuorh to him 'atonce [*sic*] . . . without the least delay'.[27] It is not clear what happened afterwards. But it seems that government meant to eliminate the practice of panyarring.

We will see that such investigations, and even prosecutions, were not always sufficient to destroy the kind of institutions with which this chapter is concerned. But in the case of panyarring they may have been. I have found no evidence of panyarring after 1903, and there are strong circumstantial reasons for suspecting that this may reflect a final demise of the institution during the first decade of colonial rule. Unlike with pawning, there was no element of complicity or even consensus between the debtor and creditor to keep cases out of the courts: by definition, panyarring was a form of kidnapping prompted by the failure of the debtor to fulfill his or her obligation. Unlike with slavery, the victims of panyarring had local supporters—the debtor or his or her kin and/or master—who would fight the case. Unlike both pawning and slavery, panyarring was already illegal before colonial rule began, despite flourishing briefly during the disorder of the mid-1880s.[28] Finally, a new alternative remedy was available to the frustrated creditor: the presentation of a promissory note at the commissioner's court.[29]

From the start, the colonial regime sought to suppress the slave trade. Besides prosecuting slave traders, the administration invited the

Basel Mission to provide a home for captives freed from slave traders. On 1 October 1896, in the words of Ramseyer, 'a caravan of 59 poor slaves—24 women and near-adult girls and 35 children—arrived'. They had all been:

> . . . wrenched off some slave traders who had dared to come near K[i]ntampo. As I have heard, these slave traders at first were deprived of their merchandise, i.e. the slaves, otherwise they could go free. But when some of them were caught again trading slaves they were taken prisoners and brought to this place. I saw a whole number of them in the house of Perempes [the Asantehene's palace], which now serves as a prison; all of them are in fetters they had used the same on their slaves.[30]

However, this large-scale action against slave traders turned out to be the last as well as the first of its kind in Asante.[31] This may have been partly because of lack of resources. In his annual report for 1898 Stewart noted that his detachment of constabulary had been reduced from 300 plus 5 officers to 185 with just one officer. 'The detachment has to provide Guards, Picquets, Convict warders, Runners, Orderlies, etc. and when these are found, very few men are left for any other duty'. It was therefore 'impossible even to send a small mission away for any object'.[32] However, the 1896 action had been near Asante's northern border, in the savanna. Perhaps the decisive phase in large-scale enforcement began in 1898, when colonial forces began to tackle the major supply routes within the Northern Territories, that is, at or closer to their sources.[33]

But slave dealing did not collapse overnight. Stewart's 1898 report stated that 'large quantities of kola' are exported to Côte d'Ivoire, and 'the exchange is slaves; this is impossible to prevent as long as the French Authorities do little or nothing to suppress slave dealing'.[34] Ten years after Britain forbade the slave trade the Omanhene of Adanse, Kobina Foli, and his elders stated 'we know that we are not to deal any more of slaves and by that [*sic*] we have not done so since Ex King Prempeh was transported. . . .'[35] That places Kobina Foli's own reign fully in the post-slave trade era. Yet a later generation of Adanse elders gave as a reason why Foli had been honoured with a black stool after his death, despite having been eventually destooled, 'his industry and effort in acquiring money and property (slaves etc.) for the stool, which made the stool gain in stature and respect'.[36] Kwame Dei of Asiwa is said to have obtained slaves, a man and a woman, from the north after he had become a sub-chief, the Akwamuhene of Dadiase. This was certainly after 1896 and possibly even after 1900.[37] Dumett reports interviewing a woman in Konongo, in 1987, who stated that she herself had been purchased as a slave while a young girl early in the new century.[38] As with earlier periods, though for partly different reasons, it is impossible to measure the size of the slave trade after the British invasion. According to a British non-government source, even in 1899 'slaves were purchased almost daily' in Kumasi,[39] though there seems to be no corroboration of this in government documents.[40] Dumett and Johnson noted that between 1902 and 1910 an average of about twelve cases a year were brought to the courts in Asante.[41] For subsequent years separate data for Asante are not always available, but the Police Department gave the number of 'crimes' (which in this context presumably means cases resulting in convictions)[42] of slave-trading in Asante specifically as five in 1919, none in 1920, and one in 1922–23.[43] In view of the government's severe lack of resources for enforcement we must assume that the great majority of cases went undetected. The Gold Coast Judicial Department itself observed that the annual number of slave-trading prosecutions was ' "wholly a function of effective policing duties" '.[44] Indeed, in 1911 and 1912 the number of cases was 'well over a hundred a year',[45] which is much more plausibly attributed to an intensified effort at enforcement than to an increase in imports.

Despite the evasion it is reasonable to assume that the flow of imported captives was reduced to the order of a thousand a year or less between 1898 and 1908. This would have been a small fraction of the level which had prevailed in the last few years before 1896, and considerably lower than the average annual rate of net imports for 1807–96.[46] As we have seen, the impact of the prohibition of slave trading on slave owners was severe enough for permission to resume trading in slaves to figure among the demands made by Yaa Asantewaa's rebels in 1900. A probable further indication of disruption to the previously abundant flow of new imports of slaves from the north was the appearance of occasional cases of child-stealing, within Asante or within the Gold Coast Colony with the victim then being sold in Asante. For instance, in 1906 there was 'A complaint . . . that a man named Kwaku Pareto[?], living at Obuasi, had stolen a small girl named Adjuah Bose from Abetifi [in Akyem, Gold Coast Colony] about two years ago and sold her'. She 'is said now to be at Fomena'.[47] In the same district, Adanse, in 1912, there was 'ample evidence that the boy AFUAKWA was in fact stolen', the alleged parents being local people. On the other hand, this time the victim was from the north,[48] which was more characteristic of the earlier flow of slaves. There was also an attempt to kidnap and sell a woman in the Wenchi zongo (the northerners' quarter of town), in January 1909, with none of the parties being

Asantes. The woman, Yamankolo, had only just arrived from Sikasso in southern Mali. But she escaped and, with the help of her brother (to whom she had been travelling) brought the case to the government.[49]

A source of new slave imports was the exiled Asante communities who returned to the country after British rule was consolidated in 1900. Among the Denyase subjects who returned from exile in Denkyira in the Gold Coast Colony in 1907 was Osei Kwame, who was to be the pioneer of cocoa farming in the village of Huntado. 'As was the custom', he brought back with him slaves whom he had acquired in exile.[50] But this source was necessarily temporary, most basically because the mass return was not repeated.

In 1927 the Fante civil servant J. C. de Graft-Johnson claimed that slave trading had been virtually non-existent in recent years. 'Police returns for the last seven years record some cases in each year of slave-dealing in the Colony and Ashanti but almost everyone [*sic*] must have been a case of pawning.'[51] The latter interpretation is dubious (courts had long shown clear awareness of the distinction), but it seems clear that, while occasional kidnaps of children might persist, organized slave trading was over by 1920—probably by 1914.

C. Slavery

Many slaves were prepared to assert control of their own destiny, and not wait for an emancipation decree. Some men escaped from their masters and joined the occupation forces. According to Stewart's report on 1898 so far 'the only recruits' for the Gold Coast Constabulary in Asante were 'run-away slaves'.[52] At this time joining up was perhaps the safest route out of slavery, given the British authorities' then practice of returning runaways to their owners.[53] By 1907, as we have seen, the colonial 'men on the spot' were under increasing pressure from their superiors to act strongly against slavery. Accordingly, it seems, the practice in such cases changed. When a chief requested the return of three runaway 'attendants' the government asked them if they wished to comply. Only one of them returned to the chief, which suggests that they had genuinely been allowed to decide for themselves.[54]

Whatever their perceptions of government policy, many slaves or people of slave descent 'voted with their feet'. For example, in 1902 the Adansehene complained to the government that 'a Bekwai slave woman named Afua Yami' had left her husband, a sub-chief of Adanse, and returned to Bekwai taking 'her four children'.[55] A more complex case arose in early 1908 in Djumo, a village in the Odumase-Bechem area of northwestern Asante.

It concerned one Adjua Badu, who had entered Kumasi as a young girl during the reign of Asantehene Kofi Kakari (1867–74). According to her own account (translated by a letter-writer into a petition to the acting chief commissioner) she belonged to a party of refugees from a civil war in her native Wassa. Having sworn to become sojourners on Asante land, the party infuriated the Asantehene by accepting an invitation to return home. The Asantehene had the elders killed and the rest detained. She was brought up as a dependent of Bantamahene Kobina Ewuah, and then married to his son Kofi Dro, who took her to 'his place called Djumo', where she had five children by him. Dro died in c.1903. His nephew and heir, Kwaku Enin, married one of her daughters. Adjua Badu felt that she herself 'took him [Enin] in substitute of my late husband'. She was to be grievously disappointed in him. In 1907 Enin asserted that she was his slave, claiming that she had been purchased by his uncle. The matter went to the court of the Bantamahene, now Nana Osei Mampon. The court rejected Enin's claim, though not before the chief had asked for and received another of Adjua Badu's daughters, Aduja Petrey, as a child bride for himself (he gave the mother only £3 in marriage payment rather than the £5 she had requested). Kwaku Enin continued his campaign: according to Adjua Badu, he demanded the £9 expenses that he had paid in marrying her daughter (implying divorce, though this is not explicit in the file). More, 'he claimed from me every property his uncle my late husband had given me including farms &c. &c. and told me to go to my country Wassah'. Then, six months after her own marriage, Adjua Petrey fell ill and Osei Mampon divorced her, claiming his £3 back from her mother, who also then incurred the cost of giving 'her to a Native Doctor to cure her'. Adjua Badu was thus in an acute predicament, from which there was only one escape. 'As I have contracted debts and I have no one in Ashanti to assist me I went to my country Wassah and reported all my troubles to the family at home. They dispatched two of my brothers' to accompany her 'with cash £50 to pay all my debts' and bring her 'home'. This was early 1908, shortly before slavery was administratively abolished in Asante.

Adjua Badu maintained that she had never been enslaved, and had stayed with her husband from choice. Evidently referring to those captured at the same time as herself, she maintained that 'all the Wassah people resident in Kumasi have returned to Wassah long ago'.[56] But Osei Mampon urged that she was indeed a slave: that having been taken captive, she was given by the Asantehene 'to a diviner for fetish consultation', and the diviner sold her to the then Bantamahene Kobina Ewuah for £4, who gave her in marriage to his son: Kofi Dro. The colonial authorities accepted Osei Mampon's argument. Chief Commissioner Fuller endorsed one of two implications that the current Bantamahene drew from this, that 'release money of £4' must be paid (to Osei Mampon) before she could go. The other implication was that her children should remain in Asante. This was apparently accepted by Acting Chief Commissioner Armitage, and it seems likely that the decision stuck, though the file leaves this slightly unclear.[57]

In some cases the initiative to depart came from the slaves's own kin rather than from the slaves themselves. Two documented instances occurred: respectively, in 1906, in a village under the chief of Manso Nkwanta; and in 1907, in the Odumase area, near Sunyani. The 1906 case concerned Jimini Yah, a Wangara woman from what is now northern Côte d'Ivoire. She had been captured by Almani Samori Ture's soldiers, and sold to a Manso Nkwanta man, who was either one Kwamin Tawiah or Tawiah's *abusua opanyin* (the head of his matrilineal segment), N'safua. Either way, she was then married to Tawiah, and had three children by him, to add to a baby she had been carrying on her back when she was captured. In 1906 she was found by her brother who redeemed her for the purchase price of £14. It is unclear whether she eventually succeeded in a long struggle to be allowed to take the children with her, against strong opposition from Tawiah and N'safua.[58] In the 1907 case 'a deputation from Mankessim', in the Fante part of the Gold Coast Colony, 'arrived at Odumase to procure the return of the descendants of a Mankessim woman who had been captured by the Ashantis over 100 years before'. On 'being given their choice . . . a certain number' of these descendants opted to go to Mankessim: to the 'intense irritation' of the Odumase 'chiefs'.[59]

Direct pressure from above, in the form of prosecutions and administrative actions by the colonial state, finally became an element of direct importance to the destiny of slaves from the later 1900s, especially after the June 1908 prohibition. For example, in 1910, despite an appeal for leniency from the Bekwaihene, the provincial commissioner sentenced two men, Kobina Pong and another, to prison for slavery and/or pawning. 'The offence was a serious one and I could not give a lighter sentence than six months imprisonment but without Hard Labour'.[60] Again, in 1915 a Bekwai sub-chief was punished in connection with the 'unlawful arrest & coercion of a "domestic" '.[61]

The suppression was by no means wholly effective. The 1908 order did not allow for compensation. Yet, as late as 1931, in Dominase and

Ofoase in Amansie, there were cases of slaves or the children of slaves paying their or their mother's purchase-price to the master. The district commissioner declared himself 'aware that by old native custom, there are many people still bound to others through ties said to be slavery'.[62] As late as 1948 one of the Asantehene's sub-chiefs, the Manwerehene, went before the Ashanti Confederacy Council of Chiefs claiming some 'slaves' and/or descendants of slaves resident in the village of Beposo near Mampon. The defendant was a nephew of the previous owner of the people, one Torpei, who had died in the mid-1920s. The issue, as the parties saw it, was whether Torpei had rescinded his original nomination of his nephew as his heir in favour of giving the slaves to Asantehene Prempe I, who in turn allocated them to the chief whom Torpei had served, the Manwerehene. Neither party, nor the Ashanti Confederacy Council of Chiefs, appears to have taken account of the fact that a grant of slaves had no meaning in colonial law and, more, that slave-holding was now entirely illegal. It was left to a British legal officer to translate the dispute into a question purely of allegiance rather than ownership.[63]

It is not surprising that some slaves should have chosen to stay with their masters even when they knew they were free in colonial law. Many had parents or spouses and children with their own ties in their present community—which for some of them was the only community they had ever known or, at least, could remember. Since slaves had enjoyed the right to own property, those who now wanted to leave would have to consider what to do about any immovable property, notably houses, and whether they could safely transport all their portable assets. Indeed, as we have seen earlier, some slaves themselves owned slaves. Torpei was an example, being the son of two slave parents as well as a slave-owner himself.[64] For many slaves dependence or security was probably more important than property. A 1969 article recounted a narrative given by a woman by then in her eighties whose face literally bore the marks of Mossi origins. Having been imported to Asante 'as a small girl', she 'eventually married her master'. She

> . . . stated that she was not ashamed of her origin; she had stayed with her lord all his life, borne him children and served him well. Even when offered the opportunity to 'free' herself, she had stayed—for what, she added, could she have left him, for in the early years of the century he was the one security she possessed.[65]

The weakening of the coercive power of the indigenous Asante state had reduced the incentive to flee even before the British occupation, and more so once the colonial commissioners offered some appeal from Asante justice. The Asantehene had renounced funerary killings—except of convicted murderers—in 1876. This must have made *nnɔnkɔfoɔ* breathe more confidently. In early 1908, though, a Mossi 'servant' in Dwaben named Nipahpawuya 'ran in to Kumasi' on the death of the omanhene, 'stating they wanted to kill him'. When a colonial official ordered him to return he refused to go and, as we will see later, was eventually allowed to stay.[66]

Others stayed in the same communities but refused to serve their former owners.[67] One informant, Mr. J. W. Owusu, put it thus: 'They didn't go away: they were there and they were not listening to instructions [laughs]'. He further stated 'In every family, there were rebels: in every family'.[68]

Still others sought to smooth their way to an independent life by offering their former owners social respect. A balance between decline in willing deference and continued reluctance to make overt defiance is indicated by a 1946 interview, given to the Ashanti Social Survey by the 'Queen Mother' of Agogo. She said that her house-maids

. . . were descendants of slaves and hostages taken in the Ashanti wars. The custom, [*sic*] has been, for each slave to send a daughter to serve the Queen Mother. Today, owing to European influence (she did not explain what she meant by this) and the desire for freedom, most parents who owe the Queen-Mother this service overlook their duty and try as it were, to vanish into the crowd. She therefore has to take the initiative to go after these girls and collect them.[69]

Showing deference was not necessarily onerous. According to the provincial commissioner of eastern Asante in 1928, 'Any young man in Ashanti if he is in debt, or wishes to make some money in order to pay the Head Rum for a wife, goes to his "Over Lord" and asks permission to go away and work, and I have never known such request to be refused'.[70]

Yet others left their former owners' communities. Indeed, it is possible that some fairly large-scale exoduses took place. In 1912 the commissioner of the southern province, Major C. E. D. O. Rew, testified that 'Villages that two or three years ago were prosperous, to my knowledge, have now dwindled down or disappeared entirely. The mines have not taken all the people, and the Chiefs cannot get young men for labour'. Rew saw this as evidence that the population of Asante as a whole was 'decreasing' due to high infant mortality.[71] The notion of decline in the overall population, though supported by the highly implausible census results from 1901 and 1911,[72] is contradicted by a lot of other evidence. This includes the testimonies of Rew's superior (the chief commissioner) and the amanhene of the three most populous chieftaincies (*aman*) in the southern province itself (Bekwai, Adanse and Kokofu).[73] There are other possible explanations of village decline or desertion. Johnson argued that the periodic abandonment and relocation of towns because of progressive degradation of the local environment was a characteristic feature of the precolonial economic history of southern Ghana.[74] In south-central Asante itself there was a recent example of existing villages being abandoned in favour of a new site closer to fresh farming land. It is said that this was how Asiwa came to be founded, in the 1890s, with the older villages of Hemtomasuaso (nearby) and Mwonwo (near Dadiase) being deserted.[75] Again, local conflicts could lead to the withdrawal of population from a village. A village that Bekwai people had built on Adanse land, presumably while the Adanses were in exile after 1886, was 'abandoned' after the return of the Adanses, who 'were always interfering' with the settlers.[76] To conclude, we cannot assume that the depopulation of villages between c.1909 and 1912 was the result of former slaves departing. But there are reasons for suggesting that this is likely, and worthy of further research. We know that many villages had consisted largely or entirely of slaves and their descendants.[77] Whereas departures by slaves living in towns might make no perceptible difference to the size of population, departures from villages, especially small ones, would be likely to cause an obvious dwindling of population. Though village abandonment was not unusual, the fact that it should occur on an apparently very noticeable scale precisely in the years immediately following the government prohibition of slavery may have more than coincidental.

The meaning of departure ranged from heading home to going to live on a Basel Mission station. The latter option was available from 1896, albeit on a small scale. Chiefs complained that in exercising it, domestic servants—some of whom they referred to explicitly as children of northern slaves (ɔdɔnkɔ-ba, sg.) had forsaken their duties in favour of living as Christian converts.[78]

We have seen that there were contrasting incentives for slaves or ex-slaves to stay, to join the Basel Mission settlements, or to return to their native or ancestral homes. But we need to examine the issue further if we are to be able to generalize about the reasons some of them took one decision rather than the other. Akosua Perbi has pointed out that, on the evidence of court cases, most of the slaves redeemed from their owners were

Akan.[79] To judge from the cases described in this chapter, the proposition may be extended to slave departures generally, though only in the form of a plausible hypothesis because the known individual cases are few. The hypothesis, which may become more adequately testable as the destinies of more individuals are uncovered in the future, is that Akan slaves or former slaves had a greater tendency to head for their natal or ancestral homes than did the apparently much larger number of slaves and former slaves who had been born in the northern savanna, or were descended from northern captives. It should be stated that it is highly likely that many northerners left Asante. But the proposition is that, compared to Akan slaves and ex-slaves, they had a greater tendency to stay in their master or former master's community, or else take refuge in a Basel Misson station. This suggestion is based on observation from the admittedly limited evidence of outcomes; the next chapter will comment on the contrasting economic incentives to go home which faced Akan—and, though we have even less evidence on their relative propensity to exit, Ewe—ex-slaves as opposed to their northern colleagues.

Certainly some Ewes and indeed northerners did leave, though not necessarily to go home, or at least not always to get so far. Salome Akosua Dua had been brought to Asante as a war captive from 'Eweland', presumably during the campaign that began in 1869. She then lived with her master, Kwesi Yentumi, at Akutuasi near Domiabra. Some time in the 1900s—but apparently before 1908—she left, evidently accompanied by her son and daughter, intending to return home. But, perhaps because of age (by 1910, at least, she was 'old and not fit to work any more') she settled in Bompata in Asante-Akyem. Yentumi asked the Dwabenhene to make the three return to him: a threat which she averted via a letter from a missionary to the chief commissioner.[80] Again, let us recall the Mossi youth Nipahpawuya, mentioned above for fleeing the Dwabenhene's funeral rites. He was one of two young male 'servants' of a Dwaben subject called Kwasi Yesireh (or Yesala) who separately escaped and made their way to Kumasi where they presented themselves to the colonial authorities. The officials handed them over to, respectively, a sergeant major from the north (Abdullai Grunshi) and the head of the Zongo (generic name for a residential district reserved for strangers, especially from the savanna). Their master sought their return or, in lieu, £18 for Nipahpawuya and £14 for the other, Doitcherow. Yesireh described the latter sum as 'being the expenses I made for the boy':[81] perhaps the purchase price. Presumably the same applied to the other sum. The £18 was paid; apparently by a man with an Akan name (Tuffuor), whose interest is unclear from the documents. But the government rejected Yesireh's claim to compensation for Doitcherow because the boy had complained that his master had ill-treated him.[82]

Taking account of such exceptions, it remains clear that Akans predominated among those who left the communities in which they had been held in Asante. Perbi explains this by physical distance, the non-Akan 'home towns' being further from where the slaves were held than the Akan ones.[83] The analysis offered in the next chapter will enable us to supplement this with a complementary economic explanation.

D. Pawnship

It is widely held for other parts of colonial Africa, and has been documented for the Gold Coast specifically, that the suppression of the internal slave trade led to a major expansion of pawn-holding, as frustrated slave masters turned to this alternative source of coerced labour.[84] It is plausible that this happened in Asante too, in the context of the shortage of new slaves and frequent departures by existing ones. Indeed, for the late 1890s and 1900s we have a gush of recorded instances of pawning. But we cannot be sure that this reflected a real rise in the frequency of the practice. It is just possible that the recorded rise was purely a function of another consequence of the colonial occupation: the increase in the volume of written records on Asante and the fact that these included a multitude of court cases involving ordinary as well as 'big' men and women. A further perspective on this matter may be gained by relating it to the evidence of trends in the monetary value of pawns and in the gender composition of the pawned population.

It will be recalled that the mid-nineteenth century pawnings were for a half *peredwan* (about £4) apiece, but that between 1883 and the end of the 1890s the scanty evidence suggested a rise to a unit loan of two *peredwan* (about £16).[85] I have corresponding information for seventeen cases between 1900 (the earliest is 1901 or 1902) and 1910. These range dramatically from £8 to possibly £26 a head, with two exceptions: one of £4 and one of £32.[86] The uncertainty of timing is too severe to permit us to trace a trend.[87] But the average size of loans on pawns appears to have been higher during 1901–10 than before 1883, or even during the late 1890s. After 1910 I have 'price' information on only two pawns: Sapon's niece, pawned for £20 long enough before 1925 to have produced three children,[88] and a child held in pawn in 1930 on a loan of £20.[89] So the monetary value of pawns may have stabilized, but if so, this was far above precolonial levels, in nominal and apparently in real terms. This conclusion is consistent with a finding of Fortes from the Ashanti Social Survey's marriage data, that the average size of individual *tiri sika* payments was higher during 1905–25 than before 1905.[90]

This increase in the monetary value of pawns has a double significance for the hypothesis of an expansion in the holding of pawns as a substitute for slaves. On one hand, it may be read as showing that the market provided the main mechanism for the transmission of the diverted demand to those who could meet it, on terms which persuaded them to do so: larger loans. This could have induced a rise in the number of new pawnings, as happened in southern Nigeria in the equivalent period.[91] If this occurred in Asante, it seems clear that the increase would have been specifically in female pawns as will be seen below. But it must be made clear that it is not definite that any increase occurred at all. For, on the other hand, the increased 'price' of pawns highlights the possibility—which appears to have been overlooked in the comparative literature—that while the demand increased, the elasticity of supply was low. Thus excess demand was channeled into inflation in the value of pawns.

Indeed, it is hard to believe that the supply of pawns was very elastic. There is no evidence that people provided pawns unless they needed money badly, and even the prospect of larger loans (often at 25 per cent flat rate interest) might not compensate for their loss of the pawn's services and their reduced share in the products of those services. Nor is there any very strong reason to believe that the need for loans became more widespread in the very early colonial period. For neighbouring Gyaman, Terray has argued that in exactly this time chiefs' courts became more ready to abuse their authority by gratuitously imposing heavy fines in order to create debtors and therefore pawns.[92] An Asante example of such judicial extortion was given in Chapter 10.[93] But in Asante the creation of severe debt via court fines was not new. In the nineteenth century, as we have seen, there were a number of much larger documented cases of fines obliging the debtors to give pawns: specifically, chiefs being forced to pawn or sell subjects and lands.[94] It is unlikely that after the British occupation, with the Asantehene exiled and the remaining chiefs' courts now constrained by colonial oversight, they could generate as many pawns as their predecessors had done, especially when the latter were being shown the way by Asantehene Kwaku Dua Panin (1834–67) or Asantehene Mensa Bonsu (1874–83). On balance, it seems most likely that both interpretations are partly true: that there was an increase in pawning in approximately the decade to 1908, driven by increased demand; but that it was far from enough to absorb all the demand that had been diverted from the slave market, and therefore suppliers of pawns were able to secure larger loans.

The inflation in monetary value seems to have been accompanied, coincidentally or otherwise, by a shift in gender composition. For 1900–1910 (more precisely, as above, 1901 or 1902 to 1910) I have found seventeen pawning transactions in which specific pawns are identifiable by gender. These involved eight males[95] and eighteen females.[96] The sample is small, but the gender composition changes in such a consistent direction that it suggests a tentative conclusion, which may be tested from an expanded data set as further cases are discovered. Whereas in the nineteenth century male pawns seem to have been about as numerous as female,[97] in the first decade of the twentieth century female pawns greatly outnumbered male pawns. This trend towards the 'feminization' of pawnship went much further after pawnship lost its legal status in 1908: as we will see shortly.

The decline in human pawnship was complex and ambiguous. As recently as c.1970, A. A. Y. Kyerematen wrote that 'Although banned, the pawning of persons is still carried out secretly'.[98] Admittedly, the initial enforcement of the ban brought moments of visibility. For instance, the local provincial commissioner warned the Adansehene in 1909:

> TOPAH and PINKRAH's case is a clear one of pawning. For nearly two years, the people have been consistently warned that pawning must be stopped or the offenders would have to go to prison. I am unable to reopen the case.
>
> 2. The Chief of Edubiasi may consider himself lucky that he was not prosecuted.[99]

But after c.1910, in other words once the prohibition of human pawning had been publicized by judicial and administrative actions, the practice rarely surfaces in the administrative and legal records. In 1928 the acting commissioner of eastern Asante commented: 'that this [pawning] still goes on is well known, and will be hard to stamp out, but I say without hesitation that it is not nearly so rife as in former years.'[100]

There was a crucial gender difference in the pattern of decline in pawnship. In a preliminary report on the matter some years ago I wrote that 'The last definite case that I have found of an adult male being held in pawn was in 1910. Further research may uncover later instances'.[101] Since then the reorganization of the national archives in Kumasi has uncovered a previously mislaid file, dated 1948, which provides one possible and one definite case of later pawning of males.[102]

In assessing the implications of this, let us begin by placing the 1948 file in context. It was created in response to a request from the Secretary of State for the Colonies in London for information to enable him to reply to an enquiry from the Anti-Slavery and Aborigines Protection Society about the continued existence of human pawning in West Africa. The district commissioners of Asante, between them, reported that they could find only two relatively recent cases. The earlier occurred in Sekyere district in c.1928.[103] One Kwaku Bekoe was pawned by his uncle to Mamponhene Kwaku Dua for a debt which had been 'presented' to the chief by one of his subjects, the original creditor. The pawn served the stool as an *ahenkwaa* (stool servant). In 1948 a later Mamponhene, who stated that he had been unaware of Bekoe's pawn status, 'has now agreed that Bekoe must be released from his obligations and have his freedom restored to him.' The district commissioner added that 'The question of the debt will have to be gone into separately'. The later instance reached the notice of the state in 1947 when Kojo Kwarteng, a licensed money-lender living in Asanso in Amansie, sued for £7.[104] This, he claimed, was outstanding from a loan of £10 with £5 interest contracted in c.1939. The defendant maintained that the principal had been only £8, and that no cash interest was due because the creditor had accepted the services of a pawn in lieu. As it happens, 'The boy stayed with' the creditor 'for only one year, and left for his home town'. Three observations should be made. First, it is likely but not certain that the pawning happened at all. In his court statement (recorded in the file) the creditor made no mention of pawning, and indeed implicitly denied it. The colonial administrators, however, wrote as if pawning had been proved, perhaps because a British magistrate's court had, on appeal, overturned the original finding (by a chief's court) in favour of the creditor. Second, the latter was clearly not prosecuted for pawning. Third, if the pawning occurred the transaction was outside Asante: at Akropong in the Gold Coast Colony, home town of both the borrower and the alleged pawn.

Paradoxically, this 1948 colonial administrative file which contains evidence only of pawning of males fits very well with the evidence from other sources that, on the contrary, the pawning of males declined fast after its prohibition, and much faster than the pawning of females (and perhaps young boys). To start with, it is striking that the administration could find only one clear-cut example of a (male) pawning transaction having taken place in relatively recent times—and that twenty years before—on Asante soil. Again, in the case of the Akropong boy pawned into Asante, it is significant that he was able to walk out just a year later.[105]

Unlike male-pawning, the pawning of women seems to have been safe from interference by the colonial authorities as long as the loan could be presented as a marriage payment, that is, as *tiri sika*.[106] This is no mere argument from silence. While the 1948 file does not mention the subject there is detailed documentation from other sources, especially the Ashanti Social Survey, that in the mid-1940s wife-pawning was widespread in Asante[107] (and in Akan society more generally).[108] Fortes stated that *tiri sika* 'is found in about one-third of extant marriages'.[109] Overall, the recorded cases of pawns seem to consist almost entirely of women and children (the latter being girls where the gender is mentioned, if we exclude cases where 'boy' appears to mean a relatively able-bodied youth). Specifically, from after 1910 I have now come across eight or possibly nine pawning trans-actions in which specific pawns are identifiable by gender. They involved only one, perhaps two, pawns identifiable as male, but nine females.[110] Two of these were pawned to their husbands. Cases of child pawning appeared in the courts at least up to 1942.[111] The quantitative pattern suggests that pawning had been 'feminized' in the sense of becoming overwhelmingly confined to females.

But this does not mean that wife-pawning continued to flourish indefinitely. From the Ashanti Social Survey's 'haphazard sample' of 608 marriages, of which 227 had involved payment of *tiri sika*, Fortes drew the provisional conclusion that the younger the respondents, both husbands and wives, the smaller was the propensity for their marriages to have involved *tiri sika*. He also concluded that the average size of *tiri sika* pay-ments had been less in the period c.1925–45 than in the previous twenty years. 'Both the amounts [of *tiri sika*] paid and the number of wives on whom [it is] paid are tending (1945) to decrease'.[112] In general it seems likely that pawns and reluctant pawn-givers were in a stronger position after pawning as such was banned. In a perhaps exaggerated way, in 1927, de Graft-Johnson urged this view for the whole of what is now Ghana:

> Today there are very probably some pawns, but without question they know they are only doing temporary service, that they are free persons and can leave at any time. Moreover the family giving and the family receiving the pawn are usually on very friendly terms, one temporarily adopting the daughter or son of the other and no crime or wrong is ever intended by either by the transaction.[113]

The different trajectories of the pawning of men, children and women after 1910 are to some extent attributable to the aims and resources of the enforcers of colonial policy. With respect to aims, the differences of outcome were partly the result of colonial officials' implicit acquiescence in wife-pawning combined with their desire to end other kinds of pawning. Regarding resources, the fact that the pawning of children outlived that of men must have been partly because the former was less visible to official gaze.

However, this was surely not the full story, either for pawning or for slavery. One has to doubt the ability of the colonial government of Asante to bring about the demise of adult male pawning, and indeed to constrain the pawning of children. In 1905 the colonial police totalled only 61, of whom 19 were specifically assigned to the railway or mines. Police were stationed only in two of the four administrative districts into which Asante was then divided.[114] It was only in 1910 that the total reached the 100 mark again, from which it climbed to pass 200 in 1921.[115] This was for a population that was probably undercounted at 406,000 in the 1921 census returns. As A. H. M. Kirk-Greene put it in a broader context, 'the police were less a presence than an earnest'.[116] Staff shortage mattered especially on issues where the government could hardly expect chiefs to be active enforcers of colonial law. This was so with pawning and slavery, in which, as we have seen, the chiefs had a vested interest; which certain of them had indeed expressed in petitions to the government. In the 1920s larger revenues enabled the government to deploy more police and administrative staff in Asante, as in the Gold Coast generally: which may have hindered pawning and what remained of slavery.[117]

As this chapter has illustrated, for Asante we are fortunate in having a variety of sources available on the ending of property rights in people on the ground; a process which, in Africa generally, is often thought to be extremely hard to document. The evidence indicates that, on the one hand, the colonial government did achieve the suppression of the slave trade, within a few years. On the other hand when Fuller claimed, in a book published after his retirement, that 'a few years sufficed to suppress both institutions [slavery and pawning] for ever',[118] he exaggerated greatly. But it could be said that in practice the gradualist policy which Armitage and himself had urged, apparently unavailingly, did take toll of slavery and pawning. The colonial courts' enforcement of promissory notes and wage contracts contributed to the realisation of the opportunities for the 'modernization' of labour and credit relationships. These opportunities, as we will now see, were created by the successful Asante adoption of cocoa farming.

13

COCOA AND THE ENDING OF LABOUR COERCION, C.1900–C.1950

This chapter examines the hypothesis that the demise of previously widespread property rights in people was the result, not only of changes in law and its implementation, but also in the economy. In the period of 'abolition' in Asante, as in the Gold Coast before it, the principal economic change was the adoption and spread of cocoa-farming.

That cocoa began to be adopted before slavery was made effectively illegal makes it interesting to examine the ending of Asante slavery as a possible case of induced institutional innovation. Can it be explained as a response to a shift in relative factor prices which made it socially efficient for the property rights regime to be changed to accommodate the new economic circumstances?[1] The spread of cocoa-farming altered the relative scarcities of labour, land and capital: and this was reflected, implicitly and explicitly, in changes in relative factor prices. Did this shift contribute to the end of slavery in Asante? A 'Third World' parallel, to judge from David Feeny's account, would be nineteenth- and early twentieth-century Thailand, where he sees a transition from rights in people to rights in land as land became less abundant.[2] Section A asks whether the concept of induced innovation can help to explain why, after waiting twelve years, the British finally introduced prohibition. In tackling that question evidence is provided about the impact of abolition on cocoa farming. This is much needed because previous publications on the history of cocoa-farming in Ghana generally have said little either way about the effect of the decline of property rights in people upon the growth of cocoa-farming.[3]

Turning from policy decisions to changes in practice, Section B examines whether the cocoa 'revolution' helped to turn mere prohibition into something approaching genuine abolition. This idea was put forward by the pioneer economic historian of British West Africa, Allan McPhee, in 1926. He asserted that the abolition of slave dealing and the legal status of slavery in 1874 in what was to become the Gold Coast Colony had 'negligible' effect until changes including 'the development of the cocoa industry' dealt it a 'staggering blow' by, he implied, creating a 'free labour market' offering 'alternative employment' to former slaves.[4] In the tradition of McPhee, but for West Africa generally, Hopkins argued in 1973 that export agriculture assisted newly emancipated slaves establish themselves as free farmers and migrant labourers. This in turn helped make it possible for slavery to be ended with relatively little social and economic disruption.[5] It was not until the 1980s that detailed work began to be published on the decline of slavery in the Gold Coast Colony.[6] Such research has enormously enriched and, implicitly, qualified McPhee's sketch, but without mentioning his hypothesis or considering the evidence on it in any detail. Section B examines the proposition for Asante, with reference to *corvée* as well as slavery and pawning. It goes on to inquire whether the growth of cocoa-farming, and related economic changes, help explain the social unevenness of the decline of slavery and pawning.

A. Induced Institutional Innovation? The Decision to Prohibit Slavery and Pawning and the Impact of Cocoa Cultivation

This section examines the British decision effectively to ban slavery and pawning in relation to the hypothesis of induced institutional innovation. The major economic change of the period was the adoption and rapid spread of cocoa production. This progressively altered the factor ratios, and is thus very much the kind of economic change that, in terms of the hypothesis, might induce institutional change. We ask first how much factor ratios had shifted by 1908. We go on to examine the contribution of various forms of coerced labour to the cocoa take-off in Asante. We then consider whether the colonial government's decision to forbid slavery and pawning, when it was eventually made, can be considered as in any sense induced by economic change within Asante.

By its nature the spread of cocoa cultivation was progressively increasing the ratio of fixed capital (mostly in the form of cocoa trees) to labour, and reducing the relative abundance of land in relation to labour.

But how far had this shift gone by the critical decision-year of 1908? To answer this question we need to estimate how much land had been put under cocoa trees by then. The basic method is to start with the annual export figures (as noted earlier, we can take exports as equivalent to output). Ideally, we would select a year in which all cocoa beans sold were the produce of trees planted by the end of the major rains in 1908, which was, in effect, precisely when the prohibition on slavery and pawning was introduced. Yet it would also be a year in which all those trees had come into full bearing. Though no such perfect year exists, we can assume that almost all the cocoa sold in 1914 came from trees planted before the prohibition; but a high proportion of these trees would not have reached peak bearing. Thus to use the 1914 crop to estimate pre-prohibition planting would be somewhat to understate the latter. To use the 1919 crop, on the other hand, would be to overstate it. Most of the trees planted before prohibition would have reached or come close to peak bearing by the time they contributed to the bumper 1919 crop, but it would have been boosted by output from newer-bearing trees planted c.1909–14. Thus the true acreage planted by the time of the ban would be represented by an output figure somewhere between the 1914 (11,819 tonnes) and 1919 (32,455 tonnes) harvests, but probably closer to the former.[7]

To obtain the acreage we divide the output by the average yield per acre. Figures for the latter, from African farms in Asante and/or the Gold Coast Colony, vary from 7 to 10 60-pound (27.2 kilogram) 'loads'. Given that much of the acreage was not yet in full bearing, it is appropriate to reject the highest of these figures. This was an estimate for Asante in 1932–33, by J. C. Muir, the head of the Ashanti Division of the Agricultural Department.[8] By that year a much higher proportion of the trees would have been at their peak. The lowest figure, which was W. H. Beckett's finding for the village of Akokoaso in Akyem in the Gold Coast Colony in the early 1930s,[9] is probably too low for our purposes. For the evidence is that yields in the early decades of Asante cocoa farming tended to be higher, as Muir's figure dramatized. The safest yield number for this period is perhaps the 9 loads per acre reported by Cardinall for 1931, apparently for colonial Ghana as a whole.[10] Assuming 540 pounds (245 kilograms) an acre, the area of bearing cocoa was 75 square miles (194 square kilometres) in 1914 and 297 square miles (769 square kilometres) in 1919. This amounted to 0.31 and 0.84 per cent, respectively, of the total surface area of Asante. Even on Beckett's 420 pounds an acre, the proportion would have been only just over 1 percent (1.07) in 1919, the first year in which such a proportion had been even approached.

Therefore, though the territory of Asante included some savanna and other land unsuitable for cocoa, including towns, it is clear that land was still relatively abundant. Virtually all the population of Asante with control over their time had free or nearly free access to land, while labour was still relatively scarce. Thus, as yet, cocoa had not changed factor ratios enough to generate a shift in relative factor prices remotely sufficient to encourage property-owners to convert themselves from masters to employers.

Consistent with this is the extensive use of *corvée* in the early colonial period, at the initiative of chiefs and of the colonial government. For this can be seen precisely as a response to the fact that the conditions which had made coercion essential to the recruitment of extra-familial labour before 1896 still obtained after it, certainly beyond 1908.[11] Admittedly, the labour requisitioned by the government was underpaid rather than unpaid (except for the post-revolt punishment tasks). For instance, in 1898 the government paid chiefs 9 pence a day, including subsistence, per worker supplied for 'a day's march averaging 18 miles' (29 kilometres).[12] It was the same government source which observed that 'the women and children . . . can make on average 9d. to 1s. a day' in gold washing, an activity which had been largely given up by men because it was harder and less profitable than rubber production.[13] So we can assume that, even aside from resentment at the colonial occupation, no voluntary labour would have been forthcoming in the dry season of 1898 at 9d. a day for such an arduous exertion as long-distance headloading. The British government thus got its labour at significantly below the market-clearing price—even for the dry season. It is harder still to envisage 9d. a day attracting labour services from Asante farmers during the rains, when planting and weeding needed to be done on their own farms to assure the adequacy of the next food harvest.

The chiefs, too, were obtaining labour at below any plausible free-market price when they called their subjects to make cocoa farms for the stool. While food crops would have been planted to shade the young plants, the rights to them would presumably belong to the chief. Let us consider Amansie district, to the south of Kumasi, a case which I have studied in detail—so far the only detailed study of the early years of cocoa production in Asante. One of the findings, from fieldwork plus some archival evidence, was that *corvée* was a major source of labour on early cocoa farms. This was so in the case of the first cocoa farm in Amansie district, Kwame Dei's at Asiwa.[14] The labour of free subjects created the first stool cocoa farm in Manso Nkwanta, which was said to be as old as any cocoa farm in the town.[15] In Esumeja, too, the early stool cocoa farm was made by communal labour.[16] Of the village of Tetekaso, in Amansie but under the Esasehene, it was said in court in 1957: 'I remember about 1911, Agyie-Tiaa was enstooled chief of Tetekaso, and two big cocoa farms were made for the Tetekaso stool'.[17] Agyie-Tiaa however denied this, claiming 'that the farms which I have are by my own labour, and nobody has made the farm[s] for me'.[18]

There are other known cases of chiefs' farms in Amansie district. It is highly likely that these too were made by *corvée*, though I cannot confirm this. In 1913 Fuller noted that Chief Owiabu of Feyase had 'made' four cocoa farms. He 'will relinquish the stool . . . and as he has disposed of 2 cocoa Plantations the remaining two will become Stool property against which Owiabu will have no claim'.[19] The Adumasahene established a stool farm as one of the first cohort of cocoa farms in the Ofoase-Kokoben area, soon after 1900.[20] At Asubina near Manso Nkwanta the chief's farm was 'about 8 years old' in 1921.[21] A stool cocoa farm was made at Amoafo: exactly when is unclear, but probably before 1914.[22] As for Adanse district, in 1911 Adansehene Kobina Foli told a commission on land tenure: 'I have a very large' cocoa farm.[23]

What of the mass of private farmers? Perhaps the most revealing context in which to consider this is the fact that cocoa was not heavily planted in Asante until shortly after the Yaa Asantewaa War. An obvious reason for this is that diffusion of the exotic crop took time. Though it had been experimented with over quite a long period in the Gold Coast, it was only in 1893 that annual exports had reached 1 tonne.[24] Further, as noted earlier, it was not until 1903 that the railway reached Kumasi, decisively improving the profitability of the crop to Asante growers. But it may well be that an additional reason was an acute shortage of labour. This was not so much because of the British moves against fresh imports of slaves: after all, Samori Toure's forces had permitted large-scale imports in the immediately preceding several years. But the colonial government's 'constant' demands for carriers (in the words of the Resident, quoted earlier) were clearly disruptive of Asante enterprise. This, in turn, helps explain why chiefs were so prominent as pioneer cocoa-farmers in Asante: they could draw on *corvée* themselves. But after the rising the Asante cocoa take-off gathered pace: initially perhaps especially in those chieftaincies, such as Bekwai, which had not revolted and therefore escaped punishment labour.

Slave and pawn labour was far more important than wage labour in the wave of planting, mainly in the southern and eastern areas, c.1900–1916, which established cocoa cultivation in Asante. Despite the shortage of new slaves and the flight of some old ones, it is reasonable to assume that slaves—including *efie nipa*, the children of slaves, as well as first-generation captives—still constituted a large proportion of the labour force. As Fuller was to note of Asante generally, 'Although the purchase of slaves had ceased since the British occupation in 1896, all families of importance owned slaves, who, in reality, formed part of the family circles'. All members of the 'family circle' who could contribute did so.[25] Kwame Dei, cocoa pioneer, was remembered as having used slaves and pawns on his cocoa farm at Asiwa near Lake Bosumtwi.[26] In 1913 the provincial commissioner in Obuasi was faced with a 'Curious claim by ex-slaves to share in profits of a cocoa farm left by their deceased master'.[27] Such a claim can only have been based on the premise that they had laboured in making or operating it. Conversely—if Amansie district, which was prominent in the cocoa take-off, was representative of the cocoa expansion generally—wage labour on early cocoa farms, when it existed at all, was limited to some casual work. Regular hired labour (six-month, annual or sharecrop) does not seem to have existed before at least 1918. By then enough trees had been planted in the district to yield over 10,000 tonnes a year when they came into bearing, a mark reached by 1921–22.[28] Overall, it is reasonable to conclude that the speed and scale of the early growth of cocoa cultivation owed much to inputs of coerced (slave, pawn and *corvée*) labour, supplementing self and free family labour, and probably co-operative work groups.

Further evidence on this comes from Fortes's notes of an interview he conducted in Asokore, in Sekyere, in 1945.

> Wealthy cocoa farmers. (They are not very willing to talk about other peo-ple[']s wealth. I asked if they knew anyone who had become wealthy only from cocoa farming.) At Nyamfa there was a man Kwame Dampa, who had very big cocoa farms wh[ich] he made in the early days. He had '[e]fie nnipa' (descendants of slaves) to work his farms and so got very rich. But if you do not have many sons or money to employ labour you can't make big cocoa farms.29

In the first twenty years or so of Asante cocoa-farming, relatively few people could have afforded regular wage labour. But those who had the services of slaves (of whatever category) and/or of pawns could nevertheless expand their cultivation beyond the scale permitted by their own labour, plus the service of free family members.

There is no evidence of Asante farmers, having established their farms, *choosing* to employ labourers rather than to own them. Their problem was that the banning of slave trading made it difficult to acquire new slaves. The price of slaves had been so low compared to the cost of regular wage labour that it is hardly surprising that there is no evidence of emancipation at owners' initiative; whereas, as we have seen, there are a number of documented cases of slaves running away. The growth of cocoa-farming was not enough to make the prohibition of slavery a 'pareto' (loserless) gain. Overall, there is no evidence of any economic pressure for abolition from within Asante: and no sign of it in the behaviour of chiefs or their free subjects; nor from the local colonial officials.

Politically, as noted in Chapter 11, it is very clear from the fairly voluminous and certainly protracted correspondence between the colonial administration in Asante and their superiors that the decision to apply the prohibition on slavery and pawning to Asante was anything but an initiative of the colonial 'men on the spot'. On the contrary, it was imposed upon them from above, and attempts to water down or re-interpret the instructions were specifically and explicitly overruled by the governor. Far from being induced by economic change, the ban was very much exogenous to Asante and even to its colonial administration.

The comparison with *corvée* is interesting. There too, the political pressure for abolition ran ahead of the availability of alternative sources of affordable labour for the tasks concerned. In the case of forced labour for road maintenance, however, the pressure was weak enough for change to be evaded to a considerable extent, until the very era of decolonization.

B. After Prohibition: Cocoa and the Uneven Decline of Coerced Labour and Property Rights in People, 1908–c.1950

Conversely, it would be a profound mistake to see the ending of slavery and pawnship as entirely the result of the colonial government's prohibition. Their actual disappearance in practice was a prolonged, complicated and ambiguous process: much influenced by the pattern of demand for labour in cocoa farming.

Even after slavery had been made effectively illegal many former slaves and descendants of slaves continued to work for their 'masters'. Those belonging to the *gyaasefoɔ* were perhaps particularly prone to continue their old tasks. Consider the property bestowed upon the abdicating Esumejahene in 1924: 'A farm has been given to the Chief & also a house & the people to [*sic*] the farm'.[30] In colonial law the farm-workers were free, but they themselves may well have understood their 'employment' in terms of status rather than contract. According to former Bekwaihene Yaw Buachie III, stool servants went on working on stool farms.[31]

We saw in the last chapter, however, that there was a gradual decline in the willingness even of the *gyaasefoɔ* to perform their 'customary' duties. When it came to cocoa labour, former owners of slaves found that even when ex-slaves had remained in the same community, they were not necessarily prepared to accept the continuation of any claim on their labour by their old masters. Osei Kwame of Huntado was unable to get any more work out of the slaves he had brought from Denkyira because 'the air of freedom was blowing everywhere', as his nephew put it.[32] The same point was made more generally by an informant in Bekwai quoted above.[33]

Thus former slaveowners found themselves obliged to look to other institutions for labour. Osei Kwame put his farm into hired hands well before his death in 1934.[34] Even on stool farms wage labour ceased to be unknown.[35] In general, the maturation of cocoa farms—many of them at least partly established and/or worked by slaves and pawns—made an alternative form of labour financially possible for 'masters' and available for 'servants'. Not that the former could necessarily rely on the latter to be their hired labourers. The acting provincial commissioner of eastern Ashanti observed in 1928 that the children of first-generation slaves 'own their own farms, and in these days plant their own cocoa'.[36]

It was shown earlier that adult male pawning seems to have been less common relative to other forms of pawning during the period c.1901–10 than it was in the nineteenth century, and that if its decline was not already absolute, it became so very soon afterwards. The contribution of pawned men to cocoa production presumably dwindled as they became fewer. The fact that the demise of the pawning of men probably began during the emergence of cocoa production, and probably also before pawning was prohibited, raises the possibility that cocoa contributed to the process. The most likely connection is the following. The new cocoa economy offered alternatives to men who previously would have accepted being pawned. They could now be casual workers and/or cocoa farmers themselves. Meanwhile it enabled richer people, who would previously have bought slaves or lent money to obtain pawns, to hire free labour instead. While at first such labour was casual, during the 1920s seasonal migrants from the savanna were frequently hired on six-month or annual contracts. However, the growth of the market for cash-crop labour was confined very largely to men.[37]

The demand for female labour continued to be concentrated in subsistence farming and the other 'reproductive' tasks. As long as pawn-wives remained numerous—as late as the mid-1940s, as shown in Chapter 12—presumably they continued to be an important part of the overwhelmingly female labour force that planted food crops such as plantain to shade the young cocoa plants and keep the farming population fed while the cocoa plants matured. Again, we have seen that by 1917 *corvée* labour in maintaining the roads—which now meant motor roads as well as paths—was left overwhelmingly to women and children. As with food crops shading young cocoa, this was a crucial but indirect contribution to the early expansion of cocoa farming; while in this phase of Asante cocoa history, direct—and directly remunerative—cocoa labour was predominantly by men.[38]

Hence while the pawns of both sexes who contributed to the development of cocoa farming helped create the conditions for the supersession of pawn by wage labour, it seems that at first this did not reduce the demand for pawn wives, nor offer alternative occupations to the women concerned. Female ownership of farms appears to have been rare during the first twenty years of Asante cocoa farming. However, as will be shown in some detail in Chapter 16, the evidence is that as cocoa cultivation expanded the number of women who owned cocoa farms increased not only absolutely but also as a proportion of all cocoa farmowners.[39] Also, it is likely that the growth of male cocoa income created economic opportunities for women in local markets, as producers of food crops and of cooked food and as traders.[40] For both these reasons it is probable that cocoa farming made a gradually increasing contribution to greater economic autonomy for women. This in turn may help to explain why, according to a former Esumejahene interviewed in 1980, the practice of pawning has died out: because the niece would refuse to be a pawn—children being no longer obedient.[41] Greater economic autonomy would also help to account for the trend which Fortes himself saw as the most important reason for the eventual decline in the frequency and average size of *tiri sika* payments: 'the control exercised over a wife by her mo[ther's] bro[ther] and other lineage kin is getting rapidly less effective. This means that a *tiri sika* loan isn't so useful now as a means of binding the woman's kin to the marriage and putting a moral obligation on them to see that the marriage holds'.[42] More to the point, *tiri sika* was less worth paying because the wife felt less obliged to her *abusua* to see the marriage through on the terms her elders had accepted on her behalf.

I have suggested elsewhere that, where it existed in colonial West Africa, relatively prosperous export agriculture gradually removed the economic basis of human pawning, in contrast to the position in the labour-exporting zones discussed by Martin Klein and Richard Roberts.[43] This applies to the cocoa-producing forest zone of Asante. Pawn-holders could use their growing cocoa receipts to become employers of wage labour or husbands of additional non-pawn wives. Even more important, borrowers were no longer obliged to use their junior matrikin as security. Instead they could borrow short on their forthcoming cocoa crops, or long on their cocoa trees.[44] The short-term variety developed first: advances given by cocoa buyers. The latter were Asante and other brokers (some were from the Gold Coast Colony, Nigeria, or the Levant). Many were financed ultimately by European companies. Such advances began in this area in the 1910s and spread rapidly in the generally quite prosperous 1920s, when cocoa buyers used this form of credit provision as they competed amongst themselves for the farmers' produce. With the collapse of cocoa prices in the early 1930s advances from buyers gave way to long-term loans from any local person with money to lend. These were secured by pledging cocoa farms, that is, handing them over as security, with their proceeds as interest.[45] During the Depression there was similarly a great surge of long-term, relatively 'lumpy' borrowing in the labour-exporting areas of West Africa examined by Klein and Roberts. But there it took the old form of human pawning. For Asante there are indications in the colonial records of a slight increase in the effectively illegal forms of human pawning.[46] Yet, though we cannot know how many instances went unrecorded, it seems that this revival of the practice was very small in volume by comparison with its resurgence in the Sahel, where many cases may likewise have escaped official notice.[47] It is significant that, as noted above, the Ashanti Social Survey found that the effectively legal—and therefore relatively reliably countable—form of pawning, the payment of *tiri sika*, actually declined during the years c.1925–45 as a whole, both in frequency and in average amount. Even if there was a net increase in human pawning in Asante during the depression, this seems to have been overshadowed by the emergence of widespread farm-pledging.[48]

Overall, by the mid-1940s the Asante transition from pawning humans to pledging farms had gone far. It seems to have happened without major disruptions, whether in the form of overt conflict or of shortages of labour or credit. This smoothness is perhaps epitomized in the fact that the same word, *awowa*, was applied to the pledging of trees as it had been to the pawning of humans (meaning literally, 'in place of').[49]

We saw earlier that it was an economic condition—the relatively high cost of labour—that motivated the colonial administration largely to uphold *corvée*, in the face of abolitionist political pressures from outside and above which were never as strong as in the case of slavery and pawning. As with the latter institutions, *corvée* made an important contribution to the spread of cocoa farming. And as with them too, the spread of cocoa gradually altered the labour market situation in the sense of making free labour a feasible alternative to coerced labour—albeit, in this case in very limited ways. The fact that the evidence of stool cocoa farms being made by the labour of subjects comes largely from before 1916 may be explained sufficiently, perhaps, by the subsequent general decline in the rate of new planting in that part of Asante. But it may also have reflected a decline in the propensity of subjects to respond positively to calls on their labour by their chiefs, a trend noted earlier in the Gold Coast Colony.[50] Indeed, by the beginning of 1931 the governor in Accra was 'given to understand that there is an increasing tendency among native communities to engage and pay a special gang to carry out' their obligations in road-maintenance.[51]

But the responses from Asante indicated that this was as yet hardly practiced north of the river Pra.[52] In March 1939 'the Oman of Essuowin' decided that inhabitants of the town should pay a tax 'to finance a Sanitary gang instead of [the Chief] calling communal labour'[53] (and it seems to have been in this period that some wage labour began to be used on stool farms).[54] Yet Esswowin was a small chieftaincy in Amansie, where, as we have seen, forced labour remained in widespread use in the 1940s for purposes including 'sanitary' work. For, as the district commissioner of Bekwai observed in 1940, 'in Ashanti there is no regular direct taxation out of which necessary communal services may be financed'.[55] It would be interesting to know if Essuowin's decision was based on the assumption that the cocoa economy was going to recover a degree of stable prosperity, and whether the policy survived the collapse of producer prices after the outbreak of war.

C. Conclusion

Having considered the process by which, and the context in which, the colonial administration made its decision effectively to prohibit slavery in Asante, we may conclude that this case exposes the limitations of the hypothesis that changes in property rights are socially-efficient responses to changes in relative factor prices. The decision was economically exogenous and involved loss to certain parties. Indeed, it is hard to see how a labour market could have been reproduced in Asante had it not been for the advent of cocoa, which greatly increased the economic rent on forest-zone land. For the first time free labour contracts were now in the mutual interests of Asante users of labour and savanna-dwellers. This is not to say that the coercion, where it was politically and practically feasible, would not still pay: as the persistence of government and chiefs with *corvée* illustrates. But, in the terms used in Chapter 8, while the Nieboer situation thus still applied, it was now in Hopkins's sense rather than Domar's: without coercion to reduce its reservation price, extra-familial labour remained relatively costly, but it was no longer so costly that coercion was necessary for the labour market to exist.

Though shifts in relative factor scarcity do not explain the colonial government's decision to ban Asante slavery, they help to explain the nature and inequalities of the subsequent slow decline. That is, with respect to the decline of slavery on the ground, as opposed to the political decision to ban it, the notion of induced innovation does have explanatory power. As McPhee implied, cocoa accelerated individuals' transitions from slave to free labour.

This in turn smoothed the local political repercussions for the colonial administrators in Asante, despite the fact that the political decision had been taken very much 'from above'. They had feared major opposition from chiefs and others for whom it entailed a loss of property. Regarding this issue as well as other aspects of early colonial rule it is not surprising that Chief Commissioner Harper, in 1921, proclaimed that 'Cocoa is the foundation of the peace and prosperity of Ashanti'.[56]

Beyond this general impact on the decline of slavery, the pattern of economic opportunities created by cocoa helped some slaves or former slaves much more than others. The result was to differentiate the process by which coercion declined on both gender and ethnic-cum-ecological lines. Most of the opportunities for regular wage employment were for able-bodied adult males. Men were more in demand for cocoa carrying and labouring, especially as at this early stage in the development of Asante cocoa culture much of the work was forest-clearance. For this reason it seems likely that, as with pawns, female and child slavery tended to outlast adult male slavery, strongly so into the 1940s. Again, in Chapter 12 it was suggested that a higher proportion of Akan ex-slaves than of northern ones returned to their to their native or ancestral homes. Besides physical distance, a reason for this may be the fact that an Akan adult could look forward to establishing cocoa farms of his, or even of her, own: whereas this would be much harder for people who had no land rights in the forest zone, and thus no direct access to the 'forest rent'. The Ewe war captives also had forest homes to go to, with land suitable for planting cocoa. It is hoped that fuller data in the future will permit us to establish whether, as the analysis here predicts, a higher proportion of Ewe than of northern ex-slaves left Asante. But it can be said that economic circumstances made it easier for Asantes rather than northerners, and for men rather than women, to achieve effective emancipation quickly.

The 'pessimistic' proposition put forward in some of the literature influenced by dependency theory is vindicated in the Asante case to the extent that coerced labour seems to have made an important contribution—along with self, family and other non-market forms of labour—to the cash-crop 'take-off'. Without the contributions of coerced labour the expansion of cocoa production would surely have been much more gradual, given the pressure on labour supplies.

Recent students of West Africa have highlighted one in particular of the theoretical disadvantages of slave labour compared to free labour: its immobility, which, it has been implied, would have hindered the economy's adjustment to the opportunities to grow crops for export. The logic of this is that the spatial distribution of slaves at the beginning of colonial rule did not coincide with the pattern of demand for labour in the emerging, geographically rather narrow, cash crop sectors. The replacement of slavery by free migrant labour is held, therefore, to have assisted the mobilization of labour for the new cash-crop economies.[57] But in Asante the mobility of free labourers was redundant in so far as the great majority of slaves in Asante had been imported from the same region from whence now came most of the annual labourers and sharecroppers.

Considering the relatively late ending of slavery and pawnship—let alone *corvée*—and the contributions of all these forms of coercion to the labour that, directly and indirectly, created the agricultural export economy of Asante, there is some validity in this West African context for the Genoveses' generalization about the 'anomaly' that 'capitalism, which rested on free labour and had no meaning apart from it . . . conquered, absorbed, and reinforced servile labour systems throughout the world'.[58]

But the contribution of coercion to the expansion of production for the market is not the full story. For the 'optimistic' liberal or market perspective is justified here to the extent that the spread of cash cropping itself contributed, directly and indirectly, to the eventual ending of slavery and human pawning and the emergence of alternative institutions in the supply of labour and credit. The benefits of cash cropping in this, as in other respects, were unevenly distributed. It was those who could participate, as owners of cocoa trees or as labourers on cocoa farms, who had the best opportunities to escape slavery and pawning, on the master's side and on the servant's side respectively.

Given that the growth of cocoa farming in Asante was largely the responsibility of the farmers themselves,[59] it is fair to conclude that the timing and smoothness of the decline of slavery and human pawning in Asante was to a large extent the unplanned result of indigenous economic activity and initiative. In the sense that slaves and pawns contributed labour directly and indirectly to the emergence of Asante cocoa-farming, they contributed to the growth of government revenue which facilitated enforcement of the laws against slavery and pawning; helped work male pawning out of a role; and assisted the eventual and gradual expansion of the economic alternatives to pawn-marriage as an occupation for women.

PART V

Social Relations of Production and Trade,
1908–1956: Towards Integrated Factor Markets?

This part describes the changing forms of ownership, control and trade in productive resources during and especially following the decline of slavery and pawnship. This history of social relations of production needs to be set in the political context of British over-rule, including the severe limits to colonial administrative capacity and, towards the end of the period, the transition towards an independent Ghanaian state. The story must also be related to the economic context of the gradual transformation of factor ratios that proceeded throughout the period (and beyond): as the area under cultivation continued to spread, cocoa trees to mature, and population to rise. The causes and implications of the outcomes defined in the chapters that follow—discussing successively the changes in the relations of land, capital and labour—will be examined in depth in Part Six. The present part thus performs the same role in our discussion of the post-1908 period as Part Two did in our consideration of the nineteenth century. As there, analysis is an essential means of establishing a consistent description amid conflicting arguments. Much of the evidence presented here is new. In the process we will reconsider the nature of British policies on market institutions in West Africa, review Polly Hill's argument that borrowers and lenders came from the same socio-economic group, and revisit the proposition that cocoa undermined the importance of the extended family in the allocation of resources. It should be noted that the cocoa trees are regarded here as capital goods rather than as land.

14

LAND TENURE:

WHAT KIND OF TRANSFORMATION UNDER CASH-CROPPING AND COLONIAL RULE?

This chapter examines the changes and continuities in the tenure of land itself, and of the rents obtained by the ultimate owners of land from its users. Section A considers a fundamental issue of colonial rule in Africa: the extent to which land was appropriated for European use. In Asante this was a potential transformation that, despite some initial facilitation by the colonial government, did not occur and was then—retrospectively, in effect—ruled out by the government. I compare the colonial government's policies regarding land alienation to Europeans and, on the other hand, to non-Asante Africans. Section B traces a crucial change that did occur: the emergence of cocoa rent, levied by land-owning chiefs on 'stranger' cocoa-farmers. I also document the consequent scramble to claim and define boundaries between chieftaincies' lands. Section C discusses British policy on land tenure, showing that the colonial government actively defended the property rights of indigenous farmers over the trees that they planted.

A. Alienation to Europeans and to Non-Asante Africans

Asante never became a 'settler' or a 'plantation' colony. But because we know how the story ended it is all the more important to appreciate that at the start it looked as if things might go in a very different direction. During the 1910s it became clear that Asante's exchange economy was fast becoming dominated by the export of cocoa grown by a multitude of Asante farmers. This outcome, which was consolidated in the decades that followed, especially the 1920s and the 1950s, was very much in line with the early public statements of the colonial regime in Asante. For example, the 1904 annual report, apparently written by Major W. B. Davidson-Houston, Acting Chief Commissioner, defined a position firmly against foreign acquisition of Asante lands.

> The secret of ensuring peace in Ashanti lies in the encouragement of trade and agriculture in the country. . . . I consider that our safest, and, therefore, wisest policy is for the Government to encourage the Ashanti in every way possible to enter into new, and improve existing trades, and also to follow agricultural pursuits to the utmost of his ability, and having done so to put a considerable portion of his profits into permanent buildings in the towns. If he does this we can fully rely upon his common sense not to risk his possessions in the future by fruitless quarrels with either the Government or his fellows.
>
> And for this reason, I am entirely averse to the Ashantis being permitted to sell or mortgage either their land or their houses to outsiders.[1]

Yet, as we will see in this section, this was hardly the whole of the government's policy on land alienation. Though it severely limited its own land acquisitions, in its actions—as distinct from its words—the administration favoured private European investors. This was true not only in mining but in agriculture too. We will also see, however, that the ultimate consequences of this de facto policy were very limited as far as indigenous land tenure was concerned. It was not to be dozens of European investors, but rather tens of thousands of Asante ones, who transformed the factor ratio in the Asante forest zone and created pressures for change in the rules surrounding the use of cultivable land.

Following the defeat of the 1900 rising the colonial government was free in British law, by 'right of conquest' to appropriate as crown property all the land, or at least all the lands of the chieftaincies who had revolted.[2] In the event it did so only for the land within a mile of the fort in Kumasi—an area which was eventually returned to the Golden Stool, in 1943.[3] Otherwise government property in Asante was to comprise piecemeal purchases of sites in district and provincial administrative centres for official buildings and for certain activities that it evidently felt needed control, such as market-places and lorry parks.[4] Beyond that, it established a network of forest reserves, primarily to conserve forests by regulating land-clearance whether for timber or cultivation.[5]

Plots within the crown's lands at Kumasi, which early in the colonial period encompassed the whole town and by the end of it covered just the now much-expanded commercial centre, were leased for building only. They could not be mortgaged or transferred without the consent of the chief commissioner. 'It is preferred that the lease be surrendered and a fresh one issued'.[6] Concessions by chiefs of land and mining rights to foreigners anywhere in Asante again required the permission of the chief commissioner.[7] Thus, on the face of it, the government's policy was strongly against large-scale European ownership of Asante lands.

Yet the government did grant long-term concessions to Europeans. The Ashanti Goldfields Corporation obtained its main concession, of 100 square miles (259 square kilometres) at Obuasi, for 99 years.[8] In the urban context of Kumasi, foreigners were actually allowed much longer leases than Asantes. In Kumasi the government would let plots 'to natives for a term of seven years, with option of renewal for a similar period'. Leases to Europeans were 'for 50 to 99 years, with option of renewal'.[9] Potentially most important, given that the overwhelming majority of the indigenous population were farmers, was the fact that the government gave concessions not only for minerals but also for agriculture. The 1903 Ashanti Concessions Ordinance permitted leases of up to 20 square miles for up to 99 years. In the event two European-owned plantations were established, both in Adanse, to grow rubber and cocoa. Both Ashanti Plantations and the Abomposu estate were granted 99-year leases under the ordinance.[10]

As the expansion of Asante-owned cocoa cultivation was consolidated, however, the administration discouraged individual European settlement. European immigrants, both workers (even skilled ones) and small investors depending on their own labour to make a profit, were warned off in the colonial annual reports on the ground that the 'country is not suitable' for them, the former being engaged in Britain when they were wanted, and the latter being without opportunities.[11] In the 1911 report Chief Commissioner Fuller spelled out that 'all work in connection with the tilling of the soil must be left to the native of the country.'[12]

The concessions system yielded rent to chiefs. In Kumasi the government leased much of its land to Kumasi chiefs for sub-division among their subjects.[13] By 1904 chiefs and wealthy commoners were rushing to put up buildings for let to European firms wanting to establish small stores in the African section of the town.[14] This enabled Kumasi chiefs—the former owners of the land—to secure some of the rents they might have enjoyed had land remained under Asante control. Under the colonial regime these rents were probably spread more widely among non-Asante Africans and Asante commoners than they would otherwise have been.

Outside Kumasi some chiefs received rent from concessions granted to European companies. The most lucrative one, for all parties, was at Obuasi. Indeed, the majority of concessions were in the south or southeast, in Adanse and Amansie districts. In 1911 the Adansehene was receiving rent from six concessions, the Bekwaihene was being paid for four, of which only the Obuasi one was actually being worked. Both stools had also given concessions which had lapsed because no rent was being paid: 'a large number' of them, in the Bekwai case.[15] The Adanse and Bekwai stools both received rent for the Obuasi concession. This was set initially, in 1897, at £100 and £66 respectively.[16] By 1914, and subsequently, Bekwai received £133 a year while Adanse got an even more meagre £66.[17] Meanwhile royalty was paid to the central, i.e. colonial, government. The rate was apparently 3 per cent initially,[18] but was raised to 5 per cent of the value of output, 'irrespective of whether the Corporation made any profit or not'. By the fiftieth anniversary of the colonial government's confirmation of the Obuasi concession the cumulative total of royalties was over £1.75 million (in nominal terms). The company had contributed a further £2 million to government revenue via export duties.[19] By the early 1950s royalties were running at about £120,000 a year, according to the local commissioner. In 1950 the government finally responded to Adanse complaints, and granted one-sixth of its royalties to the land-owning stools. As five per cent of the land belonged to Bekwai, Bekwai got five per cent of the one-sixth; while Adanse got the rest.[20] AGC also obtained and worked firewood concessions, to supply fuel to the mine.

As early as 1906 a British company applied to the colonial government for a monopoly over mahogany exports from Asante. It was rejected, apparently partly because the government believed that extensive logging would starve the nascent European gold-mining enterprises of fuel. Some small timber leases had already been granted.[21] But the proliferation of timber concessions and leases, and especially of their active use, came from the mid-1940s through the end of the colonial period. They came from both expatriate companies and individual indigenous contractors.[22] Timber trees were stool property, even when they lay within a farm, and the royalties therefore went to the chieftaincy.[23]

The general picture is that the prospect of massive land alienations, on long-term lease, to European firms looked very real in the first decade of colonial rule, and—at an individual level—was welcomed by chiefs and elders attracted by the implications for rents. Certainly the colonial government permitted European mining and planting in practice, despite 'pro-peasant' rhetoric. But as it eventuated, many concessions were either never worked or were soon abandoned. The result was that such concessions, made mostly when land was relatively very abundant, had only very localised effects on indigenous farmers' access to land. The same was true when timber rights were leased, except that where timber contractors made roads (Briscoe's lawyer claimed that the company had built 40 miles [64 kilometres] of road in Adanse in 1944–45 alone),[24] in practical terms—presumably—they facilitated the establishment of new farms.[25] Consequently they had no distinct effect on the rules surrounding the tenure of land for cultivation, except by reinforcing the effects of cocoa and increased food production in shifting the factor ratio: reducing the surplus of land in relation to labour and capital.

The issue of alienation of agricultural land to Africans from outside Asante did not arise until about thirty years into the colonial period. By this time the colonial state's law and administrative practice had followed its economic experience and solidified around the principle that land should not be alienated to foreigners. Following a number of land sales on the southern periphery of Asante to people from the Eastern Province of the Gold Coast Colony (transactions which will be examined more closely below), Chief Commissioner F. W. Applegate wrote to the Asantehene in 1936:

> It has come to my notice that certain Chiefs have sold portions of land outright. Even if native custom allows this I am sure you will agree that the transaction is to be deprecated. While the law does not allow of a foreigner taking up areas of land freehold for cultivation or for any other purpose, yet it appears that the Stools do not object to the selling of land outright to strangers. Such procedure I think you will agree is bound to work deleteriously and against the common good of Ashanti, and I am asking you to bring the question before the nation and generally to take what action you may consider advisable.[26]

This echoed a warning which Applegate had himself issued in 1928, while he was acting provincial commissioner for eastern Asante, when the sales were indeed first noticed by the administration. At that time he had been confident that the practice 'of course, is entirely contrary to Native customary law'.[27] In 1936 Asantehene Osei Prempeh II averred that it was, and warned chiefs to set their faces firmly against it: 'As this practice is exotic and against Native Custom, I should be glad if you and your Elders would take every possible precaution against the outright sale of Stool lands to strangers. . . .'[28] He reiterated the message two years later, telling the Ashanti Confederacy Council of Chiefs: 'I should like to say, that any Chief who has sold land to strangers should regret his action, and should remember that if his predecessors had sold the land he would not have got any land in his Division.'[29] This pressure was apparently successful, as we will see below. The important conclusion here is that the colonial government, and the restored Asantehene, committed themselves firmly to ending and then preventing the sale of Asante land to non-Asante Africans. In that respect the state continued the nineteenth-century Asanteman's policy of defending Asantes' monopolistic possession of the 'broad forest rent' of their territory.

B. The Impact of Cocoa on the Economic Value of Land: Rents, Boundaries, Sales

This section is organized around the basic distinction in Asante land tenure between man-made assets that stood upon the land and the land itself. It was re-emphasized by the Ashanti Confederacy Council, in 1938, in a session in which they responded to questions about 'native custom' put to them by British researchers. To the question 'Can any individual, whether a native of Ashanti or a stranger, own land as his personal property?' the unanimous answer was: 'No; individuals enjoy only surface rights but the land itself is vested in the Stool concerned.' Thus, when a farm is sold by the courts to satisfy a debt 'The purchaser of such a farm does not become the owner of the land. He enjoys only surface right, i.e. the farm, but the land is still vested in the stool of the Division [paramount chieftaincy] concerned.'[30]

Actually, as in the nineteenth century, sales of the land itself were not unknown, as was acknowledged by some of the chiefs present. The Dwabenhene testified that 'if a stool is in debt and the whole of the Division concerned [i.e. all elders] agree, part of their land can be sold or mortgaged to liquidate the debt, provided always that the land is not sold to a non-native of Ashanti.' The Adansehene, who had presided over most of the sales that Applegate had deplored, went further. He admitted: 'Recently owing to litigation about our land we incurred a heavy debt and we had to sell a portion of our land to a certain Akwapim man to liquidate the debt. We will not sell some again. We agree with the Juabenhene.' The Asantehene concluded that part of the discussion by conceding that 'In the olden days, land was sold or mortgaged in Ashanti': but it must be avoided in future.[31] So, even ownership of the land itself had not been proof against alienation. For the present discussion, however, the basic observation is that the distinction between the land itself and the 'surface' or use rights was accepted and indeed emphasized by all the chiefs. That distinction continued to be remarked upon when the colonial period was over. J. G. Amoafo, government agricultural economist for Ashanti and Brong-Ahafo, observed in 1961: 'Economic trees can be owned, separately from the land on which they stand, since land remains the sole property of the "stool".'[32] The rest of this section assesses, in turn, the extent and nature of changes in the property relations surrounding farms and the land itself. We will then consider whether the distinction itself was bridged.

There was much continuity from the precolonial kingdom in the legal categories within which rights over cultivation were defined. But key categories were far more frequently applied, and their practical importance was broadened and increased. To sell a farm was not illegal in the nineteenth century, but it is hard to conceive of circumstances in which it would have been in anyone's interests to pay for one. This changed with the arrival of cocoa cultivation.

Asante farmers got access to land for cocoa-planting within existing legal forms not previously used for commercial agriculture. First, subjects of each stool exercised their right, long-established in the setting of primarily-subsistence food farming, to plant its land. Even at the end of the colonial period, in Ahafo, a district which was a focus of the 1950s cocoa-planting boom, the basic procedure was simple: 'a local farmer may, on informing the Chief, occupy land for making a farm that is not yet occupied by another': though qualifications were beginning to be entered, as we will see in Chapter 17.[33] Second, chiefs also permitted non-subjects to farm their stool lands. Chiefs extended to cocoa beans the principle, which as we have seen was previously only relevant in the context of naturally-occurring products such as gold and wild kola, that the stool should receive a share of the proceeds, certainly when the producers were non-subjects. While it was under the established fiscal and land tenure system that would-be cocoa farmers got access to land, the fact that cocoa trees (unlike food crops) yielded a primarily, indeed purely, commercial product, and that (unlike rubber trees in the nineteenth century, at least generally) they were fully cultivated, enabled the chiefs to exact the first agricultural rent in Asante history. The government termed the payment 'tribute'. But, as an agricultural officer remarked in 1933, this so-called 'tribute' was 'actually a form of rent':[34] payment for the hire of a scarce productive resource. Finally, whereas in the nineteenth century to buy a farm would have been legal but probably pointless, cocoa made it potentially desirable.

A fundamental difference between the histories of cocoa cultivation in Akyem Abuakwa, the major 'take-off' zone of the 1890s, and in Asante, is that whereas the vast majority of Akyem cocoa output seems to have come from farms made by non-Akyems, very little of Asante's cocoa output in any period came from non-Asantes. The earliest cocoa farmers in Asante appear to have been Asantes.[35] For the end of the colonial period we have the 1956–57 survey. This enumerated a total of 17,881 male cocoa farmers, of whom 97 per cent were Asantes.[36] Nor is there any suggestion that the remaining 3 per cent were on average exceptionally big producers. The contrary is likely, as a third were from the Northern Territories,[37] and (as we will see) therefore very probably entered cocoa production as migrant labourers. From that beginning, lacking both capital and rights over forest land, it was a remarkable achievement to become a cocoa farmer (farmowner) at all. In fact it appears that not all of them were actually farmowners. For the sample of 'cocoa producing families' included caretakers working for farmers living outside the survey area, as a way of representing the latter.[38] As we will see, it is a strong assumption that most of these caretakers were from the savanna. Thus most of them were probably included in the category of 'male cocoa-farmers' from the Northern Territories. Though they were 'very few in number',[39] they may well have constituted a high proportion of the one per cent concerned.

Not only were the overwhelming majority of cocoa farmers indigenous in the sense of being Asante, in the more densely populated southern, central and eastern districts (which from 1959 comprised Ashanti Region as distinct from Brong-Ahafo Region), the bulk of the output from any one administrative district came from farmers whose birthplace, matrilineal 'home town' and chief were all from within the district.[40] As a result, most farmers were able to take advantage of their right of virtually free access to land for cultivation on the lands of the stool they served.

But, as we saw in Chapter 4, cocoa cultivation was land-extensive, and farmers expanded their individual enterprises by leap-frogging each other as the frontier of cocoa cultivation advanced west and north from Akyem Abuakwa. Most Asante cocoa farmers of the period made more than one cocoa farm, and we will see below that very often their later farms were outside their own stool's lands and, often, outside their home district. Further, at the beginning of the cocoa era the boundaries between different stools' lands were not coherently defined. Hill's observation about Akyem Abuakwa applies also in Asante: 'The boundaries . . . were literally indeterminate, in the sense that no line could be drawn such that the settlers on one side of it adhered to one stool and those on the other to another.'[41] Thus thousands of farmers planted on land which they believed—or contended or at least hoped—was the property of the stool they served. In Amansie, for example, a substantial minority of farmers planted cocoa on land which, though within the same district, was judged in retrospect—by the courts—to belong to a chiefdom other than the one to which they were respectively subject. The cumulative result was that virtually every stool in the district claimed tribute from the farmers of neighbouring stools, while some of its own subjects were liable to pay tribute to other stools. To mention a few of many instances, in Amansie district there were Kokofu farmers on land judged by the government to belong to Esumeja;[42] there were Amoafo cocoa trees on Kokofu land;[43] while Manso Nkwantas and Abores,[44] and Ofoases and Asuminias,[45] had farms on each others' lands, so that, disputes permitting, rent flowed in both directions. Again, in Ahafo district by late 1933 a total of 75 Odumasi farmers had among them nearly 68,500 cocoa trees in bearing on Dormaa lands which, assuming 500 trees per acre, implies about 137 acres under cultivation, excluding any immature trees. Meanwhile Dormaa farmers were cultivating cocoa on Wenchi and (in the Gold Coast Colony) Sefwi lands.[46]

Rent was a sufficient burden to be an incentive or deterrent in the attempts of some Asante to change their stool allegiances. According to the district commissioner of Sunyani in 1934, 'certain people living in Kwameasua', a Dormaa village, 'discovered or were told' that their ancestors were Kokofus who had been captured by the Dormaas in war. They had been 'given land to settle on and in recent years had become possessed of large cocoa farms in respect of which they of course paid no tribute, as they were considered to be and [were] treated as Dormaa citizens'. About half of them proceeded to transfer their allegiance from Dormaa to Kokofu. The Dormaahene told them that, accordingly, they would have to pay him tribute: 'as a result only some three or four men and their families still said they proposed to serve Kokofu'.[47]

Much of the cocoa planting in Ahafo was the work of migrant farmers from central and southern Asante. For them, in contrast to those who planted within the district in which they grew up, legal liability for tribute was hardly avoidable. It was thus a cost of production that they would have had to take into account from the conception of their venture. In the mid-1940s Fortes was told in the village of Kwotei, near Kumasi, that the cocoa farms which most of the villagers had created in Ahafo 'are owned on tenancy from the local chiefs. Cocoa tribute per tree is paid'.[48] For Asante farmers a kind of progression was commonly involved, especially for those from the eastern and southern districts. They would make their first cocoa farms on land that they knew, or hoped, was securely the property of 'their' chieftaincy. Later, in search of still-vacant fertile land, they would accept 'stranger' status by planting on the land of other chieftaincies, often many kilometres away. The sequence is illustrated by Kwaku Gyekye and Kojo Bah, two brothers from the village of Ofoase-Kokoben in Amansie, who I interviewed in 1980. Both made their first cocoa farms on land that was under the undisputed ownership of the stool they served. They moved on, in about 1925–26, to make additional farms on land at a place called Wawase which their stool claimed but which (after a long dispute which we will examine later) was eventually declared by the courts to belong to a neighbouring stool, to whom they then had to pay rent. Gyekye made his next cocoa farm in c.1949 in a place, Nerebehi, which was indisputably another stool's land though still within Amansie. Finally, in the 1950s, each of them planted cocoa much further afield (and westwards), in the Teppa area (Bah) and in Sefwi-Wiawso (Gyekye).[49]

I have emphasized that charging rent on agricultural produce and selling farms were changes of practice but not of form, in that both were provided for in the land tenure rules of the nineteenth-century kingdom. There were, however, attempts to modify these rules through formal innovation, whether disguised or overt. Armitage told the West African Lands Committee in 1913 that 'in every case when cocoa was started', subjects as well as strangers were required to pay the stool one third of their cocoa harvest. After that, in some chieftaincies at least, subjects had evidently obtained some relief: by 1913 'A member of the tribe would probably come to an agreement with the chief'.[50] Levying the one-third payment on one's own subjects would have been an innovation for most if not all chiefs: in the most comparable earlier cases, those of gold, kola and rubber, it had usually been demanded only of strangers.[51] Soon afterwards the colonial government firmly forbade chiefs from levying 'cocoa tribute' on their own subjects. The chief commissioner himself made an unambiguous innovation in 1910, by reducing the rate of 'cocoa tribute' from a third to a tenth. In 1913 he made it a fixed rate, of a penny per bearing tree, which at the time was about five per cent of producers' receipts. This new institution was sooner or later 'domesticated' into Asante speech under the name *nkapre* ('literally meaning "pennies"').[52] These colonial interventions will be documented, and discussed in more detail, in the next section in the context of colonial policy.

As the cocoa trees planted in the early years of Asante cocoa cultivation matured, so did the number of farmers liable to 'tribute'. Meanwhile, lower cocoa prices entailed a severe rise in rent as a proportion of the gross income of stranger-owned farms. From 1916 onwards prices were usually much lower than in 1913. So the flat rate of a penny a tree had the opposite effect on the rent-payers' burden from that intended. The latter years of the First World War brought a spate of cases of farmers unable to pay in full.[53] Government estimates put 'tribute' at, implicitly, 47 per cent of the producers' gross receipts in 1921, and at nearly 60 per cent in 1933.[54] Two years later stranger-farmers at Dormaa in western Asante actually petitioned for a return to the old one-third rate, because the penny rate exceeded it.[55]

While there is much evidence of the penny rate being enforced in most years, colonial administrators were prepared to intervene to reduce it during recessions. In 1919 the commissioners' courts tended to arrange some remission when chiefs brought before them farmers who had defaulted during times of low cocoa prices.[56] In 1933 the government suggested that the rate be reduced to a halfpenny south of Kumasi and a farthing (a quarter-penny) north of it.[57] The difference was presumably intended to reflect the lower prices received by producers relatively remote from the railway, and the lower average incomes of farmers in 'young' cocoa districts (those with a relatively high proportion of trees yet to bear). The proposal was accepted by the chiefs, though not always without pressure from the government.[58] The reduction proved indeed to be temporary because prices revived somewhat.

Chiefs themselves had not necessarily been able or willing to enforce the penny rate in all cases. In 1927 the district commissioner of Bekwai noted after a day of court-work:

> Several claims re cocoa tribute on land which is alleged not to be under dispute. The chiefs seem particularly helpless in these matters and one sometimes wonders if they are as helpless as they seem. I rather think they are.[59]

For Asante-Akyem the acting district commissioner reported in 1933:

> 1. I have enquired regarding tributes paid by Cacao Farmers and am informed there is a very well known Ashanti Custom or habit of 'begging for small reduction' which if done in the proper manner and sufficient grounds being shown is usually successful and in view of this all Chiefs show a reluctance to show their minds before being begged.
> 2. All Chiefs are only too well aware that times are hard and money scarce and the majority are willing to make concessions. . . .
> 3. The 1d a tree tribute is, I think, rarely paid. The more usual form of tribute is to divide the farm into three parts when it has reached maturity and give one third to the Stool.[60]

But in Amansie, for instance, there is no evidence that the one-third system operated in this period. On the contrary, there is evidence of the penny rate being applied literally. For example, in 1927 a court bailiff collected one penny per tree (before authorisation) from stranger-farmers on Asuchem land, while the Amoafohene asked the district commissioner for permission to collect a penny a tree from Sanfo farmers on his land.[61] In the documented cases in which the land-owning chief agreed to compromise, he insisted on getting a high proportion of the penny rate, and used it as an explicit norm from which concessions might be considered. Thus when the Manso Nkwantahene, Kobina Atta, agreed to the 1933 general reduction to a halfpenny rate, he added:

> But I wish to make matters plain to you that from since Two Years now the Abori people have failed to pay this tribute of £500 per annum which the matter went before the Kumasihene and I reduced same to £350.0.0. which at present they have only paid £200 on a/c leaving balance unpaid. The Akrampa Winisu people also refused entirely to pay Tribute of which Your Worship's directed me to Summons them before my Oman Council and same has been carried out and have obtained Judgment and am only wanting to apply for writs of Fi Fa[62] against their properties.
> After these are collected I shall then reduce to 1d per Tree to half please.[63]

One penny per tree was again 'the current rent' by 1936, when the Ashanti Confederacy Council debated a proposal to reform it, but reached no conclusion.[64]

The period from the outbreak of the Second World War to decolonization saw the biggest fluctuations in real producer prices of the entire colonial period: variations which stretched the notion of a penny norm to the breaking-point (see Fig. 15.2 below). Given the extremely low war-time prices it was not surprising that, in March 1941, the Ofoasehene appealed to the government against his subjects farming on Esumeja land having to pay a penny per tree. The assistant district commissioner minuted that a penny 'is excessive but the Essumegahene [*sic*] tells me no farmers are so assessed.'[65] This indicates both the willingness of chiefs to accept pleas for 'small reduction', and of the administration to press for such concessions if necessary. In April 1946 a colonial court set the rate on those farms at a quarter-penny per tree:[66] evidently now the prevailing rate. In March 1948 the Esumeja stool was apparently claiming a penny a tree from the Ofoases, but the latter's solicitor was able to cite an Ashanti Confederacy Council proclamation that the rate should be one-eighth of a penny.[67] With real producer prices shooting up, however, the Confederacy Council doubled the rate with effect from the 1950–51 season.[68]

In the 1950s two trends were apparent in the rate of cocoa rent. One was pressure from landowning stools against any uniform rate across Asante. The chief and elders of Nkwanta, in Sunyani district, were not satisfied with the rise approved by the Confederacy Council and tried to impose a much higher local rate. The Techiman authorities did likewise, demanding 2 pence a tree.[69] In the latter case, at least, a compromise was finally agreed by all parties in February 1954, of three-quarters of a penny: still well above the Confederacy Council's standard.[70] The other trend was for the 'penny' system—even in fractions—to give way altogether to a restoration of 'share' rates. 'It may be a sixth or one-third and the proportion is determined by a number of economic factors, viz, the nature of the land as to whether it is "virgin", proximity of the land to motorable roads, and the relative demand for land in that particular area. . . . At Fomena [Adanse], for example, strangers pay initially an amount of about £2.8/- and then, one-third of the proceeds of produce annually when the cocoa farm is bearing.'[71] In 1961 it was reported that the penny system 'is not widespread and seems to be falling into disuse'.[72] The variation within the share system suggests that this may have been more than simply a revival of pre-1913 practice, but rather evidence of greater institutional flexibility in responding to economic pressures, including changing producer prices and the availability of land in the locality concerned.

From the start of the cocoa era, the opportunity and threat of cocoa rent gave chiefs incentives to claim as much land as they could and gave many farmers reason to maintain that their trees stood on their own stool's land rather than on that of a neighbour. To be sure, as we saw in the last chapter, throughout the first planting boom the land under cocoa remained far less than the available land suitable for the purpose, even in the older cocoa districts. On a static analysis this would imply that the marginal product of land remained zero. But the land surplus was shrinking steadily and, with thousands of farmers simultaneously clearing land and planting trees during the 'take-off' of Asante cocoa-farming, chiefs and subjects acted as if to anticipate scarcity. Already in 1910 Rew, the commissioner of the southern province, commented on accusations of trespass made by the Kokofus against the chief of Prahsu that 'the cause of these complaints was probably the presence of gold on the land and its usefulness for cocoa, and for agricultural purposes in general'.[73] In 1928 a group of farmers on land at Oyoko and Dadease near Kumasi stated that 'Owing to Cocoa trees planted by us on the said land' no fewer than three chiefs laid claim to it, besides 'the rightful owner'.[74] In 1914 Chief Commissioner Fuller had stated that 'The enhanced value of land is the cause of 90%' of 'inter-tribal' disputes in Asante.[75] Several years later he wrote 'Litigation is beloved by the ASHANTIS, and land disputes form a large proportion of court cases, owing to the accruing value of the soil for planting purposes.'[76] These disputes created a new and pressing need for an innovation in Asante land tenure, in practice if not in conception: the laying down of precise and continuous boundaries between chieftaincies. As we will see shortly, the colonial administration sought to do this, though found it a vexatious task.

As under the precolonial kingdom, there were cases of land itself— not just farms—changing hands for money. In the eighteenth and nine-teenth centuries these were usually in settlement of a debt arising from a fine imposed on a provincial chief by the Asantehene. The colonial-period cases arose in a different context.

In 1937 the acting chief commissioner remarked on an 'influx of farm-ers from the Eastern Province of the Gold Coast Colony in search of new farming areas. Adansi and Bompata [in Asante Akyem] are the two areas principally affected by this invasion up to the present and the extent to which alienation of land to strangers has taken place is not accurately known.'[77] We noted Applegate's opposition to such sales above. A 1928 file shows that land had been sold to Akwapims by the *amanhene* of Adanse and Banka in Adanse district; by the Omanhene of Obogu in Asante-Akyem dis-trict; and separately by a sub-chief of Obogu, the Bansohene.[78] The lands sold by the Oboguhene were 'near' and 'towards' Prasu[79] in Adanse. Indeed, most of the sales seem to have occurred in Adanse district, which led to, and was documented by, a 1947 report on land disputes in Adanse which noted that there had been a series of land purchases by people from the Gold Coast Colony. These were primarily Akuapems, also Krobos and Gas.[80] The acqui-sitions can be seen as a northern extension of the famous cocoa migration in the Eastern Province of the Colony, perhaps partly as a response to the out-break of swollen shoot disease there.[81] The extent of the land purchases is unclear. In the one case for which the report gives figures for the dimensions they work out at over 14 square miles (36 square kilometres). For this the agreed price was £995,[82] implying a rate of £71 per square mile (2.59 kilo-metres). Agreed purchase prices are given for four other complete sales, and for part of a fifth. The six prices total £6,641.[83] If £71 per square mile was the mean rate, this would imply that over 93 square miles (241 square kilo-metres), amounting to nearly 6 per cent of the surface of Adanse district, was alienated. Even allowing for a few further sales in Asante-Akyem, the proportion of Asante land as a whole which was sold to non-Asante Africans must have been far less than one per cent.

It may well be that the area sold was even less than this. A price of £71 per square mile is far lower—probably by a factor of about nine on average—than the cost of the land bought in the original cocoa-farming migration into Akyem Abuakwa.[84] Part of the difference is accounted for by the fall in cocoa prices between the two periods, by between two and three times. This may be assumed to have depressed estimates of the long-term return on cocoa. Another part is explained by Akyem Abuakwa being closer to the coast than Adanse, so that transport costs would have been lower, and producer prices therefore higher. Even so, £71 per square mile may well have been lower than the average cost per unit area of these Adanse purchases. If so, the area involved was even less than the already relatively tiny total estimated above. Whatever the precise figure, it is clear that the sale of land to outsiders was very largely, perhaps entirely, confined to the south and southeastern marches of Asante, and accounted for a negligible proportion of Asante's cocoa lands. In this there is a further fundamental contrast with the history of cocoa cultivation in Akyem Abuakwa, which was literally founded in outright sales by Akyem chiefs and elders to stranger farmers.[85]

It was still possible for Asantes themselves to buy Asante land outright, though this was very rare. When Asante farmers acquired cocoa land outside their own stool's lands they did so—almost invariably—by renting the use rights. By 1949 the Ashanti Confederacy Council declared that land for cocoa farming could be bought legally by an individual.[86] This was not the revolutionary step it might appear, heralding the coming of individual private ownership of land itself. For the ruling stipulated that the land would thereby become the property of the stool of the paramount chief served by the purchaser. The latter could found his own village on the land, enjoy the lowest rank in the hierarchy of territorial chieftaincy, that of *odekuro* (village headman), and demand rent/tribute from settlers.[87] This kind of land purchase does not resemble the coerced 'market in towns and villages' of the previous century in that the sales would not necessarily be the result of political manipulation. On the other hand, it is hard to find actual examples of this happening, presumably because chiefs and elders were generally very reluctant to sell. The strongest parallel with precolonial patterns is that the purchasers envisaged by the Ashanti Confederacy Council's ruling would have something in common with the pioneer entrepreneur-chiefs, the *abirɛmpɔn* who founded so many Akan settlements and states.[88] But the context was now different: the existing chiefly hierarchy offered such individuals a defined but humble slice of rights and recognition.

The closest parallel with the nineteenth-century pseudo-market was a sale of land in June 1923 at Ahinsan near Dompoase in Adanse. The background was that the nephew of the *odekuro* of Ahinsan 'was employed as a Storekeeper' by one of the [European] firms. Evidently he received stock on credit from the firm. For this he was guaranteed by Omanhene of Adanse, Kobina Foli, who was in turn 'indemnified . . . against loss' by the *odekuruo*. Then the storekeeper defaulted; the firm sued; the Omanhene paid; but the *odekuro* failed to reimburse him. The Omanhene himself now sued, and won judgment against the *odekuro* for over £2,200. The village and its lands, which included a mining concession, were auctioned by writ of 'fi: fa:'.[89] The buyer, Kwami Akowuah, received 'a Certificate of title signed by His Honour the Circuit Judge Ashanti.' Akowuah, from nearby Brofoyedru, was a nephew of Adansehene Kobina Foli himself. According to the district commissioner, 'Kwame Akowuah is not a chief in any way, but claims that under the writ he has purchased the land outright and can do as he pleases with it.' Specifically, he 'has been treating the people on this land as "Strangers"' and, on pain of eviction, levying the penny per cocoa tree charge on them ('perfectly' illegally, according to a judge:[90] presumably because he was not a chief and they were not strangers). For [two] years they paid, but then refused, pointing out that the (now former) *odekuro*'s debt had been a personal not a stool one.[91] Finally, in July 1926, following a suggestion from the chief commissioner, the Omanhene effectively bought the land from his nephew (for just under £2,012)[92] and agreed to 'restore [to] the [new] Odikro, Elders and people all rights which they enjoyed prior to the seizure and sale of the said land'. This restoration, however, was conditional on the villagers first reimbursing him by paying '1d per year for every Cocoa tree in bearing on the said land and all other monies and tribute from the said land' until the amount was cleared. The villagers accepted this.[93] That is, they agreed to buy back from the omanhene, for their village stool, rights and powers which had been sold over their head to begin with. In 1925 the acting circuit judge noted that the district commissioner 'informs me that he has some reason to believe that' Akowuah 'is merely a man of straw and that the real purchaser is the judgment Creditor himself':[94] the Omanhene. In this story there is much in common with the earlier history of rent-seeking exploitation of court judgments; except that in the early 1920s, before the restoration of the Ashanti Confederacy, the accumulation was by members of a local provincial elite rather than by members of the metropolitan circle surrounding the Asantehene.

Let us move from land to farms. The first cocoa trees in Asante had hardly come into bearing when they started to be bought and sold. In 1907 'Mr. Harold—[second name illegible] of Kumasi purchased some Cocoa plantations in the neighbourhood of Fomena'.[95] Six years later the Kumasi Council of Chiefs complained 'that Plantations are constantly changing hands even without their knowledge'.[96] Unfortunately we do not have figures for such sales because farm ownership was generally not registered. In 1920 a Kumasi chief, Nana K. Yebuah of Taffo, sold a cocoa and rubber 'plantation' (5,000 trees of each: probably about 20 acres) situated at Taffo Nkwanta, just outside the then town limits to one Alfred Kwaku Duah, otherwise known as A. B. Thompson, for £1,400.[97] There are a handful of documented instances of cocoa farms being sold in later decades. In Wenchi district it was reported in mid-1933 (the information being collected evidently by chiefs' clerks) that three 'persons' in Wenchi division itself, but none in Techiman, had sold their cocoa farms 'to people who do not live in the Division' concerned. The period covered by the enquiry was not specified.[98] But the lively market in farms of 1913 seems to have no parallel later. One may surmise that during the cocoa 'take-off', when relatively few farmers had bearing trees, there was considerable demand for them from people wanting a short cut to ownership. In a sense the demand for bearing trees continued, but it was now met largely through indebted farms. People with ready cash could obtain farms on pledge, or buy them at public auction when defaulters' farms were sold by court order. Given that cocoa farms were capital goods, we will consider this further in Section C. But it is relevant in this section because the particularity of trees as capital goods is that their ownership conveys de facto use rights over the land, denying its use to others.

Cocoa greatly reduced the practical importance of the distinction between ownership of the land and of what stood on it (except regarding liability to rent). By planting cocoa trees a farmer was doing more than exercising use rights. The trees would occupy the land for decades, and their owner would have the right to replant the plot when the trees died or were felled. The Kumasi chiefs made a related point when, in 1913, they called for the right to tax sales of cocoa farms. As before, individuals had the right to sell their self-made property. But to sell a tree-crop farm is to sell the use of the land on which it stands, for the productive life of the trees and potentially beyond. Therefore, if the self-made property was a cocoa farm, the individual who sold it thereby usurped the right of the stool to dispose of land to new users. The government noted 'The Chiefs . . . argue that if individuals sell their Plantations for considerable sums of money, a proportion should go to the Owners of the Soil, as the latter are effectually debarred from the use of the land'.[99]

Cocoa trees, when mature enough to form a shade canopy, denied space for food farming while simultaneously depleting Ruf's 'forest rent'. The Kumasi Confederacy Council's geographically broader and more powerful successor, the Ashanti Confederacy Council of Chiefs, did prohibit the making or extension of cocoa farms from 1938 (applied in some areas only in 1939) to 1946. We will examine this episode in Chapter 17. But reforms which might internalize the external costs of cocoa planting, and release market pressures to encourage more economical use of resources, were neither proposed from 'below' nor imposed from 'above'.

C. Colonial Land Policy: The Administration as Defender of Cocoa Farmers' Property Rights

In 1911 Chief Commissioner Fuller made a partly misleading statement to the Belfield Commission on land alienation:

> According to native custom there is no such thing in Ashanti as individual ownership in land, and such as occurs at the present time has come into existence under British occupation . . . In connection with . . . cocoa plantations difficulties arose owing to insecurity of tenure. We had to make a rule that where a man had properly planted a plantation it should be regarded as his own, so as to give him the fruits of his labour. That was the beginning of individual ownership.[100]

Actually it was not the beginning of individual ownership of farms: that was well-institutionalized under the pre-colonial kingdom. In the nineteenth century there were even cases of politically-favoured individuals acquiring lands; which would be their own during their lifetimes, as with farms.[101] It was also not true that the government had intervened, as Fuller himself later made clear when questioned by the West African Lands Committee.[102] But what was true was the administration's claim to defend the property rights of farmers in the farms that they had made. This has been obscured in the literature by a concentration on the regime's non-promotion of individual title over land itself.

The colonial government accepted the principle that a stool had the right to levy rent ('cocoa tribute') on non-subjects farming cocoa on its land. But it sought to limit the amount that farmers had to pay. Fuller initiated the policy, which in this case was different from that followed south of the River Pra. When cocoa 'tribute' began to be levied, the rate was the traditional Akan *abusa*, one third of the proceeds.[103] In the Gold Coast Colony this became, in the words of an agricultural officer reviewing events from c.1940, 'the most widely used basis' for determining rent. But in Asante these 'natural developments . . . were overshadowed' by action taken by the local administration.[104] In 1911 Fuller told Belfield that he had 'made a rule' that the rate should be 'one tenth, instead of one third, which is enormous'.[105] Two years later Fuller adopted a proposal from the acting police magistrate, G. R. Griffith, that chiefs should be allowed to charge not more [?] than one penny per bearing tree per year, which was estimated to 'amount to 5%'.[106] The same motivation was apparent twenty years on. In 1933 the government insisted upon temporary reductions because of the Depression. The following year Chief Commissioner Jackson instructed the district commissioner in Sunyani to 'inform the Omanhene and Elders of the Dormaa Division that I must express surprise at their attitude in not entertaining the request for the cacao tribute to be reduced since every other chief in Ashanti has already agreed as a temporary measure to such a reduction.'[107]

British officials also insisted that it was only stranger-farmers who should pay rent at all: subjects of the land-owning stool should be exempt. The evidence on this is initially ambiguous. When Armitage testified in 1913 that chiefs had levied rent on their own subjects, and in some cases perhaps still did so, he left it unclear whether the government had a policy on this. In any case, the practical importance of a payment imposed only on trees that had come into bearing would still have been relatively small as of 1913. But after this the evidence is clear. There were isolated attempts by chiefs to obtain rent from cocoa farms made by their own subjects: but the colonial government would not permit them. In 1915 the Omanhene of Bekwai was accused of 'collecting a penny a tree on cocoa grown by your own people'. The provincial commissioner reminded him that rent was payable only by strangers.[108]

This raised the question of whether subjects of one sub-chief were liable to pay 'tribute' on farms made on the land of another sub-chief under the same omanhene. In December 1914 the provincial commissioner for southern Asante was asked about it while he was visiting Kokofu. He decided no, as all 'contributed to the stool expenses' but that 'a small rent, which in this case I fixed at £2. should be paid.'[109] In 1929 Adansehene Kobina Foli and his elders passed a bye-law prohibiting 'the system which has been practised by chiefs, Adikro and others as power to levy especial tributes on the subjects of Adansi having farms on their lands for the payment of debts of their Stools'.[110] It will be recalled that both the omanhene himself, and his nephew, had followed this practice themselves only a few years before. In a perfect example of what has been called 'the invention of tradition'[111] the declaration went on: 'In these Bye-laws Adansi Customs prove that it is not customarily legal for a chief of a sub-division to levy a tribute on a subject of any other chief in Adansi having farms for the payment of his stool debt.'[112]

The issue was raised again in 1946, in a different form. The chief and sub-chiefs of Odumase, near Sunyani, wrote to the district commissioner 'to inform you that we have all come to an agreeable conclusion that the Sub-Chiefs should collect the cocoa tribute in the form of sheep (Adwantwire) yearly from the citizens to signify the ownership of [the] portion of land entrusted to [the] individual Sub-Chief [concerned]'.[113] The 'customary sheep' (perhaps more precisely rendered *dwantwere*) was a concessionary, almost token, rent which an authoritative source later described as 'generally offered to' those strangers who had already assimilated to the extent of 'making donations during funeral ceremonies, paying local taxes and, perhaps, have owned a house or married from the village'.[114] Thus the implication of the Odumase chiefs' use of the term was that the rate they imposed would be less than the usual penny rate paid by ordinary strangers. Yet the justification they offered for introducing the charge was precisely that farmers from neighboring sub-divisions did not contribute to local revenues.[115] Hence, in this case, it was evident to both the farmers concerned and the government that there would be nothing token about the sums, whatever label they bore. By their 'agreeable conclusion' the Odumase chiefs were effectively proposing to increase their revenues at the expense of Odumase subjects. There were vigorous petitions of protest from the latter to the commissioner, which were presumably behind his subsequent remark that 'If this tribute is collected I am afraid the young men [commoners] will object to contributing towards stool debts and levies'. In other words, if denied their right as citizens to rent-free farming on chieftaincy lands, they would repudiate the fiscal obligations of citizens.[116] The government refused the chiefs permission to implement their resolution. In the words of the new district commissioner, 'I have to inform you, once and for all, that the answer is NO'.[117]

The colonial ban on stools imposing 'cocoa tribute' on their own subjects left chiefs with one avenue for extending their rent-gathering nets: to define or re-define residents of immigrant descent, however distant, as strangers. In 1920 the new chief commissioner, C. H. Harper, blocked that avenue when he ruled against a chief who claimed cocoa tribute 'from a community of Ashantis who had been settled on his land for about 200 years'. They 'originally paid tribute of 12 yams, two pots of palm oil, and eight loads of snails'. If cocoa tribute applied to them, they would owe £2,000 a year, though the chief 'was prepared to accept less'. Harper, acting in his judicial capacity, held that these long-established 'settlers could not be regarded as strangers'. In his annual report he commented:

> The cocoa industry is the result of individual toil, individual enterprise, individual energy. Cocoa is not found wild in the earth like minerals. Land has to be cleared, seeds or cuttings obtained and planted, the farm has to be cared for, the crop picked and prepared and then transported. All the work is done by the farmer himself and his family, or at his own sole expense.
>
> It is neither natural justice nor good faith that they should now be called upon to pay a heavy tax merely on the ground that by their own energy and enterprise they are making valuable use of land which has been in their occupation all these years.[118]

Thus the colonial administration saw itself as having a duty to defend the incomes of those who had invested in agriculture against the attempt of chiefs to extract rent (both in the sense of a charge for the use of land and in the sense of 'economic rent'). It specifically protected farmers' ownership of the cocoa trees against acquisitive chiefs, whether or not the farmers had lost legal disputes over related but distinct matters such as liability to rent.

In 1916–17 the chief commissioner dealt with the case of a 7,000-tree cocoa farm which had been established by a married couple from Nsuta on land in Adanse district. The land-owning chieftaincy was Asecherewa, which 'served' Ankase. After the husband died his widow, Abena Denta, inherited the farm. But the Asecherewahene evidently coveted the farm itself. He refused to accept rent from her, seized the farm and burnt the buildings that they had apparently built on it. Fuller intervened. 'I cannot allow plantations to be forfeited like that', wrote he to the Ankasehene, and ordered the latter's sub-chief to accept the standard rent of a penny per tree from Abena Denta. On the other hand, when Abena Denta, whom Fuller described as 'an obstinate party', herself refused these terms he permitted her to be evicted from the farm.[119]

The principle behind Fuller's original intervention was upheld by the state after his retirement, both by the British themselves and by the Asantehene and his court following the 'restoration of the Ashanti Confederacy' in 1935. Indeed, it faced a challenge immediately following the restoration. A group of farmers in Dormaa, in the words of the Asantehene Agyeman Prempeh II, 'transferred [or restored] their allegiance' from the Dormaahene 'to the Oyoko Stool of Kumasi'. The farmers themselves complained that the Dormaahene 'unlawfully and contrary to the native customary laws has taken possesssion of our Cocoa farms cultivated on his lands'. The Asantehene and the British administration insisted that, while these farmers were now liable to pay cocoa tribute to the Dormaahene, they could not be dispossessed.[120] Again, in November 1945, for example, judgment was given by the Asantehene's court in a test case brought by one Kweaku Nesemfoo. He was one of 53 subjects of the Ofoase stool (along with the above-mentioned Bah and Gyekye) who had been farming cocoa on the Wawase land, which was claimed by both Ofoase and Esumeja.[121] The two stools had disputed the ownership of the land from before 1916, possibly as far back as c.1900.[122] This issue was appealed all the way from the Chief Commissioner's Court via the West African Court of Appeal to the Privy Council in London. The latter found for Esumeja, in 1939. The Esumejahene, victorious after so many years and having incurred several thousands of pounds of debt, proceeded to send in his bailiff. He evicted the Ofoase farmers and, over the next several years, harvested the pods from the trees they had planted. Nsemfoo's protest, however, was successful, the venue this time being the Asantehene's 'A' Court. In words put to the defence by one of the presiding judges (the Kyidomhene of Kumasi), the Privy Council's judgement 'vested only the ownership of the land in you', not that of the farms and buildings that had been made upon it. Providing they fulfilled their obligations to the landowning stool their ownership of the farms was legally secure.[123] The result was that Esumeja had to pay compensation to Nsemfoo and his neighbours.[124]

So the state protected and enforced the claims of individual farmers to continued possession of their farms. The colonial administration also recognised another aspect of ownership, the right to sell, and insisted that the sellers should enjoy the whole of the receipts. In 1913 the members of the Kumasi Council of Chiefs seem to have been unanimously in favour of a proposal from one of their number that where a stool had permitted a non-subject to make a cocoa farm on its land, and the farmer later sold the farm to another stranger, part of the proceeds should be paid to the chief. In the discussion proportions ranging from an eighth to a quarter were 'proposed as purchase tax'. Then Chief Commissioner Fuller intervened to convert the proposed tax into a mere fine on cases where 'plantations change hands *without the consent of the Chief*' [emphasis in the original], and at the rate of only 'one tenth of the purchase price'. His amendment was politely adopted by the Council.[125]

The colonial state's record in providing institutions for reducing the costs of enforcing contracts and settling disputes over land was mixed. The delineation of chieftaincy boundaries was an essential step in this direction. But its impact was severely limited by resource constraints, which meant that the early lines were drawn by the commissioners themselves. These judgments necessarily lacked legal expertise and, often, topographical precision. As a result, in the view of Chief Commissioner Maxwell in 1925, they were open to the challenges to which increasingly they were being subjected in court. He declared that 'The day of executive decisions with regard to land is finished and in the writer's opinion should never have been started'.[126] That was easy to say after the event. As recently as 1919 the Acting Director of Surveys, in Accra, had turned down an urgent request from the administration in Kumasi for a surveyor: 'owing to a shortage of staff, it is at the moment impossible to place a Surveyor at your disposal.' He elaborated in a later letter: 'I am 8 European Surveyors short of my full establishment and, until some of these arrive, it will not be possible for me to do much work in Ashanti. Also I am extremely short of experienced Native Surveyors.'[127] Even after 1925 progress, though real, was insufficient to prevent the continuation and reproduction of land disputes. In 1940 a colonial official commented that 'most stools in Ashanti have land cases pending or in progress'.[128] One reason for this was that the colonial regime did not borrow from British law the notion of a 'statute of limitations', that is, a limit on the time after the relevant events that a suit, such as a claim to land now occupied by someone else, could be brought.[129]

The colonial state offered cheaper justice; but perhaps only during its early years, when the commissioners acted as judges, with their own courts from which lawyers were excluded.[130] We noted in Chapter 3 that it was only in 1933 that lawyers were permitted to practise in courts in Asante. Fuller, writing in retirement at the beginning of the 1920s, commented with particular reference to land cases: 'Litigants are only too ready to take their complaints to the Commissioners, who, they well realise, will mete out strict justice at but slight cost to the parties.'[131] Even then legal costs were evidently much higher when cases went to courts where the parties were allowed to hire lawyers to represent them, as happened on appeal beyond the Chief Commissioner's court. Partly because of this, litigation between stools over boundaries became a notorious source of heavy chieftaincy debt.[132]

Despite the colonial government's evident commitment to defend farmers' property rights it never introduced a scheme, whether voluntary or compulsory, for the registration of title to farms. This was despite repeatedly considering it; we will examine the policy debate in Chapter 17. Here it should be noted that such a step would not necessarily have involved extending farmers' ownership to the land itself—a measure with which it is often confused. Meanwhile individual Asante farmers commonly took the initiative in seeking written documentation of their title. The provincial surveyor for Ashanti observed in 1930 that 'For some considerable time past, individual farmers have been having plans of their farms prepared' and then endorsed by the local chief 'to the effect that the farm, purported to be shown, is the property of the individual usually named on the face of the plan.' The intention was that the document could then be 'attached to deeds of mortgage or some such instrument' as security for loans. He cited letters complaining about the practice from the district commissioners in Obuasi, Bekwai and Juaso. The district commissioner for Kumasi, J. R. Dickinson, confirmed that 'It is certainly a very common practice now'. He added that 'I have occasionally come across cases when farmers have said they desired the plans not for borrowing purposes but so that they should form documents of title.' The farmers were vulnerable to quacks, according to the Provincial Surveyor: 'A considerable number of these plans, in fact, I would say, the majority, are at present prepared by unauthorised Surveyors, and clerks of any description.' Estimates of the fees charged ranged, he said, 'from £5 to £20'; Dickenson said 'I have usually been told by the people presenting the plans that they paid from £10 to £15 for same'.[133] The most basic technical deficiency of the diagrams was that they were (as C. K. Meek put it later with reference to the same practice in the Gold Coast Colony) 'merely ground plans' which failed to show the location of the farm.[134] Despite the evident thirst for documentation, outside the urban setting of Kumasi it remained the case to the end of the colonial period, in Asante as well as further south, that (in the words of Meek's authoritative survey of colonial land law at the end of the Second World War) 'No indefeasible title based on a Government survey can, in fact, be obtained'.[135]

In summary, to a large extent colonial officials defended farmers' interests against the chiefs in the latter's role as potential or actual landlords. They also tried, though not particularly successfully, to reduce transactions costs in land disputes. But they made no effort to secure farmers' titles by registration.

D. Conclusion

The long-established distinction in Asante land tenure, between ownership of the soil and ownership of crops planted in it, was maintained throughout the period. Within that institutional framework major changes occurred in the volume and character of land transactions. The adoption of cocoa had made cultivation rights economically valuable. Land-owning chiefs sought to charge farmers, for the first time, economically-significant sums for the enjoyment of such rights. Meanwhile a market in cocoa farms developed. Sales of land itself, in contrast, were rare except on the southern periphery of Asante, and there they were eventually suppressed.

The traditional view of colonial administrations in British West Africa as being socially conservative, anxious both to keep out European settlers and planters and to moderate or curtail the development of capitalist relations in African agriculture, is not all wrong but does require much modification in the light of the evidence for colonial Asante. At first the administration was willing to issue large agricultural concessions to British investors: policy hardened against them only when the competitive weakness of these plantations became apparent. A more timely intervention against the alienation of land was the administration's pressure on southern Asante chiefs to stop their land sales to farmers from the Eastern Province of the Gold Coast Colony. Even in this case, though, as will see in Chapter 17, the scale of the phenomenon was anyway likely to have been very limited beyond the southern marches of the former Asante kingdom. What should be observed, in relation to the main argument of this book, is that the colonial state helped sustain the Asante monopoly of direct access to the forest rent against African—but not European—competition.

The colonial administration also tried—in this case, consistently and apparently effectively—to defend farmers' property rights over the trees they had planted. It insisted that rent was payable only by 'stranger' farmers rather than by a chief's own subjects. It ensured that farmers kept their farms even when their chief had been defeated in litigation over the ownership of the land. It refused to allow chiefs power to control the market in farms. Finally, it attempted to define chieftaincy boundaries, which at least in principle would reduce the risk and transactions costs of investing in planting cocoa trees on previously disputed land. The one step that the colonial state did not take in establishing and securing private property rights in farms was to register title. We will consider why not in Chapter 17.

15

CAPITAL AND CREDIT:

LOCKING FARMS TO CREDIT

The widespread planting of cocoa trees created a stock of fixed capital with no parallel in the previous history of Asante. Issues of ownership arose, especially in the contexts of divorce settlements and inheritance. As far as the supply of working capital and consumption credit was concerned there were three fundamental, and related, qualitative changes during the colonial period.

The first was a transition from lending on people to lending on the crops and farms of the new agricultural export sector. In Part IV we examined one side of this, the decline of human pawning. Though, as we saw, that process was drawn out to mid-century, the spread of lending on cocoa assets began soon after the prohibition of pawning in 1908. In the rural economy perhaps the most conspicuous trend of the 1910s–30s was the growth of agricultural indebtedness, in the sense of borrowing on the security of cocoa farms or future cocoa crops. There were two main types of such loans, which were usually short-term and long-term respectively. An 'advance' was payment in advance for—and thus credit on the security of—a forthcoming crop. A 'mortgage' was where a loan was secured on a cocoa farm. Given the distinction in Asante land tenure between the land itself and what grew on it, this meant specifically the cocoa trees rather than the land beneath. Mortgages can be subdivided to distinguish between a 'charge', where the debtor was to deliver to the lender part or all of the crop for a fixed period of years or until repayment was complete, and a 'pledge', where the farm itself was handed over to the creditor for a fixed number of years, or until the principal was repaid (interest and/or principal might or might not be met from the farm proceeds).[1] As we will see in Chapter 18, this distinction has important implications for markets and social welfare.

The second major change was related in the sense that it began, to a large extent, as a response to the growth of cocoa output: for the first time Western suppliers of finance became quantitatively significant in Asante. Shortly after Asante began producing cocoa European produce-buying companies began to offer credit on forthcoming crops. They were later backed, in some limited cases, by British banks seeking a slice of the cocoa economy.

The final major change was the creation of new lending institutions by the state. In the colonial period this was motivated to a large extent by a desire to combat the widespread indebtedness of cocoa farmers to private lenders. For this reason the colonial agriculture department established cooperatives, from the late 1920s. The same reason was given in the 1950s when parastatal agencies, controlled to a large extent by Kwame Nkrumah's now-ruling party, offered funds to relieve farmers' debts. If this third change was causally related to the first, in a sense it complemented the second. With the establishment of state lenders the 'formal' financial sector was extended and consolidated. Indeed, the Cocoa Marketing Board ultimately took over (though not necessarily on as large a scale) the forward-purchasing role previously played by the European cocoa-buyers. The institutional impact of Western lenders outlived their funds, for the partial withdrawal of Western lenders in the era of decolonization was accompanied by their replacement or takeover by Western-style ('formal' or 'organized') lending institutions under African management and ownership.

So far in this chapter we have outlined the major changes of the period and defined the main forms of credit contract. Section A examines the Asante evidence on the contentious issues of changes in the ownership of capital: the possible decline of matrilineal and male monopolies of the non-market means of acquiring ownership of existing cocoa trees. Section B considers the various sources of loans, highlighting the contribution of African capital. Elaborating from this, Section C scrutinises the relative wealth and poverty of indigenous lenders and borrowers within Asante society. Section D explores the changing volume of lending and borrowing over time, distinguishing cycle and trend. Section E draws together the evidence regarding colonial policy on property rights in capital within the rural economy.

A. Fixed Capital: The Ownership of Cocoa Trees

We have already noted that the first cocoa trees in Asante had hardly begun to bear before the trees themselves became a commodity. In the longer term, however, buying and selling of farms was to be much less common than the use of farms as collateral on loans. Farm mortgaging will be described in detail in a later section. Here we will focus on the claims of wives and children (especially sons) to ownership of cocoa farms originally made in the name of their husbands or fathers respectively. On this there are two classic propositions in the specialist literature.

The adoption of cocoa farming has been seen as a revolutionary force in Asante, undermining matrilineal and patriarchal ownership of property. Hill wrote that 'In matrilineal cocoa-growing societies the most extraordinary change, so far as sedentary (non-migrant) cocoa farmers are concerned, is in the extent to which women evolve into independent (cocoa) farmers on their own account'.[2] Busia, writing in mid-century, noted what he saw as a trend for cocoa farms to be inherited by a man's sons rather than his kin, such as his nephews, and quoted a farmer at Daho near Mampon as saying '*Cocoa sɛɛ abusua, paepae mogya mu*', 'Cocoa destroys kinship [the matrilineage], and divides blood'.[3] The two transitions, whether real or just perceived, overlap in that a shift away from matrilineal inheritance could favour both sons and wives of deceased men.

The evidence on the respective rates of establishment of cocoa farms in the names of men and women will be detailed in the next chapter, because it relates closely to the domestic division of labour. We will see there that the incidence of female ownership of cocoa trees tended to rise, relatively as well as absolutely, as cocoa cultivation in general expanded. On the other hand, the level remained low in relation to male ownership. Thus Hill's observation is supported, but the change described was perhaps not 'extraordinary'. Here, we consider what happened to cocoa-farm properties once they had been established: the disposal of ownership, at the break-up of a marriage or on the death of a male farmer.

In 1942 the Ashanti Confederacy Council passed a proposal from the Asantehene that 'when a person makes a gift of his own personal or self-acquired property to his children or to any other person in the presence of accredited witnesses, whether the relatives of the donor approve of it or not, it becomes valid'.[4] Three years later Fortes's team carried out a sample survey of the ownership of cocoa farms in several parts of Asante. This is the best available evidence about the extent of change on the ground during the colonial period; albeit too soon to see much impact from the Confederacy Council's decision. Fortes's estimate was that, judging by outcomes, 'matrilateral rights' were as powerful as 'patrilateral claims' in the transmission of cocoa farms.[5] As far as the expectations of the young were concerned, 'In the mid-forties it was still taken for granted that a man's sons would have far less chance than his brothers and nephews of becoming the owners of cocoa farms and other productive resources in his possession, even if the sons had helped their father to exploit and maintain these resources'.[6] The surveys also revealed variations between districts. Among the sampled areas, matrilineal inheritance was weakest in the area of Asokore and Efiduase in Sekyere (Mampon) district. There, of a sample of 262 cocoa farms 75 [28.6 per cent] had been transmitted 'from a previous generation of owners'. Among these 42 (56 per cent) had passed matrilineally, while 33 (44 per cent) had been gifts from fathers. The matrilineal principle was strongest in Asante-Akim, where 60 [26.3 per cent] out of 228 farms 'had passed from a previous generation', 45 (75 per cent) of them by matrilineal inheritance and 15 (25 per cent) by paternal gift.[7] Busia remarked 'I chose to spend most of my time in Mampong' during his fieldwork,[8] which was in 1941–42.[9] Though Fortes was 'tutor and friend' to Busia,[10] there is no indication in Busia's book, published in 1951, that he had been acquainted with these particular results of Fortes's 1945 research, which were themselves not published until after Busia's book had appeared. Thus Busia's impression of a decisive shift from 'lineage to individual claims of ownership'[11] appears to have been over-generalized. For the 'destruction' of Asante matrilineal inheritance by cocoa we should read 'potential weakening'. How far that potential was realised was a matter of intense conflict, at interpersonal, judicial and legislative levels.

Considering the evidence on change, both classic propositions are partly justified, and partly exaggerated. In Chapter 18 we will consider the nature and economic implications of the prolonged and agonised controversies within Asante society, during the colonial period, over the property claims of both wives and sons.

B. Sources of Credit: African and European, Formal and Informal

This section examines the respective role of different categories of credit-suppliers. The most striking theme is the importance of African (private) capital as a major (though not the main) source of advances on crops, and as the main source of mortgages on farms, even after the state intervened to reduce or take over such debt in the 1950s.

The suppliers of credit could be sub-divided in various ways. It is tempting to do it by sector, 'formal' and 'informal', or by contrasting European and African suppliers. These divisions are cumbersome, however, because the reality was complex. Should European produce-buying companies who gave advances to Africans be regarded as 'formal'-sector lenders? They were not specialist financial institutions, but they were incorporated under 'formal' company law and they themselves received credit from British banks. Again, the distinction between European and African suppliers of credit is compromised by precisely such advances, which were mostly—though far from entirely—originated by European cocoa-buying companies but which reached the farmers through African intermediaries. A distinction according to the term of the loan would also require qualification, in that short-term loans could become long-term if they were not repaid. But this distinction remains the simplest and, as we will see, it turns out to be very significant in that the economics of the main form of short-term credit, crop advances, was importantly different from those of the main form of long-term loan, farm mortgages. The definition of 'short-term' loans used here, which fits cocoa advances, is those originally due to be repaid by the end of the coming or current cocoa-marketing season.

For centuries European merchants had given advances to African intermediaries at the coast. But, except perhaps to a small extent during the rubber trade,[12] there seems to be no evidence that such credit reached producers in Asante until advances began to be given on cocoa. So far, the earliest evidence of such advances relates to the years after European merchants had begun to establish branches around Asante. This move by European traders into Asante followed rather than led the planting of cocoa trees in the former kingdom. For most firms, indeed, it came only after Asantes had begun to offer for sale the produce of those trees.

There is a documented case as early as 1908 of the Dwabenhene, no less, asking for and receiving £100 worth of goods from the African Association (a British trading company) as an advance on 'produce such as Cocoa or rubber'.[13] That he asked for an advance may suggest that the practice of European firms giving such credit in Asante was already established. The application was to the company's branch in Kumasi;[14] indicating that there was as yet no branch in Dwaben. I have examined the evidence available for south Asante, that is Amansie and Adanse districts, in some detail. The earliest case to come to light there so far is a '£200 advance' given, apparently for cocoa produced in the Kokofu area, by an agent of the Basel Mission Trading Company in Bekwai. The beans were due to be delivered in October 1913.[15] The case appears in the colonial records only because a dispute arose (the Kokofuhene tried to stop cocoa being taken to Bekwai). It is likely that advances had already been under way for a few years; but only a few. For as late as 1907 only one European buyer, the Ashanti and Obuasi Trading Company, was established in Adanse district while none were represented in Amansie. It will be argued below, from the fuller evidence about advances that is available for later years, that the European firms gave advances only when competition between themselves for the farmers' produce obliged them to do so. From this perspective it would be very surprising if advances were given before the beginning of effective competition between European buying firms. It appears that as soon as more than one such merchant was buying in a particular area, however, advances proliferated. Thus in 1914 Miller Brothers, who by then had set up in Adanse in competition with AOTC, had 'several debt cases' before the provincial commissioner's court at Obuasi.[16] If they were like the majority of the firms' debt suits in subsequent years, they would have included some about advances on cocoa.

Import-export merchants did not remain the only exporters of cocoa from Asante, and cocoa exporters were not quite the only possible source of advances. Certain of the chocolate manufacturers entered the Gold Coast to buy cocoa beans for themselves rather than via the European merchants. Cadbury, the largest of these entrants, originally adopted a policy of refusing to give advances, which is not surprising. As we will see in Chapter 18, even the merchants were individually inclined not to offer advances; and they had the compensation, not available to the manufacturers, that some of any credit they dispensed would be spent in their own stores. By the time Cadbury started buying cocoa in Asante, it had been obliged to follow the competition and offer advances, on a limited but gradually increasing scale.[17]

The banks did not generally give advances to cocoa brokers or farmers, but the Bank of British West Africa's records show their branches in Asante dispensing large amounts of credit as 'advances against produce in store'. The customers were European merchant firms: presumably the advances were to cover the costs of their stocks before they could make money on them overseas. The Kumasi branch of the BBWA gave out £106,187 of such advances in 1920–21, rising to £411,927 in 1926–27 (much of the rise being a function of the producer price). In the latter year, for example, their main client was Frames Agency which took £276,000, followed by the Anglo Guinea Company with £54,000 and, among others, G. B. Ollivant with £13,640.[18]

When European cocoa-buyers gave advances, it was almost always not to farmers themselves but to brokers. Much of this credit eventually reached the producers, either from the original broker or via further intermediaries: sub-brokers and even sub-sub-brokers. Correspondingly the cocoa beans, when ready, were moved through the same chain in the opposite direction. Many brokers appear to have been specialists (among whom were non-Asantes, from as far afield as the Levant as well as Nigeria).[19] But many others, probably including most of the smaller brokers, were also farmers: relatively large farmowners, for whom it was worthwhile to take their own beans to market and who built a broking business around this, bulking and marketing the beans of neighbours. In the village of Huntado in Amansie, for example, 'The rich farmers they were the brokers'. They advanced money to poor farmers in the off season and were repaid in cocoa at harvest-time. One such sub-broker was Osei Kwami, the first and, at the time of his death in 1934, still the largest cocoa-farmer in the village.[20] He left 3 farms totalling 5,800 trees.[21] He diversified into brokerage, giving advances to 'selected' farmers and selling his accumulated beans to a broker at the nearest large marketing centre, Anwiankwanta, from which it went 8 kilometres to the European firms in Bekwai.[22] Some chiefs (a category which itself overlapped with that of farmers) ran brokerages, giving advances to their clients. Two sub-chiefs of Esumeja, Kweku Wereku and Kwasi Gyimah, between them sued three people before the local Native Tribunal in March–April 1931 for sums given as advances for cocoa that they had failed to supply.[23] This gives plausibility to a claim made by the European firms during the 1937–38 hold-up that 'Many [chiefs] are actual brokers, and many indulge in large-scale loans on the farmers' crops'.[24]

There has been an impression that the ultimate source of advances was always European. This view was implied at the time by W. R. Danby, head of produce-buying in Kumasi for the biggest cocoa-buying company, the United Africa Company (UAC). He wrote in 1933 that 'if advances were stopped by the Firms in Ashanti then this practice would automatically die out'[25] (unless he meant that independent African and Levantine buyers would no longer need to offer credit themselves if their European competitors desisted from doing so). Yet five years later the Nowell Commission on the marketing of cocoa concluded that 'A large part of the advances before the season is made by [African and Levantine] buyers from their own capital'. Such buyers, the Commission specified, included not only individuals whose main occupation was cocoa-buying but also money-lenders and farmers.[26] It seems most unlikely that this contribution of African capital to the pool of advances had originated only after 1933 or only outside Asante.

The indigenous supply of advances expanded during the 1937–38 cocoa hold-up, responding to a situation in which most farmers had received no income during the very season which they normally relied upon to pay their bills. Beckett, the government agricultural statistician, made the following comment about what is now southern Ghana as a whole, implicitly including Asante: 'During the present Hold Up, the system of advances had [*sic*] enlarged, big farmers and also many others (clerks etc) not usually associated with cocoa marketing have advanced money at about 5/- per load to farmers in need of cash: they have not yet been able to remove the cocoa from the farmers' hands.'[27]

The role of African capital increased during the war, especially in relative terms. In c.1945 an experienced observer, who had been a district commissioner in 'ten cocoa Districts' and professed particularly detailed knowledge of Asante, wrote that advances 'are given on request or pressed upon farmers formerly from firms['] money but since the wartime control more usually from profits accrued to brokers from previous seasons.'[28] One B. K. Nsiah recalled working as a cocoa weighting clerk in the 1944–45 buying season with what was clearly a small African enterprise, the Ashanti Farmers Agency in Kumasi. This firm regularly gave 'cash advances' to its brokers.[29]

After the government introduced a state monopoly of cocoa exporting, in 1939, European firms continued to buy produce: as Licensed Buying Agents on behalf of the state. They continued in this role to just beyond the end of the colonial era. By then, though, they were being increasingly challenged in the produce market by the state-backed cocoa cooperative societies and by the state-owned (and CPP-run) Cocoa Purchasing Company (hereafter, CPC). The cooperatives' lending operations, however, even more than their purchasing activities, had developed only slowly. As the veteran commissioner later commented, 'In the early stages of the [co-operative] movement, loans were small in total and mostly for expenses of cultivation'.[30] They were also relatively few. In 1934–35 the cooperatives supplied less than 3,400 loans for the whole of southern Ghana,[31] roughly one loan per hundred cocoa-farmers. This increased gradually, but for most farmers it was really only in the mid-1950s that state-sponsored organizations became an alternative source of credit to the European merchants. In 1955–56 some 2,000 members of the Ahafo Co-operative Union alone received, between them, £48,750 in advances. Compared to the 1930s and 1940s, this was proliferation. But the cooperatives' advances continued to be small in relation to the value of the cocoa purchased: about £1 million in this case.[32] Meanwhile, however, the marketing board had been distributing advances much more lavishly via the CPC. More will be said about the latter shortly.

Whereas foreign capital was the ultimate source of most of the short-term credit secured on cocoa, Asante capital was overwhelmingly the major source of farm-mortgage finance.[33] In terms of rules, the pledging of tree-crop farms was very much the equivalent or continuation of the pawning of people. Economically, it would have been pointless to lend on farms until a kind of farm existed that yielded cash over years to come. With the establishment of cocoa farms in the 1900s and the colonial prohibition of debt bondage in 1908, it is not surprising that instances of farm pledging occurred even by 1914. That, presumably, is what the chief commissioner meant when he gave evidence to the West African Lands Committee in 1912. Asked 'Has the pledging of land for money crept in at all?' Fuller replied 'Yes, there have been a few exceptional cases'.[34] Consistently with this, elders of Amoafo, in Amansie, testified in 1980 that farm-pledging had begun soon after cocoa started bearing and people therefore realised that it was a good source of income.[35] In Asante-Akyem in 1917 the district commissioner noted that 'Kwasi-Koko appears to have pledged his cocoa farms for £60, and the farm has been seized by one man called Akajo of Fomansu who lent him the money.'[36]

In this context it is ironic but not necessarily coincidental that the individual who (as we have noted) first planted cocoa in Amansie district, Kwame Dei of Asiwa, eventually found himself something of a pioneer also of debt secured on cocoa farms.[37] In 1903 he was made Akwamuhene of Dadiase. He eventually became heavily indebted and was destooled. In 1920, some years after his death, his nephew and heir Yaw Jumbo brought a case before the commissioner's court at Obuasi claiming ownership of those farms made by Dei before his elevation (Jumbo accepted that those his uncle had made during his reign belonged to the stool). The defendant was the current Akwamuhene, who had possession of all Dei's farms. It was shown in court that several of Dei's creditors had outstanding claims apparently secured on the farms in dispute. A settlement was reached under which Jumbo's ownership was recognized subject to his clearing the debts. In 1922 he returned to court, this time in Bekwai, to sue several parties for trespass on the farms. He was unable to prove that he had paid the debts and lost the case. What appears to have happened is that because he had not cleared the encumbrances the Akwamu stool (now under yet another chief) had continued to work the cocoa trees and harvest their produce. Certain of the outstanding creditors had done the same. It is not explicit in the court record that the trees had been formally pledged to them, but in any case they acted as if they had been. This time the judgment went against Jumbo, leaving the creditors free to harvest. They comprised men from Asiwa and neighbouring villages and towns. Their occupations were mostly unspecified. The exception was a cocoa farmer, Kobina Edu, lender of £30. Meanwhile Kweku Apiadu, described as a storekeeper, had stood surety for one of Dei's other borrowings. He eventually paid £50 of the debt of £70, but secured reimbursement from Gyima, the new holder of Dei's sub-chieftaincy stool, who described the reimbursement as 'on behalf of this farm'. Both Apiadu and Edu were nephews of Dei.

As in this case, so with the proliferation of farm-pledgings that were to follow, the creditors were almost always indigenous. Their social and economic profile will be examined in some detail in the next section. Asante private lenders remained the principal suppliers of loans on mortgages until the decade of decolonization, when the politics of lending and debt changed.

In 1945 the government set up a committee to consider a proposal that part of the marketing board's surplus be used to relieve agricultural indebtedness. In the event the Puckridge Committee was primarily concerned with short-term debt, proposing loans for up to nine months.[38] Perhaps more fundamentally, it wanted all cocoa farms to be surveyed.[39] It seems to have been the general sense of political urgency, rather than expert reflection, which gave new impetus to the case for facilitating a drastic expansion of formal-sector loans. In 1948 the Watson Commission, investigating the causes of the riots that had taken place in Accra and other towns (including Kumasi) earlier that year, recommended that the Cocoa Marketing Board create a Cocoa Farmers Bank. This would take over farmers' existing mortgage loans, compulsorily, at a price fixed by the Board, while giving loans at 3 per cent to farmers.[40] The Colonial Office in London and the administration in Accra seem to have been anxious to be seen to act on as many of the recommendations as possible.[41] The commissioners had not suggested that there was any direct causal link from agricultural indebtedness to the violence and political discontent (an element in which was opposition to the government policy of cutting out cocoa trees to contain swollen shoot disease). But the proposal of mortgage relief was accepted and persevered with despite subsequent expert advice to the contrary.[42] Watson's recommendation was finally implemented in late 1952, by when executive power was in the hands of Nkrumah's joint African-British administration. Under its auspices the marketing board created a government buying agency, the CPC, with a Loans Agency whose official brief was the Watsonian one of relieving farmers of debt owed to moneylenders. In just under a year, to 21 September 1954, it was given £1.9 million by the marketing board to lend to farmers. A further £900,000 followed within the next 6 months.[43] The marketing board also provided money to the cooperatives to enable them to offer their members relatively long-term loans on the security of their farms. Interest was to be only 10 per cent a year. These loans were limited to £1,500 per borrower, and were intended to be for medium rather than really long periods (they were available on 2, 3 and 5-year terms). According to Bray, 'Loans granted through the Teppa Union of Co-operative Societies grew from £48,000 in 1953–54 to £77,000 in 1955–56.'[44]

The Loans Agency also had a party-political mission. Krobo Edusei, the government Chief Whip and the leading CPP figure in Asante, described the company as 'the atomic bomb of the Convention People's Party'.[45] Most of the kilotonnage was supplied by the Loans Agency. After an outcry from the opposition and pressure from London the government in Accra ordered an independent enquiry into allegations against the CPC, notably that the Loans Agency had distributed funds on political rather than commercial criteria, favouring those belonging to the United Ghana Farmers' Council, which was effectively a CPP subsidiary. The Jibowu Commission upheld the complaints. It found that the CPC had not only given loans exclusively to CPP supporters but in many cases had failed to seek their repayment.[46] For their part the opposition in Asante, the National Liberation Movement, was said to have persuaded Cadbury to provide farmers with loans in return for promises of support for the NLM.[47] As for the cooperatives, while their procedure for granting loans—'on the basis of recommendations and guarantees given by the local committees'[48]—was in principle well-designed to reflect locally-available information on the creditworthiness of the recipients, it had the potential to be incorporated in politically-driven patronage networks. Shortly after independence in 1957 the government liquidated the CPC but transferred responsibilities to the United Ghana Farmers Council itself.[49]

Despite the publicity and politics surrounding the 'formal sector' interventions in the rural credit market in the run-up to independence, informal lenders remained quietly predominant. The 1956–57 budget survey of cocoa-farming families reported the distribution of creditors for the 123 families in their sample who had 'pledged' at least one farm (the authors used the term 'pledging' apparently as co-extensive with mortgaging in general). In 9 cases the creditor was a cooperative society; in 19 it was the CPC; in 16 it was 'Firms & Brokers'. This left 79 cases (64 per cent) in which the creditor was 'Other'. By default, this latter category must have comprised the same kinds of indigenous lenders who had been virtually the sole lenders beforehand. Members of this category had supplied all ten of the loans which were six or more years old (therefore taken out before c.1950) and 61 per cent of the 'younger' loans.[50] Thus, despite the entry of various 'formal sector' lenders, 'informal' ones continued to be the most common sources of long-term credit on the security of farms. This is testimony to the size of indigenous savings and to the capacity of indigenous credit institutions to attract them—a capacity to be analyzed in Chapter 18.

As the earlier reference to 'recognised money lenders' illustrates, the credit economy—even the indigenous credit economy—was not quite confined to cocoa-based transactions. Though cocoa cases predominate among the suits for repayment of debts in court records, there are occasional cases from other trades. For example, one before the DC's court in Bekwai in 1922 concerned £7 of 'dried & smoked snail' sold on a fortnights' credit.[51] It is also possible that rotating credit societies existed, providing means by which people who owned little or no cocoa—most obviously, the majority of women—could ease their liquidity constraints. We will return to this in Chapter 18.

C. Credit between Asantes: The Rich were the Lenders, The Poor were the Borrowers?

Hill has argued strongly over the years, with particular reference to Ghanaian cocoa-farming, that in relatively poor rural economies lenders and borrowers come from the same socio-economic groups, and that the roles of debtor and creditor are temporary and reversible.[52] The Ghanaian national archives provide quantitative data from colonial government investigations in various districts in 1933–34. Together with the 1956–57 survey, this source enables us to consider Hill's thesis in some detail.

In early July 1933 the Wenchi district commissioner sent to Kumasi what were clearly intended as comprehensive lists of the names of those

Table 15.1. Borrowers and lenders on cocoa in Wenchi district, 1933[1]

Division	Techiman	Nkoranza	Wenchi
(A) Advances			
Total 'advance' takers	92	–	19
Advance-takers with male day-names	86	–	19
A-takers with female day-names	2	–	0
A-takers with no day-name given	4	–	0
Total transactions	128	–	–
Total advance-givers	59	–	–
Advance-givers with male day-names	54	–	–
A-givers with female day-names	4	–	–
A-givers with no day-name given	1	–	–
(B) 'Mortgages' (Pledges)			
Total 'mortgage' borrowers	117	32	51
Mortgage borrowers with male day-names	107	32	49
M-borrowers with female day-names	5	0	1
M-borrowers with no day-name given	4	0	1
Total transactions	131	34	–
Total mortgage lenders	93 (= 92 'firms')*	33	–
Mortgage-lenders with male day-names	75	30	–
M-lenders with female day-names	12 (= 11 'firms')*	1	–
M-lenders with no day-name given	6	2	–

* There was one pair of joint-lenders; the other 'firms' were individuals.

who borrowed and lent on cocoa farms (pledges or, as the source has it, 'mortgages') from the three divisions (paramount chieftaincies) in the district, Techiman, Nkoranza,[53] and Wenchi. The information was compiled by chiefs' clerks (to judge by the signatures). He also provided information on cocoa crops (advances), but only for Techiman and Wenchi, and in the latter case only on borrowers rather than lenders. The above table summarise the data on the ratios of borrowers to lenders and on the gender composition of each group.

A preliminary observation is that the average size of an individual advance was small compared to an average cocoa-farm 'mortgage'. Presumably the minimum efficient size of a farm mortgage was much larger than that of an advance,[54] while a pledge was secured on the capital value of the farm rather than merely on the current crop. According to data collected as part of the 1933 survey, in Techiman 'division' the average amount of the 128 individual cocoa advances was £0.54; of the 131 individual 'mortgage' loans on cocoa farms, £7.46. Some farmers received more than one advance or pledge loan. The average of the total advances received by those who obtained them was £0.75; the corresponding figure for those with 'mortgages' was £8.35.[55]

The suppliers of short- and long-term credit to cocoa farmers constituted overlapping but largely different categories, to judge from the Techiman data. Relatively few of those named as mortgage-givers to cocoa-farmers in this division, the only one for which such data exist, appear also on the list of brokers distributing cocoa advances. Even assuming that the same name implies the same person, only 14 people were among *both* the 93 mortgage-lenders and 59 forward-buyers. This contrasts with a statement the same year, by the acting commissioner of Kumasi district, that 'mortgagors' of cocoa farms 'are usually Cacao brokers as well.'[56] Brokers were among those able and willing to lend long as well as to supply (or, most commonly, pass on) advances; but they were a minority within what turns out to have been a larger, more diffuse group of mortgage suppliers. The average number of advances per advance-giver was 2.2; the average number of mortgages per mortgage-lender was 1.4. Those who received advances were overwhelmingly male: a total of 105 were identified as such in Techiman and Wenchi districts, compared to just two identified as women. Women were slightly more heavily represented among suppliers of advances, at four rather than two. This fits what we know of the gender distribution of cocoa-farm ownership in this period: most owners were men, and they had most of the access to advances on crops.[57]

Mortgage-lending (or pledging) was strikingly widespread: there were a lot of suppliers of this kind of loan, mostly lending relatively modest sums to very few people. If we combine the totals for Techiman and Nkoranza divisions (the two for which we have the relevant data), for five loans there were an average of four different lenders; and for nine borrowers, an average of eight lenders. In Techiman (the only division for which we have the information) the total lent/borrowed was £976.75, making an average of £8.35 per debtor and £7.46 per transaction. The largest debt/loan was £109, but this was an outlier indeed: the second biggest was £70, the third £50. At the opposite end of the scale there were six loans of less than one pound, each of them being the borrower's only identified mortgage. The very smallest was for eight shillings (£0.40).[58]

In January 1934 a commissioner submitted to higher authority a small 'selection' of 'typical' cases of cocoa-farm pledging from Amansie. It comprised six debtors with a total of eight pledge loans. The average loan was £36.22, the average debt per debtor was £48.22 (with a range from

£11 to £101.75).[59] The average size of these loans was thus several times that for Wenchi district. Much of the difference can be related to the small size of the 'sample', and raises questions about its typicality—given the contrast with the seemingly comprehensive information from Wenchi district. But part of it can be attributed to variations in the pattern of demand for loans. Amansie farmers recieved high producer prices (because transport costs to the coast were much less, especially as their district was crossed by the Kumasi-Sekondi railway) while also tending to have a higher proportion of bearing cocoa farms. These conditions would have made it easier for farmers to raise larger loans. On the supply side, the small scale of the creditors' mortgage-lending in Wenchi district suggests that very few, if any, of them were specialist moneylenders. This observations is consistent with observations elsewhere in Asante, including Amansie, whose commissioner commented that 'the recognised money lenders in this District do not willingly accept cocoa farms as security, preferring something more substantial such as houses or ornaments.'[60]

The mortgage-lenders were not only relatively small but also overwhelmingly local, as far as can be determined. Of the 126 such creditors of farmers in Techiman and Nkoranza divisions, all have Akan names with the partial exception of one Kwami Mosi, who presumably hailed from what is now Burkina Faso but (perhaps reflecting long residence) had adopted an Akan day-name. Nkoranza is the only division for which the 'village' of the lender is given. Of the 33 mortgage-givers one is identified as non-Asante: specifically, as a Fante. The others included three from what is now Ashanti Region: from Asante Akyem, 'Ashanti' (Kumasi?) and Ejura respectively. The remaining 29 were all from villages or towns in Nkoranza or an immediately-neighbouring division.[61] Local provenance of mortgage-lenders was also shown in the above-mentioned much smaller, and selected, sample for Amansie district. In the latter all the creditors came from villages or, in one case, a town (Bekwai) within the district.[62]

All the parties in the small 'selection' of 'typical' pledging cases from Amansie appear to have been male.[63] The much fuller pledging data from Techiman and Nkoranza divisions, taken together, show a total of five women borrowers and 13 female lenders, two of whom operated as a pair (Table 15.1 [B]). For Techiman only we have information on the sums involved. There 12 women (10 individuals plus the pair) lent a total of £115 in 14 transactions. The mean loan by female creditors was a third larger than that of creditors as a whole. But this reflected two or three particularly large lenders. Only one woman, Afia Twimpro, gave more than one mortgage loan (she gave four, of £12, £6, £3 and again £3). The biggest loan was the joint effort, by Akosua Tamia and Akosua Nketia, of £50. Seven of the other women lent sums in the range £2–£4.[64]

The overall conclusion which emerges from the 1933–34 evidence is that, in the words of the acting commissioner for Bekwai (Amansie) district, 'Investigation seems to show that the practice of lending money against the Cacao crop as security is not particularly centred in any individuals, any farmer having ready money being apparently willing to lend provided the terms are sufficiently in his favour.'[65] This observation helps to make sense of the finding that women were more common as lenders than as borrowers. We know that women faced specific labour constraints when they wanted to enter cocoa-farming. But any woman with some cash could lend at interest, as a substitute or alternative to cocoa farming. Again, the apparent rarity of brokers as mortgage-lenders in Techiman compared to Kumasi district may well be no illusion. To anticipate a point which will be documented in Chapter 18, it may reflect the greater independent wealth of brokers in a relatively long-established cocoa district (Kumasi) as against an area on the cocoa frontier, in which a particularly high proportion of the advances which brokers made to farmers constituted 'retailing' of credit given to themselves by the European firms.[66] Hill's view that lenders and borrowers were not structurally or permanently different from each other in their general economic and social positions is upheld thus far.

The 1956–57 survey provided a detailed cross-section of the economic profile of borrowers and lenders. The data are presented in Fig. 15.1. It can be seen that cocoa-farmers across the size spectrum borrowed: which again fits Hill's position. The very richest farmers were the biggest borrowers. But with lending it is different: though lending and income are not

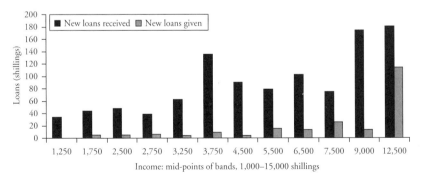

Figure 15.1. Cocoa-farming families' income and loans in Asante, 1956–57.
Source: Ghana, *Survey of Cocoa Producing Families in Ashanti, 1956–57*, Table 25.

closely related across the middle bands of the spectrum, the richest farmers were by far the biggest lenders, while the poorest did not lend at all.

D. Dynamics of Cocoa Crop Advances and Farm Mortgages: 'Cycle' and Trend

Earlier we considered the origins of cocoa crop advances and farm mortgages: let us now examine the evidence about their incidence over subsequent decades. The basic problem is that our most detailed evidence is in the form of snapshots: cross-sections at particular moments. This makes it difficult to distinguish fluctuations from any trend. But we can progress by relating this survey evidence to that obtained from archives and interviews. Before we focus on the evidence about advances and mortgages themselves it is important to put them in the context of the available data on fluctuations in nominal and real cocoa prices. The available evidence on this was summarised in Table 3.1. Here, Fig. 15.2 depicts the year to year variations in the nominal prices of cocoa and of textiles ('clothing, leather and textiles'), from Kay and Hymer's index numbers. While they moved roughly in parallel, the cloth-purchasing power of cocoa was relatively high during the first planting boom, to 1916, and still more so in the early 1950s. Conversely, it was at its lowest during the Second World War.

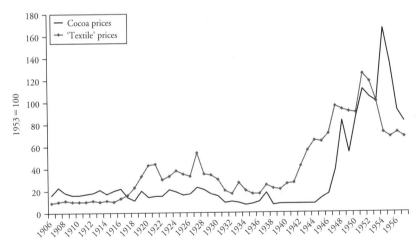

Figure 15.2. Kay-Hymer price indices of Ghana cocoa exports and 'textile' imports, 1906–57.
Source: As for Table 3.1.

The first observation to make about the incidence of new crop-advances and of farm-mortgages is that both varied with the price of cocoa; but in opposite directions. These relationships were noted by W. S. D. Tudhope, the colonial Director of Agriculture, in March 1919, primarily with reference to the Gold Coast Colony.

> In practically every district instances are found of mortgaged farms or of debts, although I have less evidence to show that it is at all common in Ashanti. The practice is not new but it seems to have enormously extended during the recent dull times, and as might be expected the granting of advances on prospective crops has latterly been, I believe, entirely suspended.[67]

The context makes clear that by 'the recent dull times' he meant the last three crop-years of the First World War, which were characterised by low cocoa prices.[67] A similar combination of a fall in crop advances and a rise in farm mortgages occurred in the depression of the early 1930s. This was noted, for Ghana generally, in a periodical published by the Department of Agriculture. Mortgaging 'appears to be on the increase', whereas 'The older system by which the money-lender regarded the loan as an advance against future cacao is becoming less common . . .'[69]

This time the story applied firmly to Asante as well as further south. In May 1933, replying to an enquiry from the government, the heads of produce-buying of two of the European firms represented in Kumasi indicated that the volume of advances was down. W. R. Danby of UAC thought that 'little or no advances will be given this season for various reasons'. Using the word 'mortgages' confusingly to refer to advances (that is, to the forthcoming crop being 'mortgaged'), he added 'at the present time there is less cocoa being mortgaged than has been the practice during the past six years': years when the price had generally been higher. C. L. Devin, of The Commonwealth Trust Limited (with phrasing that discreetly avoided any indication that his own firm might ever have given advances), remarked that the present commercial 'uncertainty has without doubt caused the closing of one source of supply of borrowed money: some buying firms, I am given to understand, have in the past been in the habit of advancing against the next crop, but it is safe to assume that these firms are no longer willing to do so'.[70] Meanwhile, while farm pledging appears to have been relatively uncommon before, by 1933 the situation had changed radically.

Before considering more general evidence, let us return to the farms that Kwame Dei made. The district commissioner of Bekwai noted that

'The Elders of that small stool Essiwa [Asiwa] under Dadiasi want to borrow £600 on their cocoa farms'.[71] This presumably meant stool farms,
otherwise it would have been no business of the commissioner. Asiwa's
original and (especially in view of the decline of *corvée*) probably only
stool farms were those made by Kwame Dei. This time the Asiwa farm
mortgages were far from isolated. The DC noted that 'The Licensed
Surveyor has been making plans of cocoa farms in the District, for farmers who use them for the purpose of security'.[72] More systematic data
come from the one detailed cross-sectional study of the incidence of agricultural indebtedness over a crop year, across the Gold Coast and Asante
cocoa belt. This was carried out for the government in 1933 (the 1932–33
season) by a combination of agricultural inspectors and district commissioners. They appear to have proceeded by asking chiefs to report, and
supplementing this information with the views of European merchants,
together with figures from cooperative societies and from some individual
farmers.[73] A 'questionnaire was completed for villages distributed
throughout the cocoa areas'. For 'Ghana' as a whole, the survey covered
the sale of 45,700 tonnes of cocoa,[74] 17.6 per cent of the total.[75] For
Amansie 'reports from Chiefs indicated that at least one third of the
farmers have one or more farms mortgaged, for periods of one to ten
years . . .'[76]

The same cyclical relationships are apparent in the late-colonial
period, the era of the marketing-board monopoly of cocoa exporting,
from 1939 onwards. During the war real producer prices were very low;
and we have noted that African brokers, lending from their own capital,
were said to be the main suppliers of advances. Part (only) of this was by
default, reflecting a major reduction in advance-giving by European
firms. As with the African brokers, though in the opposite direction, the
European produce-buyers' behaviour partly reflected an underlying shift
in the amount of advances they would offer at any given producer price.
But they were also responding to low prices in the same way as they had
in earlier decades. The net effect was that advances were relatively few
during the war. By contrast, the impression from scattered evidence in
the Fortes Papers and other sources, which we will examine in related
contexts in Chapter 18, is that pledging was at a very high level during
the war.

By comparison with the war years it appears that pledging was reced-
ing drastically in 1956–57, while (more cautiously) it seems that advances
were more abundant. For this crop year we have a further snapshot
of the volume of advances and mortgages, in the form of the survey of

cocoa-farming families in Asante. This investigation found that the frequency of 'pledging' was relatively low. Only 2.1 per cent (123) of the 5,838 'farms' owned by the members of the 1,620 families in the budget sample were recorded as 'pledged'.[77] By this time the vast majority of cocoa farmers were free of mortgages. On the implausibly extreme assumption that no family had pledged more than one farm the proportion of families whose own farms were pledge-free would have been 92.4 per cent. The real proportion must have been higher still. Unfortunately the survey did not collect the corresponding information on advances. It did find that more money was owed for crop advances than on pledged farms at the beginning of the cocoa season and, as might be expected, that the reverse applied at the end of the season. On 1 September 1956 the average debt for a sample size of 1,303.5 families was 493 shillings (£24.65) on pledged farms, 522 shillings (£26.1) on crop advances, and 288 shillings (£14.4) on 'other' loans. At 31 March 1957 the average debt had fallen to 273 and 161 shillings (£13.65 and £8.05) for pledges and advances respectively, and to 140.5 shillings (£7) for 'other' loans.[78] The number of families in debt had also fallen over the season: from 1,303.5 to 574.5 (after adjusting for sampling error). That is, from 80.5 per cent to 35.5 per cent of the overall budget sample of 1,620. Given the incidence of pledging noted above, the most likely interpretation of the figures for the overall proportions of indebted families is that advances were considerably more common in 1956–57 than in 1933 or during the war years; while the incidence of farm mortgages less than a quarter of that estimated in 1933 and apparently greatly declined since c.1945. Much of this can be explained in cyclical terms. Though cocoa producer prices were lower in 1956–57 than for several years, they were very much higher (in nominal and real terms) than during the First World War or the 1930s Depression: as well as compared to 1939–45.

To summarize the evidence on incidence so far, it seems that the proportion of cocoa beans bought in advance was strongly and positively related to the price of cocoa; while, conversely, the number of cocoa farms mortgaged rose strongly when cocoa prices were depressed. The fact that the latter relationship was more strongly manifest in Asante in the early 1930s than in the 1910s shows, however, that variations in the extent and form of indebtedness over time were not solely related to the prevailing price of the produce. We also need to explore the likelihood that the incidence of both types of 'cocoa credit' in the late colonial period reflected not only the variations in the real producer price but also various 'parametric shifts'. To separate trend from cycle we need to take up a neglected task: that of exploring change over the period in the supply and demand schedules, respectively, for advances and for mortgages. That is, in the quantity of advances (or mortgages) that would be offered (or demanded) at each possible cocoa price.

The data on advances are fragmentary, but a comparison of the approximate level of advances during two periods of low cocoa prices is possible and revealing. We can compare Tudhope's report of 1919 with the 1933 survey. Unlike the latter, Tudhope's conclusions, from his own wide-travelling individual investigations on foot and bicycle,[79] do not purport to offer quantitative precision. Thus a subtle variation between the two years would be undetectable. There is, however, a clear contrast which is significant because in other key respects the two periods are similar. Both were characterized by relatively low cocoa prices. From July to September, when the bulk of off-season advances would probably have been given, the mean monthly price at the point of shipment in 1932 was 209 d. [£0.87] per 60-lb. (27.2 kg.) load. For the years for which data compiled in the same way are available, 1927–28 to 1937–38, the mean of the corresponding means was 312.09 old pence (£1.30). In six of these crop years the mean July–September price was higher than in 1932–33: in four it was lower.[80] As we have seen, in both periods the level of advances given and received was down on the immediately preceding years of higher prices. Yet there was a striking difference. Whereas Tudhope had reported that advances were 'entirely suspended' in the earlier hard times, the 1933 survey found that they had been given on a quarter of the crop: 25.4 per cent of the 45,700 tonnes covered (for Ghana as a whole) 'had been sold in advance'.[81] In the case of Amansie the acting district commissioner and the agricultural inspector had asked chiefs to report on the matter, and obtained 'more definite figures from Co-operative societies and [from some] farmers'. It 'was universally admitted' that advances 'are commonly received . . . As far as could be ascertained at least one third of the farmers were in the habit of receiving such advances.'[82] This is the more surprising because, if anything, farmers faced more unfavourable barter terms of trade in the Depression than in the wartime recession. The general producer-price level in 1932–33 was slightly *below* what it had been during 1915–16 to 1917–18, while textile prices were higher. Part of the contrast can be accounted for by Tudhope exaggerating slightly[83] and by a scarcity of cash during the war years concerned: little coin was imported and farmers were resistant to the introduction of paper currency.[84] But the difference between the war years and the early 1930s is too great to be fully explained thus. It points to the conclusion that the schedule of advances had risen: a higher volume of advances would be offered at each price level, other things being equal.

We have already seen that for Asante farm mortgages seem to have been far more common in 1933 than in c.1917–19. In view of the qualitative observations made at these times, quoted above, there appears to have been a significant rise in the quantity of farm mortgages for each drop in the price level. To pursue our enquiries further we need to ask whether these upward movements in the schedules of advances and of mortgages were on the demand or the supply side, or both. This we will do in Chapter 18, having put the question in context by examining the motives for advances and pledges.

Did these trends, underlying the cocoa-price fluctuations, towards higher levels of lending and borrowing on cocoa continue to the end of the colonial period? The matter is complicated and much of the evidence indirect. In the case of advances there are several reasons why one might expect that the upward trend would continue. For a start, it may well be that by 1956–57, with the economic harshness of the war years well behind, African private buyers had more working capital from which to give advances. The same might be said of the European produce-buyers, though with the opposite chronology: their profit margins were presumably well defended during the war by the marketing board's quota system which guaranteed the perpetuation of their respective prewar shares of the crop; whereas in the decade of decolonization they faced increasing competition from African private and, especially, state buyers. Finally, the political imperative to offer more credit to farmers had been put into effect by the cooperatives and especially by the marketing board and its agencies. Yet there was during the war, at least, a major counterveiling pressure pressing down on the supply schedule of cocoa advances. The very fact that the European firms' quotas were pre-determined meant that they barely had to compete to secure produce.[85] During the decade of decolonization, however, the level of competition seems to have built up again, as cooperatives and, temporarily, the CPC challenged the European firms. The latter needed to be able to secure produce in order to justify their long-term future as licensed buyers for the board. Even so, the level of advances given in 1956–57 was hardly impressive for a year of such high producer prices, by historic standards. Perhaps the demise of the CPC reduced the pressure on its former rivals to give generous credit.

It is clear from the 1956–57 evidence, presented above, that the level of mortgage debt was considerably reduced by the end of the period. This may well be sufficiently accounted for by the very favourable producer prices; but they were reinforced by the state's efforts at debt relief. Pledging, however, was far from doomed.[86]

E. Colonial Policy on 'The Problem' of Agricultural Indebtedness

The introduction of promissory notes helped creditors to use the courts in enforcing payment. Armitage observed in 1907 that 'promissory notes . . . can easily be drawn up for illiterate natives, now that Licensed letter writers are to be found throughout Ashanti . . .'[87] British courts enforced creditors' claims, not only in principle but in practice. Reading among the vast quantity of suits for recovery of loans or other debts one gets the clear impression that the overwhelming majority were decided in favour of the plaintiff. Many of these cases were brought by European trading firms, but many others were brought by African—usually Asante—creditors.

But, especially from the 1920s to the end of colonial rule, British officials deplored 'The Problem of Indebtedness', in Asante and in the 'Ghanaian' cocoa belt generally.[88] Specifically, this meant advances on cocoa crops and mortgages of cocoa farms.[89] Two particular themes emerged from the chorus of disapproval. One was concern that advances (and the pledging of farms) removed the incentive to producers to maximise the quality of their produce.[90] This suggestion struck a nerve in the colonial government, especially the agriculture department, which had long feared that cocoa exported from the Gold Coast might eventually lose its market because of inadequate quality control. The other theme was the risk that the debtors might be dispossessed of their holdings. In 1940 a commissioner warned that unless land litigation was 'curtailed the future of the independent peasant family farming its own holding will be jeopardised by debt and the subsequent foreclosure and purchase of the farms by money lenders and Cocoa brokers'.[91]

In 1930 a provincial commissioner commented: 'This mortgaging is bad, but we can't prevent it.'[92] Nevertheless, attempts were made to reduce indebtedness by both the administration and the Department of Agriculture. Commissioners on tour tried moral suasion: preaching against it to elders.[93] In 1933 courts were empowered to reduce 'excessive' interest rates. Implementing this policy, the acting district commissioner of Bekwai, for example, wrote to all government-recognised chiefs' courts ('Native Tribunals') in the district in July 1933 observing that 'As you are well aware, the rates of interest charged by Money Lenders in Ashanti are often ridiculously high and most unfair'. He drew their 'attention' to the Loans Recovery Ordinance, under which 'any Court or any Native Tribunal before which any claim for recovery of money lent is brought, may, if it considers the interest charged to be excessive, alter the interest to an amount which the Court or Tribunal considers reasonable'. Again, if a borrower complained of being charged excessive interest, the court or tribunal could cancel the original agreement and substitute one it deemed reasonable. The commissioner also asked that all the chiefs' subjects be informed of the ordinance.[94] In 1941 the Moneylenders' Ordinance fixed a maximum of 15 per cent interest on a secured loan. Four years later a commissioner with long experience in Asante reported that the ordinance '[is] largely ignored', except that it 'has created amongst the more knowing a practice of always falsifying the document by including the 50% interest as principal.' He cited an instance: 'Loan of £200 put down as £300 and lender (having unwisely pleaded guilty) convicted. Two documents one drawn up in the bush another 2 weeks later in Kumasi on the same transaction showing the alteration.'[95] While the occasional law-breaker might be caught, it seems clear that such prosecutions did not affect the general level of interest paid: as will be seen in Chapter 18.

Meanwhile, the reduction of indebtedness was one aim of the Department of Agriculture's promotion of farmers' marketing cooperatives in the 1930s in all cocoa-growing areas of Ghana.[96] The Director of Agriculture, Auchinleck, was quoted in 1938 as denying 'that there is any need for outside assistance in financing the crop'. Rather, all credit transactions should be between farmers themselves, within the institution of cooperatives.[97] The cooperative program was given its main official momentum in the 1930–31 crop year,[98] though in the 1929–30 season there was already one cooperative society in Amansie, in the village of Pekyi, supervised by the Department from Kumasi.[99] But the cooperatives were poorly equipped to provide an alternative to the moneylenders. They were largely self-financing, restricted their lending mainly to short-term credit for directly 'productive' purposes (i.e. investments likely to lead to repayment of the loans), had a strict ceiling on the amount that an individual member could borrow (initially £10, later doubled) and would not accept farms as collateral. Moreover, they were instituted from above with little spontaneous support among farmers, and in the early years the farmers who joined them seemed to give low priority to keeping them solvent.[100] In the 1933–34 season there were only 667 members of cooperative societies in Amansie,[101] the population of which was recorded as 76,366 in the 1931 Census. As late as March 1952 membership of cocoa cooperatives had climbed only to 18,398 members in Ghana as a whole. During the 1951–52 season the membership received a total of £215,000 in loans from the societies,[102] an average of £11.68 per head. Nearly 89 per cent of this had been repaid, and the rest 'was not necessarily overdue'.[103] The cooperative movement was progressing, but it remained a sideshow in the rural credit market. Its membership was only a few per cent of all cocoa farmers, and the loans it supplied them in 1951–52 equalled just 0.68 of one per cent of the total producer revenue from that year's cocoa crop.[104]

In 1948, after decades of government concern about the 'problem of indebtedness', the commission investigating the causes of the riots commented that the 'mortgaging' of cocoa 'presents the worst features of usury'.[105]

F. Conclusion

The main form of capital goods in the new cash-crop economy was the cocoa tree. Because the creation of cocoa farms was to a great extent a function of labour inputs, the social organization of family labour potentially conditioned the distribution and disposal of farm property. This was only 'potentially', because these property rights were bitterly disputed. Wives struggled to find enough of their own labour-time to create cocoa farms for themselves; widows and divorcees argued for a share in the cocoa farm(s) they had helped their husbands to make. The overall female share in cocoa-farm ownership rose as time went on, for reasons we will explore further below. But it remained comparatively small. Relatedly, the system of matrilineal inheritance was gradually weakened over the period, to the—as yet modest—benefit of widows and sons.

The period saw a revolution in rural credit: it became specifically agricultural, with the emergence and proliferation of short-term lending on the security of forthcoming cocoa crops, and of long-term lending on the security of cocoa farms, which were usually transferred to the creditor's possession. In this chapter we have sought to track the changing incidence of both forms of indebtedness, and to distinguish their basic determinants. Contrasting cyclical patterns were indicated: the incidence of advances being positively related to the current price of cocoa, whereas pledging of farms was common in recession years and receded in prosperity. We also sought to disentangle the cyclical pattern from long-term changes in the supply schedule of each kind of cocoa credit. For instance, it seems that the amount of credit, of both kinds, that was on offer at any given level of cocoa price rose markedly from the 1910s to at least the 1930s. Whereas cocoa advances were part of the cocoa-buying system, financed primarily—though increasingly less predominantly—by the European buying firms, the taking of farms on pledge was widely practised by anyone with money in the local economy. Whether these developments should be seen as a cure for the chronic liquidity-shortages of a poor rural economy, or evidence of usury, will be examined in Chapter 18.

Finally, the state increasingly sought (from a variety of motives) to regulate the capital market (like the labour market). It tried in vain to restrict interest rates. Of rather more practical importance, the colonial administration, and perhaps even more so the joint-rule government led by Kwame Nkrumah, tried to create and expand formal-sector avenues for supplying credit to farmers.

16

FREE LABOUR:

FAMILY WORKERS, THE SPREAD OF WAGE CONTRACTS, AND THE RISE OF SHARECROPPING

The purpose of this chapter is to document and clarify the variety of ways in which labour was put to work in the cocoa economy after the prohibition of slavery and pawning. The first three sections consider the importance of non-market inputs: from the farmer and from his or her spouse (a matter to be related to the gender distribution of farm ownership); from children; and from the cooperative work (*nnɔboa*) group. We then consider the origins of a wage labour market in rural Asante, initially in carrying and on the mines, c.1900–c.1920; describe the spread of regular wage labour, from c.1916 to the mid-1930s, mostly recruited from men, and mostly from the savanna; and document a remarkable transition from regular wage-labour to sharecropping contracts, from the late 1930s onwards. Finally, we examine state policy on rural labour.

A. Self and Spouse Labour in the Context of Mostly Male Ownership of Cocoa Farms

The most widespread form of cocoa-farm labour, throughout the period, was the farmer him or herself. In gender terms, the vast majority of the early cocoa farmers were male. Though female cocoa farmownership rose gradually throughout the period, by the end of it women were still very much a minority among cocoa farmers. The next most widespread category of cocoa labour was that of help from spouses. The implication of the distribution of farm ownership is that in the great majority of cases this meant wives helping husbands rather than the other way round. The key point about women's labour inputs on cocoa farms is that for most women cocoa production was a residual claim on their time.

Women started and finished the period with a primary commitment to reproductive responsibilities in the broadest sense, while men concentrated on extra-subsistence activity. Earlier I argued that this was so in the nineteenth century (Chapter 6), and we will see here and in Chapter 18 that this basic distinction remained true throughout the period and beyond. But, as Allman wrote of matriling, it is important to 'historicise' such durability: it was not immutable, it was fought over and partly reconstructed during the period.[1] Gracia Clark, and also recently Allman and Tashjian, argue that women increasingly took over food trades in the 1920s and 1930s, which men had largely abandoned in order to take up cocoa farming. Their evidence is from extensive oral research. Though Clark does not specify the individual sources for particular statements, the overall argument is persuasive.[2] It should be remembered, though, that women were active in at least some food trades in the nineteenth century. For example, they seem to have monopolised the fish trade from Lake Bosumtwi.[3] Again, if their share of food trading rose in the twentieth century, it had done so decisively by 1920 at the latest, when Chief Commissioner Harper, reporting the results of an internal inquiry, commented that 'The traffic is almost exclusively in the hands of petty traders, mostly women'.[4] On this chronology, the shift was swift indeed: but that is possible, given the rapid growth of the cocoa industry, and of male commitment to it.

The most important change, and the subject of the most significant conflict, was women's involvement, in addition to their food-growing and child-rearing responsibilities, in labour on, and even ownership of, cocoa farms.

The evidence indicates that in the early years of cocoa farming in Asante women owned only a very small proportion of cocoa farms. The introduction of cocoa to Asante has only been studied in detail for Amansie, one of the two oldest cocoa-growing districts.[5] It seems that all the individual pioneer farmowners there were male, beginning with the abovementioned Kwame Dei of Asiwa, who was the first to plant cocoa in Amansie.[6] Women were important participants in the process, but not as farmowners. It was 'the wife and children of Kwame Dei', for example, who carried out the 'peddling of the pods' over 'about 6 years', thereby turning

Dei's farm from a local novelty into a major centre of diffusion. They 'travelled all over Ashanti and the Western Province [of the Gold Coast Colony]'.[7] Somewhat later, both women and men from Bekwai walked to Akyem Abuakwa and returned carrying pods on their heads in order to plant the seeds on Bekwai land. This must have been in the late 1900s or so, because at the time cocoa was already being produced in Bekwai, but still in such small quantities that pods commanded a price high enough to justify this arduous journey to buy them in what was then the cocoa heartland. At least one of the women involved, Afua Fofie, made a farm of her own near her home village of Begorase.[8] It is clear from the report of an African travelling inspector of the Department of Agriculture, Mark Alexis, that female ownership of cocoa farms existed in Amansie by 1921. Arriving at Asubina, a village near Manso Nkwanta, he found that the 'Chief and nearly all the farmers are absent. I addressed three men and a number of women, the latter were interested in cocoa farming as some owned farms.'[9] But that he should remark on the female presence suggests that it was unusual.

A more specific insight into the dynamics of women's cocoa-farming is provided by the late T. E. Kyei, mentioned earlier as Fortes's principal research assistant. He has left a remarkable memoir of his youth, including his childhood living on his father's cocoa farm near Agogo in the 1910s. He recalled that cocoa then was:

> mostly grown by men in virgin forests some distance away from the town. Enterprising women, particularly those elderly and unattached ones, made their own cocoa farms alongside the men.[10]

A quantitative perspective on the relationship between the spread of cocoa growing and the growth of female property in cocoa farms is provided by the findings of two surprisingly neglected surveys made by the Department of Agriculture in different parts of Asante in the later 1920s. In 1925–26, in the context of a programme of inspecting farms for pests, a 168 square-kilometre (65 square-mile) area of Asante-Akyem district was studied, 'comprising the cacao-growing areas of Konongo, Patriensa, Juansa, Bompata, Adomfe and Juaso'. This district was chosen in the belief that it contained the oldest cocoa trees in Asante.[11] In contrast, in 1928–29 the cocoa-growing villages of the four districts of the Western Province of Ashanti, broadly representing the newer cocoa areas, were examined.[12] The surveys, directed respectively by A. C. Miles and J. C. Muir, both claimed to be comprehensive: albeit the former only within its study area,

Table 16.1. Gender of farmers (owners) and size of cocoa farm in Asante-Akyem, 1925–26[1]

Farm-size (acres)	Median of size-class	Number of farms	Male farmers	Female farmers	Total farmers	Female as proportion of all cocoa farmers (%)
0.00–0.99	0.5	1,299	359	198	557	36
1.00–1.99	1.5	476	240	43	283	15
2.00–3.99	3.0	271	242	29	271	11
4.00–6.99	5.5	96	88	8	96	8
7.00–9.99	8.5	27	27	0	27	0
10.00–12.99	11.5	7	7	0	7	0
13.00–15.99	14.5	2	2	0	2	0
16.00–18.99	17.5	2	2	0	2	0
19.00–20.99	20.0	3	3	0	3	0
21.00+		1	1	0	1	0
Total		2,184	971	278	1,249	22

[1] Data from Miles, 'Size of cacao farms in Ashanti', 55. The percentages were recalculated from his absolute numbers.

which however included the bulk of the district's cocoa trees. According to Miles, 'Every cacao plot' within the study area in Asante-Akyem was included, while in western Asante Muir's team conducted 'house to house' visits to 'each cacao producing village in the Province'.[13] Muir attempted to predict future yields; a particularly difficult task on which his figures turned out to be highly inaccurate.[14] But the figures provided by both studies on cocoa farmers (farmowners) as a proportion of the population may be accepted as a general indication of the reality.[15]

Female cocoa farmers constituted 3.46 per cent of the total population of the study area in Asante-Akyem, while cocoa farmers as a whole made up 15.54 per cent.[16] The proportion of women cocoa farmowners in the population of cocoa-growing villages in each district was correlated with the proportion of all cocoa farmowners in the population, with a correlation coefficient (R) of 0.76. For the four western districts it was higher, at 0.97. Another measure, for which no data are available for Asante-Akyem, is the correlation between the ratio of women cocoa farmowners to total population and the proportion of farmowners with bearing farms, the coefficient (for the four western districts) being 0.99.[17]

Though the number of districts is small, the correlations are close enough to permit a tentative conclusion, that the more widely cocoa farming had been adopted by a particular population (whether composed of people

Table 16.2. Female and all cocoa farmers (owners) in western Asante, 1928[1]

District	Kintampo	Wenchi	Sunyani	Ahafo
Female cocoa farmers	57	478	3,301	1,215
All cocoa farmers	1,759	3,662	11,066	3,344
Female farmers with bearing cocoa	11	162	1,179	482
All farmers with bearing cocoa	573	1,647	5,987	1,936
Total adult population of cocoa-growing villages	4,804	9,762	23,097	8,382
Total population of cocoa-growing villages	8,884	17,919	43,143	13,293
Cocoa farms per 1,000 population	198	193	251	256
All cocoa farmers/total population	19.80%	20.44%	25.65%	25.16%
Farmers with bearing cocoa/total population	6.45%	9.19%	13.88%	14.56%
Female as proportion of all cocoa farmers	3.32%	13.05%	29.83%	36.33%
Female proportion of all farmers with bearing cocoa	1.92%	9.84%	19.69%	24.90%
Female cocoa farmers/adult population	1.19%	4.90%	14.29%	14.50%
Female cocoa farmers/total population	0.64%	2.67%	7.65%	9.14%

[1] Data from Muir, 'Survey of cacao areas – Western Province, Ashanti', *Bulletin of the Department of Agriculture, Gold Coast*, vol. 22 (1930), 63–64. See also Muir, 'Crop surveys', 179. In the three asterisked rows most of the figures differ very slightly from – and correct – the corresponding entries in the table in Austin, 'Human pawning', 142. That was based on ratios presented by Muir himself ('Survey of cacao areas', 61, 63; 'Crop surveys', 173, 177). The present table is based upon recalculation from his absolute numbers.

native to the area and/or of strangers), the higher was the proportion of women among the growing number of cocoa farmowners and, to judge from the western Asante data, among the increasing number of farmowners with bearing trees.[18] The reasons for this will be examined in Chapter 18. It should be noted, though, that the rate of adoption of cocoa in a district was not simply a function of time, otherwise Asante-Akyem would have had the largest proportion of cocoa farmowners.[19]

Despite the gradual increase in female ownership of cocoa farms, the proportion of such farms owned by women remained small. Of the 53 Ofoase farmers evicted from Esumeja land in 1939 none appear to have been female. Certainly, of nineteen whose full names are given in a petition all were male.[20] Of a handful of Esumeja farmers expelled from Ofoase land in retaliation, however, at least one was a woman.[21] In a 1945–46 survey of Asokore, Fortes and Kyei found that of 246 adult females 44 'either farmed cocoa or owned cocoa farms'. Fortes did not report a precise figure for the corresponding number of men in the same categories, but it appears to have been of similar magnitude: of 200 adult males, '30 are cocoa farmers' while 'a number of others have an interest in or are owners of cocoa farms'.[22] This relative equality is exceptional in the evidence. It may have been related to Asokore's position on the northern edge of the ecological zone in which cocoa trees would grow; where other activities were perhaps as or more remunerative for those whose time was relatively free to take advantage of them. As late as 1974, a sample survey, based on purchasing records, of 3,726 cocoa farmowners from Ghana as a whole found men outnumbering women by nine to one.[23]

Not only did woman tend to own fewer farms than men, their farms tended to be smaller. Miles's Asante-Akyem survey of 1925–26 provided figures for the size of individuals' cocoa farm holdings. In just over a third of the cases these comprised more than one plot. He calculated that the average area of cocoa owned by female farmers in the study area (1.13 acres) was only 40 per cent of the average for male farmers (2.8 acres).[24] Again, while for both sexes modal ownership was less than an acre, this represented 71 per cent of the female owners compared to 'only' 37 per cent of males. No woman owned as much as 7 acres, whereas 42 men (4.3 per cent of male owners) owned more,[25] the largest holding being 27 acres (10.9 hectares).[26]

The most ubiquitous source of cocoa-farm labour was specifically the male farmer on his own farm. That is, we have seen that the overwhelming majority of cocoa farms before at least the 1930s were owned by men, and the evidence is that, chiefs (and the richest commoner farmers) apart, farmowners laboured on their own farms.[27] Direct cocoa labour was done by males, while women's contributions focussed on the shade crops, which were also food crops. Interviewed in 1980, Nana Frema II, an old woman of Jacobu in southern Amansie, described her own experience in helping her husband to make a farm at Esasi, and implied that it typified the division of labour in Asante in the period: the husband was responsible for clearing the land, the wife for planting shade crops, which were also food crops: cocoyam and plantain.[28] The same pattern emerges from Kyei's account of his upbringing on a cocoa farm near Agogo in the 1910s.[29] The woman also had the primary responsibility for weeding, although the man would help if the task was too large for her alone.[30] Bray's survey in Ahafo, data for which were collected in the years 1956–c.58, found that 104 'farmers', all presumably men, were assisted on their cocoa farms by 186 'wives'.[31] Given the findings summarized in this paragraph male farmers may be assumed to have worked more hours on their cocoa farms than their wives did, especially on the cocoa plants and trees themselves. On the other hand, because of polygamy, the number of wives making *some* contribution on their husbands' cocoa farms, directly and/or by food-farming of shade crops, exceeded the number of married male farmers.

B. Rise and Decline in Children's Contributions to Family Labour in Agriculture?

This section considers labour inputs from children, including those who were nearly or actually full-grown but not yet working much for themselves. The discussion can be organised around two hypotheses. The first is that as the cocoa era continued there was a decline in the share of family labour in the total of cocoa-farm labour inputs. We will see below that there was no tendency towards the creation of a wage-dependent proletariat within indigenous Asante society. But the growth of the labour market offered opportunities which junior members of cocoa-farming families might reasonably prefer to unwaged work for their fathers. As school capacity expanded, more and more parents themselves had reason to direct their children's time into 'human capital formation' rather than cocoa labour. The second hypothesis is that labour inputs from matrilineal relatives (especially, male farmers being helped by their sisters' sons) declined over the period.

The only direct evidence of apparent decline in family labour inputs on cocoa farms that I have found is the following statement in a report on the 1928–29 survey of western Asante:

> until recently, when transport facilities to Kumasi were vastly improved, cacao growing tended to be a family rather than a personal form of occupation. This . . . is changing, and at present there is an increasing tendency for individuals of a family to make their own farms and to employ labour. . . .[32]

However, the fact that expanding cocoa output was associated with increased use of hired labour does not necessarily mean that family labour inputs fell absolutely. In his interviews in the mid-1940s, Fortes found that the farmers from Kwotei used some family labour *in addition* to wage labour on the 'very big' cocoa farms they had established around Bechem in Ahafo. He was told that 'Some of the farmers live in Ahafo but most of them live at Kwotei & go to their farms with their families periodically when there is work to be done, especially during harvest time'.[33] In general hired labourers were purely supplementary to family labour, rather than a partial replacement for it. While the terms available to cocoa labourers gradually improved from the late 1930s onwards, farm ownership remained preferable to farm employment. Farmowners' sons continued to have a strong interest in helping their fathers directly, with the expectation of being rewarded with help in establishing their own first farms during their fathers' lives, quite apart from the issue of inheritance.

On the other hand, the growth of schooling offered the prospect of earnings beyond those available in cocoa farming. Fortes's impression in 1946 was that 'any Ashanti who can afford to do so directs his children's education and upbringing in such a way as to qualify them for any other occupation than cocoa farming'.[34] As an indication of farmers' intentions this requires two qualifications. First, for 'other' should be substituted 'more lucrative'. As Fortes noted, Asantes treated cocoa farms as 'any other piece of productive capital'.[35] Second, Fortes himself found in Kwotei that although the villagers were devoting much of their cocoa receipts to the building of a school, 'They are proud of their cocoa farms & say they want their children to take up cocoa farming'.[36] But certainly a successful school career would equip the child for work outside farming. Even in 1937 farmers' sons were beginning to enter government service.[37]

School itself reduced the amount of time children had available to help on farms. Bray's survey in Ahafo in 1956–c.58 found that of 839 offspring of cocoa-farming families 30 had finished school and 239 were at school.[38] Thus 32 per cent of them had been or were unavailable for farm work on school days. Moreover, this figure understates the effective share of potential labour time denied to the farm by the classroom because many of the remaining 68 per cent would have been too young to be either at school or contributing significantly to farm labour.

Family labour remained extremely important to the end of the period and beyond. Husbands cleared land for wives to plant food crops; wives helped husbands on cocoa farms. Youths, male and female, likewise assisted on their parents' cocoa farms; young men sometimes helped their mothers' brothers. Labour contributions on the senior generation's farms were stemmed, though not in all cases stopped, when the younger individuals established their own farms and households. Conversely, in his fieldwork in the mid-1940s Fortes was told, in an old cocoa-growing area, that young men were growing up to find that all the land suitable for cocoa in the locality was already cultivated.[39] This presumably led some to work longer for their elders in the hope of securing the inheritance of their maternal uncle's cocoa trees or aware that 'At times a kind father gives his sons farms before he dies.' Not that these youths were trapped in family service: 'many' of them migrated for several months of the year to launch their independent cocoa-farming activities in a younger cocoa area, while others became sharecrop labourers responsible for 'the cocoa farms of people who are too old to farm'.[40] Any overall decline in farm labour inputs per child would have been more than balanced by the growth of population until the provision of universal primary education in the 1960s. But it seems safe to assume that for the increasing minority of farming households that included school children, the current and future inputs of child labour in agriculture of all types was in decline, if only per capita and cohort by cohort.

When children assisted their seniors, was it their parents or, in the case of boys, their mothers's brothers whom they helped? Kyei recalled his own mother helping hired labourers to convey his grandmother's cocoa beans from her own farm (which was in the same area) 'to the Cadbury and Fry yard at Asokore'.[41] My own fieldwork in Amansie indicated that the farmowner's children were a standard part of the early cocoa farm workforce.[42] On the other hand, nephews (sisters' sons) helped the farmowner in some cases but not all. In Esumeja it was reported that nephews did not work on their uncles' farms; in Amoafo, that they did so sometimes (and in Asikaso in southeast Amansie, much the same).[43] Kwame Dei of Asiwa and Osei Kwame of Huntado were helped by their respective nephews.[44] In Sanfo nephews were first described as part of the labour force, but then omitted in a description of the same a moment later in the same interview.[45] This suggests that cocoa farmers got less help from nephews than from sons in that village. That pattern seems to have been taken further by the end of the colonial period. Bray's Ahafo survey, cited above, reported 151 'sons and daughters' working for those 104 male farmers.[46] It is striking that Bray and his local research assistant, B. M. Agyare, did not find it necessary to have a category of 'sister's sons and other matrilineal relatives'.

This does not mean that sister's sons had disappeared permanently as a source of labour. This was shown by Christine Okali's study of Dominase, a small settlement of migrant-farmers in Ahafo which was founded only in 1959. Survey evidence was collected in 1971–73. Forty-one male and eight female farmers had received labour assistance from relatives on 53 and 11 cocoa farms respectively. The women had had no help from 'matrikin' apart from their own 'Offspring/grandchildren', who had helped on five of their farms. But just over half of the men's cocoa farms had had inputs from their owners' 'matrikin' (mostly sister's sons, presumably): four times as many as had received labour from the men's own offspring.[47] How many hours this amounted to is unknown; Okali commented that 'wives were the only persons who were in a position to have assisted with labour on farms over a comparatively long period'.[48] It may be that sisters' sons helped in this case in response to their uncles having particular difficulty in affording hired labour. For the farms were immature or, even at the time of the survey, only fairly recently beginning to produce income; real producer prices had been much lower during the lifetime of Dominase than for several years before Bray's survey; and some of the farm labour force had been bid away to the towns or, in the case of non-Ghanaians, expelled under the 1969 Aliens' Compliance Order.[49] Thus a deterioration in the position of employers on the labour market may have stimulated the use of matrilineal links to recruit labour, at least short-term.

Overall, it is clear that it was very common for children, especially sons, to contribute much of their labour to their seniors' (especially their fathers') cocoa farming. It seems likely, from the circumstances, that the free children were required to put in more farm labour to offset the adverse effects of the decline of slavery and pawning. Finally, the conjugal unit was much more important for labour than the matrilineal one. Two observations on this must be emphasized. First, the same was true in the nineteenth century. Second, the role of sister's sons as labourers may have been reduced further by or during the buoyant cocoa market that accompanied the end of the colonial period; but it would be ahistorical to interpret this as a permanent social or 'structural' shift rather than a contingent one.

C. Nnɔboa: The Cooperative Work Group

Non-family labour was available through institutions which involved neither the wage-labour market nor slavery and pawning. When additional labour was required on non-stool cocoa farms, the institution of the cooperative work group was invoked.[50] We are fortunate to have, now, a marvellously detailed recollection of *nnɔboa* fairly early in the cocoa era. This comes from Kyei's memoirs, here referring apparently to about the mid-to-late 1910s. He lived with his parents and siblings in a 'cottage' or hamlet amid the cocoa farms.

> Reciprocal services were rendered between members of the cottage community. By some mutual agreement, one 'family' might work one day on another's farm, say, on bush-clearing (*adɔ*), tree-felling (*abue*) or seedling-planting (*atɔdwe*), such service to be returned another day. This system was called *nnɔ-boa*.

Cocoa pod-splitting day (*kookoo-bɔ da*) was a grand occasion of recipro-cal service, when almost all farmers in the neighbourhood went to help a fellow farmer to split his/her heaped cocoa pods for fermenting. Early in the morning of a *kookoo-bɔ* day, men, women and children—all in a cot-tage—proceeded to a specially prepared spot on the farm for the splitting of the beans (*kookoo-abɔyɛ*). There they met to work communally. All sat around the mountain-heap of cocoa pods. The men-folk did the splitting of the pods with cutlasses (matchets) while women and children did the scooping of the beans from pods into baskets. The contents of filled baskets were emptied into a shallow pit lined with fresh plantation or banana leaves. When all pods had been split, the heap was covered with more plan-tation/banana leaves and left for about five or six days to ferment.[51]

There is also evidence of the use of *nnɔboa* labour in early Asante cocoa-farming from oral testimonies I collected in Amansie. In Sanfo *nnɔboa* groups performed all the operations of harvesting: plucking and breaking of pods, and carrying to market.[52] In Jacobu they did the breaking but not the plucking.[53] In Asikaso they were involved not only in harvesting but also in weeding, and even land-clearance and planting.[54]

For the mid-1940s there is a contemporary account, given to the Ashanti Social Survey, of the exchange of labour at cocoa harvest.

The splitting business is usually done in groups by the farmers. About twenty farmers decide to go and split one farmer's cocoa pods and the next day they go to the second man's farm to do the same. Women and children also help . . . While men are splitting the pods the women and the children may also be removing the beans from the pods into some baskets. When this is over the real farmer plus his assistant put the beans on some plantain broad leaves and cover them too.[55]

From the same years there is also evidence of a hired-labour variation on reciprocal labour, which will be detailed later.

Finally, the range of forms of cocoa labour extended to at least one case of what might be called congregational labour. Certainly it was not *nnɔboa*, nor was it service to the chief. A Methodist catechist in Jacobu named Mensah made (or had made for him) five cocoa farms there from the 1900s to the 1910s and beyond. The bulk of the work on the last four of them was done voluntarily, and without pay, by Church members.[56] The evidence comes from oral testimony. I have found no evidence of this kind of rela-tionship in missionary records. There may well have been other cases, but it is reasonable to assume that it was rare in the cocoa economy as a whole.

D. The Origins of Wage Labour, to c.1916–18: Short-Term Contracts

Wage-labour emerged rapidly in colonial Asante, but it was only some years after the 1908 prohibition of slavery and pawning that regular contracts (for the whole of the main-crop season or for the whole year), as distinct from short-term, casual ones, appeared in farming.

Asantes offered their services to the European-owned gold mines early on. The 1904 annual report on the colony commented that 'The Ashantis having taken kindly to work at the mines, labour [for the mining companies] throughout the year—with the possible exception of the six or eight weeks of seed-time at the beginning of the rains—has been plentiful.'[57] In 1906 four 'young men' from Kokofu asked for employment at the Obuasi mine, which the District Commissioner duly arranged with the manager.[58] In the agricultural economy the evidence of wage contracts before the First World War relates to carrying dried cocoa beans to market. The same source indicates that the headloading of cocoa was the first occupation in the emerging cocoa economy to become dominated by northern labourers: seasonal migrants from the savanna. Already in 1910, for instance, the charges made by local porters for carrying cocoa from Bompata to Kumasi were being undercut by 'the Northern Territory carriers who came in increasing numbers each year, (and) carried three full loads for the rate laid down for two'.[59] The presence of Mossi cocoa carriers, whether seasonally resident or in transit, was noticed in the provincial commissioner's diary with reference to specific places in Adanse and Amansie in the 1910s.[60] By 1919 Bekwai had a sizeable community of Hausas and Mossis engaged in cocoa carrying.[61]

From Kyei's memoirs it appears that around Agogo labourers were hired to do much of the carrying of produce to market, but that they were not employed in farming. Certainly that was so with his father's cocoa-farming.[62] A similar picture emerged from my fieldwork in Amansie. In some places in the district, including Bekwai, hired labour was not used on farms, as distinct from in carrying, until after 'the Influenza' of 1918,[63] or indeed until the 1920s.[64] In the twin village of Ofoase-Kokoben it was not used during at least the first few years of cocoa farming.[65] In other villages it was used but only in a limited role, contracted to perform specific heavy tasks: land clearance[66] and, at Sanfo, also weeding.[67] Overall, there is no evidence of what we might call 'regular' (six-month, annual or sharecrop) hired labour in this precocious cocoa-farming district before at least 1918. Meanwhile the era of generally high produce prices that had characterized the launch of cocoa-farming in Asante ended in 1916. Whether there was a causal relationship between trends in produce prices and in farm labour contracts, and if so what it might be, will be considered in Chapter 19. Those employed in the early, casual, cocoa-farm labour force comprised both Asantes and northern migrants. At Huntado, Osei Kwami employed locals,[68] whereas at Sanfo the labourers were northerners. The latter pattern was to be multiplied many times in the years that followed, for casual and especially for regular contracts.

E. The Spread of Regular Wage Contracts, c.1916–19 to Early 1930s

It was thus after the early cocoa boom that regular wage-labour spread rapidly on farms. Its timing can be broadly determined by comparing employers' responses to the cocoa depressions of 1921 and 1930. In the former, farmers generally responded to the low cocoa prices by reducing labour inputs: suspending planting, allowing weeds to grow, and leaving pods unmarketed. Retrenchment, however, was confined to non-wage labour (notably their own) and casual wage-labour. The question of what to do about regular wage-workers did not arise. We have detailed reports, for Amansie district, from agricultural officers' tours made at this time. They do not mention such workers,[69] while a survey of production costs in the district referred to hired labour only in the context of thrice-yearly farm 'clearing', that is, weeding; which implied casual labour.[70] By the time of the next major price-fall this had changed. Farmers emerged from the 1930–31 main season having realised their lowest prices for at least six years.[71] Further, some had found their crops spoiled as a result of their having participated in the cocoa hold-up of that season, which was initially firm in Adanse and in Manso Nkwanta. A legacy of the season was a series of court suits by northern labourers claiming unpaid wages from farm-owners in South Asante.[72] For every northern worker who took his complaint to court, there were probably several who did not. This is especially likely because the court of first instance was the local chief's tribunal, which they might well have expected to be unsympathetic.[73] These complaints suggest that regular wage labour was now part of the cocoa-farm labour force. Thus it appears that this form of labour developed, in agriculture, from 1918 but especially between 1921 and 1930.

For Amansie the colonial records take us some way towards greater precision about the process. In 1923–24 three men (on separate occasions) identified themselves as cocoa labourers living in the villages of Bogyawe, Boni and Patase respectively.[74] However, they may have been cocoa carriers rather than farm-workers. Two labourers who were definitely employed on farms appear in the district commissioner's 'Complaints' file: Kofi Buachie, a stranger, though by his name not a northerner, was share-cropping in the Denyase village of Bisiase from 1925; while a local woman, Yaa Aduwa, accepted a year's farm-employment on the (unfulfilled) condition that the owner 'would pay my debt of seven pound[s] . . . and . . . present to me four pounds'.[75] Informants in Bekwai and in Asikaso stated that wage-labour began on cocoa-farms around their settlements respectively during and 'after' the influenza year of 1918. In Asikaso the workers were northerners, usually on annual contracts. In Esumeja, where daily wage-labour began in the 1920s, it was said that annual labourers arrived in the early 1930s.[76] To judge from the oral testimonies, Buachie and Aduwa were rather unusual among farm wage-labourers at the time in not being northerners,[77] in one of them being female,[78] and in one of them share-cropping. Overall, both archival and oral evidence give the impression that in Amansie employment of regular hired labour on cocoa farms was widespread by the early 1930s, and that most of the workers concerned were migrants from the savanna. To judge from the oral testimonies cited above, hired labourers had become almost synonymous with northerners.

It was not just in a relatively long-established cocoa-growing area like Amansie that wage labour proliferated during this period. I have already quoted the report of the 1928–29 survey in western Asante which stated that there was 'an increasing tendency' for cocoa-farmers to use hired rather than family labour. A particular example of this comes from rather later, in the mid-1940s. Rather than referring to local farmers, however, it concerns farmers from one of the older cocoa areas who reinvested some of the proceeds of their existing cocoa farms in the creation of new ones on the planting frontier in the west. Fortes was told that the Kwotei farmers who had made cocoa farms in Ahafo 'All employ labourers to work their farms.' Most of the farmers were said to have 'very big' farms there. 'The wealthiest of them, Abubreso, has a farm which yields 1,000 loads'.[79]

These Kwotei farmers had a noteworthy variation on *nnɔboa*. On their Ahafo cocoa farms 'the farmers cooperate in the sharing of labour. When harvesting time comes neighbours lend one another labourers to assist in the harvesting. Nothing is paid for this but there is reciprocal mutual aid'.[80] It is not clear whether the labourers concerned were on wage terms, or whether they were among the—by then—growing numbers of sharecroppers.

F. Transition to Sharecrop Labour, 1930s–1950s

In 1938 the Chief Inspector of Labour, J. R. Dickinson, produced a major report on hired labour. For Asante he first described the average pay and conditions of annual and seasonal labourers. He added that 'there is an interesting variation of this kind of agreement when the labourer or labourers, instead of a fixed wage, receive one third of the proceeds of the produce from the particular farm on which they have been working. This is the "Abusa" system.'[81] The evidence from detailed enquiries which I made at the level of a single district, Amansie, indicates that the 1930s did indeed see the start of a trend for long-term wage contracts to be replaced by a managerial form of sharecropping, whereby the worker operated the farm for a season, mostly receiving part (usually a third, *abusa*) of the crop. Oral testimonies date the appearance of *abusa* labour in specific Amansie towns and villages from 1930 to 1940.[82] Sharecropping also begins to appear regularly in the written sources for the district from the mid-1930s. There were two *abusa* labourers on a Huntado farm in 1934,[83] while sharecroppers from Gyaman were working on Kokofu lands in 1935.[84] The shift from wage to sharecrop terms appears to have accelerated over the next several years. In 1946 the official in charge of a government enquiry into farm labour in Asante as a whole reported that sharecropping 'is having a phenominal [*sic*] popularity in these days, and a tendency to eclipse all other forms of labour contract'.[85] Fifty-nine per cent of the 3,607 reported contracts for the 1946–47 season were for sharecropping.[86] In the same year the President of the Manso-Nkwanta-Abori Co-operative Society stated that 'We have no labourers under Annual Contract in the area at all. The boys working in our farms at present are all under the "Abusa" system.'[87]

The dominance of sharecropping lasted to the end of the colonial period. The 1956–57 family budgets survey provides data on labourers employed by cocoa farmers.[88] It shows that sharecroppers ('caretakers') were the category of hired labourer most used by all but the smallest farmers with bearing trees. Only farmers producing less than about 20 loads a year (roughly the output of a single hectare) employed sharecroppers less than they did another category of labourer. The latter category was 'temporary labourers'. Hence, farmers of all size-classes employed, on average, more sharecrop than regular-wage labour. Though the sample was stratified, the results relevant to the present discussion were weighted to reflect the actual size of the sample, yielding means for the sample as a whole.[89] The average for all cocoa-farmers in the sample of 1,620 families was 1.2 sharecroppers compared to 0.2 regular wage-workers ('permanent labourers').

Of the various possible sources of bias in the selection of the sample,[90] only one seems likely to have significantly affected this result. Whereas the 1,620 families in the household budget sample included only those with bearing cocoa trees (though including those who had non-bearing trees as well), in Asante sharecropping was used mainly on bearing farms (though by no means always, as will be seen in Chapter 19). The above-quoted president of Manso-Nkwanta-Abori Co-operative Society had commented that the work of *abusa* labourers 'comprises the weeding of the under shrubs in the farms, collecting the crops, drying the beans, and carrying same from the farm to the village.'[91] This association with mature farms is reflected in the English word which was used for *abusa* men by some Asantes and in the 1956–57 survey.[92] Conversely, 'caretaker' hardly seems the word to apply to someone making a new farm. For a specific example let us return to the two brothers from Ofoase-Kokoben whose vigorous cocoa-farming careers were outlined above. Kwaku Gyekyi and Kojo Bah's practice was to use wage labourers to supplement their own and their conjugal families' energies in making new cocoa farms; then hand them over to *abusa* caretakers when the trees started yielding.[93] While sharecroppers may have done some work on non-bearing farms, it is reasonable to assume that wage labour was much more important on such farms than it was, in mid-century, on bearing ones. Thus the ratio of sharecropping to regular wage contracts on Asante cocoa farms as a whole was presumably a bit less than the six to one found on bearing farms. But there is no obscuring the fact that sharecropping had become overwhelmingly the main institution of extra-familial labour.

Finally, the 1956–57 survey confirms what is also clear from the accumulation of other evidence from various sources that, nearly half a century after the prohibition of slavery, free hired labour in general was a mainstay of the Asante rural economy. Already in c.1945–46 the Ashanti Social Survey had conducted sample surveys in Ahafo and Sekyere districts. Fortes commented in an unpublished note:

> Figures from different areas [of Asante] show that approximately 30% of cocoa farms are worked by either caretakers or labourers. That is to say, approximately one farm in three is not worked by the farmer himself with or without the assistance of his family or labourers. Our figures suggest that hired labour is used in working at least 40% of cocoa farms in Ashanti, but I am of opinion that this is an underestimate.[94]

The 1956–57 survey, the first relatively comprehensive study, reported that the ratio of hired labourers (wage and sharecrop combined) to farmers was nearly two to one (the weighted average for the sample was 1.89).[95] Thus the often-quoted finding of a 1950 United Nations report, that five-sixths of labour in Gold Coast cocoa production came from family as opposed to hired labour, appears very wide of the mark: certainly in relation to Asante, which was then the largest cocoa-producing region.[96]

G. Colonial Policy on Free Labour

In 1912 the local provincial commissioner, Rew, wrote to the Adansehene to ask if he could supply a plantation owner with 'about 50 labourers to work on his rubber plantation'.[97] It would be misleading to describe this as forced labour: unlike perhaps in the Northern Territories,[98] in Asante chiefs did not necessarily regard commissioners' requests as implicit commands, and in any case the likes of the formidable Nana Adansehene Kobina Foli of Adanse were not reticent about arguing with the colonial government. Further, the proposed wage rate of 1/3d a day[99] was about the current market rate. But the commissioner's letter may be assumed to have strengthened the plantation owner's chance of securing labour, and of doing so through a single 'bulk order'. I have not managed to discover the outcome of this letter, but it can only be seen as supportive of European agricultural enterprise.

It was probably the European firms, in commerce as well as in mining, that the administration had in mind when it intervened to extend the rights of employers over the time of their employees. When the omanhene of Kokofu died in 1913 the provincial commissioner visited the town where he was 'assured' by the elders that 'the [funeral] custom should be no hindrance to trade and that no Kokofu should be ordered to Kokofu from the mines.'[100]

In the late 1930s a change of imperial labour policy was implemented with the formation of a Labour Department. In November 1937 unlicensed recruiters were banned from the Northern Territories.[101] This was followed by the promulgation of a Labour Code under which it was made compulsory for employers to register migrant labourers as either 'recruited' or 'contracted', and contracts had to be witnessed by a government official.[102] Though this applied to African employers as well as European, the Department focussed its activities on the large-scale European employers, public and private. This was perhaps all that its staff numbers equipped it to supervise, and it was also potentially the most politically sensitive area of labour relations. Even at the end of the colonial period an academic observer could write of Ghana as a whole that 'the labour problem in cocoa farming . . . seems to be regarded, at present, as rather outside the field of industrial relations'.[103]

H. Conclusion

The fundamental change in the labour market during the period was the rise of free labour. The combination of declining legal opportunities for labour coercion and the expansion of producers' purchasing-power through cocoa cultivation drove the emergence and proliferation of hired labour. By the end of colonial rule farmowners were outnumbered nearly two to one by their regular hired labourers. The hiring of labour supplemented rather than replaced the use of self and family labour. Indeed, it is by no means clear that, in absolute terms, the overall volume of family labour inputs in agriculture contracted during the period. The nineteenth-century division of tasks between males and females continued to be the basic feature of the organisation of family labour: males directing most of their efforts towards extra-subsistence activities while women gave priority to food-growing, cooking and child-rearing. Again as before, the conjugal unit was much more frequently the source of labour services than the matrilineage: though there are some indications that, compared to sons, sister's sons were less likely than before to provide such inputs. The reciprocal labour institution, *nnɔboa*, was an important means of convening labour in peak times, perhaps especially for the smaller farmers who could not afford much hired labour. Some of the hired labour services were provided by Asantes. This was primarily in short-term casual or contract jobs; though, especially as land for new farms became scarce towards the end of the period, some local youths accepted regular contracts working for existing farmowners. The vast majority of the regular labourers were migrants from the northern savanna: broadly, from the areas from which captives had been imported in the past. The meanings of 'free labour' will be further explored in Chapter 19, particularly in relation to perhaps the major surprise of this period: the fact that the spread of annual wage contracts succumbed, from the mid-1930s, to what became an overwhelming trend towards sharecropping as the standard form of regular (season- or year-long) labour contract.

Finally, the state increasingly sought to regulate the labour market, especially in that the colonial administration sought to ensure that northern migrants received their wages. In this respect it may have contributed a bit towards the gradually strengthening bargaining position of northern labour in the Asante market, which we will discuss in Chapter 19.

PART VI

Freedom and Forest Rent, 1908–1956

This part seeks to explain the trends and patterns identified in Part Five and to explore their implications. The basic process in the making of a cocoa-based economy was the application of labour to land to create fixed capital. The organization of each of the next two chapters, on land and capital, follows the stages of the tree-farm cycle: from establishment, through maturity, to the consequences of the longevity of cocoa trees. In doing so, we examine the emergence of a recognisably contemporary 'less-developed' economy, and reflect on the problems involved for participants and observers. These include the long-running controversy over colonial 'failure' to introduce compulsory land titling, and the beginnings of a historic transition towards land scarcity: the latter creating possible opportunities for the capture of economic rents by those who control access to land, and the problem of finding rules to reconcile the interests of living individuals with those of society as a whole and of future generations. On the perennial controversy over agricultural indebtedness we inquire into the competitiveness of credit markets, and the social implications of the specific institutions involved. In this matrilineal society, we examine the dynamics of female cocoa-farming, and consider the legal and social struggles over the rights of divorced and widowed women, and their children, to shares in their husbands' cocoa farms. The shifts in property rights and factor markets had profound consequences for the ways in which chiefs sought to maintain their economic position within Asante society. This is treated in the context of the chapter on land, because the basic move was from rights in labour to rights in land as the economic base of chieftaincy.

In what was still a labour-scarce economy, the changes in labour relations are arguably the most important. Chapter 19 examines the basic but neglected question of why the ending of slave and pawn labour was followed not by a shrinkage of extra-subsistence production as coerced sources of extra-familial labour dried up, but rather by the development of free wage labour, including annual contracts. The chapter goes on to try to explain arguably the most remarkable trend of the period: the displacement of regular wage contracts on cocoa farms by sharecropping.

17

LAND IN A TREE-FARM ECONOMY

Section A reflects on access to land for cocoa: why permission to plant it was generally granted easily and cheaply; why—in contrast—the extension of cocoa cultivation was banned c.1939–46; and how far the rules on access, and their effects and their changes, can be understood in the framework of the rational-choice theory of the evolution of land tenure. Section B analyses the institution of rent charged on bearing cocoa farms. Section C examines the colonial policy debate, and the continuing scholarly argument, over the economic case for the establishment of more sharply defined individual rights in land. In this context, Section D asks whether the property rights regime evolved so as to create incentives for the sustainable use of the forest environment, or whether the progressive depletion of the Asante forest rent continued throughout the period without effective institutional restraints. Section E discusses the implications of the changes in social relations of production for the respective economic positions of commoners and chiefs.

A. Establishment of New Cocoa Farms: Access to Land for New Planting

There is much that needs explanation about the rules on access to land for planting cocoa during the colonial period. For most of it, as we saw in Chapter 14, access was almost automatic and was virtually free. Subjects of the land-owning chieftaincy paid no rent, while non-subjects ('strangers') seem to have found it easy to obtain permission to plant from the host chief, in return for which—at least until the last years of the period, as we will see, in Ahafo—they made only token payments until the trees came into bearing. Yet, paradoxically, there was a six-year period during which the creation or extension of cocoa farms was forbidden by the Ashanti Confederacy Council of Chiefs. Also requiring explanation is the striking contrast between the terms on which chiefs accepted stranger farmers in Asante (lease) compared to the scene of the original Ghanaian cocoa 'take-off', Akyem Abuakwa (sale). The main aims of this section are to explain these phenomena and to explore their implications, notably how far the land tenure regime facilitated or impeded the 'socially'-efficient allocation of land during this era of transformation in land use. All this was premised on the failure of European planters, and the consequent preservation of indigenous ownership of Asante lands.

There was some inconsistency between the public statement by Acting Chief Commissioner Davidson-Houston in 1904, advocating the encouragement of Asante agriculture and the prohibition of land alienation to non-Asantes, and the colonial government's acceptance of long-term alienation of land to Europeans under the concessions system.[1] The clash may be seen, at one level, as a conflict between political and economic considerations. Given the administration's concern about the political risks of land alienation to foreigners, the fact that it was willing to grant long-term leases and other help to European entrepreneurs, not only for commercial premises but also for mining and even plantations, can be attributed most plausibly to economic motives. Government revenue, and employment and income for Asantes, would benefit from European investment. European planters might act as exemplars of best practice, most obviously in planting rubber trees rather than simply tapping wild ones, as Asante rubber producers were doing. While there were only a handful of plantations the political risk was low, and indeed chiefs were pleased to have the rents. It must be said, however, that had European entrepreneurs been more successful, the general economic and revenue case for letting them continue to acquire land would have become stronger, while any attempt by the government to prevent this would have faced political opposition from within Britain. As yet the scale of such alienations was relatively small, and British officials—certainly most of those on the spot—hoped that Asante would be an economically viable part of the empire without large-scale alienation of land to foreigners. But their policies left open the possibility that the future would be dominated by mineowners and planters.

Thus, the Asante case supports a general proposition that revisionist writers have put forward about 'peasant' colonies: that the 'West African

Lands Policy' was not imposed at the start, but emerged through interaction between the parties involved.[2] The European plantations struggled for profitability,[3] while European gold mining became established only at Obuasi and, later and on a comparatively small scale, at Konongo. It was this relative commercial failure by European enterprise that left the field dominated by the proliferation of African—mostly Asante—owned cocoa farms. That Asante lands remained overwhelmingly in Asante ownership was not the result of a prior commitment of British policy. Rather, it was the outcome of economic competition which resolved the conflict between political and economic imperatives in colonial policy.

In trying to explain why access to land was so easy and cheap, both during the 'take-off' in the early colonial period and during the second planting boom of the 1950s, it is important to remember that the rules which permitted this were inherited from the nineteenth century, from the pre-colonial kingdom. But that is hardly a sufficient explanation, as these rules could have been changed. Indeed, the Council's prohibition did so, or at least had the legal effect of cancelling the generosity of the older rules. So let us focus on the exception that changed the rules: why was cocoa-planting banned, to what effect, and why did the ban not last?

In February 1919, shortly before land clearance would begin in preparation for the new planting season, Adansehene Kobina Foli informed the colonial administration that he had banned the making of new cocoa farms in Adanse. He explained that this was 'Because the cocoa farmers has maken the cocoa farm in all land. . . . our children can't get field to make farms for food to support theirself the time will come [*sic*]'.[4] The provincial commissioner expressed sympathy with the chief's aims but vetoed his threat to punish offenders.[5]

The fact that it was the *oman* of Adanse which took unilateral action is surprising in the sense that the Adanse had a long history of being exceptionally political decentralized, compared to the major provincial *aman* of Asante such as Mampon, Dwaben and Bekwai. The Adansehene's paramount authority was resented by some of the chieftaincies under him, notably Akrokerri. In this context it is highly likely that the omanhene's rule would have been defied by some of the sub-chiefs had it not been vetoed from above. It may be that this defiance of the logic of collective inaction is attributable to the individual character and calculations of the redoubtable Nana Adansehene Kobina Foli.[6] The fact that other *amanhene* did not do what he did in 1919, however, makes situational sense. To prohibit new cocoa plantings was a self-denying ordinance for any chieftaincy, since it meant foregoing future revenue from the cocoa 'tribute' paid by strangers, and from the levies paid by citizens. This, in turn, could imperil the chances for the stool and its subjects in future legal disputes, notably over land. Moreover, planting by the stool's own subjects might consolidate its claim to own disputed land. Thus there were very strong motives for individual *aman* to leave farmers free to plant cocoa. In this context it may be significant that the next action, and the first Asante-wide one, to curtail the spread of cocoa trees waited until after the establishment of the Ashanti Confederacy Council in 1935. The restoration of an indigenous central authority reduced the organizational obstacles to state action to curtail the spread of cocoa trees.

On 14 March 1938 the Ashanti Confederacy Council made an order prohibiting the creation of new cocoa farms.[7] The director of agriculture commented that 'the initiative has come spontaneously from the chiefs themselves.'[8] In view of the centrality of cocoa to the livelihood of both individuals and chieftaincies it may seem remarkable that such a drastic measure could be passed and implemented without major organized opposition and massive defiance on the ground. Resistance was surely muted by the context in which the council met: the great 1937–38 cocoa hold-up was still in progress, with farmers refusing to sell cocoa to European firms. It would have been further quietened by the context in which, as it turned out, the ban operated for most of its existence: the Second World War, during which the government gave itself a statutory export monopoly over cocoa, and real producer prices were the lowest they had been since cocoa was introduced into Asante. Thus the incentive to plant was reduced by a combination of low current prices and uncertainty about the future of both the price and the organization of cocoa marketing. Further, farmers' capacity to invest was limited by their relatively low current incomes.

But the evidence is that the ban both made some difference to the level of planting, and also encountered some defiance. The chiefs themselves seem to have been readier to pass a collective decision than to enforce it on their own particular subjects. To give their wish legal effect, the Confederacy Council had resolved that each Native Authority (*omanhene* and elders) should issue an order with effect from 1 January 1939.[9] Some did so, but not all. In one of the most heavily-planted districts, Amansie, it was 22 September before the Omanhene of Bekwai did likewise.[10] The annual report on soil erosion for 1939 proclaimed that the rules 'have in general been operated with success and have resulted in a real curtailment of this pratice' (of 'cutting down of forest for planting new cocoa farms').[11] In 1940 the chief commissioner asked district commissioners to report on the effectiveness of the ban. The acting district commissioner for Bekwai was echoed by most of his colleagues when he replied that the prohibition:

1. has undoubtedly resulted in a real curtailment of the practice of cutting down forest for planting new Cocoa farms in this district.
2. It is probable that no new Cocoa farms have been made since the beginning of last year, although the destruction of forest for food farms of course continues.[12]

Essentially the same was said even for the more rapidly-expanding newer cocoa areas further west. From Goaso the assistant district commissioner wrote:

> I have the honour to report that the Ashanti Confederacy Council's decision is being obeyed in Ahafo. Only a general statement can be made, but it would seem that cocoa farmers pay great attention to the Council's decisions and, if there is evasion, it is on a very small scale.[13]

In March 1946 the Ashanti Confederacy Council softened its policy. Under the Cocoa (Control of Planting) Order, 1946, new cocoa farms were allowed provided that the farmers first obtained permits 'issued by the Confederacy Council on the advice of the Department of Agriculture'. People 'owning or operating' more than fifty acres were not eligible to apply, and no-one granted a permit was to plant more than ten acres. The stipulated penalties for illegal planting were the uprooting of trees at the farmer's expense, and a fine of £5 or, in default, two months imprisonment.[14] On the other hand, effectively there were to be no further prosecutions of offenders against the 1938 prohibition.[15]

Pressure for further relaxation did not come only from farmers in the more densely-cultivated districts. A letter from a school teacher requested a permit 'to carry on with the making' of cocoa farms in his home village, Noberko, in the Goaso area: 'as I have not a single cocoa farm that may support me in my old age, I realise that life would be miserable in the near future if I abuse the present chance and look down upon such a glorious and interesting work of the country.'[16] An indication of the scale of the pent-up demand for new farms in western Asante came in a request by the Dormaahene: 'As the time for the cultivation of forests is getting due, I wish to have 500 copies of the Permits for the planting of new cocoa trees in my areas.'[17]

In assessing the practical impact of the Confederacy Council's ban on the extension of the area under cocoa we need an idea of the extent of the planting that is likely to have taken place in the absence of the ban. It is clear from the statistics that the volume of planting was fairly closely related to the real price of cocoa.[18] Merrill Bateman has compiled estimates of the real producer price and the cost of planting in Ghanaian cocoa farming from 1900 onwards. According to his figures, during the six planting seasons when the ban was officially in force throughout Asante, 1940–45 (crop years 1939–40 to 1944–45), there was actually a net disincentive to plant cocoa: the cost of planting exceeded the real price of cocoa in terms of its import-purchasing power. Indeed, according to these estimates the crop season in which the ban was partially lifted was the one before it became profitable again—on current prices—to plant cocoa.[19]

A rough estimate of the amount of planting in one year may be obtained from the growth in sales several years later, to allow for the maturation of trees. From Table 17.1 we see that annual sales for the above-mentioned six crop years during which the ban on planting was law across Asante averaged 82,500 tonnes. For the next six years (1945–46 to 1950–51), during which productive capacity would have been raised progressively as any trees planted in spite of the ban began to bear, the average was 109,200 tonnes. For the following six years, during which output would have been further boosted by the growing maturity of any trees planted during the ban, the annual mean was nearly 115,600 tonnes. It should be noted that wartime sales may have been held down by farmers deciding not to market (or to complete the production—including harvesting and fermentation—of) all the beans that matured on their trees; so low were the producer prices. After all, there is no reason to think that productive capacity fell between the mid-1930s and the war years, yet average annual output for the six crop years before the ban was applied everywhere had averaged 87,200 tonnes. But, even allowing for some planting during the 1930s, the figures clearly imply that there must have been further planting during the war: otherwise it would be almost impossible to account for the scale of the post-war growth in marketed output.

Clearly, farmers in what became the separate regions of Ashanti and Brong-Ahafo, and especially in the latter, did not act on the net disincentive to planting that Bateman's figures describe. It is possible that Bateman's price figures underestimated the net incentive to these farmers, perhaps because he relied on the Accra retail price index in calculating the real value of the producer price of cocoa. Yet, as noted in Chapter 3, it is probable that the retail prices facing Asante farmers followed similar trends.

Table 17.1. Cocoa sales and incentives to producers in Asante, 1933–57

Year	Real producer price £/ton	Planting costs £/ton	Price incentive	Ashanti sales	Brong-Ahafo sales
1933–4	50.5	67.0	−16.5	71	
1934–5	62.5	68.0	−5.5	86	
1935–6	68.3	68.0	0.3	91	
1936–7	143.4	69.0	50.0	91	
1937–8	72.2	69.0	3.2	75	
1938–9	61.9	70.0	−8.1	101.1	
1939–40	57.2	70.0	−12.8	73.8	
1940–41	41.3	71.0	−29.7	82.3	
1941–2	44.6	72.0	−27.4	89.6	
1942–3	37.1	73.0	−35.9	72	
1943–4	37.1	74.0	−36.9	78.2	
1944–5	57.3	75.0	−17.7	91.3	
1945–6	65.1	76.0	−10.9	94.9	
1946–7	115.3	77.0	38.3	79.6	
1947–8	156.6	78.0	50.0	69.9	36.1
1948–9	273.4	79.0	50.0	81.9	44.0
1949–50	140.2	80.0	50.0	73.1	42.9
1950–51	186.7	81.0	50.0	77.7	45.0
1951–2	217.5	82.0	50.0	60.5	37.2
1952–3	191.6	83.0	50	77.7	40.6
1953–4	197.4	84.0	50	60	42.5
1954–5	184.2	85.0	50	69.1	43.0
1955–6	203.7	86.0	50	67.8	51.3
1956–7	87.0	87.0	50.0	78	54.9

Units: Sales are in tons. Brong-Ahafo sales are includes in 'Ashanti' sales until 1947–8. Real producer price and planting costs (both estimated) are in £ per ton, as is price incentive. The latter variable is the difference between the first two, except that Bateman treats it as having a maximum value of £50, since his 'analysis indicated that this . . . is the level at which farmer's resources are exhausted',[1] meaning, presumably, that this incentive was sufficient to induce the farmer to devote invest all available resources in planting. The planting costs series is highly stylized: see comment in text. The price, planting costs and price incentive figures are for Ghana generally.

[1] Ibid., 319.

Source: Merrill J. Bateman, 'An econometric analysis of Ghanaian cocoa supply', in R. A. Kotey, C. Okali and B. E. Rourke, eds, *Economics of Cocoa Production and Marketing* (Institute of Statistical, Social and Economic Research, University of Ghana, Legon, 1974), Tables A1 and A2.

A greater weakness with Bateman's incentive calculations is that the 'cost of planting' series is not based on direct measurement[20] and is therefore unlikely to have any close relationship to the situation on the cocoa frontier. Above all, farmers' previous experience would have told them that current prices were hardly a reliable guide to future ones, and they may well have realised that some sort of recovery was likely after the war. The crucial point is that the Council's ban was defied on a fairly large scale, even when the financial incentive to do so—though presumably still positive—can only have been modest. Even if the district commissioners were correct that the prohibition stopped the creation of new farms in 1939 and 1940, it did not do so for long.

The story of the chiefs' proscribing cocoa planting out of concern for its medium and long-term opportunity costs helps us understand why such bans were, over the colonial period as a whole, unusual and unsustained. Even if it had been in the collective interest to stop the extension of the area under cocoa there was a double free-riding problem to be solved. For both at the level of individual farmers and of many individual chieftaincies there were still private gains to be made from adding more cocoa trees. For all the chiefs to adopt the ban therefore required a political feat. But it was only temporary and had little apparent effect on the volume of planting during the years concerned. Thus free-riding by individual farmers appears to have been little checked. In retrospect, the perception which motivated the bans may seem overly pessimistic. Even after 1946 the expansion of the cocoa acreage does not appear to have compromised the basic food security of Asante residents, though it impelled a partial shift from a favourite starch staple, plantain, to a less favoured one, cassava. Indeed, the second great planting boom in Asante's cocoa history solved any short-term shortage of plantain and other foodcrops that could serve also as shade crops.[21]

In general it is not difficult to provide an economic explanation for the continuation of the liberal practices on access to land which had been inherited from the nineteenth century. As we have seen, land was relatively abundant during the cocoa take-off and this remained the case beyond the colonial period. To put it another way, in terms of land use the opportunity cost of creating cocoa farms was very low, except perhaps for the production of food once the expansion of cocoa cultivation had itself slowed. Fortes and his colleagues conducted a survey, presumably in c.1946, of the means by which cocoa farms had been acquired.[22] They sampled 231 cocoa farms in the Sekyere district (Asokore, Efiduase and Akyinakrom) and 151 in Ahafo. As might be expected from its reputation as a land-surplus area attracting migrants from older cocoa-farming districts, over three-quarters (76.8 per cent) of the Ahafo farms had been made by their owners. What is striking is that the 'self-made' proportion was almost as high (at 71.4 per cent) in Sekyere. For this was an older cocoa area, closer to Kumasi and, not least, one situated on the northern fringe of the forest zone, so with easily exhaustible supplies of suitable land.

Only relatively late in the period, and relatively mildly as yet, did there begin to emerge signs of actual or incipient economic pressure, a logic of scarcity, which might in the longer term motivate changes to a more restrictive land tenure system. We have seen that by the mid-1940s in an old cocoa-growing area most young men now had to wait for their fathers or uncles to give or leave them a cocoa farm before they could acquire one: the local supplies of suitable land were already in use.[23] According to Amoafo in 1961, 'today, forest land appears to be relatively scarce' in Ashanti Region, though in 'relatively fair supply' in Brong-Ahafo. In the former 'The original practice whereby a farmer established his right to a holding by clearing a virgin land no more exists.'[24] For would-be planters in the older cocoa areas the solution was migration. As we have seen, it was resorted to on a large scale when the cocoa price climbed in the 1950s. Even on the moving cocoa frontier, however, signs of pressure emerged. From a survey of six Ahafo villages from c.1956 to c.1958,[25] Bray found that both farmers and landowning chiefs were acting to anticipate an eventual shortage of land.

> In present conditions of approaching land scarcity consequent upon the competition for land on the part of immigrant farmers, the citizen has evolved methods of acquiring land which have changed the pattern of land settlement in the area. Instead of beginning his clearing operations near the clearing of other farmers, the ambitious citizen will go off into the wilderness and make his farm there. By doing so he is free to advance in all directions.[26]

Telling the same story in 1965 for Nkrankwanta, a village in the Dormaa area which had seen much cocoa planting after 1945, George Benneh wrote that 'In certain cases people even clear plots of land which they do not intend to cultivate during the current farming season with the sole aim of staking their claims over them'.[27] Though the sentence is in the present tense, the context does not suggest that this was solely a post-independence phenomenon. It may possibly explain an institutional innovation reported in 1961. 'In certain parts of Ashanti, featuring Offinso State, a system has emerged which seeks to allocate land of a definite size to individuals. This would reduce tendencies towards inequalities in the distribution of land and speculation'.[28]

Again, Bray wrote in 1958–59 that 'at present, owing to the scramble for land' some farmers were resorting to the 'not popular' method of clearing land only very partially in order to claim larger areas than they would otherwise have time to do.[29] Thus the land-extensive approach to cocoa farming was here given a further push. As usual in Asante (and West African) history it was an efficient response to the prevailing set of relative factor scarcities, but in this case it was an institutional tactic (to secure a resource) as well as a technical one. Meanwhile:

> Farmers have also evolved short cut methods of acquiring a title to [the use of] a particular piece of land. Farmers may agree to divide up an area of land by cutting and clearing a swath around the boundary of the area they wish to farm and the title to farm would lapse should the farmer not justify or perhaps reassert his claim by further operations there within two or three seasons. Alternatively, farmers who do not have the funds to bring farms into planted cocoa as quickly as they wished may clear an area of undergrowth. Even though they do not plant a crop thereafter they acquire by this means an indefinite title to the area so cleared.[30]

The Ahafo chiefs also responded to the situation. Some stool land was 'kept intact from farming operations in order to satisfy future claims of those who may be away from the tribe'.[31] More dramatically, stranger-farmers could no longer obtain land for merely symbolic payment. They had to pay 'substantial sums' or a share of the cocoa trees. 'In these villages of West A   .⹀i', wrote Bray, to obtain 'a permanent right of usufruct over the land' ...e stranger farmer had to give the local stool one third of 'the developed farm' or pay 'substantial sums'.[32] This can be seen as taking further the transition from the 'penny' rate (back) to the share system that was happening widely in Asante.[33] This shift fits well the theory of induced institutional innovation. When land scarcity approached, people changed their behaviour within the existing rules in order to secure their land rights, whether as farmers on behalf of themselves and their heirs or as chiefs on behalf of absent subjects. They also changed the rules (or possibly invoked previously unenforced ones, as may have been the case with the division of stranger farms) to ensure that the chieftaincy captured a substantial share of the gains from bringing the land into cultivation. Further, this ensured that the private cost to strangers of acquiring land roughly reflected the opportunity cost to the local community.

We have seen that throughout the period, with small exceptions in Adanse, land in Asante was made available to 'strangers' for cocoa farming only on lease and usufruct terms rather than by sale of the land itself. The question is why was this so, considering that in the Gold Coast Colony cocoa cultivation had been pioneered by stranger-farmers buying land from Akan chiefs and elders, in Akyem Abuakwa. The movement of farmers to clear and plant away from their home areas was a major dynamic of the expansion of cocoa cultivation in Asante, as further south. Admittedly, most of the 'stranger' farmers were fellow Asante, but if that had made a difference, one would expect that it would have facilitated outright sale rather than excluded it. It has been suggested that the difference reflected learning from experience,[34] but the chronology does not fit. For the contrast between sales in Akyem and leases in Asante was present long before the cocoa migration in Akyem was over.

A more persuasive approach to the issue is that offered by George Benneh. Drawing comparisons across the Ghanaian cocoa belt, he argues that when a community provided land for migrants (strangers), whether they did so on lease or sale terms was determined by the extent to which the paramount chief was able to assert control over his sub-chiefs, preventing them from selling land for local profit, as the sub-chiefs had done in Akyem Abuakwa.[35] To put it in 'new institutionalist' language: where central authority within an *oman* was powerful, it overrode the free-riding temptations to which sub-chiefs were subject. Relating this hypothesis to the Asante experience, it can account for the fact that Adanse was the exception to the Asante rule: because of the historic weakness of the Adanse stool in relation to what it (and the colonial government) considered to be its 'sub'-chieftaincies. On the similar exceptionalism of the Omanhene of Obogu and his sub-chief the Bansohene, Benneh's approach might prompt the plausible speculation that their 'free-riding' behaviour was facilitated by the constitutional circumstances of the early colonial period: specifically, the combination of the British elevation of the Obogu stool to the status of paramountcy and the absence of a central chiefly authority until the restoration of the Asantehene in 1935. Obogu was by no means unique in this respect, but the other newly-created *amanhene* did not have land on the border with the Gold Coast Colony. By the time Akwapim migration might have affected them, the general policy against such sales had been reinforced. Once the office of Asantehene was restored in 1935, Benneh's hypothesis would predict leases rather than sales in Asante: which is exactly what happened. If the hypothesis has a weakness, it is for the early colonial period, in which the authority of Kumasi over the provinces was officially non-existent and in practice relatively weak. Yet the strength of the Asante state was far from extinguished by the exile of its head. The same centripetal tendencies that led to the restoration of the Asantehene may help to explain why almost all the provincial chiefs resisted sale of land to non-subjects.

For completeness it should be noted that the case of Banka, another exception to the Asante resistance to land sales, is equally explicable by more than one hypothesis. Though the town is said to have originated as an Asante (specifically, Kokofu) settlement,[36] by 1935 it was considered by the colonial government to have such strong informal links with Akyem Abuakwa that it was not consulted about whether the Ashanti Confederacy should be 'restored', nor indeed was it included in the restored confederacy. In the words of a post-colonial government memorandum, it was 'within Ashanti for geographical reasons only'.[37] The liberal position which its chiefs adopted on land sales could be plausibly attributed to political distance from Kumasi, in line with Benneh's explanation; and/or to cultural similarity with Akyem Abuakwa where so many land sales to outsiders had occurred.

Can we conclude that, in the terms of the evolutionary theory of land tenure, the rules of access to land for planting facilitated the socially-efficient use of resources over the period? Additionally or alternatively, can it be said that any changes in the rules were induced correctives to the emergence of discrepancies between relative factor scarcities and the existing institutions? Certainly the long-established rules on access to land for planting facilitated the widespread adoption of a crop whose opportunity cost, at least over the timescale of the colonial period, was demonstrably outweighed by the increase in income that it brought most of the population. This inherited tenure system facilitated socially-widespread access to land, though to take advantage of it required at least some prior assets of labour and capital. That access to land was made expensive for strangers participating in the 'scramble for land' with which the period closed in Ahafo can indeed be seen as an induced response to the fact that forest land was beginning to acquire scarcity value. Finally, the chiefs' attempts to stop the extension of cocoa cultivation, though rather ineffective and largely premature with respect to the food-security concern that inspired them, raise the question of the long-term implications of cocoa farming: to which we will return later in this chapter.

B. Bearing Farms: Cocoa 'Tribute'

In seeking to explain the existence, form and variations of cocoa 'tribute' (rent), it is useful to consider how effectively this can be done in 'new institutionalist' terms. The right of stools to demand from strangers a share of any wealth made from the natural resources owned by the stool was, as we have seen, well established in the nineteenth century. It was entirely predictable, from a rational-choice perspective, that this right should be exercised in relation to cocoa trees. They occupied stool land, depleted its natural fertility, and in doing so made money for the farmers. Strangers were, by their situation, politically vulnerable to such fiscal demands. With a tree crop they were trapped by the rental character of cocoa output: once the tree was there, it would be wasteful to abandon it because it would keep on bearing even if the cultivators left. The fact that trees did not run away and could not be concealed (providing the chief's bailiff was prepared to walk far enough) meant that in principle cocoa tribute was cheap to collect.

That the colonial government, and later the Ashanti Confederacy Council of Chiefs, should endeavour repeatedly to reduce the rate of 'tribute', temporarily or permanently, is less predictable in terms of the theory. By definition, these steps reduced stool revenues: which was not only bad for the chiefs themselves but likely to make them less effective instruments of colonial 'indirect rule'. On the other hand, the reductions took place during years of falling or still relatively low cocoa prices, when it was difficult and expensive to enforce payment. It could be argued that in such circumstances reductions were necessary in order to maintain the confidence of farmers in the cash crop. Because 'tribute' was in force throughout the period, litigation and local politics permitting, its application was no retrospective extortion by the landowning chiefs. Rather, the fact of the rent was a predictable cost (except for those who had planted on the mistaken assumption that the particular land they used belonged to the stool they themselves served). But the fluctuations in the world price were very hard to predict, and, as we saw in Chapter 14, the result in some years was that the rent became very burdensome on producers. In this context it may have been enlightened (long-term) self-interest on the part of the state, both indigenous and colonial, to try to ensure that the stranger-farmers continued to cultivate.

The proposal of a one penny per bearing tree rent which Fuller accepted was put forward by Griffith in August 1913 on the grounds that it was low enough not to cause 'injury to the industry' and that the fact that the rate was fixed would encourage farmers to increase their output per tree. He may perhaps have been influenced by T. E. Fell, the provincial commissioner of western Asante, who earlier that year had ruled that stranger-farmers should be charged rent on the land they leased rather than on the 'the amount of cocoa produced from their farms'. In itself Fell's initiative had no practical effect because the chief commissioner reminded him gently that government policy was precisely that 'tribute' should be paid by strangers (in Fell's phrase) on 'the cocoa which they themselves have grown'.[38] In retrospect both the notions of charging by tree and by area appear irrelevant to raising total factor productivity given the abundance of land and the weed-reduction argument for close spacing of trees. It is worth noting that sixty years later the CPP government legislated to fix the rent (this term now replaced 'tribute') paid by stranger-farmers, at five shillings per acre. It could be argued (though it was still debatable) that by then the diminution of the land surplus and the availability of insecticide sprays (favoured by wider spacing) had made charging by area 'socially efficient'.[39]

Griffith also thought that 'The smallness of the Rent and the prominence of the penny as a coin might also, in the long run, tend, [*sic*] to reduce prices and to promote thrift . . .'[40] In short, he wanted reform to stimulate higher output, productivity and savings. Again, as we have seen in passing, Harper in 1920 believed that an extension of rent to long-established settlers would have been damaging to the cocoa industry.

For the colonial administrators of Asante, though, the pragmatic economic case for ensuring incentives to producers sufficient to maintain the growth of prosperity in the society and of customs revenue to the government was supplemented by an individualistic sense of economic morality, or at least a moral contention in favour of producers against what would now be called, in a generic as well as a specific sense, rent-seekers. When Fell made his short-lived ruling he wrote to a chief that 'Men have to work hard to make a cocoa farm and it is not right that they should be taxed by the payment of tribute for the cocoa which they themselves have grown. In this way cocoa is different from rubber which grows wild in the Forest. . . .'[41] Indeed, the one-third rate imposed on rubber in the late nineteenth century was continued during the colonial era, notably during the Second World War when there was a mini-boom in response to exceptional demand for West African supplies of this strategic commodity after Japan occupied Malaya.[42] In 1921 Harper pronounced that 'Cocoa is the foundation of the peace and prosperity of Ashanti'.[43] Taking this together with his decision and commentary of the previous year against the imposition of tribute on 'strangers' who had been resident for several generations[44] we may conclude that, like his predecessor Davidson-Houston, Harper believed that prosperity would only be translated into political stability if the mass of the population continued to have effective rights of access to land.

Harper's decision may have helped ensure that what Stefano Boni, in an incisive study of the western Akan district of Sefwi, has called 'the emergence of the permanent stranger'[45] tended to happen also in Asante. We saw in Chapter 5 that previously in Asante (as in Sefwi), late-coming groups would be offered land virtually free and would be accepted as members of the community, providing they did not challenge the claims of the original landholders to sovereignty over lands and stool. The colonial government's insistence that chiefs could not impose cocoa rent on their own subjects created a fiscal incentive for chiefs to close the door to assimilation; even before land became scarce and the question of competition between subjects and strangers might arise. Yet, though it is hard to find specific examples, assimilation did not die out following the adoption of cocoa-farming, to judge from a minute by Asantehene Osei Prempeh II in 1946: 'Some stools treat strangers farming on their lands as citizens, and make them enjoy the same privileges as the Stool subjects enjoy and share equally with the Stool subjects any debt incurred by the Stool on whose land they farm.'[46]

Cocoa rent could be seen as a means of arranging that the gains from the use of what might be seen as a common resource (stool lands) were not monopolized by a private interest, the farmer, but were shared with the host community (or at least, its political authority). In this sense, the fact that the colonial government forbade chiefs from levying cocoa rent on their own subjects could be regarded as wasteful. Again, the fact that the rate was fixed, whether relatively or absolutely, meant that it did not adjust automatically or precisely to fluctuations in the cocoa price and therefore in the opportunity cost of the farmer's use of the land. But it could be argued that the produce price changed so continuously that it was in the farmers' interest to be facing a stable rent demand: providing it was not fixed at too high an absolute level. We have seen that chiefs and commissioners did respond to sustained price falls by lowering the rate. Conversely, the fact that in the 1950s, real producer prices having bounded upwards, chiefs generally restored share-rates—especially the old, pre-Fuller, one-third rate—could be seen as a relatively efficient response to the growing value of use rights over land suitable for cocoa. In this respect, and generally for this section, 'New Institutionalism' raises pertinent questions and accounts for much of the evidence.

C. Cocoa Trees and the Political Demand for Individual Title to Land: Internalizing the Externalities?

Periodically the colonial administration faced the argument that the long-term success of cocoa farming required the creation of individual ownership of land. Already in 1912 the authors of the Belfield Report observed that cocoa was making rapid 'headway' in Asante,

> and the necessity for creating a form of land tenure in the nature of individual ownership is therefore becoming apparent. At present a member of the tribe may occupy and plant the tribal land free of charge, and subject only to the liability to deliver a portion of his produce to the chief . . . but he holds no title to the land, and appears to have no power to dispose of it in his lifetime, neither can he ensure continued possession by his family after his death. If the people are really going to take seriously to planting enterprise, they will have to admit into their system of land tenure an exclusive right to land, which has only been recognised up to the present time in the case of concessions to Europeans.[47]

Belfield seems to have missed the Asante distinction between ownership of the land and ownership of farms on it. It was to be clear to Fuller in 1913, if not earlier, that cocoa farms could be and were being sold.[48] In a 1918 dispatch Fuller, nevertheless, favoured a strengthening of individual ownership, 'for toil, enterprise, energy and forethought will otherwise pass by unrecompensed'. But he was vague about what he wanted— 'modified individual possession'—and saw it as a matter for the future.[49] Meanwhile the expansion of cocoa cultivation proceeded, as was recognised in the West African Lands Committee's draft report of 1916. For West Africa generally the committee observed that it was 'inaccurate to contend that systematic cultivation of crops for export is necessarily inconsistent with the native system of tenure'.[50] For Asante specifically, on the evidence of their cross-examination of the most senior commissioners, they concluded that 'the cocoa industry is proceeding at a great pace without threatening to dislocate native social life'.[51]

This colonial policy debate continued in the 1920s.[52] Lieutenant-Colonel R. H. Rowe, Surveyor-General of the Gold Coast from 1920 to 1927, led a campaign—regarding Asante as well as the Gold Coast Colony—for 'a change to definite individual ownership of land' to guarantee security for investments.[53] He maintained that this was already the direction of change on the ground. With 'whole communities specialised' in the production of cocoa, 'vast areas today are under cultivation. The areas available for the casual agriculturalist are becoming restricted and *the whole tendency is towards individual ownership by native proprietors*' (his emphasis). Yet, he lamented, 'In many cases . . . land which apparently is "individually owned" is merely occupied by the individual during his lifetime and reverts to the Tribe, Stool or family on his death'. Moreover, tenure was insecure because of difficulty in definitively ascertaining and registering ownership.[54] The 'gradual attainment of individual ownership and civilised forms of owning and leasing land, is an advance brought about by economic necessity and must inevitably be introduced with the full development of any country.' Government action to make individual land ownership definitive was ultimately 'inevitable, unless development of the country's resources and its commerce is to be hampered and retarded'.[55]

Against this battled Rattray, in his role as official government anthropologist in Asante, both in administrative memoranda and in a book published in 1929.[56] In the latter he made the implicit criticism that 'consideration' of the land tenure issue 'is being allowed to drift' in British West Africa generally. He warned against the 'insidious' danger that stool lands would 'gradually become the freehold property of individuals'.[57] This would 'destroy the already dwindling power of the chiefs'[58] and diminish 'the small landholder class, which from an economic standpoint is the very backbone of this country'.[59] For with freehold tenure, 'almost certainly' the temptation of 'immediate pecuniary advantage' would lead individuals to sell to African speculators.[60] The result would be 'the creation of a landless class' who would eventually become 'paupers'.[61]

By 1944, however, a later advocate of Rowe's general position felt confident enough to assert that the intellectual argument for it had been won. In a memorandum G. W. Stackpoole, the Commissioner of Lands for the Gold Coast, averred that 'The benefits to the community accruing from the adoption of registration of title to land are well appreciated by all advanced Colonial Administrators and economists'. More specifically, he insisted that 'The various official publications upon the subject in this Colony published over a number of years indicate a sustained solidarity of opinion in favour of the adoption of registration', the only division being about the extent and form in which it should be adopted.[62] Yet the very next year the Lands Department insisted that there was no government 'proposal to institute registration of title in Ashanti'.[63] Moreover, the Survey Department 'confirmed . . . that it would be impossible' for them 'to undertake' the preparation of a cadastral plan. Hence any registration scheme would have to be in a watered-down form.[64]

In 1948 the Watson Commission, set up to investigate the causes of the 1948 riots in the Gold Coast, sought to reconcile two potentially contradictory lines of argument. On the one hand, it asserted that:

> The general fear of the African in the Colony and Ashanti today undoubtedly is that if alienation of tribal lands continues unrestricted there is a great

danger that a landless peasantry may result. The situation of Africans in other parts of the Continent is cited with telling effect. However remote that may be we are of the opinion that some positive steps should now be taken to prevent the possibility of an avaricious chief, with the assent of venial (*sic*) elders, effectively alienating tribal lands for personal gain or some temporary enrichment of the tribe.'[65]

On the other hand, Watson maintained that 'Insecurity of land tenure militates at every turn against the better utilisation of land', and commented that 'It appears to be said with some truth, that a purchaser of land in the Gold Coast buys not the land but a lawsuit.'[66] Thus the commission seemed to believe both that land was too freely sold, and that the rights of the buyer were insecure. Apparently to reconcile this contradiction, the commission recommended reform to ensure that 'tribal lands' were alienated only for approved purposes, that payment for the alienation went to the selling community as a whole, and that the purchaser on these terms would enjoy indefeasible title. But agriculture was not among the 'approved purposes' (which comprised the construction of homes and factories).[67] It should be noted that the two large boxes of memoranda received from the public in Asante contain no evidence of fear of landlessness.[68] The Commission's references to sales of land [itself], and specifically to opportunistic sales by free-riding chiefs and elders read primarily as comments on Akyem Abuakwa. By contrast, as we have seen, such sales in Asante had been merely 'peripheral', literally and metaphorically. It may be said that Watson picked up threads from both sides of the long-running debate among colonial policy-makers. But, as noted above, the commission also specifically wanted to see credit made more easily available to farmers. Given this, the overall effect of the report's comments on land tenure was probably to strengthen the lobby for land registration.

In 1951, a few months into the formal decolonization process, Sir Cecil Trevor, reporting on banking conditions in what was to become Ghana, stated that 'the insecurity of land tenure' and, relatedly, 'the lack of security' for loans were the 'principal obstacles in the way of the extension of credit'.[69] Moreover, he implied that he had been told that the government was going to take remedial action. He 'understood that Government intend in due course to have a complete survey made of the country and to register each owner's right and title to his properties'. The context suggests that he meant that individual ownership of land, as distinct from farms, would be established. Even if he meant simply that titles to farms—usufructory rights over land—would be registered, making it safer and cheaper to lend on such collateral, he recognised that 'this will take many years to complete'.[70] His report did not specify the source of his impression, but his interviewees in June–July 1951 included Kwame Nkrumah and the relevant ministers in his joint-rule administration, plus the British governor. No such exercise went ahead, whether because of the administrative and financial burden or for political reasons.[71]

Still within the decolonization phase, the distinguished West Indian economist W. A. Lewis, who had worked as an advisor to the Colonial Office and had produced a major report on the Ghanaian economy in 1953, expressed the view that indigenous systems of property rights were obstacles to economic development.[72] Five years after independence the Division of Agricultural Economics of the Ministry of Agriculture, while conceding that 'the present land tenure arrangements of this country are flexible and in no way seem to hinder progress in agricultural development', insisted that 'at the same time much better planning of land use would be achieved if certain lines of reform were encouraged, such as the registration of title'. This 'should start with the family units and finally develop to individual registration'.[73]

Retrospective academic assessments of the social efficiency of the land tenure system in the context of cash crops have varied. Cocoa farming in colonial Ghana, admittedly specifically in the Eastern Province of the Gold Coast Colony rather than in Asante, has been seen as having been facilitated by flexibility of the indigenous land tenure system. In this respect the rational-choice 'evolutionary' literature on African land tenure, published in the 1970s and 1980s, took its cue from Hill's field research in the late 1950s and early 1960s, which highlighted indigenous institutions of group land-purchase.[74] In the 1990s, however, Kathryn Firmin-Sellers offered a more pessimistic perspective. She argued, again for the Gold Coast Colony, that the colonial state had failed to deliver the political conditions for socially-efficient institutional change. As a result property rights had been and remained insecure and this was, she contended, a major deterrent to agricultural investment.[75] In the rest of this section we will consider the evidence for Asante about how flexibile and, especially, how secure were property rights in farms and land; the role of the colonial state in defining and securing such rights or 'failing' to do so; and the effect of the land tenure system on agricultural investment.

The near-absence of land sales in Asante means that Hill's emphasis on land-purchasing arrangements as evidence of the flexibility of indigenous land tenure does not find a parallel north of the River Pra. As we have seen, this difference can be explained in political terms. But it is also true that there was no compelling economic need for stranger-farmers to be able to buy land outright when they could obtain use rights for land on which to plant trees that would last for decades. The same applies to citizen-farmers. In that sense, the Asante practice was flexible enough not to obstruct economic expansion.

Before going further it is crucial to ask exactly what was insecure. In Asante, and in Ghana generally, the essence of this insecurity was simply that titles were not registered:[76] at least not until the later years of the colonial period and then only voluntarily and, as we have seen, with very doubtful legal effect.[77] For Asante especially it is important to distinguish the absence of title to farms from the absence of permanently fixed boundaries between different chieftaincies' lands. The litigation that brought uncertainty and not infrequently heavy bills to farmers was most commonly over the ownership not of their farms but over that of the land they stood on. Thus what was at stake was not the farms themselves but their liability to rent.

What explains this contrast between the extent of practical insecurity of property in tree-crop farms and in land itself? It was made possible by the now-familiar distinction in indigenous land law between ownership of the soils and of what was planted in or made upon them. As to what made it happen, we can discern both micro-economic and political-economy influences. The relative abundance of land reduced the importance of use rights over any particular plot: why argue over any one when more were available? But once cocoa trees had been planted, their ownership was valuable. At this level security of property rights was decisively upheld by the colonial government. Commissioners in Asante, as was shown in Chapter 14, were determined to protect farmers' ownership of the trees they had planted. This prevented certain chiefs from appropriating farms, and preempted the possibility that the scope of inter-stool land disputes would expand to include title over farms as well as over the land itself. It left open the field of disputes within farming 'households' over who had helped to make the farm and whether such help entitled the giver to a share of the asset so created. Hence the cases brought by women for part of their former or deceased husband's cocoa farms. But such cases, though important for defining the rules which would be followed in others which did not reach the courts, usually involved claims over only one or a few farms. In contrast, the disputes over chieftaincy boundaries often affected many farms and, supported as they were by the funds and credit of the contending stools and their subjects, could be extremely expensive in legal fees and in interest on loans taken out to meet such fees. As we have seen, the colonial state sought to settle such cases and avoid similar ones in future by defining stool boundaries. It did not take the further steps, implicitly envisaged by Belfield and urged by Rowe, of strengthening individual titles by registering them and also extending them from use rights to ownership of the soil. Such measures, once they had been applied in detail, would presumably have reduced uncertainty and transactions costs for future cocoa planters and other agricultural investors.

The colonial administration's caution partly reflected its anxiety to avoid further social differentiation among the African population. The possibility that a free land market would lead to the emergence of a large class of landless labourers was not appealing to the likes of Rattray, whose 'ideal for these people' was 'each man working his own holding'.[78] Cardinall declared in 1927 'that peasant proprietorship gives the greatest happiness to the greatest number, which . . . economically sound or unsound, is what every Government desires'.[79] There was also a powerful practical problem: the likelihood that the immediate effect of a general titling would be to induce a storm of litigation, as individuals sought to preempt others or to get their claims defined and secured before they were preempted themselves. Thus a compulsory titling scheme would have greatly increased farmers' transactions costs in the short term, before reducing them in the longer term. This was one of the reasons given by a governor of the Gold Coast, A. R. Slater, in 1931, for proposing the discontinuation of the policy debate on registration of title. Another was concern that to tell the Africans that they 'must prove and register their titles' would lead many of them to suspect that the government was planning to expropriate land.[80]

So what was the relationship between (in)security of property rights and the rate of investment in agriculture? During the 'take-off' in Asante there was genuine confusion and much litigation over chieftaincy boundaries. For many farmers the legal finding that they were on the wrong side of a boundary, and therefore liable to rent ('tribute') probably came as a shock. But such was the uncertainty about where lines should be drawn that we must assume that other farmers decided to plant first and argue afterwards.

By the time of the second boom lines had been drawn and re-drawn, argued and argued over. Thus the ownership of the land was now reasonably clear. The fact that proprietorship rested with chieftaincies rather than with individuals meant that to assert effective ownership of a plot it was necessary to clear and, better still, plant on it. In a context of approaching land-scarcity this rule gave an incentive to farmers to plant extensively. We saw that this appears to have happened in Ahafo. In that respect the absence of individual title to land actually contributed to the investment boom. But the quantitative impact of this interesting paradox was presumably small because extensiveness made economic sense anyway. The incentive probably had more effect on where cocoa trees were planted than on the number of them.

There is a gender dimension to the security of ownership in cocoa trees which has been surprisingly neglected in the literature. According to the rational-choice theory of property rights, insecurity deters investment. This prediction fits the fact that wives' contributions to the making of their husbands' cocoa farms primarily took the form of planting their own food crops to shade their husbands' cocoa plants, rather than putting their labour directly into the creation of assets in whose ownership they had no guarantee of participating. It should be remembered, though, that this can only have been part of the story. The evidence can be accounted for sufficiently in terms of the division of labour.[81]

Crucially, it is evident that the land tenure system(s), both in the Gold Coast Colony and in Asante, offered cocoa farmers what they regarded as sufficient security of tenure to make very widespread long-term investments. Almost tautologically, the dramatic speed and scale of the 'take-off' of cocoa planting from the 1890s in the Colony and from 1900 in Asante, and again of the second planting boom of the mid 1950s to early 1960s, could not have happened had farmers been fearful for the security of their ownership over the trees themselves.

This discussion has two major implications for the general issue of the interactions between colonial policy, indigenous land tenure, and economic development. The first—to reinforce a point that emerged from Chapter 14—is that the emphasis on the social conservatism of colonial policy on West African land tenure has been overdone. It is not just that, as a generation of scholarship has emphasized in many contexts, the colonial state did not simply preserve 'custom' but also defined or redefined it selectively, and then often sought to fossilize it in the face of economic and political pressures for change.[82] This claim does indeed apply in the Asante case, at least in the specific sense that the colonial administration, apparently from a mixture of ideological and economic considerations, chose to enforce and perhaps reinforce 'customary' land tenure; just as it frustrated the attempts of chiefs to extend cocoa rent to their own subjects. But more, the colonial state took serious steps to facilitate indigenous agricultural investment and ensure that farmers could keep the assets they made. In North's terms, they reinforced institutions (the farmers' property in what he or she had planted) and literally delineated property rights (chieftaincy boundaries) with the effect of reducing transactions costs. The second implication is that in the context of agricultural expansion in a land-surplus economy, even with that surplus diminishing, the strengthening and extension of individual titles to land itself were proved unnecessary by the fact that the second great expansion of cocoa cultivation, in the 1950s, happened without them. The same applies to titles to farms, in that the state's 'neglect' to introduce an official voluntary scheme, let alone a compulsory one, did not prevent that massive planting boom.

Let us put both historical findings together and relate them to the broad theories. The optimists, including the agrarian populists, are partly vindicated, in that the 'indigenous' land tenure system repeatedly proved to permit, even to facilitate, widespread and rapid expansions in the capital stock. Part of this, as Rattray noted, was thanks to the 'Akan-Ashanti' legal distinction between ownership of the soil and ownership of what was planted in it. This permitted 'the free interplay of capital . . . without jeopardising the land',[83] i.e. the use rights of the above-mentioned 'small landholder class'. But the populist view needs to be qualified by recognition that the institutions concerned were not simply a legacy of the precolonial period, nor did they 'evolve' in the way they did without colonial intervention. The rational-choice theory of induced institutional innovation is at least consistent with the evidence. This is so positively in that the state did the most important things that it could have done to ensure that the expansion of cocoa cultivation proceeded. It is also true negatively, in that the efficiency argument for further delineation of individual property rights turns out to have been weak, in view of the great planting booms that occurred. The shift in relative factor scarcities was not enough to have made it efficient to introduce compulsory titling, given that the reform would itself have been costly to the farmers (especially if it induced a wave of litigation, leading to long-term debts). Hence the absence of such a measure is what would be expected on an essentially economic analysis. Paradoxically, the more complex political economy account proposed by Firmin-Sellers seems to miss the main story: one of economic success.

This achievement was despite the lack of credit to farmers from banks. This gap—for whatever it was worth—may indeed be sufficiently attributable to the banks being deterred by the absence of registered individual title to farms.[84] However, the high unit cost of dealing with relatively small but sometimes complicated transactions would have been a major constraint in any case. Both obstacles to bank credit were spelled out by the Paton Report, which 'With all respect' urged the government to drop its commitment, made in response to the Watson Report, to establish an agricultural bank.

the foundation of bank credit is security, and in the specialised field of agricultural banking the first prerequisite is an unassailable and easily enforceable title to land. There is no system of land registration in the Gold Coast and the tenure of agricultural land is complex and flexible. The uncertainty and obscurity surrounding land tenure is such as to make land a completely unsatisfactory form of bank security. There is thus no basis for an agricultural bank. In the second place, experience in other countries has shown that an agricultural bank is not a suitable agency for the making of loans to thousands of simple and illiterate peasants scattered over wide areas.[85]

D. Property Rights and the External Costs of Cocoa Cultivation

Here we explore the tenurial implications of the decline of soil fertility under cocoa—the capture of the 'forest rent'—and of the diminishing area of land available for food farming, which was described in Chapter 3. Both trends can be seen as imposing internal and external costs, the distinction being that external costs are imposed on parties not directly involved in the economic activity or transaction. In this case the costs were internal to the extent that it was the current generation of cocoa-farming families that suffered the beginning of falling yields of beans and a choice between a less attractive diet and (presumably) higher food prices. The costs were external to the extent that they were borne by other consumers of food and by future generations of farmers. Such a situation was a potential 'tragedy of the commons', in Hardin's phrase.[86] This is a classic free-rider problem, where the interests of society as a whole are not reflected in the structure of incentives to individuals, with the result that the rational pursuit of individual self-interest leads to an outcome that is collectively damaging.

The issue of inter-generational conflicts of interests raises the question of whether cocoa farmers invested in improving the quality of land. To clarify the point it is useful to distinguish economic rent, defined earlier,[87] from 'rental', defined as the total income paid for the hire of an asset. Rental could include a return on capital invested in improving the asset, for example, in improving the quality of land. In this case, Bray viewed farmers' planting of cocoa trees as a way of improving the quality of the land.[88] But it is more appropriate to consider the trees as capital goods rather than as a characteristic of the land. For (as noted earlier) they undoubtedly have the characteristics of fixed capital, and the problem is precisely that they degrade the long-term fertility of the soil. I have found no evidence of cocoa farmers as individuals (as opposed to chiefs trying to restrict cocoa planting)[89] putting labour or capital specifically into ways of preserving or restoring the fertility of the land under their trees. This contrasts with the behaviour of African farmers faced with relatively poor soils and/or local demographic pressure on land.[90] But it is hardly surprising in the situation they faced: with fresh land available and the optimality—given the structure of costs facing them—of the land-extensive method of cultivation. Hence rental plays no part in the story here.

In contrast to rental, the economic rent on land is the income arising from merely holding the land and allowing it to be used. For this reason economic rent has often been argued to be parasitic, a reward for passive landlordism. On the other hand, neoclassicists tend to see it as socially constructive, because it allows the user of an asset to be made to pay for using it, and is thereby a deterrent to the overuse of natural resources. That is, it gives the user an incentive to work the asset sustainably rather than, in the case of land, simply extracting every last bit of fertility and thereby degrading it. Within this framework it could be argued that the cocoa rent system offered a partial antidote to the risk of cocoa-borne free-riding, in that rent was imposed only on cocoa farms, rather than on any use of land which was suitable for cocoa farming. In other words the system discriminated against the financially lucrative crop in the interests of food security. But it only did so as far as 'stranger'-owned farms were concerned. The absence of a universal rent charge on land suitable for cocoa meant that there was no incentive for subjects of the respective stools to avoid planting every acre they could: thereby 'crowding out' other crops, in both space (current food crops) and time (future crops). In Coase's terms, the way to avoid external costs is to delineate exclusive property rights, and establish a free market in them.[91] Thus if stool lands were divided between individual cultivators, each would have an incentive to avoid unsustainable exploitation of the soil. If they had some land under cocoa, they would have an incentive to keep other land fallow. In practice, from the start of the cocoa era in Asante the colonial administration was determined, apparently for political reasons, to prevent chiefs from charging their own subjects rent.

Rather, chiefs later attempted a state solution: anticipating Hardin's approach[92] and—it may be noted—acting in the tradition of the Agogohene's limitation of the snail-gathering and bat-hunting seasons reported in Chapter 10. The problem they addressed, however, was the second of the two free-rider issues noted above: the risk that (mature) cocoa would crowd out food growing. Twice chiefs, individually or collectively, took the drastic step of prohibiting the extension of cocoa cultivation. If property rights are rights to use assets in permitted ways, then restrictions on the kind of crop that may be grown limit property rights in land. As we have seen, the 1917 initiative by a single omanhene in south Asante was vetoed by the colonial government. Just over two decades later, the Ashanti Confederacy Council's ban evidently carried the support of the commissioners. But it was crude, especially in that it was unsuited to the particularly abundant land conditions of the western districts. Crucially, even though it was applied only in a six-year period of particularly low cocoa prices, it was quite extensively evaded.

That failure probably did little environmental harm at the time. But both free-rider problems remained for a future in which they would be reinforced by a new cocoa planting boom and an unprecedented rise in population. This remained essentially a long-term problem. As of 1971 (and indeed beyond), the post-colonial Ministry of Agriculture could observe that in Ashanti Region 'Almost universally, reliance is placed entirely on the bush fallow for the maintenance of fertility.'[93] The need, anticipated by Bray and others, for an eventual transition to a more intensive form of cultivation in which labour and capital would have to be invested in restoring soil fertility rather than relying almost exclusively on natural fallowing, would come to pass. But as of 1956–57, not yet.

E. Land and the Implications of Changing Social Relations of Production for the Position of Chiefs

We know that in the nineteenth century there were crucial differences between chiefs and commoners in their options in and requirements from the markets and other institutions through which productive resources could be obtained. Commoners' share in economic activity seems to have increased during that century of structural change in the international position of the Asante economy and state. But chiefs retained key powers and privileges. During the colonial period, as we have seen, chiefs lost most of their privileges in labour supply: completely, in the case of access to new captives; not in principle but to a great extent in practice in the cases of *corvée* and in services from the *gyaasefoɔ*. We have seen that the colonial administration frustrated chiefs' attempts to apply 'cocoa tribute' to their own subjects, to tax the new market in cocoa farms, and to appropriate farms that non-subjects had 'illegally' created on their stool lands. Thus even their control over the allocation of usufructory rights was restricted by colonial overrule. They also found themselves drawn into costly boundary litigation among themselves. Having thus highlighted these elements of decline, the rest of this section is devoted to two aims. The first is to specify, in some detail, certain ways in which the chiefs' position was shored up during the period: especially through the ownership of cocoa farms and the rent charged on non-subjects' farms. The second is to reflect on the implications of all these changes for the workings of the institutions surrounding the mobilization of factors of production.

The chiefs' right to *corvée* may have been a dwindling asset in the context of cocoa farming and colonial authority but we saw in Part Four that some chiefs used it to give themselves a head start in the cocoa era. Again, in Chapter 14 we observed how stool revenues came to be boosted by rent charged on 'stranger's' cocoa farms. Further, I will argue below that because of cocoa the chief's role as guardian of his subjects' rights to free use of land became newly significant as a source of justification and legitimation for chiefly authority.

A corollary of chiefs' entitlement to labour from their subjects to make cocoa farms was that the farms were made for the chiefdom not the chief. As such, 'chiefs' farms' were considered (certainly by the subjects) to belong to the stool and not to the chief as an individual. The chief could not alienate them without his elders' approval, nor keep them if he abdicated or was destooled. By the 1940s, however, there was a clear tendency for chiefs to assert private ownership over 'their' cocoa farms (and other assets), despite opposition from subjects.[94]

Even before that, in several respects the chiefs were the effective owners of stool farms. Not merely were they the custodians, they were also the immediate and principal beneficiaries of the proceeds. In the case of Amansie, which I have studied in some detail, a number of chiefs were amongst the earliest and largest of cocoa-farming entrepreneurs, in the sense of commanding and organizing the establishment and extension of cocoa farms. In Chapter 13 we noted a number of specific cases of 'chiefs' farms' established by 1914. In 1924 the Asuminahene was 'given' a farm on abdication, following a dispute over whether certain property, perhaps including the farm, belonged to him or to the chiefdom.[95] In 1930 the District Commissioner of Bekwai remarked: 'The Ex-Odikro of Mim has been accused by Mim Tribunal of pledging stool farms a[s] security for private loans. I have little doubt of the truth of the accusation.'[96] Again, four of the Adumasa farmers evicted from the Wawase lands after the Esumejahene won possession of the land are referred to as being a chief or regent. It is surely no coincidence that, of the nineteen farmers for whom figures are available, these four were among the six largest owners of cocoa farms on the land concerned. The biggest producer (with 525 loads) was officially titled 'Chief' in 1947. The next largest (260) had apparently been succeeded by the third (190) as Odekuro of Kokoben. The sixth largest (85) was the Regent of the stool they all served, Adumasa.[97] There is no suggestion in the available evidence that any of the farms were stool rather than personal property.

In 1938 destoolment charges were brought against Denyasehene Kwesi Aduonin II. One charge implied that not all chiefs were dedicated guardians of the stool's farms: 'Wilfull neglect to maintain the Stool Cocoa farms at Nminiamina'. Another supports the proposition that chiefs were tending to assert private ownership over cocoa farms, and indicates an additional means by which such farms could be acquired in the first place: 'Not rendering accounts of the proceeds of cocoa farms confiscated from Kwesi Marfu and one at Huntadu.'[98] Admittedly, confiscation was exceptional (and the reason for it in this case is unknown). Routinely, however, stools inherited any farm whose owner died without known heirs (presumably because he was a stranger). This latter rule probably accounts for the following item in a 1938 list of the stool cocoa farms of the town of Essuowin: 'deceased Tei Kwabena's farm [at] Akrukroso—[annual yield] 20 loads.'[99]

The major distributional consequence of cocoa rent was to give chiefs a share in the cocoa income. It is important to emphasize this, which was in counter-balance to the unfavourable effects on their material base of the ending of slavery and the decline of *corvée*. As a bonus, for some chiefs cocoa 'tribute' helped to consolidate the allegiance of their people, in that it gave those of 'stranger' descent an incentive to maintain their status as subjects of the chieftaincy on whose lands stood the majority of their bearing cocoa: which, more often than not, would be where they lived.

Cocoa rent created a major set of transaction costs, in that it inspired intense litigation between chieftaincies and between communities via their chiefs. This was especially concerning where chieftaincy boundaries lay, as this determined who should pay rent to whom. In 1945 the Havers Commission, set up to investigate indebtedness arising from legal expenses, concluded:

> It is abundantly clear from the evidence that the majority of States in the Colony and in Ashanti have been, and many still are, in debt. Though there are other contributing factors, litigation is undoubtedly the main cause of

the indebtedness. Stool debts caused by litigation generally arise out of litigation over land and particularly out of boundary disputes.[100]

In Asante, wrote a commissioner in 1940, the chief 'is bound by custom and public opinion to fight any land case to the limit of his stool's credit.'[101] Havers amplified this observation:

> a Chief would run the risk of destoolment if he did not take every step, which his subjects thought could be taken, to defend the Stool land. He is therefore compelled, even in cases where he does not consider the chance of success is favourable, to carry the litigation to its utmost limit[102]

The legal bills were indeed a major source of debt for chieftaincies and for subjects required to contribute to levies (occasional taxes) to meet them.[103] For some stools the costs surely more than off-set the extra income that they had derived, directly and indirectly, from the cocoa industry.

But for the position of chiefs in the communities concerned there was another side to the financial burden of land litigation.[104] The commissioner quoted above continued:

> The development of the Cocoa industry was carried out by independent small peasant farmers on land held in trust for them by their Stool. From the Stool the small farmer's security of tenure is safeguarded by customary law; the authority of the local chief . . . is derived, in the eyes of his subjects, from his position as trustee for their land; the subjects['] allegiance to their chief is derived mainly from their tenure of stool land.[105]

Both sentences were exaggerations. But though the chief's position as trustee for the community's land was long-established, it had never been of such practical peacetime importance before the coming of cocoa. For the first time, subjects' scope for cultivation was effectively limited by stool boundaries, with the accompanying threat of heavy rent or eviction for farmers judged to be on the wrong side of them. Thus the role of land-trustee became much more immediate and important as a source of chiefly authority in a period in which its other sources had been diminished (his religious authority by the spread of Christianity, his political legitimacy by colonial overrule).[106]

The net result of the changes discussed in this section was fundamentally to alter the impact of chieftaincy in the allocation of productive resources. The assertion by chiefs of private claims on what had been considered stool property, and above all the loss of most of their privileged access to cheap labour, made their economic activities far less distinct from those of their subjects. The indigenous state became considerably less important as a producer and trader in the economy. But its role in the allocation of land acquired much greater practical importance than before the cocoa era, even though the exercise of that responsibility was restricted in certain respects by colonial overrule. In their capacity as rule-makers, chiefs showed themselves willing to take a long-term view of the implications of the changing pattern of land use and to impose restrictions in order to safeguard their peoples' future. In their sources of revenue they had become rent-takers; but, in some of their policies, they showed themselves to be more than rent-seekers.

F. Conclusion

The indigenous land tenure system seems not to have been a significant barrier to the rapid growth of export agriculture. The main qualification is the heavy transactions costs that arose from the initial lack of defined chieftaincy boundaries: which the colonial state sought to remedy. Again, on the face of it the absence of a statute of limitations could also have deterred investment. But the established Asante distinction between ownership of the land itself and ownership of farms, backed (as seen in Chapter 14) by the colonial state's defence of farmers' property rights over what they had planted, meant that farmers could have confidence in the institutional security of their tree-planting (risks of fire, crop disease and falling world prices were harder to control). The case for compulsory registration of title was made repeatedly and vigorously in internal colonial policy debates over the decades, and has been put in the academic literature since. But in the Asante case it is likely that the additional security was not worth the costs of delivering it: which would have been very heavy in relation to the fiscal and human capital resources available.

The induced innovation theory provides an interesting angle on the evolution of cocoa rent. On some aspects of this story, though, what the theory offers is critical commentary rather than explanation. The fact that such a rent was imposed is explicable in terms of the theory, as is the observation that over the years the actual rates charged varied broadly in the same direction as the real producer price of cocoa. Even the nominally fixed penny rate was modified in practice by the concessions made by chiefs (partly under government pressure) in years of recession. The theory is less useful when we seek to explain why the colonial government barred chiefs from imposing cocoa rent on their own subjects. To be sure, this can be accounted for in political terms: but a theory based on the notion that change is a response to opportunities for economic gain appears to add nothing in this case.

The exemption of citizens from cocoa rent could be said to have the disadvantage that it entailed that, unlike strangers-farmers, citizens paid nothing for using chieftaincy land in a way which progressively diminished its fertility and, in the medium and long term, reduced the quantity of land available for food-growing. The imposition of rent would have been a way of internalising some of the social costs of cocoa production through the price mechanism. When the Ashanti Confederacy Council of Chiefs resorted to quantitative controls, banning new planting of cocoa, the measure took no account of drastic variations in the extent of land scarcity/surplus in different parts of Asante, and had little effect on the rate of planting. It was evaded and, anyway, was imposed during a time of low real cocoa prices and was lifted just as incentives to plant began to revive.

On the question of why in Asante, unlike in Akyem Abuakwa, land was mostly made available to strangers though lease rather than purchase, part of the explanation is that, given the distinction between ownership of the land and of assets made on it, purchase was unnecessary for secure investment. But this is an insufficient explanation because some sales did occur, albeit in the 'exceptions that prove the rule': chiefdoms on the southern margin of the former Asante kingdom. In accounting for this I argued that the most persuasive framework is provided by Benneh's hypothesis that the incidence of sales was inversely related to the degree to which sub-chiefs are under the control of superior chiefs. Asante's relatively high degree of political coherence, even before but especially after the restoration of the Confederacy in 1935, largely averted the 'risk' of large-scale land sales to outsiders. This account fits the rational-choice theory of collective action, and is an example of where Bates and Firmin-Sellers are right in emphasizing the need for a political dimension to any rational-choice explanation of institutional change.[107]

Finally this chapter has pointed to certain advantages, fiscal and political, which chiefs derived from the institutional changes and pressures of the period: which qualifies the usual picture of profound decline in their status and wealth.

18

CAPITAL IN A TREE-FARM ECONOMY

This chapter begins by trying to explain how the making of cocoa farms was financed, considering the rapidity of the expansion and the long gestation of this kind of investment. Section B analyses the working capital requirements of bearing farms and the capacity of such farms to attract credit in the form of advances for forthcoming crops. It goes on to examine the question of usury and efficiency in the market for short-term agricultural credit. The following pair of sections explore the implications of the longevity of cocoa trees, as opposed to annual crops. Section C considers the effects of cocoa farming on wealth, in the sense of the creation of valuable legacies, inspiring conflict over the disposal of property on divorce or death. Section D investigates the impact of cocoa farms as assets in the credit market: the creation of a new and major form of mortgage lending, which raised important issues for welfare and possibly longer-term economic development. Throughout the chapter issues of market operation and imperfection are raised, and we note their implications for rational-choice theories, and consider in what respects (if any) these theories illuminate the evidence.

A. Establishment of New Cocoa Farms: Economies in, and Provision of, Working Capital

The fact that cocoa-planting was an investment with a several-year gestation might, in other circumstances, have made the supply of working capital a major constraint upon the expansion of cultivation. Yet we can be brief in trying to explain how Asante farmers financed the making of their cocoa farms, because their working-capital problems were eased and generally overcome by means which we have already considered in other contexts. The liberality of the rules on acquiring land meant that there was no need to pay for the use of land, at least (in the case of 'strangers') not before the trees were bearing and could therefore (usually) pay for themselves. This left the issue of how to finance and equip the labour force until the trees began to yield.

In this context it is important to note that the structure of costs that the first generation of Asante cocoa growers faced in establishing their first cocoa farms was different from that encountered by most of their successors, or by themselves when multiplying their farms. Once a farmer had a bearing cocoa farm, or had financial assistance from a relative who had one, the receipts from the mature farm could be used to meet the living expenses of family labour and if necessary to pay wages. But the main costs facing the pioneers were fixed rather than variable. Regular wage labour was neither available no affordable. Labour for particular tasks might perhaps be obtained from casual wage labourers or by reciprocal exchange with neighbours, as we will discuss below. But overwhelmingly the early labour force was a stock rather than a flow: the farmer did not go out and hire labour but deployed the workforce he had already assembled, free and otherwise. Here the legacy of accumulation from the nineteenth-century exchange economy was critical. The proceeds of the gold, kola, rubber and other trades enhanced the capacity of individual commoners, as well as chiefs, to invest in the new crop. Besides having financed the acquisition of imported captives, these activities directly or indirectly contributed to the supply of cutlasses and other tools used by the new cocoa-farmers.[1] Finally, the practice of planting tall foodcrops to shade young cocoa, described in Chapter 4, was a double economy for farmers in that it both limited the weeding and reduced the cash requirements of feeding the workforce.

B. Bearing Farms: The Advances System

Cocoa Advances

This section examines why advances were wanted and offered. The members of the European cocoa-buying cartel argued that until their 1937 agreement 'a far larger proportion of the crop than is justified has been bought on credit'.[2] But these firms themselves had been the major source of such credit, via their advances to brokers. So why did they give them?

P. T. Bauer, in his classic *West African Trade* (1954), emphasized the efficiency of the prewar marketing system, asserting that 'Buying the crop by paying advances was simply a method of financing the harvesting and movement of a seasonal and expensive crop with European capital'.[3] Let us then consider the hypothesis that advances were essential if the crop was to be harvested, fermented and delivered to the European buying stations. The crop-year 1936–37 provided an accidental test of what would happen in the near-absence of advances. The banks had seriously underestimated the demand for money and therefore had not imported enough cash to enable the firms to give advances on anything like the scale that they envisaged.[4] Yet not only did the crop come in to the European buyers, the volume for Asante equalled the record (set the previous year) at 92,000 tonnes, while for Ghana as a whole a new record was set, of 305,000 tonnes. Thus it is clear that advances were not necessary to finance the crop as a whole. This conclusion is reinforced if we recall the empirical observation, made in Chapter 15, that advances were made much more extensively when the cocoa price was high than when it was low: indicating that the scale of advances, absolutely and as a proportion of all sales in a crop-year, was a function of the spot price rather than being a precondition of supply.

There is a qualification to be entered, and one which is particularly important for Asante: it appears that advances were necessary for financing local cocoa marketing—though not production—at the economic and geographic margin. The necessity for advances to brokers in new cocoa areas, which almost by definition tended to be distant from the buying centers and outside the main road network, was noted in Cadbury's internal reports of the early 1930s. As a chocolate manufacturer, Cadbury distinguished itself from the import-export houses, its main rivals for produce, partly by trying to avoid giving advances.[5] But it found that 'small cash advances are inevitable' when dealing with the brokers who operated in these relatively new and 'far off' areas of cocoa production. Crops were offered for sale in 'very small lots' over 'very long distances and wide areas', and transport involved the [head-loading] of cocoa 'many miles along bush paths'. Thus the front-line brokers faced relatively high unit costs, while being themselves often short of funds compared to the local brokers in longer-established cocoa areas, where there had been more opportunity for 'accumulation of wealth among the brokers'.[6] To judge from the 'natural experiment' of the 1936–37 crop year, noted above, this specific need for advances in frontier areas is unlikely to have affected overall 'Ghanaian' output by more than a few per cent. But it would have had a rather greater proportional impact within Asante, because Asante had a disproportionately large share of the frontier areas of cocoa production. To gauge the impact of this we need to place Asante's marketed output in 1936–37 in the context of the rapid expansion that had been evident in immediately preceding years. The trend of growth in Asante cocoa output in the 1930s exceeded that of Ghana as a whole, because its cocoa-tree stock was relatively young and therefore much of it was only gradually coming into bearing. This catching-up process is illustrated in the table below.

Hence under normal conditions Asante output can be expected to have risen further in 1936–37, rather than merely matching the 92,000 tonne mark set the year before. The relative shortfall does not seem to be attributable to, for example, an abnormal difference in weather between Asante and the Gold Coast Colony. It can, however, be attributed to the effects of the credit famine in hindering marketing in cocoa 'frontier' areas, especially in western districts (now within Brong-Ahafo Region). There is also an indication (which will be illustrated below) that liquidity was particularly short in Asante compared to the Gold Coast Colony: which could have aggravated the plight of brokers and farmers in 'far off' areas.

The main finding remains: advances were unnecessary for cocoa production, that is, either credit was not required to finance production from currently-bearing trees, or it was obtained by other means. But how could farmers manage without credit? The Nowell commissioners declared themselves 'satisfied that under conditions of cocoa farming on the West Coast little financing of the crop is really necessary, since labour appears usually to be paid by a share in the proceeds of the crop or by wages as the crop is harvested.'[7] It will be argued here that the commissioners were exactly wrong in their conclusion but exactly right in their premise. That is to say, 'financing of the crop' was indeed necessary in production: to cover the costs of the labour force, whether family or hired, between cocoa harvests;

Table 18.1. Asante cocoa sales: selected years[1]

Year	1910	1919	1932–33	1938–39
Tons	1,900	31,900	72,000	101,100
Share of 'Ghana' total	8.3%	18.1%	28.2%	33.9%

[1] Calculated from *ARA*, various years; Kay with Hymer, *Political Economy of Colonialism*, 336–7; Bateman, 'Econometric analysis of Ghanaian cocoa supply', 315.

but that the essential finance was provided in the form of credit from the suppliers of labour themselves.

Food crops were either supplied by the farmowner or grown by the cocoa-farm labour force themselves, on immature cocoa farms (where plantain and cocoyam could be grown to shade the young cocoa plants) and/or on dedicated plots.[8] But that left the cost of purchased items, the importance of which was underlined by the hold-up movement itself in 1937. The producers' strike was to be accompanied by a consumer boycott of imports. Though the farmers were to forego new imported textiles or metalware, exceptions were specifically made (in the words of a resolution of the Ashanti Farmers' Union) for 'Salt; soap; matches, Tobacco; Kerosene; petrol; Sardines; (Provisions) medicine, cutlasses; sugar; and such and such other personal necessaries indispensable to life' (*sic*).[9]

The cash element in the working-capital requirement was met, in effect, by credit provided to the farmers (in the sense of farmowners) by the labourers themselves; whether the workers were hired or domestic, and including those farmers who worked their own farms. There were exceptions: some employees were paid monthly, but the farmers concerned evidently had unusually deep pockets.[10] It seems to have been standard practice for labourers on seasonal or annual contracts, not to mention sharecroppers and family workers, to receive cash only when the crop was sold: typically after six months' work.[11] We might assume that it was the practice of some employers to lend their workers small sums to tide them over until the crop was sold. But this remains to be documented and the scope for it was very restricted as the farmers faced the same seasonal liquidity crisis (indeed, most farmers did some of their farm labour themselves). The farmers' liquidity squeeze would have been alleviated whenever they themselves received advances from brokers. But as we have seen for 1936–37, such alleviation was not indispensable. On the contrary, a record crop could be produced in a year of exceptionally low advances. Rather, workers supplied their inputs (in weeding on—especially—immature farms, in harvesting, fermenting and carrying the produce) very largely on terms which amounted to interest-free credit. The cost to the suppliers of labour could be in cash, if they themselves had to borrow at interest. But the most evident cost was non-monetary: the need to postpone expenditure. Though labourers received some credit from traders,[12] whether interest-free or otherwise, the telling point is that most sales of consumer items took place during the cocoa-buying season rather than being spread throughout the year[13] as presumably they would have been had the timing of sales matched the timing of the needs or desires they met.

It may be asked why farmer-cultivators and their domestic and hired labour-forces were prepared regularly to give their labour on several months' credit. Up to a point they had little choice: abstractly, because capital was even scarcer than labour. But when payment to hired labourers was delayed even longer than usual, they reacted strongly. We will see in the next chapter that there were bitter cases of labourers being left unpaid by their employers, especially in the low-price era of the 1930s and, even more so, the early 1940s. The 1937–38 hold-up ended with great hardship for many labourers, paid late and only in part if they were paid at all. We will see in the next chapter that such experiences were a major reason for the labourers' insistence on switching from wage to sharecropping contracts.

So why did farmers take advances, given that the price at which crops could be sold forward was less than the price that the buyer expected would prevail by the time the pods were ripe? Because most of the cocoa-farmers' income came in during little more than six months of the year, there was a major demand for credit in its classic role of smoothing the distribution of consumption over the year. The work that was done in maintaining farms during the off-season was, in effect, labour provided on credit: whether by the farmer working for himself, or his wife or children or sharecroppers. But if credit was available on the next crop, it would be tempting to take it: even at what might turn out to be a high de facto interest rate. Liquidity was literally at a premium: a point we will return to below.

If advances were generally unnecessary for cocoa production, and if its marketing only required advances at the margin, why did the European firms give them, especially on what was frequently a vast scale? The volume of advances was determined proximately on the supply side (how much the firms wanted to dispense) rather than on the demand side (how much credit would the farmers have liked to receive). Ultimately, it responded to the state of the produce market, reflected in the cocoa price. For the produce-buying firms as a whole the decision to supply advances was discretionary; but as long as the market remained competitive, they forced each other individually to offer advances in their struggles to secure produce. European merchants themselves attributed the abundance of advances to 'Intense competition between the merchants for cocoa tonnage'.[14]

That competition should oblige them to offer advances suggests some inelasticity in the response of cocoa supply to price. It was in the nature of a tree crop that the supply of produce was largely inelastic with respect to price movements over periods shorter than it took a seedling to develop into a bearing tree. Hence, when world cocoa prices were relatively high, merchants in Ghana could—and because of competition amongst themselves, did—offer more attractive terms to obtain produce from brokers, who in turn did the same in relation to farmers. Because liquidity was a chronic problem for farmers, the provision of advances was a key part of these more attractive terms. One could say that there was a 'rental' element in the extraction of advances by farmers: advances were a response to the short-term inelasticity of cocoa output. But it should be emphasised that this was not sufficient to make advances cheap: in the context of the extreme shortage of liquidity for most of the year, the farmers' 'enjoyment' of rent was limited to the fact that advances were available at all.

The finding that the quantity of advances was essentially determined by the extent of competition among the produce-buyers provides an explanation for a phenomenon observed in Chapter 15: the pro-cyclical character of advances, that is, the tendency for their volume to rise relatively as well as absolutely when the produce price rose. Competition among buyers was a key reason for the rise in the supply schedule of advances (which was also shown in that chapter). Before elaborating on this, it must be emphasized that there were other sources of upward pressure on that schedule.

The long-term tendency for bank facilities to improve was probably one: by easing liquidity constraints on the cocoa-buying companies, thus making it easier for them to buy forward. However, changes in bank branch networks were themselves partly 'cyclical' or, at least, influenced by changes in the volume of trade. The two commercial banks operating in Asante (and in Ghana generally) opened branches outside Kumasi after the First World War. But this was only in one town, Bekwai: the Bank of British West Africa in 1919 and the Colonial Bank, i.e. Barclays, in 1921.[15] Both branches closed during the Depression, in 1932.[16] The banks' second and more vigorous attempt to establish themselves outside the Asante capital waited until the mid-1950s. Then a cocoa boom combined with a strictly non-cyclical influence, decolonization (specifically, the pressure it created on banks to show that they were serving the African population), to encourage them to extend their networks. In February 1956 Barclays opened agencies (their minimum level of presence) in Konongo, Bekwai and Tepa; while BBWA opened in the latter town on the same day.[17]

A more widespread and probably more important source of the greater underlaying availability of advances was what E. J. Organ of Cadbury had called in 1932, in a phrase quoted above, the 'accumulation of wealth among the brokers'. The firms implicitly testified to this in the arguments they put forward in 1937–38.[18] To this may be added the process of accumulation through farming too. For it is essential to remember the growth of Ghanaian, and especially Asante, cocoa output during this period. Despite the vicissitudes of the price, many thousands of people evidently got richer over the period: and some were apparently willing to invest their own capital in advances, in order to establish or expand a broking business. Relatively few Africans seem to have put their savings into banks at this stage. The manager of the Kumasi Branch of BBWA reported that the 1926–27 financial year had seen a rise in the number of fixed deposit accounts held with them, the increase being 'in amount £7,269 and in number 18. We are pleased to say that about half of this amount is on account of African Customers'.[19] By the end of the colonial period the level of Africans' bank deposits had risen greatly. At mid-December 1955 Barclays in Kumasi (again their only branch in Asante) had 5,814 savings accounts. We do not know how many of these were held by Africans but the total 'non-African' (mainly Levantine and European) population of the town was only 1,320:[20] by no means all of whom would have banked with Barclays. The implication is that several thousand Africans (including Fante clerks and other non-Asantes) had opened savings accounts with one or other of the banks in Kumasi by the end of the period. Much of the money was presumably derived directly or indirectly from the cocoa industry. But until the 1950s, at least, advances or pawning/pledging seems to have been a much bigger outlet for Asantes' savings. Conversely, the annual accounts of the BBWA in Kumasi indicate that bank lending to Africans, at least before the Second World War, was restricted to a very few mortgages, all of which can probably be assumed to be secured on urban buildings.[21]

Even more than the increased wealth of some Africans, competition among the European firms drove the advances system, helping to explain the rise in the supply schedule. It seems likely that when such competition led to freer distribution of advances it was not always easy or costless to put into reverse later, because expansions racheted up the level of advances which brokers (and thence farmers) expected and on which they would try to insist thereafter. Such competition is particularly relevant to explaining the rise in the supply schedule that seems to have occurred between the First World War and the early 1930s. William Cadbury complained, apparently in 1930, that the United Africa Company and other merchants 'have gone much further in this loan system. Almost all the trade in their stores is done on credit . . . and very large sums are advanced to brokers or farmers on mortgage or prospective crops. Our loans are made at the beginning of the cocoa season (September–October); U.A. and others in June–July;

already (February) demands from brokers are being placed and considered by U.A. for next season'.[22] Admittedly, part of the tendency Cadbury described is attributable to 'cyclical' influence in the sense of being a response to the relatively high produce prices of the later 1920s. But part of it is attributable to specific business strategies, notably UAC's apparent attempt to eliminate its main rivals or oblige them to forego competition for collusion.[23]

The finding that advances were unnecessary as working capital to producers and to most brokers makes it possible to understand why the European firms decided to eliminate or reduce their own giving of advances when they had (or thought they had) the chance to do so. Twelve such firms, who together accounted for 94 per cent of the cocoa shipped from Gold Coast ports in 1936–37, formed a buying agreement (or 'pool', to use the colloquialism of the time) to run for four crop years starting with 1937–38.[24] This was by no means the first pool in the Gold Coast cocoa trade but, because it contained all the major competitors, it was the first with a real chance of decisively changing the marketing system.[25] It was precisely the 'problem' of competition among themselves for tonnage that the 1937 buying agreement addressed: it removed competition among its signatories not only over price but also over volume. Under it quotas as well as uniform prices were agreed, and any firm buying more than its quota had to dispose of it to rivals in deficit according to a formula based on the uniform price.[26] The European firms believed that under this scheme they could avoid or minimize the provision of advances to brokers.[27] They could thus escape their own 'prisoner's dilemma': under which, though they would all be better off if they stopped giving advances, none dared abstain in case a competitor persisted. As it turned out, the pool ran into more effective opposition than the firms anticipated: in the form of the 1937–38 'hold-up', which paralyzed the cocoa trade for most of the season. Moreover, to the fury of the firms, the local colonial administration—whom they had not consulted before introducing the buying agreement—adopted a position of 'neutrality'.[28]

Like the European firms, in principle the African and Levantine brokers could have avoided giving advances had they arranged to eliminate competition among themselves. They could have jointly refused to buy forward whether from their own capital or with advances that they had themselves received from the European companies. But the sheer number of brokers meant that such cooperation would be expensive and difficult to agree and enforce. For Ghana as a whole, Nowell estimated that there were 38,500 cocoa brokers of all sizes.[29] This implies about

11,600–12,100 in Asante if the ratio of brokers per tonne exported in 1936–37 and 1937–38 was the same in Asante as elsewhere (probably it was slightly higher, because of production being, on average, more dispersed geographically).[30] Even greater numbers of farmers managed to mount the hold-ups, admittedly, but they had the chiefs to help enforce discipline and deter individuals from breaking ranks. The chiefs would have been unlikely to support a brokers' cartel against the interests of the farmers, who constituted most of their subjects. Moreover, a high proportion of the brokers were themselves farmers.[31] Finally, if the European firms failed to elicit the unambiguous support of the colonial state, there was no chance of the brokers doing so.

As it happened, an exogenous event delivered the European firms from the need to compete vigorously with each other, for several years. With the outbreak of war in 1939 the British government introduced a state monopoly of cocoa exports, with the former exporters continuing to operate, but now as licensed buying agents of the marketing board. For several years the crop was allocated among the different firms, each of whom had a fixed quota which was the same as their prewar market share. Thus the goal of eliminating effective competition, which the firms had failed to achieve with the 1937–38 'pool', was awarded to them primarily out of administrative convenience propelled by wartime exigency. During the war, as we noted in Chapter 15, the Europeans left it to African brokers to finance most of such advances as were given from the latter's own retained profits. It may be asked why the brokers themselves gave advances in these circumstances. This may be attributed in part to competition among the brokers themselves. But, also, it must be remembered that real producer prices were exceptionally low during the war, as low or lower even than in the early 1930s. In this situation some farmers surely did need credit if they were to produce very much cocoa: as we saw was the case with farmers and brokers in the newer cocoa areas even in the relatively high-price year of 1936–37. Even so, the brokers could afford to be choosy about how much and to whom they gave advances. The Fortes Papers include a couple of loose sheets listing farmers, their requests for advances, and the amounts they were given. They evidently relate to the activities of an individual broker in the Sekyere/Asante Akyem area in June–August 1945. In all, 49 farmers asked the broker for advances: 15 received nothing, while all the rest got less than they had requested.[32]

The years from the war to Ghana's formal independence saw at least a partial revival of competition for produce, intensified by the enlarged operations of the co-operatives and the entry of the marketing board's own buying agency, the CPC (short-lived though its existence was; under that name at least). We saw in Chapter 15 that advances were widely given in 1956–57. But the survey which showed this also indicated that farmers now enjoyed greater liquidity during the early months of the cocoa season than seems to have been the case in earlier decades. Payments to labour (wage and sharecrop combined) during each of the six main months of the cocoa-selling season varied only from 23 to 26 per cent of the gross farming income of the employers' families. The peak of farmers' incomes was in November and December. In absolute terms payments to labour were at their highest in the same months, though as a proportion of farmers' receipts the peak came in January and February (26 per cent, compared to 23–24 per cent in November and December).[33] The implication is that—because, presumably, of the high real producer prices of the mid-1950s—labourers no longer had to allow their employers several months' credit.

Did the Brokers Extract Economic Rents?

Let us now ask whether the market for advances was imperfect in the specific sense that it enabled brokers to extract economic rents from the other parties in the trade. The concept of rent seems the most rigorous way of formulating an enquiry into the truth of two clichés from the discourse of European merchants and officials: that the returns on advances given by brokers to farmers tended to be usurious; and that the brokers exploited the advances they themselves received from the European cocoa-buyers to extract windfall gains by inflating the price they obtained from the firms. When the firms maintained that they gave advances to secure tonnage, they were thinking not of farmers but of brokers. Advances were a key part of 'competitive bidding for the services of middlemen with connexions in wide areas . . . who were thereby in a position to offer attractive tonnage.'[34] Bauer thought that it 'plainly impossible' that the middlemen could have exploited the firms or farmers in view of 'the severe competition among middlemen and the ease of entry into their ranks'.[35] But it was more complicated than that. Let us define the specific possible mechanisms of rent-extraction and then consider the evidence on each of them.

The accusation that the brokers used the advances system to exploit the farmers was made, for example, in a statement drafted on behalf of the cocoa-buying firms as a defence of the 1937 buying agreement: 'The uncurbed activities of brokers facilitated by uncontrolled competition among the merchants militates [*sic*] against the best interests of the farmers.'[36] The Nowell Commission, whose findings were generally more negative than positive as far as the European firms were concerned, nevertheless agreed with them that buying cocoa in advance at a reduced price 'is usually to the detriment of farmers'.[37] The firms claimed that not only would forward sales be at a big discount from the spot price, but that the spot price regularly appreciated during the season: a predictable rise on which those who had sold in advance necessarily missed out. The contention rested upon the assumption that: 'Advances are obviously made on a conservative estimate of the ruling price when marketed, with the result that except in abnormal seasons such as the present the farmer not only fails to realise the market value of his cocoa, but is debarred from participation in a price increase.'[38]

Such a price increase might be expected on the familiar argument that agricultural prices tend to rise as the harvest approaches, responding to the progressive depletion of stores from the previous harvest. It should be noted, though, that while this model would apply very well to a crop whose market was entirely domestic and which was not supplied from any other source, it may be less applicable to a crop which was so heavily traded internationally, such that its ultimate users could draw upon supplies from producers whose seasons did not entirely coincide. However that may be, the firms contended that brokers engaged in self-fulfilling speculation on the price, driving it upwards while the pods ripened. I have presented and discussed this proposition in detail elsewhere, using sources from other parts of southern Ghana as well as Asante. In the present context, the key observation to make is that figures on average monthly cocoa prices (at Accra) are available for the six years to 1936–37. These permit analysis of price movements between the period during which most advances were given (in the latter months of the cocoa off-season), and the period during which the bulk of the crop was marketed. The conclusion which emerges is that over the six years rises and falls almost exactly balanced out. Any 'speculation' on prices was, at least in retrospect, no more than that.[39] So far, so good for Bauer's dismissal of any claim that the brokers exercised power over prices.

If the brokers could not count on a rise in the price of cocoa between the time they made their advance purchases and the time the produce was ready, their only possible opportunity to extract economic rent from farmers through the advances system must have been at the original contract. The evidence about how much the forward price was discounted from the then spot price is fragmentary. The most comprehensive data come from the survey of indebtedness for the 1932–33 crop year.[40] The survey found that in the advance sales the average price per 60-pound (27.2 kilogramme) load was 5s/2d [£0.26], whereas 'the average ruling price' (presumably the price paid eventually for the rest of the crop) was 9s/- [£0.45].[41] The price difference—the gross return to the buyer/lender—was thus 73.1 per cent. Of this, 4.3 percentage points can be attributed to a rise in the spot price between the time when most advances were made and the time when the bulk of the produce was marketed. If the forward purchase is regarded as a loan, the implicit rate of interest (the portion of the produce price that the farmer gave up in return for the credit)—leaving out the rise in the spot price—was 68.8 per cent. And this was on advances whose average period was 'probably 2 to 3 months'. In interpreting this we should keep in mind the possibility that when the forward sales were made both parties expected the cocoa price to fall. Certainly, this figure for an isolated crop year is even higher than the kind of figures indicated by individual cases.

An example of these cases can be found in testimony prepared by John Holt's for presentation to the Nowell Commission. This included a statement by George Yebuah, an African produce buyer employed by the company in Kumasi. He had twenty-one years of experience in the trade and had worked for various firms. Speaking not of his own advance-giving, which was to brokers, but rather of advances given to farmers themselves, Yebuah stated that the amount of an advance payment 'is usually arrived at by taking the price at the moment of the advance less one or two shillings' per load.[42] From a rough calculation, relating 'less one to two shillings' to the prices paid in the preceding several seasons,[43] this would often amount to 10–20 per cent over the period of the loan, which could well be the equivalent of an annual rate above 50 per cent. Can such high interest rates be explained without invoking usury, that is to say, the extraction of economic rent? Could they, in particular, be explained as socially-efficient, competitive-market responses to a situation in which lenders faced major risks while the opportunity cost of cash was very high?

On risk, the crucial question is whether the brokers were able to hedge their advances against a fall in the cocoa price between advance and delivery or whether the implicit interest rate included a risk premium. The issue of hedging turns on the terms on which European firms gave advances to brokers; and on how effectively they were enforced. The most authoritative contemporary investigations of the economics of cocoa in colonial Ghana very clearly implied (though none were explicit) that the European firms did not give their advances on the basis of a discount from the current spot price.[44] This was, in a sense, 'because' they did not give them on the basis of a fixed price at all. Rather, they advanced a sum of money, to be repaid in produce to the value of the cash lent. This is the implication of the firms' claim, quoted earlier in this section, that the brokers stood to lose from the tumble of prices in 1937. It is confirmed by evidence of contracts revealed in court cases brought by firms against defaulting brokers.[45] The price per unit of cocoa would be whatever price the firm was then paying for delivered produce. The implication is that the brokers, even those who were re-advancing the firms' money rather than using their own, were contractually obliged to accept the full risk (or gain) of a change in price. Yebuah was explicit: 'the person advancing the money [directly to the farmer, i.e. the broker] takes the risk of a rise or fall in the market price.'[46] If this is the full story, the significance of the spot price at the time the broker bought the farmer's cocoa was merely that, as Yebuah (and a colleague of his, Joseph Mensah)[47] indicated, it was used as the reference price from which a discount was made: it did not affect the ultimate return on the sum advanced. Moreover, given the absence of hedging and the presence of big fluctuations in prices, it would follow that much of the brokers' modal return on advances could be accounted for as a risk premium.

There is no doubt that cash was extremely scarce, and in that sense the opportunity cost of a loan was high. This was epitomized by the fact that 'Gold Coasting' apparently still paid: the practice of buying goods from a European firm on credit and selling them quickly, even at a loss, in order to get cash which was then lent out at sufficient interest to pay the original debt and still be in surplus. This can be seen in the internal correspondence of John Holts, one of the major import-export companies, in 1939. Mr. Goddard, its agent in Accra, wrote to his head office in Liverpool in 1939 on the issue of 'produce advances', that is, advances in kind:

> We fully appreciate your concern in regard to the possibility of the restricting of cash advances for Cocoa being followed by the far greater evil of merchandise obtained on credit terms being used for the financing of the crop. You are quite correct . . . that there is, on the Gold Coast, a sharp division between the functions of goods distribution and Cocoa collection—it is a very rare thing to find a Cocoa broker handling merchandise, but in Ashanti there was in the past, a practice of advancing to Chiefs of villages and large farmers quantities of corrugated iron in lieu of cash. These goods were distributed by them as advances and Cocoa collected eventually in payment.[48]

Two months later Goddard indicated that produce advances were no longer merely a thing of the past. That day, at a meeting of general managers of the European firms in Accra:

> We tackled the subject from the point [*sic*] of long credit terms extended on building materials, it being certain that the bulk of this material was

Gold Coasted and used as produce advances. This is particularly prevalent in B.M.T. [British Mandated Togoland] where by far the bulk of cement and galvanised iron is sold on six months credit terms, it is also very bad in Ashanti.[49]

In this context one would expect that liquidity would command a premium. This, along with risk, makes high interest rates relatively plausible even within Bauer's proposition that the market was highly competitive.

Let us now consider this notion directly. Bauer's premise, that the number of brokers was very high and that entry was easy, fits well with the evidence. To receive credit from a European firm it was necessary to become a broker or storekeeper. A prospective entrant was required to find a relative or patron to act as surety: but this does not seem to have been hard to do[50] (as we have noted, thousands managed it). The supply of credit from indigenous African sources was at least elastic enough to respond to the cash famine in the latter stages of the 1937–38 hold-up.[51]

For interest rates to include an element of economic rent the supply of credit would have to have been less than fully price-elastic. For the European cocoa-buying firms the supply of cash was relatively elastic, whether obtained from the turnover on imported goods or from head office or on credit from the banks. But, as some of them discovered first-hand, they were not in a position to lend efficiently to individual farmers. Nowell reported:

> The firms themselves sometimes advance money direct to farmers . . . but . . . it has been admitted to us that this system has not been very successful since, in view of the type of security available, the firms are not prepared to offer as much direct to farmers as are the brokers. We had evidence that farmers who approach a firm for advances may be directed to put their application through one of its brokers, who will then take the responsibility of repayment.[52]

Brokers might be able to use intimate local knowledge to assess the risk of default,[53] thereby partly overcoming the problem of satisfactory security. In any case they might well be willing to accept a farm as collateral, which firms would be reluctant to do. Brokers might also cope more efficiently with the smallness of individual transactions. Thus the supply of advances from European firms to African farmers was channelled by the brokers. This was surely in the interests of all three parties, especially given positive transactions costs and imperfect information. In principle, though, it is possible that the brokers' screening did not simply adjust for imperfections, but also created new ones by permitting individual brokers—especially those best-placed to obtain funds from the firms—to achieve considerable bargaining power in relation to particular farmers. This could be translated into supplying the latter with advances on terms which included a rent.

Moreover it is conceivable that, despite the ease of entry at the bottom of the tonnage range, at any given time few farmers had the equity or contacts with the firms to enter the advance-giving or advance-channeling market on a significant scale. Brokers ranged 'from the farmer who sells his neighbour's crop along with his own to the large independent African or Syrian broker, who may have a capital of some thousands of pounds and handle up to 5,000 tons a season.'[54] To judge from Nowell's rough estimate for Ghana as a whole, in Asante probably only about 450–500 brokers bulked what was sold to them by most of the rest.[55]

If brokers were accused of profiteering from price rises at the expense of the producers, they were also alleged to abuse price falls, thereby capturing what we would now call 'economic rents'. To some extent, claimed the European firms, 'brokers have been able to dictate selling prices to merchants by reason of the power placed in the[ir] hands by cash advances'.[56] This was through a practice which the European firms called 'over-declaration', described as follows:

> On a drop in price brokers have been allowed to declare as stocks in their hands tonnages in excess of those actually existing. This has enabled the broker to continue buying at the higher price ruling before the change long after the home market price has justified. In most cases this abuse has been rendered imperative to the competitive firms and a certain source of revenue to the brokers by the existence [*sic*] of a cash advance. The firm has either had to accept a loss on the purchase of the cocoa or a loss on the advance.[57]

Circumstantially this is highly plausible, at least as a move that individual brokers might make occasionally. What made it possible was the fact that the firms could not afford to supervise the brokers to ensure that they complied fully with the contract. Specifically, the cost of such supervision would defeat the purpose of using intermediaries to bulk the produce. Hence firms could not know whether a broker's declaration of how much he had bought at what price was accurate or not. It is a feasible case of asymmetric information creating 'moral hazard': the conditions for post-contractual opportunism by an agent at the expense of a principal. Direct evidence is, in the nature of the case, limited—either way. But the papers of John Holt of Liverpool, one of the cocoa-buying firms, offer first-hand contemporary testimonies that the practice actually existed. According to Yebuah:

> In the days before the [1937–8] pool it was possible for a broker to be given a price on one day and the next day the price dropped. Immediately I have sent a messenger or a notice to the bush advising the broker of the drop in price. In some instances the broker has returned some four to seven days afterwards saying that he has spent the whole of the money advanced to him in buying cocoa at the old price, and I had to accept cocoa from him also at the old price.
>
> Whenever there is a price drop or a price increase, the farmer in the bush is aware of it always within twenty four hours of it being known in Kumasi.
>
> Prior to the Pool it was a common occurrence for the old price (i.e., in the event of a drop in price) to be paid in the bush for one or even two weeks after the drop in price had become known.[58]

Mensah (who had six years experience as a salaried buyer with various companies) observed that when the price rose the brokers to whom he had given advances would only sell cocoa to him at the new price; whereas when the price fell they would insist on receiving the old price.[59] The company's buying records provide further evidence, for December 1936, of the firm repeatedly paying the old price for cocoa delivered after price falls.[60]

The implications of over-declaration are more radical than simply that brokers thereby captured rent at the expense of the firms who gave them advances. To the extent that brokers could rely on being able to over-declare they were hedged against price falls when they bought forward from farmers; while remaining free to capture the whole of any price rise. Because they had thus transferred the risk to the European firms, the implicit rate interest rate they obtained from African farmers would not include a risk premium. If the interest rate was high, it was because it included a large rent.

But was such exploitation of farmers and firms sustainable? We can envisage that it was in the short term, mainly during high-price buying seasons. In this context Bauer's picture of perfect competition among brokers would not apply at the micro level of the individual produce buyer competing for beans on behalf of his company against the representatives of more than a dozen rival firms in one of dozens of buying centres. For such a buyer it would be essential to hang on to the services of the small number of individual brokers, personally known to him, whom he could trust to deliver large tonnages, even if the price of giving them no reason to take their cocoa elsewhere was to turn a blind eye to suspected over-declarations. It may be highly significant that the quantitative confirmation that over-declaration existed comes from the 1936–37 season when prices were exceptionally high and, despite the dips, were generally rising exceptionally fast.[61] The fact that, as we have seen, the firms themselves thought that the brokers faced big losses because of the subsequent drastic slide in prices implies that even they believed that brokers would not be able to get away with over-declaration in a bear market. Thus for brokers reliable hedging was conditional on a favourable price environment. It also seems unlikely that it could be sustained over several seasons in succession without firms seeking alternative brokers. In this longer-term context Bauer's assumption seems sound.

If over-declaration enabled brokers to capture economic rent, it was at the expense of the European firms rather than the African farmers. That, at least, is the implication of Yebuah's sentence, quoted above, about 'the old price' being commonly 'paid in the bush for one or two weeks after the drop in price had become known'. This makes circumstantial sense: whereas the firms depended (at local level) on the services of specific brokers, farmers had much more choice. In late June or early July 1933 in Techiman division 91 farmers were recorded as having sold their forthcoming cocoa crop while still on the tree. Many of them took advances from more than one broker: there were 125 combinations of farmer and broker. One Kwame Dro divided his forward sales (totaling 34 loads, equivalent to the produce of about four acres) between no less than six different buyers.[62] In this context the farmers were in a stronger competitive position than the European companies. This may be why the Adansehene was able to report from a public meeting in 1933: ' "The Oman . . . observed that there be no support for the farmers to cease this adoption [*sic*] of giving their cocoa while on trees for money of 2/- or 4/- per load" '.[63]

We have seen that the question of whether brokers extracted rents at the expense of firms and farmers has more than one part. The over-declaration mechanism did provide brokers with opportunities to gain— relatively modest—rents from firms, though not from farmers. Even these opportunities were probably confined to individual crop-years in which bull-market conditions were both perceived and real. Otherwise it seems that competition between brokers was sufficient to prevent them from capturing significant rents.

C. Capital Goods after Divorce and Death: The Claims of Wives and Children to Cocoa Farms in a Matrilineal Society

We saw in Chapter 15 that there is a long-established view that cocoa brought a shift from matrilineal inheritance to inheritance by widows and sons. I argued that, while such changes were facilitated—though not required—by a ruling of the Ashanti Confederacy Council in 1942, the evidence suggests that such transitions had occurred only in part by the end of the colonial period. This section emphasizes the severity of the conflicts involved, within families and househlds and among legislators, and examines the arguments and their possible economic implications.

There is plenty of evidence of widowed and divorced women claiming a share in the cocoa farms—the capital goods—they had helped their husbands to make. These claims were based specifically on the proposition that labour deserved reward and created the right to benefit from the assets that it had helped to create. However, this needs to be seen in context of women's view of marriage in general. Among other things, the marriage relationship was seen as an economic arrangement. A wife expected some cash contribution from her husband, and cloth too. In a petition to the chief commissioner in 1936, Akosua Birago of Asante-Akyem put it thus:

> if a man marrys a woman he has to provide the said wife with cloth, daily subsistence and in short anything of vital importance for the said marriage. The woman also has to be very serviceable to the said husband in making farms, petty-trading and shortly anything of benefit to the said husband.[64]

The likes of Akosua Birago expected a return from their help to their husbands in making farms: and her husband eventually gave her part of the cocoa farm they had made.[65] An indication that wives expected to benefit as of right from their husbands' cocoa farming receipts is given by alleged reactions to the government decision to freeze the producer price in 1954. 'There have been suggestions that farmers obtained credit on the expectation of a £7/10/-d. price and now cannot meet their obligations and that their wives were now deserting them.'[66] Even if these 'suggestions' were mistaken, the fact that they were made is evidence that wives believed that they were entitled to benefit materially from their husbands' cocoa income. The strength of women's sense of economic entitlement from husbands is highlighted by Allman and Tashjian's evidence of women in the interwar period protecting themselves from unrewarded labour on their husbands' cocoa farms by, in some cases, refusing to marry a man who expected it or resorting to divorce.[67]

These claims by women were not without some acceptance among men.[68] The case of Abena Denta, the Nsuta woman farming on Adanse land in 1916–17, was introduced in Chapter 14. Its relevance here is that, at this comparatively early date in the history of Asante cocoa-farming, she had inherited a 7,000 tree cocoa farm which had belonged to her late husband, and which she had helped him to make. Though she was eventually dispossessed, this was not by her husband's kin and not because anyone questioned her right to inherit. Rather, it was because she refused to pay rent to the landowning chief.[69] Again, in Amansie district in 1925, upon divorce Adjuah Aboaku apparently had no difficulty in securing one of the three cocoa farms she and her husband had made.

> one Kweku Nkrumah of Domi in Bekwai District was my husband and about one year . . . ago, the marriage between ourselves was dis[s]olved and at the divorcement the husband presented me one cocoa farm at Nkrumaku out of the three cocoa farms I made with him for my trouble. Drink was offered by me and was drunk over this matter by the arbitrators.[70]

But women's claims also faced a great deal of resistance. The view of many male elders about wives' relationship with their husbands' cocoa farms was perhaps epitomized in a statement by one of Rattray's informants in 1925, which emphasized continuity with previous economic practice. Having said (as quoted in Chapter 6) that when wives accompanied husbands in precolonial long-distance trade, 'all the profits she makes are the husband's', the informant added: 'This is carried over to day in cocoa farms a wife helps her husband all the year but all the proceeds are husbands [*sic*]. He will give her a small gift if he wants'. The same applied to the 'help of children on cocoa farms'.[71] In reporting his 1928–29 survey Muir noted that 'in several villages of the Berekum Division females are not allowed to possess cacao farms'.[72] Even Adjuah Aboaku's former husband allegedly changed his mind about allowing her one of the farms they had made when it began to prosper.

> At the time of presenting this cocoa farm some of the plants were in unhealthy condition and seeing that by my effort all the plants are now in good condition and for that the said ex-husband Kweku Nkrumah is claiming the whole farm from me and is making false allegation that he only presented me twenty plants whereas in truth and fact it is not so.[73]

In 1930 the district commissioner of Bekwai noted one day in his official diary that he was dealing with two appeals from divorced women 'dissatisfied at not receiving a portion of their late husbands' cacao farms'.[74] These cases seem to have been appeals from the Native Tribunals of Manso Nkwanta and Bekwai respectively. In the former case the chief's court had evidently found against the woman, for the commissioner wrote that he upheld their judgement 'as the woman insisted on the divorce without reasonable grounds'.[75] In the other case the chiefs were divided. It involved the village of Offoase, whose 'Ohene . . . is very anxious that a woman of his people recently divorced should not be granted a portion of her husband's cacao farm—as in his opinion it is customary [*sic*: presumably meant 'contrary'] to the Ofuasi custom and [would] create a bad precedent. The woman appealed to the Bekwai Elders who disagreed'.[76] However, the provincial commissioner 'Reversed their decision that a divorced woman has by customary law a claim to a portion of her late husband's cacao farms'.[77]

Allman and Tashjian have shown recently that it was only in the 1940s that 'many' women began to bring such cocoa-farm claims, arising from divorce, to chiefs' courts; and that it was only in the 1950s that they began to have much success there. Even so, there remained a wide variation in outcomes indicating an 'utter lack of consensus over how divorced women's complaints should be treated.'[78]

In the Ashanti Social Survey's investigations in Asante-Akyem in the mid-1940s Fortes and Kyei compiled a file of notes of interviews with widows. These women testified to immense suffering at the hands of their deceased husbands' kin, partly explained or rationalized by an expectation that a surviving wife may have been responsible for the husband's death. Invariably they reported having been expelled from their husband's house, with the children, and being denied any share in the cocoa farms that they claimed to have made with him.[79]

On the attitude of chiefs' courts towards widows trying to keep one of her late husband's farms, Fortes stated: 'In the cases of which I have records, the court has invariably ruled in favour of the legitimate matrilineal heir—but with an exhortation, on the grounds of equity and common decency, for some concession to be made by the heir to the dispossessed wife.'[80]

The same institutional forces that hindered the growth of female ownership of cocoa-farms also constrained their size. Because most women could make cocoa farms for themselves only during such times as they could find between or after fulfilling what for them were prior obligations, and because they inherited mere fractions of the farms they had helped their husbands to make, the average size of cocoa farms owned by females was bound to be less than that of cocoa farms owned by males. In part this disadvantaged position was self-reinforcing: being absolutely or at least relatively short of bearing cocoa farms at any one time, women were less likely than men to be able to hire labour to make good this deficiency in the future.[81]

For a later period, the 1960s and early 1970s, Okali's research provides evidence about the dynamics of female cocoa farmownership among the matrilineal Akan in Ghana. She used court records and survey data, the latter including a study of a new cocoa-growing community of 'stranger'-farmers at Dominase in Ahafo. She found that women owners of cocoa farms were most likely to be widows, divorcees or co-wives. They acquired a share of their late or former husband's cocoa farms in return for having helped to make them, or they took advantage of being able to concentrate on working for themselves, either wholly or because of the relative autonomy of being a co-wife, to make cocoa farms of their own. In contrast, a sole wife would have lacked the time to do so, after helping her husband and performing her other duties.[82] This recalls Kyei's observation, quoted in Chapter 16, that those women who were among the first generation to make cocoa farms in that locality, tended to be 'elderly and unattached'.

At this stage it is illuminating to return to the 1928–29 survey. The evidence presented in Chapter 16 showed that, in a given community, the proportion of cocoa-farms owned by women was correlated with the extent of cocoa-farm ownership in the community, and with the proportion of all farmers who had bearing cocoa. That is to say, the longer and 'broader' that cocoa-farming had been established, the higher was the share of women in the ownership of cocoa trees. The figures are presented in graphical form in Fig. 18.1 (see next page).

An explanation can now be proposed. Given the frequently documented propensity for Ghanaian cocoa farmers to make more than one cocoa 'farm', contiguous or otherwise,[83] and the absence of economic advantages of scale,[84] it is a safe generalization that the spread of cocoa farming involved both an increase in the number of farmowners and an increase in the average number of cocoa farms per owner. This implies that the higher the proportion of cocoa farmers in such a village, the higher would be the average number of farms per farmowner. We may assume that the more cocoa farms that men acquired per head, the greater became the average propensity of men to give, concede or leave one of them to their wives, divorced wives or widows. Again, the more farms a husband had, the more likely it became that one (or more) of his co-wives, having first helped him to make cocoa farms, would then find the time to make one for herself.

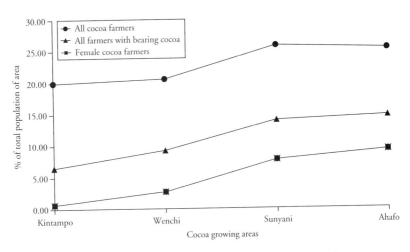

Figure 18.1. Cross-sectional evidence on the dynamics of female cocoa farming: western Asante, 1928–29.
Sources: As for Tables 16.1 and 16.2.

One motive for a wife to do this, in addition to more obvious ones, would be to secure her economic position in case her husband reinvested some of his cocoa income in another marriage. Indeed, we may assume that the more farmers there were with bearing farms, the more male farmers there would be seeking additional wives. Since co-wives tended to have more time free from assisting their husbands, this in turn probably enabled more women to make cocoa farms of their own. Finally, the longer the time since a farmer made his first farm, the greater the chance that he would have divorced or died, raising at least the possibility of part of his estate coming into the possession of his widow or former wife.

To turn from wives to sons, Busia tells of a man who on his deathbed, in 1942 (near Wenchi?), 'made a dying declaration giving one of his cocoa-farms to his son, and swore an oath enjoining his brother, who was his successor [in terms of matrilineal inheritance] to see that the gift was hon-oured'. Such a departure from matrilineal inheritance was valid only with the formal consent of the matrikin. After the death the successor 'refused, with the concurrence of the other members of the family', to follow his dead brother's stipulation. Three months later the inheriting brother himself died, as a result of a fall from a roof when fighting a fire.

Before he died, he told his family that he believed his deceased brother was summoning him to the spirit world to answer for his conduct in not honouring his brother's death-bed declaration. The general belief was that his death was due to his failure to carry out his deceased brother's instructions. The next successor to the property duly gave the cocoa-farm to the son to whom it had been left.[85]

Before its 1942 decision to allow fathers to give self-acquired property to their children 'or any other person' whether his matrikin approved or not,[86] the Ashanti Confederacy Council had repeatedly debated the issue, with Asantehene Prempeh II proposing reform, while the next highest-ranking chief, the Mamponhene, led the resistance.

This transfer of capital goods to sons on death, contested as it was, can be seen as a step on from the nineteenth-century practice of fathers giving sons trade goods to launch them on their economic careers. From 1958 we have a detailed record of a chief's court, at Esumeja in Amansie, endorsing the innovation. The plaintiff, Kofi Adu, successfully sued his father's sister's daughter for trespass. Both parties, like Adu's late father Kwame Danso, were farmers at Esumeja. The starting-point of the case was that Danso had left all his cocoa farms to his sons, daughters and wives: to the evident unhappiness of the defendant.[87]

In Chapter 15 we noted the Ashanti Social Survey's evidence of variations between two districts in the proportion of cocoa-farm inheritance cases which had followed the matrilineal pattern. However, 56 per cent of a sample of 75 and 75 per cent from a sample of 60 are not striking extremes. For what it is worth, Fortes explains the variation between districts largely by relative difference from 'urban social and economic forces', Asante-Akyem being about twice as far from Kumasi as the Asokore-Efiduase area. He also characterised the latter as 'an area of falling productivity', presumably in cocoa farming.[88] Fortes's notion of urban influence is left vague, while Asante-Akyem's extra distance from Kumasi was offset by the fact that it was spanned by the main Accra-Kumasi road. It is also unclear what significance he attached to falling productivity in cocoa-farming. Furthermore, while yields on old farms in Mampon district were liable to decline earlier than in Asante-Akyem because, being near the savanna, the former had relatively poor soils for cocoa, yields in the latter were suffering from its status as perhaps the oldest cocoa-growing district in Asante, with much old stock, some of which was now infected with swollen shoot disease. The absence of a strongly plausible hypothesis to account for the observed variations in the survey findings strengthens the suspicion that any real variations in inter-generational transmission patterns between districts was minor.

This section has explored the changing interaction between the provision of inputs, specifically of labour, by members of the farmowner's conjugal and matrilineal families, and the effect of this on the acquisition of property rights. It has argued that Hill's proposition about the growth of female farmownership in matrilineal cocoa-growing societies is accurate as a description of the eventual outcome, but requires modification in two important respects. First, the growth in female farm ownership of cocoa farms began very slowly, and was strongly opposed. Second, by the end of the colonial period, and indeed much later, it was still the case that much less of the capital value of cocoa farms was under female than under male ownership.[89] However, the prolonged struggle of widowed and divorced women for shares in cocoa farms which they had helped their late or former husbands to make is a vivid and important example of a theme emphasised by Allman and Tashjian: women participating strongly in the making of their own histories.[90]

Cocoa farming greatly heightened the divergence between the economic interests of wives and children, on the one hand, and the matrilineage on the other, in the disposal of the assets of a divorced or deceased husband. There was intense resistance to departing from matrilineal inheritance. But by the 1940s the cause, previously fought for by individual women in local courts, had attracted the support of the Asantehene. The rule-change that he pushed through the Ashanti Confederacy Council did not compel a general shift to the conjugal family as the unit of inheritance. Nor does it appear to have led to one. But the most plausible overall conclusion is that there was an increase, by the end of the colonial period, in the frequency with which wives and possibly sons inherited capital assets from men. This is broadly in line with the findings of Allman and Tashjian, in an excellent recent discussion which draws heavily on their own interviews.[91] My understanding from fieldwork in Amansie in 1980[92] is that the formal rules of inheritance changed little during the colonial era, but that the relative frequency with which different rules are applied shifted— at the expense of matrilateral inheritance, even if the latter remained common. In the early 1980s I frequently heard criticisms of the matrilineal system from both men and women. In 1985 the Provisional National Defence Council government made a clear legislative attempt to secure rights of inheritance for children and surviving spouses.[93] How far it worked within Asante society is beyond the scope of this study.

On the whole cocoa farming enabled Asante rural producers to increase their income and wealth. Thus the conflict over the gender division of cocoa property was a struggle over an enlarged pool of wealth. To the extent that the adoption of cocoa farming led to a greater frequency of productive assets being transmitted to the next generation by paternal gift rather than matrilineal inheritance, this experience matches Goody's hypothesis (discussed earlier in a pre-colonial context) that when the value of legacies increases, inheritance practices become more restrictive, reducing the dispersion of estates and promoting the concentration of wealth.[94]

D. Long-Term Lending and Welfare: The Pledging of Cocoa Farms

Pledging Cocoa Farms to Avoid Credit Rationing?

Responding to the long-bearing lives of cocoa trees, the mortgaging of cocoa farms was usually a vehicle for long-term loans. We may ask why Asantes borrowed and lent long-term in the rural economy of the colonial period. For long-term credit at high interest rates presents to the borrower the risk of a self-perpetuating drive towards penury, and to the lender the likelihood of not being repaid.

During the second half of the colonial occupation, as we saw in Chapter 15, there was intense concern among British officials and commentators over indebtedness among cocoa farmers. The debate between and around the colonial policy-makers over the efficiency and exploitativeness of indigenous credit arrangements has echoed since in the academic argument over whether the colonial changes promoted entrepreneurship or simply rentiership. From a dependency theory perspective, Rhoda Howard restated the view of a usury-ridden, rentier-dominated countryside, within the context of an externally-dependent economy in which world price fluctuations were a source of the demand for credit and foreign firms, ultimately, a source of its supply.[95] Cowen and Shenton have shown that British banks in West Africa were keen to expand their business with Africans, including lending to them: providing the colonial governments made the institutional reforms that would have lowered the risk of default and the cost of pursuing defaulters.[96] Whether private enterprise or government was to blame, the colonial legacy has been widely seen as inadequate for the efficient promotion of economic development. Specifically, commentators have pointed to the continued fragmentation of the capital market, including the persistent overlap between consumption and production loans, and the lack of any pronounced flow of agricultural savings into productive investment in other sectors.[97]

Such characteristics of the colonial cash-crop economy of Asante (and of Ghana generally and of much of West Africa) as widespread indebtedness and high interest rates are paralleled in many other countries in that period and to the present. We may identify several themes in the debate about how such phenomena should be understood. One is the sense that high interest rates were (are) indeed usurious, that is, that they included a very large element of economic rent. In that sense they were 'exploitative' even in neoclassical terms. The ultimate result was a transfer of assets from poor to rich. The fact that indebtedness widespread among farmers underlines the enormity of the problem. We will see shortly that, in colonial Ghana generally, officials argued in addition that indigenous credit arrangements were inefficient in their effects on the quality and quantity of output.

Hill offers a more optimistic assessment, from an agrarian populist perspective. To elaborate on my earlier summaries of her position, she has interpreted the case of Ghanaian cocoa as evidence for her general challenge to the conventional assumption that moneylending in rural communities in Africa and Asia has been, and is, usually a symptom or a cause of poverty. She argues where farms were mortgaged, they were usually mortgaged to fellow farmers. Thus each farming debt was also a farming credit. While debt was widespread it was functional to the operation of the local rural economy rather than being a cause or index of cumulative impoverishment of part of the population. She maintains that interest rates charged by moneylenders were much lower in real than in nominal terms, primarily because interest was often fixed at the start rather than accumulating over time, and that lenders rarely foreclosed.[98]

A still more upbeat note was sounded from a radical free-market perspective in the 1950s and 1960s. Peter Bauer and Hlya Myint pointed to elements of competitiveness and efficiency in credit markets in West Africa and other 'developing' regions; which they believed were hampered by the interventions of post-war and post-colonial governments in the name of promoting development. While, as we have seen, Bauer emphasized the ease of entry into the ranks of African brokers and lenders before the introduction of statutory marketing in 1939, Myint insisted that high interest rates mainly reflected 'a real shortage of savings' and 'the extra risks and costs of lending money to a large number of small borrowers'.[99]

A more nuanced framework is offered by work in economic theory in the 1980s and since, introduced in Chapter 2, which accepts that markets tend to be imperfect, focuses on information problems as the major source of imperfection, and highlights institutional arrangements which it sees as responses to those problems. The fundamental characteristic of borrowing in such settings, according to the theory, is what has become known in the literature, with nice irony, as 'limited liability': re-payment is ultimately optional because the creditor cannot effectively and/or cheaply enforce it. As Kaushik Basu summarises it in a slightly different context, 'The *limited liability axiom* asserts that if *i* has some financial commitment towards *j* (for example, a loan to be repaid or rent to be paid) but happens to be bankrupt, then *j* has to forego his claim'.[100] These studies report that, while indebtedness is widespread and the risk of bankruptcy high in the informal sectors of contemporary less-developed economies, default rates on informal-sector loans tend to be very low despite asymetric information. The explanation suggested in this literature is that lenders find strategies which keep default rates down. The basic one is to ration credit, such that only some of those would-be borrowers with the means to make the required payments on a loan actually receive one.[101] The credit market is segmented, creating local monopolies. These, as much or more than the risk of default, result in high interest rates.[102]

Let us begin the empirical discussion by asking two basic questions. The first is why borrowers sought long-term loans: specifically, what were the needs or desires for liquidity that motivated them to pledge cocoa farms? The second is why lenders lent: which we will approach by considering their behaviour and their interests given the structure of the contract. I will then present the main argument of this sub-section. This is that the nature of the usual kind of mortgage contract in Asante, specifically the fact that it took the form of a pledge rather than a charge, together with the physical characteristics of cocoa trees, which made them long-term capital assets, provided a solution to the 'limited liability' constraint on lending. Hence credit rationing was unnecessary. We will go on to consider the workings of the farm-mortgage market in relation to issues of welfare and exploitation.

It is much easier to list than to measure the kinds of spending for which farmers were prepared to take the portentous step of borrowing comparatively large sums at interest; a particularly alarming act when repayment was made more difficult by the transfer of a cocoa farm to the lender's possession. It is useful to distinguish three broad categories, all of which are attested to in the sources.[103] First, expenditure to finance cocoa production: to pay labourers and/or establish a new farm.[104] Second, litigation over land, including payment of contributions by subjects to meet the legal expenses of a stool boundary dispute. Such expenditure could be classified as, in part, indirectly or potentially 'productive' in an economic sense: for the outcome might determine whether the farmers concerned were deemed to be 'strangers' on the land on which they were farming and, therefore, liable to pay rent. Finally, there was expenditure which, in economic terms, was 'consumption': notably spending on subsistence, housing, medicines and social rites of passage. According to information collected by three farmers' co-operative unions in Asante (Ahafo, Bekwai and Kumasi districts) in c.1955, 40 per cent of farmers' indebtedness was for 'farming' expenses, i.e. the first category. This figure may well be misleadingly high. Though the debts concerned were far from being exclusively owed to the co-operatives, the respondents were presumably members of cooperatives. Given that the cooperatives' policy was to urge—and give loans for—only 'productive' borrowing, respondents may well have been reluctant to admit to having borrowed for other purposes. The policy faced severe 'moral hazard'. An experienced administrator expressed 'a purely personal opinion': of 'doubt as to the percentage of cases in which loans have actually been used for the purposes [for which they were] nominally requested.'[105] In analysing the causes of debt a further complication is that the immediate purpose for which money is required may not be the reason why the sum had to be borrowed. In 1935 the chief of Bechem claimed that the 'annual cocoa tribute' that his subjects had to pay for farming on Dormaa-Wam land 'has created and maintained the basis of our present chronic indebtedness'. This was in the context of a plea for the tribute demand to be reduced.[106] Besides the special pleading, his statement is interesting because it raises the possibility that rent demands may have been the basis of indebtedness, in the sense of impoverishing the farmers whether or not the sums they borrowed were used specifically to pay rent.

Overall, it seems clear that directly productive expenditures constituted very much the minority of the immediate sources of borrowing. This is what most of the—as has been emphasized—admittedly problematic sources indicate. But, further, it is hard to believe that the circumstances allowed anything else. For the high interest rates would make it extremely hard for the borrower to make a profit on the deal. Rather, the terms make it likely that this kind of borrowing was often prompted by desperation rather than strategic calculation. Another possibility, rather than rational desperation, was profligacy. The chief commissioner observed in his annual report for 1932–33 that mortgaging of cocoa farms ' "has not occurred so frequently in the Juaben Division" '. He attributed this ' "to the fact that the Omanhene himself is always notified of every debt incurred by his sub-chiefs' Stools and insists on all his subjects reporting any debt over about £2 or £3 to his Chief before a loan is effected and [that] the document is witnessed by that Chief or some of his elders. This prevents rash loans on the part of the young men and in the case of a properly witnessed loan secures help." ' Later in 1933 the government encouraged chiefs to make this general practice.[107]

The very fact that much borrowing on pledged cocoa farms was to finance 'consumption' (enforced or otherwise) rather than directly productive investment was itself good reason for the lender to be wary. The fact that the borrowing was usually not going to be self-financing made the likelihood of default very high. But the system of pledging—the fact that the collateral, itself a productive asset, was handed over at the time of the loan—would have reassured the lender. This point will be taken further below.

In exploring what the lenders wanted from such a deal, or more precisely, what incentives faced them and what preferences they revealed, we have evidence about the structure of the contract and the choices made by some creditors in response to default. A snapshot of contracts is available from the same camera that we used on interwar advances: the 1933 survey. In Adanse the main form of mortgaging was for the farm to be pledged for five years. The lender took over the farm and kept its receipts as interest. If the principal was not repaid in time, he became the owner.[108] This system was 'very common' also in Kumasi and Mampon districts.[109] In Amansie, according to 'reports from Chiefs', 'the commonest system' was:

> that the whole or part of the crop is taken each year as interest, the amount of the loan remaining unchanged. In a very few cases part of the proceeds of the sale of the crop go to pay off a portion of the principle [*sic*] amount so that the loan is definitely liquidated at the end of a stated period of years.[110]

A similar picture emerged in the mid-1940s from the Ashanti Social Survey's work, which in this respect had focused on the samples of farms in Sekyere and Ahafo districts that we already considered in other contexts. An unpublished memorandum in Fortes's papers, evidently by himself in c.1946, commented as follows:

> The conditions attached to mortgages on farms vary greatly and no general rule exists. The commonest practice is for the mortgagee to take over the farm completely and harvest it until it is redeemed, the annual crop being regarded as interest on the loan. The loan may bear a monetary interest in addition. One practice, however, is for the mortgagee to harvest the farm

and set aside a proportion of the actual proceeds as repayment of the loan. Though this is not common farmers are strongly in favour of regularising this practice by legislation.[111]

The Ashanti Confederacy Council had recommended in 1943 ' "that the secured farm may be in the possession of both lender and borrower" '.[112] If so, as the quotation from the Fortes Papers illustrates, this does not appear to have been implemented on the ground. By the mid-1950s, to judge from the 1956–57 survey, mortgaging of cocoa farms was synonymous with 'pledging'.

The author of an article in a colonial Department of Agriculture publication commented in 1934 that the increase in farm mortgaging (which the writer confusingly termed 'crop mortgaging') was because 'it produces a certain and definite return to the money-lender', while the decrease in advances against future cocoa was 'because of the relative ease with which the farmer can evade repayment.'[113] The writer mistook cycle for trend, in that (as we saw in Chapter 15) no such long-term switch from crop advances to farm mortgages was under way. But the comment contained a major insight. From the perspective of potential lenders, the great virtue of the system of pledging farms was that it overcame the 'limited liability' problem. Because the farm—which was both collateral and a means of paying interest and principal—was handed over to the creditor, the latter was secure against default by the debtor. Pledging therefore reduced or removed the incentive to ration credit. The lender might lack information on the trustworthiness of the borrower, and might have found it expensive to chase him should he default. But these issues did not arise because the means to secure payment of interest and principal were put into the possession of the creditor at the start.

In some African settings it is/was not unusual for creditors to avoid or postpone foreclosure, in order to maintain a patron/client relationship and/or to continue enjoying interest payments.[114] In Asante the pledging contract removed a major incentive to foreclose: because the creditor was already in possession of the security. In this context it is almost surprising that foreclosures did occur. In 1933 it was reported in Kumasi district that 'Many mortgages are never redeemed and the farms are sold under writs of Fi: Fa.'[115] This is confirmed by a file containing details of over a dozen such sales from late 1929 to early 1933, from Kumasi and Amansie districts.[116] The Sunyani district commissioner stated in May 1933 that in the preceding seven months he as Deputy Sheriff had seized twelve cocoa farms under writs of *Fi: Fa*.[117] We noted in Chapter 15 that in July 1933 the commissioner for Wenchi district sent to Kumasi a detailed tabulation of indebtedness among cocoa farmers. In Wenchi division [oman] itself nine farmers unable to repay loans had suffered their farms being 'taken over by mortgagors', though this had not happened in at least one of the other two divisions of the district, Techiman and Nkoranza.[118] In the Wenchi case the source does not state whether foreclosure was by legal process, but the other examples show that the creditors, assuming they were equipped with promissory notes, received the backing of the courts. Providing the mortgage was a pledge, they were doubly secure: they enjoyed the proceeds of the farm and could hold onto it unless and until the debt was cleared. If, on default, they wished to retrieve their cash and reinvest, the state would enforce their right to do so by arranging the sale of the collateral.

On the face of it, farm-pledging in Asante looks like a case of inter-linked factor markets,[119] like the credit institution which preceded it, human pawning, by which the lender obtained both interest and labour. But with pledging the appearance is deceptive. For the structure of the contract was such that for the term of the loan the creditor's interest in the farm that he (as it usually was) took over was limited to precisely that: to secure interest on his loan by harvesting and selling the produce and, usually, additional interest paid in cash directly from the borrower. So for the lender the transaction was confined to the market for credit and capital, not for land or labour. Legally, the land itself was not the borrower's to alienate. Economically, to use lending on cocoa farms as a means to acquire land (use) rights would make little sense as alternative means of obtaining land were available which were much more secure. That the pledging contract did not involve interlinking of factor markets makes sense in terms of the neoclassical explanation of interlinking, as an instrument to make possible deals which would otherwise not happen. For in this case, pledging itself was that instrument.

Let us turn to the implications of cocoa-farm pledging for welfare and 'social efficiency'. How widely available was long-term credit through this means, and at what cost? By definition, to borrow on the security of a cocoa farm you had to own one. This precluded young men who had yet to establish one. More so, the gender distribution of cocoa farms implies that most such credit went to men. Farm-pledging by women may be assumed to have risen, but only gradually and slightly, as the female share in cocoa-farm ownership edged upwards. The pattern was not changed by the entry of 'formal-sector' lenders into the market for long-term credit. In 1953 thirteen cocoa farmers from Beposo near Mampon received loans from the Cocoa Purchasing Company: twelve men, one woman.[120] This admittedly small sample illustrates that women could get such loans; and that, relatively, very few of them did. In the CPC case this may have been the bias, conscious or unconscious, so often attributed to formal institutions during this period. But the proportion is not unexpected given the male predominance in cocoa-farm ownership, even by the decolonization era, coupled with the CPC's aim of relieving farmers' existing indebtedness by displacing private lenders.

Was lending on pledged farms 'usurious', in the sense of extracting economic rent? A basic problem in addressing this question is that it is hard to be sure how high interest rates actually were, in annual terms. According to Bray, writing shortly after the end of colonial rule, 'Interest rates jumped to their present level in 1937', that level being fifty per cent 'without strict regard to the time period involved'.[121] It seems that Bray was wrong about an enduring change having occurred in 1937, for interest rates had been as high or higher in at least some earlier years as they were to be afterwards. This is not to dispute that there was a jump in 1937, but it was apparently a temporary movement: presumably in anticipation of and/or in response to the cocoa hold-up, during which cash was exceptionally scarce. During the 1933–34 enquiry it had been reported from Amansie that:

> In view of the varying yields of farms it is impossible of course to arrive at an accurate idea of the rate of interest obtained, but in one specific case the interest on a loan of £13 is given as 17 loads per annum, which, assuming a price of 8/- per load, works out at approximately 50% per annum.[122]

As it happens, over the next several years prices were at least as high as during the 1933–34 season. This implies that the interest rate in this case would have been over 50 per cent a year. We have already seen that the risk *of* default was high: especially where, by handing over a cocoa farm, the borrower surrendered a productive asset with which he or she might otherwise have raised the means to repay. But for the creditor the risk *from* default was low, because he already had the farm. In view of this the general level of interest rates does seem to have been very high, despite the concessions made in individual cases. This picture is consistent with Bray's data from a quarter of a century later, presented in Table 18.2. This summarises the size and terms of the loans owed by 73 farmers in Ahafo who were in debt at the end of the cocoa season.

Table 18.2. Credit, debt and interest in relation to source of loan among cocoa-farmers in Ahafo, c.1957–58[1]

Source of loan	Local farmer or relative	Money lender	Cooperative Society	Cocoa Purchasing Company
Loan received (principal)	£18,013	£1,650	£160	£1,450
Amount repayable (principal + interest)	£21,994	£2,725	£160	£1,625
Interest/principal	22.1%	65.2%	Nil	12.1%
Share of source in total principal	84.5%	7.8%	0.8%	6.8%

[1] Data from Bray, *Cocoa Development in Ahafo*, Table VI. Bray does not specify which season, but it was either 1956–57 or 1957–58 (see ibid., i, 1). It seems most likely that a survey on such a sensitive subject as debt would have been carried out later rather than earlier in the research, to allow time for Bray's field assistant, B.M. Agyare, to win the confidence of informants (cf. ibid., 50).

As with (and related to) foreclosure, the annual interest rate was effectively at the creditor's discretion. Bray's observation that the standard rate in Ahafo in the late 1950s, though ostensibly high at 50 per cent, was a fixed sum not related to a specific term, is anticipated in a more detailed description from c.1945, by a colonial administrator.

The normal interest is 50% to be paid together with the principal within 1 year or less. However this is seldom done nor does either party indeed expect it to be performed. Then follows a series of annuam [*sic*] borrowings which result in payments of about one tenth or so of the amount being received as 'drink' without reducing the original debt. Then if further delayed interest of a further 50% may be charged on the original making 100% but save with a few of the biggest moneylenders interest beyond this is not charged in cash and arrangements are then made for gradual repayment.[123]

Hence the annual rate of interest demanded depended on whether and when the creditor chose to foreclose.

It is reasonable to suggest that he or she would be influenced in this by the social relationships involved and by the nature of the contract. The two might overlap. This may be what was meant by Chief Kobina Yebua in 1919, petitioning the government for relief from his debt of £545 owed to the estate of B. C. Asafu-Adjaye, when he lamented: 'It is only by the death of the lender that I have lost all the advantages to which I should be entitled as an Ashanti money borrower having already suffered the disadvantages of the situation.' He had mortgaged his cocoa and rubber (mostly the former by now, to judge from his letter) plantation on the outskirts of

Kumasi for a flat-rate loan. It is easy to read too much into what may have been special pleading, and his main claim was that the lender had died before he found a mislaid document proving that the debt (comprising two loans) was only £400, including interest of £130.[124] But it may be remarked that had the creditor rather than his heir been making the decision, he might well have allowed the account to remain open which, given that the interest was not accumulating, would have been to the borrower's advantage. Where, unlike in Yebua's case, the contract took the form of a pledge rather than a mortgage possession of the farm removed urgency from the demand for interest separate from that provided by the farm's crop.

Clearly, this was not a fully integrated market in which the law of one price prevailed. In this context simple models—whether of usury, friendly accommodation, or perfect competition—are inadequate. The supply of long-term loans in rural Asante is better seen as involving a range of relationships variously combining elements of competition, social obligation and elements of predation. Schematically, we can see this range as having two regions: one a competitive market in which farmers lent among themselves, the other a multiplicity of highly imperfect micro markets and individual relationships between the most desperate borrowers (those lacking alternative lenders) and professional moneylenders. In their different ways all responded to the scarcity of liquidity.

We have seen that credit between farmers was by far the largest portion of long-term rural lending. That it was a competitive market is evidenced by the very fact that average interest rates could be as low as 22 per cent in an economy in which capital was still relatively scarce, and in which institutional constraints were such that the banks would not lend on farms. The conditions that facilitated the existence of a competitive market were the combination of widespread ownership of potential collateral (especially bearing cocoa trees) with a wide distribution of potential lenders. This would be the market segment in which farmers borrowed from farmers (and other non-specialist lenders) who had no particular social obligation towards them: on the security of pledged cocoa farms. These farmers would all be 'local' in Bray's terms: partly because there would be no need for either party to go far afield; and partly because only locals would have the information necessary to assess the risk of default well enough to consider offering a loan. Given that a nominal interest rate was set by custom (the 50 per cent rate),[125] one would expect that fluctuations in the balance between supply and demand would be felt in the periods which creditors allowed for repayment and in the handling of default. In this market (or market segment) the actual average annual interest rates would often be well under 50 per cent. If they were still high, from the perspective of a borrower, that was because liquidity was so scarce.

In other long-term credit transactions—the second 'region' of long-term credit supply and indebtedness in the rural economy—the degree of competition would have been much less. Some borrowers took advantage of their familial or other social relationships to obtain loans on concessionary terms, in some cases perhaps interest-free. At the other extreme some would lack access even to the competitive market because they had no bearing cocoa farm to pledge; or needed to retain such cocoa trees as they possessed to provide some sort of income; or had cocoa trees to pledge, but not enough to cover the sum required. Such borrowers would have to pawn 'unproductive' chattels such as jewelry, or face especially high interest rates in the context of credit rationing. Some might well find themselves facing a local monopoly, in which only one person was willing to lend to them at all. In those settings the interest paid would have included an element of economic rent. This may well have been the case with Owusu Nyantakyi, a major moneylender based in Kumasi, whose clients in 1945–46 included the five most indebted people in the village of Adeɛbeba, on the outskirts of Kumasi.[126]

It is pertinent to ask why specialist moneylenders were so comparatively unimportant as lenders on cocoa farms. In 1934 a commissioner observed that 'the recognised money lenders' in Amansie district 'do not willingly accept Cacao farms as security preferring something more substantial such as houses or gold ornaments.'[127] The veteran district commissioner quoted in Chapter 15 observed in c.1945 that 'Syrians . . . dislike dealing in farm property and specialise either in the town house property, or valuable trinkets.'[128] The local lenders—anyone with cash to spare—had a decisive edge over the specialists in that they had, precisely, local knowledge and could use local social ties to bring moral suasion to bear in the event of default. The lack of concentration among the local part-time lenders, by making for considerable competition in local credit markets, probably reduced the many borrowers' sense of being exploited: a matter to which we will return shortly.

It should be added that the professional lenders' share in the long-term debts of cocoa farmers was surely not static. We have seen that it was small both in our 'depression' snapshot from 1933–34, and in our 'boom' one from c.1957–58. But on the analysis offered here it is a reasonable prediction that, should adequate evidence surface to test it, it will be found that a higher proportion of farmers' debts, in both volume of loans and in total value, were owed to specialist lenders in the former period.

The logic of this prediction is simple: with a smaller volume of output and lower producer prices in the 1930s, a higher proportion of cocoa farmers would have needed loans, but fewer fellow-farmers were in a position to lend. Thus more would have been forced to seek out the professionals.

To complete the contrast between farmer-lenders and specialist lenders let us consider their respective aims. Judging from their behaviour, for the 'professional' lenders the object of the business, as McCaskie argues, was to maintain an inflow of interest. Such lenders seem to have invested little in working any cocoa farms they took on pledge,[129] and they had nothing to gain from foreclosing on a farm: in both cases, because this would slow/lower the return on their capital. Hence their preference for maintaining a usurious relationship rather than losing the client. But for the much larger category of farmers prepared to lend when they had money available, the acquisition of another cocoa farm, temporarily or permanently, was potentially attractive. They were themselves used to mobilizing labour to work cocoa farms: one more would be an extension of their own main business. Hence the mixture of lenders who would not foreclose and lenders who did; besides the majority of long-term lenders, who had no need to foreclose because they already possessed the farm on pledge.

Self-Perpetuating Debt and Permanent Dispossession?

This sub-section pursues the issue of usury further. We begin by asking how far lending at interest on the security of pledged farms was socially accepted within the rural communities. In this context we explore the significance of the local provenance of most of the creditors. We go on to consider the borrowers' own problem of 'moral hazard': the risk that creditors would neglect the farms they held as security. We then consider whether the pledging of cocoa farms was a self-perpetuating form of long-term indebtedness; assess how the overall level of pledging changed during the period; and examine whether indebtedness tended to result in the permanent dispossession of the borrower.

In his microhistory of the above-mentioned Adeɛbeba, McCaskie presents a typology of sardonic terms for different kinds of loan, terms which were apparently in use in the mid-1940s.[130] There was a kind of short-term loan whose urgency was implied by its familiar name '*fɛm*, a usage that implied the sense of being pressed upon or squeezed'; another contract was '*fifiri* ('Fafafiri'), literally, "sweating"', under which the lender was entitled 'to revise interest or repayment conditions every three months'; then there was '*huru*, literally the "jumping" loan in which compound interest might be charged at . . . 50 per cent every six days'. According to McCaskie, 'Worst of all loans was *afaaseduru*—the "laxative"—an agreement that imposed such high interest charges that trying (and failing) to repay them "purged" the borrower of all money without ever reducing the principal.'[131] The word for moneylender was *ɔkyekyefo*, literally 'he who binds'.[132] Kyei recalled that 'To go to a money-lender to raise a loan was a dreaded evil.'[133]

Yet there is evidence, specifically from the 1930s and 1940s, that in Asante the lending of money on cocoa was widely accepted as legitimate by those whom the government regarded as its victims: the farmers. We have already seen this in the case of advances. In respect of both farm-mortgaging and advances, Nana Osei Agyeman Prempeh II, the 'Kumasihene', told the acting district commissioner of Kumasi in 1933 'that he is well aware of the pernicious effect of it all, but it is now so widespread that interference by him would be an extremely unpopular move'.[134] These quotations are not necessarily in contradiction. Kyei's recollection may have reflected attitudes to the predicament of borrowers without access to friendly relatives or to the competitive sector of the market, while the 1933 statement may have reflected attitudes to the latter sector. Again, it is possible to dread a visit to the dentist without disputing the social value of dentistry. Thus, while debtors surely did not welcome the levels of interest rate which British officials regarded as usurious—and McCaskie's lexicon from Adeɛbeba confirms this—they do *not* seem to have been widely regarded as in any sense illegitimate.

After all, unlike the banks and even some of the specialist moneylenders, the pledgee was at least willing to accept as security and as payment of interest and perhaps also of principal, the one large asset that many farmers had to offer. Even a heavily indebted individual whose collateral was apparently a Kumasi house (which might have been more attractive to bankers) rather than a cocoa farm, affirmed that ' "usurers are needful to everybody here (in Adeɛbeba) and are good helpers with the trials of life" '.[135] While many people may have dreaded having to borrow, there does not seem to have been general disapproval of moneylending as such, nor of taking farms in pledge. This, as much as the technical problems of enforcement, helps to explain the general ineffectiveness of colonial anti-usury legislation (which was reported in Chapter 15).

Less easy to reconcile with a consensual view of moneylending is what the Ashanti Social Survey was told in Akyenakrom, about 17 kilometres southeast of Kumasi, in 1945–46.

> I was surprised to hear that despite the huge debt that the people in this village owe and the fact that they are unable to pay the debt, no one has

been compelled to mortgage or sell his farm. The farmers think it is a disgrace to sell or mortgage one's farm and it is therefore the last thing to do. For this reason I did not meet even a single case of mortgaged or sold farms.[136]

Pledging of farms was so widespread, however (hence Fortes's surprise, presumably), that even if the visiting researcher was given the full story in this village, it does not seem to have been generally the case that moneylenders (at least non-specialist ones) were pariah figures. This was partly because of acceptance of their role, and partly because, as we saw in Chapter 15, they were not identifiable as a social minority because moneylending was widely distributed through the community.

Colonial officials tended to regard moneylenders not only as usurers but also as parasites, in that they saw creditors' acquisition of farms as a recipe for under-investment in production.[137] They argued that the creditor who took over a farm on pledge had little or no incentive to invest resources in its long-term maintenance. Both in Asante and further south evidence accumulated that cocoa-farmers' creditors preferred merely to harvest the farms they acquired from debtors, rather than invest in their maintenance.[138] This may be partly accounted for by the cyclical dimension of farm-pledging: the prevailing low producer prices, which had often helped to bring the original farmowner into debt himself, discouraged the lender from long-term investment in the farm. It also surely reflected a calculation based on the lack of economies of scale in cocoa farmownership. Cocoa farming might provide a good income by village standards, but larger fortunes required diversification and an emphasis on activities which were more likely to yield high returns on large sums invested, such as produce-buying and—up to a point—moneylending. However, the officials' criticism is highly plausible. The pledging contract gave creditors incentive to harvest any current crop. But any long-term investment that they made would be wasted if the debt was cleared and the farm redeemed. Yet in the case of cocoa it is doubtful that neglect of maintenance would have seriously impaired the long-term potential of the farm.[139] This appears to be a case where, in terms of efficient use of resources, the contract was flawed because it created moral hazard: but the practical consequences were fairly minor. So, as we have noted, were those of the Confederacy Council's recommendation of 1943 that mortgaged farms should be jointly held by lender and borrower. This step had been taken precisely ' "As it has been found that some lenders do not take reasonable care of mortgaged farms in their possession and as such farms deteriorate while in their hands . . ." '[140]

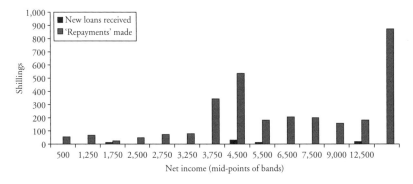

Figure 18.2. Cocoa-farm mortgages in Asante, 1956–57: 'repayments' (including interest?) and new borrowing.
Source: Ghana, *Survey of Cocoa Producing Families in Ashanti, 1956–57*, Table 32.

Usurious relationships are traditionally considered to be self-perpetuating. The Watson Report levelled precisely this charge. 'Of the variety of mortgages in the Gold Coast there is no end. They usually, however, have one feature in common—the unlikelihood of the borrower ever escaping from the clutches of the lender.'[141] This view fits Bray's sample: of 74 cocoa-farmers in debt at the beginning of the cocoa season, 73 were still in debt at the end.[142] But Bray himself, having reviewed the extent and terms of each debt, concluded 'Taking it over all, debt is not a serious problem'.[143] Decisively, the pessimistic argument surely falls when one considers the much larger survey conducted across the 1956–57 season. As Fig. 18.2 shows, indebtedness decreased greatly during these six months.

Is it possible to offer an overview of the changes in the level of cocoa-farm pledging over the period? It was argued in Chapter 15 that the changing incidence of farm-pledging had two basic dimensions. One was a pro-cyclical pattern: more mortgages in a depression, less in a boom. The other was a long-term rise in the supply schedule, as the population of potential lenders grew richer and more numerous, albeit at a very uneven rate of progress. It remains to account for these phenomena and for certain exceptions or qualifications.

That the demand for loans should rise when average incomes fell is not surprising, especially in the case of relatively large loans: the kind of loans for which it was often necessary to provide as security so comparatively large a productive asset as a cocoa farm. For the demand for lumpy expenditure was relatively income-inelastic: funerals had to be properly performed even in economic recessions. One would expect that in such circumstances the supply of loans from those with cash reserves would increase, in that the real value of cash balances rises when prices are generally falling. The latter was especially the situation in the early 1930s Depression because of the sharp fall in the prices of imports. But this would not have applied in wartime when, partly because of shipping shortages, cocoa export prices were down but import prices were up. For Asante specifically, there are two additional reasons why the 1916–19 slump in cocoa prices did not trigger a wave of farm mortgages similar to that which occurred in the early 1930s. One is that for borrowers a partial alternative existed in that wife-pawning was still not impossible. The other is that Asante cocoa output was still very much in the 'take off' phase, with a very high proportion of farms yet to come into substantial bearing. Such farms would not be as attractive to most potential lenders as the more mature farms which were already predominant in the older cocoa-growing areas south of the Pra.

The grounds for thinking that there was a long-term upward shift in the supply schedule are the same as for advances, which were discussed above. Why then was the level of pledging apparently much higher in 1933–34 than in 1956–57? Partly for cyclical reasons: the former being a depression year, the latter a boom one (albeit slightly less so than the immediately preceding seasons). The same relationship was noted among cocoa-farmers in southwest Nigeria for much the same period: a major survey there in the early 1950s found evidence that long-term indebtedness had fallen during the recent years of relatively high producer prices.[144] But it must also have reflected the effects of the CPC/CMB campaign to relieve indebtedness.

Let us now assess how far indebtedness really was a motor of 'proletarianisation', driving struggling farmers out of the cocoa-produce market altogether: at least before the easier conditions of the 1950s. We need first to consider the evidence of farm-pledging leading to the permanent loss of the farm to the debtor, either because the account was never settled or, more usually, because it was settled by the sale of the farm in response to the borrower defaulting.

The temporary alienation of farms, which mortgaging often involved, could become permanent. This was testified in Amoafo[145] and we have noted it in the case of various foreclosures. In principle Asante land law allowed the original owners the chance to recover their former property, but this seems largely to have been a dead letter when default led to farms being auctioned by court order. Indeed, long before a pledging case reached that stage the borrower might consider the farm—now, after all, in the creditor's possession—irretrievable. Fortes commented that 'Many farmers tend to think of farms they have mortgaged as being permanently lost to them' (which he thought led to concealment of the full extent of mortgaging).[146]

Indeed, the Fortes Papers show that the permanent alienation of farms was much more widespread than one would think from reading Hill's accounts of rural indebtedness. In presenting the evidence let us start with a micro-level illustration of the dynamics of the process and proceed to an overview. One Yaw Basare of Asokore, Fortes was told in 1945–46, 'used to advance money to people on [the] security of farms and [is] said to have bought many farms that way.'[147] The Papers include a list of 27 writs for the sale of property used to secure loans issued by the district commissioner of Sunyani from 16 February 1943 to 21 March 1945. There were 13 in 1943 (from 16 February onwards) and 13 in 1944.[148] In that rural area it is likely that all the properties were cocoa farms. To what scale of alienation, overall, did such cases amount? Fortes noted, in an unpublished memorandum reflecting on his and his colleagues' survey, that 'the proportion of farmers who have lost one or more farms by mortgage appears to be considerable. The information we have is not conclusive but it suggest[s] that the proportion is of the order of 20%–30%.' To him, 'The surprising thing is the low proportion of farms that are admitted to have been acquired by mortgage'. That proportion was only 3.9 per cent in the sample of 231 farms in Ahafo and Sekyere. 'Miss Ady's figures confirm this. The highest proportion (7%) occurs in the Fwidiem area.'[149]

On reflection, Fortes's puzzlement was perhaps unnecessary. As we know, farmers generally planted cocoa in more than one—often several—sites during their careers. There was also ambiguity and inconsistency about the usage of 'farm': about whether the word referred to all trees which the same owner planted contiguously, or whether each year's new plantings at a given site constituted a separate 'farm' (as with Gyekyi and Bah handing over 'farms' in this sense to caretakers, in annual succession as each cohort of trees matured).[150] Thus the average number of farms per farmer was much more than one, even under the more restrictive definition, let alone in the 'annual plantings' sense. This affects the interpretation of the figures reported above. For illustration, let us assume that farmers averaged five 'farms' (in whichever sense) each and that 20 per cent of farmers lost one farm via pledging/purchase; the farms being ultimately acquired by existing 'farmers', in that most if not all such acquirers would own at least one other farm already. By implication, the proportion of farms acquired by pledging/purchase would be only a fifth of a fifth: four per cent. Thus the apparent contradiction between the numbers of farmers who said they had lost and gained farms, respectively, through indebtedness was probably not real.

Closer inspection of the Ahafo-Sekyere data suggests an important refinement. In the older cocoa-farming area, Sekyere, 5.6 per cent (13 of 231) farms had been acquired by mortgage or purchase. In the younger area, Ahafo, the figure was only 1.3 per cent (two of 151). This would seem to reflect the fact, noted earlier, that bearing trees were more acceptable in pledges than immature ones. It must be said, though, that Ady's figure of seven per cent does not fit this hypothesis: for Fwidiem (Hwidiem) is itself in Ahafo. Unfortunately I lack further information on Ady's work which might enable us to resolve this.

Overall, it seems that many farmers—between a third and a fifth of all Asante cocoa-farmers, according to Fortes in c.1946—lost at least one farm permanently as a result of pledging. But only a much smaller minority would have lost every cocoa tree they possessed. Even those who did had a way back in to cocoa-farmownership. While fresh land continued to be available somewhere, albeit at a cost, the accumulation of farms by creditors in the older Asante cocoa-growing areas was not sufficient to drive the defaulted debtors into any sort of a proletariat. A former agricultural officer stated:

> I found before I left [c.1931] that many farmers had to give up their farms near Kumasi owing to debts and naturally moved well away to start farming afresh . . . The number of farmers [*sic*] already in the hands of moneylenders was increasing to an alarming extent. The farmer with his usual outlook simply turned to planting more cacao.[151]

The growth of cocoa-farming indebtedness constituted a major advance of capitalism in that it involved the widespread earning of interest on capital, and the transfer of farms through the market. It led, however, not to proletarianization but to what appeared to many to be a usurious rentier economy. But this characterization understates the degree of competition—and also some conciliation—within it; and the continuing opportunities for a fresh start in agricultural self-employment on the cocoa frontier.

E. Conclusion

This chapter has sought to unravel the determinants of change and continuity in the social mobilization of capital in the cocoa-fueled rural economy of colonial Asante: specifically, during the decline and after the demise of pawnship. It has also considered the welfare implications of the story. Substantively, a recurrent theme has been the extent and nature of market 'imperfection'. Theoretically, we have continually asked whether rational-choice theories, such as the notions of induced institutional innovation, of principal-agent problems and of economic rent, can help us make sense of the evidence, and what the evidence implies for the theories. On all this there will be more to say in the final chapter; but the major findings and immediate implications of this one should be summarised here.

The emergence of the two major forms of 'cocoa credit', crop advances and pledging of farms, is easy to explain in terms of induced innovation: as responses to the new economic value of both the crop and the capital goods that yielded it. Other rational-choice concepts are useful in analysing these credit relationships. I argued that only a relatively small part of the incidence of advances is attributable to production and marketing costs. Most of it was a function of competition for crop share. Hence the quantity of advances was low when such competition was reduced or absent. I also argued that, given that the distribution of advances from European firms to farmers was mediated by a myriad of brokers, Bauer was right that advance-takers faced a competitive market. But he overlooked one phase of the credit-produce buying cycle in which, it seems, local monopolies did occur, at least in the short run. Specifically, in falling markets brokers could use the device of 'over-declaration' to capture rents at the expense of European merchants.

The Asante variation on farm-mortgaging is particularly interesting in the context of recent economic models in which creditors reduce the risk of default by lending to only some of those who are economically 'eligible' to receive them. Under the pledging system the lender took possession of the farm, thereby guaranteeing himself both interest and collateral. In principle, this removed the need to ration credit. This explains why, in depression, so many cocoa-farmers (perhaps a third of them) were able to obtain mortgages. The latter point brings us to a further finding: that almost as many people lent on the security of cocoa farms as borrowed on it. The overwhelming majority of creditors seem to have been local, mostly cocoa-farmers themselves. This is as Hill would have thought, though, unsurprisingly but unlike in her argument, they seem to have been the richer farmers. The fact that the pledge-takers were mostly farmers rather than being specialist merchants or moneylenders helps to explain a striking contrast with south India. In the world Depression of the early 1930s agricultural prices tumbled in south India as they did in Asante. In south

India agricultural credit dried up: informal bankers such as the Nattukottai Chetties found that they could not sell on the lands they were rapidly accumulating from defaulting borrowers—and the last thing they wanted was for their capital to be immobilized.[152] In Asante, in contrast, the level of long-term lending rose drastically. The main difference was that cocoa farmers were willing to have more farms. The fact that cocoa is a tree crop is also relevant: in that the capital value of a tree-crop farm is not simply a function of the current price of the produce.

It is very hard to identify the real interest rates on long-term loans in Asante: there was usually a fixed nominal rate of 50 per cent, unrelated to term, but the rates actually paid per year were adjusted by negotiation. Unlike the short-term credit market (advances), the long-term credit market was segmented, with loans often being intertwined with social relationships. But the largest segment does seem to have been competitive, such that it would be misleading to conclude that the whole market was ridden with usury. Indeed, in contrast to that stereotype, to pledge away a farm was by no means necessarily to be sucked into self-perpetuating debt. On the contrary, the level of farm-'mortgage' debt fell drastically in the high-price years of the mid-1950s. Yet, by its nature, pledging—like its predecessor, human pawning—reduced the options available to the borrower for repayment, as it deprived the debtor of a productive asset. This was the social cost of avoiding the need for credit rationing. The government (colonial and then joint-rule) was increasingly determined to provide and enlarge formal-sector sources of credit to farmers. In this context, as we saw earlier, officials considered the introduction of compulsory registration of titles to farms (and/or land itself). Here it is only necessary to comment that this reform would surely have been insufficient to make lending on farms profitable to the banks, or indeed, to any potential lender lacking the information and transaction-cost advantages of a neighbouring farmer.

Let us turn to distributional aspects of the discussion. However high the interest rates, cocoa farmers at least gained access to credit from a variety of sources: from European merchants (ultimately), from fellow farmers and (in kind, and interest-free), even from their own labourers. Because most cocoa farms were owned by men, it was mainly men who were in a position to take advantage of these opportunities. Over the period, though, there were heated contests over inheritance and related issues. By the 1950s a trend had emerged for inheritance of cocoa farms to be more restrictive, benefitting widows and sons rather than matrikin: as is consistent with the Goody hypothesis that richer societies and families tend to transmit property within narrower channels than poorer societies and families.

19

FREE LABOUR:

WHY THE NEWLY-EMERGED REGULAR WAGE CONTRACTS WERE ECLIPSED BY SHARECROPPING

Two key questions arise about the emergence of free labour. One is why regular hired—voluntary—labour developed at all. This basic question for Sub-Saharan labour history[1] is particularly stark for Asante, given the argument of Chapter 8 that the nineteenth-century labour market there depended for its very existence upon an element of coercion. The other question, which applies also to the other major cocoa-growing countries in West Africa, is why the rise of wage labour turned out to be so halting. In particular, why was the spread of regular (six-month, annual or permanent) wage contracts followed by their replacement with sharecropping tenancies—contrary to the general historical expectation, shared by many influenced by Marx or Marshall alike, that if sharecropping existed it would be a transitional stage towards pure wage contracts.

The preliminary question, fundamental as it is, can be addressed succinctly. Much of the literature on the formation of wage-labour forces in twentieth-century Africa points to the imposition of direct taxation by colonial regimes as the key which enabled employers to unlock labour 'reserves', obliging communities who lacked the facilities to engage in remunerative export agriculture at home to export (male) labour temporarily, often seasonally, to the nearest cash-cropping zone.[2] But this cannot be the main explanation here, as much of the labour came from the Northern Territories, where direct taxation was imposed only in 1936[3]—after the flow of migrant labour south to Asante and the Gold Coast Colony was already long-established and prolific. The workers from French West Africa were under fiscal pressure, in that they needed money to pay the poll tax imposed by the French authorities. But their presence outside French territory was itself an act of defiance. They chose to cross the border to avoid forced labour (until the abolition of the latter in 1946), and to seek higher wages on African-owned farms in colonial Ghana; wages to enable them to meet the French tax demand and have some import-purchasing power left over.[4] At a micro level migrant labourers were free to approach any one of many thousands of potential employers.

For Asante, as was argued in Chapter 13 in the context of the decline of slavery, the key to the emergence of a hired labour force was the adoption of cocoa farming. Bearing cocoa trees enabled Asante farmers to attract voluntary labour from the savanna, in exchange for a share of the 'forest rent'. But not all the voluntary, extra-family labour in the Asante cocoa economy came from these northern migrants. We saw in Chapter 16 that Asantes themselves offered their own labour services, not only in reciprocal exchange but also for hire. Why was this, in what was still broadly a land-surplus economy?

Section A examines the demand for labour: not as an aggregate, but rather asking how overall demand translated into demand for different kinds of labour, in the sense of labour from different social and contractual categories. We will see that farmers preferred to use their own labour, and then that of members of their conjugal and lineage families. The resort to hired labour was to supplement, not to replace, own and family labour; to enlarge the labour force, not to increase its average productivity. Section B analyses extra-familial labour services by Asante workers: the paid varieties, whose existence defied a European perception that Asantes were culturally resistant to accepting the role of employee; and the Asante reciprocal labour institution, *nnɔboa*. We ask whether, in the face of the cash-crop revolution, *nnɔboa* evolved into a disguised form of hired labour, or rather remained resiliently reciprocal. Section C asks why the proliferation of regular wage contracts was eclipsed by a spread of sharecropping contracts. Section D draws together the implications of the preceding discussion for issues of social efficiency and market imperfection.

A. From Demand for Labour to Demand for Particular Labour Relationships

The Inelasticity of Supply of Self and Family Labour

The ubiquity of 'self' labour—the fact that the farmer relied first on his or her own labour, unless wealth made this unnecessary or until old age made it unrealistic—is easy to explain in the sense that with oneself, by definition, principal-agent problems do not exist. But for production on more than the smallest scale, 'own labour' was naturally insufficient.

Help from a spouse was an obvious resort. We have seen that in Asante cocoa farming owners were usually male, especially in the early years but also even at the end of colonial rule. Thus the labour of owners' 'spouses' in cocoa growing mainly meant that of wives. If the supply of the farmowner's own labour was subject to an absolutely inelastic ceiling, that of his wife or wives was relatively inelastic. For while he might acquire a few additional wives, for married women inputs into cash-cropping were limited to time left over from prior obligations.[5]

For as in the nineteenth century, women's first responsibilities were considered to be child rearing and the supply of both food crops and cooked food.[6] Foodcrop farming remained (as Kyei recalled from the 1910s) 'a woman's occupation', except for men's role in felling trees and clearing land.[7] These priorities severely constrained the amount of time women could put into their own cocoa farming. When women did make farms it seems that they had to economize on labour inputs even more than did the men. According to Muir, female cocoa farmers 'are notoriously careless in the preparation of their produce'.[8] One might dismiss this statement as the product of bias, whether on the part of Muir or his informants. But it is perfectly plausible that women cocoa farmers economised on inputs of their own labour into cocoa farming even more than men did: not out of carelessness but out of a rational sense of priorities. The form taken by wives' assistance on their husbands' cocoa farms fits this picture. They concentrated on planting food crops which would provide shade for immature cocoa trees.[9] Thus women's contributions to making cocoa farms were crucial: but they were residual and, as we have seen, sufficiently indirect to leave scope for husbands to dispute its implications for ownership.

Labour inputs from other members of the conjugal and lineage families were also limited, by the relatively inelastic number of eligible individuals and by their other obligations and their own interests. Thus, within this category we have seen that sons seem to have been the most common providers of labour inputs. Yet only for a number of years was a son likely to be both old enough to be of much help to his cocoa-farming parent and not yet ready to withdraw that help in order to become a cocoa farmer in his own right.

The Demand for Hired Labour—a Supplement to Self and Family Labour

We saw in Chapter 16 that hired labour was recruited almost always from outside the family (conjugal and matrilineal): long-term labourers came overwhelmingly from beyond Asante, while Asantes who hired out their labour seem to have done so normally for strangers. The distinction between familial and hired labour, in the context of cocoa farming, leads us to the question of whether, when farmers hired labourers, they did so simply to raise farm output by supplementing their own and their spouses' efforts, or in the hope of higher productivity.

It is easy to assume that farmers' motive for 'switching to hired labour from family labour' was to 'increase the rate of financial return'.[10] In Chapter 4 we considered the 1956–57 survey figures, which on first glance support the proposition that such a switch would indeed have improved efficiency. But on closer examination, it was argued, this support collapses.[11] Turning to the oral testimony of a veteran farmer, Kwaku Gyekyi of Ofoase-Kokoben insisted that hired labour—from the savanna—was unskilled. To ensure that the cocoa and shade-crops were planted correctly he and his brother used only their own and their wives' and children's labour in planting. They restricted their use of hired labourers in the establishment of new farms to clearing land for planting and to weeding afterwards.[12] Again, in view of Muir's criticism of the quality of wives' labour on their husbands' cocoa farms it is interesting that this agricultural officer was similarly unimpressed with hired labour. Reporting his survey of cocoa production in Western Ashanti in 1928–29, he lamented the trend for family farming of cocoa to give way to the employment of 'labour which is deplorably inefficient and is seldom supervised. This is resulting in lack of attention to ordinary sanitation measures, such as removal of diseased pods and branches, and to the improper fermentation of cacao'.[13] The implication of his remarks is that the use of any labour other than that of the farmowner himself entailed serious 'moral hazard.' But there was no alternative, if output was to be expanded beyond the minimum. This observation fits the example of Kwotei, noted earlier.[14] The same applies to the evidence on the general pattern of demand for hired labour, both over time and in cross-section.

We saw in Chapter 16 that during the early, rapid, expansion of the cultivated area up to c.1916 labour was hired only as a short-term supplement to the energies of the farmer, of (probably) his wife (or wives) and children, and of *nnɔboa*, in meeting the particularly heavy demands of clearing forest or harvesting. The rapid spread of the employment of wage labourers in the following two decades was partly to fill the gaps left by the erosion of earlier—coercive—forms of extra-familial, non-reciprocal labour (slaves, pawns, and perhaps *corvée*). Family and *nnɔboa* labour were not enough.[15] The growth of labour-hiring also partly reflected demand from men who were for the first time expanding their operations beyond the capacities of themselves, their family workforces, and indeed of *nnɔboa*.[16]

It may seem paradoxical that it was not during the era of high producer prices but rather during the subsequent years of fluctuating and generally low prices, from 1916 to the early 1930s, that hired labour became established and spread rapidly, within Asante cocoa-farming. This paradox can be resolved in three main ways. First, as we have seen, the process of the decline of slavery and pawnship obliging large users of labour to seek free hired labourers took time even after the 1908 prohibition of those institutions. Second, in much of western Asante real producer prices seem generally to have reached record levels during the 1920s, because of the new and increasing availability of motor transport. Thus the quotation in Chapter 16 about better transport as the source of the switch to wage-labour is plausible.[17] The higher producer prices which entailed lower transport costs could have given many farmowners the cash to hire labour for the first time, enabling them to replace slaves and pawns and/or to expand labour inputs beyond the limits of family labour. Third, the level of potential demand for labour on existing farms was a function of the extent of previous planting; while how far this was translated into effective demand was a function of the current producer price. Hence the rapid expansion of regular wage employment on Asante cocoa farms in the 1920s, especially, was founded on the preceding wave of planting—creating a level of demand which could not be met solely from household sources, however broadly defined.

When prices were particularly low, the expansion of labour-hiring was indeed interrupted or temporarily put into reverse. When the producer price fell, farmers had to make do with less—or without—hired help. In July 1931, with the real producer price very low, the Department of Agriculture remarked: 'In some areas cutlassing of the undergrowth in young and medium-aged farms has been delayed, partly owing to the unusually wet weather and partly because some farm owners, who usually employ hired labour, are doing the work themselves this year'.[18] This flexibility in farmers' use or non-use of hired labour is further evidence that the hiring of labour remained supplementary to the use of self and family workers.

This pattern of hired men being used as a supplement to whatever non-wage forms of labour were still available was indeed very common in the Ghanaian cocoa industry generally in the late 1920s and 1930s,[19] although some farmers had adopted what the Nowell Commission called 'the complete use of hired labour'.[20] One of the examples the commission probably had in mind was Osei Kwabena, an Asante who gave evidence to them. He claimed to produce 500 loads (13.6 tonnes) of cocoa a year, apparently entirely through hired labour.[21] But it should be cautioned that the farmers had an interest in exaggerating their costs of production, in order to strengthen the case for higher producer prices.

To sharpen our understanding of the relationship between farm size and the composition of the labour force let us now adopt a cross-sectional perspective. The crucial distinction is illustrated by a study carried out in the late 1920s of the cost structure of the operations of three Asante cocoa-farmers. The two larger ones used regular hired labour. The smallest 'Having little capital . . . has only employed labour to help with the heavier stages'.[22] While, as in the previous century, the area a farmer cultivated was proximately determined by the amount of labour he applied, the size of the workforce was now limited only by his capacity to hire 'free' labourers. This capacity in turn consisted of working capital in the form of cash, or, more commonly, of fixed capital in the form of bearing cocoa trees that would yield the beans which would be sold to provide the cash to pay the accumulated wage bill.[23]

We noted in Chapter 4 that the distribution of rural output among producers was distinctly unequal.[24] Most farmers with relatively small farms probably used *nnɔboa* and/or causal wage labour, but they neither needed nor could afford to hire regular wage labourers. In Beckett's survey of the Akyem village of Akokoaso in the Gold Coast Colony, a community with a high proportion of relatively small producers, 88 per cent of farmers hired casual labour at some stage during the year.[25] The larger a farmer's cocoa production (which would almost invariably be divided between a gradually increasing number of farms), the higher the proportion of labour inputs which would have to be obtained from regular hired labourers. For example, in 1934 George Yebuah, a produce-buyer for Holts in Kumasi, established a 28-acre (11.3 hectares), 15,000 tree farm. As of 1938 he employed 10 annual labourers on this farm.[26] The general relationship is very strongly visible in the budget survey at the end of the colonial period, as can be seen from Fig. 19.1. As Bray put it with reference to his study of Ahafo in the later 1950s, 'Farmers employ labour because their farms are too large to be worked by family labour only'.[27]

It is a reasonable assumption that the same logic applied to food farming, where individuals managed to practice it on a sufficiently large commercial scale. Some of those farming at Wawase took advantage of it being less than 15 kilometres from the food market of Bekwai, and less

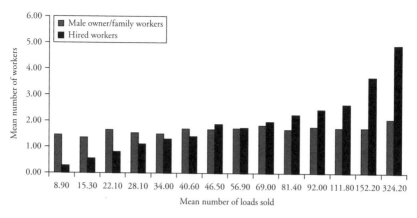

Figure 19.1. Male owner/family and hired workers on different sizes of bearing cocoa farm, Asante 1956–57.
Source: Ghana, *Survey of Cocoa Producing Families in Ashanti, 1956–57.*

than 30 kilometres from the market in Kumasi.[28] To take an extreme example, Kwame Akowuah's cocoa farm there produced 52 loads a year, which in the 1930s would rarely have fetched more than £35. Yet Akowuah's lawyer claimed that he had 30 foodstuff farms, from which he made at least £600 a year. It seems safe to assume that he employed labourers.

We should make explicit the observation that female farmowners generally accounted for a relatively small proportion of the employment of hired labourers—at least, of regular as opposed to casual (task or day) labourers. During the nearly six years from 22 October 1943 to 15 September 1949 the district commissioner at Bekwai approved a total of 47 contracts between the owners of cocoa farms in Asante (and in one case, an Asante owner's cocoa farm elsewhere)[29] and regular labourers (all with northern names). Among the 45 different employers only three were women. Together they hired just four of the total of 85 workers.[30] This small proportion would seem to be a logical consequence of women's relatively small share of ownership of cocoa farms—especially of the larger farms.

To conclude, hired labour was employed as a supplement to family labour rather than an alternative to it: individual farmers' demands for the services of hired labourers were a function of their need for labour inputs beyond the 'unpaid' supplies already available to them. 'Unpaid' might include reciprocally exchanged. The cocoa acreages of the smaller farmers neither required nor generated the income to hire regular wage labourers. When their own and their family's labour was insufficient for particularly heavy tasks they could still rely on *nnɔboa* and casual wage labour—both to be discussed in the next section. The exception that 'proves the rule' seems to have been very large farmers, who may have felt that family labour could make so little difference relative to the sum of their labour requirements that they might as well rely completely on hired labour. Overall, when labour was hired on cocoa farms it was employed to increase not the rate of financial return but simply its total. As in the nineteenth century, so in the cocoa era, the accumulation of wealth on even a modest scale required labour additional to conjugal resources. This applied with a new distinctness as slavery and—very gradually—pawning ceased to be available as sources of wives.

B. Asante Labour Outside the Family

Reciprocal Work Parties

The *nnɔboa* system may well have been used much more often as demand for cocoa labour rose and the availability of slave and pawn labour declined.[31] At a minimum it remained a feature of labour mobilization throughout the period. It was called upon for particularly heavy tasks, notably breaking of harvested pods.[32] Did farmers value it as preferable to hiring labour, or did it become a form of hired labour itself?

In some parts of Africa the cash-crop 'revolution' of the early colonial period led to work parties being transformed into disguised wage employment. Tosh has argued that whether work parties remained reciprocal or were transformed into quasi-wage labour was determined by the type of reward given to members of the group for their labour. Where the food and drink was merely a token, and the real reward was the exchange of labour, the institution was resistant to economic and social differentiation. Where the food and drink was regarded as payment in kind, only those wealthy enough to cater for a party were able to summon such a work-group. In this context the work party became an object in a process of polarization among farmers: between rich ones who hired it, and poor ones who themselves constituted a labour pool.[33]

The reciprocal character of the Asante institution of *nnɔboa*, as remembered from the 1910s, is conveyed in the passage from Kyei's memoirs of childhood quoted in Chapter 16. The passage continues:

> *Kookoo-bɔ* day was a pleasurable occasion of work and eating. Palatable dishes were prepared to serve the visiting helpers, and all had enough to eat

to their fill. The food that I enjoyed most was boiled plantain served with *nkontomire* and corned beef stew.[34]

Despite the gastronomic delight of the occasion, the capacity to provide food seems never to have displaced the capacity to exchange labour in determining who could call on *nnɔboa* services. That *nnɔboa* continued as a reciprocal exchange of labour was emphasised to me by several elderly informants in Amansie.[35] As it was put in the village of Sanfo, near Bekwai, in 1980, the principle of *nnɔboa* was 'today I work on your farm, tomorrow you work on mine'.[36]

In this context, presumably it was most used by poorer farmers, with relatively little or no access to family help or hired labour. It must have helped such people adopt cocoa production, especially by easing their way through seasonal bottlenecks of labour demand: as with Kyei's father. Not that farmers without 'permanent' hired labour remained dependent on reciprocal services: as we have seen, casual labour was also available for hire. On the question of the creation of a proletariat, it may be said that *nnɔboa* helped poorer Asante farmers avoid having to give up independent cash-crop farming and sell their own labour. In this sense too there is no evidence of reciprocity becoming transformed into wage labour during the colonial period. This reflects the fact that virtually all Asante had access to land (including for cocoa, sooner or later) and therefore retained options outside the labour market.[37] Conversely, wage labour itself became the object of reciprocal exchange. As we have seen, there is a documented case of wealthy stranger-farmers in Ahafo sending their respective labourers to help in rotation on each others' farms.[38]

But a statement volunteered by an elderly informant, in Kokofu in 1987, suggests that the causal and historical relationship was almost the opposite from that envisaged by Tosh. To my surprise—and not in answer to a question about it, since no such question had occurred to me—he said:

> *Nnɔboa* is better than *Adopaa*. With *adopaa*, the individuals involved had to be paid e.g. 6 pence a day for each participant. Later, it was realised that the *nnɔboa* system is better since that does not involve any monetary remuneration. The *nnɔboa* system originated from the *adopaa* system.[39]

It would be unwise to build much about the general history of *nnɔboa* in Asante from a single source. But it is a significant comment in a cross-sectional as well as a dynamic context. For it confirms that reciprocal labour was preferable to wage labour for farmers with little cash: providing that the partners had confidence in each other, which they generally seem to have done.[40]

Asantes as Hired Labourers

There was a long-standing perception among European observers that free Asante were unwilling to serve as manual labourers. Fortes wrote in the 1940s that Ramseyer and Kühne, 'writing in Kumasi' in the 1870s, 'often remark that no free-born Ashanti will stoop to menial labour, and this holds to a great extent to-day. And the Kumasi pattern goes right through the country. It is found in the mining towns and in the cocoa villages.'[41] If so, it is a puzzle to explain why in fact, as we saw in Chapter 16, considerable numbers of Asante were willing to work in the European-owned gold mines. We also have to explain why Asantes provided short-term wage labour for produce-carrying and on cocoa farms—all this from as early as the 1900s.

The European reports of free-born Asante disdain for performing manual labour for someone else are unlikely to have been completely wrong, for the association of such a role with slave or pawn status would have been pervasive in the 1870s and well remembered in the 1940s. However, the European perception of Asante attitudes may have been a poor guide to their behaviour, especially that of what was, after all, the minority of the population who at any given moment were willing to take even part-time hired employment. That minority may have taken a different view from the majority or, whatever their values, acted pragmatically.[42]

Another possibility, perhaps stronger, is that disdain for labouring in the service of another was a stance associated specifically with (social) adulthood. Hence temporary work for others may have been considered appropriate for able-bodied but unmarried people: youths in a social and usually, though not always, biological sense. *Adopaa* groups were an institutionalised form of youthful paid labour. A further hypothesis is that the early Asante wage-labour force was drawn from the poorer and lower-status ranks of society, comprising former slaves and pawns, and people of slave descent. It is even possible that some of the earliest wage-contracts of the colonial period, perhaps before 1908, may have involved 'slaves and pawns contracted out by their owners who received their wages', as Pepe Roberts has speculated for neighbouring Sefwi-Wiawso.[43] There was, as we have seen, a nineteenth-century precedent for this practice. The issue cannot be resolved at present for lack of direct evidence.

What can be said is that it makes circumstantial sense to assume that most of the Asante wage-workers were socially junior. This would apply to youths of 'free' descent as well as to people of slave origin. Members of both these categories might have little to lose in social respect from selling their labour for short-term tasks. They would have money to gain, given that they were not yet in a position to enter cocoa-farming or other enterprises for themselves: at least, not on a scale sufficient to preclude other opportunities to earn. From the perspective of their seniors such side-activities could be accommodated providing their obligations (to work for their parents, for example) were not neglected.

Some Asante males continued to treat wage-earning as an option for themselves, albeit as a short-term occupation, even when cocoa-farmownership had become very widespread in their communities with northerners predominating among those offering their labour services. In June 1938, in the aftermath of the pool and the protracted hold-up of the cocoa season before, the Kokofuhene said 'that most of his youngmen have given up cocoa farming this year and have gone to work at Begosu (Marlu Mines, Limited)',[44] probably in obtaining firewood (rather than in mining). The reference to 'cocoa *farming*'(emphasis added) almost certainly indicates that the chief meant small farmowners rather than labourers. We saw earlier, however, that it was not unknown for Asante youths, born too late to be able to find land locally to start their own cocoa farms, to become sharecrop-labourers.[45] Again, in the 1956–57 survey of cocoa-farming families 878 Asantes, 844 of them male, were recorded as agricultural labourers. The latter constituted 2.3 per cent of the Asante men in the sample.[46] Indeed, in a survey of Hwidiem in Ahafo in 1954–55, Hill had found that 35 (27.5 per cent) of the 142 *abusa* labourers were Akans, mostly Asantes, 'probably mainly not local.'[47] Presumably they came from more densely-cultivated areas, and hoped ultimately to own cocoa farms themselves.

I have suggested that the paradox of Asantes themselves supplying hired labour in the face of apparently strong social attitudes may be resolved by the proposition that the Asantes who performed the work were mostly social juniors: either temporarily (being young and unmarried) or perhaps permanently, if they were of slave descent. An economic question remains: why would anyone be prepared to work for someone else in a land-surplus economy?

Part of the answer is that conditions were changing. By the 1940s in at least one of the older cocoa-growing areas cultivable land was now scarce, hence the willingness of some youths to work on others' farms as sharecrop-labourers, presumably until they acquired cocoa trees of their own via migration or inheritance. But this does not account for wage work in earlier decades, or in those districts where land was still surplus to beyond the end of the colonial era. In this context too, however, factor ratios had changed since the adoption of cocoa. Before the tree crop, farmers lacked the capital goods to enable them to pay a capital-less labourer from within the forest zone more than he could make by using his own land rights, his own access to the forest rent. In contrast, possession of bearing cocoa trees enabled farmers to pay wages high enough to attract the labour services of youths who as yet had no bearing cocoa trees of their own—albeit, usually attracting them only for short periods. Asante youths evidently worked for their fathers, or for themselves, for much of the year, thereby investing, indirectly or directly, in their own future stocks of bearing trees. Accordingly, it was left to labourers with no land rights in the forest zone—with no direct access to its rent—to supply the regular, season-long, part of the new, free, extra-familial labour force that emerged in the 1920s.

C. Northern Labourers and Asante Employers: Wage Work, Bargaining, and the Shift to Sharecrop Contracts

This section seeks to explain why the spread of regular wage-labour gave way to the widespread adoption of sharecropping. The most obvious theoretical reason for adopting sharecropping would be a desire by farmers to delegate the risk entailed in price fluctuations.[48] For Ghanaian cocoa-farmers specifically, Jonathan Frimpong-Ansah assumes that farmers' motive for 'adopting share cropping' was (again) to 'increase the rate of financial return'.[49] Both propositions make plausible hypotheses; but the evidence, as we will see, contradicts them. We will ask first at whose initiative the change took place; and then consider their motives, and why the other side came to terms.

Could the change have been consensual? In principle it might have reflected the gradually increasing average age of the Asante cocoa-tree stock during the 1930s and early 1940s. For, as we have seen, sharecroppers were to work primarily on bearing farms. But this will hardly do as an explanation of the adoption of the institution in view of the fact that Asante cocoa farmers had managed to pass 70,000 tonnes a year with seemingly negligible use of sharecroppers. Thus the annual labour that sharecropping replaced must itself have been employed mostly on bearing farms. Again, the dominance of sharecropping continued throughout the wave of new planting by and during the 1950s. An early contemporary observer of the change did indeed interpret it as consensual. Dickinson remarked of *abusa* in Asante, as of May 1939, that 'In the cases which have come to my notice this [system] appears to be fairly satisfactory from the point of view of both master and servant'.[50] But colonial officials soon had reason to revise this perception.

A government labour officer in charge of an enquiry into farm labour in Asante reported in 1946 that share-cropping 'it is said, does not economically work in the best interest of the farmer'.[51] Informants in Esumeja, interviewed in old age in 1980, volunteered that the farmers had been 'cheating the labourers'. The latter forced the change upon the farmers, who accepted it for lack of alternative recruits.[52] Likewise, in Sanfo it was said that sharecropping was accepted by farmers because they could not get labourers on other terms.[53] Back in 1946 the labour officer implied that the labourers generally had come to distrust annual contracts: ' "The Yearly Contract" system is gradually disappearing, due mainly to the sad experience labourers have, in the past, had, in getting their cash earnings paid regularly at the expiration of their term of contract . . .'[54] In addition, by insisting on sharecropping labourers stood to gain a much higher proportion of farm income. The President of the Manso-Nkwanta-Abori Co-operative Society himself employed *abusa* men:

> I expect to get approximately 108 loads. My two labourers jointly will get 36 loads or the equivalent cash value of £46 16/- (cocoa being sold at 26/- a load here) i.e. £23 8/- to each of them for only eight months work, instead of the basic wage of £5 to which each of them would be paid had they been employed under a 'Yearly Contract' system.[55]

One third of the farm-income from 54 loads would be less than £5 only if the price fell virtually to 5s 6d a load: a price-level which was rare even in the depressed interwar period.

In this context it was no coincidence that, as Nicholas Van Hear as shown, attempts by Asante and other cocoa-farmers and middlemen to recruit directly in the north increased in the mid-1930s, and continued during the war despite government restriction.[56] Evidently some employers were very dissatisfied with the terms on which spontaneous migrants insisted, for they sought to bypass them by obtaining labour directly in the north on wage terms. An International Labour Office inspector, sent to the Gold Coast to investigate the welfare of labour, travelled up the road from Kumasi to the north. Among the farmers and specialist recruiters he met was a 'well dressed African, bringing a party down by lorry, [who] said that he employed twelve men on his cocoa plantation, receiving food, quarters, and a uniform (he was an ex-soldier) and £2–10s in cash at the end of their service.'[57] But in the context of the labour market as a whole such efforts seem ultimately to have been a sideshow besides the general push for share-cropping on the labourers' side.

But this begs the question of why the farmers, faced with this unwelcome change, did not offer higher regular wages—and paid on time—in order to preserve the wage system. In principle, the latter was perfectly capable of delivering for the labourers the same level of income as the sharecroppers received in an average year. Under perfect competition the wage rate would equal the marginal product of labour (MPL).[58] In a context in which harvest size and produce price could each be regarded as fluctuating randomly, and given that wages were fixed at the start of the crop year, this would mean the MPL for an average year. This would present employers with no problems—it would indeed strike the optimal balance between cost and incentive—providing the relevant markets were complete and perfect, or at least not significantly distant from these ideal types. The farmer could maintain his normal expenditure level (including paying the wages) year in year out either by saving in the good times to offset deficits in the bad or by borrowing in the bad and repaying in the good. But, as we have seen, interest rates were very high. A succession of poor years would oblige almost any farmer to pledge his farms, thereby making it extremely hard to clear the debts. In these conditions the rational farmer would not optimise in the marginalist sense of equating his (average-year) marginal costs and (average-year) marginal revenue.[59] It is interesting to note that though there seems to be no evidence of farmers in the 1930s offering annual wages that would approximate to an average-year MPL, there were examples—rare in Asante—of relatively high fixed rates for piecework, which can be seen as a variant on that hypothetical strategy. Dickinson wrote in 1939:

> During my travels in the Eastern province of the Colony I came across a form of contract which is not common in Ashanti. In the Birim District a labourer will be engaged at the beginning of the season at so much a load. Last season the amount was 3/- and it must have been difficult, owing to the fall in price later in the season, for the farmer to have fulfilled his obligations.[60]

Dickinson's forebodings about the system may have been justified. Van Hear quotes several cases of labourers' complaints of non-payment by southern employers from the Labour Department's diary for Bolgatanga district in 1941. Two of these, each involving two unfortunate labourers, were for arrears due under the *appa* (piece work) system. For example, in one of them ' "2 labourers were refused payment of 14/- by an employer of Mampong, after completion of a contract under the *Appa* system." '[61] It is unclear whether these piecework cases were from the Mampon in Akwapim in the Gold Coast Colony or from Mampon in Asante. Either way, the case illustrates the riskiness of this kind of contract to both parties. This helps to explain its rarity; at least in Asante.[62] High fixed wages were unusual and, in any case, frequently went unpaid. Rather, as we saw in Manso Nkwanta, wage rates were generally below *abusa* earnings. It is reasonable to assume that regular annual wage rates—those superseded by *abusa* terms—were significantly less than the marginal product of labour in an average year. By the late 1930s the labourers were no longer willing to accept them.

But the farmers could not commit themselves to paying higher rates without knowing what the season would bring. For them, it appears, sharecropping was a reluctant compromise: costing them more on average but without the risk of being trapped into having to pay high wages in a disastrous year. There was also the bonus that it reduced supervision costs because it made the labourers' earnings proportional to their effort. There is irony here, in that the traditional neoclassical criticism of sharecropping is precisely that it reduces incentive, and therefore raises supervision costs, because the worker only gets part of his marginal product.[63] But in this case, as we have seen, it appears that the labourers had been getting still less of the average-year marginal product under the wage regime. It must be reiterated that, for the employers, any increase in incentive resulting from the change of contract was merely a bonus. Had it been their main consideration, presumably, they would have favoured the change instead of opposing it.

An additional consideration, which may help to explain why farmers accepted the northern labourers' demand for sharecrop contracts in the 1930s, is that in that decade there were successive attempts by most of the European cocoa-buying companies to force down the produce price by forming buying agreements (known as 'pools') among themselves. Thus on top of the usual random variation of prices was the fear that they were subject to systematic downward pressure, which would penalize any employer who had fixed the amount he would pay his labourers before knowing what price would be offered. Indeed, in some years farmers collectively refused to sell to European firms, in organized response to the pools. After a very localized hold-up at Manso Nkwanta in 1927, larger numbers of Asante farmers were involved in wider but still limited hold-ups in 1930 and 1934–35, before the comprehensive one of 1937–38, which held firm across almost all the Ghanaian cocoa belt for most of the buying season.[64]

From the labourers' perspective sharecropping offered substantially higher average-year earnings. But it had other features which may have made it more attractive compared even to higher fixed wages, had the farmers been prepared to concede the latter. There was the non-monetary advantage of freedom from supervision until the harvest was ready to be divided. But also, or more than that, a sharecrop contract improved the probability that the worker would be paid on time and, indeed, at all. For sharecropping gave labourers a greater opportunity to enforce the payment of what was due to them. Like annual-wage labourers they were there at the harvest; unlike them, the sharecroppers were directly entitled to part of it.

This was important because examples of the 'sad experience' noted above are not infrequent in the sources. It is clear that labourers were highly concerned about it. Dickinson noted 'a growing tendency in Ashanti for the labourer other than the purely temporary one to be engaged on a written agreement, the form of which has become almost stereotyped by the local letter writer. It generally provides a clause whereby one of the parties may sue the other who breaks the agreement in any court he may chose.' Some northerners had indeed taken their defaulting employers to court,[65] whether armed with such paper or not. Others applied physical pressure. The Mamponhene claimed that 'very often they [the labourers] threaten to kill their employers if they are not paid.' This was in 1937 at a public meeting of chiefs and massed cocoa farmers in front of the Chief Commissioner and representatives of the European cocoa-buying companies. The head of the Asante farmers' association, on the same occasion, went a step further. 'Some people employ about 30 labourers others about 2 . . . If at the end of the month the farmer is unable to pay his labourers, in some cases he is killed by them.'[66] In this context the switch to sharecropping is a case of an institutional change which presumably reduced transactions costs by removing the need for labourers to threaten—or use—coercive and mutually-dangerous measures to get what they were owed. Sharecropping offered a (partial) solution to the labourers' moral hazard problem. This reduction in contractual uncertainty balanced, to some extent, the production uncertainty which the sharecroppers took over from the farmers.

The proviso was that the crop was indeed sold, and on time. There is no reason to believe that sharecroppers were completely immune from the widespread suffering among northern labourers during the latter stages of the 1937–38 holdup. The sale of the crops was delayed and in some cases the produce deteriorated, reducing the amount received for the eventual sale if the transaction took place at all. Many labourers were forced to stay away longer from their savanna homes than they wanted to do, and then to return with little or sometimes no money.[67] This case illustrates that sharecropping was indeed an incomplete answer to the threat of employer default. But it would appear to have been a large part of the answer, to judge from the persistence with which northern labourers continued to push for share terms in the following years.

Persistence often requires a different explanation from origin. As before, the pressure for sharecropping contracts came from the labourers rather than the employers. For the mid to later 1950s Bray noted that farmers [still] complained that *abusa* terms were very costly.[68] But evidently they had to accept them; otherwise they could not retain their labour forces. There was 'some tightness in the rural labour market'. Specifically, 'Farmers . . . state that they cannot get annual labourers or that they run away'.[69] In this case, the question is how to explain why farmers continued to agree to sharecrop terms—and so frequently—in the era of statutory marketing, when produce prices were fixed in advance for the season. This reduced production uncertainty diminished such advantage as sharecropping had had for employers. Admittedly, farmers' confidence in prices remained fragile during the first six years of statutory marketing because the system had been introduced as a wartime expedient in 1939. During the war real prices were very low and there was the spectacle of the government, having bought the crop, burning some of it for lack of shipping space.[70] But when statutory marketing was consolidated in peacetime, with the establishment of the Cocoa Marketing Board in 1947, an important element of uncertainty had been eliminated from farmers' calculations. Yet harvests still fluctuated, and loans were still expensive and often hard to repay (though the question of repayment did not necessarily arise for some potential CPP voters in the mid-1950s).[71]

From the labourers' perspective, fixed produce prices reduced a major disadvantage of sharecropping, and thus presumably strengthened their inclination towards such contracts. Again, the fact that the 1937–38 holdup was not repeated meant that the risk of non-payment or late payment was now mainly from individual delinquent farmers, rather than from collective action. Thus the problem arose in the form to which share contracts provided a relatively efficient solution. Indeed their proliferation helps to account for the disappearance by the later 1950s of 'forced' credit, extracted by farmowners at the expense of labourers.[72]

It may be that by the mid-1950s a further advantage of sharecropping, to both sides, had emerged. The higher average-year earnings that the *abusa* system had brought northern labourers made it more likely than before that they could afford to marry. The share contract gave an incentive to a male labourer to supplement his own efforts with conjugal help. Bray noted that 'Abusa [men] also have wives and children working for them, especially in gathering, breaking pods and headloading the harvest.'[73] A specific example is Musa Moshi, from near Ouagadougou, who was helped by his wife and children during his work as an *abusa* man on a farm near Dominase, in Amansie, in the late-colonial period.[74]

Moreover, the balance of bargaining power in the labour market stayed with the labourers, in that farmers could not afford all the labourers they required. In elaborating on this it is necessary to distinguish various influences on the supply and demand schedules for labour. It should be noted that certain demographic and institutional changes favoured the employers in that, by themselves, they would have led to more northern labourers being willing to accept employment at any given wage rate. The population of the neighbouring savanna areas was rising. It is possible that this was not entirely exogenous to the expansion of Ghanaian cocoa farming. For it has been argued that the earnings opportunities for male migrant labourers encouraged the continuation of social arrangements conducive to a high birth rate among migrants' families, such as early age of female marriage, even when death rates fell.[75] If so, there may have been a causal relationship in West Africa between expanding commercial opportunities in the forest zone and expanding families in the savanna. Institutionally, the creation of the Labour Department and the subsequent state attempts to regulate labour contracts may have given labourers and prospective labourers more confidence in the labour market.

On the other hand, in the short term the sufferings endured by labourers as a result of the 1937–38 cocoa hold-up deterred some from returning to the cocoa farms. After the war, two major long-term influences took hold. One was competition from an adjacent cash-crop economy: the post-war take-off of Ivoirian cocoa production attracted migrant labourers from northern Côte d'Ivoire and what is now Burkina Faso who had previously headed for Asante and beyond. In the year to the end of March 1938 nearly twice as many French as British subjects (67,317 against 34,574) had taken the ferries south from the Northern Territories.[76] There is a tentative indication that the proportion of migrants from French colonies had fallen by 1956: the preliminary enumeration for the 1956–57 survey recorded as agricultural labourers nearly five times as many Northern Territories men as 'Others', the latter category being the only one used into which French subjects could fit. The qualification is that the data were collected during a time of year (mid-May to end-July) when the majority of migrant labourers would have been absent. So the absolute numbers were comparatively small (1,404 British, 296 French subjects).[77] The apparent decline in the proportion of French subjects among the hired labour force would have been exaggerated *if* they were less prone to stay on in (or return early to) Asante than their counterparts from the Northern Territories. But it seems unlikely that any such difference would have been great enough to account for the drastic reversal in proportions between the 1937–38 and the 1956–57 figures.

The second powerful long-term influence was the growth of competition for labour from outside cocoa production. This was fuelled by the marketing board system, in that much of the share of the world price withheld from the producers was spent ultimately in ways that created urban employment; thereby enlarging the market for food crops. This trend was evident in the late colonial period; though it was pushed much further afterwards, particularly when to the marketing board surplus was added the implicit taxation of a largely non-convertible and increasingly over-valued currency (starting with monetary independence in 1964–65, and at its height between 1975 and 1983).[78] The significance of this in the present context is that, while Asante cocoa farmers had to make concessions to obtain labour during the late colonial period, their bargaining position was to deteriorate much further during the subsequent era of 'state-led' development policies. A 1970 survey found that more than two-fifths of Ghanaian cocoa-farmers did not employ permanent labour (annual or sharecrop), but that nearly two-thirds of these farmers wanted to do so.[79] Part of the labour-scarcity recorded then can be attributed to an exogenous event, the expulsion of illegal aliens in 1969.[80] Yet by 1974, when legal migration (from within and without Ghana) might have been expected to have made up that particular shortfall, a survey of 'Bekwai Zone' (slightly larger than, incorporating most of, Amansie) found that 'only 3 per cent' of 'the farming population' were hired labourers (the majority of these being share-croppers). The 'farming population' was, admittedly, broadly defined: including non-cocoa producers and farmowners too old for manual work. Even with that qualification, it was clear that the long-term decline in farmers' ability to attract wage-labourers and, by the 1970s, even sharecroppers,[81] left the farms, by default, increasingly in the 'domestic mode of production' rather than the capitalist one.[82] Whether this trend was reversed following the adoption of 'Structural Adjustment' in 1983, an integral part of which was a drastic reduction in explicit and implicit taxation of export producers, needs to be considered elsewhere.

But in a broad sense the institution of hired labour has maintained a dominance established in its heyday within cocoa-farming. Despite population growth—partly offset by rising school enrollment—the domestic labour force never sufficed to compensate for the loss of outside workers. Wage-labour continues to represent an opportunity cost which the returns for domestic labour cannot equal. The irony is that, from the 1940s and especially from the mid-1960s to the early 1980s, the wage opportunities which drew away the potential domestic workforce were mainly outside agriculture, yet were largely financed, directly or indirectly, by government exactions from the nation's cocoa earnings.

In an earlier work I remarked that the northern labourers achieved the shift to sharecropping, thereby winning higher incomes and greater autonomy at work, despite the absence of a trade union and, initially, in the face of persistent unemployment among northern labourers in the cocoa belt.[83] But given that they were paid well below their average-year marginal product before, it is equally striking that it took several years of annual contracts before they obtained something closer to it. In 1920 Governor Guggisberg said that ' "during the last two or three years, the NTs [Northern Territories] native has not rushed blindly into work in the South. He wants to know where he is going and what he is going to do. In fact, he has learnt to pick and choose, *and to know his own value in the labour world*" ' (Guggisberg's emphasis).[84]

In the event it took rather longer for northerners to *get* their 'own value in the labour world'. In the early years after the prohibition of slavery, and with the slave trade to Asante only a generation or less behind them, northerners who ventured into Asante may well not have felt themselves in a secure bargaining position. An anonymous publication of c.1937 included a pair of photographs (Plates 19.1 and 19.2) depicting the happiest of relations between a cocoa farmer, who may very well have been an Asante, and a northern labourer whose facial markings would have led him to have been routinely described as an ɔdɔnkɔ in the recent past.

Relations were by no means always harmonious, though the worst incident did not stem from farm-labour relations. In 1919 there was a riot in Bekwai against Hausas and Moshis, who were working as cocoa carriers.[85] Eleven men were killed and thirteen badly wounded. All the victims were northerners.[86] The violence was triggered by a gambling dispute,[87] but the rapidity and scale with which it escalated suggest that intercommunal relations were already very tense: which is hardly surprising in view of the recent history. As we have seen, employer-employee relations were not infrequently conflictual during the next twenty years. But the northern labourers gradually achieved more in the multitude of employment negotiations that took place each season between farmers and migrant workers, the latter offering their services as individuals or in small groups.

Plate 19.1. 'A labourer from the North is employed during the cocoa season'.
Source: Photograph by P. B. Redmayne in Anonymous, *The Gold Coast: General & Historical; Timbers; Cultivated Resources* (London, n.d. but c.1937), 'Cultivated Resources', 20.

Where one farmer gave way, both sides in other potential deals would no doubt hear about it, increasing the chance that other farmers would be obliged to follow suit. The network of zongos no doubt helped the flow of news among muslim northerners,[88] while others, notably Frafras and Dagaras, presumably relied on their dispersed networks of kinship and

Plate 19.2. 'The cocoa farmer of the forest zone'.
Source: as for Plate 19.1.

ethnicity.[89] Besides these matters of information and of the social context in which deals were struck, it is crucial to emphasize that the underlaying conditions in the labour market were moving in favour of those who offered their services for hire: in the interwar period and over 1908–56 as a whole. As time went on slave and pawn labour was decreasingly available, while the area under cocoa increased.

   Analyses of sharecropping have tended to be clouded by conflation of its different varieties, including in studies of Ghanaian cocoa farming.[90]

This is partly induced by the nature of the phenomenon. Sharecrop deals, by definition, bridge the markets in different factors. But it is essential to recognise that the significance of the 'one third' deal varies historically with the economic contexts in which it has been made. Hill noted that in the Gold Coast Colony share-croppers were commonly employed at an early stage in the local development of cocoa-farming, especially by Akuapem farmers. There the farmers seem to have used sharecropping primarily to spare scarce working capital. The newly-employed labourer would be entitled to all the crop he plucked from the owner's existing farm, on condition that he assisted the owner to establish new ones. As the yield of the original farm increased, the labourer's share would be reduced: to a third, and perhaps later to a (smaller) fixed sum per load (*nkotokuano*).[91] In Asante, by contrast, sharecropping became popular only after the original 'take-off' of cocoa planting was already over. Sharecrop contracts were wanted by the labourers not by the employers. Moreover, they were reluctantly accepted by the latter not because of a shortage of capital specifically but because of a combination of the rising bargaining power of labourers; production uncertainties; and imperfections in the markets for credit, labour and produce. The Asante case seems to have close parallels, not with the original cocoa boom in the Gold Coast Colony, but with southeastern Côte d'Ivoire in the 1940s–50s and southwestern Nigeria in the 1970s–80s, in both of which cocoa-farmers had to concede to migrant labourers the substitution of sharecrop for regular wage contracts.[92]

As an epilogue to this section, we may see a further round in the labourers' negotiation of successively more favourable terms in the appearance, some years after Ghana's independence, of a kind of share-tenancy arrangement known as *yemayenke*. Its defining feature is division, not of the harvest, but of the farm. The landlord-employer gives half the cocoa trees, or the general use rights over half the land, in return for the tenant-labourer conducting all phases of farm work, from clearing and planting through to harvesting. Tsutomu Takane, who carried out a field study in the southwestern Asante village of Nagore in 1995, found it common there and further south in Ghana.[93] Takane does not examine the origins of the institution, and his sample is confined to tenants working at the time of his study. Among these, the first to secure a farm-dividing contract was a northerner called Amadu, who said that he came south to Nagore in 1958, and worked as an annual labourer before obtaining a *yemayenke* deal in 1964.[94] The fact that this type of contract is not mentioned in Dorothy Dee Vallenga's (admittedly brief) account of her study of labour contracts in Brong-Ahafo, using Labour Department files for 1957–69,[95] supports the view that it was indeed rare in the 1960s. The emergence of such an arrangement suggests even greater bargaining power for labour than was the case in the last twenty years of colonial rule. On the other hand, a departure from the trend examined in this chapter is the fact that many of the tenants (it is not clear how many) are Akan rather than northerners, to judge from their names.[96]

D. Land and Freedom: 'In this Ashanti . . . the cocoa-farmer employs labourers for whose labour he has to pay . . .'[97]

These words express fundamental truths about the 'mature' cocoa economy of Asante. The most basic is that hired labourers had become a crucial component of the labour force. They had replaced slaves and pawns as overwhelmingly the main source of the additional labour which a producer needed if he or she was to expand output beyond a very modest level. Principals had to buy the services of labourers instead of being able to buy the labourer, as in the previous century; or to summon the labour of those they had purchased in the past, as during the 'take-off' phase of cocoa cultivation.

Labourers were now unlocked from legally subordinate relationships. Hired labour appeared in the form first of casual, and then of regular, wage contracts. Its spread was a function, in the long term, of the growth of output; and in the short term, of the price of cocoa. Casual labour continued to be employed after the spread of regular contracts, primarily though not exclusively by small farmers, who were probably also the category of farmer who relied most on the institution of the co-operative work group, in which farmers exchanged labour in rotation. Employers of regular wage labour were normally medium and large farmers. Asante wage labourers on cocoa farms worked mostly on casual (day or contract) terms, were young, and were less numerous. In contrast, the workers who took regular contracts were overwhelming from the savanna. The key to the latter relationship was the economic rents on forest land created by the adoption of cocoa farming: rents which were large enough to make free labour contracts mutually rewarding. In a sense, therefore, migrant labour perpetuated one of the characteristics of the internal slave trade, namely the disadvantaged position of northern labourers in relation to forest-zone masters/employers. From a different perspective, writers influenced by dependency theory have maintained that the labourers' retention of a safety-belt in the form of access to land and the assistance of family labour had the ironic effect of permitting their exploitation; by enabling employers to pay male labourers more cheaply than the market would otherwise have borne.[98]

It has been argued here that the fact that the northern labourers were now free of physical coercion, in law and mostly in fact, mattered. Indeed, it was of critical importance, along with the fact that they had *not* been 'freed' from rights of access to land in their home areas. Contrary to the dependency-theory argument, the ability of labourers to draw upon these extra-market resources gave them more bargaining power than that 'enjoyed' by archetypically 'proletarianized' labour. The combination of such resources with legal freedom enabled them to capture much of their 'own value in the labour world', to use Guggisberg's phrase. This bargaining power was progressively strengthened during the period. The strongest evidence of this is that the labourers secured successively more favourable contracts from farmowners. They did not limit their efforts to enforcing their wage contracts. Above all, they achieved a structural innovation: the gradual replacement, from the middle 1930s, of annual wage contracts by a managerial form of sharecropping. It is clear, from both archival and oral sources, that the impulse for the adoption of sharecropping came from the labourers themselves. Under this arrangement, they not only obtained greater autonomy but also greater security of payment and, in almost all years, a higher share of farm income. In other words, they gradually won a larger share of the economic rent on cocoa land.

They earned enough to save. We have seen that in the later 1950s, with sharecropping the main form of regular labour and real producer prices high, if labourers waited until the end of the season for the bulk of their cash this was now—it seems—from choice. From the evidence of farmers—admittedly, rather than labourers themselves—interviewed for Bray's study, it appeared that 80 per cent of labourers' earnings were:

> available for the purchase of durable assets at the end of a year. If that seems a very high proportion of savings, the cash saving motive which impelled the labourer to migrate in the first place should be recalled and so should the fact that [cash] earnings are supplemented, perhaps more than doubled in the normal case, by the value of food and lodging given.[99]

This is not to say that all of them saved every available penny to buy such items as clothes, bicycles and the ingredients for bridewealth. In 1938 the government did a detailed budget survey of government workers, especially of unskilled labourers, who in this study, like their counterparts on cocoa farms, came overwhelmingly from the savanna. Dickinson commented:

> It is surprising how the cost of living varies with the individual. One man will spend only 3d per day on food whilst another, earning the same pay, will spend 10d. Some men will spend considerable sums on luxuries, palm wine, tobacco, women and clothes, whilst others stint themselves to an unreasonable degree.[99]

By the time of Bray's study it can be said that northern labourers had the opportunity to save—or spend at their discretion—a high proportion of their cash earnings.

The author of a contemporary study of northern labour in Ghana, 1953–55, lamented that for the migrant cocoa-worker 'no progress is possible: on his twentieth stay, the cocoa migrant gains no more than on his first'.[101] Yet a few did manage to become cocoa farmers in their own right: accessing the 'forest rent' directly, even before *yemayenke* terms were available. Two were recorded in Hwidiem in 1954–55: northern labourers who had become owners of cocoa farms.[102] Another example was the above-mentioned Musa Moshi. About 1956, having worked for the same farmer for seventeen years as an *abusa*-caretaker on a cocoa farm near Domi-Koniago in Amansie, he reminded his employer that on the latter's death he was liable to be evicted. He asked the farmer for some land and was granted it[103] (this being, presumably, land which the farmer had already obtained from the stool he served). He went on to establish five more cocoa farms 'in different places but in [the] same locality'.[104] A more dramatic example of economic and social mobility was noted by Bray. This concerned a man from northern Nigeria 'who came to Ahafo over twenty years ago', i.e. in the late 1930s at the latest.

> "He does not intend to go back and, in fact, he is regarded as a native. He started life as an ordinary labourer, then became an abusa, then 'cocoa broker' and is now a cocoa receiver for Messrs. Cadbury & Fry. His annual cocoa purchase is over 240 tons. He took up farming barely six years ago; his first two farms yielded 17 loads in 1955, and three farms 47½ loads in 1956. This year (1957), he hopes to get over 100 loads. . . . He has two taxis and three one ton passenger lorries."[105]

In the context of the literature, the eclipse of regular wage contracts by sharecrop terms is doubly remarkable. As Robertson has emphasized, this sequence contradicts the traditional assumption that sharecropping is a precapitalist or at best a transitional institution on a unilinear path to capitalism.[106] Equally interesting is the fact that, as we have seen, the pressure for this change came, not from the employers, but from the labourers themselves. Rather than seeking to increase their profit margin or avoid risk, the farmers were making a concession under pressure. This confounds the association, sometimes made, of sharecropping with exploitative relationships only a stage better than slavery.[107]

Like the migrant labourers, bankrupt Asante farmers did not face full proletarianization: we have seen that they retained access to land somewhere, whether inside or outside the cash-crop belt. It was partly for this reason, presumably, that the work party system in Asante remained a reciprocal exchange rather than evolving into a disguised form of wage labour.

Contrary to a common view, the interaction of market and non-market institutions in the labour market worked, on the whole, against the interests of indigenous rural capitalists and, by exerting downward pressure on one of the parameters of the cocoa supply schedule, also against those of foreign merchant capitalists. This was because physical coercion had been eroded and was being eliminated, while the indirect compulsion imposed by immersion in the market, that is by proletarianization, had not occurred and was not under way. The argument here can be represented in a pair of diagrams.

Figure 19.2 depicts the structure of the labour market in rural Asante in the era of free labour. Already in the 1920s to mid-1930s the picture contrasted in fundamental respects with the nineteenth-century market in imported captives portrayed by Figure 8.1. With much less extra-economic coercion being involved in recruitment, the price of labour was now paid in money wages. On the vertical axis 'price' means the real wage (the monetary

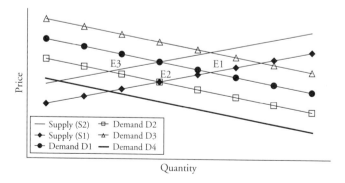

Figure 19.2. A model of the post-slavery labour market in Asante: occcasional clearance.

value of the labourer's earnings divided by the price of consumption goods) per unit of labour. The horizontal axis shows the quantity of labour forthcoming at each real wage rate. As before the adoption of cocoa-farming, the reservation wage—the minimum required to induce anyone voluntarily to sell his or her labour—was relatively high, because everyone had some access to land and, for northern Ghanaians until 1936, as for Asantes, there was no direct taxation. The latter did not apply to French subjects, but they faced a longer, riskier and perhaps more expensive journey to enter Asante. It is likely that the reservation wage was also kept high, in the early years after slavery, by trepidation among some northerners as to how they might be treated in Asante. But, compared to the nineteenth century, *effective* demand—demand backed by means of payment—for labour had increased enormously (curve D^1), because cocoa had boosted the productivity of agriculture in the forest zone, thus making employment there more worthwhile for cash-seekers from outside that zone. Given the supply curve S^1, how many labourers would be hired in a given year would depend on the cocoa price, the main short-term determinant of the demand curve. D^1 illustrates the relatively buoyant later 1920s (with employment high at E^1). D^2 depicts the depressed early 1930s, when fewer labourers were hired (E^2) and, especially when cocoa prices fell during the period of employment, they faced a significant chance of not being paid.

Working through Figure 19.2 we can also reflect on the Asante rural labour market in the era of sharecropping. To an extent, one would expect the reservation wage to have fallen, because of the introduction of direct taxation in the Northern Territories, making it essential to acquire cash, and as memories of violence by Asantes against northerners receded. But on the other hand, and very strongly, from the later 1930s savanna labourers reacted strongly against experiences of money wages that went unpaid in low-price years and which tended to be significantly below their average-year market value. Hence their insistence, with progressively increasing effect, on the substitution of sharecrop for wage terms. By implication, the effect of this would be to shift the labour supply schedule outwards: fewer labourers, if any, were willing to accept any given rate of real earnings (S^2). With the 'depression' demand curve, D^2, this implies even fewer labour hirings (E^3). Indeed, if we were to depict a wartime demand curve it would have been lower still, reflecting record low real producer prices, even if the Ashanti Confederacy Council ban on cocoa planting had little effect.

After 1945, as we have seen, there were other pressures on the supply schedule facing would-be employers of farm labour in Asante: pressures in opposite directions. Population growth pushed the schedule upwards;

increasing competition for labour from the Ivorian forest zone, and the growth of employment opportunities within Ghana but outside cocoa production, pressed it downwards. The schedule must have moved continuously, but its basic characteristic in the sharecropping era, of being relatively low such that in most years significant numbers of employers were unable to make all the hires they wanted, is still represented by S^2.

During the 1950s, especially, cocoa producer prices were high, giving farmers the purchasing power to secure much larger labour inputs—a higher proportion of whom now came from the Ghanaian savanna, rather than from across the border—which, collectively, permitted the massive expansion of planting and, to 1966, of output. If this—by historical standards—exceptionally strong effective demand can be represented by D^3 (for 'c.1956–57'), the subsequent weakening of effective demand for cocoa labour, as the purchasing power of the cocoa producer price shrank, is illustrated by the low position of D^4 (for 'c.1980').

The argument here fits W. A. Lewis's observation, made with reference to the Gold Coast (Ghana) generally, that 'there is a shortage of adult male labour . . . in the sense that at the current level of wages employers cannot get all the labour they want, in spite of the fact that there is considerable immigration from French Territories'.[108] Though the parameters thus moved continually throughout the period, the overall structural evolution of the relationship between employers and workers in rural Asante after slavery and pawning can be put like this: with the decline of physical coercion, and without the economic pressure that proletarianization would have entailed, the cocoa labour market—in Asante and, indeed, in Ghana generally—could only clear when effective demand was exceptionally high.

Having emphasized the bargaining power of labourers in the post-slavery era, it is important to underline the fact that they remained at a basic disadvantage, in terms of physical geography and property rights. There is an instructive contrast with certain men from the forest region of what is now the Volta Region of Ghana who, early in the twentieth century, worked as migrant labourers on cocoa farms in Akyem Abuakwa. They served as labourers on cocoa farms because they had no cocoa of their own. But when they returned home they brought planting materials with them. A few years later, they were cocoa farmers in their own right.[109] This opportunity was not open to labourers from the savanna. They could bring back knowhow, cash and cocoa seedlings: but the latter would never thrive. Except for the very few who were eventually given land-use rights in Asante, they could not access Ruf's 'forest rent' as principals; they had to do so as agents. That this outcome was institutionally rather than 'naturally' determined was underlined by President Houphoet-Boigny's promise of 'land to the tiller' to encourage migrants to work the Ivoirian forest lands.[107] Even by the end of the colonial period, the northern labourers in Asante, despite the gains they had made in the cocoa-labour market, still obtained substantially smaller shares of cocoa-farm earnings than the Asante farmers did.[108] Dependency writers and other critics of migrant labour have tended to focus too narrowly on labour relations.[109] For, as the comparison shows, the long (or even short)-term results of the labour contract depended crucially on the broader setting of property and power in which it took place. This context determined, to a very large extent, whether the migrant labourer was likely to remain precisely that.

20

CONCLUSION

This final chapter summarises and integrates the preceding discussion (Section A), then considers the implications for students of African history and social science theory (Section B).

A. Overview

This section briefly recalls the major contextual changes over the period and then restates the main argument within a broadly narrative structure.

Contexts

1807–1956 was a period of profound changes in the size and form of the demands for the products of the soil, agricultural and mineral; in the ways in which those demands were met; and in the identity, structure, resources, ideology and behaviour of the state.

The Asante rural economy expanded greatly in the volume and value of its output between the closing of the Atlantic slave market and the achievement of Ghanaian independence. Among many set-backs the most severe was the temporary exodus of much of the population following the Asante civil war of 1883–88, and the episodes of low real cocoa prices during the 1930s world depression and the world wars. Yet the underlying trend was decisively upward. Part of the growth in volume of agricultural output can be attributed to the demand and, later, the labour supply effects of natural increase in population, which was a feature from the end of the 1918 influenza pandemic onwards, and probably also occurred in earlier, shorter, episodes. The main motor of the growth in extra-subsistence output, however, was the successive changes in the composition of exports: the large rises in kola and gold exports between 1804 and 1874; the late-nineteenth century rubber boom; above all, the introduction and very widespread adoption of cocoa growing during the colonial period; and as a supplement, the emergence of timber exporting in the mid-twentieth century. Though this sequence of shifts owed much to declines in the prices received for the current staples, the main dynamic was the seizure of a series of new opportunities, mostly by Asante principals. The evident increase in food production during the colonial era was partly a response to the growth in the food market caused by the expansion both of the immigrant labour force in cocoa farming and trading, and of the buying power of the domestic cocoa economy as a whole. Much of the rise in rural output should be attributed to higher productivity, based on innovation in the choice of products which permitted better use of the relatively abundant factor of production: the natural resources.

There is no doubt that the expansion of production also involved a vast increase in the quantities of resources employed within the rural economy. The main components of this growth of imports were more intense use of forest land, capturing the forest rent in both the broad and narrow senses of the term; greater use of imported captive or, in the twentieth century, voluntary immigrant labour; a huge increase in the supply of credit from buyers to producers during times of rising prices; and, as a result of the combination of these dynamics, the creation during the colonial period of a vast stock of fixed capital in the form of cocoa trees.

The Asante Kingdom, Its Resource Endowment and Property in People, 1807–96

We are now in a position to survey the institutional forms in which this massive mobilization of factors occurred, beginning with the situation that prevailed by the first decade of the nineteenth century. There was a factor market in labour, but not in land, and labour was bought and sold by the person rather than by portions of labour-time.

This can be seen as a response to two phenomena which, at one level, were environmental and by extension economic. The first was the characteristic factor ratio, given the technologies in use: under which land was abundant relative to capital and labour, and the creation of capital goods was largely a function of labour inputs. So, at the busiest parts of the agricultural year—especially the bottleneck of the planting season—the supply of labour was the sole constraint on the expansion of output.

The other was the heterogeneity of land in the broad economic region of which Asante was part, and specifically the possession by Asante of much of the richest non-moveable resources. Asante possessed a very large 'broad forest rent' in agricultural and mining terms. The significance of these phenomena, however, cannot be fully understood in ecological and economic terms alone. Let us follow through the economic logic, and then place it in political context.

Given that the land tenure system gave virtually everyone access to land for cultivation, we might expect that there would also have been no labour market in the nineteenth century. For amid such physical and institutionalized abundance of land, and with economies of scale absent in production, there would be too little occupational specialisation to generate a market for goods sufficiently remunerative to make it profitable for a producer to employ a labourer on any terms that it would be profitable for the labourer to accept. Indeed, there is no clear evidence of wage labour existing in this economy before the British occupation. Evidently, the reservation wage was greater than the marginal value product of labour. If anyone was going to work for anyone else in this setting non-market mechanisms would have to be involved. Such instruments ranged from social obligation to physical coercion.

The most pervasive principle on which such labour was organized was gender, especially within the conjugal family. Most of the labour-time of men was available for extra-subsistence activities, under a division of tasks in which women and children did most of the domestic work and most of the food-farming other than clearing land. In this setting a male household head could increase his productive assets, both for the current generation and beyond, by additional marriages. But marriages themselves were costly, and in any case further additions to the current workforce were desirable both as manifestations of achievement and as means of further enrichment in production and commerce, whether, for example, in supplying the Kumasi food market or in export-import trade.

In this situation the demand for extra-familial labour could not be matched with supply without at least an element of coercion. Force was conspicuous in the flow of captives purchased from the northern savanna. More subtly, it was an aspect of the pawning of members of the indigenous population, though imported slaves could also be pawned. Coercion was not always physical. An Asante pawn was expected to feel a strong sense of family obligation in consenting to being exiled by her (or his) elders, in principle just temporarily, to become a labouring extra within a strange household.

On slavery, the argument presented in Chapter 8 is that in nineteenth-century Asante coercion was a necessary condition of labour being cheap enough for there to have been a labour market at all. The use of force in the acquisition and retention of slaves lowered the supply price of labour to the point at which supply could intersect with demand. With both slavery and pawning the pattern of transactions displays the defining characteristic of genuine markets: a tendency towards price-equalisation as a result of competition. Relatedly, the available evidence indicates that sums paid for slaves or loaned on pawns moved in response to changes in the balance of supply and demand.

Having linked coercion and markets, let us consider more generally the political economy of the institutional response to the prevailing factor ratio. Natural abundance can be turned into artificial scarcity. The 'natural' land surplus would not have 'translated' into a system of property rights under which land was effectively a free good (for all food-farming uses, and for most cash-earning uses by subjects of the landowning chieftaincy), had the state been able and willing to impose a different set of rules. The political requirements for such a 'translation' were the absence or non-use of coercive and ideological means (administrative, judicial, military) to alter the institutional 'responses' to the factor ratios. The reality was that, at least until 1874, the Asante central government was very powerful in terms of ability to send an army to force a neighbouring ruler to pay tribute. It was strong internally, too, in its capacity to impose draconian punishment on exemplary offenders, from individuals to rebel chieftaincies. It could be said that the Asante kingdom—and the subsequent colonial regime—was acutely strong, in the sense of being able to defeat rebellions or opposing armies. But both states were chronically weak in the sense of lacking the resources to dominate everyday decisions at village and family level around the country. Admittedly, as Wilks has shown, by the nineteenth century the Asantehene presided over a considerable administration.[1] Again, as McCaskie has detailed, it strove to achieve ideological hegemony over its population, by projecting the most vivid sense of its overwhelming might through cultural means including elaborately choreographed public performances.[2] Yet the state did not possess the tax base or (chicken and egg: a self-enforcing equilibrium) the army of officials or tax farmers that would have been necessary to deny virtually free use of land to the mass of free subjects.

Nor was it in its interests to try to change this. The 'broad forest rent' offered by Asante's soil and mineral endowment, still only comparatively lightly exploited, provided a militarily strong state with the opportunity to convert environmental favour into economic rent: to capture economic rents on top of natural resource rents. Going with rather than against the grain of the prevailing demographic and ecological conditions was not only the easier option, but one which delivered material advantages to the free Asante population generally, and to its upper echelons particularly. To imagine the Asante state not intervening in the economy would be a bad counterfactual because it would not be a remotely credible alternative to what it actually did. Needing revenue, possessing military power, it had both motive and opportunity to alter certain of the conditions under which both Asantes and their neighbours obtained their livelihoods. A less far-fetched alternative would have been for the Asantehene and chiefs to try to extract economically significant payments for access to land; rather as East European rulers and ruling classes did (at about the same time as the Akan states emerged) in imposing serfdom in their own land-surplus economies. But instead of striving, say, to turn free (if subject) cultivators into serfs, the Asante government used its coercive powers for the kind of intervention for which it was best suited, and which would consolidate its political base by benefitting its own free citizens as well as chiefs and officials. That is, foreigners were denied access to Asante natural resources except in return for a substantial tribute or rent: and, in practice, foreign labour was combined with Asante agricultural and mineral resources usually in the role of slaves.

For much of the nineteenth century the Asante kingdom had a monopoly of kola in its immediate economic region, and a near-monopoly of gold ore, and presumably was able to extract an economic rent accordingly, at least on kola. More importantly, and much more enduringly, people from less ecologically-favoured areas—the neighbouring savanna—had no practical chance of accessing the resources of the Asante forest zone except on terms that favoured the Asantes. The nature of those terms changed over the whole period discussed in this book, according to shifts in state policy that themselves were conditioned by the changes in the identity and nature of the state. Under the precolonial kingdom of Asante the only realistic chance for northerners to work in the Asante forest was as slaves. The state permitted and participated in the import of captives and their incorporation in Asante society as slaves (*nnɔnkɔfoɔ*), a status under which their labour was available to chiefs' establishments and commoners' households. The *nnɔnkɔfoɔ* were able to limit the extent of their exploitation to some degree, especially by the threat or use of flight. But, to judge from the rough calculations that are possible with turn of the century (c.1900) data, it is clear that slave labour was extremely cheap compared to the price that free labour would have commanded for any tasks except short-run work during the agricultural off-season.

The era of the Asante equivalent of 'legitimate commerce', from the beginning of the end of the Atlantic slave trade to the colonial occupation, was characterised by a significant increase in the exploitation of Asante's 'broad' forest rent: specifically with respect to the endowment of kola, rubber and gold. There was considerable demand for labour: for producing and trading both exports and goods for the internal commodity market. This induced greater use of slaves in production for the market as well as in other roles. Much of the extra-subsistence economic activity was in the hands of commoners, especially married men drawing on the labour of their conjugal families and seeking to acquire slaves and pawns. It appears that the majority of slaves imported into Asante were female, but there seems to have been a rough balance between male and female pawns, which suggests that labour as such, rather than the possibility of additional wives, was the major advantage sought by male pawn-takers. By the end of the period, the growth of the commoner stake in the commodity economy had had its first significant political consequences, in the movement to overthrow what the rebels perceived as the over-taxing, over-fining Asantehene Mensa Bonsu in 1883. This was the beginning of a defining feature of Asante political economy which lasted until 1956: protest and rebellion by coalitions of export suppliers and chiefs against any major attempts at what they considered to be organised extortion.

Cocoa, Colonialism and Institutional Change, 1896–1956

The imposition of colonial over-rule and the Asante adoption of cocoa coincided rather closely in time though, as will be highlighted later, the causal relationship between the two was weaker than might be supposed from this. What matters here is that the period inaugurated by these fundamental political and economic changes was characterized by major shifts in the institutional settings in which labour, land and capital were put to work.

The most fundamental innovation, though slow and uneven as it was happening, amounted to a transformation when completed: the ending of physical coercion of labour. In 1908 the state effectively (in terms of both court and administrative policy) relocated property rights over someone else's labour—at least outside marriage—from ownership of the person to a contractual claim on part of his or her time. The process by which prohibition of slavery and pawning was converted into genuine abolition was also the process by which these old institutions were replaced by new practices: wage labour and the use of (cocoa) trees and forthcoming (cocoa) crops as collateral for loans. By the end of the period, in a further change whose significance will be emphasized below, regular wage contracts (six monthly or annual) had themselves to a large extent been displaced by the development of sharecropping. Meanwhile, for the first time, elements of a factor market in land had appeared: not the buying and selling of land itself, but the mortgage and purchase of tree-crop farms, and the payment of rent by 'stranger' farmers to land-owning chieftaincies for the use of cultivable land (for cocoa).

Before trying to define the causal relationships between these institutional innovations and the spread of cocoa farming we need to specify the economic implications of this crucial addition to the crop repertoire. The adoption of cocoa was a response to an exogenous change: the appearance for the first time of an export market for a crop that would grow on Asante soil. The result was steadily to reduce the previously great abundance of land in relation to labour. This happened directly and immediately as fresh forest land was put into cultivation: permanently at that, rather than to be farmed and then fallowed as in the food-crop rotation. In the longer term there was a further, indirect, addition to the area under cultivation: as cocoa production and trading attracted net immigration, the demand for food rose. While part of this was met from neighbouring savanna areas, much of it was supplied from within the Asante forest zone. By the middle of the twentieth century land rotation cycles in food-farming in the longer-established cocoa-producing districts were becoming shorter, and relatively infertile land was being pressed into cultivation. Besides the increasing pressure on land, cocoa brought other important changes in factor inputs. It entailed a vast increase in what is properly regarded as fixed capital formation: the creation of capital goods in the form of cocoa trees. It also increased labour inputs, which, contrary to proponents of the vent-for-surplus model, could not come mostly from the surrender of leisure, as there is little evidence that a significant 'leisure reserve' existed. Rather, much labour-time was obtained by reducing or abandoning existing economic activities, especially in the dry season. But, as in the nineteenth century, to expand the workforce beyond familial resources required the importation of labour from the savanna. With slave trading (as distinct from slave-holding) being strongly suppressed from the beginning of the colonial occupation, such imports would have to be voluntary.

As before, the capacity of Asante users of labour to pay for it was based on the value of their produce from the forest-zone lands, much of that value being specifically 'forest rent'. Asante cocoa-farmers had to share some of the 'narrow' forest rent (i.e. from cocoa) with chiefs and brokers (though chiefs and Asante brokers were also cocoa-farmers themselves), and with European merchants and the colonial and transitional governments. Part of the 'broad' forest rent was also captured, using more capital-intensive means, by European mining companies, principally Ashanti Goldfields Corporation at Obuasi. But the overseas demand for cocoa enormously increased the economic value of Asante's broad forest rent, hence the willingness of Asante villagers to abandon gold mining within their lands in favour of cocoa cultivation. As a permanent crop, however, cocoa broke the pattern of ecologically sustainable cultivation characteristic of the precolonial period, under which soil fertility was restored by long fallowing. Thus it steadily reduced the remaining forest rent, in both senses of the term.

Let us now focus on the relationship between these resource implications of the spread of cocoa farming and the institutional changes. Was the adoption of cocoa endogenous, in the sense of being determined by the then-existing system of property rights in the factors of production? Clearly the growth in the world demand for cocoa was exogenous as far as Asante was concerned. One could argue that the importation of planting materials in response was part of a longer-term pattern of Asante entrepreneurship facilitated by the property rights system in a broad sense: a pioneer who made money could keep most of it, at least till his death, and/or use it to obtain respect and status. But it would be stretching the claim too far to link it to specific rights over productive resources.

From the point at which cocoa-planting material reached Asante, however, the production 'take-off' was made easier by the social forms in which productive resources were made available. The expansion occurred within the pre-existing arrangements. It was encouraged by the tenure system under which Asantes paid nothing, or merely token amounts, for access to land on which to plant cocoa. It was further facilitated by the fact that, in the case of slaves (first or later-generation) and pawns, the initial supply-price of labour had been reduced by coercion and, except with some pawns, had already been paid. To be sure, the bulk of labour inputs during the early wave of planting, into the 1920s, evidently came from within the conjugal family: male farmowners working for themselves, helped by their sons and with wives and daughters planting foodcrops to shade the young cocoa plants. But farmers operating on a larger scale relied on slave and pawn labour or, if they were chiefs, summoned their subjects to make the farm on behalf of the chiefdom. Moreover, it seems clear that slave-ownership and pawn-taking had themselves not uncommonly been the paths by which free Asante men had obtained wives (or additional wives) and, thereby, children.

Conversely, cocoa had a major effect on the micro-institutional changes that followed during the colonial period. Admittedly, the colonial prohibition of slavery and pawning was itself exogenous in relation to cocoa and to Asante society. Cocoa was already being widely planted by 1908 without wage labour being used by farmers. The proposal to act against coercion of labour was opposed by Asante chiefs and by the colonial 'men on the spot', and—twelve years after the imposition of British rule—was finally imposed on the local commissioners by higher authority in Accra and London. Yet once the ban on slavery and pawning was introduced, cocoa enormously smoothed the way to their supersession by regular hired-labour and by alternative forms of collateral. Earnings from cocoa enabled Asante farmers, for the first time, regularly to afford wages high enough to attract voluntary recruits. This is a key point which, in the context of Ghanaian cocoa, has been largely neglected since it was first asserted by McPhee (in relation to the Gold Coast rather than Asante) in 1926. Moreover, the opportunity to earn wages, or to farm cocoa for oneself, gave some slaves a genuine alternative to staying on with their master after 'emancipation' in 1908. Though farmers still lacked individual title to the land on which their farms stood, cocoa trees became acceptable collateral to moneylenders (though not banks, when and where the latter made their relatively isolated appearances). The fact that cocoa was both a tree and a cash crop made cocoa farms a relatively durable and marketable capital asset in a sense in which a farm composed of annual food crops was not.

But if cocoa growing—its opportunities and proceeds—made the ending of slavery and pawning easier and faster, the social relations within which it was adopted ensured that the process of abolition was extremely uneven in terms of gender and chronology. Pawning continued to be common after 1908, but now only for women and children, and among the latter, mostly girls. It was not until mid-century that female pawning seems genuinely to have reached the point of near-disappearance. Slavery endured after 1908 on a smaller scale than pawning, but the logic of survival and decline was similar in both cases. Adult male slaves or pawns were far more conspicuous, socially, than non-free women who could be classified as wives and their pawn or slave status made to seem invisible, or perhaps but a technicality, from the perspective of the short-staffed colonial administration. Perhaps more important was the fact that the economic opportunities which cocoa farming created for former slaves and pawns, or for slaves and pawns thinking of leaving their masters, were real mostly for (able-bodied) males. Even if a woman could find employment as a cocoa-farm labourer, or (as was much more likely) had access to land which she could plant with cocoa, in practice, in this period, she would usually be constrained from taking these apparent opportunities because of prior obligations to children and husband in the growing and preparation of food and in child-rearing. It was only gradually that women were able to establish rather more lucrative niches within the cocoa economy: providing services (such as food crops or cooked food) for a market whose buying power had expanded because of cocoa, or eventually becoming cocoa farmowners themselves.

Much the same institutional constraints, and the accumulated effect of their operation in the preceding period, meant that even women who had been neither pawns nor slaves very rarely enjoyed the same access as men to the productive resources necessary to exploit the potential of cocoa-farming. The fact that women generally entered the cocoa era having had less opportunity than men to build up capital made it impossible for most of them to obtain labour through the market, a resort which (whether the labour was free or coerced) might otherwise have enabled them to circumvent the restrictions on the disposal of their own labour-time. Consequently the female share in farm ownership was very small, as late as the 1920s. Over the decades it increased gradually, principally through certain specific mechanisms whose salience itself reflected both the past and the continuing constraints on women's access to labour and capital. In principle a woman might establish a farm herself. In practice this appears to have been a real possibility mostly for widows, co-wives or spinsters: such women tending to have more time to work for themselves. Members of the first two of these categories who established farms in their own names usually did so for the first time generally when they were relatively old, having already helped their present or former husband to establish his own cocoa farms. Women in the third category tended to lack capital and to have their own time committed to the support of relatives, and in any case, as Allman has shown, they were under great social pressure not to remain unmarried.[3] In some cases a woman obtained title to a cocoa farm second-hand, in an immediate legal sense: getting a minority share of the farms that had belonged to her now deceased or divorced husband, in recognition of her own contribution to making them. It must be emphasized that the right of widows or female divorcees to such a share was strongly resisted by chiefs and elders in the 1910s–30s, in chieftaincy courts and outside, but seems to have been more established by the end of the colonial period.

There were important institutional changes which can be said to have been 'induced' by the spread of cocoa cultivation. Forward sales/advances to producers already existed in Asante's precolonial trade. But the extremely widespread cultivation of a relatively lucrative cash crop gave most households an option for obtaining credit in smaller lumps than human pawning had permitted. This can be seen as a genuine advance in farmers' welfare, especially as an examination of the evidence undermines the claim, widely made by European cocoa-buying firms in the 1930s, that the advances system was manipulated by middlemen in a monopolistic fashion to extract economic rents from the producers (though there is evidence of rents being captured by brokers from the European firms). The basic limitations were the fact that, by definition, advances were given only to farmowners (therefore mostly male and almost exclusively Asante) and that their supply was largely confined to years of comparatively high cocoa prices, when the buying firms were competing intensely for produce.

It was a similar story with the use of cocoa farms as collateral in place of people, except that here the physical characteristics of the crop do not account for the particular form which such lending took. The predominance of pledging, involving the transfer of the asset to the creditor for the duration of the loan, over mortgaging was a direct continuation from the era of human pawning of the Asante/Akan concept of *awowasi*. This had major consequences, because it removed the risk from default as far as lenders were concerned. It thus made it safe to lend to someone over whom the creditor had no particular social hold. In short, while it did not literally encourage impersonal lending—lending relationships were basically face to face—it meant that the long-term credit market in this particular 'Third World' agrarian economy was not fragmented into a multitude of micro-monopolies. There was a segment that was so divided: where 'usury' was the rule. But it seems that most cocoa-farmowners could avoid it, and instead borrow from a richer or at least more 'liquid' neighbour.

Meanwhile the rule that non-subjects of the particular land-owning chieftaincy should pay the chief a substantial proportion of their cash winnings from Asante lands as 'tribute' was extended to cocoa. Despite the formal continuity, this was a fundamental change. For the first time cultivation rights were the subject, not merely of token payments in recognition of the rights of the owner of the soil, but of the payment of economically significant sums: for the hire of a factor of production which was now scarce enough to have a market value. The charging of 'cocoa tribute' led to legal disputes between groups of farmers and the chief they 'served' on one side, and the rent-charging chief on the other, usually over which chiefdom owned the land on which the farms stood. Virtually every land-owning chieftaincy was involved in such litigation during the colonial period (many of them in several cases, a high proportion of which were pro-tracted over many years).

The most important point about land in the colonial period, how-ever, was that despite its decreasing abundance virtually all adults had access to it somewhere, and to varying degrees. It is in this context—one to be defined in political economy terms, not simply in economic ones— that we can appreciate the significance of the decline and ending of slav-ery and pawning. The fundamental significance of 'free labour' in Asante, as became observable from the 1930s, was that it was genuinely free in the sense that labourers had a real choice.

The nature and extent of the choices were, it must be emphasized, highly unequal. For Asante women the options were generally less lucra-tive than for Asante men, while northern women were most unlikely to share the fruits of Asante cocoa farms except as part of the household workforces of northern men hired as sharecroppers by Asante farmowners. Northerners in general, though no longer at risk of enslavement, could share the forest rent only at arms-length in the sense that they lacked own-ership of farms or soil. This was one reason why, even by the very end of our period, farmowners made substantially more from cocoa than did labourers. But the migrants from the savanna retained rights of access to land in their home areas, and this gave them a basic bargaining power in the forest zone. Moreover, from the 1930s through the 1950s there were a series of upward pulls on the labour demand curve: from the further extension of the area under cocoa in Asante and, to a lesser extent, the rest of the Ghanaian forest zone; from the growth of the urban labour market and, relatedly, food-crop production for the towns; and from the emer-gence of an Ivoirian market for cocoa labour, bolstered by Houphoet-Boigny's promise of land rights in the cocoa-growing areas. Meanwhile there was little prospect of bankrupt Asante farmers swelling the supply of labourers. If a farmer suffered foreclosure on his existing cocoa trees he could simply start another cocoa farm.

In this comparatively—and (on the whole) increasingly—favourable bargaining situation, the migrant labourers obtained successively more desirable terms of employment on Asante farms, thereby increasing their share of the forest rent, in both senses of the term. The period of prolifer-ating wage contracts, especially annual ones, from the late 1910s to the mid-1930s, had occasionally been disfigured by suspicion and even violence between northern labourers and their Asante hosts and employers. Even so, we must not forget that for the labourers annual contracts were a fundamental qualitative, as well as a quantitative, improvement on the slave status which had accompanied the earlier use of northern labour in the Asante forest zone! From the later 1930s onwards regular wage contracts were replaced by a managerial form of sharecropping. In the post-colonial period the terms of these contracts were themselves gradually made more generous to the sharecropper. Where the nineteenth-century state had used coercion to lower the supply price of labour enough (more than enough) to make it pay for Asante principals to obtain labour through the market, the twentieth-century state left it to market forces. With most potential labourers continuing to have the alternative of working for themselves, during and after colonial rule cocoa farmowners could not be confident of securing all the labour they wished to hire except when the real producer price of cocoa was exceptionally high. Despite the concessions they had made on the structure of contracts, when the state imposed very low real producer prices in the 1970s and early 1980s Asante cocoa farmers were to find it harder than ever to secure satisfactory supplies of hired labour.

Having considered the implications of the decline of coercion for markets, let us explore further the institutional response to the changed and changing factor ratio of the cocoa era. If the imposition of cocoa 'tribute' (rent) was a 'reflection' of the fact that land now had a market value, the mirror was a distorting one in that the fixed-rate payment system allowed only a rough relationship with the varying value of the service (the supply of land) involved. Again, while the frequency of litigation about chieftaincy boundaries was a response to their new economic value, investments (primarily tree-planting) to realise that potential were made expensive and risky by the very fact of such frequent litigation. The absence of a statute of limitations (for example, restricting the length of time after an alleged trespass within which a boundary case could be brought) is a specific example of an indigenous law that, while innocuous in the context of annual crops, contributed to the potential for tenurial instability in the new era of permanent crops. Critics of the government's land policy, from within the colonial service, argued with some exasperation that the system of tenure that would most efficiently accommodate the growing pressure on land was some sort of individual title to defined areas. This would encourage banks and other formal lenders to offer credit to producers at much below the rates demanded by informal moneylenders. Most basically a free land market, with transactions costs and risk reduced by a system of universal registration, would stimulate the transfer of assets (cocoa trees) from less to more efficient farmers. In the light of Ruf's recent analysis, if not necessarily at the time, it could also be argued that maximizing the property rights of the individual farm owner would maximize the farmer's incentive to avoid unnecessary degradation of soil fertility.

A fundamental land market reform would have required a government able and willing to carry it out. It is wise to be cautious in generalising about why the colonial regime did not act on the urging of the advocates of such reform. For this policy was made and then maintained over successive generations of decision-makers, through rather different political and economic and ideological settings. Indeed in the early years of colonial rule in Asante, as in the Gold Coast, the administration actually permitted experiments in plantation agriculture by European investors. The policy of 'defending' African proprietorship in Ghana was definitively established only after European planters had tried and failed commercially. But, once the 'West African Lands Policy' had become orthodoxy, three elements stand out as recurrent and important in the reasoning behind the rejection, by the administrations in Accra and Kumasi, not merely of European settlement but also of an open land market among African agriculturalists. These were administrative (ultimately fiscal), political and economic: that land titling and related reforms were costly, dangerous and unnecessary. The most prosaic was not necessarily the least important: the very high administrative cost of a detailed and definitive survey. The government was hampered by a shortage of surveyors even in conducting the much less ambitious project, carried out over many years, of defining chieftaincy boundaries. The political consideration was the fear that easy foreclosure and sales of land would result in a polarization between richer and poorer Asantes, with the latter becoming destitute and therefore, colonial officials feared, potentially either criminals or rebels. The economic point was that an active and open land market, and even definitive individual title, was unnecessary to the well-being of the rural economy. The great cocoa-planting boom of c.1901–16 had occurred without it, and the same was to happen in the middle and later 1950s. The problems of the intervening decades had more obvious (and more important) causes than the above-mentioned institutional imperfections.

Thus the colonial regime was, most of the time, 'conservative' on land alienation, though its courts upheld creditors' proven claims and permitted the surrender or sale of cocoa farms in settlement of debts. What is often overlooked is that the colonial government also took active steps to protect the investments of the individual cocoa farmers. First, it defended them from eviction. Drawing on the Asante distinction between ownership of the soil and ownership of what is planted on it, the administration generally refused to allow the victors in inter-chieftaincy land cases to remove the losing side's farmers from their farms. Second, it prevented chiefs from charging their own subjects the 'tribute' imposed on non-subjects. Third, over a number of years it demarcated the boundaries between chieftaincies in an attempt to reduce litigation between them—much of the costs of which were being borne ultimately by the farmers on each side. Finally, on several occasions the colonial administration or, later, the Ashanti Confederacy Council of Chiefs took steps to reduce the rents paid by 'stranger' farmers, either during cocoa-price recessions or permanently.

The absence of registered title in rural land helps to explain why it was only Asante creditors, rather than Levantine or European ones, who acquired farms. This outcome would have pleased the colonial administration which, apart from its initial willingness to accept European planters, was keen to see the continuation of the Asante monopoly of Asante farms. In this sense there was still an element of economic rent in Asante cocoa earnings, into the 1950s and beyond. As before, northerners could find land in the Asante forest zone only as agents rather than principals: though now free from coercion. This conditioned the distribution of the 'producers'' share of Asante's forest rent between farmowners and labourers, to the benefit of the former.

The sharp increase in the rate of depletion of Asante's broad forest rent which was entailed by the adoption of cocoa had a dialectical relationship with the coercion of labour. Slaves and pawns assisted the rapid adoption, but cocoa-farming and the income it generated greatly facilitated the freeing of labour—eventually for women pawns and slaves as well as their male counterparts. By mid-century not only were slavery and pawning very largely over—though the memory of the former remains important to this day in such contexts as chieftaincy succession—but a significant minority of women had managed to begin to improve their access to productive resources within the rural economy. In short, the forest rent was being shared more widely among the contributors to the Asante rural economy.

Also by mid-century, however, there were signs that the forest rent was beginning to approach exhaustion in the older and more densely-populated cocoa-growing districts. The Ashanti Confederacy Council's 1938–46 ban on new cocoa planting was in force in a period when few people were planting anyway, and was withdrawn before the price was right for the next planting boom. But it is a clear indication that many chiefs realised that the era of land abundance was virtually over. There remained some scope for new planting in the western districts, but mid-century can be seen as the beginning of a long transition, still under way, from extensive to intensive farming in the Asante forest zone: a transition which reflected the progressive exhaustion of the forest rent, and created incentives for further changes to the institutions within which land, labour and capital were put to work.

It is appropriate to end this narrative section with reflections on periodization. The organization of the book has reflected the view that 1896 and 1908 are the years that can most meaningfully be invoked to signal turning-points. The latter signifies the beginning of the end of slave and pawn holding. Though not in itself important for land tenure, it was only shortly after this that the proliferation of mature cocoa farms reached the stage of provoking the first colonial interventions to try to limit chiefs' claims to 'tribute' from them. No subsequent year, or short period, was so important across the range of factors of production: the mid-1930s inaugurated a new era in labour contracts, but not in the social relations surrounding land or capital, despite the continuing processes of change in which they too were involved.

In a book that spans the traditional historiographical divide of the onset of colonial rule, it may seem ironic to insist that that date marked a watershed. Two observations should be made. One is that it is only by considering the decades—not merely the few years—before and after the colonial invasion that its significance can be properly determined. The other, more important in the Asante context, is that the beginning of the colonial period was also the beginning of a longer era, that of the cocoa economy. Colonial rule accelerated the spread of cocoa within Asante, especially via the investment in the railway, but Asantes, not British, were the agents of the diffusion and adoption of cocoa. As we have seen, this agricultural innovation had profound implications for resource use, and for the institutions in which resources were used.

B. Implications

In commenting on the broader theoretical and historiographical implications of the discussion we must remember that this is a story not of creation but of change. That is, it is not an account of the 'emergence' or 'development' of property rights, still less of markets, in the factors of production. These existed already by 1807: albeit in 'pre-modern' forms. Rather, the issue is how they changed over the next century and a half in the context of the intensification of land use that resulted from the emergence and development of export agriculture and from (partly related) population growth. The remaining comments will be organized in two sub-sections: the first focused on theories, historiography and debates; the second an attempt to place the main findings of this book in relation to the history of capitalism.

Recent Themes and Old Debates: Integrations

In retrospect, much of the analytical ambition of this book is integrative: to span the traditional chronological divide in African historiography; to draw ideas from the recent concerns of historians and social scientists and to use them to improve our understanding of older concerns; to try to transcend the stand-off in a classic debate between economic 'determinism' and cultural-political 'choice'; and to bring together, selectively but also (and unashamedly) eclectically, insights from conflicting theoretical traditions. Methodologically, the study has combined qualitative and quantitative methods and used a wide range of primary sources. Further, in an era in which intellectual markets often seem ever more minutely segmented, with many (thankfully, far from all) scholars separating themselves into mutually-disregarding groups, I have sought to integrate as precisely as possible analytical abstraction and the histories of specific, named, individuals.

The chronological balance of this book has been slightly telescoped in favour of the twentieth century, ultimately for source reasons. Yet I have devoted much space to the nineteenth century, and sought to add to our empirical knowledge and analytical understanding of it. This is both 'for its own sake' and, as I hope has been demonstrated, because it really is true that one cannot get more than the most superficial and misleading understanding of Asante's experiences with cocoa and under colonial rule except by relating them to the preceding history. Certainly the discussion here has not simply 'covered' the late precolonial and colonial period: the analysis offered of the latter has been based squarely on a specific account of the former. As I hope is clear from the synthesis in the preceding section, the argument about forest rent and about coerced and free labour unites as well as differentiates the sub-periods within the era of Asante's emergence as an agricultural export economy.

This book has addressed a classic, if understudied, problem. In so doing I have drawn on recent themes in the general historiography of Africa, not to pursue them separately, but rather as sources of inspiration for fresh work on long-standing but ever-contentious issues. One such theme is gender. Whether in the history of slavery, pawning, free labour, family labour, self-employment, of access to credit, of opportunities to use land and to form fixed capital—in all these cases much of the analysis here has turned on the self-consciously different treatment of and opportunities for men and women within Asante society over the period. Again, I have tried to treat ecology as an integral part of the study of scarce resources and their exploitation: to relate it to economics and political economy. The key tool here has been Ruf's concept of 'forest rent', which I have stretched to coin the term 'broad forest rent', as distinct from his cocoa-specific or 'narrow' sense of the term. This notion enables us, precisely, to bridge ecological and economic approaches, and in a way that is historically appropriate because it captures the particular type of economic growth that was achieved by Asantes in the late precolonial and colonial periods: one that can only be understood within the context of environmental constraints. The logic is likely to be applicable to other cases where depletable resources happen not to be in a forest zone: 'forest rent', or rather its progressive exhaustion, is simply a specific application of what environmental economists call 'user cost': 'the sacrifice of future use caused by using up a unit of an exhaustible resource today'.[4]

The argument on the economics of slavery in Chapter 8 should be commented upon in this sub-section, because it is an attempt to resolve the non-meeting of minds on this issue between explanations grounded in the price theory of market economics and, on the other hand, 'old institutionalist' approaches, whether marxist or substantivist, based on the social and political parameters of economic calculation. In applying to West Africa the Nieboer hypothesis that slavery simply made labour cheaper, inducing employers to prefer it to the alternative of wage-labour, Hopkins explicitly insisted on the reality of 'deliberate choice on the part of African employers' between slave and wage labour. Goody, Cooper and Thornton replied that choice was unreal, for social and cultural reasons.[5] The discussion here included what I believe is the first (albeit tentative) attempt to quantify the relative costs of slave and free labour in precolonial West Africa. The conclusion, from this and importantly also from qualitative sources, is that in the Asante case, wage labour was not a practical alternative: but that this was for economic rather than cultural reasons. While in some other historical cases slaves and wage labourers were available as alternatives to employers/owners, in this case slaves (or pawns) were the only affordable labourers besides additional wives (who were likely to be slaves or pawns anyway). Empirically, it is particularly interesting that the admittedly fragmentary figures confirm what qualitative sources imply, that the price of slave labour was very low compared to the reservation wage of free labour. This point is well established in the context of the external slave trade: slave labour being cheaper than free labour for European planters in the Americas.[6] But the fact that it should also be true within West Africa is strong evidence that market interpretations of 'internal' slavery have much to offer, at least for the nineteenth century. But what kind of market interpretation? It should be noted that, on this point, the argument presented here is not a neoclassical one: in that it includes the proposition that one of the factors (land) had no price, and in its conclusion that the 'choice' of slave rather than wage labour was—in an economic sense—no choice at all. Colin Leys has asked rhetorically: 'Rational Choice or Hobson's Choice?'[7] Slavery in nineteenth-century Asante is precisely a case where the *economic* logic of rational choice led to a form of Hobson's choice.

The Nieboer hypothesis could be described as a 'new institutionalist' idea before the school, in that it is an example of the attempt to extend economising logic to explain the rules surrounding economic activity as well as the size and characteristics of the activity itself. Throughout the book particular propositions from the dependency, marxist, agrarian populist, and new institutionalist traditions (as described in Chapter 2) have been related to Asante evidence, considered as sources of possible historical insight, and tested where possible in specific historical contexts. Here it is appropriate to offer some observations about the most relevant general arguments of these traditions in relation to the story presented above. Brief comments on key dependency, marxist and populist propositions will be incorporated into the final sub-section. Let us reflect first on the new institutionalist approach, which is particularly pertinent not only in the sense that it has been the most influential in economic history, including of Africa, over the last twenty years but also because its evolutionary theory of property rights provides the most detailed theoretical model for us to consider in relation to the historical evidence.

In the context under consideration the theory offers insight without sufficiency. It provides a framework within which possible economic explanations can be pursued to their limits individually and related to each other coherently. The notion of economic rent, like the Nieboer hypothesis, is a valuable analytical tool in the setting of Asante economic history and, though too old to be specifically a 'new institutionalist' idea, can be integrated into a general rational-choice political economy approach. The same might be said of McPhee's view that cocoa contributed enormously to the decline of slavery on the ground in the Gold Coast Colony.

This argument has been applied here to Asante, refined, and related to gender differences. The very notion of conflicting interests within the same household lay outside market economics until recently, yet is easily thinkable from a 'new institutional economics' perspective. Again, NIE draws valuable attention to an issue that is fundamental in many contexts, that of divergence between incentives to individuals and the interests of groups or society as a whole (the free-rider problem). A related general concept, not specifically from NIE but part of the same general project of making the rules endogenous, is principal-agent theory, whose exploration of potential obstacles to efficient cooperation between employer/master/lender and worker/slave/pawn/debtor has been highly relevant, explicitly or implicitly, in many contexts in the substantive chapters.

But we have also seen that the rational-choice approach to political economy, whether by economists or political scientists, has serious limitations as a source of explanation in the history under discussion. The single most important institutional innovation of the entire period, the ending of slavery, was initiated (though not completed) by a government decision which was not endogenous in the sense of being induced by changes in relative factor prices within the Asante economy. Rather, it was imposed from higher up the imperial hierarchy. It is possible that the decision could be explained as an endogenous response to factor price shifts on a scale broader than Asante, or colonial Ghana, or indeed British West Africa as a whole. But it is equally possible that it could be explained by phenomena which were, at least in part, irreducibly cultural or political. Again, the rational-choice 'logic of collective action' predicts that large numbers of individually poor or small-scale operators are likely to be relatively ineffective in expressing and enforcing their joint interests compared to small numbers of individually wealthy people. Yet in colonial Asante we have the examples of both Asante women and northern men who, separately, succeeded in winning improvements in the terms on which they contributed labour to cocoa farming despite being poor and numerous. Indeed, while there may have been informal solidarity between individuals and among groups, in neither case is there evidence of any organized attempt to win concessions through collective action. In particular the case of the male migrants, who achieved particularly large concessions, confounds the assumption that free-riding by individuals would prevent the group from securing the best available terms. To conclude, the new institutionalism is based on the worthy methodological principle of seeking the most parsimonious explanation. But when applied to experience it runs into not only the problem that it may be indeterminate in the sense that its logic is compatible with more than one outcome,[8] but also that there are relatively few sufficient causes in history.[9]

Further, the case examined here highlights the fact that property rights affect economic outcomes not only through their effect on incentives but also through their implications for the distribution of power: in the sense of confirming if not determining who would be the principals, who the agents, and what the (im)balance of bargaining power would be.[10] 'New Institutionalism' focuses upon systems of property rights as incentive structures, and much in this study has illustrated the pertinence of that insight. But the incentive set facing those who possessed the relevant natural resources offered very different opportunities and dangers to the incentive set facing those who, under the distribution of property underpinned by the coercive capacity of the state, lacked ownership of a share in the 'broad forest rent'.

Asante Factor Markets and the History of Capitalism

Let us now discuss some of the major changes examined in this book in relation to the history of capitalism in Africa and more generally. We can begin by returning to the Genoveses' remark, quoted in Chapter 13, that 'capitalism, which rested on free labor and had no meaning apart from it . . . conquered, absorbed, and reinforced servile labor systems throughout the world', and indeed 'created new ones'. In Asante we see that slavery and pawning were indeed 'reinforced' by Asante's post-1807 commitment to producing 'legitimate' commodities for export, in the sense that the demand for extra-familial labour was met by further acquisitions of slaves and pawns. This picture must be modified in two ways, both of which, but especially the second, highlight the specificity of (this) African experience. First, the pull of the external market not only encouraged more slave purchases and more lending on pawns, it also seems to have stimulated at least a partial re-orientation of the nature and uses of slavery and pawning in Asante: a greater emphasis on their economic (and specifically market-oriented) uses. Second, much of the export production served, not the industrial or industrializing economies overseas, but rather an expanding regional economy relatively nearby, centred on the Sokoto Caliphate. The Genoveses' 'pessimism' is further borne out by the early years of the colonial period, when the remarkable speed of the spread of cocoa-planting owed much to the availability of slave and pawn labour. On the other hand, as noted in the previous section, the work of those slaves and pawns contributed—as it turned out—to their own emancipation in the sense that cocoa money ameliorated the pain for masters and increased the opportunities for independent work for former slaves and pawns.

Chapter 19 queried the assumption that the growth of wage labour was a natural corollary of other 'modernizing' processes. 'The labour question' for Asante farmers[11] was whether they would be able to recruit extra-familial labour once slave imports ceased, and if so whether on wage terms or something less in their favour, such as sharecropping. In the event, with the establishment of cocoa growing, what one might call the 'Nieboer problem', of a prevailing factor ratio and production function within which wage labour was not mutually profitable to providers and users of labour services, seemed to have been overcome. Yet, as recalled in the previous section, employers faced major problems. Their labour demands were fully effective, it seems, only in years of exceptionally high cocoa prices, when they could afford to attract the labour they required. This case conflicts with the 'articulation of modes of production' thesis, widely adopted by dependency writers in the 1970s and since, that in 'peripheral' economies capitalism preserves precapitalist institutions such as the family farm and extracts from them labour and goods at below any competitive market price.

Sharecropping has often been regarded as a transitional institution, doomed to disappear when 'the transition to capitalism' is completed. In Asante cocoa-farming, however, it was regular wage labour that proved to be the transitional institution under which extra-household labour was recruited in the years between the end of slavery and the rise of share-cropping. This is significant theoretically because it shows that the transition to specialized wage labour markets can, historically, be anything but unilinear. This observation, like the one in the preceding paragraph, is consistent with the agrarian populist rejection of any assumption that the inevitable and imminent fate of 'peasants' is to become polarized between employers and proletarians.

A related though different argument can be made about the significance of cocoa farm-pledging. In one respect this practice, new in itself but fashioned within an established institutional template, fits a dependency interpretation, for the transition from lending on the security of persons to lending on crops and farms represented a shift from a form of general rural credit/debt to a specifically agricultural one. This was a response to the shift in the structure of the economy, as the relatively diversified nineteenth-century economy was superseded by the cash-crop economy of the colonial era. But specialization, if it raises average income, may reduce risk more than it increases it. Pledging farms did not doom farmers struck by the vicissitudes of the international cocoa market to self-perpetuating poverty and exploitation. To be sure, it gave those who had money opportunities to make more, but the evidence is that most would-be borrowers were able both to find a lender and, ultimately, to pay off the loan. In this sense it reinforces the picture of active economic life, which can be associated with Hill's 'dynamic' variant on the agrarian populist tradition, in which the mass of the population engaged in small-scale accumulation as well as in survival.

Colonial regimes in West Africa have often been seen as socially conservative, less keen to promote free markets than to preserve what they perceived—or 'constructed'—as older, more paternalistic relationships. There is much in this book to confirm this view, notably the reluctance of British officials in Asante to implement the imperial commitment to abolish slavery. But we have also seen that the administration not only permitted European planters to try their luck, but also, and much more successfully, took a series of measures to secure the property of individual African cocoa farmers. Rather than running a 'sustained campaign against the cocoa industry', as Kay argued, colonial officials sought (albeit often with misguided advice) to protect Ghana's comparative advantage.[12]

Finally, the experience of northern—and Asante—labour on Asante cocoa farms underlines—but by contrast—the pertinence of Marx's notion of the double-edged character of 'free labour'. He wrote that:

> Free labourers, in the double sense that neither they themselves form part and parcel of the means of production, as in the case of slaves, bondsmen, &c., nor do the means of production belong to them, as in the case of peasant-proprietors; they are, therefore, free from, unencumbered by, any means of production of their own. . . . The capitalist system pre-supposes the complete separation of the labourers from all property in the means by which they can realise their labour.[13]

In colonial Ghana, however, freedom from physical coercion was not associated with that 'freedom' from possession of land or capital which would deny the worker any alternative to seeking paid employment. The weakening and ultimate ending of the property rights of slave owners really did transform the situation facing, in particular, young men from the savanna areas near the Asante forest zone. It gave them bargaining power, which they used to raise their incomes and, from the 1930s, to establish some control over their work process. It is important to observe that this bargaining power was based not only on the ending of property rights in humans, but also on the fact that individual property rights in land were not established, and specifically not in the areas which the free migrant labourers called home. The real foundation of the bargaining power of labour was not its relative scarcity as such, but their continued access—physical and institutional—to land. Thus, the northern labourers, and indeed indebted Asante farmers, gained from the 'failure' to extend individual property rights. Conversely, this fact that emancipation was not accompanied by proletarianization constrained the supply of hired labour during the colonial period, and has continued to do so. This has been a central problem for the long-term profitability of cocoa farming in Asante, as in Ghana generally.

It illustrates Cooper's remark that the development of capitalism in Africa has been hindered by the resistance which 'Africa's spaces and Africa's social structures' have offered to exploitation, indigenous or foreign.[14] This must be coupled, however, with the equally important observation that Africans have combined their spaces and social structures, and changed both, in the process of accumulating productive wealth: as in the development of Asante's agricultural export economy over the nineteenth and early twentieth centuries.

ABBREVIATIONS USED IN THE NOTES

AF	Austin Fieldnotes
Ag	Acting
ARA	*Annual Report on Ashanti*
ARG	Ashanti Records Group (signifies a file in the Ashanti Office of PRAAD, in Kumasi: in the post-1996 file-numbering system)
Asst	Assistant
BMA	Basel Mission Archive
CCA	Chief Commissioner of Ashanti
CS	Colonial Secretary
CEPA/CSPA/CWPA	Commissioner Eastern/Southern/Western Province of Ashanti
DC	District Commissioner
DLB	Duplicate Letter Book
JAH	*Journal of African History*
MRO	Manhiya Record Office (the Asanthene's Record Office)
NAGK	National Archives of Ghana, Kumasi (use of this abbreviation signifies a file which I have not found, as yet, in the post-1996 file-numbering system).
PC	Provincial Commissioner
PRAAD	Public Relations and Archives Administration Department (formerly National Archives of Ghana)
PRO	Public Record Office, Kew, U.K.
RB	Record Book

NOTES

Chapter 1

1. E.g. Frederick Cooper's remarkable trilogy (New Haven), *Plantation Slavery on the East Coast of Africa* (1977), *From Slaves to Squatters* (1980), and *On the African Waterfront* (1987).

2. Notably David E. Ault and Gilbert L. Rutman, 'The development of individual rights to property in tribal Africa', *Journal of Law and Economics* 22:1 (1979), 163–82; J. Marvin Bentley and Tom Oberhofer, 'Property rights and economic development', *Review of Social Economy* 39 (1989), 51–65; and at some length, by Kathryn Firmin-Sellers, *The Transformation of Property Rights in the Gold Coast* (Cambridge, 1996). These deal exclusively with land tenure.

3. Jean Allman and Victoria Tashjian, '*I Will Not Eat Stone*': *A Women's History of Colonial Asante* (Portsmouth NH, 2000); Sara S. Berry, *Chiefs Know Their Boundaries: Essays on Property, Power, and the Past in Asante, 1896–1996* (Portsmouth NH, 2001); T. C. McCaskie, *Asante Identities: History and Modernity in an African Village 1850–1950* (Edinburgh, 2000).

4. Kwame Arhin, *West African Traders in Ghana in the Nineteenth and Twentieth Centuries* (London, 1979). This focuses on the Asante trade with the north of Ghana.

5. The most extensive survey is Frederick Cooper, 'Africa and the world economy', *African Studies Review* 24:2/3 (1981), 1–86; reprinted with postscript in Cooper and others, *Confronting Historical Paradigms: Peasants, Labor, and the Capitalist World System in Africa and Latin America* (Madison, 1993).

6. An outstanding example is T. C. McCaskie, *State and Society in Pre-Colonial Asante* (Cambridge, 1995).

7. Much of the best economic history published in these years is also, and has been received as, social history: which ameliorates, but also illustrates, the sidelining of economic history as such.

8. This emphasis is exemplified by Frederick Cooper, *Decolonization and African Society: the Labor Question in French and British Africa* (Cambridge, 1996).

9. Epitomized by the founding of the first journal to be published outside Africa dedicated to the study of contemporary African economies: the *Journal of African Economies*, published by Oxford University Press from 1992.

10. This is even true of the better efforts at the exceptionally difficult task of analysing 'economic change in world history', such as E. L. Jones's book with that sub-title, *Growth Recurring* (Oxford, 1988).

11. As a recent article in a 'mainstream' disciplinary journal illustrates: E. W. Evans and David Richardson's on the concept of economic rent, applied to the Atlantic slave trade ('Hunting for rents: the economics of slaving in pre-colonial Africa', *Economic History Review* 48 [1995], 665–86). The comparison is with the important work of Avner Grief: e.g. Grief, 'Microtheory and recent developments in the study of economic institutions through economic history', in David M. Kreps and Kenneth F. Wallis (eds), *Advances in Economics and Econometrics*, Seventh World Congress, Vol. II (Cambridge, 1997), 81–113.

12. Thomas S. Kuhn, *The Structure of Scientific Revolutions* (Chicago, 2nd edn, 1970).

13. The text mentioned being R. H. Coase, 'The problem of social cost' (1960). This and his other seminal essay, 'The nature of the firm' (1937), are conveniently reprinted in Coase, *The Firm, the Market, and the Law* (Chicago, 1988). For a survey of the new institutionalism see Thráinn Eggertsson, *Economic Behavior and Institutions* (Cambridge, 1990). See, further, John N. Drobak and John V. C. Nye (eds), *The Frontiers of the New Institutional Economics* (San Diego, 1997).

14. Nancy Folbre, 'Hearts and spades: paradigms of household economics', *World Development* 14:2 (1986), 245–55; also Folbre, 'Cleaning house: new perspectives on households and economic development', *Journal of Development Economics* 22 (1986), 5–40.

15. Robert H. Bates, *Markets and States in Tropical Africa* (Berkeley, 1981); *Essays on the Political Economy of Rural Africa* (Cambridge, 1983); *Beyond the Miracle of the Market: the Political Economy of Agrarian Development in Kenya* (Cambridge, 1989).

16. Jean Ensminger, *Making a Market: the Institutional Transformation of an African society* (Cambridge, 1992); Firmin-Sellers, *Transformation of Property Rights in the Gold Coast*.

17. Joseph E. Stiglitz, 'The new development economics', *World Development* 14:2 (1986), 257–65.

18. Debraj Ray, *Development Economics* (Princeton, 1998); Pranab Bardhan and Christopher Udry, *Development Microeconomics* (Oxford, 1999).

19. Paul Bohannon and George Dalton, 'Introduction' to their (eds), *Markets in Africa* (Evanston, 1962); Karl Polanyi, *Dahomey and the Slave Trade: an analysis of an archaic economy* (Seattle, 1966); Paul and Laura Bohannon, *Tiv Economy* (Evanston, 1968).

20. A. J. Latham, 'Currency, credit and capitalism on the Cross River in the pre-colonial era', *Journal of African History* (hereafter *JAH*) 12 (1971), 599–605; A. G. Hopkins, *An Economic History of West Africa* (London, 1973), esp. ch. 2; Paul E. Lovejoy, 'Interregional money flows in the precolonial trade of Nigeria', *JAH* 15 (1974), 563–85; Lovejoy, 'Polanyi's "ports of trade": Salaga and Kano in the nineteenth century', *Canadian Journal of African Studies*, 16:2 (1982), 245–77; Robin Law, 'Posthumous questions for Karl Polanyi: price inflation in pre-colonial Dahomey', *JAH* 33 (1992), 387–420.

21. The most famous instance is one of the earliest: Polly Hill's *The Migrant Cocoa-Farmers of Southern Ghana* (Cambridge, 1963; 2nd edn, Hamburg and Oxford, 1997).

22. Mark Granovetter, 'Economic action and social structure: the problem of embeddedness', *American Journal of Sociology* 91:3 (1985), 481–510. See also Jean-Philippe Platteau, 'Behind the market stage where real societies exist', *Journal of Development Studies* 30:3 (1994), 533–77 and 30:4 (1994), 753–817; Avner Offer, 'Between the gift and the market: the economy of regard', *Economic History Review* 50 (1997), 450–76. A clear statement, in case-study form, of the argument for continuity in this sense in economic history is Philip T. Hoffman, Gilles Postel-Vinay and Jean-Laurent Rosenthal, 'Information and economic history: how the credit market in old regime Paris forces us to rethink the transition to capitalism', *American Historical Review* 104 (1999), 69–94.

23. E.g. see Platteau, 'Behind the market stage where real societies exist'.

24. Allman and Tashjian, *'I Will Not Eat Stone'*. See also Allman's 'Of "spinsters", "concubines" and "wicked women": reflections on gender and social change in colonial Asante', *Gender and History* 3:2 (1991), 176–89; Allman, 'Rounding up spinsters: gender chaos and unmarried women in colonial Asante', *JAH* 37 (1996), 195–214; and related papers cited later in the present study. Important new evidence was presented in Victoria Beardslee Tashjian, 'It's Mine And It's Ours Are Not The Same Thing: a History of Marriage in Rural Asante, 1900–1957', Ph.D. dissertation (Northwestern University, 1995).

25. For an Africanist survey see William Beinart, 'African history and environmental history', *African Affairs* 99:395 (April 2000), 269–302.

26. Hopkins, *Economic History of West Africa*.

27. Hans P. Binswanger and John McIntire, 'Behavioral and material determinants of production relations in land-abundant tropical agriculture', *Economic Development and Cultural Change* 36:1 (1987), 73–99.

28. Geoffrey M. Hodgson, *Economics and Institutions* (Cambridge, 1988), 173.

29. Cf. Gareth Austin, 'Indigenous credit institutions in West Africa, c.1750–c.1960', in Austin and Kaoru Sugihara (eds), *Local Suppliers of Credit in the Third World, 1750–1960* (London, 1993), 139.

30. As distinct from 'parallel' markets which arise 'to evade government controls' (Christine Jones, David L. Lindauer and Michael Roemer, 'Parallel, fragmented, and black: a taxonomy', in Michael Roemer and Christine Jones (eds), *Markets in Developing Countries* (San Francisco, 1991), 4.

31. For an introduction to the usage of the term in new institutionalist (which the author confusingly calls 'neoinstitutionalist') economics see Eggertsson, *Economic Behavior and Institutions*, 33–40.

32. 'Opportunity cost': the cost of the opportunity foregone.

33. Cf. Coase's definition: 'the difference between what a factor of production earns in the activity under discussion and what it could otherwise earn' ('Notes on the problem of social cost', in Coase, *The Firm, the Market, and the Law*, 163). A clear exposition of the concept of economic rent, followed by a historical application, is provided by Evans and Richardson, 'Hunting for rents'.

34. 'Marginal product': the output gained from applying one extra unit of the resource concerned.

35. Paul M. Romer, 'The origins of endogenous growth', *Journal of Economic Perspectives* 8:1 (1994), 3–22.

36. Cf. Donald N. McCloskey, 'The economics of choice', in Thomas G. Rawski (ed.), *Economics and the Historian* (Berkeley, 1996), 135–36.

37. François Ruf, 'From forest rent to tree-capital: basic "laws" of cocoa supply', in Ruf and P. S. Siswoputranto (eds), *Cocoa Cycles: the Economics of Cocoa Supply* (Cambridge, 1995), 6–7. See, further, Ruf, *Booms et crises du cacao: les vertiges de l'or brun* (Montpellier, 1995); William Gervase Clarence-Smith and François Ruf, 'Introduction', to Clarence-Smith (ed.), *Cocoa Pioneer Fronts* (London, 1996).

38. Francesca Bray, *The Rice Economies: Technology and Development in Asian Societies* (Oxford, 1986); Kenneth Pomeranz, *The Great Divergence: China, Europe, and the Making of the Modern World Economy* (Princeton, 2000); Kaoru Sugihara, 'The East Asian Path of Economic Development: a Long-Term Perspective', *Discussion Papers in Economics and Business*, Graduate School of Economics, Osaka University (Osaka, 2000).

39. Denmark had withdrawn from slave trading with effect from 1 January 1803, which is relevant because Danish merchants were among those who bought captives from Asante traders. But the annual volume of slaves (not all of whom were from Asante suppliers) carried from the Gold Coast in Danish ships was very low after 1792: at most one or two ships a year (Georg Norregård, *Danish Settlements in West Africa 1658–1850* [Boston, 1966: Danish original, 1954], 177–78). In view also of Britain's naval interdiction of continental European shipping during the Napoleonic war (e.g., not a single ship could be sent from Copenhagen to the Gold Coast while Britain and Denmark were at war, 1807–14: ibid., 177), the British abolition law, which came into effect on 1 January 1808, was far more important for the Asante economy than the pioneering Danish one. Longer term, what was decisive about the British decision to withdraw from the trade was not simply the size of the British market share, but the fact that British naval and diplomatic pressures were then used to induce other shippers to desist.

40. Gareth Austin, ' "No elders were present": commoners and private ownership in Asante, 1807–96', *JAH* 37 (1996), 1–30. Also Austin, 'Between abolition and *jihad*: the Asante response to the ending of the Atlantic slave trade, 1807–1896', in Robin Law (ed.), *From Slave Trade to 'Legitimate' Commerce: Commercial Transition in Nineteenth-Century West Africa* (Cambridge, 1995), 93–118. See, further, pp. 90–91, 94 below.

41. Austin, ' "No elders were present" '. The point is enlarged somewhat in ch. 3 below.

42. On this watershed see Gareth Austin, 'National poverty and the "vampire state" in Ghana: a review article', *Journal of International Development* 8:4 (1996), esp. 562–63.

43. R. S. Rattray, *Ashanti* (Oxford, 1923); *Religion and Art in Ashanti* (Oxford, 1927); *Ashanti Law and Constitution* (Oxford, 1929).

44. Theodore H. Von Laue, 'Anthropology and power: R. S. Rattray among the Ashanti', *African Affairs* 75, 298 (1976), 33–54; T. C. McCaskie, 'Rattray and the construction of Asante history: an appraisal', *History in Africa* 10 (1983), 187–206.

45. References to their work are given in context below.

46. K. A. Busia, *The Position of the Chief in the Modern Political System of Ashanti* (London, 1951), esp. 125–28, 200–205.

47. Wilks, *Asante in the Nineteenth Century: the Structure and Evolution of a Political Order* (Cambridge, 1975; 2nd edn with new preamble, 1989), 73–74.

48. Ghana, Office of the Government Statistician, *Survey of Cocoa Producing Families in Ashanti, 1956–57* (Accra, 1960). As far as I am aware, only one previous study has used this extremely rich source: Barbara Ingham, 'Ghana cocoa farmers—income, expenditure relationships', *Journal of Development Studies* 9:3 (1972), 365–72, who used it to investigate farmers' propensities to save or to consume their income.

49. Ghana, *Survey of Cocoa Producing Families in Ashanti, 1956–57*, 2.

50. Ibid., 2–3. The qualification to randomness is that 'After the selection a few very isolated districts were discarded and replaced by substitutes as it was not practicable for interviewing teams to visit them, but these changes were small and not sufficient to affect the random quality of the sample' (ibid., 3).

51. Ibid., 3.

52. Ibid., 3.

53. One qualification: besides 'farmers' (farmowners), caretakers (sharecroppers) working for farmers living outside the survey area were included 'to cover the case of farmers who had no chance of being recorded in the enumeration, but it turned out that they were very few in number' (ibid., 3). Their rarity is just as well because their inclusion biases the

sample downwards, in terms of the average size of farmers' cocoa output, because it implicitly omits any farms they owned outside the survey area.

54. Ibid., 7. The 1956–7 survey concentrated on cash transactions, but the difficulty in defining households in Asante was noted a decade earlier by Fortes in his contribution to a joint paper. In many cases uncooked food passed daily from husband's house to wife's house, while cooked dishes moved in the opposite direction. Further, 'the food that thus enters a matrilineal household is not consumed only by the recipient', but 'shared with other members of the unit'. Fortes commented that 'This makes the study of family budgets a task requiring much patience and ingenuity . . .' (M. Fortes, R. W. Steel and P. Ady, 'Ashanti survey, 1945–46: an experiment in social research', *Geographical Journal*, cx:4–6 [1947], 168–69).

55. It is depressingly common for 'household' to be left undefined in economic surveys which use it as a basic unit, as if Fortes had laboured in vain. An instance of this sin in a more recent survey of cocoa-farmers in Asante is the otherwise useful paper by Simon Commander, John Howell and Wayo Seini, 'Ghana', in Commander (ed.), *Structural Adjustment and Agriculture: Theory and Practice in Africa and Latin America* (London, 1989), 107–26.

56. Ghana, *Survey of Cocoa Producing Families in Ashanti, 1956–57*, 10.

57. That is, the main part of them, available in Cambridge University Library. At the time of writing the rest of Fortes's Ashanti Social Survey (ASS) papers, together with the ASS papers of one of Fortes's partners in the Survey, Robert Steel, are not as yet in the public domain, and I have not had access to them. They have been used in the books of T. C. McCaskie, cited above (and who deserves recognition for retrieving the Steel papers from obscurity).

58. Formerly entitled simply and proudly the National Archives of Ghana; recently succumbed to bureau-speak as PRAAD (the Public Records and Archives Administration Department).

59. I drew attention to the scholarly neglect of the bulk of the archive in Gareth Austin, 'The Kumase branch of the National Archives of Ghana', *History in Africa* 13 (1986), 383–89. In 1996 the archivists undertook a complete re-cataloguing, so that it became, for the first time, systematically ordered. In the process some previously mislaid files were evidently found. One possible cause for concern in this admirable and much-needed reform is that some files were apparently 'weeded' during the process. For an introduction to the new classification system see Thomas K. Aning, 'Re-opening of National Archives of Ghana—Ashanti Regional Archives, Kumasi', *Ghana Studies Council Newsletter*, 11 (Spring/Summer 1998), 8–9. In this book the new classification numbers are used where I have them (they all begin with the letters ARG). Where I have not found a new classification number I give the old (these are signalled by 'NAGK', standing for the former name of the archive: National Archives of Ghana: Ashanti Regional Office, Kumasi).

60. In particular, some of the contents of the Asantehene's Record Office at Manhyia, Kumasi. Examples of this are noted by Ivor Wilks, *Forests of Gold: Essays on the Akan and the Kingdom of Asante* (Athens OH, 1993), 122 (nn. 34, 36). See also n. 57 above.

61. As with Otumfuo Nana Agyeman Prempeh I, *'The History of Ashanti Kings and the Whole Country Itself' and Other Writings*, ed. A Adu Boahen, Emmanuel Akyeampong, Nancy Lawler, T. C. McCaskie, and Ivor Wilks (Oxford, 2003).

62. In this book such words as 'reveal' and 'recovery' (of history, experience) are used broadly, qualified by recognition that—as most historians have accepted since long

before the relativist trends of the last quarter-century—sources do not speak for themselves: historical research is 'constructionist' in the sense that observation does not precede the start of conceptualization.

Chapter 2

1. For recognition of the parallel see, e.g., Vernon W. Ruttan and Yujiro Hayami, 'Toward a theory of induced institutional innovation', *Journal of Development Studies* 20:4 (1984), 204–5. The canonical reference is Karl Marx, 'Preface' to *A Contribution to the Critique of Political Economy* (1859). An accessible English edition, from which the quotation is taken, is Marx, *Early Writings* (introduced by L. Colletti, transl. R. Livingstone and G. Benton: London, 1974), 425–26.

2. John Sender and Sheila Smith, *The Development of Capitalism in Africa* (London, 1986); also Bill Warren, *Imperialism: Pioneer of Capitalism*, ed. by John Sender (London, 1980).

3. For a relatively recent statement by a dependency writer who made a celebrated if tentative conversion to a marxist analysis of Africa's economic history (at least for Kenya) but who later reverted to much of his original radical pessimism, see Colin Leys, 'Confronting the African tragedy', *New Left Review* 204 (1994), 44–45.

4. E.g. Samir Amin, *Unequal Development: an Essay on the Social Formations of Peripheral Capitalism* (Hassocks, Sussex, England, 1976; French edn, 1973), 328–29. On Ghana specifically this view was expressed by Rhoda Howard, *Colonialism and Underdevelopment in Ghana* (London, 1978) and Beverly Grier, 'Underdevelopment, modes of production, and the state in colonial Ghana', *African Studies Review* 24 (1981), 21–47. These works are to some extent in the tradition, not only of Latin American dependency theory, but also of A. T. Nzula, I. I. Potekhin and A. Z. Zusmanovich, *Forced Labour in Colonial Africa*, ed. R. Cohen, transl. H. Jenkins (London, 1979; Russian edn, 1933), especially (on West Africa) 46, 49.

5. Claude Meillassoux, 'From reproduction to production: a marxist approach to economic anthropology', *Economy and Society* 1 (1972), 102–3; Harold Wolpe, 'Capitalism and cheap labour-power in South Africa: from segregation to apartheid', *Economy and Society* 1 (1972); Henry Bernstein, 'Notes on capital and peasantry', *Review of African Political Economy* 10 (1978), 72. This model was applied to Ghanaian history by Grier, 'Underdevelopment', 25, 37–38.

6. Bernstein, 'Notes on capital and peasantry', 72; Rhoda Howard, 'Formation and stratification of the peasantry in colonial Ghana', *Journal of Peasant Studies* 8 (1980), 68–69, 73; Beverly Grier, 'Contradiction, crisis, and class conflict: the state and capitalist development in Ghana prior to 1948' in Irving Leonard Markovitz (ed.), *Studies in Power and Class in Africa* (Oxford, 1987), 28; Grier, 'Underdevelopment', 33.

7. Beverly Grier, 'Pawns, porters, and petty traders: women in the transition to cash crop agriculture in colonial Ghana', *Signs* 17:2 (1992), 304–28; reprinted in T. Falola and P. Lovejoy (eds), *Pawnship in Africa: Debt Bondage in Historical Perspective* (Boulder, 1994), and in P. Lovejoy and T. Falola (eds), *Pawnship, Slavery, and Colonialism in Africa* (Trenton NJ and Asmara, 2003).

8. E.g. Patrick Harries, 'Kinship, ideology and the nature of pre-colonial labour migration', in Shula Marks and Richard Rathbone (eds), *Industrialisation and Social*

Change in South Africa (Harlow, 1982), 142–66; William Beinart, *The Political Economy of Pondoland 1800–1930* (Cambridge, 1982).

9. Notably in the work of E. P. Thompson, a major influence on African labour historiography (see the comments of Frederick Cooper, 'Work, class and empire: an African historian's retrospective on E. P. Thompson', *Social History* 20 [1995], 235–41). Also in that of Robert Brenner: 'Agrarian class structure and economic development in pre-industrial Europe', *Past and Present* 70 (1976), 30–75 and 'The origins of capitalist development: a critique of neo-smithian marxism', *New Left Review* 104 (1977), 25–92.

10. Jean-Philippe Platteau, 'The evolutionary theory of land rights as applied to Sub-Saharan Africa: a critical assessment', *Development and Change* 27 (1996), 29–30.

11. Hill, *Migrant Cocoa-Farmers of Southern Ghana*.

12. Hill, *Development Economics on Trial: the Anthropological Case for a Prosecution* (Cambridge, 1986), 81. Further references will be given when Hill's position is elaborated and discussed in relation to the Asante evidence, in later chapters.

13. A. F. Robertson, *The Dynamics of Productive Relationships: African Share Contracts in Comparative Perspective* (Cambridge, 1987), 53–79. An earlier formulation was Robertson, '*Abusa*: the structural history of an economic contract', *Journal of Development Studies* 18:4 (1982), 447–78.

14. See esp. Wilks, *Asante in the Nineteenth Century*; Wilks, *Forests of Gold* (Athens OH, 1993), 127–88; Arhin, 'Some Asante views of colonial rule: as seen in the controversy relating to death duties', *Transactions of the Historical Society of Ghana* 15 (1974), 63–84; Arhin, 'Trade, accumulation and the state in Asante in the nineteenth century', *Africa* 60 (1990), 524–37; McCaskie, 'Accumulation, wealth and belief in Asante history', Part I, *Africa* 53:1 (1983), 23–44; McCaskie, '*Ahyiamu*—"a place of meeting"': an essay on process and event in the history of the Asante state', *JAH* 25 (1984), 169–88. Recently T. C. McCaskie has produced a major new reading of the state's hegemony over Asante society, focussed on the intellectual categories in which it was expressed and sustained: McCaskie, *State and Society*. For further references see Austin, ' " No elders were present" '.

15. See p. 13.

16. Arhin, 'Some Asante views of colonial rule'.

17. G. B. Kay, 'Introduction' to his *The Political Economy of Colonialism in Ghana* (London, 1972), 3–37; Anne Phillips, *The Enigma of Colonialism: British Policy in West Africa* (London, 1989).

18. M. P. Cowen and R. W. Shenton, 'Bankers, peasants, and land in British West Africa 1905–37', *Journal of Peasant Studies* 19:1 (1991), 26–58. For a different perspective see Chibuike Ugochukwu Uche, 'Foreign banks, Africans, and credit in colonial Nigeria, c.1890–1912', *Economic History Review* 52:4 (1999), 669–91.

19. For more on the notions summarized in the next paragraph see Eggertsson, *Economic Behavior and Institutions* and also works by the founding fathers of the evolutionary theory of property rights, whose models are inevitably slightly conflated in my brief exposition: Harold Demsetz, 'Toward a theory of property rights', *American Economic Review* 57:2 (1967), 347–59; Douglass C. North and Robert Paul Thomas, *The Rise of the Western World* (Cambridge, 1973); Ruttan and Hayami, 'Toward a theory of induced institutional innovation', 203–23.

20. Property rights authors formulate this step in the reasoning in a variety of ways, but it seems to me that the most precise way of putting it is in terms of social efficiency prices. Here I draw on Frank Ellis's exposition of the concept in a different

but related context, that of the relative efficiency of small and large farmers: Ellis, *Peasant Economics: Farm Households and Agrarian Development* (Cambridge, 1988), 201–3.

21. Note that his actual marginal product (in both quantity and value) would be less than it would be if factor prices reflected the new scarcities. This is because, as the old factor prices still prevail, profit-maximizing entrepreneurs would continue to combine factors in the old proportions. So, in our example, they would use too much labour and too little land. To put it another way, the actual marginal product of labour would be less than its 'social' marginal product, if the latter is defined as the opportunity cost of using a unit of labour in its existing use, under the established but now socially inefficient property rights regime, rather than using it in proportions that reflect the new scarcities.

22. Anne O. Krueger, 'The political economy of the rent-seeking society', *American Economic Review* 64:3 (1974), 291–303; Kevin M. Murphy, Andrei Schleifer and Robert W. Vishny, 'Why is rent-seeking so costly to growth?', *American Economic Association Papers and Proceedings* (1991), 409–14.

23. See, e.g., Douglass C. North, *Institutions, Institutional Change and Economic Performance* (Cambridge, 1990).

24. Bates, *Markets and States in Tropical Africa*; Murphy, Schleifer and Vishny, 'Why is rent-seeking so costly to growth?'

25. For a clear introduction see Ellis, *Peasant Economics*, 150–4, and Ray, *Development Economics*, 561–72. I thank Richard Palmer-Jones of the University of East Anglia for advice on the literature.

26. See Pranab K. Bardhan, 'Interlocking factor markets and agrarian development: a review of issues', *Oxford Economic Papers* 32 (1980), 82–98; Kaushik Basu, *Analytical Development Economics: the Less Developed Economy Revisited* (Cambridge MA, 1997), 267–316; Clive Bell, 'Credit markets and interlinked transactions', in Hollis Chenery and T. N. Srinivasan (eds.), *Handbook of Development Economics* (Amsterdam, 1988), vol. I, 764–830. For an attempt to relate this literature to West African economic history see Austin, 'Indigenous credit institutions in West Africa', 117–30.

27. Avishay Braverman and Joseph E. Stiglitz, 'Sharecropping and the interlinking of agrarian markets', *American Economic Review* 72 (1982), 695–715; also M. G. Quibria and Salim Rashid, 'The puzzle of sharecropping: a survey of theories', *World Development* 12:2 (1984), 103–14. See, further, Keijiro Otsuka, Hiroyuki Chuma and Yujiro Hayami, 'Land and labor contracts in agrarian economies: theories and facts', *Journal of Economic Literature* 30 (1992), 1965–2018.

28. For this pessimistic interpretation see Amit Bhadhuri, 'The method of usury', in his *The Economic Structure of Backward Agriculture* (London, 1983), 69–84.

29. North, *Institutions, Institutional Change and Economic Performance*, 98.

30. Mancur Olson, *The Logic of Collective Action* (Cambridge MA, 1965); Olson, *The Rise and Decline of Nations* (New Haven, 1982).

31. Bates, *Markets and States in Tropical Africa*, esp. 88–95; Bates, *Essays on the Political Economy of Rural Africa*, 78–82, 124–25). He qualifies this contention with the observations that in electoral politics numbers are a virtue, and that small suppliers may be more economically mobile if their sunk costs are relatively as well as absolutely low. See, esp., Bates, *Beyond the Miracle of the Market*, 86–89.

32. On Olson's work see Ronald Rogowski, 'Structure, growth and power: three rationalist accounts' in Robert H. Bates (ed.), *Toward a Political Economy of Development* (Berkeley, 1988), 300–330, at 306–10. For an empirical problem for Bates in interpreting the political economy of cocoa in colonial Ghana see Gareth Austin, 'Capitalists and chiefs in the cocoa hold-ups in South Asante, 1927–1938', *International Journal of African Historical Studies* 21 (1988), 92–93.

33. For an interesting exploration of this framework to a neighbouring colony within what became Ghana see Firmin-Sellers, *Transformation of Property Rights in the Gold Coast*.

34. For a stimulating application of bargaining ideas to the political economy of colonial Ghana, albeit on an issue not directly involving production relations, see Rod Alence, 'The 1937–38 Gold Coast cocoa crisis: the political economy of commercial stalemate', *African Economic History* 19 (1990–91), 77–104.

35. Pauline E. Peters, 'Is "rational choice" the best choice for Robert Bates? An anthropologist's reading of Bates' work', *World Development* 21:6 (1993), 1063–76. Cf. Mark Granovetter, 'The sociological and economic approaches to labor market analysis: a social structural view', in Granovetter and Swedberg, Richard, (eds), *The Sociology of Economic Life* (Boulder, 1992), 233–63. See further, in an African context, Jane Guyer, 'Wealth in people, wealth in things—introduction', *JAH* 36 (1995), 83–90.

36. The problem is recognised from within new institutionalism by North, *Structure and Change in Economic History* (New York, 1981), 45. For a broad attack on neoclassical conceptions of rationality and agency in the name of a *non* rational-choice 'institutionalism' see Hodgson, *Economics and Institutions*. For recent economists' doubts about rational choice, drawing partly on new work in cognitive psychology, see Richard H. Thaler, 'Doing economics without *homo economicus*', in Steven G. Medema and Warren J. Samuels (eds), *Foundations of Research in Economics: How do Economists do Economics* (Cheltenham, England, 1996), 227–37; Andy Clark, 'Economic Reason: the interplay of individual learning and external structure', in Drobak and Nye, *Frontiers of the New Institutional Economics*, 269–89.

37. Cf. A. G. Hopkins, 'Rationality and technology in African history', *Technology and Culture* 16:4 (1975), 462.

38. To adapt a phrase from Milton Friedman, 'The methodology of positive economics', in his *Essays in Positive Economics* (Chicago, 1953), 14. For a critique of Friedman's classic essay see Hodgson, *Economics and Institutions*, 28–35, 48–50.

39. For vent-for-surplus approaches see, most notably, H. Myint, *The Economics of the Developing Countries*, revd edn (London, 1973), 29–40, and R. Szereszewski, *Structural Changes in the Economy of Ghana, 1891–1911* (London, 1965). For problems, see Polly Hill, review of Szereszewski in *Economic Development and Cultural Change* 16:1 (1967), 131–37; Barbara Ingham, *Tropical Exports and Economic Development: New Perspectives on Producer Response in Three Low-Income Countries* (London, 1981); J. Hogendorn and M. Goldberg, 'Origins of the Gold Coast cocoa industry: example of a vent-for-surplus?', *Itinerario* 6:2 (1982), 46–58; Gareth Austin, 'Rural Capitalism and the Growth of Cocoa Farming in South Ashanti, to 1914' (Ph.D. thesis, University of Birmingham, 1984), 347–449. For a revised version of the model see Francis Teal, 'Growth, Comparative Advantage and the Economic Effects of Government. A Case Study of Ghana' (Ph.D. thesis, School of Oriental and African Studies, University of London, 1984).

Chapter 3

1. For 1750–1874 there is Joseph Raymond LaTorre, 'Wealth Surpasses Everything: an Economic History of Asante, 1750–1874' (Ph.D. thesis, University of California, Berkeley, 1978).

2. This book focuses on the Asante forest heartland: on the administration of Asante's tributary empire see Emmanuel Terray, *Une histoire du royaume abron du Gyaman: des origines à la conquête coloniale* (Paris, 1995), 521–44.

3. There has been a major debate about the significance of these creations, in particular about whether they should be regarded as part of a bureaucratic revolution in government, as Wilks urged, or as a manifestation of patrimonialism. The original article was Wilks, 'Aspects of bureaucratization in Ashanti in the nineteenth century', *JAH* 7 (1966), 215–32. For an excellent survey see Larry W. Yarak, *Asante and the Dutch, 1744–1873* (Oxford, 1990), 17–27. See further, Wilks, 'What manner of persons were these?', *Forests of Gold*, 241–328.

4. Wilks, *Asante*, 106–9; Wilks, 'Golden Stool', 6; LaTorre, 'Wealth Surpasses', 129–31; T. C. McCaskie, 'Office, land and subjects in the history of the Manwere *fekuo* of Kumase', *JAH* 21 (1980), 189–208.

5. The general point is well conveyed by the map in Thomas J. Lewin, *Asante Before the British: the Prempean Years, 1875–1900* (Lawrence KS, 1978), 140–41.

6. See Wilks, *Asante*, esp. 46–48.

7. See, esp., Lewin, *Asante Before the British*.

8. McCaskie, '*Ahyiamu*—a place of meeting'.

9. Ivor Wilks, 'Asante at the end of the nineteenth century: setting the record straight', *Ghana Studies* 3 (2000), 13–59.

10. The Gold Coast Colony, declared in 1874, comprised only the forts and settlements. But in the same year Britain extended the legislative authority of the Colony over the adjacent, much more extensive, Protected Territories.

11. For details see William Tordoff, *Ashanti Under the Prempehs, 1888–1935* (London, 1965), 139–46.

12. On the political and administrative consequences of the Asantehene's exile, and the origins and implementation of the restoration, see Tordoff, *Ashanti Under the Prempehs*, 147–66, 173–84, 205–15, 226–46, 322–414.

13. For an Ahafo case-study of the conflicts following from the creation of Brong-Ahafo region (1959) see John Dunn and A. F. Robertson, *Dependence and Opportunity: Political Change in Ahafo* (Cambridge, 1973), 224–77. For a useful summary of which chief served which, from 1935 until and beyond the Nkrumah era, see ARG 2/3/1/11, 'Memorandum on Brong-Ahafo Lands and Kumasi Lands in Brong-Ahafo' (anonymous and n.d., but evidently by an official in the regional administration, 1966 or slightly later).

14. David Kimble, *A Political History of Ghana 1850–1928* (London, 1963), 325, 532. For the internal colonial-government debate on the issue see PRAAD Accra ADM 12/5/16 'Admittance of lawyers to Ashanti'.

15. For discussion of aspects of the court system see Victoria B. Tashjian, 'The diaries of A. C. Duncan-Johnstone: a preliminary analysis of British involvement in the "native courts" of colonial Asante', *Ghana Studies* 1 (1998), 135–50.

16. For a recent discussion of the incidence of death duties, with references to earlier literature, see Austin, ' "No elders" '. The rents will be detailed in chapter 5.

17. For details see Rattray, *Ashanti Law*, 107–19; Kwame Arhin, 'The financing of the Ashanti expansion (1700–1820)', *Africa* 37 (1967), 283–91; Wilks, *Asante*, 64–71, 431–45; LaTorre, 'Wealth Surpasses', 216–97; Claude-Hélène Perrot, *Les Anyi-Ndenye et le pouvoir aux 18e et 19e siècles* (Paris, 1982), 94–97; Terray, *Une histoire du royaume abron du Gyaman*, 547–54.

18. Wilks, 'Golden Stool'.

19. McCaskie, *State and Society*.

20. School of Oriental and African Studies Library, University of London, Methodist Missionary Society Archive, Picot to Boyce, Cape Coast, 3 May 1876, quoted in McCaskie, *State and Society*, 140.

21. For discussion of the significance of funerary killings in precolonial Asante see, in particular, Rattray, *Religion and Art in Ashanti*, 105–9; Clifford Williams, 'Asante: human sacrifice or capital punishment?', *International Journal of African Historical Studies* 21 (1988), 433–41; Ivor Wilks, 'Asante: human sacrifice or capital punishment? A rejoinder', *International Journal of African Historical Studies* 21 (1988), 443–52; Wilks, 'Space, time, and "human sacrifice"', in Wilks, *Forests of Gold*, 215–40; and for the broader ideological and political context, McCaskie, *State and Society*.

22. For a vivid example see T. C. McCaskie, 'Time and the calendar in nineteenth-century Asante: an exploratory essay', *History in Africa* 7 (1980), 179–200; see, further, McCaskie, *State and Society*.

23. E.g., see Busia, *Position of the Chief*, 24–25, 43.

24. Ibid., 42–43.

25. Claude-Hélène Perrot and van Dantzig, Albert (eds), *Marie-Joseph Bonnat et les Ashanti: Journal (1869–1874)* (Paris, 1994), 616; Rattray, *Ashanti Law*, 314, 343.

26. T. Edward Bowdich, *Mission from Cape Coast Castle to Ashantee* (London, 1819: reprint, 1996), 260. For more evidence of variation see Austin, 'Rural Capitalism', 109n.

27. E.g. M. J. Field, *Search for Security: an Ethno-Psychiatric Study of Rural Ghana* (London, 1960), 29, 87; Gareth Austin, 'Moneylending and witchcraft: the moral economy of accumulation in colonial Asante', paper presented at the Modern Economic History Seminar, London School of Economics, May 2003.

28. Busia, *Position of the Chief*, 26–39.

29. Ibid., 31. For a magnificent study of the festival in its broad political, social, cultural and ideological context see McCaskie, *State and Society*.

30. See pp. 212, 218–19, 239.

31. E.g. Public Record Office (PRO) CO96/662, X.7792, 'Memorandum' by Chief Commissioner of Ashanti (CCA), John Maxwell, for Mr Ormsby Gore's visit, 31 Dec. 1925.

32. See Rod Alence, 'Colonial government, social conflict and state intervention in Africa's open economies: the origins of the Ghana Cocoa Marketing Board, 1939–46', *JAH* 43 (2002), 397–416.

33. Methodist Missionary Society Archive, Box 597, Thomas Birch Freeman papers, manuscript of unpublished book by Freeman entitled 'Reminiscences and Incidents of Travels and Historical and Political Sketches in the Countries Bordering on the Gold and Slave Coasts and in Ashantee, Dahomey, etc.' (n.d. but c.1860), p. 133. On the working of the gold-dust monetary system see LaTorre, 'Wealth Surpasses', 181–89.

34. Cruickshank, *Eighteen Years on the Gold Coast of Africa* (London, 1853: reprint, 1966), 2 vols, II, 42–46: quotes from pp. 45 and 42 respectively.

35. Wilks, *Asante*, 420–21.

36. Perrot and van Dantzig (eds), *Marie-Joseph Bonnat et les Ashanti: Journal*, 640–1.

37. Wilks, *Asante*, 35–36, 434.

38. Bowdich, *Mission*, 255–57.

39. T. E. Bowdich, 'Remarks on civilization in Africa', in his *The British and French Expeditions to Teembo with Remarks on Civilization in Africa* (Paris, 1821), 18. Bowdich there gives the date as 1818, but his book makes clear that it was the previous year. He emphasises that he was present at the proclamation, and he had left Kumasi finally before 1818 began (Bowdich, *Mission*, 255–56 and passim).

40. Paul E. Lovejoy, *Caravans of Kola* (Zaria, 1980), 14–17; Austin, 'Between abolition and *jihad*', 99–100.

41. PRO CO96/293, H. M. Hull to Colonial Secretary (CS), Cape Coast, 14 May 1897, enclosed in GCC No 212 of 27 May 1897. For the political context see Wilks, *Asante*, 51, 579, 584.

42. Cf. Lovejoy, *Caravans of Kola*, 11–12, 19 and 'Polanyi's "ports of trade"', 253–55, 258.

43. Wilks, *Asante in the Nineteenth Century*, 20, 55, 270–71, 685, 690.

44. On the latter see, e.g., J. S. Hogendorn and H. A. Gemery, 'Continuity in West African monetary history', *African Economic History* 17 (1988), 138–39.

45. On railways in general see Christian E. Tsey, 'Gold Coast Railways: the Making of a Colonial Economy, 1879–1929' (Ph.D, University of Glasgow, 1986).

46. E.g. PRO CO96/662, X.7792, 'Memorandum' by CCA, 31 Dec. 1925 (see p. 466 n. 31), p. 14.

47. Kay, *Political Economy of Colonialism*, 22–25.

48. NAGK D1913, 'CCA's Tour of Inspection to the South Eastern (*sic*) and East of Ashanti—Report On' (Ashanti MP 8/12), F. C. Fuller to CS, Kumasi, 25 March 1912. For an overview of government policy on roads and lorries see Simon Heap, 'The development of motor transport in the Gold Coast, 1900–39', *Journal of Transport History* 11:2 (1990), 19–37.

49. See the breakdown of government expenditure in Kay, *Political Economy of Colonialism*, 360–75.

50. On such offences by soldiers, see *Annual Report on Ashanti* [hereafter *ARA*] for *1905*, 12; on those by carriers accompanying British commissioners, see T. E. Kyei, *Our Days Dwindle: Memoirs of My Childhood Days in Asante*, ed. by Jean Allman (Portsmouth NH, 2001), 107.

51. Gareth Austin, 'Mode of production or mode of cultivation: explaining the failure of European cocoa planters in competition with African farmers in colonial Ghana', in W. G. Clarence-Smith (ed.), *Cocoa Pioneer Fronts Since 1800* (Basingstoke, 1996), 154–75.

52. Emmanuel Akyeampong and Pashington Obeng, 'Spirituality, gender and power in Asante History' *International Journal of African Historical Studies* 28 (1995), 481–508.

53. Wilks, *Asante*, 676–79 (Wilks used the term 'standing army', but his specific description does not indicate that troops were permanently assembled, except in the case of Asantehene Mensa Bonsu's northern riflemen, noted below); McCaskie, *State and Society*, 85–6. See, further, Emmanuel Terray, 'Contribution à une étude de l'armée asante', *Cahiers d'études africaines* 16:61–2 (1976), 297–356.

54. McCaskie, *State and Society*, 84–85, 98.

55. Wilks, *Asante*, 535–39; Austin, ' "No elders" ', 24–25.

56. Wilks, *Asante*, 616–21; Terray, 'Contribution à une étude de l'armée asante', 346–48.

57. And it appears not to have survived his fall (Terray, 'Contribution à une étude de l'armée asante', 348).

58. See p. 275.

59. Ivor Wilks, 'On mentally mapping Greater Asante: a study of time and motion', *JAH* 33 (1992), 175–90; reprinted in Wilks, *Forests of Gold.*

60. Ivor Wilks, 'Dissidence in Asante politics: two tracts from the late nineteenth century', in I. Abu-Lughod (ed.), *African Themes* (Evanston, 1975), 47–63 (reprinted with some changes in Wilks, *Forests of Gold*).

61. For a general discussion of the agrarian implications of fiscal self-sufficiency in colonial Africa see Sara Berry, *No Condition is Permanent: the Social Dynamics of Agrarian Change in Sub-Saharan Africa* (Madison, 1993), 22–42.

62. For a broader picture see A. H. M. Kirk-Greene, 'The thin white line: the size of the British colonial service in Africa', *African Affairs* 79:314 (1980), 25–44.

63. For a case-study see Dunn and Robertson, *Dependence and Opportunity*, 286–313.

64. Austin, 'Capitalists and chiefs'.

65. Cf. Dunn and Robertson, *Dependence and Opportunity*, 125–26.

66. For a partial illustration see Busia, *Position of the Chief*, 38.

67. Austin, ' "No elders were present" ', esp. 24–25.

68. Austin, 'Capitalists and chiefs'.

69. The major study of the NLM is Jean Marie Allman, *The Quills of the Porcupine: Asante Nationalism in an Emergent Ghana* (Madison, 1993). See also Richard Rathbone, 'Businessmen in politics: party struggle in Ghana, 1949–57', *Journal of Development Studies* 9:3 (1973); Rathbone, ' "The youngmen and the porcupine" ', and reply by Allman, in *JAH* 32 (1991), 333–38.

70. For an Ahafo case-study of this era, see Piet Konings, *The State and Rural Class Formation in Ghana* (London, 1986), 104–39.

71. For elaboration on the theme of this and the next three paragraphs see Austin, 'Between abolition and jihad'.

72. Timothy F. Garrard, *Akan Weights and the Gold Trade* (London, 1980), 158–66.

73. LaTorre, 'Wealth Surpasses', 380.

74. Cruickshank, *Eighteen Years*, II, 278.

75. Ivor Wilks, 'Asante policy towards the Hausa trade in the nineteenth century', in C. Meillassoux (ed.), *The Development of Indigenous Trade and Markets in West Africa* (London, 1971), 126, 129–30.

76. Ibid., 125, 127–28, 130–31, 135–36.

77. Lovejoy, *Caravans of Kola*, 11, 114–16.

78. LaTorre, 'Wealth Surpasses', 365.

79. Cruickshank, *Eighteen Years*, II, 244.

80. LaTorre, 'Wealth Surpasses', 439, 446.

81. See Wilks, *Asante in the Nineteenth Century*, 267–68, 270, 276, 690. I say 'almost' because of the caption to an illustration in an 1873 newspaper showing 'Northern merchants in Kumasi market' (reproduced without comment in Garrard, *Akan Weights and the Gold Trade*, 65).

82. Austin, 'Between abolition and jihad'.

83. Austin, ' "No elders" ', 8–10.

84. Ibid., 8.

85. Austin, ' "No elders" ', 8, 12. The Bowdich reference is *Mission*, 323–24. Cf. A. Riis's *Journal* of his visit to Kumasi, 1839–40, entry for 4 Jan. 1840. I am grateful to Larry Yarak for providing me with this extract, which was translated from the German by Anja Schwalen.

86. Austin, 'Between abolition and jihad', 107–9.

87. British Parliamentary Papers, C.4477, *Further Correspondence Regarding the Affairs of the Gold Coast* (London, 1885), p. 91: Captain Brandon Kirby's report on his mission to Kumasi, Accra, 15 April 1884.

88. Raymond Dumett, 'The rubber trade of the Gold Coast and Asante in the nineteenth century', *JAH* 12 (1971), esp. 94–95; Kwame Arhin, 'The Ashanti rubber trade with the Gold Coast in the eighteen-nineties', *Africa* 42 (1972), 32–43; Arhin, 'The economic and social significance of rubber production and exchange on the Gold and Ivory Coasts, 1880–1900', *Cahiers d'études Africaines* 20:77–78 (1980), 49–62.

89. *Annual Reports on Ashanti* (hereafter *ARA*s) for the years concerned.

90. As distinct from 'semi-cultivated', defined above, p. 64.

91. Austin, 'Rural Capitalism', 442–48.

92. Gold Coast Government, *ARA for 1921*, 7; PRO CO96/662, X.7792: 'Ashanti'. Memo. by the Chief Commissioner for Mr Ormsby Gore's Visit, 31 Dec. 1925.

93. *ARA for 1921*, 7.

94. *ARA for 1917*, 4.

95. *ARA for 1923–1924*, 9 (on means of transport, see also *ARA for 1919*, 8).

96. A. C. Miles, 'Cola survey: eastern Ashanti area, and a general review of the cola industry', *Bulletin of the Department of Agriculture, Gold Coast*, vol. 23, *Year-Book 1930* (1930), 135–43; on the methods, see also J. C. Muir, 'The cola industry in the Western Province of Ashanti', *Bulletin of the Department of Agriculture, Gold Coast*, vol. 22, *1929 Year Book* (1929), 218–24.

97. Austin, 'Rural Capitalism', 441.

98. Miles, 'Cola survey', 142.

99. Muir, 'Cola industry', 219.

100. NAGK D133, 'Diary—Bekwai District' (EP 9/29), entry for 23 Jan. 1931.

101. On the beginning of Asante cocoa growing see Austin, 'Rural Capitalism', 225–29, 273. See, further, M. P. Frempong, 'A history of the Presbyterian church at Bompata in Asante-Akyem' (translated from Twi by E. A. Kyerematen), *Ghana Notes and Queries* (June 1972), 21; A. C. Miles, 'The size of cacao farms in Ashanti', *Bulletin of the Department of Agriculture, Gold Coast*, vol. 22 (1929), 54. For reports of pre-1900 starts in Amansie and even in northern Asante, before 1900, see, respectively: Anonymous, 'Oldest cocoa farm in Ashanti', Gold Coast Department of Agriculture, *Monthly Newsletter*, I, 11, 30 Nov. 1947, 24–26; Hill, *Migrant Cocoa-Farmers*, 167n.

102. Smuggling of cocoa across the international border with Côte d'Ivoire does not seem to have been an issue during the colonial period, at least in Asante (in contrast to the 1970s and early 1980s in particular).

103. The figures in this paragraph and the next are as cited for Table 3.1, for the years concerned.

104. E.g. E. V. T. Engmann, *Population of Ghana 1850–1960* (Accra, 1986), 92–93, 95; T. E. Hilton, *Ghana Population Atlas* (Achimota, Ghana, 1960), 30.

105. Engmann, *Population of Ghana*, 132 (table); Hilton, *Ghana Population Atlas*, 30.

106. Calculated from Ghana, *Survey of Cocoa Producing Families in Ashanti, 1956–57*, Table 2. I use 'Asante' here to comprise three categories distinguished in the table: Ashanti, Brong, and 'Other Ashanti'.

107. Stated in or calculated from ibid., Table 3. There were also 23 poultry farmers. 'Asante' defined as above.

108. The correlation was not perfect (NAGK Bekwai DAO File 35, 'Cocoa Crop Report', United Africa Company agent, Bekwai, to District Commissioner [DC]: Bekwai, 2 Oct. 1931), but there seems no doubt that it was strong, as is illustrated by the 'over-declaration' issue discussed later, pp. 371–73.

109. See G. B. Kay, *The Political Economy of Colonialism in Ghana* (London, 1972), statistical abstract prepared with Stephen Hymer, Table 20a.

110. Calculated from Ghana, *Survey of Cocoa Producing Families in Ashanti, 1956–57*, Table 47.

111. *ARA for 1910*, 20.

112. *ARA for 1908*, 9. On weaving from imported yarn in Ghana generally see Rajiv Ball, 'The State and the Development of Small-Scale Industry in Ghana Since 1945' (Ph.D. thesis, London School of Economics, 1997), 40–41.

113. Calculated from Ghana, *Survey of Cocoa Producing Families in Ashanti, 1956–57*, Tables 2, 3. 'Asante' here to comprise three categories distinguished in the table: Ashanti, Brong, and 'Other Ashanti'.

114. Ball, 'State and the Development of Small-Scale Industry in Ghana', 40–42, 60–61.

115. As n. 106 above.

116. Ghana, Office of the Government Statistician, *Labour Statistics, 1959* (Accra, 1960), 7, cited in Ball, 'State and the Development of Small-Scale Industry in Ghana', 70.

117. Austin, 'Rural Capitalism', 439.

118. AGC's royalties over that period totalled £1.75 million. Royalties were initially 3, later 5 per cent of output. See below, ch. 14. On aspects of the history of AGC see T. C. McCaskie, 'The creation of Ashanti Goldfields Corporation, Ltd., ca.1890–1910', *Asantesem* 9 (1978), 37–55; Jeff Crisp, *The Story of an African Working Class: Ghanaian Miners' Struggles 1870–1980* (London, 1984); Raymond E. Dumett, 'Sources for mining company history in Africa: the history and records of the Ashanti Goldfields Corporation (Ghana), Ltd.', *Business History Review* 62:3 (1988), 502–15; Dumett, *El Dorado*, 280–83; Sarah Stockwell, *The Business of Decolonization: British Business Strategies in the Gold Coast* (Oxford, 2000), esp. 80–84, 165–95, 234–36. Ayowa Afrifa (London School of Economics) is currently preparing a business history of AGC for a Ph.D.

119. See ARG 2/5/3/6 'Timber Concessions General'.

120. Dunn and Robertson, *Dependence and Opportunity*, 77–84. Dunn and Robertson's brief case-study of logging in Ahafo remains a valuable exception to the neglect of this industry's history, which Raymond E. Dumett is currently addressing. See his preliminary paper, focussed on southwest Ghana, 'Tropical forests and West African enterprise: the early history of the Ghana timber trade', *African Economic History* 29 (2001), 79–116.

121. F. R. Bray, *Cocoa Production in Ahafo, West Ashanti* (cyclostyled: Faculty of Agriculture, University of Ghana: Achimota, 1959), 7.

122. Rhodes House Library, Oxford: MSS Afr.s.873, Goldie-Scott papers: Obuasi Sub-District Handing-Over Report by W. Norton L. Goldie-Scott, 8 Aug. 1952.

123. On the very small African share of timber exports, in Ghana as a whole, a convenient reference is the documents reproduced in Kay, *Political Economy of Colonialism in Ghana*, 76–77, 93.

124. ARG 2/5/3/6, e.g. pp. 205, 279.

125. See Dunn and Robertson, *Dependence and Opportunity*, 82–84.

126. *ARA for 1920*: 10–11; James Wilson Brown, 'Kumasi, 1896–1923: Urban Africa during the Early Colonial Period' (Ph.D., University of Wisconsin, Madison, 1972), 106–7.

127. E.g., on demand from northerners resident during the cocoa season in a market town, presumably as labourers, see NAGK D1144 'Bekwai Market', Minute by G. Puckridge, Acting (Ag) DC Bekwai, to Ag DC Obuasi, Bekwai, 31 July 1923.

128. *ARA for 1920*, 10. Cf. *ARA for 1921*, 8, and *ARA for 1922–23*, 12. The latter reports give the impression that rice growing in the district was no longer confined to 'immigrants'.

129. *ARA for 1920*, 10.

130. Food production as a corollary of young cocoa farms during this boom was emphasised by Bray for western Ahafo though, as he noted, transport costs might mean that the shade crops 'may or may not be fully harvested' (Bray, *Cocoa Production in Ahafo*, 4, 31, 35 'bis' [sic]). In these years there was also much new planting in the older-established, more densely-populated cocoa districts of eastern and central Asante (as can be deduced from the growth of output in the future Ashanti Region, as distinct from Brong-Ahafo, shown in Table 11.2 below). So even there, despite further rises in population, the food supply situation was probably alleviated.

131. E.g. *ARA for 1920*, 11. See Gracia Clark, *Onions Are My Husband: Survival and Accumulation by West African Market Women* (Chicago, 1994), 316–22; Allman and Tashjian, *'I Will Not Eat Stone'*, 13–16. See further, ch. 16.

132. Calculated from Ghana, *Survey of Cocoa Producing Families in Ashanti, 1956–57*, Tables 2, 3. The proportions are the same (when calculated to one decimal point) if only Asantes ('Ashanti', 'Brong' and 'Other Ashanti') are included, leaving out the small minorities of immigrants.

133. Computed from ibid., 33–34.

134. As Claude-Hélène Perrot wrote of Anyi society (eastern Ivory Coast): Perrot, *Les Anyi-Ndenye*, 31–34 (quote at p. 31); for Asante specifically see Busia, *Position of the Chief*, 28, 30, 36.

135. Ivor Wilks, 'Land, labour, capital and the forest kingdom of Asante: a model of early change', in J. Friedman and M. Rowlands (eds), *The Evolution of Social Systems* (London, 1978), 487–534, reprinted with revisions in Wilks, *Forests of Gold*; Ray A. Kea, *Settlements, Trade, and Polities in the Seventeenth-Century Gold Coast* (Baltimore, 1982), 85–94. For an archaeological perspective see Peter Shinnie, 'Early Asante: is Wilks right?' in J. Hunwick and N. Lawler (eds), *The Cloth of Many Colored Silks: Papers on History Ghanaian and Islamic in Honor of Ivor Wilks* (Evanston, 1996), 195–203.

136. See LaTorre, 'Wealth Surpasses', 427–35.

137. Ibid., 136–37.

138. NAGK File D133 (EP 9/1929): Commissioner's Diary, Bekwai District, entry for 5 Aug. 1930. For another instance, from the same war, see Native Tribunal of Kumasi, Kwadjo Agyekum v. Yah Mainoo, 5 Sept. 1935 (copy in Herskovits Memorial Library, Northwestern University: Ivor Wilks Papers). For examples from the 1770s and 1780s,

respectively, see D. J. E. Maier, 'Military acquisition of slaves in Asante', in D. Henige and T. C. McCaskie, *West African Economic and Social History*, 123.

139. Wilks, *Asante*, 83–85; Maier, 'Military acquisition of slaves', 123.

140. Wilks, *Asante*, 90.

141. Marion Johnson, 'The population of Asante, 1817–1921: a reconsideration', *Asantesem* 8 (1978), 22–28 (quotation, 25).

142. Cardinall, *The Gold Coast, 1931* (Accra, n.d.), 144n.

143. Colony of the Gold Coast, *Report on the Census for the Year 1901* (London, 1902), 4.

144. R. W. Steel, 'The population of Ashanti: a geographical analysis', *Geographical Journal*, 112:1–3 (1949), 64; cf. Johnson, 'Population: a reconsideration', 22.

145. *ARA for 1911*, 16.

146. See the census reports for the years concerned, also *ARA for 1911*, 16. See also the comments of Cardinall, *The Gold Coast, 1931*, 146–47; J. C. de Graft-Johnson, 'The population of Ghana 1846–1967', *Transactions of the Historical Society of Ghana* 10 (1969), 5–6.

147. *ARA for 1921*, 29.

148. de Graft-Johnson, 'The population of Ghana 1946–1967', 8; more emphatically, Engmann, *Population of Ghana*, 101–2.

149. Ibid., 109–13.

150. Wilks, *Asante*, 90.

151. Ivor Wilks, 'The population of Asante, 1817–1921: a rejoinder', *Asantesem* 8 (1978), 33.

152. Wilks, 'Population', 34, and *Asante*, 91–92, 569–70, 579, 582, 703; Lewin, *Asante Before the British*, 91, 102, 117, 128, 144, 147, 155; for Denyase see Austin, 'Rural Capitalism', 97 n. 47.

153. See, e.g., *ARA for 1907*, 9–10. For a pre-1896 return see Lewin, *Asante Before the British*, 167–68.

154. See the census reports and, further, Brown, 'Kumasi, 1896–1923', 54, 57, 59–60, 93, 102–3, 107–8, 181–87.

155. For a discussion of the contemporary debate in relation to south Asante see Austin, 'Rural Capitalism', 375–78.

156. *ARA for 1911*, 16–17.

157. *ARA for 1918*, 18–19.

158. K. David Patterson, 'The influenza epidemic of 1918–19 in the Gold Coast', *JAH* 24 (1983), 495–96. See also James W. Brown, 'Increased intercommunication and epidemic disease in early colonial Ashanti', in Gerald W. Hartwig and K. David Patterson (eds), *Disease in African History* (Durham NC, 1978), 190–92.

159. E.g., see Cardinall, *The Gold Coast, 1931*, 146–47, 150.

160. de Graft-Johnson, 'The population of Ghana 1846–1947', facing p. 6. The 'North' comprised the Northern Territories and the northern part of former British Togoland, the 'South' meant the Gold Coast Colony plus the southern part of former British Togoland.

161. The 1960 ' "census date was chosen in the dry season when most of the farmers and many of the migrant farm labourers were expected to be in their homes" ' (Ghana, *Population Census of Ghana*, I, xvi, quoted by de Graft-Johnson, 'The population of Ghana 1846–1947', 8–9). Actually, the dry season was precisely the period when seasonal migrants were most likely to be away from the north and at work harvesting cocoa in Asante and further south. The 1948 census was taken as far as possible on 8 Feb., i.e. in the same season.

162. See Chs 16 and 19.

163. This was not constant because of boundary alterations which, however, did not affect the forest zone. See Bening, 'Evolution of the administrative boundaries of Ashanti'. Total area was 24,379 square miles at the time of the 1931 and 1948 censuses.

164. On deduction of the 'urban' population cf. Ghana, *Survey of Cocoa Producing Families in Ashanti, 1956–57*, 2, 5.

165. Because of the numerous rivers and streams it seems that the population of the Asante forest-zone was at least free of guinea worm, a scourge of rural productivity as well as health where people depend on ponds for water. This, at least, seems a reasonable deduction from a discussion of the disease (in the setting of the Accra plains) by Donald W. Belcher, Frederick K. Wurapa, William B. Ward and Irvin M. Lourie, 'Guinea Worm in Southern Ghana: its epidemiology and impact on agricultural productivity', *American Journal of Tropical Medicine and Hygiene*, 24:2 (1975), 243–49. A study in the northern savanna fringe of Asante is reported by David Scott, 'An epidemiological note on guinea-worm infection in north-west Ashanti, Ghana', in *Annals of Tropical Medicine and Parasitology* 54 (1960), 32–43.

166. M. R. Talbot and G. Delibrias, 'Holocene variations in the level of Lake Bosumtwi, Ghana', *Nature* 268 (1977), 723. For context see Sharon E. Nicholson, 'The methodology of historical climate reconstruction and its application to Africa', *JAH* 20 (1979), 31–49.

167. According to the maps in H. O. Walker, 'Weather and climate' in J. Brian Wills (ed.), *Agriculture and Land Use in Ghana* (London, 1962), 13–14.

168. On which see D. A. Lane, 'The forest vegetation', in J. Brian Wills (ed.), *Agriculture and Land Use in Ghana* (London, 1962), 160–69; J. B. Hall and M. D. Swaine, 'Classification and ecology of closed-canopy forest in Ghana', *Journal of Ecology* 64 (1976), 913–51; Claude Martin, *The Rainforests of West Africa* (Basel 1991; transl. L. Tsardakas).

169. George C. Musgrave, *To Kumassi with Scott* (London, 1896), 108.

170. As C. C. Wrigley put it with reference to different kind of forest, but the same point applies here (review of Vansina's *Paths in the Rainforest* in *JAH* 33 [1992], 129).

171. Rhodes House Library, MSS Brit. Emp. S311(9): typescript mss. by T. F. Chipp, 'The Gold Coast Forest', n.d., pp. 9–10 (a note on the cover indicates that the mss. was published as *Oxford Forestry Memoir* 7, in 1927).

172. Joseph Dupuis, *Journal of a Residence in Ashantee* (London, 1824: reprint, 1966), 65–66; Wilks, 'Land', 501, 503.

173. Marion Johnson, 'Elephants for want of towns', in Christopher Fyfe and David MacMaster (eds), *African Historical Demography* II (Edinburgh, 1981), 322.

174. Dupuis, *Journal*, 65–66.

175. H. Brammer, 'Soils', in Wills (ed.), *Agriculture and Land Use*, 92–95; cf. William Allan, *The African Husbandman* (Edinburgh, 1965), 225.

176. Cf. Brammer, 'Soils', 94–95.

177. Wesleyan Methodist Archive, School of Oriental and African Studies Library, University of London: Coppin's Journal, Book VI, p. 30.

178. Compare P. H. Nye and D. Stephens, 'Soil fertility', 137, and A. Foggie, 'The role of forestry in the agricultural economy', 229, both in Wills (ed.), *Agriculture and Land Use*; see also Wilks, 'Land', 492–94.

179. Allan, *The African Husbandman*, 228.

180. Wilks, 'Land', 500.

181. Bowdich, *Mission*, 29.

182. Thomas Birch Freeman, *Journal of Various Visits to the Kingdoms of Ashanti, Aku, and Dahomi in Western Africa*, 118.

183. British Parliamentary Papers, C.3386, *Further Correspondence Regarding Affairs of the Gold Coast* (1882), 'Report by Captain Rupert La Trobe Lonsdale, of his Mission to Coomassie, Salagha, Yendi, &c. October 1881 to February 1882', 59.

184. W. Hutton, *A Voyage to Africa* (London: 1821), 202, cf. 285.

185. Rhodes University Library, Grahamstown, South Africa, Cory MS 15, 'Journal of the Rev. George Chapman', 1843–57, p. 166. I am grateful to the librarian for supplying me with a copy.

186. Wilks, 'Land', 492–95, 500.

187. Johnson, 'Elephants for want of towns', 317–18, 329–30.

188. See Raymond E. Dumett, *El Dorado in West Africa: the Gold-Mining Frontier, African Labor, and Colonial Capitalism in the Gold Coast, 1875–1900* (Athens OH, 1998), 29–32, 35, 37.

189. LaTorre, 'Wealth Surpasses', 381; Bowdich, *Mission*, 334.

190. E.g. Perrot and van Dantzig (eds), *Marie-Joseph Bonnat et les Ashanti: Journal*, 636–37.

191. See T. C. McCaskie and J. E. Wiafe, 'A contemporary account in Twi of the *Akompi Sa* of 1863: a document with commentary', *Asantesɛm* 1 (1979), 74.

192. LaTorre, 'Wealth Surpasses', 66; Kwame Arhin, 'Market settlements in north-western Ashanti: Kintampo', *Research Review* (Institute of African Studies, University of Ghana), *Supplement 1, Ashanti and the Northwest*, ed. J. Goody and K. Arhin (1965), 143.

193. Marion Johnson, review of Lovejoy, *Caravans of Kola*, in *African Economic History*, 11 (1982), 203.

194. Basel Mission Ghana Archive (henceforth BMA), Begoro Station Correspondence, Mohr to Basel, 28 Sept. 1881. Translated by Veit Arlt, Ph.D student at the University of Basel. For the context of the passage see Paul Jenkins, 'Abstracts of Basel Mission Gold Coast Correspondence' (cyclostyled: Basel, n.d.), 151.

195. Cf. 1929 observation about the elasticity of kola supply in western Asante quoted earlier in this chapter.

196. Austin, 'Rural Capitalism', 279–81, 446.

197. On soil fertility in the two districts see the map in K. B. Dickson, 'Cocoa in Ghana' (Ph.D. thesis, University of London, 1960), 3.

198. Cf. S. N. Adams, 'Soils and manuring', in Wills (ed.), *Agriculture and Land Use*, 268.

199. Perrot and van Dantzig (eds), *Marie-Joseph Bonnat et les Ashanti: Journal*, 643.

200. Kyei, *Our Days Dwindle*, 126.

201. Austin Fieldnotes (AF): interview with Mr P. Osei and Mr J. W. Owusu in Bekwai, 14 May 1980; also with Nana Frema II (and Nana Adu Darkoh II), Jacobu, 2 Sept. 1980; compare interview with Nana Kwabena Ntiamoah, Gyaasehene of Bekwai, 29 August 1982.

202. NAGK Bekwai File 118, 'Colonial Developments', Ag. DC Sinclair to CCA, Bekwai 7 April 1940.

203. McCaskie, *Asante Identities*, 48.

204. Cf. Timothy C. Weiskel, 'Toward an archaeology of colonialism: elements in the ecological transformation of the Ivory Coast', in D. Worster (ed.), *The Ends of the Earth* (Cambridge, 1988), 141–71.

205. See Walker, 'Weather and climate', esp. Table 26.

206. Austin, 'Rural Capitalism', 403–49.

207. For a detailed examination of nineteenth-century labour use, for southern Asante, see ibid., 106–46.

208. For reflections on this in relation to some African cases, see Robert H. Bates, 'Capital, kinship, and conflict: the structuring influence of capital in kinship societies', *Canadian Journal of African Studies* 24:1 (1990), 145–64.

209. In exceptional cases, much longer still: the main determinant being soil conditions (R. A. Lass, 'Replanting and rehabilitation of old cocoa farms', in G. A. R. Wood and R. A. Lass, *Cocoa* [4th edn, Harlow, 1985], 210–11).

210. E.g. K. Y. Daaku (ed.) *Oral Traditions of Adanse* (Institute of African Studies, University of Ghana, Legon, 1969), 111, 139, 151; Bowdich, *Mission*, 25.

211. The former description is from Kwame Arhin, 'Succession and gold mining at Mansu Nkwanta', *Research Review* (Institute of African Studies, University of Ghana) 6:3 (1970), 106; the latter from Daaku, *Oral Traditions of Adanse*, 301. See, further, Dumett, *El Dorado in West Africa*, 53.

212. See Arhin, 'Succession and gold mining', 105; Dumett, *El Dorado in West Africa*, 57–58.

213. C. H. Armitage and A. F. Montanaro, *The Ashanti Campaign of 1900* (London, 1901), 239. On the origin of the mine see Wilks, *Asante*, 436.

214. See Wilks, *Asante*, 1–39.

215. Peter R. Gould, *The Development of the Transportation Pattern in Ghana* (Evanston, 1960), 23, 25, 27; Kay, *Political Economy*, 20–24.

216. See Heap, 'Development of motor transport in the Gold Coast'.

217. *ARA for 1923–1924*, 24.

218. Brown, 'Kumasi, 1896–1923', 101–2.

219. *ARA for 1927–28*, 8.

220. See Ch. 15.

Chapter 4

1. The subject would be appropriate for a book to itself. The purpose of this chapter is to lay foundations for the analysis of property and markets in factors of production which will follow in the remaining chapters. I intend to pursue the main arguments presented here in more detail, and in some cases in much broader geographical contexts, in later writings.

2. Hopkins, *Economic History of West Africa*, 8–77.

3. Philip D. Curtin, 'The lure of Bambuk gold', *JAH* 14 (1973), 623–31.

4. Ibid., 631.

5. J. F. V. Phillips, *Agriculture and Ecology in Africa* (London, 1959), 160–61.

6. Kyei, *Our Days Dwindle*, 225.

7. Hopkins, *Economic History*, 15, 24–25, 38. Hopkins makes this point specifically by comparison with land, that is, of the two it was the supply of labour that was the constraint on output. He did not comment on capital in this context, though noted in passing that it was scarce (p. 71).

8. To say that labour was scarce in relation to complementary inputs does not imply that it was always expensive in the sense of having a high opportunity cost.

9. Indicatively, this distinction is not made in the major syntheses of African economic history, such as Ralph A. Austen, *African Economic History* (London, 1987); Hopkins, *Economic History of West Africa*; Paul Tiyambe Zeleza, *A Modern Economic History of West Africa*, I, *The Nineteenth Century* (Dakar, 1993). See also the comment in the first paragraph of this section on Curtin not making the distinction.

10. M. D. McLeod, *The Asante* (London, 1981), 152.

11. Ibid. 153; Angela W. Browne, 'Rural industry and appropriate technology: the lessons of narrow-loom Ashanti weaving', *African Affairs* 82:326 (1983), 30; Bowich, *Mission*, 309.

12. Marion Johnson, 'Ashanti craft organisation', *African Arts* 13 (1979), 60–63, 78–82; Browne, 'Rural industry and appropriate technology'.

13. *ARA for 1898*, 223. Cf. Curtin, cited above.

14. Introduced at pp. 32–33 above.

15. See Ch. 3 above. The point is made more fully in Austin, 'Rural Capitalism', 106–46.

16. Ibid., 267, 285–86; cf. Gould, *Development of the Transportation Pattern*, 25, 27.

17. J. C. Muir, 'Survey of cacao areas—Western Province, Ashanti', *Bulletin of the Department of Agriculture, Gold Coast* vol. 22 (1930), 59.

18. Shares calculated from Cocoa Marketing Board purchases. Merrill J. Bateman, 'An econometric analysis of Ghanaian cocoa supply', in R. A. Kotey, C. Okali, and B. E. Rourke (eds), *Economics of Cocoa Production and Marketing* (Legon, 1974), 315.

19. Sharon Stichter, *Migrant Laborers* (African Society Today series: Cambridge, 1985), 53.

20. Austin, 'Rural Capitalism', 417 (for details see ibid., 383–95, 408–27).

21. Ibid., esp. 429–49.

22. Ibid., ch. 11.

23. This paragraph is based on Austin, 'Mode of production or mode of cultivation', 164–68; cf. R. H. Green and S. H. Hymer, 'Cocoa in the Gold Coast: a study in the relations between African farmers and agricultural experts', *Journal of Economic History* 26 (1966), 307–9.

24. On mobility in Asante cocoa-farming see Austin, 'Rural Capitalism', 252–59, 316–20, 335–42. For reflections on the significance of mobility in relation to rural entrepreneurship in southern Ghana generally, see Gareth Austin, 'New Introduction', 2nd edn of Polly Hill, *Migrant Cocoa-Farmers of Southern Ghana* (Hamburg and Oxford, 1997), xviii–xix; Austin, 'African rural capitalism, cocoa farming and economic growth in colonial Ghana', in Toyin Falola (ed.), *Ghana in Africa and the World: Essays in Honor of Adu Boahen* (Trenton NJ and Asmara, 2003), 440–42.

25. This sentence and the rest of the paragraph are based on Austin, 'Mode of production or mode of cultivation', 165–68.

26. Cambridge University Library, Manuscripts Department, Add 9359: Meyer Fortes's papers from the Ashanti Social Survey (hereafter Fortes Papers), 8.7, 'Notes on Kwotei Village', n.d. but c.1945–46.

27. Gold Coast, *Enquiry into the Gold Coast Cocoa Industry, Final Report*, 14.

28. PRO CO964/17, Kojo Dukwoh to Secretary of [Watson] Commission, Kumasi 19 April 1948.

29. To use Douglass North's phrase from a different context: North, 'The New Institutional Economics and Third World Development', in Harriss, J., Hunter, J. and

Lewis, C. M. (eds), *The New Institutional Economics and Third World Development* (London, 1995), 18.

30. See G. A. R. Wood, 'Establishment', in Wood and R. A. Lass, *Cocoa* (4th edn, Harlow, 1985), 144–45. Close-spacing has advantages for yield in reducing exposure to intense sunlight and, relatedly, to excessive loss of moisture, plus avoidance of severe insect attack (M. Wessel, 'Shade and nutrition', in Wood and Lass, *Cocoa*, 166–72).

31. Austin, 'Mode of production or mode of cultivation', 167.

32. Quoted in Kay, *Political Economy of Colonialism*, 248 (from a Gold Coast Legislative Council debate, 1916). Cf. Green and Hymer, 'Cocoa in the Gold Coast', 309.

33. See R. A. Lass, 'Labour usage', in Wood and Lass, *Cocoa*, 239–41. The labour input figures they report, however, exaggerate the disadvantage because they include time spent weeding 'the food crops planted with the cocoa' (ibid., 241), a task necessary whether cocoa was planted or not.

34. G. A. R. Wood, 'Establishment', in Wood and Lass, *Cocoa*, 145; cf. J. C. de Graft-Johnson, *African Experiment: Cooperative Agriculture and Banking in British West Africa* (London, 1958), 53. See further, Austin, 'Mode of production or mode of cultivation', 167.

35. H. C. Sampson and E. M. Crowther, 'Report on cocoa production and soil fertility problems', in *The West Africa Commission 1938–1939: Technical Reports* (London: Leverhulme Trust, 1943), 27.

36. Austin, 'Mode of production or mode of cultivation'.

37. AF: interview with Nana Osei Kofi, former Amoafohene, 6 May 1980.

38. These figures were given by one official in defining the aims of his tour (D574 'Mr. J. S. Martinson': report on tour in Ashanti by H. G. S. Branch, 14 Aug.–20 Sept. 1912).

39. NAGK RAO Files on Shelves 14 & 15, 52, 'Cocoa—fermented and unfermented—indiscriminate purchase of': Martinson to CCA, 31 Dec. 1908. Also Ag Director of Agriculture to CCA, Kumasi 16 Oct. 1912. For Asante generally it was stated in the *Report of the Agricultural Department for 1910* that 'farms are being formed with the trees planted at wider distances apart' (p. 14). D574 'Mr. J. S. Martinson': report on tour of instruction Nov.–Dec. 1912 by E. Buckmire, and Martinson's diary for Aug. 1912.

40. For Ghana generally, Austin, 'Mode of production or mode of cultivation', 168; for Asante specifically, Austin, 'Rural Capitalism', 407–8.

41. *ARA for 1920*, 9; see also Green and Hymer, 'Cocoa in the Gold Coast', 312.

42. ARG 9/12/1 'Cocoa': 'Ashanti Rule No. 2 of 1936', encl. in DC Bekwai to chiefs, Bekwai 31 August 1936.

43. Austin, 'Mode of production or mode of cultivation'.

44. The plantation was at Kpeve, in Southern British Togoland, now part of the Volta Region of Ghana. The case is examined in Austin, 'Mode of production or mode of cultivation', 159–60.

45. PRO CO96/768, 'Cocoa—(Cacao) Diseases of', A. F. Posnette, 'Transmission of "Swollen Shoot" disease of cacao', 16 Feb. 1940. For an account of the history of this research, limited by non-use of the archival sources, see Francis Danquah, *Cocoa Diseases and Politics in Ghana, 1909–1966* (New York, 1995), 60–68, 72.

46. PRO CO964/17, Dukwoh to Secretary of Watson Commission, 19 April 1948.

47. H. Toxopeus, 'Planting material', in Wood and Lass, *Cocoa*, 85–87.

48. See R. A. Kotey, C. Okali and B. E. Rourke (eds.), *Economics of Cocoa Production and Marketing* (Legon, 1974), 96, 321.

49. E. E. N. A. Bonaparte, 'An agronomist's assessment of recent research findings and their implications for cocoa production', in Kotey, Okali and Rourke (eds), *Economics of Cocoa Production and Marketing*, 73–85.

50. This is implied by Bateman, in that he does not mention new varieties when discussing tree stock (Bateman, 'Econometric analysis of Ghanaian cocoa supply', 290–91). It is also implied by Leston, who despite firmly downplaying the contribution of insecticides to the output boom of the late 1950s and early 1960s does not mention improved planting materials as part of his alternative explanation. On the contrary, he implicitly equates the new cocoa with Amelonado (D. Leston, 'The diseconomy of insecticides in cocoa production in Ghana', in Kotey, Okali and Rourke (eds), *Economics of Cocoa Production and Marketing*, 101).

51. Bateman estimated the average supply capacity of Ashanti and Brong-Ahafo regions as 107,100 tons (108,900 tonnes) for that year, and attributed 1.59% of this to insecticide use. Actual crop sales were 135,000 tonnes (Bateman, 'Econometric analysis of Ghanaian cocoa supply', 289, 293, 301, 304–5, 321). For a sceptical assessment of the impact of insecticides, albeit more in the long than in the short term, see Leston, 'Diseconomy of insecticides in cocoa production in Ghana', 96–104.

52. Leston, 'Diseconomy of insecticides in cocoa production in Ghana'.

53. S. A. Oni and J. Adubi, 'The economics of fertiliser use in cocoa production', in Kotey, Okali and Rourke (eds), *Economics of Cocoa Production and Marketing*, 86–95.

54. Bray, *Cocoa Development in Ahafo*, 2. In context, the 'country' he meant appears to be Asante rather than Ghana generally, though the comment would also have been true of Ghana as a whole.

55. Ibid., 2.

56. Teal, 'Growth, Comparative Advantage and the Economic Effects of Government', 64.

57. Cardinall, *The Gold Coast, 1931*, 86. Cf. W. H. Beckett, *Akokoaso: a Survey of a Gold Coast Village* (London, 1956: 1st edn, 1944), 70. For oral testimonies from Amansie district see Austin, 'Rural Capitalism', 389–90.

58. Szereszewski, *Structural Changes*, 22, 75 (also 51, 137).

59. This is reflected in the predominance of labour in the evidence on planting and maintenance costs of cocoa farms in Asante and in Ghanaian cocoa farming generally during the period. For an 'estimate based on a farm in Ashanti' see Cardinall, *The Gold Coast, 1931*, 86–90: quotation at p. 87. The Kpeve plantation, noted above, provides a vivid example from another part of Ghana (Austin, 'Mode of production or mode of cultivation', 159–60).

60. Though an opportunity cost emerged when land began to become scarce in the older cocoa districts, a process noted in Chapter 3.

61. Implied in Bray, *Cocoa Development in Ahafo*, 2.

62. Hopkins, *Economic History of West Africa*, esp. 124–28.

63. See Robin Law (ed.), *From Slave Trade to 'Legitimate' Commerce*, esp. 11–15; Martin Lynn, *Commerce and Economic Change in West Africa: the Palm Oil Trade in the Nineteenth Century* (Cambridge, 1997), 58–81.

64. The quotation is from an informant in Sodua quoted in Daaku, *Oral Traditions of Adanse*, 358. On Kwaku Akore and other examples of individuals honoured for wealth in Adanse, see ibid., 59–60, 73, 93–94, 109, 203–4, 212, 282, 314, 345, 348, 362. It is difficult—and misleading—to separate trade from market-oriented production in these careers. I single out Akore here because in his case trade, especially in rubber (hence late

nineteenth-century), seems to have been the main path to wealth (ibid., 203–4). For a broad discussion of commoners' access to wealth in nineteenth-century Asante generally, see Austin, ' " No elders were present" '.

65. See Chs 15 and 18 below.

66. For a detailed first-hand account, admittedly five years after Ghanaian independence, see the fieldnotes on Kumasi Central Market presented in Polly Hill, *Indigenous Trade and Market Places in Ghana 1962–64* (Jos, Nigeria, 1984). For a major study of Kumasi Central Market, focussed on c.1979–90 but carefully contextualised historically, see Clark, *Onions are My Husband*.

67. The first point is evident, the second is the impression conveyed by the specialist studies, though they are not explicit: Arhin, 'Market settlements', 143–44; Lovejoy, *Caravans of Kola*, 21–22. On rubber see Dumett, 'Rubber trade', esp. 94–95; and Arhin, 'Economic and social significance of rubber', esp. 52–54, 61.

68. Dumett, 'Precolonial gold mining and the state in the Akan region: with a critique of the Terray hypothesis', *Research in Economic Anthropology* 2 (1979), 44–47; compare Emmanuel Terray, 'Long-distance exchange and the formation of the state: the case of the Abron kingdom of Gyaman', *Economy and Society* 3 (1974), 327–28; and Terray, 'Gold production, slave labor, and state intervention in precolonial Akan societies: a reply to Raymond Dumett', *Research in Economic Anthropology* 5 (1983), 101–6.

69. Dumett, *El Dorado in West Africa*, 55–56, 62–63; quote at 55.

70. Arhin, 'Market settlements', 136–37, 143–45; Arhin, 'Succession and gold mining', 107–9; Arhin, 'Gold-mining and trading among the Ashanti of Ghana', *Journal des Africanistes* 48:1 (1978), 92–93; Raymond E. Dumett, 'Traditional slavery in the Akan region in the nineteenth century: sources, issues, and interpretations', in D. Henige and T. C. McCaskie (eds.), *West African Economic and Social History: Studies in Memory of Marion Johnson* (Madison, 1990), 17–18; Dumett, 'Rubber trade', 12 (1971), 94–95; Arhin, 'Economic and social significance of rubber', 52–54, 61.

71. E.g. Clarence-Smith (ed.), *Cocoa Pioneer Fronts since 1800.*

72. It is important to avoid simply assuming that the productivity of any single factor, in this case labour, can be taken as emblematic of total factor productivity (overall efficiency), i.e. output divided by the sum of all factor inputs.

73. Figures depicted are calculated from Ghana, *Survey of Cocoa Producing Families in Ashanti, 1956–57,* 56–57.

74. T. Killick, 'The economics of cocoa', in W. Birmingham, I. Neustadt and E. Omaboe (eds), *A Study of Contemporary Ghana*, Vol. I, *The Economy of Ghana* (London, 1966), 389. I reached a similar conclusion in a survey of much of the subsequent literature (Gareth Austin, 'The political economy of small and big farmers in Ghanaian cocoa farming, c.1890–1992', paper for SOAS-LSE international conference on Cocoa Production and Economic Development in the 19th and 20th Centuries, London, Sept. 1993).

75. For a clear presentation see Ellis, *Peasant Economics*, 201–8.

76. Teal, 'Growth, Comparative Advantage and the Economic Effects of Government', 67–68.

77. See Bateman, 'Econometric analysis of Ghanaian cocoa supply', 315. As elsewhere in this volume, 'Asante' refers to both Ashanti Region and Brong-Ahafo Region.

78. Calculated from Ghana, *Survey of Cocoa Producing Families in Ashanti, 1956–57,* 6.

79. Calculated from ibid., Table 7.

80. For a positive case-study that supports the proposition of scale-neutrality in Ghanaian cocoa farming, see Austin, 'Mode of production or mode of cultivation', 169–70.

81. By which I mean goods that could be sold, whether a particular good was or not, and whether on domestic or in export markets (gold dust is an example).

82. Austin, '"No elders were present"'.

83. I made this point in a conference paper (Austin, 'Political economy of small and big farmers in Ghanaian cocoa farming'). Stefano Boni (University of Modena) and I are now undertaking a more thorough investigation of the matter.

Chapter 5

1. Unremarked except for LaTorre, 'Wealth Surpasses', 130, who makes a similar point though does not refer to the historiography.

2. Rattray, *Ashanti*, 221, 233–34, and *Ashanti Law*, 346–47, 356, 357; likewise Busia, *Position of the Chief*, 43–44.

3. Rattray, *Ashanti*, 216–17; *Ashanti Law*, 358, 360–61; Busia, *Position of the Chief*, 43.

4. Wilks, *Asante*, 106–9; LaTorre, 'Wealth Surpasses', 130, 170; McCaskie, 'Office, land and subjects', 192, 194–98.

5. Rattray, *Ashanti Law*, 15, 340, 342, 347–48, 354–55; Ashanti Confederacy Council of Chiefs, 'declaration of custom', 1938, quoted in J. N. Matson, *A Digest of the Minutes of the Ashanti Confederacy Council from 1935 to 1949 Inclusive: a Revised Edition of Warrington's Notes on Ashanti Custom Prepared for the Use of District Commissioners* (Cape Coast, n.d.), 18–19.

6. Rattray, *Ashanti Law*, 352–53.

7. Wilks, *Forests*, 99; Rattray, *Ashanti Law*, 342. The Twi maxim itself I quote from Wilks; Rattray's version being slightly different.

8. Classic statements are Rattray, *Ashanti Law*, 346, 361, 363; Busia, *Position of the Chief*, 43–44, 51, 56. See also A. A. Y. Kyerematen, *Inter-state Boundary Litigation in Ashanti* (Leiden, n.d. but early 1970s), 36. Armitage in 1913 testified to the West African Lands Committee that in Asante land was regarded only as stool property, not family property (West African Lands Commission, *Minutes of Evidence*, pp. 429–30, 4 June 1913).

9. Rattray, *Ashanti*, 232.

10. Ibid., 236–37 (quotation, p. 237).

11. Wilks, *Asante*, 106–9; T. C. McCaskie, '*Ahyiamu*—"a place of meeting"', 170–78.

12. Wilks, *Asante*, 106–9; McCaskie, 'Office, land and subjects', 192, 194–98; McCaskie, '*Ahyiamu*—"a place of meeting"', 170–78.

13. McCaskie, '*Ahyiamu*—"a place of meeting"'.

14. Wilks, 'Golden Stool', 29–30 (the quotation is from p. 30).

15. Rattray, *Ashanti*, 229, cf. 226.

16. Rattray, *Ashanti Law*, 356–57.

17. Ibid., 356; Busia, *Position of the Chief*, 51, 199.

18. Busia, *Position of the Chief*, 125.

19. Rattray, *Ashanti*, 232.

20. Ibid., 231.

21. Rattray, *Ashanti Law*, 341. See also Wilks, *Asante*, 109.

22. Busia, *Position of the Chief*, 52–53.

23. LaTorre, 'Wealth Surpasses', 124.

24. Ibid., 130.

25. See p. 40.

26. Daaku, *Oral Traditions of Adanse*, 16.

27. On the last point see McCaskie, '*Ahyiamu*: "a place of meeting"', 175–76.

28. E.g. see Daaku, *Oral Traditions of Adanse*, 139, 157, 211.

29. Ibid., 205.

30. Ibid., e.g. 108, 196. Dumett, 'Rubber trade of the Gold Coast', 96; Arhin, 'Ashanti rubber trade', 35.

31. LaTorre, 'Wealth Surpasses', 249; Daaku, *Oral Traditions of Adanse*, pp. 22, 69, 122, 139, 151, 211, 353.

32. Arhin, 'Economic and social significance of rubber production', 52 (no source given: presumably oral testimony).

33. Kyei, *Our Days Dwindle*, 88.

34. Daaku, *Oral Traditions of Adanse*, 153. Cf., slightly less clearly, Arhin, 'Market settlements', 143.

35. AF: interview with Nana Kojo Appiah Darko II, Regent of Manso Nkwanta, Manso Nkwanta, 23 July 1980.

36. AF: interview with Opanyin Kofi Agyepong and Nana Baffuor Asare Bediako, Akwamuhene of Dadiase, Asiwa, 1 Sept. 1982.

37. Hopkins, *Economic History*, 126.

38. Austin, 'Between abolition and jihad', 106.

39. See pp. 64–65 above.

40. Arhin used the word in this sense in 'Ashanti rubber trade', 41, cf. 35.

41. Rattray, *Ashanti*, 230.

42. Kyerematen, *Inter-state Boundary Litigation*, 39.

43. Rattray, *Ashanti*, 224–25; Busia, *Position of the Chief*, 47.

44. Rattray, *Ashanti Law*, 355.

45. C.K. Meek, *Land Law and Custom in the Colonies* (London, 1968 ed.: 1st edn, 1946).

46. See Wilks, 'Land', 500–501, reprinted with revisions in Wilks, *Forests*, 55–56; McCaskie, *State and Society*, 57. Wilks's source note simply refers the reader to another essay which, however, does not deal with this specific point; while McCaskie cites documents in his personal possession.

47. Wilks, 'Land', 501 (*Forests*, 56).

48. Wilks, 'Land', 500 (*Forests*, 55); cf. McCaskie, *State and Society*, 57.

49. Wilks, 'Land', 500; McCaskie, *State and Society*, 36–37.

Chapter 6

1. On slaves, women and children see Rattray, *Ashanti Law*, 40, 336–37 and 337 respectively; on children and slaves, also LaTorre, 'Wealth Surpasses', 112, citing an interview in Amoafo in 1975.

2. For a succinct critique of the stereotype see Anne Whitehead, 'Wives and mothers: female farmers in Africa', in A. Adepoju and C. Oppong (eds), *Gender, Work and Population in Sub-Saharan Africa* (London, 1994), 36–37.

3. Allman and Tashjian, '*I Will Not Eat Stone*', 61. For a critical view of this contention, and of Allman and Tashjian's view that this gave way to a more unilineal flow of labour from women to the assistance of their husbands, see Stefano Boni, 'Twentieth-century transformations in notions of gender, parenthood, and marriage in Southern Ghana: a critique of the hypothesis of "retrograde steps" for Akan women', *History in Africa* 28 (2001), 17–18.

4. R. S. Rattray Papers (hereafter Rattray Papers), Manuscript Collection of the Royal Anthropological Institute, housed in the Museum of Mankind, London, MS 107:3, p. 1809.

5. Wesleyan Methodist Archive, School of Oriental and African Studies library: Coppin's Journal, Book VI, 29.

6. AF: interview with Nana Owusu Sekyere, Chief Linguist, and Opanyin Kwesi Kaabi, Kokofu, 12 May 1980. Victoria Tashjian's informants in 1990 made the same point (Tashjian, ' "It's Mine" and "It's Ours" Are Not the Same Thing', 148). I was asking specifically about the time before cocoa was introduced, in a locality where this meant before the Yaa Asantewaa war of 1900. The focus of Tashjian's dissertation is on the early colonial period. As she points out in a slightly different context (ibid., 145–46), if free husbands' contributions to food-farm labour changed in the early colonial period this is much more likely to have been an increase rather than a decrease: because of the declining contribution of slave and pawn labour.

7. For women planting and looking after the crops, AF: interview with Nana Sekyere, and Opanyin Kaabi, Kokofu, 12 May 1980.

8. LaTorre, 'Wealth Surpasses', 113, makes this point, though does not specifically document it.

9. Coppin's Journal, Book VI, 29.

10. Wilks, 'Land', 497–508 (quotation, 504); reprinted in *Forests*, 51–63 (quotation at p. 59). I have argued that Wilks's simulation makes mistaken assumptions about which crops were grown, but this would not alter the assumptions about labour requirements enough to affect the conclusions here (Austin, 'Rural Capitalism', 114–18).

11. Wilks, 'Land', 506–7 (*Forests*, 62–63).

12. For house-building as men's work see Coppin's Journal, Book VI, 29: Rattray Papers, MS 107:3, 1809.

13. Quotations from Rattray Papers, MS 107:3, 1809.

14. T.B. Freeman, *Journal of Various Visits*, 31.

15. Ibid., 31.

16. Coppin, Journal, Book VI, 29; Rattray Papers, MS 107:3, 1809–10.

17. Rattray, *Religion and Art*, 139.

18. Rattray, *Ashanti*, 105.

19. Wilks gives an instance of a spectacularly successful female entrepreneur from the late eighteenth century (Wilks, *Asante*, 694–95).

20. On spinning see Rattray Papers, MS 107:3, 1809.

21. AF: interview with Nana Sekyere and Opanyin Kaabi, Kokofu, 12 May 1980.

22. Rattray Papers, MS 107:3, 1809.

23. AF: interview with Nana Sekyere and Opanyin Kaabi, Kokofu, 12 May 1980.

24. Rattray, *Religion and Art*, 301.

25. Rattray Papers, MS 107:3, pp. 1809–10.

26. Rattray, *Religion and Art*, 301.

27. Arhin, 'Market settlements', 143.

28. Rattray, *Ashanti Law*, 336.

29. This fits, e.g., Busia, *Position of the Chief*, 47.

30. Arhin, 'Succession and gold mining', 107; Daaku, *Oral Traditions of Adanse*, 118.

31. Arhin, 'Succession and gold mining', 107; Daaku, *Oral Traditions of Adanse*, 139.

32. To judge from, e.g., Daaku, *Oral Traditions of Adanse*, 69, 204, 261; AF: interview with Nana Kojo Appiah Darko II, regent of Manso Nkwanta, 23 July 1980.

33. Rattray Papers, MS 107:1, p. 1656.

34. Arhin, 'Succession and gold mining', 107. Reasons for this will be considered later, pp. 171, 173–74.

35. Ibid., 107.

36. Kwame Arhin, 'Peasants in 19th-century Asante', *Current Anthropology* 24:4 (1983), 472. Arhin did not specify his source, so it was presumably oral testimony.

37. See below, 313–14.

38. Ken Swindell, *Farm Labour* (Cambridge, 1985), 141.

39. Peter Geschiere, 'Working groups or wage labour? Cash-crops, reciprocity and money among the Maka of southeastern Cameroon', *Development and Change* 26 (1995), 503–23: quotations from pp. 504, 506 (see also 513–14).

40. Kwame Arhin, 'Aspects of the Ashanti northern trade in the nineteenth century', *Africa*, 40:4 (1970), 371.

41. J.G. Christaller, *A Dictionary of the Asante and Fante Language called Tshi* (Basel Evangelical Missionary Society: Basel, 1881), 335.

42. P. 16 above.

43. See below, 317.

44. From archival sources the most I would hope for is a passing reference or two in mission archives or in colonial-period court records.

45. Rattray, *Ashanti*, 227.

46. Coppin's Journal, Book VI, 34–36, 39.

47. Wilks, *Asante*, 35–36, 434.

48. Daaku, *Oral Traditions of Adanse*, 356, cf. 337–38.

49. Ibid., 58.

50. Dumett, 'Precolonial gold mining and the state'; Dumett, *El Dorado*, 71–72.

51. Rattray, *Ashanti Law*, 114.

52. Arhin, 'Aspects of the Ashanti northern trade in the nineteenth century', 366.

53. René Baesjou, 'Introduction' to his (ed.), *An Asante Embassy on the Gold Coast: the Mission of Akyempon Yaw to Elmina, 1869–72* (Afrika-Studiecentrum: Leiden, 1979), 27.

54. The source is K. Sapon, formerly *batahene* (head of the state traders) of Mampon, one of the major Asante chieftaincies, who was interviewed by Rattray in 1925. Rattray, *Ashanti*, 110; for the notes of the interview, see Rattray Papers, MS. 107:2, pp. 1770, 1774–78.

55. Arhin, 'Economic and social significance of rubber', 53.

56. PRO CO96/293, H.M. Hull to Colonial Secretary, Cape Coast, 14 May 1897 (not 27 May as cited by Arhin), encl. in GCC No 212 of 27 May 1897.

57. Ibid.

58. Ibid.

59. The qualification 'almost' being because Arhin refers to 'hired labour' in carriage, without specifying sources, but apparently using oral testimony from 1965 or later (Arhin,

West African Traders, 10, 14: compare p. xii in the same work). Dumett, 'Rubber trade', 95n, writes of money wages being paid to Gyaman and Grunshi carriers in the Asante rubber trade. But this was over a year into the colonial period in Asante; also, I have been unable to find the observation in the source cited (PRO CO 96/293, Report encl. in Maxwell to Colonial Office, 27 May 1897).

60. ARG 1/2/30/1/2 'Domestic Slavery in Ashanti' (specialists may note that this is the file that, before the 1996 re-organization of the Kumasi branch of what was then called the National Archives of Ghana, was classified as D234 'Slaves and Pawns'): Petition of 'Kings, Chiefs and Head men of Adansi' to Governor, Fomena, 30 Nov. 1906.

61. Rattray, *Ashanti Law*, 37.

62. NAGK D905, 'Complaining of His Captive Woman Taken to Wassaw by Certain Men Without His Knowledge', Bantamahene Osei Mampon to CCA, Kumasi, 20 June 1908.

63. On northern predominance among tribute slaves see Wilks, *Asante*, 66–68, 164, 197, 246, 305–7, 706; LaTorre, 'Wealth Surpasses Everything', 407. There are abundant references to purchased slaves being from the savanna, some of which are cited elsewhere in this chapter. I am not aware of any evidence of Akan (or other forest-zone) captives being traded to Asante.

64. Noted by Cruickshank, *Eighteen Years*, II, 244–45; Rattray, *Ashanti Law*, 35–36; McCaskie, 'Office, Land and Subjects', 192.

65. Paul Jenkins, 'Abstracts of Basel Mission Gold Coast Correspondence' (cyclostyled: Basel, n.d.), 128, 143, 168, 189 (latter relating to slaves held in Asante; quoted below, 120). In Kumasi in 1872 two imprisoned Basel missionaries bought an Ewe slave (from 'Ahudome'), probably captured (like the missionaries) in the Asante invasion of Ewe in 1869. He too 'could not speak Ashantee . . .' (Friedrich August Ramseyer and Johannes Kühne, *Four Years in Ashantee* [London, 1875], 168).

66. Cf. Wilks, *Asante*, 706.

67. On the mission generally see LaTorre, 'Wealth Surpasses', 409–14 and Yarak, *Asante and the Dutch*, esp. 109–11. I have followed the more recent account, Yarak's, where they differ. For a fuller discussion of Dutch recruitment in Ghana, see Larry W. Yarak, 'New sources for the study of Akan slavery and slave trade: Dutch military recruitment in Asante and the Gold Coast, 1831–72', in Robin Law (ed.), *Source Material for Studying the Slave Trade and the African Diaspora* (Centre of Commonwealth Studies, University of Stirling: Stirling,1997), 35–60.

68. LaTorre, 'Wealth Surpasses', 412–20, on which the rest of this paragraph is based.

69. Given that these 46 were variously of Hausa, Borno, Adamawa, Yoruba and northern Togolese origin.

70. 'Mr. Hutchinson's diary' in Bowdich, *Mission*, 393.

71. Donna J. E. Maier, 'Asante war aims in the 1869 invasion of Ewe', esp. 237–39, 242.

72. LaTorre, 'Wealth Surpasses', 420; see also p. 409.

73. Rev. J. Leighton Wilson, *Western Africa: Its History, Condition, and Prospects* (New York, 1856), 178. The author had spent nearly 20 years in West Africa, visiting 'every place of importance' along the coast, though he appears not to have visited Asante.

74. Marion Johnson, 'The slaves of Salaga', *JAH* 27 (1986), 341–62 (quotation at p. 346).

75. Kwasi Boaten, 'Trade among the Asante of Ghana up to the end of the 18th century', *Research Review* (Institute of African Studies, University of Ghana), 7: 1 (1970), 36. See also Arhin, 'Aspects of the Ashanti northern trade', 365.

76. ARG 1/2/30/1/2, C. H. Armitage, memo. to F. C. Fuller, quoted in full in Fuller to Ag Governor, 'Memorandum in Connection with Domestic Slavery', 5 Aug. 1905.

77. Bowdich, *Mission*, 323. T. B. Freeman implicitly accepted that commoners owned slaves when he questioned whether they, like chiefs, were allowed to sacrifice them at funerals (T. B. Freeman, 'Reminiscences and Incidents', p. 38, 38b).

78. See the Boaten quotation above. Cf. K. Poku, 'Traditional roles and people of slave origin in modern Ashanti—a few impressions', *Ghana Journal of Sociology*, 37; cf. Arhin, 'Aspects of the Ashanti northern trade', 365.

79. Bowdich, *Mission*, 317.

80. Ramseyer and Kühne, *Four Years in Ashantee*, 29.

81. Rattray, *Ashanti Law*, 38.

82. Wilks, 'Land', 523 (*Forests*, 81).

83. Fortes Papers, 9.2, 'A very short account about the poor family Bretuo' (Aug.–Sept. 1945).

84. BMA, D1, 86, N. V. Asare, 'Annual Report about Kumase Congregation', Kumase, 20 March 1907. All the quotations and statements of fact in the following account of Donko's marriage are from this source. The statement about the approximate date of the pawning is derived by working backwards from the date of Donko's wife's death, which was not later than 1906. They had 'lived together for a considerable length of time' since marriage; he had redeemed her from pawnship 'when she became fit for marriage'; and had been a pawn since she was 'a small girl'.

85. Cruickshank, *Eighteen Years*, II, 243–44.

86. We owe Rev. Asare's rendition to the fact that, after sentence had been passed, he repeatedly visited Donko and eventually baptised him.

87. McCaskie, 'Office, land and subjects', 192.

88. Rattray, *Ashanti Law*, 92.

89. Meyer Fortes, 'The social background', in Frank Lorimer et al., *Culture and Human Fertility* (UNESCO: Paris, 1954), 293–94.

90. Busia, *Position of the Chief*, 22; Rattray, *Ashanti Law*, 203.

91. Rattray, *Ashanti*, 43.

92. For more on the origin of the term and the organization of the institution, see McCaskie, *State and Society*, 284.

93. Rattray, *Ashanti Law*, 229.

94. Ibid., 229.

95. Ibid., 92, cf. 156.

96. ARG 1/2/30/1/2, Petition of 'Kings, Chiefs and Head men of Adansi' to Governor, Fomena, 30 Nov. 1906.

97. Rattray, *Ashanti Law*, 229.

98. Fortes Papers, 8.9, notes of interview with Queen Mother of Agogo, Jan. 1946.

99. Rattray, *Ashanti Law*, 228–29. He would give the *gyaasehene*, the sub-chief responsible for the *gyaase*, a present of a *peredwan*: [conventionally] £8 (Rattray, *Ashanti Law*, 229).

100. AF: interview with Nana Kwabena Ntiamoah, Gyaasehene, 27 Aug. 1982, Bekwai.

101. Bowdich, *Mission*, 335, cf. 323.

102. Coppin's Journal, Book VI, 42.

103. Bowdich, 'Remarks on civilisation in Africa', 18.

104. Jenkins, 'Abstracts of Basel Mission Correspondence', 189: Dilger's report of a journey to Agogo, 17 March 1884.

105. D. J. E. Maier reports a similar phenomenon in the last quarter of the nineteenth century in the Kete-Krachi area, which by then was outside Asante control. Large-scale immigration (of fugitives from Asante after the 1874 war and the abortive Dwaben rebellion that followed) coupled with a growth of the town as a centre of long-distance trade led to the emergence of a substantial market for food, which, according to Maier, was supplied using northern slaves on sharecropping terms (D. J. E. Maier, *Priests and Power: the Case of the Dente Shrine in Nineteenth-Century Ghana* [Bloomington, 1983], 33–36, 108).

106. Wilks, 'Land', 500, reprinted in Wilks, *Forests of Gold*, 56.

107. Bowdich, 'Remarks on Civilisation in Africa', 18.

108. The argument here may seem ironic in view of Marshall's argument that sharecropping dilutes the incentive to the worker because the latter receives only a fraction of the marginal product of labour (see below, 415, 542 n. 62). But in this case the alternative was that the slave would not necessarily get anything of his or her marginal product.

109. Lovejoy, *Caravans of Kola*, 16, 22.

110. Bowdich, 'Remarks on civilisation in Africa', 18.

111. Bowdich, *Mission*, 332–33, quote at 333.

112. Wilks, *Asante*, 65–68, 164, 170, 177–78; Maier, 'Military acquisition of slaves', 128–29.

113. On war and tribute as sources of slaves see Arhin, 'Financing of the Ashanti expansion', 290; Wilks, *Asante*, 177, 197–98, 499, 674–75, 680; Maier, 'Military acquisition of slaves'; LaTorre, 'Wealth Surpasses', 301–6, 406–7.

114. LaTorre, 'Wealth Surpasses', 414.

115. Ibid., 407, quoting H. Pel, *Aanteekeningen gehouden op eene Reis van S. George d'Elmina naar Coomassie* (Leiden, 1842?), 24.

116. Wilson, *Western Africa*, 178. His chapters on Asante appear to be based on English-language books and on what he was told, presumably in English, on the Gold Coast. Thus it seems unlikely, though not impossible, that his direct or indirect source was the Dutch recruiters of 1837–42.

117. See the Terray-Dumett debate referred to in Ch. 4; see also Kwame Arhin, 'Market settlements', 143–5, and Arhin, 'The political economy of the expansionist state', *Revue française d'histoire d'Outre-Mer*, 68 (1981), 17, 24.

118. See Jenkins, 'Abstracts of Basel Mission Correspondence', 306, 308.

119. 'Autobiographical reminiscences of an Asante slave, "Mose"', translated by D. Maier-Weaver from *Der Evangelische Heidenbote* (1892), *Asante Seminar* 3 (Northwestern University: Evanston, 1975), 19–20. On his name, see the exegesis by T. C. McCaskie, 'Death and the *Asantehene*: a historical meditation', *JAH*, 30 (1989), 418–19, which I follow largely.

120. 'Autobiographical reminiscences of an Asante slave', transl. Maier-Weaver, 20.

121. Wilks, *Asante*, 302.

122. Daaku, *Oral Traditions of Adanse*, 38, 173, 303; Agnes A. Aidoo, 'Political Crisis and Social Change in the Asante Kingdom, 1867–1901' (Ph.D. dissertation: University of California, Los Angeles, 1975), 2 vols, II, 608. For archival evidence of Samori's captives being sold to Asantes, see the case of a Wangara mother and child from

what is now northern Ivory Coast documented in ARG 1/2/30/1/8 'Respecting "Slave Dealing" Recently Occurred at Sefwhi'.

123. ARG 9/2/2, 'Kokofu Subjects on Dorma Land', 20 April to 21 Nov. 1935.

124. PRO CO96/312: statements enclosed in Ag Governor to Secretary of State, 21 Feb. 1898. For an analysis of the economic implications of the file see Arhin, 'Economic and social significance of rubber'.

125. PRO CO96/293: statement by Kwamin Diaba, Debrisu, 14 Jan. 1898 (encl. in Governor to Secretary of State, 21 Feb. 1898).

126. Arhin, 'Economic and social significance of rubber', 57.

127. Arhin, 'Ashanti rubber trade', 42; Arhin, 'Economic and social significance of rubber', 59 (from which the quote comes).

128. Arhin, 'Economic and social significance of rubber', 59; Arhin, *West African Traders*, 52–53.

129. Daaku, *Oral Traditions of Adanse*, 45.

130. LaTorre, 'Wealth surpasses', 408, citing an interview with the then Amoafohene.

131. Arhin, *West African Traders*, 43–44, 46–47.

132. Fortes Papers, 8.39, Notebook entitled 'Asokore Bima II', recording testimony of Kwasi Frompong (*sic*), n.d. but c.1946.

133. As was noted in a study of the Salaga market by Emmanuel Terray, 'Réflections sur la formation du prix des esclaves á l'intérieur de l'Afrique de l'Ouest précoloniale', *Journal des Africanistes* 52, 1–2 (1982), 136–38.

134. In interpreting the appendix note that the price observations vaguely dated 'late nineteenth century' may well refer to years before 1895–96.

135. See p. 9.

136. LaTorre, 'Wealth Surpasses', 414.

137. Albeit one that his master chose to restrict by going to a shrine and having the boy declared to be 'a present of grace from the god, so that the master should have the protection of the god; therefore the slave was not allowed to be sold or exchanged unless another more powerful god consecrated it and the name changed again.' Later his master 'brought me to the god Tano and requested him that I take my name again so that he . . . could exchange me for another slave.' But Tano declined, saying ' "This person is your god-person (i.e. your blessing)." ' ('Autobiographical reminiscences of an Asante slave', transl. Maier-Weaver, 19).

138. Rattray, *Ashanti Law*, 40–41 (*Akoa didi me a, na wo wura, okom de no a, ne die no afuhye*). It should be noted that the word *akoa* denoted a 'subject' rather than specifically a slave, but doing his fieldwork less than twenty years after the colonial prohibition of slavery, Rattray was presumably able to hear the proverb used in the context of slavery.

139. Maier, 'Military acquisition of slaves', 129.

140. Representatives of European governments who visited Salaga in 1887 and 1888, respectively, estimated that 15,000 or 20,000 slaves were sold annually in the market there: for destinations in Togoland and the Gold Coast—though constrained by colonial actions against the slave trade, at least in the Gold Coast—as well as, indirectly, in Asante (Johnson, 'Slaves of Salaga', 341). This was, as indicated earlier, only one of the routes by which slaves reached Asante after 1874.

141. John Frederick Maurice (but published anonymously), *The Ashantee War: a Popular Narrative* (London, 1874), 271.

142. Rattray, *Ashanti Law*, 49; Rattray Papers, MS 107:3, p. 1807, testimony of 'K. S.' This was presumably the above-cited K. Sapon, formerly *batahene* of Mampon, as these

notes are among Mampon material, and Sapon is named as informant in a slightly earlier interview.

143. 'Autobiographical reminiscences of an Asante slave', transl. Maier-Weaver, 20; McCaskie, 'State and society, marriage and adultery: some considerations towards a social history of pre-colonial Asante', *JAH* 22 (1981), 477–94; Rattray Papers, MS 107:3, p. 1807, testimony of K. S[apon]; Rattray, *Ashanti Law*, 51; Arhin, 'Market settlements', 144–45; Arhin, 'Succession and gold mining at Manso-Nkwanta', 108.

144. Arhin, 'Market settlements', 143–44.

Appendix to Chapter 6

1. Johnson, 'Slaves of Salaga', 349. As the repeated references will show, this table owes much to the late Marion Johnson's research on Salaga market.

2. LaTorre, 'Wealth Surpasses', 440–41; Terray, 'Réflections sur la formation du prix des esclaves', 140–41.

3. Bowdich's Asante figure; those from Barter, Daaku, the Fortes papers, the national archives of Ghana, Jenkins' *Abstracts*, Kirby, 'Mose'; and a second observation from Rattray (p. 36).

4. Jan Hogendorn and Marion Johnson, *The Shell Money of the Slave Trade* (Cambridge, 1986), 125–47, 194–98.

5. LaTorre, 'Wealth Surpasses', 207–8. LaTorre is wrong, however, in quoting 4,200 cowries to the *ackie* (of which more shortly) for 1888. Von Francois (as cited below), who visited Salaga that year, specifies that the rate was 1,000 to the mark which, on the mark/pound/*ackie* ratios used by LaTorre (and in Table 6.1 here), implies 4,500 cowries to the *ackie*.

6. Marion Johnson, 'The cowrie currencies of West Africa', Part 2, *JAH* 11 (1970), 345, 346; Marion Johnson (ed.), *Salaga Papers*, Vol. I (Legon, 1966).

7. Reported in Johnson, 'Slaves of Salaga', 345–46.

8. David Asante's report on his journey to Salaga, 1877, in Jenkins's *Abstracts*, 79. See, further, Terray, 'Réflections sur la formation du prix des esclaves', 138.

9. J. C. Muir, 'Cola industry', 219.

10. See Garrard, *Akan Weights and the Gold Trade*, esp. 233–35, 239, 256–57, 268, 332–33, 338.

11. Bowdich, *Mission*, 330.

12. Ramseyer and Kühne, *Four Years in Ashantee*, 303.

13. Wilks, *Asante*, 729.

14. Ramseyer and Kühne, *Four Years in Ashantee*, 303.

15. LaTorre, 'Wealth Surpasses', 207.

16. Ibid.

17. LaTorre interprets this as a price within Asante (LaTorre, 'Wealth Surpasses', 440), but in context it seems more likely that Bowdich meant purchases in 'the interior' in the sense of further from the coast than Asante (see Bowdich, *Mission*, 333).

18. However, Larry Yarak suggests that this may be a coast rather than an Asante price, and that it may have been exaggerated by the exchange rate between goods and gold quoted by the Dutch governor (personal communication, 28 April 2001).

19. Yarak, 'New sources for the study of Akan slavery', 49; cf. LaTorre, 'Wealth Surpasses', 440.

20. Source specifies that the sale of 'Mose' in Asante preceded the death of Asantehene Kwaku Dua Panin, which happened in 1867.

21. At the mark-pound-*ackie* conversion rates generally used in this table 200 marks is 43.51 *ackies*. But it is most likely that the source rounded to '200 marks' a price that— assuming the transaction did indeed occur in Asante—was actually 1.25 *peredwan* (45 *ackies*). For there was a convenient gold weight, *osua ne dwoa*, that was effectively 0.25 *peredwan* (see Timothy F. Garrard, 'Studies in Akan goldweights [3])', *Transactions of the Historical Society of Ghana* 14:1[1973], 6–7).

22. See pp. 41, 47 for the policy of excluding northern traders from Asante markets, which was followed from c.1840 to nearly 1874.

23. This was Adjua Badu, taken captive in Kumasi during the reign of Asantehene Kofi Karikari (1867–74) (D905) and mentioned in passing above, p. 115. That she was sold, and for that price, is according to the Bantamahene in 1908. This was disputed both by Adjua Badu herself, who claimed she was never enslaved, and by her son-in-law and self-proclaimed master, Kwaku Enin, who asserted that his late uncle had paid £16 (2 *peredwan*, presumably) to buy her in order to make her his wife. At minimum, these numbers could be taken as an indication of the kind of sums paid during living memory. However, £16 is higher than any confirmed price of which I am aware for the entire century, even if it included a marriage payment. Of the three stories (summarized in Ch. 12 below), the chief's version seems to me the most likely, and gains a little further plausibility from having been accepted by the colonial authorities, who showed themselves on other occasions well capable of rejecting a chief's claims. Her own account seems too good to be true, given her alien origin and the Asantehene's lethal fury.

24. According to Ramseyer and Kühne themselves one *ackie* exchanged for one Spanish or American dollar, at least on the coast (*Four Years in Ashantee*, 304).

25. See n. 24.

26. In practice the range of variation would have been less. The source specified that the price of a load of kola 'varied from as much as a *nsoansafa* to a *nsoansa* of gold-dust (i.e. from 5s. to 10s. [£0.25–0.50] according to the season's crop' (Rattray, *Ashanti Law*, 110). We may assume that if a massive harvest drove the value of kola down to the bottom of its range in terms of gold it would not simultaneously rise to the top of its range in terms of slaves.

27. As previous note.

28. £3–7 is reported again in 1896 by Major C. Barter, 'Notes on Ashanti', *The Scottish Geographical Magazine* 12:9 (1896), 456, whose account of the 'Hinterland of Ashanti' was based on 'the most recent reports by English travellers in this region' (ibid., 455), and so may have been merely repeating Ferguson.

29. The victim said 'I was born in Jimini at the back of Bodookoo', and was captured 'when Samory came and made war and broke our country', and was sold by her captors (ARG 1/2/30/1/8: statement by Yah Jimini, Obuasi, 11 November 1905). Samori Ture's invasion of the Gyaman state was in 1895.

30. Assuming the £14 'expenses' for which a redemption fee of the same amount was later paid comprised solely the purchase price. The price was probably paid in cloth. The captive herself later said that warriors of the Almami Samori Ture 'sold me to Kwamin Tawiah, who gave cloths for me and took me to be his wife' (ARG 1/2/30/1/8: statement by Yah Jimini, Obuasi, 11 November 1905). Arhin found from fieldwork that 'Asante rubber traders obtained war captives against strips of "grey baft", calico', the latter being the material in which the Almani's army were clothed (Arhin, 'Ashanti rubber trade', 36–38). Arhin's

informants in Dormaa told him that a slave at Bonduku was then four pieces of cloth ('much less after a particularly successful Samory expedition'). This quantity of cloth cost 10 shillings (£0.50, A2.2) at Cape Coast, a small fraction of the amount paid for Yah Jimini: but, crucially, we are not told what the price of cloth was in the interior, except in terms of slaves.

31. According to the source, slaves cost between *kokoa* and *benaa*. Ramseyer and Kühne (*Four Years in Ashantee*, 303) describe the former gold weight as equivalent to 5 1/4 British old pence (£0.022) the latter as two gold ounces or £7 4 shillings (£7.2).

Chapter 7

1. Christaller, *Dictionary*, 105; cf. 618.

2. Ibid., 618.

3. Arhin, 'Aspects of the Ashanti northern trade', 369n, citing a personal communication from Professor Nketia.

4. Hill, *Migrant Cocoa-Farmers*, 215. Hill has an appendix on 'Linguistic economics', derived from Christaller (ibid., 214–17).

5. This seems to be implied by, for instance, Kwame Arhin's use of, and commentary on, Christaller in an article presenting results from Arhin's own fieldwork, 1965–67, on the Asante kola trade (Arhin, 'Aspects of the Ashanti northern trade', 369).

6. Christaller, *Dictionary*, 122, 438.

7. Wilks, *Asante*, 615, 636, 650–55; Aidoo, 'Political Crisis and Social Change', II, 381–82, 609–11.

8. Wilks, *Asante*, 646–47; Aidoo, 'Political Crisis and Social Change', Vol. II, 609–10. The reason the Bekwaihene was able to offer to lease out Obuasi in the first place was that Bekwai forces had occupied Adanse during the civil war, forcing the Adansehene into exile. Cade took the precaution of signing leases from both the Bekwai and Adanse chiefs in 1895 (Wilks, *Asante*, 646). Following the British occupation the Adansehene returned to resume his position on the ground.

9. See Kirby, 'A journey to the interior of Ashanti', 449; Peter C. Garlick, 'The development of Kwahu business enterprise in Ghana since 1874—an essay in recent oral tradition', *JAH* 8 (1967), 467; Daaku, *Oral Traditions of Adanse*, 150.

10. Garlick, 'Development of Kwahu business enterprise', *JAH* 8 (1967), 467.

11. AF: interview with Nana Kojo Appiah Darko II, Regent of Manso Nkwanta, in Manso Nkwanta, 23 July 1980.

12. Bray, *Cocoa Development in Ahafo*, 46.

13. Hull to CS, 14 May 1897, cited p. 467 n. 41 above.

14. Daaku, *Oral Traditions of Adanse*, 69 (Akrofoum), 217 (Ataase Nkwanta) and 261 (Fumso). The last source mentioned nephews as well as sons as recipients.

15. Arhin, 'Aspects of the Ashanti northern trade', 365 (quoting his informant).

16. *Royal Gold Coast Gazette*, 34, 9 Aug. 1823.

17. See Austin, 'Indigenous credit institutions in West Africa, c.1750–1960', 102–3.

18. Robin Law, 'Finance and credit in pre-colonial Dahomey', in Endre Stiansen and Jane I. Guyer (eds), *Credit, Currencies and Culture: African Financial Institutions in Historical Perspective* (Uppsala, 1999), 34.

19. Bowdich, *Mission*, 257.

20. LaTorre, 'Wealth Surpasses', 194.

21. Hull to CS, 14 May 1897.

22. See p. 41 above (Ahafo); Stefano Boni, 'A precolonial, political history of the Sefwi Wiawso oman', *Ghana Studies* 4 (2001), 166–67; Wilks, *Asante*, 289, 289–90n., 303 (Sefwi) and 294–97 (Wenchi).

23. Hull to CS, 14 May 1897.

24. *Sika nko adidi nsan mma kwa*, in R. S. Rattray (ed. and transl.), *Ashanti Proverbs* (Oxford, 1916), 162.

25. Thomas C. McCaskie, 'The Paramountcy of the Asantehene Kwaku Dua (1834–1867): a study in Asante political culture' (Ph.D. thesis, University of Cambridge, 1974), 40–42. The primary source is the *Royal Gold Coast Gazette*, 1823–24.

26. Daaku, *Oral Traditions of Adanse*, 174.

27. Ibid., 314.

28. Bowdich, *Mission*, 295. This passage is quoted below, p. 187.

29. ARG 1/2/30/1/2, Memo. from C. H. Armitage to CCA, quoted in Fuller's memo. to Ag Governor, 5 August 1905. Rattray describes the procedure in *Ashanti Law*, 368–69. A specific case is documented—albeit for a later period—in NAGK D2018 'Respecting Kwasi Amofa, Changing Security from Chief of Droboso for Yaw Mani's debt' (Ashanti MP 531/08), [1908]. This relates to a Wenchi man, Kwasi Amofa, who borrowed £70 from a man in Mampon in 1907, for which 'The chief of Droboso stood security . . . as Kwasi Amofa was a leading personage in his village'. But then (probably in 1908) Amofa moved to Tekyiman, and the Drobosohene withdrew his security.

30. Rattray, *Ashanti Law*, 369.

31. Ibid., 369–70.

32. Ibid., 369–70n.

33. Bowdich, *Mission*, 293.

34. Ibid., 370.

35. Ibid., 257.

36. Rattray, *Ashanti*, 234, and *Ashanti Law*, 370.

37. British Parliamentary Papers, C.4477, *Further Correspondence Respecting the Affairs of the Gold Coast* (London, 1885), 22: Samuel Rowe, Governor, to Earl of Derby, Accra, 12 Jan. 1884.

38. Jenkins, 'Abstracts of Basel Mission Correspondence', 188: Dilger's report of a journey to Agogo, 17 March 1884.

39. *The Western Echo* (Cape Coast), no. 1, 18 Nov. 1885.

40. Rattray, *Ashanti*, 232–36.

41. Ibid., 234.

42. Rattray, *Ashanti Law*, 367–68.

43. NAGK D2486 (34/1927) (EP 52/N/31), Petitions General: Petition of Chief Kofi Dompeh, Oyokohene, to Commissioner of the Eastern Province of Ashanti, Kumasi, 22 Feb. 1929.

44. See Rattray, *Ashanti Law*, 19–20; see also 48–55.

45. Ibid., 8: Rattray Papers, MS 107:3, p. 1803. Much earlier, Bowdich wrote that if a man returned from a prolonged absence to find that his wife had remarried, he had the right to pawn the children of her second marriage (Bowdich, *Mission*, 260). This can be seen as compensation by her *abusua* for the loss of the wife they had given him.

46. Rattray later contradicts himself by saying that Asante fathers could never pawn their sons (*Ashanti Law*, 16). Twenty years before, the missionary Edmond Perregaux had

written that a father could pawn his child with the consent of the mother and [maternal] uncle, while a mother could pawn her child providing the father agreed. His language suggests an equality between these two possibilities (see Perregaux, 'Chez les Achanti', *Bulletin de la société neuchateloise de géographie*, 17 [1906], 154–55). But Perregaux seems to have been misled by what was clearly his own unacknowledged source, a passage in A. B. Ellis's *The Tshi-Speaking Peoples of the Gold Coast of West Africa* (London, 1887), 294–95. A few pages further on Ellis himself emphasized the primacy of the *abusua* in pawning (*Tshi-Speaking Peoples*, 298). He did state that it was possible for fathers to pawn children, subject to their matrikin's consent, and that a mother needed the father's consent before pawning their child (*Tshi-Speaking Peoples*, 295). But his own knowledge of the matter probably derived from Fante rather than Asante practice, as did his knowledge of Akan society and culture generally. On his lack of Asante sources, see Ray Jenkins, 'Confrontations with A. B. Ellis, a participant in the scramble for Gold Coast Africana, 1874–1894', in *European Sources for Sub-Saharan Africa Before 1900: use and abuse*, edited by Beatrix Heintze and Adam Jones, a special issue of *Paideuma: mitteilungen zur kulturkunde*, 33 (1987), 321–23.

47. ARG 1/2/30/1/5, esp. statements by Kobina Fosu, an Odumase 'linguist' (spokesman), and by Chief Kusi, the new Ankobeahene, before the district commissioner of Kumasi, 21 March 1908. There is a recorded instance, from approximately the second quarter of the nineteenth century, of a girl being pawned by her maternal grandfather, who could not have belonged to the same *abusua*. But this could be accounted for by the grandmother being a slave (see below), an interpretation which is strengthened by the fact that the pawn's own daughter was later 'purchased'. For the case, without sources but free of my reading of it, see Asante Collective Biography Career Sheet No. 68, prepared by I. Wilks, *Asantesem: The Ashanti Collective Biography Project Bulletin*, 10 (1979), 37. There was also a case which came to court in 1930 of a child being pawned by her uncle and grandfather (SCT 205/160 Bekwai Magistrate's Court, Criminal Record Book [RB], p. 7). We may assume that the uncle was her mother's brother. If the grandfather's consent was involved, rather than his role being to give advice or mediation, this would also be consistent with the rules of *awowasi* if her mother was a slave. If this was not so, a need for the grandfather's consent could be reconciled with the matrilineal principle if he was also her maternal granduncle: in other words if she was the product of a familiar arrangement in Asante, the cross-cousin marriage between son and sister's daughter (Rattray, *Religion and Art*, 317–31).

48. NAGK D1573 'Return of a Girl Named Ekua Misa to Wenchi' (1910), Fell, Commissioner of the Western Province of Ashanti (CWPA), to CCA, Sunyani, 12 July 1910.

49. ARG 1/2/30/1/2, e.g. Petition of 'Kings, Chiefs and Head men of Adansi' to Governor, Fomena (Ashanti), 30 Nov. 1906.

50. ARG 5/1/6 'Quarterly Intelligence Reports S.P.A' (contains several files, in some disorder), untitled sub-file of petitions, Kwamin Obenney to DC, Abodom, 7 Aug. 1905.

51. For the principle see Rattray, *Ashanti Law*, 48n.

52. Ibid., 44, 48, 52–53.

53. Ibid., 40.

54. Her son said that he was with his mother when she was first pawned, and remembers that it was before the war with the British, though he had earlier stated that it was during the reign of Asantehene Mensa Bonsu, which began in 1874 (ARG 1/2/30/1/7: the quotations are from Kweshi Dwamena to DC, Kumasi 9 March 1908, and statement by Dwamena, n.d. but evidently also 9 March 1908).

55. ARG 5/1/6, untitled sub-file of petitions, Kwamin Obenney to DC, Abodom, 7 Aug. 1905.

56. ARG 1/2/30/1/2, Adansi petition, 30 Nov. 1906.

57. ARG 1/2/30/1/2, Fuller to Ag Governor, 5 Aug. 1905; Rattray, *Ashanti Law*, 47, 50.

58. Rattray, *Ashanti Law*, 47–55.

59. Rattray Papers, MS.107:3, p. 1803.

60. Musa Dagarti's published memoir does not indicate how long he was in pawn, except that the fact that it gives no information at all about his period as a pawn suggests that it was short. What it makes explicit is that between his redemption and May 1883, there was time for him to be sent by his master to Akyem to buy salt; run away (as we have seen), go to Fanteland where he 'took up my residence at Akramang' and there 'learned witchcraft and spirit-banning', meet Christians while he was on a trip with his 'amulets and charms' (evidently to practise his new profession), and move to Asamang to join the congregation there. See 'Autobiographical reminiscences of an Asante slave', transl. Maier-Weaver, 20.

61. Conventionally £8, more strictly £8.15 in this period. See p. 129 above.

62. ARG 1/2/30/1/5, esp. Kwesi Peyso, Omanhene of Odumase, to DC of Western Ashanti, Sunyani, 21 Sept. 1907.

63. In the event, either the creditor 'refused to keep the woman' (according to the debtor) or she 'refused to stay with me' (according to the creditor). She returned home, and the creditor eventually secured full payment by presenting a promissory note to the colonial court. (ADM 53/4/1 Obuasi Civil RB 1904–7, p. 279, Kwesi Mpong v. Kofi Berukyi, 25 July 1905.) It seems likely that the promissory note, dated Jan. 1903, was made when the pawning arrangement collapsed (cf. ADM 53/1/2 Obuasi Duplicate Letter Book (DLB) 1905–6, p117, C. H. Armitage to Bekwaihene, Obuasi, 25 July 1905).

64. PRAAD Accra ADM 46/1/1 Moinsi Hill/Obuasi DLB 1902–4, p. 243, Armitage to King of Bekwai, Obuasi 1 Dec. 1903.

65. ADM 53/4/1 Obuasi Civil RB 1904–7, pp. 156–57, Yao Donkor v. Eduo Acheampong, 20 Dec. 1904.

66. Wilks, *Asante*, 50–51.

67. ARG 1/2/30/1/2, Ag DC to CCA, Nkoranza, 20 Nov. 1906. In the same period Perregaux also stated that interest was often required before the creditor would return the pawn. He added that the rate was normally 50% (Perregaux, 'Chez les Achanti', 154). However, on both points he appears to have been paraphrasing an earlier description of Akan pawning given by Ellis (Ellis, *Tshi-Speaking Peoples*, 295). Thus it seems unlikely that Perregaux had independent information on the matter. Ellis himself almost certainly relied on data about Fante rather than Asante practice (see n. 46 above).

68. PRAAD Accra ADM 53/4/1 Obuasi Civil RB 1904–7, pp. 69 (Dadzi v. Shou), 168 (Foli v. Gimson), 187 (Forsu v. Cobina), 200 (Sackey v. Malobriah), 212 (Pobee v. Sawah), 263 (Quashie v. Armah), 274 (Frank v. Arkim[?]), 279 (Mpong v. Berukyi), 357 (Pobee v. Akosua), 366 (Asare v. Assiama).

69. Ibid., Soden to CCA, Obuasi, 11 Dec. 1906.

70. Ibid., Armitage memo. quoted in Fuller to Ag Governor, 5 Aug. 1905.

71. Perregaux, 'Chez les Achanti', 116. This passage, or specifically the link between child-betrothal and pawning, is one which I have not found in any of the books on the Gold Coast which Perregaux used, and from which he was not above plagiarizing and translocating apparently uncritically to Asante (see n. 46 above). Perregaux had considerable

direct experience in Asante (see the preface to 'Chez les Achanti' by the editors of the journal). Hence it is reasonable to accept his observations when they appear to be independent of previous authors.

72. Rattray, *Religion and Art*, 78, 101.

73. Ibid.

74. Rattray, *Ashanti Law*, 48.

75. Meyer Fortes, 'Analysis and description in social anthropology', Presidential Address to the British Association for the Advancement of Science, Section H (1953), reprinted in Fortes, *Time and Social Structure and Other Essays* (London, 1970), 142–43; Fortes, 'Kinship and marriage among the Ashanti' in A. R. Radcliffe-Brown and Daryll Forde (eds), *African Systems of Kinship and Marriage* (London, 1950), 281; cf. J. W. A. Amoo, 'The effect of Western influence on Akan marriage', *Africa*, 14 (1946), 230, 235.

76. Fortes Papers, 8.1, 'Ashanti Marriage Data', comprising tables and an incomplete memo. by Fortes entitled 'Ashanti Marriage Statistics'.

77. Contrary to the suggestion of Grier, 'Pawns, porters, and petty traders', 326–27, based on a comparison of passages in publications by Rattray and Fortes. This proposition is completely undermined if (as in the present discussion) one takes account also of other work by Rattray, and, even more so, Fortes's unpublished papers from the Ashanti Social Survey. For specifics see Gareth Austin, 'Human pawning in Asante, 1800–1950', in T. Falola and P. Lovejoy (eds), *Pawnship in Africa: Debt Bondage in Historical Perspective* (Boulder, 1994), 125–26, 149 (reprinted in P. Lovejoy and T. Falola [eds], *Pawnship, Slavery, and Colonialism in Africa* [Trenton NJ and Asmara, 2003]); also p. 231 below.

78. Meyer Fortes, 'Analysis and description in social anthropology', Presidential Address to the British Association for the Advancement of Science, Section H, (1953), reprinted in Fortes, *Time and Social Structure and Other Essays* (London, 1970), 142–43; Fortes, 'Kinship and marriage among the Ashanti' in A. R. Radcliffe-Brown and Daryll Forde (eds), *African Systems of Kinship and Marriage* (London, 1950), 281; cf. J. W. A. Amoo, 'Effect of Western influence on Akan marriage', 230, 235.

79. Rattray, *Ashanti Law*, 48–51.

80. P. 101 above for the general principle. For its application to the property of wives and children see Rattray, *Ashanti Law*, 336–37.

81. Rattray, *Ashanti Law*, 49.

82. Ibid., 49n.

83. Ibid., 49–50.

84. Ramseyer and Kühne, *Four Years in Ashantee* (1875), 260, quoted by Aidoo, 'Order and Conflict', 23. Aidoo cites the New York edn; I confess I have been unable to find the sentence in the London edn.

85. Lewin, *Asante Before the British*, 154.

86. AF: note of conversation with Nana Akomeah, former Krontihene of Bekwai, 27 Aug. 1982. In his very last years Nana Akomeah was unable to recall this point when I asked him to record it on tape, in 1987. But he expressed it with characteristic clarity, and at his own initiative, in 1982.

87. For the latter see McCaskie, *State and Society*, 40, citing papers in his own possession. For the other cases see Asante Collective Biography Career Sheet 68, prepared by I. Wilks, Asantesɛm 10 (1979), 37; ARG 1/2/30/1/7.

88. For clarification of the units involved see the appendix to Ch. 6.

89. McCaskie, 'State and society, marriage and adultery', 493–94.

90. BMA, D1, 86, N. V. Asare, 'Annual Report about Kumase Congregation', Kumase, 20 March 1907.

91. PRAAD Accra 53/4/1 Obuasi Civil RB 1904–7, pp. 87–92: Akwesi Kwatchie v. Akwa N'bu, 15 Oct. 1904.

92. ARG 1/2/30/1/5, esp. K. Fosu's statement of 21 March 1908.

93. Raymond Dumett and Marion Johnson, 'Britain and the suppression of slavery in the Gold Coast Colony, Ashanti, and the Northern Territories', in Suzanne Miers and Richard Roberts (eds), *The End of Slavery in Africa* (Madison, 1988), 94–95.

94. In some cases £10 (or £20) to redeem a pawn may have represented one (two) *peredwan*(s) plus 25% interest (see the earlier discussion of interest rates).

95. For the units see Garrard, 'Studies in Akan goldweights (3)', 6.

96. Asante Collective Biography Career Sheet 68, prepared by I. Wilks, *Asantesem* 10 (1979), 37; McCaskie, 'State and society, marriage and adultery', 493–94; Rattray Papers, MS.107:3, p. 1803; PRAAD Accra ADM 53/1/2 Obuasi DLB 1905–6, p. 27, C. H. Armitage, DC, to Omanhene of Kokofu, Obuasi, 26 June 1905; ADM 53/4/1 Obuasi Civil RB 1904–7, p. 279, Kwesi Mpong v. Kofi Berukyi, 25 July 1905; NAGK RAO Files on Shelves 12 and 13, No. 80 (Ashanti M.P. 274/06), 'Kobina Nkrumah, Kumasi, 29th April 1906, Requesting Return of His Daughter', statement by Chief Kofi Mintah before DC of Southern Ashanti at Fomena, 18 May 1906; ARG 5/1/6; SCT 205/160, Bekwai Magistrate's Court, Criminal RB, p. 7; D133, Bekwai DC's Diary, 3 Oct. 1930; ARG 1/2/30/1/2, Ag CWPA to Ag CCA, Sunyani, 22 Jan. 1908; ARG 1/2/30/1/5; D1486 'Complaint from King of Wenchi'; D1573 'Return of a Girl', Fell to CCA, Sunyani, 12 July 1910; ARG 1/2/30/1/7.

97. PRAAD Accra ADM 53/4/1 Obuasi Civil RB 1904–7, pp. 156–57, Yao Donkor v. Eduo Acheampong, 20 Dec. 1904; ARG 1/2/30/1/7, DC, Kumasi, to DC, Western Ashanti, 16 March 1908; McCaskie, *State and Society*, 40; NAGK D2593 'Respecting Redemption'; NAGA 53/4/1 Obuasi Civil RB 1904–7, pp. 87–92, Akwesi Kwatchie v. Akwa N'bu, 15 Oct. 1904.

98. For the exception see McCaskie, *State and Society*, 40. Two cases (in the sense defined earlier) arose from the same original debt (McCaskie, 'State and society, marriage and adultery', 493–94). For the remaining cases see Asante Collective Biography Career Sheet 68, prepared by I. Wilks, Asantesεm 10 (1979), 37; ARG 1/2/30/1/7.

Chapter 8

1. H. J. Nieboer, *Slavery as an Industrial System* (The Hague, 1900), 383–84, 420–27 (in revd edn, 1910, pp. 387, 418–24; page references below are to the original). Nieboer's own formulation was that 'slavery as an industrial system' (p. 421) was only likely to exist where the slave-owning population enjoyed 'open resources among which subsistence is easily acquired', [because] it is only such a population for whom, 'generally speaking, the keeping of slaves is economically profitable' (p. 426).

2. Evsey D. Domar, 'The causes of slavery or serfdom: a hypothesis', *Journal of Economic History* 30 (1970), 18–32.

3. Hopkins, *Economic History of West Africa*, 23–27.

4. Ibid., 37–39; quotation at p. 39.

5. Ibid., 24 (cf. 26).

6. See, e.g., the bibliographies in Paul E. Lovejoy, *Transformations in Slavery: A History of Slavery in Africa* (Cambridge, 1983); Patrick Manning, *Slavery and African Life* (Cambridge, 1990); Claude Meillassoux, *The Anthropology of Slavery: The Womb of Iron and Gold* (Chicago 1991, transl. by A. Dasnois from French original, 1986)); Martin Klein, *Slavery and Colonial Rule in French West Africa* (Cambridge, 1998).

7. The one systematic case-study of which I am aware is David Northrup, 'Nineteenth-century patterns of slavery and economic growth in southeastern Nigeria', *International Journal of African Historical Studies* 12 (1979), 1–16. Northrup's method is to distinguish three different systems of slavery in different parts of the study-region, and to relate variations in their institutional characteristics and in their reported incidence with variations in population density and demand for labour. Northrup's analysis is perceptive and suggestive, but does not address the issues of choice considered here in Sections B and C below; nor does it examine the production function(s) in any detail, nor attempt to quantify labour costs.

8. Nieboer, *Slavery as an Industrial System*, e.g. 426–27; Domar, 'Causes of slavery or serfdom', 31–32; Hopkins, *Economic History of West Africa*, 24n.

9. Nieboer, *Slavery as an Industrial System*, 423, 426, 427.

10. E.g., see Lovejoy, *Transformations in Slavery*, chs 8, 9; Manning, *Slavery and African Life*, 140, 142–44; several of the contributions to Law (ed.), *From Slave Trade to 'Legitimate' Commerce*.

11. Domar, 'Causes of slavery or serfdom', 19–20.

12. Defined p. 11 above.

13. Stephen H. Hymer, 'Economic forms in pre-colonial Ghana', *Journal of Economic History*, 30 (1970), 34.

14. Domar himself noted the tax option ('Causes of slavery or serfdom', 19). See, further, Stanley Engerman, 'Some considerations relating to property rights in man', *Journal of Economic History*, 33 (1973), 58–59.

15. Jack Goody, 'Slavery in time and space', in James L. Watson (ed.), *Asian and African Systems of Slavery* (1980), 16–42; cf. Frederick Cooper, 'The problem of slavery in African studies', *JAH* 20 (1979), 108.

16. John Thornton, *Africa and Africans in the Making of the Atlantic World, 1400–1680* (Cambridge, 1992), 74–76.

17. Standard interest-group theorists' arguments about the free-rider problem as an obstacle to effective cooperation among members of large groups—arguments which are debatable in some other contexts—would appear to apply strongly in this. See Olson, *Logic of Collective Action*; Bates, *Essays on the Political Economy of Rural Africa*.

18. Pp. 36, 100–102 above.

19. Stanley Engerman, 'The economics of forced labor', *Itinerario* 17 (1993), 63.

20. P. 43; cf. p. 275 below.

21. Pp. 38, 40 above.

22. An incisive recent essay re-interprets the material base of the Asante state as tribute or taxation supplemented by rent extracted from a coerced tenantry, the latter comprising slaves and their descendants: Larry W. Yarak, 'Slavery and the state in Asante history', in J. Hunwick and N. Lawler (eds), *The Cloth of Many Colored Silks: Papers on History and Society Ghanaian and Islamic in Honor of Ivor Wilks* (Evanston, 1996), 223–40. As will be apparent, I place much more emphasis on the scale and importance of slavery

per se: especially the exploitation of first-generation slaves, by commoner households as well as in chiefs' establishments.

23. Wilson, *Western Africa*, 178.

24. P. 112.

25. Pp. 315–16, 410–12.

26. McCaskie, *State and Society*, 96.

27. Cf. Emmanuel Terray, 'La captivité dans le royaume abron du Gyaman', in C. Meillassoux, *L'Esclavage en afrique précoloniale* (Paris, 1975), 441–43.

28. 12 old pence ('d.') made one shilling ('s.'), of which there were 20 to the pound.

29. Garrard, *Akan Weights and the Gold Trade*, 148–49, citing F. Hart, *The Gold Coast: its Wealth and Health* (London 1904), 111, 131–34. There is a further useful discussion, focussed on the Wassa district of western Ghana, in Dumett, *El Dorado*, 76–78.

30. *ARA for 1898*, 221.

31. Szeresewski, *Structural Changes in the Economy of Ghana*, 138, asserts that 1/- a day was 'standard' on the Gold Coast (apparently including Asante) in 1911. In two different individual instances European planters in Asante paid 1s 3d. a day, in one case specifically including a 3d. subsistence allowance (NAGA ADM 53/1/10 Obuasi DLB 1911–12, p. 240, PC to Adansehene, 10 Feb. 1912; West African Lands Committee, *Minutes of Evidence*, 402–3, 21 March 1913).

32. (1953 = 100). Kay, *Political Economy of Colonialism in Ghana*, Table 20c, p. 332.

33. Garrard, *Akan Weights and the Gold Trade*, 148.

34. Ibid., 148.

35. Lovejoy, *Caravans of Kola*, 22.

36. Ramseyer and Kühne, *Four Years in Ashantee*, 2nd German edn, 290, extract transl. by Marion Johnson, in Johnson, *Salaga Papers*, I, p. SAL/32/1.

37. Terray, 'Réflections sur la formation du prix des esclaves', 134.

38. See esp., pp. 121, 127, 188, 192, for discussion of the methods used by masters to try to overcome their agency problem. Conversely, given the argument above that economies of scale were absent in production, I am unpersuaded that the fact that slaves could be concentrated made for higher productivity per head—which is implied in Terray's pioneering discussion ('Réflections sur la formation du prix des esclaves', 130–31). Indeed, if there was such a productivity advantage, and it was big enough to reduce significantly the cost of producing goods, one would expect slave prices to have been substantially higher than they were.

39. See Table 8.1 and Appendix to Ch. 6.

40. Rattray Papers, MS 106, 2032.

41. Cardinall, *The Gold Coast, 1931*, 78.

42. Freeman, *Travels and Life in Ashanti*, 489.

43. Great Britain, *Annual Report on the Social and Economic Progress of the People of the Gold Coast, 1936–7* (London, 1937), 23. Similar sentences appear in the reports for 1935–6 (p. 22) and 1937–8 (p. 32).

44. ARG 1/2/30/1/2: Petition of 'Kings, Chiefs and Head men of Adansi' to Governor, Fomena, 30 Nov. 1906.

45. Domar, 'Causes of slavery or serfdom', 19.

46. Introduced in Chapter 2, pp. 30–31.

47. ARG 1/2/30/1/2, Petition of 'Kings, Chiefs and Head men of Adansi' to Governor, Fomena, 30 Nov. 1906.

48. ARG 1/2/30/1/2, 'Executive Instructions with Regard to "Pawns" and "Slaves" in Ashanti', anonymous and n.d., but probably Nov. or Dec. 1907.

49. BMA, D1, 86, N. V. Asare, 'Annual Report about Kumase Congregation', Kumase, 20 March 1907.

50. See Ellis, *Peasant Economics*, 151–2; Kaushik Basu, *Agrarian Structure and Economic Underdevelopment* (Chur, Switzerland, 1990), 72–73.

51. 'Executive Instructions', cf. in the same file, C. H. Armitage, Ag CCA, to Ag Colonial Secretary, Kumasi, 20 May 1908.

Chapter 9

1. Arhin, 'Succession and gold mining', 107.

2. See pp. 107–10.

3. Coppin's Journal, Book VI 29.

4. Ibid., 30.

5. Ibid., 29.

6. Quoted above, 108.

7. While the Igbo case was different again. See Robin Law, 'Introduction', to Law (ed.), *From Slave Trade to 'Legitimate' Commerce*, 18–19, and the chapters by Law and by Susan Martin in the same volume.

8. Outlined above, pp. 13, 90–91, 94.

9. Barter, 'Notes on Ashanti', 453.

10. Arhin, 'Peasants in 19th-century Asante', 473.

11. Ibid., albeit not citing sources specifically for the period. In the mid-1940s Fortes noted the frequent sight of meals being carried from wives' houses to their husbands' houses (Fortes et al., 'Ashanti Survey, 1945–6', 168).

12. Arhin, 'Succession and gold mining', 107.

13. Jack Goody, *Production and Reproduction: a Comparative Study of the Domestic Domain* (Cambridge, 1976); quotation from p. 20.

14. Rattray, *Ashanti Law*, 336.

15. I owe my information on this case to the generosity of Jean Allman, who found it in MRO, Yaa Bosuo v. Odikro Kwabena Nketia, in the Kumasihene's court, 24 Jan. 1929, on appeal from the Gyasi tribunal. I base the approximate dating on the fact that Akosua Krah reached puberty shortly before ' "the Kokofu rising" ': presumably a reference to the final phase of the civil war, in 1888, when Kokofuhene Osei Asibe fought for the Golden Stool for himself (see Wilks, *Asante*, 578–82).

16. For Atipimoa see p. 144. For other examples of female pawn-takers see NAGK D1573 'Return of a Girl', Fell to CCA, Sunyani, 12 July 1910 and ARG 1/2/30/1/2, Ag. CWPA to Ag. CCA, Sunyani, 22 Jan. 1908. For female pawn-givers see McCaskie, 'State and society, marriage and adultery', 494 and NAGK RAO Files on Shelves 12 and 13, No. 80 (Ashanti M.P. 274/06), 'Kobina Nkrumah, Kumasi, 29th April 1906, Requesting Return of His Daughter', statement by Chief Kofi Mintah before DC of Southern Ashanti at Fomena, 18 May 1906. On both see ARG 1/2/30/1/7.

17. See pp. 107–10.

18. The children would still belong to the mother's lineage not to the father's. It is possible, however, that a debt owed to the father by his wife's *abusua* strengthened his rights over the children, providing the parental relationship was pawn-marriage rather than pawn-concubinage (Rattray, *Ashanti Law*, 50n, 52).

19. Ibid., 48–52.

20. Terray, 'Captivité', 440.

21. Rattray Papers, MS 107:1, p. 1647 (my interpolations). For some reason this passage is crossed out, but otherwise looks like any other of his notes. It is not clear who his informant was, but from the position of the note in the sequence the interview appears to have taken place on Mampon lands in 1925.

22. Rattray, *Ashanti Law*, 39.

23. Ibid., 39.

24. Wilson, *Western Africa*, 181.

25. LaTorre, 'Wealth Surpasses', 138, citing his 1975 interview in Amoafo.

26. Daaku (ed.), *Oral Traditions of Adanse*, 22 (Fomena), 277 (Hweremoase).

27. *ARA for 1898*, 225–26 (quotation on 225).

28. Ibid., 226.

29. Maurice, *The Ashantee War*, 271.

30. See pp. 131–32.

31. I excluded the pawns identified by the Ashanti Social Survey's study of marriage, since by its nature it would have identified only female pawns. Any husbands who had been pawns would probably have been redeemed or redeemed themselves before marriage. In any case, within the Asante institutional context, their pawning would not have been part of the marriage arrangements, and therefore would have been outside the scope of the enquiry.

32. The following improves upon the preliminary results presented in Austin, 'Human pawning in Asante', 127–28.

33. The following pawns: Mose ('Autobiographical Reminiscences', transl. by D. Maier-Weaver, 20); Enieni and Kwaku Ntwiaa (McCaskie, 'State and society, marriage and adultery', 493–94); Kwesi Dwamena (ARG 1/2/30/1/7); the father of the late Nana Opoku Akumiah, former Krontihene of Bekwai, sent by Omanhene of Bekwai to be pawned to chief of Elmina to finance purchase of guns and ammunition to fight the Adanses [1886] (AF: Nana Akumiah in conversation, 27 Aug. 1982); Kojo Mensah, Bohah, Osei Yaw, Kwasi Adai, Kwaku Jemfi (ARG 1/2/30/1/5).

34. Dufie (Asante Collective Biography Career Sheet 68, prepared by I. Wilks, *Asantesem* 10 [1979], 37); Yaa Odom (McCaskie, 'State and society, marriage and adultery', 493–4); Atta (once or twice) and in the second transaction (which may in fact have been outright sale: see below), Amba N'sia (ARG 1/2/30/1/7); an unnamed paternal aunt of the late Nana Opoku Akumiah, former Krontihene of Bekwai, sent by Omanhene of Bekwai to be pawned to chief of Elmina to finance purchase of guns and ammunition to fight the Adanses [1886] (AF: notes on conversation with Nana Akumiah, 27 Aug. 1982); young woman redeemed from pawnage by Kwadwo Donko, as noted in Chapter 7 above; Akua Addy (twice, if the payment of her redemption money by the man who then became her husband, Akwesi Kwatchie, was payment of head money, so that their relationship should therefore be regarded as pawn marriage—which seems the most likely interpretation): NAGA 53/4/1 Obuasi Civil RB 1904–7, pp. 87–92, Akwesi Kwatchie v. Akwa N'bu, 15 Oct. 1904); Amankwa, Kra Montrisu, Eku [Akua] (ARG 1/2/30/1/5).

35. Kwadwo Donko's future wife; and those cited above from ADM 53/4/1, pp. 87–92 and ARG 1/2/30/1/5.

36. ARG 1/2/30/1/2, C. H. Armitage, memo. to CCA, quoted in Fuller's memo. to Ag. Governor, 5 Aug. 1905.

37. Rattray, *Ashanti Law*, 48.

38. ARG 1/2/30/1/: the quotation is from K. Fosu's statement of 21 March 1908.

39. Another possibility is that the supply of female pawns was indeed more elastic than that of males, but not by enough to be reflected in 'price' differences. This is possible if market valuations tended to be rounded to relatively large monetary units, as suggested in Chapter 7. In this context, marginal preferences for pawns of one sex rather than the other would not often be expressed in 'price'. It is more likely that they would have resulted in differences in the relative number of males and females pawned; but differences too slight to be reflected in the very crude quantitative picture that emerges from the data I have assembled.

40. Cf. Rattray, *Ashanti Law*, 52.

41. For both sides of this issue see Paul E. Lovejoy and Toyin Falola (eds.), *Pawnship, Slavery, and Colonialism* (Trenton NJ, and Asmara, 2003).

Chapter 10

1. I put this case first in Austin, 'Human pawning in Asante'.

2. Arhin, 'Market settlements', 144–45.

3. Terray, 'La captivité', 402.

4. Arhin, 'Market settlements', 144–45. Arhin did not specify that the lenders he described were commoners, but this seems clear from context.

5. G. C. Musgrave, *To Kumassi with Scott* (London, 1896), 117.

6. On Asante participation in that trade see LaTorre, 'Wealth Surpasses', 421–35.

7. Ibid., 425–27, 439–43. As LaTorre notes, Gold Coast slave prices recovered somewhat after c.1820, but on his data they seem never to have returned to their levels of c.1770–1807.

8. On commoners' acquisition of slaves see pp. 117–19, 124; on commoners' general acquisition of wealth, see 13, 90–91, 94.

9. Arhin, 'Market settlements', 144–45.

10. Fortes Papers, 8.2 Supplementary Ntes on Marriage and Divorce Questionnaire. The Twi sentence has a range of closely-related possible meanings. I am grateful to the following native speakers for assistance with this: Ayowa Africa's mother, and at the University of Ghana Dr Amos Anyimadu and Professor Kwasi Yankah, who supplied the translation finally used here.

11. Bowdich, *Mission*, 317.

12. As with the title of *safohene* which in Adanse was conferred on commoners who made fortunes. In the specific case mentioned in Daaku's collection of oral traditions and testimonies, that of Kwame Akowuah, the honour was awarded 'after the white men came' (Daaku, *Oral Traditions of Adanse*, 362). But the same title had been awarded before colonial rule to Kwame Akore (ibid., 348), and presumably the same adultery fee privilege came with it.

13. See above, p. 113.

14. See appendix to ch. 6.

15. For the late precolonial period see: Arhin, 'Market settlements', 144; Arhin, 'Succession and gold mining', 107. For the early colonial years see ARG 1/2/30/1/2, Soden to CCA, Obuasi, 11 Dec. 1906.

16. An example of this will be given in Section B (p. 195).

17. For the evidence of importation by these two means see Maier, 'Military acquisition'.

18. Bowdich, 'Remarks on civilisation in Africa', 18.

19. Oddly, in his pioneering study of Akan slavery, Norman Klein interpreted Bowdich's reference to the dispersal of slaves surplus to the export (or re-export) trade in the 1810s as evidence of 'the beginnings of the large-scale spread of "domestic slavery"', though he recognised that the 'breakup of the system of state slavery did not follow immediately', (A. Norman Klein, 'Inequality in Asante: A Study of the Forms and Meanings of Slavery and Social Servitude in Pre- and Early Colonial Akan-Asante Society and Culture' [Ph.D. thesis, University of Michigan, 1980], 2 vols, I, 99, 127). But there is no suggestion in Bowdich (or other sources) that chiefs' slave-holding declined in absolute terms: on the contrary. I agree with Klein that the post-1807 period saw the beginning of (or at least a great increase in) widespread small-scale, commoner ('domestic') slave-holding (see, further, ibid., Chs 4, 5). But, as indicated in the text, I do not base this on the Bowdich quotation. For overviews of Klein's analysis see his 'West African unfree labor before and after the rise of the Atlantic slave trade', in L. Foner and E. Genovese (eds), *Slavery in the New World: A Reader in Comparative History* (Englewood Cliffs NJ, 1969), 87–95; and Klein, 'The two Asantes: competing interpretations of "slavery" in Akan-Asante culture and society', in P. Lovejoy (ed.), *The Ideology of Slavery in Africa* (Beverly Hills, 1981), 149–67.

20. Bowdich, *Mission*, 259.

21. Ibid., 259; see further, McCaskie, 'State and society, marriage and adultery', 490–91, and Jean Allman, 'Adultery and the state in Asante: reflections on gender, class, and power from 1800 to 1950', in J. Hunwick and N. Lawler (eds), *The Cloth of Many Colored Silks: Papers on History and Society Ghanaian and Islamic in Honor of Ivor Wilks* (Evanston, 1996), 34–35.

22. Allman, 'Adultery and the state', 33–37.

23. McCaskie, 'State and society, marriage and adultery', 490–91; cf. Barter, 'Notes on Ashanti', 453.

24. Bowdich, *Mission*, 295.

25. His emphasis. T. B. Freeman, 'Reminiscences and incidents', p. 38b.

26. Wilks, 'Space, time, and "human sacrifice"', 221, 227. As a correspondent of *The Times* of London commented, more generally, ' "human sacrifice . . . is, granting the theory on which it is based, a most rational custom" ' (Winwood Reade, *The Story of the Ashantee Campaign* [London, 1874], 360–61, quoted by Wilks, ibid., 226).

27. Wilks, 'Asante: human sacrifice or capital punishment?', 448.

28. Ibid., 449.

29. McCaskie, *State and Society*, 297.

30. This general proposition is put forward by Wilks, 'Asante: human sacrifice or capital punishment?', 449–51. I inserted the qualifier 'hard-working' in view of McCaskie's observation referenced in the preceding note.

31. Austin, 'Between abolition and jihad', 102–3.

32. See pp. 143, 144.

33. Kyei, *Our Days Dwindle*, 88, 89.

34. For a major statement see Igor Kopytoff and Suzanne Miers, 'African "slavery" as an institution of marginality', in Miers and Kopytoff (eds), *Slavery in Africa: Historical and Anthropological Perspectives* (Madison, 1977).

35. A. N. Klein, 'Inequality in Asante', I: the longer quotation is from p. 237, while his Ch. 3 is devoted to 'state slavery'.

36. Cf. Paul E. Lovejoy, 'Fugitive slaves: resistance to slavery in the Sokoto Caliphate', in Gary Y. Okihiro (ed.), *In Resistance: Studies in African, Caribbean, and Afro-American History* (Amherst, 1986), 71–95.

37. Implied in Terray's hypothesis, discussed later in this chapter, that the weaker the coercive power of the slave-holding state, the more assimilative the form of slavery it practised.

38. Rattray, *Ashanti Law*, 48n.

39. Ibid., 44, 48, 52.

40. Ibid., 44.

41. Ibid., 51.

42. A. A. Y. Kyerematen, 'Ashanti Royal Regalia: their history and functions' (University of Oxford D.Phil. thesis, 1966), 90, quoted in Wilks, *Asante*, 693.

43. ARG 1/2/30/1/2, Petition of the Omanhin and Chiefs of Mansu Nkwanta, 19 Feb. 1908.

44. Rattray Papers, MS 107:3, p. 1807; cf. Rattray, *Ashanti Law*, 50–51.

45. Ibid., 51; Rattray Papers, MS 107:3, p. 1951.

46. Rattray Papers, MS 107:3, p. 1951.

47. Rattray, *Ashanti Law*, 51.

48. On the issue of whether, and if so in what sense, functionalism was an instrument of colonial rule in Asante see von Laue, 'Anthropology and power: R. S. Rattray among the Ashanti'. For an impassioned rejection of any suggestion of colonial government influence on the content of anthropologists' output, see Meyer Fortes, 'The prologue: family studies in Ghana 1920–1970', in C. Oppong (ed.), *Domestic Rights and Duties in Southern Ghana* (Legon, 1974), 4–5.

49. ARG 1/2/30/1/2, C. H. Armitage, DC of Bekwai, Memo. to CCA, quoted in full in CCA to Ag. Governor, 'Memorandum in Connection with Domestic Slavery', 5 Aug. 1905.

50. Rattray, *Ashanti Law*, 38.

51. See Poku, 'Traditional roles and people of slave origin', 36–37.

52. NAGK Bekwai DAO File 39, 'Native Tribunal Ohene of Essumeja' (54/1927), Nana Kobina Karikari, Esumejahene, and elders to DC, Esumeja, 26 Nov. 1931. The loan was 'still outstanding'. A possible alternative interpretation is that the owner was obliged to lend the slave the money for the funeral, but this fits less well with the wording ('Kwesi Kyei was compelled by the said Yao Krah to raise loan of £10 for the purpose of making her funeral custom'). It seems most likely that the reference to the loan being outstanding was meant with the sense of Kyei having been unable to repay it. This would highlight what the authors evidently considered as the unfairness of Kyei being denied head money.

53. Bowdich, *Mission*, 260.

54. Rattray, *Ashanti Law*, 42.

55. See pp. 118–19.

56. Wilks, *Asante*, 86.

57. LaTorre, 'Wealth Surpasses', 96.

58. K. Poku, 'Traditional roles and people of slave origin', 35–36. One hears anecdotally of occasional cases where practice is said to have departed from the rule (as was illustrated by ibid., 37).

59. Ibid., 36–38.

60. A detailed account is provided by Akosua A. Perbi, 'A History of Indigenous Slavery in Ghana from the 15th to the 19th Centuries' (Ph.D., University of Ghana, 1997).

61. Wilks, *Asante*, 461–63, 464n. The quotation is from Asantehene Osei Agyeman Prempeh II in an interview with Wilks in 1958, quoted in ibid., 461.

62. Fortes Papers, 9.2, 'Akyinakrom. Donkor. Land': 'The reason why Fathers are inherited by their sister's sons' by Samuel Fosuhene, Wesley College, Kumasi, 30 Aug. 1945.

63. Wilks, 'Golden stool', 8–16; LaTorre, 'Wealth Surpasses', 99–104; Austin, 'Rural Capitalism', 196–98.

64. Malcolm D. McLeod, 'Gifts and attitudes', in E. Schildkrout (ed.), *The Golden Stool: Studies of the Asante Center and Periphery* (New York, 1987), 189–90.

65. Wilks, 'Golden stool', 5. In reporting his fieldwork referred to above, Arhin observed that for the late nineteenth century that 'what the older Ashanti regarded as the real measure of wealth' was 'his hoard of gold dust' ('Market settlements', 145).

66. Wilks, 'Golden Stool', 7.

67. Amit Bhadhuri, 'On the formation of usurious interest rates in backward agriculture', *Cambridge Journal of Economics*, 1 (1977), 341–52. However, Bhadhuri's explanation of this phenomenon, which is based on his idea that the creditor undervalues the security, is different from the one advanced here.

68. Rattray Papers: MS 107:4, p. 1950. Cf. Rattray, *Religion and Art*, 78.

69. Rattray Papers, MS 107:3, p.1803, testimony of K. S[apon]. Cf. Rattray, *Ashanti Law*, 50.

70. Rattray, *Ashanti Law*, 21, 37.

71. On a related issue, Orlando Patterson in *Slavery and Social Death: a Comparative Study* (Cambridge MA., 1982) relies on Rattray for his account of pawning in Asante (p. 124). His general view, which he applies specifically to Asante, is that debt-bondage becomes true slavery if the debt is not repaid. This overlooks the fact that however old the debt became, it remained alive. Asante was a major exception to Patterson's view that debt-servitude was 'almost never inherited by the debtor's children' (p. 9). As noted above, *awowa* status certainly could be inherited, by children, nephews and nieces within the same *abusua*. Since second-generation non-slave pawns were, by definition, performing a duty to their matrilineages, in turn they continued to await redemption by their kin. Thus, the pawn too remained socially 'alive', in contrast to the position of slaves (such as *nnɔnkɔfɔ*) who, as Patterson memorably put it, characteristically suffered 'natal alienation' and 'social death' (ibid., pp. 5–8). On the other hand, an *abusua* that despaired of raising the money to redeem a pawned member had the option of selling her or him (see immediately below).

72. ARG 1/2/30/1/7.

73. Rattray, *Ashanti Law*, 53.

74. Ibid., 37; Rattray Papers: MS 107:3, pp. 1807–8.

75. Rattray, *Ashanti Law*, 53.

76. NAGA ADM 53/4/1 Obuasi Civil Record Book 1904–7, pp. 156–57: Yao Donkor v. Eduo Acheampong, 20 Dec. 1904.

77. The quotation is from 'Hutchinson's Diary' in Bowdich, *Mission*, 379.

78. Ibid., 381–82.

79. Bowdich, 'Remarks on civilisation in Africa', 18.

80. Ibid., 18–19.

81. Klein, 'Inequality in Asante', I, 99.

82. Bowdich, *Mission*, 149–50.

83. Ibid., 119–20. See Wilks's comments in *Asante*, 706–9.

84. On those motives see Wilks, *Asante*, 529–39, 701–3, 709–11; Austin, ' "No elders were present" ', 22–26.

85. See p. 123.

86. Wilks, 'Asante: human sacrifice or capital punishment?', 449–50; largely reproduced in 'Space, time, and "human sacrifice" ', 224.

87. Bobieh (ARG 1/2/30/1/5), esp. K. Fosu's statement of 21 March 1908); Yaa Penim (PRAAD Accra ADM 53/4/1 Obuasi Civil RB 1904–7, p. 279, Kwesi Mpong v. Kofi Berukyi, 25 July 1905); and an anonymous pawn from Gyaman (NAGK D2593 'Respecting Redemption', Minute for CCA to CWPA, [Kumasi], 28 Jan. 1909).

88. Rattray, *Ashanti Law*, 55.

89. See p. 14.

90. NAGK Obuasi DAO File 16, 'Kumasi Villages in S. D. A.', DC Ashanti (CCA's Office) to CSPA, Kumasi, 9 March 1909.

91. See, e.g., Rattray, *Ashanti Law*, 132–33.

92. See Terray, 'La captivité', 444.

93. Nieboer, *Slavery as an Industrial System*, 423 (in 1910 edn, 422).

94. Meillassoux, *The Anthropology of Slavery*, 307–8; Martin Klein, *Slavery and Colonial Rule in French West Africa*, 13, 263.

95. As seems to have happened (see p.121 [and 104]).

96. See p. 144.

97. See p. 141.

98. See Wilks, *Asante*, 636–37, 651–54. Whether the political conditions for the scale of investment required for railway-building could have been brought about in a still-independent Asante state is beyond the scope of this study.

PART 4

1. In contrast to a lengthy series of publications on the ending of slavery in the Gold Coast Colony (for a merely illustrative, partial list ch. 13, n.6), published work on the ending of slavery in Asante is limited to a 5-page section of Dumett and Johnson's 1988 essay 'Britain and the suppression of slavery' in Ghana as a whole (a section based largely on my own PhD thesis of 1984, as they graciously made clear), and to Akosua Perbi, 'The abolition of domestic slavery by Britain: Asante's dilemma', *Legon Journal of the Humanities* 6 (1992), 1–23. The decline of pawning has been discussed in Austin, 'Human pawning in Asante', 137–44.

Chapter 11

1. See pp. 24–25, cf. p. 27.

2. E.g. C. Harrison, T. W. Ingawa and S. M. Martin, 'The establishment of colonial rule in West Africa', in J. F. Ade Ajayi and Michael Crowder (eds), *History of West*

Africa, II (2nd edn: Harlow, 1987), 511, 513; Richard Roberts and Suzanne Miers, 'The end of slavery in Africa', in Miers and Roberts (eds), *The End of Slavery in Africa* (Madison, 1988), 21, 27; Phillips, *Enigma of Colonialism*, 28–29; Patrick Manning, *Slavery and African Life* (Cambridge, 1990), 161–62; and most fully, Paul E. Lovejoy and Jan S. Hogendorn, *Slow Death for Slavery: the Course of Abolition in Northern Nigeria, 1897–1936* (Cambridge, 1993), 27–29, 65–97.

3. NAGK Bekwai File 21, 'Kokofu and Dadiase Riots', Treaty of Friendship and Protection between Britain and Kokofu, 10 Feb. 1896: the other treaties are identical on this point.

4. ARG 1/2/30/1/2, Fuller to Ag Governor, 5 Aug. 1905, 'Memorandum in Connection with Domestic Slavery in Ashanti'.

5. Ibid., Minute by Ag Attorney-General to CS, 14 May 1907, forwarded in CS to CCA, 22 May 1907.

6. Ibid., Fuller to CS, 1 July 1907.

7. Implied by Armitage in his memo. Quoted by Fuller, 'Memorandum in Connection with Domestic Slavery in Ashanti'.

8. Brown, 'Kumasi, 1896–1923', 52, citing NAGK SCT 204/1, Cantonment Magistrate's Court, Reg. vs. Asari Kouko, 23 Aug. 1898.

9. For a full account see Austin, 'Rural Capitalism', 471–85.

10. ARG 1/2/30/1/2, 'Instructions with regard to PAWNS and DOMESTIC SLAVES in Ashanti', enclosed in Ag CS to CCA, Accra, 17 June 1908. They were circulated around the administration in Ashanti via CCA to PCs and others, Kumasi, 22 June 1908.

11. Gold Coast Government *Gazette*, July–December 1930. See further Perbi, 'History of Indigenous Slavery in Ghana', 324–29; John Grace, *Domestic Slavery in West Africa with particular reference to the Sierra Leone Protectorate, 1896–1927* (London, 1975), 255n.

12. ARG 1/2/30/1/12 'Return of Salome Akosua Dua and her children to Kripe': CCA to Rev. Otto Schimming, Abetifi, 15 Feb. 1910. Fuller's emphasis.

13. *ARA for 1908*, 25.

14. ARG 1/2/30/1/12: CCA to Rev. Otto Schimming, Abetifi, 15 Feb. 1910.

15. ARG 1/2/30/1/2 DC Obuasi to CCA, 13 Sept. 1907.

16. Ibid., Ag CCA, draft 'Executive Instructions with regard to "Pawns" and "Slaves" in Ashanti', enclosed in Ag CCA to Major Bryan, Ag Governor, 3 Feb. 1908.

17. ARG 1/2/30/1/2, Ag CCA to Ag CS, 20 May 1908.

18. As n. 4 above.

19. By this time it seems that administrators, at least within the Gold Coast and Ashanti, could write to each other in the confidence that their correspondence would not be published in the British parliamentary papers, as had been the case in the preceding era of remarkably 'open' government.

20. PRO CO96/258 W. E. Maxwell to Lord Ripon, Accra, 13 June 1895.

21. This was in line with at least some of the advice he got from within the Colonial Office. See Lewin, *Asante Before the British*, 188–89.

22. CO96/258 J. Chamberlain to Maxwell, 6 Sept. 1895.

23. CO96/260 'Instructions for Captain Stewart and Mr. Vroom' by Maxwell, Cape Coast, 23 Sept. 1895, encl. in Maxwell to Chamberlain, 26 Sept. 1895 (which also encloses Maxwell to 'King of Kumasi', 23 Sept. 1895).

24. CO96/359 Hodgson to Chamberlain, Kumasi, 16 April 1900; BMA, D1, 73c, 'Short Report about our Mission to Nkoranza in the present Rising', by J. A. Hanson,

Catechist, Nkoranza-Obo, 20 Sept. 1900; and 73c, Perregaux to Law(?) [from content of letter, evidently addressee was a British officer or official], Abetifi, 12 June 1900.

25. ARG 1/2/30/1/2, Fuller, Memo. on Domestic Slavery, 5 Aug. 1905.

26. Ibid., Fuller to Governor, Minute, 12 Dec. 1905.

27. Ibid., Soden to CCA, Obuasi, 11 Dec. 1906.

28. Ibid., CCA to CS, 18 April 1907.

29. He gave an account of his experiences in Armitage and Montanaro, *The Ashanti Campaign of 1900*. He actually led the expedition which attempted to find and capture the Golden Stool, in implementation of the governor's demand for its surrender: the provocation which precipitated the rising.

30. ARG 1/2/30/1/2, Armitage, Ag CCA, to Ag CS, Kumasi, 20 May 1906.

31. NAGK D3 Ag CS, Minute, 3 July 1908. This document is reproduced in Arhin, 'Some Asante views of colonial rule', 74.

32. ARG 1/2/30/1/2 Soden to CCA, Obuasi, 11 Dec. 1906.

33. Ibid., CCA to Ag CS, 1 Nov. 1907.

34. Ibid., Fuller, Memo. on Domestic Slavery, 5 Aug. 1905; cf. Fuller to CS, Kumasi, 18 April 1907.

35. Ibid., Armitage to Major Bryan, Ag Governor, Kumasi, 5 Jan. 1908: cf. Ag CCA to Ag CS, Kumasi, 20 May 1908.

36. Ibid., Ag CCA to Ag CS, Kumasi, 20 May 1908: cf. Armitage to Major Bryan, Ag Governor, Kumasi, 5 Jan. 1908.

37. Ibid., Ag CCA, draft 'Executive Instructions': cf. Ag CCA to Ag CS, Kumasi, 20 May 1908.

38. Ibid., Soden to CCA, Obuasi, 11 Dec. 1906.

39. Howard Temperley, 'The ideology of antislavery', in David Eltis and James Walvin (eds), *The Abolition of the Atlantic Slave Trade* (Madison, 1981), 29.

40. David Eltis, 'The abolitionist perception of society after slavery', in J. Walvin (ed.), *Slavery and British Society, 1776–1846* (London, 1982), 195–213, 255–62; Seymour Drescher, 'Abolitionist expectations: Britain', in Howard Temperley (ed.), *After Slavery: Emancipation and its Discontents* (London, 2000), 41–66.

41. *ARA for 1897*, 84.

42. Ibid.

43. PRAAD Accra ADM 46/1/1, pp. 270, 277: Davidson-Houston to CCA, Moinsi Hill, 16 May 1903; Davidson-Houston to Kokofuhene, 22 May 1903.

44. See pp. 42, 218.

45. See pp. 42, 112.

46. The text is reprinted in G. St. J. Orde Browne, *The African Labourer* (London, 1967: 1st edn, 1933), 216–17.

47. On the convention see Cooper, *Decolonization and African Society*, 29–30; for the Gold Coast Colony see Kwabena Opare Akurang-Parry, 'Colonial forced labor policies for road-building in southern Ghana and international anti-forced labor pressures, 1900–1940', *African Economic History* 28 (2000), 1–25.

48. Gold Coast, *The Laws of the Gold Coast 1936* (4 vols), (Accra, 1937), I, 1142.

49. Quoted by Akurang-Parry, 'Colonial forced labor policies for road-building', 24–25.

50. This logic was set out clearly, and largely explicitly, in a long memo by the Ag Commissioner of Central Province in the Gold Coast Colony. PRAAD Accra ADM 11/1/1058 'Forced Labour', Lynch to Secretary of Native Affairs, Cape Coast, 29 Aug. 1930.

51. PRO CO96/826/7, note by G. Foggon for proposed meeting with Mr Gbedemah, 18 July 1951; CO96/826/8, Foggon to M. Tennant, London 22 Aug. 1951, encl. revised CO memo. on 'Direction of Labour'. The July document is reproduced in Richard Rathbone (ed.), *Ghana* (British Documents on the End of Empire. Series B, Vol. I, 2 parts), Part 1 (London, 1995), 347–50.

Chapter 12

1. E.g., see Poku, 'Traditional roles and people of slave origin', 36.

2. Relatedly, at the beginning of the 1970s church elders in Asante Akyem were prepared to acknowledge that many of the original members were former slaves, but 'clearly did not feel it an appropriate subject for insertion in a published history' of their church (Paul Jenkins, 'A comment on M. P. Frempong's history of the Presbyterian church at Bompata', *Ghana Notes and Queries*, June 1972, 26).

3. Poku, 'Traditional roles and people of slave origin', 36. See also pp. 115, 118–19 above.

4. Perbi, 'Abolition of domestic slavery', 17–18.

5. Poku, 'Traditional roles and people of slave origin', 36–37.

6. Ibid., 36–37; Perbi, 'Abolition of domestic slavery', 16–17.

7. See the observations on this repository above, p. 17.

8. Jenkins, 'Comment on M. P. Frempong's history of the Presbyterian church at Bompata', 26.

9. Roberts and Miers, 'End of slavery in Africa', 54.

10. *ARA for 1908*, 223.

11. *ARA for 1897*, 84.

12. PRAAD Accra ADM 52/5/6, Ejura (Mampong) District RB, Jan. 1912 to May 1923, entry on food supplies initialled by Rattray, 1912.

13. *ARA for 1898*, 223. See also Robert Earl Hamilton, 'Asante, 1895–1900: prelude to war', Ph.D. dissertation (Northwestern University, 1978), 337–38, 352–53.

14. CO96/359 Hodgson to Chamberlain, Kumasi, 16 April 1900. For a detailed description of the colonial government's forced labour regime in these years see Hamilton, 'Asante, 1895–1900', 345–50, 353–64.

15. See p. 212.

16. Quoted in *ARA for 1923–24*, 26.

17. *ARA for 1923–24*, 25.

18. PRAAD Sunyani RG 2/1/2 'Tributes General', Ohene Yeboa Yaw to DC Sunyani, Boma 14 Dec. 1926.

19. On the spread of cocoa production see p. 50.

20. NAGK D651 'Motor Roads Constructed By Chiefs—As to Government Monetary Assistance': CCA to Colonial Secretary, 3 May 1917.

21. See p. 213.

22. See pp. 107, 110.

23. ARG 9/7/2 'Labour Complaints', Ag DC to CCA, Bekwai, 17 Aug. 1940.

24. See ARG 9/7/2: DC to CCA, Bekwai, May [no date given] 1946.

25. PRAAD Accra ADM 46/1/1 Moinsi Hill/Kwissa Duplicate Letter Book (DLB) 1902–4, pp. 262–63, C. H. Harper, Assistant (Asst) DC, Saltpond to DC, Cape Coast,

Saltpond, 9 April 1903; and enclosed statements by King Kofi Ahinkora, Akyem Swedru, 5 April 1903, and by Kofi Akinkora and Kobina Atchempon, 9 April 1903.

26. ADM 46/1/1, p. 261, Davidson-Houston to CCA, Moinsi Hill, 9 May 1903.

27. Ibid., p. 290, Davidson-Houston to King of Bekwai, Moinsi Hill, 1 June 1903.

28. See pp. 141–42.

29. As Armitage noted (ARG 1/2/30/1/2 DC Obuasi to CCA, 13 Sept. 1907).

30. BMA: 'Unermartetes Entftehen eines Sklavenheims' ('The unexpected origin of a hostel for slaves'), *Der Sklavenfreund* 13 (March 1897), 129–36 (quotations from p. 130 and 133 respectively). The translation here is by Veit Arlt (University of Basel).

31. To judge from later items in the BMA, and from the fact that the government's annual report on Asante for 1898 stated that 'we have been able to send' to the Basel Mission's slave-home 'all the children taken from the slave dealers', but gave the number of children currently in the home as 25 plus two young men, representing the opposite of an increase on the original level. The report stated that a grand total of 25 women had been sent there: implying at most one addition since the start (*ARA for 1898*, 225–26: quotation at p. 225).

32. Ibid., 223.

33. Dumett and Johnson, 'Britain and the suppression of slavery', 102–3, 105.

34. *ARA for 1898*, 221.

35. ARG 1/2/30/1/2, Adanse petition.

36. Daaku, *Oral Traditions of Adanse*, 14.

37. AF: interview with Opanyin Kofi Agyepong and Nana Baffuor Asare Bediako, Akwamuhene of Dadiase, Asiwa, 1 Sept. 1982.

38. Dumett and Johnson, 'Britain and the suppression of slavery', 109n.

39. *The African Times* (1 Feb. 1899), 25, quoted by Hamilton, 'Asante, 1895–1900', 350–51, and Klein, 'Inequality in Asante', II, 144–45.

40. Hamilton, 'Asante, 1895–1900', 352.

41. Dumett and Johnson, 'Britain and the suppression of slavery', 100n, citing Gold Coast *Judicial Department Reports* for the years shown.

42. The nature of slave-trading accusations was that the issue before the court was usually not who had committed an undoubted crime, but whether a crime had been committed: whether what the accused had done constituted slave trading.

43. PRO CO98/34 and C098/38: Reports on the Police Department for 1920 (p. 9) and 1923–24 (p. 24) respectively.

44. Gold Coast, *Judicial Department Report for 1909*, 16, quoted in Dumett and Johnson, 'Britain and the suppression of slavery', 84.

45. Dumett and Johnson, 'Britain and the suppression of slavery', 100n, citing *Judicial Department Reports*.

46. See, further, Hamilton, 'Asante, 1895–1900', 352. For pre-1896 volumes see pp. 115–17, 122–26.

47. PRAAD Accra ADM 53/1/3 Obuasi DLB 1906, p. 91, Armitage, Commissioner of the Southern District of Ashanti to Adansehene, 30 March 1906.

48. ADM 53/1/11 Obuasi DLB 1912, p. 181, Commissioner of the Southern Province of Ashanti (CSPA) to CCA, 14 May 1912.

49. ARG 1/2/30/1/10 'Forwarding copies of notes of evidence held by Commr: Western Province respecting alleged selling of a woman named Yamankolo in the Wenchi Zongo'.

50. AF: Interview with Mr Kojo Asiedu, Huntado, 11 July 1980.

51. PRAAD Accra ADM 11/975, 'Memorandum on the Vestiges of Slavery in the Gold Coast' by J. C. de Graft-Johnson, Assistant Secretary for Native Affairs (Accra, Oct. 1927), 17.

52. *ARA for 1898*, 224.

53. See p. 206.

54. NAGK D2470 'Requesting Return of Subjects from Akrokerii' (25 Feb.–27 March 1907).

55. PRAAD Accra ADM 46/1/1 Moinsi Hill/Kwissa DLB 1902–4, p. 73, Armitage to Yaw Boakyi, Bekwaihene, Moinsi Hill, 8 July 1902.

56. NAGK D905 'Complaining of His Captive Woman Taken to Wassaw by Certain Men Without His Knowledge': Adjua Badu to Ag CCA, Kumasi, 19 May 1908.

57. D905: Bantamahene Osei Mampon to 'High Commissioner' (sic), Kumasi, 15 and 18 May 1908; Minute by CCA, Fuller, 19 June 1908.

58. ARG 1/2/30/1/8 'Respecting "Slave Dealing" Recently Occurred at Sefwhi (619/08).'

59. *ARA for 1907*, 9.

60. PRAAD Accra ADM 53/1/7 Obuasi DLB 1910, p. 283, Provincial Commissioner (PC), C. Rew, to Bekwaihene, Obuasi, 11 Aug. 1910.

61. ADM 46/5/1, PC's Diary (Southern Province, Obuasi) 1913–17, 25 Oct. 1915. The entry implies, however, that the punishment was imposed primarily because the offender diverted money to this purpose from a public fund in aid of the British war effort.

62. The DC intervened to stop the payments since slavery was illegal: Bekwai File 39, Esumejahene and elders to DC, 26 Nov. 1931, and DC to Esumejahene, 9 Dec. 1931.

63. NAGK RAO Files on Shelves 14 and 15, No. 2041, 'Slavery' (1950), enclosing extract from Chief Commissioner's File 0114.SF1, p. 21: Ag JA [Judicial Advisor?] to Assistant CCA, 31 July 1948.

64. Ibid., Ag JA to Assistant CCA, 31 July 1948.

65. Poku, 'Traditional roles and people of slave origin', 36.

66. ARG 1/2/30/1/9 'Asking that two servants of Akwasi Yesala, who have deserted, should be ordered to return to their master': minute dd. 10 March 1908.

67. An example of this from Huntado, Amansie, will be given below, p. 243.

68. AF: interview with Mr. J. W. Owusu, Bekwai, 30 Sept. 1987.

69. Fortes Papers, 8.9, notes of interview with Queen Mother of Agogo, Jan. 1946.

70. ARG 1/23/30/1/13 'Domestic Slavery', Ag CEPA to CCA, 5 Jan. 1928.

71. Great Britain, *Report on the Legislation Governing the Alienation of Native Lands in the Gold Coast Colony and Ashanti* (the Belfield report), Cd. 6278 (London, 1912), Notes of Evidence, 90.

72. See pp. 57–59.

73. Belfield, *Report*, Notes of Evidence, 88–89, 97–98.

74. Johnson, 'Elephants for want of towns'.

75. AF: interview with Opanyin Kofi Agyepong and Nana Baffuor Asare Bediako, Akwamuhene of Dadiase, Asiwa, 1 Sept. 1982.

76. PRAAD Accra Obuasi DLB 1905–6, C. H. Armitage, DC to CCA, 1905 (day and month illegible).

77. See p. 119–20.

78. De Graft-Johnson's 'Memorandum on the Vestiges of Slavery' (cited above, 508 n. 51), 14.

79. Akosua Perbi, 'Abolition of domestic slavery', 10.

80. ARG 1/2/30/1/12. Quotation from Rev. Otto Schimming to CCA, Abetifi 14 Jan. 1910.

81. ARG 1/2/30/1/9. The quotations are from Yesireh to CCA, Kumasi 1 July 1908.

82. Ibid.

83. Perbi, 'Abolition of domestic slavery', 10.

84. For the Gold Coast Colony see Dumett and Johnson, 'Britain and the suppression of slavery', 94–5, 106. For cases elsewhere in Africa see E. Adeniyi Oroge, '*Iwofa*: an historical survey of the Yoruba institution of indenture', *African Economic History* 14 (1985), 75–106 (reprinted in P. Lovejoy and T. Falola [eds], *Pawnship, Slavery, and Colonialism in Africa* [Trenton NJ and Asmara, 2003]). See the comments of Toyin Falola and Paul E. Lovejoy, 'Pawnship in historical perspective', in Falola and Lovejoy (eds), *Pawnship in Africa*, 18–20 (reprinted in Lovejoy and Falola [eds], *Pawnship, Slavery, and Colonialism*).

85. See p. 148.

86. NAGK CCA 4/691 'Enquiry Respecting a Boy Kwaku Premang Pawned to Kwasi Adaye for £18 by one Boshi' (Ash.M.P.605/07); PRAAD Accra ADM 53/4/1 Obuasi Civil RB 1904–7, pp. 156–57, Yao Donkor v. Eduo Acheampong, 20 Dec. 1904, and p. 279, Kwesi Mpong v. Kofi Berukyi, 25 July 1905; ADM 53/1/2 Obuasi DLB 1905–6, p. 27, C. H. Armitage, DC, to Omanhene of Kokofu, Obuasi, 26 June 1905; NAGK Obuasi DAO File 26 'Quarterly Intelligence Reports S.P.A.'; RAO Files on Shelves 12 and 13, No. 80 (Ashanti M.P. 274/06), 'Kobina Nkrumah, Kumasi, 29th April 1906, Requesting Return of His Daughter', statement by Chief Kofi Mintah before DC of Southern Ashanti at Fomena, 18 May 1906; ARG 1/2/30/1/2, Ag CWPA to Ag CCA, Sunyani, 22 Jan. 1908 (which includes both the £4 and £32 pawns); D1486 'Complaint from King of Wenchi'; D1573 'Return of a Girl'; ARG 1/2/30/1/7, DC, Kumasi, to DC, Western Ashanti, 16 March 1908; D2593 'Respecting Redemption'.

87. This is especially so in a case mentioned in ch. 7, where we know that redemption was proposed in 1903 but do not know when the pawning took place. The principal quoted in the letter from the DC, who acted as messenger/intermediary, was a mere £6 (albeit at 25 per cent interest) for 'Abina Antu with her two children'.

88. Rattray Papers, MS 107:3, p. 1803.

89. NAGK SCT 205/160, Bekwai Magistrate's Court, Criminal RB, p. 7; D133, Bekwai DC's Diary, 3 Oct. 1930.

90. Fortes Papers, 8.1, incomplete memo. by M. Fortes entitled 'Ashanti Marriage Statistics'.

91. See Lovejoy and Falola (eds.), *Pawnship, Slavery, and Colonialism in Africa*, chs. by Oroge, Byfield, and Falola.

92. Terray, 'La captivité dans le royaume abron du Gyaman', 402–3.

93. See p. 195.

94. See pp. 36, 100–101.

95. Young boy pawned in Kumasi, apparently in 1901 or 1902, by chief of Jiasi to Kwesi Adaye who took him to live in Tekyiman area (NAGK CCA 4/691 'Enquiry Respecting a Boy Kwaku Premang Pawned to Kwasi Adaye for £18 by one Boshi' (Ash.M.P.605/07); Kwame Obenneh and his brother, who was pawned twice (NAGK Obuasi DAO File 26 'Quarterly Intelligence Reports S.P.A.'); Akwasi Ajeiman (NAGK D2593 'Respecting Redemption of Certain Nyami People With Kofi Poku, Subject of Chief Kobina Kokofu' [1909]; Akwesi Nyami and Kobina Nketea, in separate transactions (ARG 1/2/30/1/2, Ag

CWPA to Ag CCA, Sunyani, 22 Jan. 1908); Cobina Piatin (PRAAD Accra ADM 53/1/7 Obuasi DLB 1910, p. 79, Ag CSPA to Omanhene of Adanse, [Obuasi], 29 April 1910).

96. Yaa Penim (PRAAD Accra ADM 53/4/1 Obuasi Civil RB 1904–7, p. 279, Kwesi Mpong v. Kofi Berukyi, 25 July 1905; ADM 53/1/2 Obuasi DLB 1905–6, p. 117, C. H. Armitage to Bekwaihene, Obuasi, 25 July 1905); daughter of Yaw Donkor (ADM 53/4/1 Obuasi Civil RB 1904–7, pp. 156–57, Yao Donkor v. Eduo Acheampong, 20 Dec. 1904); Effia Siriki (NAGK D1486 'Complaint from King of Wenchi Against the King of Kokofu' [1905], and PRAAD Accra ADM 53/1/2 Obuasi DLB 1905–6, p. 27, C. H. Armitage, DC, to Omanhene of Kokofu, Obuasi, 26 June 1905); Akua Addai, Kra, Abena Apete (NAGK D2593 'Respecting Redemption'); Ekua Wusunah (NAGK RAO Files on Shelves 12 and 13, No. 80 [Ash. M.P. 274/06], 'Kobina Nkrumah, Kumasi, 29th April 1906, Requesting Return of His Daughter Ekua Wusunah From Kofi Mintah of Borfi Sangu'); 'two maid servants' belonging to Nsuta Queen Mother's stool (NAGK D2386 'Requesting Return of Two Servants from the King of Nsuta' [1906]); Akua Misa (NAGK D1573 'Return of a Girl' [1910], Fell to CCA, Sunyani, 12 July 1910); Amah Jambea, Ambah ___ [?], Efua Nehifie, Akua Nooa and Awu[?] Oyeh, in a total of at least three separate transactions (ARG 1/2/30/1/2, Ag CWPA to Ag CCA, Sunyani, 22 Jan. 1908); Adjuah Tenene (ARG 1/2/30/1/7); Abina Achiri (PRAAD Accra ADM 53/1/7 Obuasi DLB 1910, p. 42, Ag CSPA to Ag Cantonment Magistrate, [Obuasi], 16 April 1910); Adjuah Poh (ADM 53/1/7, Obuasi DLB 1910, p. 79, Ag CSPA to Omanhene of Adanse, [Obuasi], 29 April 1910).

97. See pp. 177–78.

98. Kyerematen, *Inter-State Boundary Litigation in Ashanti*, 110.

99. ADM 53/1/6 Obuasi DLB 1909–10, p. 211, PC to Adansihene, Obuasi, 12 Aug. 1909. ADM 53/1/7 Obuasi DLB 1910 contains documentation of official enquiries into specific cases of suspected pawning (pp. 42, 79, 91, 192).

100. ARG 1/23/30/1/13, Ag CEPA to CCA, 5 Jan. 1928.

101. Austin, 'Human pawning in Asante', 138, cf. 127. The case concerned is recorded in PRAAD Accra ADM 53/1/7 Obuasi DLB 1910, p. 79, Ag CSPA to Omanhene of Adanse, [Obuasi], 29 April 1910.

102. ARG 1/2/30/1/18 'Pawning of persons as security for debt' (1517). Compared to my preliminary account, the figures below also include an additional case of female pawning, the information on which was kindly provided by Jean Allman: Manhiya Record Office (MRO), Yaa Bosua v. Odikro Kwabena Nketia, in Kumasihene's court, 24 Jan. 1929.

103. The following account is drawn from ibid., Ag DC to CCA, Mampong 5 Oct. 1948.

104. The following description is derived from ibid., Ag DC to CCA, Bekwai, 8 Sept. 1948.

105. As a self-pawned man did in 1905, though his complaint was about the creditor's abuse of the deal rather than about pawning as such (NAGK Obuasi DAO File 26, 'Quarterly Intelligence Reports S.P.A.' [contains several files, in some disorder], untitled sub-file of petitions, Kwamin Obenney to DC, Abodom, 7 Aug. 1905).

106. Grier, 'Pawns, porters, and petty traders', 327; and implied by Amoo, 'Effect of western influence', 235.

107. Fortes, 'Analysis and description', 137, 142–44. Fortes began his Asante fieldwork in 1945.

108. Amoo, 'Effect of western influence', 230.

109. Fortes, 'Analysis and description', 142–43; cf. Amoo, 'Effect of western influence', 230, 235.

110. The male cases are from the 1948 file discussed above. Female cases: Yaa Krah (NAGK D2307 'Re Yaw Poku's Wife (Yaa Krah)' [1919]); niece of Rattray's informant K. S[apon] (Rattray Papers, MS.107:3, p. 1803); 'a female child' pawned in village of Agwafo in Bekwai District (NAGK SCT 205/160, Bekwai Magistrate Court, Criminal RB, p. 7; D133, Bekwai DC's Diary, 3 Oct. 1930); 'two girls from Adumasa' pawned to mother of Mr. J. W. Owusu (AF: interview with Mr. J. W. Owusu, Bekwai, 30 Sept. 1987); Ama Gyanfuah and Afua Marnuh (NAGK Obuasi DAO File No. 1632, 'Kojo Pong's Cocoa Farms 1933'); pawn-wife referred to in Gwendolyn Mikell, *Cocoa and Chaos in Ghana* (New York, 1989), 116–17; daughter of the slave Akosua Krah, allegedly pawned before the influenza pandemic, i.e. 1918 (MRO: Yaa Bosua v. Odikro Kwabena Nketia, in Kumasihene's court, 24 Jan. 1929).

111. Dunn and Robertson, *Dependence and Opportunity*, 360.

112. Fortes Papers, 8.1, incomplete memo. by M. Fortes entitled 'Ashanti Marriage Statistics'.

113. de Graft-Johnson's 'Memorandum on the Vestiges of Slavery', 19.

114. *ARA for 1905*, 17–18.

115. *ARA*s for the years concerned.

116. Kirk-Greene, 'The thin white line', 40.

117. See the tables in Kay, *Political Economy of Colonialism in Ghana* (prepared in collaboration with Stephen Hymer), 334–35, 348, 364.

118. Sir Francis Fuller, *A Vanished Dynasty: Ashanti* (London, 1921), 220.

Chapter 13

1. For a fuller summary of the theory see pp. 27–33 above.

2. Feeny, 'The decline of property rights in man in Thailand, 1800–1913', *Journal of Economic History* 49 (1989), 285–96.

3. Neither 'slave' nor 'pawn' appear in the index to the classic study, Hill's *Migrant Cocoa-Farmers*. They are mentioned in the text, but not as sources of labour. See Gareth Austin, 'Introduction' to 2nd edn of Hill, *Migrant Cocoa-Farmers* (Hamburg and Oxford, 1997), xvii.

4. Allan McPhee, *The Economic Revolution in British West Africa* (London, 2nd edn 1971, with an introduction by A. G. Hopkins: 1st edn, 1926), 252–3.

5. Hopkins, *Economic History*, 228.

6. Gerald M. McSheffrey, 'Slavery, indentured servitude, legitimate trade and the impact of abolition in the Gold Coast, 1874–1901: a reappraisal', *JAH* 24 (1983), 349–68; Dumett and Johnson, 'Britain and the suppression of slavery'. See, further, Kwabena Opare Akurang-Parry, 'Colonial modes of emancipation and African initiatives', *Ghana Studies* 1 (1998), 11–34; Kwabena Opare-Akurang, 'The administration of the abolition laws, African responses and post-proclamation slavery in the Gold Coast, 1874–1940', in S. Miers and M. Klein (eds.), *Slavery and Colonial Rule in Africa* (London, 1999), 149–66; Trevor Getz, 'That Most Perfidious Institution: the slow death of slavery

in nineteenth century Senegal and the Gold Coast' (Ph.D. dissertation, School of Oriental and African Studies, London, 2000); Trevor Getz, 'A "somewhat firm policy": the role of the Gold Coast judiciary in implementing slave emancipation, 1874–1900', *Ghana Studies* 2 (1999), 97–117; Peter Haenger, *Slaves and Slave Holders on the Gold Coast* (eds J. J. Shaffer and Paul E. Lovejoy, transl. Christina Handford) (Basel, 2000).

7. Because cocoa cultivation was so new in Asante we can assume that there were no trees too old to bear, though we could allow a few additional square miles for farms planted in what turned out to be unsuitable locations or which had been abandoned, at least temporarily, because of disease or infestation.

8. NAGK D4B, 'Cacao', Muir to Asst CCA, Kumasi, 28 Jan. 1933.

9. Beckett, *Akokoaso*, 70.

10. Cardinall, *The Gold Coast, 1931*, 90. For a fuller discussion of the variables affecting yield, especially the age of the trees and what we know about them in this geographical and historical setting, see Austin, 'Rural Capitalism', 389–91.

11. Cf. the general comment of Hopkins, *Economic History*, 25–26.

12. *ARA for 1908*, 223.

13. See p. 162.

14. AF: interview with Opanyin Kofi Agyepong and Nana Baffuor Asare Bediako, Akwamuhene of Dadiase, Asiwa, 1 Sept. 1982. For a preliminary account of Dei's role in the spread of cocoa farming to Asante see Austin, 'Rural Capitalism', esp. 225, 228, 229, 250–52, 308.

15. AF: interview with Nana Kojo Appiah Darko II, Regent of Manso Nkwanta, Manso Nkwanta, 23 July 1980.

16. AF: interview with Nana Kofi Agyeamang, former Omanhene, Esumeja, 5 May 1980.

17. MRO Kumasi State Council RB No. 10, Case of Opanyin Kwasi Agyei-Tiaa, Odikro of Tetekaaso, Plaintiff, vs. Agyeman Manu and 14 others, all of Tetekaaso (1957), p. 437, testimony of Yaw Ntem for the defendants, 1 May 1957.

18. MRO Kumasi State Council RB No. 10, Kwasi Agyei-Tiaa vrs. Agyeman Manu and others, p. 445, plaintiff cross-examining.

19. NAGK D4A 'Demarcation of Boundaries & Land Disputes', Fuller, 'Feyiasi Stool Case Deposition of Owiabu', 27 Oct. 1913.

20. AF: interview with Nana Kweku Gyekyi, Ofoase-Kokoben, 28 July 1980.

21. NAGK D2168, M. Alexis (travelling inspector of agriculture), Diary of tour in Manso Nkwanta district, May–June 1921.

22. AF: interview with Nana Osei Kofi, former Amoafohene, 6 May 1980.

23. Belfield, *Report*, Notes of Evidence, 98.

24. Hill, *Migrant Cocoa-Farmers*, 177.

25. AF: interview with Mr J. W. Owusu, Bekwai, 30 Sept. 1987; also interview with Mr B. Osei and Mr J. W. Owusu, Bekwai, 14 May 1980.

26. AF: interview with Opanyin Kofi Agyepong and Nana Baffuor Asare Bediako, Akwamuhene of Dadiase, Asiwa, 1 Sept. 1982.

27. PRAAD Accra ADM 46/5/1 PC's Diary (Southern Province, Obuasi), 1913–17, 24 Oct. 1913.

28. Austin, 'Rural Capitalism', 227.

29. Fortes Papers 8.32, 'Discussion with K. Boateng, Sanahene [treasurer], and Yaw Agyekum', Asokore, 8 June 1945.

30. NAGK Bekwai File 634, 'Handing-Over Notes' of Captain O. F. Ross, Ag DC, Obuasi, 22 Sept. 1924.

31. AF: interview with Nana Jonah Samuel Eddo Senior (stool title Yaw Buachie III), former Omanhene of Bekwai, Bekwai, 30 Aug. 1980.

32. AF: interview with Mr Kojo Asiedu, Huntado, 11 July 1980.

33. AF: interview with Mr J. W. Owusu, Bekwai, 30 Sept. 1987, quoted above, p. 227.

34. NAGK Bekwai File 86; AF: interview with Mr. Kojo Asiedu, Huntado, 11 July 1980.

35. AF: interview with Nana Jonah Samuel Eddo Senior (stool title Yaw Buachie III), former Omanhene of Bekwai, Bekwai, 30 Aug. 1980.

36. ARG 1/2/30/1/13: Ag Commissioner of the Eastern Province of Ashanti (CEPA) to CCA, 5 Jan. 1928.

37. See p. 317 below, also p. 321.

38. See Chs 16, 19.

39. See pp. 304–9.

40. Judith A. Byfield has documented this process for southwestern Nigeria, in the case of *adire* cloth, dyed by women in Abeokuta. Demand for their product rose until the 1930s with the growth of (predominantly male) cocoa income in both Nigeria and Ghana (See Byfield, *The Bluest Hands: A Social and Economic History of Women Dyers in Abeokuta (Nigeria), 1890–1940* [Portsmouth NH, 2002], xxii, 138–9, 199–203). Women traders in Asante, as elsewhere, would have shared in the proceeds.

41. AF: interview with Nana Kofi Agyeamang, former Omanhene, Esumeja, 5 May 1980.

42. Fortes Papers, 8.1, incomplete memo. by M. Fortes entitled 'Ashanti Marriage Statistics'.

43. Austin, 'Indigenous credit', 125–27; Martin A. Klein and Richard Roberts, 'The resurgence of pawning in French West Africa during the Depression of the 1930s', *African Economic History* 16 (1987), 23–37 (reprinted in revised form in Falola and Lovejoy, [eds], *Pawnship in Africa* and in Falola and Lovejoy [eds], *Pawnship, Slavery, and Colonialism*). The argument that follows was first put in Austin, 'Human pawning in Asante, 1850–1950', in Toyin Fayola and Paul E. Lovejoy (eds), *Pawnship in Africa: Debt Bondage in Historical Perspective* (Boulder, 1994), 143–44.

44. This will be examined in detail in Chs 15 and 18.

45. A transition from advances to pledging seems to have happened earlier in those parts of what was now the Gold Coast Colony in which cocoa farming itself had begun earlier than in Asante. See, e.g., W. S. D. Tudhope, *Enquiry into the Gold Coast Cocoa Industry, Final Report* (Gold Coast Government, Sessional paper IV: Accra, 1919), 17.

46. NAGK SCT 205/160, Bekwai Magistrate's Court, Criminal RB, p. 7, and D133, Bekwai DC's Diary, 3 Oct. 1930; NAGK Obuasi DAO File No. 1632, Kojo Pong's Cocoa Farms 1933 (sic: file mistitled, and original file number missing), item 174, Memo. by DC Obuasi to DC Bekwai, 24 Sept. 1932. The second case may have been panyarring rather than pawning, but that seems rather unlikely since panyarring had been illegal since the previous century (pp. 141–42 above). A further case apparently dating from this period is reported in AF: interview with Mr. J. W. Owusu, Bekwai, 30 Sept. 1987.

47. It should be noted that cash-cropping and labour-exporting zones interacted: which may account for the allegations that during hard times beyond the cocoa belt in the north of Ghana, Asante labour-recruiters took children from needy families there as pawns.

See Nick Van Hear, 'Child labour and the development of capitalist agriculture in Ghana', *Development and Change*, 13 (1982), 504–5.

48. See pp. 295–96.

49. E.g., see Rattray, *Ashanti*; Kyerematen, *Inter-state Boundary Litigation*, 110n. For detail on the terminology of cocoa farm pledging, see ibid., 101–4.

50. Mate Kole, Konor of Manya-Krobo, said in 1907: 'our people . . . do us no service as in olden time' ('Economic History of the Gold Coast 1874–1914: Select Documents', originally compiled by H. J. Bevin and extended by R. Addo-Fening, stencilled, Department of History, University of Ghana [Legon, 1981], 268, criticism by Mate Kole of Native Jurisdiction Bill 1906). In 1912 he said that this was because the time was absorbed in government road and sanitation schemes ('Economic History: Select Documents', 264, extract from Legislative Council Minutes of 28 Oct. 1912). Not that anyone's whole time was thus occupied: rather, presumably, subjects were only prepared to devote a given amount of time to state labour of any sort: if the government occupied that time, the stool was the loser. In that sense, they put their own work before that of the stool.

51. NAGK D658 'Upkeep of "Political" Roads by Chiefs and Payment of Labour Thereof' (EP 1/1931): CS to CCA, Accra 9 Jan. 1931.

52. Commissioners' responses in D658.

53. NAGK Bekwai File 77, Assuowinhene to DC, 18 March 1939.

54. AF: interview with Nana Jonah Samuel Eddo Senior (stool title Yaw Buachie III), former Omanhene of Bekwai, Bekwai, 30 Aug. 1980. It is possible that a later date was meant.

55. ARG 9/7/2 AgDC to CCA, Bekwai, 17 Aug. 1940.

56. *ARA for 1921*, 5.

57. Hopkins, *Economic History*, 225; Swindell, *Farm Labour*, 117.

58. Elizabeth Fox-Genovese and Eugene D. Genovese, *Fruits of Merchant Capital: Slavery and Bourgeois Property in the Rise and Expansion of Capitalism* (New York, 1983), vii.

59. Austin, 'Rural Capitalism', 224–86.

Chapter 14

1. *ARA for 1904*, 14.

2. As was proposed by the outgoing governor, Hodgson, on returning to the coast after being besieged in the British fort at Kumasi by the rising which his demand for the Golden Stool had precipitated. His successor said no (Kimble, *Political History of Ghana*, 322).

3. Berry, *Chiefs*, 79.

4. See, e.g., PRAAD Accra ADM 52/5/9 Mampong District Land Terrier [1930–36].

5. See, e.g. T. F. Chipp, *The Forest Officers' Handbook of the Gold Coast, Ashanti and the Northern Territories* (London, 1922); Cardinall, *The Gold Coast, 1931*, 97–98.

6. Belfield, *Report*, 91–92 (quote, 92), evidence of Gordon Riseley Griffith, DC, Ashanti [Kumasi] and Ag Police Magistrate, Kumasi.

7. This was formalised by the Ashanti Concessions Ordinance of 1903.

8. For an account see McCaskie, 'Creation of Ashanti Goldfields', 42.

9. Belfield, *Report*, 92, Griffith's evidence.

10. Austin, 'Mode of production or mode of cultivation', 163–64.

11. *ARA for 1910*, 21; similar wordings in other years.

12. *ARA for 1911*, 24.

13. On urban and peri-urban land use and tenure see Berry, *Chiefs*; also McCaskie, *Asante Identities*.

14. See, e.g., *ARA for 1904*, 14, which is quoted later in this chapter.

15. Belfield, *Report*, Notes of Evidence, p. 97, Yao Boatchi, Bekwaihene, and Kobina Foli, Adansehene.

16. Kimble, *Political History of Ghana*, 24n; McCaskie, 'Creation of Ashanti Goldfields', 40.

17. NAGK Files on Shelf No. 7, No. 107, 'Mining Rent to Bekwai and Adansi due by Ashanti Goldfields Corporation Ltd', memo. by CCA, 28 Feb. 1914; cf. Minute (by CCA?) dd. 27 Feb. 1920: 'These rents should be paid out in the ordinary way—£133 to Bekwai, and £66 to Adansi . . .'

18. McCaskie, 'Creation of Ashanti Goldfields', 42.

19. Guildhall Library, London: Ashanti Goldfields Corporation papers (hereafter 'AGC Papers'), 'A Short History of Ashanti Goldfields Corporation Ltd., 1897–1947: issued to the members to commemorate the Corporation's Jubilee' by G. W. Eaton Turner, p. 19.

20. Rhodes House MSS Afr.s.873: Obuasi Sub-District Handing-Over Report by W. Norton L. Goldie-Scott, 8 Aug. 1952; also Stockwell, *Business of Decolonization*, 80–81.

21. ARG 1/15/3/1 'Establishment of a regular mahogany forestry industry'.

22. Cf. pp. 53–54. See, further, ARG 2/5/36. From 1950 there was also a diamond concession in Adanse. On timber and diamond rights in Adanse see Rhodes House MSS Afr.s.873, Goldie-Scott's handing-over reports for 1952 and 1953.

23. E.g. PRAAD Sunyani, RG 9/1/34 'Cocoa Tribute': J. K. Owusu, State Secretary, Techiman Local Council to government agent, Wenchi district: Techiman 27 Feb. 1954.

24. ARG 2/5/3/1 'Jimachi Timber Concessions (R. T. Briscoe Ltd.)': J. J. Peele & Co. to CS, 12 Jan. 1946.

25. The benefits were not always mutual. Mim Timber Company's lawyer complained that 'farmers who in clearing their farms burn down trees indiscriminately' had preempted the timber companies' enjoyment of their own concession rights (ARG 2/5/3/7 'Mim Timber Co. Ltd'), H. V. A. Franklin to Asantehene, Accra 21 Oct. 1951).

26. MRO SB15 'Ash. Land Tenure' (26/46), Ag. CCA to Asantehene, Kumasi 12 Feb. 1936.

27. ARG 3/3/52 'Alienation of Lands—Ashanti', Ag CEPA to DCs, 5 July 1928.

28. MRO SB15, Asantehene to chiefs, Kumasi 2 June 1936.

29. ARG 1/3/5/3 'Native Land Tenure—General': Extracts from Minutes of Third Session of the Ashanti Confederacy Council, Manhyia, Kumasi, 7–23 March 1938.

30. Ibid.

31. Ibid.

32. ARG 2/3/1/6 'Ministry of Agriculture: Economic Aspects of Land Tenure Arrangements': J. G. Amoafo, 'Economic Aspects of Land Tenure Arrangements in Ashanti/Brong Ahafo Regions' (April 1961), p. 3.

33. Bray, *Cocoa Development in Ahafo*, 19.

34. ARG 1/12/1/33 (formerly NAGK D4B), 'Cacao', J. C. Muir to Assistant CCA, 'Memorandum: tribute paid by farmers', 28 Jan. 1933. Muir's memo is also in PRAAD Sunyani RG 2/1/2, 'Tributes General'.

35. Certainly as far as has been researched so far (Austin, 'Rural Capitalism', 250–55).

36. 'Asante' in this context meaning 'Ashanti', 'Brong' and 'Other Ashanti' combined; 'cocoa farmers' including—and mostly comprising—'food and cocoa farmers'). See

Ghana, *Survey of Cocoa Producing Families in Ashanti*, 33. The figures for female 'cocoa farmers' are potentially very misleading, as noted in ch. 3. For what little it is worth, less than 2% of those recorded in this category (including 'food and cocoa farmers') were non-Asante (Ibid., 34).

37. Computed from same page.

38. See pp. 459–60 n. 53.

39. Quoted above, 459 n. 53.

40. Austin, 'Rural Capitalism'.

41. Hill, *Migrant Cocoa-Farmers*, 139.

42. PRAAD Accra ADM 46/5/1, 17 Feb. 1915.

43. NAGK Bekwai File 634, Ross's 'Handing-Over Notes', 1924.

44. PRAAD Accra ADM 46/5/1, 24 June 1917; ADM 46/5/2, 23 May 1927; ARG 1/12/30, Manso Nkwantahene to DC, 29 Feb. 1933.

45. ADM 46/5/1, 14 June, 16 July 1917; ADM 53/5/1, 10 Jan. 1918.

46. PRAAD Sunyani RG 2/1/2: Odumasehene to DC Sunyani, Odumase 11 Dec. 1933 (with enclosed lists of farmers); Dormahene to DC Sunyani, Sunyani [21?] Dec. 1930. Number of trees is implied in the former letter: it states total tribute due, at one penny per tree, as £285/4s/6d.

47. ARG 9/2/2 'Kokofu Subjects on Dorma Land', Sanderson to CCA, 17 Aug. 1935.

48. Fortes Papers, 8.7, 'Notes on Kwotei Village', n.d. but c.1945–46. See p. 80 above.

49. AF: interviews in Ofoase-Kokoben on 28 and 30 July 1980 with, respectively, Nana Kwaku Gyekyi and Opanyin Kojo Bah.

50. Great Britain, Confidential Print, African (West), No. 1047 West African Lands Committee, *Minutes of Evidence, etc* (London, 1916), p. 429.

51. See pp. 102–3.

52. ARG 2/3/1/6 Amoafo, 'Economic aspects of land tenure in Ashanti/Brong Ahafo', 1.

53. NAGK D886 (cf. PRAAD Accra ADM 53/5/1, 15 Aug. 1918, 18 March 1919).

54. *ARA for 1921*, 6–7; ARG 1/12/1/33 'Cacao' (formerly NAGK D4B). Memo. by J. C. Muir, i/c Ashanti Division, Department of Agriculture, to Asst CCA, 28 Jan. 1933.

55. ARG 2/1/2: Kwaku Buadie and five others to Dormahene, Kumasi 16 Oct. 1935.

56. NAGK D866.

57. ARG 1/12/1/33: Muir's memo. of 28 Jan. 1933; Ag DC to Asst CCA, 25 March 1933, enclosing replies from chiefs of Bekwai, Denyase, Kokofu and Manso Nkwanta.

58. Ibid.: Muir's memo. of 28 Jan. 1933; Ag DC to Assistant CCA, 25 March 1933, enclosing replies from chiefs of Bekwai, Denyase, Kokofu and Manso Nkwanta; PRAAD Sunyani RG 2/1/2, esp. CCA to DC Sunyani, Kumasi 16 Jan. 1934.

59. PRAAD Accra ADM 46/5/2, 21 April 1927.

60. ARG 1/12/1/33, Ag DC Asante-Akyem to Asst CCA, 31 March 1933.

61. PRAAD Accra ADM 46/5/2, 16 Feb. and 30 July 1927.

62. Writ of *fieri facias*: court order requiring the sale of property to meet a debt.

63. ARG 1/12/1/33, Manso Nkwantahene to DC, 29 Feb. 1933.

64. Matson, *Digest of the Minutes of the Ashanti Confederacy Council*, 17.

65. ARG 9/3/2 'Essumeja—Ofuasi Land Dispute': Kweku Boaten II, Offuasehene, to DC Bekwai: Senfi, 20 March 1941.

66. Ibid., Judgment of Ag CCA in CCA's Court, Kumasi, 25 April 1946, in Nsemfoo [and others?] v. Essumejahene.

67. Ibid., Heward Mills to DC Bekwai, Kumasi, 22 March 1948. See also 'Particulars of Tribute due to Esumeja Stool by Nsemfoo and Others', encl. in E. O. Asafu-Adjaye to DC Bekwai, Kumasi 19 Feb. 1948.

68. PRAAD Sunyani RG 2/3/17 'Land Tenure "Land Tribute"', Takyimantiahene to DC Sunyani, Takyimantia, 26 April 1951; RG 9/1/34 'Cocoa Tribute': Samuel Attoh, Solicitor, to Techiman Local Council, Kumasi 19 Dec. 1952.

69. RG 2/3/17 'Land Tenure "Land Tribute"', Takyimantiahene to DC Sunyani, Takyimantia, 26 April 1951; RG 9/1/34.

70. RG 9/1/34, esp. J. K. Owusu, State Secretary, Techiman Local Council to Government Agent, Wenchi, dd. Techiman 27 Feb. 1954, enclosing 'Memorandum of Agreement', [Techiman] 16 Feb. 1954.

71. ARG 2/3/1/6 Amoafo, 'Economic aspects of land tenure in Ashanti/Brong Ahafo', 2.

72. Ibid., 1.

73. NAGK D4A 'Demarcation of Boundaries & Land Disputes' (1909–15), executive decision 'Respecting Chempoh Land' by C. Rew, CSPA, 18 Dec. 1910.

74. NAGK D862 'Yaw Boatin v. Kobina Safu et al.: Claim £600 estimated tribute due on Cocoa', Yao Adu, Yao Amponsa et al. to Commissioner, Central District of Ashanti, Kumasi 4 July 1917.

75. *ARA for 1914*, 22.

76. Fuller, *A Vanished Dynasty*, 330.

77. Gold Coast Government, *Annual Report on Soil Erosion in the Gold Coast, 1937* (Accra, 1938), 2.

78. ARG 3/3/52, esp. 'Notes by District Commissioner' [last page(s) missing, but 1928].

79. Ibid., 'Notes by District Commissioner'.

80. Mrs J. M. Matson, 'Report on Land Disputes in the Adansi Division, Obuasi District, Ashanti' (originally enclosed in Gold Coast No. 62 of 24 March 1947: copies are held in the Balme Library, University of Ghana). In addition, during the early 1930s people from Brenasi, south of the Pra, crossed the river and appropriated some land, part of which they may have proceeded to sell to a Ningo (from the coast east of Accra) (ibid., 30).

81. Made famous by Hill, *Migrant Cocoa-Farmers*, who however emphasised the small size of migration from the Eastern Province into Asante (237–38).

82. Matson, 'Report on Land Disputes', 19.

83. Ibid., 9, 16, 19, 20.

84. The figures which Hill put forward, cautiously, for the cost of individual lands ranged from £0.30 to £1.60 per acre (Hill, *Migrant Cocoa-Farmers*, 49–50, 57–58), i.e. £192 to £1,024 per square mile (£74–£395 per square kilometre). She suggested that the cost in the Nankese area about 1896 averaged about £1 per acre (ibid., 49: cf. 50, 57–58), i.e. £640 per square mile (£247 per square kilometre).

85. Hill, *Migrant Cocoa-Farmers*.

86. Matson, *Digest of the Minutes of the Ashanti Confederacy Council*, 72–73.

87. Ibid.

88. Cf. Wilks, *Forests of Gold*.

89. NAGK D972 'Sale of Land Dompoasi under FiFa' (113/26).

90. Ibid., Ag Circuit Judge Ashanti to CCA, Kumasi 14 April 1925.

91. Ibid., L. W. Judd, DC, to CEPA, Obuasi 31 March 1926.

92. Ibid., 'Agreement', in DC's Court, Obuasi, between Kwame Akowuah of Brofoyedru and Omanhene Kobina Foli, 13 July 1926; DC to CEPA, Obuasi 2 June 1926.

93. Ibid., 'Agreement' in DC's Court, Obuasi, between Omanhene Kobina Foli and the [new] odekuro and elders of Ahinsan, 13 July 1926.

94. Ibid., Ag Circuit Judge Ashanti to CCA, Kumasi 14 April 1925.

95. PRAAD Accra ADM 53/1/4 Obuasi DLB 1907, p. 440, Report on the Southern District of Ashanti for the Quarter ending September 30th 1907, by Captain C. H. Armitage, DC.

96. D2743 'Rent Payable to Chiefs': CCA to CS, 6 Oct. 1913.

97. NAGK D1609 'Claim for compensation for her son A. B. Thompson's plantation situate within the town area of Kumasi' (217/1924): esp. Thompson to CCA, Kumasi 20 April 1923; F. W. Applegate, President, Kumasi Public Health Board, Administrative Branch, to CCA, Kumasi 25 Feb. 1926. There is some suggestion in the file that Yeboah and/or Thompson claimed the land as well as their private property, during the periods when they respectively owned the farm. This is possible, especially as Thompson would have had an incentive to do so when, later, he sought compensation from the government when the city boundaries were extended to include his farm. But if so, he was obliged to abandon the claim (D1609: Memo by Ag Police magistrate to CCA, Kumasi 18 Sept. 1919; Minute by J. M[axwell], CCA, 5 April 1926). The price may have been influenced not only by the agricultural assets but by the prospect of compensation or by the general rise in urban land values (cf. D1609 Minute by Ag CEPA to CCA, 2 May 1924).

98. ARG 1/12/1/33, enclosures in DC to Asst CCA, Wenchi, 7 July 1933.

99. NAGK D2743, 'Rent Payable to Chiefs by Cocoa Planters' (Ashanti M.P. No. G188/1913) CCA to CS, 6 Oct. 1913.

100. Belfield, *Report*, Notes of Evidence, 87.

101. Pp. 35–36, 100–101.

102. West African Lands Committee, *Minutes of Evidence*, 168.

103. West African Lands Committee, *Draft Report*, 98.

104. Rhodes House Library, University of Oxford: Afr.s.1105, Hay, 'Payment of Cocoa Tribute'.

105. Belfield, *Report*, Notes of Evidence, 87 (cf. 166). Cf. NAGK D2743 'Rent Payable to Chiefs', CCA to CS, 6 Oct. 1913.

106. NAGK D2743 'Rent Payable to Chiefs': the proposal is in G. R. Griffith, Ag Police Magistrate, to CCA, 29 Aug. 1913.

107. PRAAD Sunyani RG2/1/2, CCA to DC Sunyani, Kumasi 16 Jan. 1934.

108. PRAAD Accra ADM 53/1/15 Obuasi DLB 1914–15, p. 314, PC to Bekwaihene, Obuasi, 12 Jan. 1915.

109. ADM 46/5/1 PC's Diary (Obuasi), 7 Dec. 1914; cf. entries for 16 and 17 Feb. 1915.

110. NAGK D972, bye-laws 'signed' (marked) by Omanhene Kobina Foli and elders of Adanse, Fomena 3 April 1929.

111. Terence Ranger, 'The invention of tradition in colonial Africa', in Eric Hobsbawm and Terence Ranger (eds), *The Invention of Tradition* (Cambridge, 1983), 211–62.

112. D972, Adanse bye-laws, 3 April 1929.

113. PRAAD Sunyani RG 2/3/17: Chiefs Kwasi Apraku and Yaw Awua to DC Sunyani, Sunyani, 24 June 1946. See likewise Krontihene Kofi Asante of Odumase to DC, Sunyani, 28 March and 16 July 1946, and 13 March 1947.

114. ARG 2/3/1/6 Amoafo, 'Economic aspects of land tenure in Ashanti/Brong Ahafo', 1.

115. PRAAD Sunyani RG 2/3/17: Chiefs Kwasi Apraku and Yaw Awua to DC Sunyani, Sunyani, 24 June 1946; Krontihene Kofi Asante of Odumase to DC, Sunyani, 28 March 1946, 16 July 1946, and 13 March 1947.

116. Ibid., quotation from W. H. K. Littlewood, DC, to Asantehene, Sunyani 26 June 1946; for petitions from Odomase subjects see Detective Sergeant Payne, Kwasi Amankwa, Kojo Nimo and others to DC Sunyani, Odumase, 10 June 1946 and Yaw Donkor, Kwaku Addae and others to DC Sunyani, Fiapre, 17 June 1946.

117. Ibid., S. K. Anthony, DC, to Krontihene of Odomase, Sunyani, 8 April 1947.

118. *ARA for 1920*, 23.

119. NAGK D2469 'Abina Denta—Cocoa Plantation on Asecherewa Land', 20 June to 25 Sept. 1917.

120. PRAAD Sunyani RG 2/1/2, Yaw Twumto to Asantehene, Kumasi 24 July 1935; with minutes by Asantehene, 3 Aug. 1935, and reply by DC Sunyani, 10 Aug. 1935.

121. ARG 9/3/2. For the 53, see enclosure in item 104, Petition by Kwaku Nsemfoo and others to the Governor, dd. Kumasi, 20 Sept. 1944.

122. Ibid., Esumejahene Kobina Karikari and elders to DC, dd. Esumeja, 9 Sept. 1941.

123. Ibid., enclosure in item 128, Copy of Proceedings in Kwaku Nsemfoo of Kokoben v. Nana Gyebi Ababio II, Esumejahene, in the Asantehene's A Court, Kumasi. Judgment given 9 Nov. 1945. The same principle can be seen in an executive decision of 1927, when a commissioner decided that the Adanse stool owned land on which Abodom farmers had established cocoa farms. He stipulated that they 'are not to be dispossessed or molested. They will pay to the Omanhin of Adansi the Customary tribute' (NAGK SCT 30/5, p. 167: C. E. Rew, CSPA, boundary decision headed 'Adansi-Abodom', Kumasi 19 Nov. 1927).

124. ARG 9/3/2, various items.

125. NAGK D2743, minutes of Kumasi Council of Chiefs' 'Meeting held on the 2nd October 1913'.

126. PRO CO96/662 Memo. by CCA, 31 Dec. 1925.

127. NAGK file 'Lands Dispute—Ashanti' (no archive file number on cover, but original colonial number L55/1919): Ag. Director of Surveys to CCA, Accra, respectively 13 Aug. and 17 Sept. 1920.

128. NAGK Bekwai 118, Sinclair, Ag DC, to CCA, Bekwai 7 April 1940.

129. Meek, *Land Law and Custom*, 24–25.

130. Legal fees aside, cases held in Kumasi involved transport and maintenance costs for provincial litigants (for an example see Berry, *Chiefs*, 38). In principle, though, this was not new: albeit the transport costs took a different form from when cases were brought to the capital during the pre-colonial kingdom.

131. Fuller, *A Vanished Dynasty*, 330.

132. For boundary litigation as a source of stool debt see Kwame Arhin, 'The pressure of cash and its political consequences in Asante in the colonial period', *Journal of African Studies* 3:4 (1976–77), 461–66; Berry, *Chiefs*, 38–39.

133. ARG 1/1/125 'Surveys of Lands in Ashanti': Provincial Surveyor Ashanti to CCA, Kumasi 12 Nov. 1930; J. R. Dickinson, DC, to CCA, Kumasi 10 Jan. 1931.

134. Meek, *Land Law and Custom*, 171; Provincial Surveyor's letter, 12 Nov. 1930, cited above.

135. Where compulsory registration of deeds was introduced in the former crown lands in Kumasi in the 1940s (Meek, *Land Law and Custom*, 171n).

Chapter 15

1. Gordon R. Woodman, 'Developments in pledges of land in Ghanaian customary law', *Journal of African Law* 11 (1967), 8–26; Kyerematen, *Inter-State Boundary Litigation in Ashanti*, 102–4.

2. Polly Hill, 'The West African farming household', in Jack Goody (ed.), *Changing Social Structure in Ghana* (London, 1975), 131.

3. Busia, *Position of the Chief*, 125–27; quotation from p. 127.

4. Ibid., 125–27. The quotation from the Minutes of the Confederacy Council is, again, on p. 127.

5. Fortes, 'Ashanti patrilateral kinship and its values', in his *Kinship and the Social Order: The Legacy of Lewis Henry Morgan* (London, 1970), 206.

6. Ibid., 207.

7. Ibid., 206.

8. Busia, *Position of the Chief*, x.

9. Ibid., ix.

10. Ibid., xii.

11. Ibid., 125.

12. See p. 136.

13. File 'Enquiry held on the disturbance at Juabin' (570/09): J. B. Hayford, ex King's Clerk, to CCA, Kumasi 26 May 1908. The file is enclosed, apparently by accident, within the covers of ARG 1/2/5/9 'Claim of subjects from Konongo by Chief Kobina Kokofu and others'.

14. Ibid.

15. PRAAD Accra ADM 46/5/1 PC's Diary, Southern Province of Ashanti, 14 Oct. 1913.

16. Ibid., 14 Dec. 1914.

17. Southall, 'Cadbury on the Gold Coast', 109–11.

18. Guildhall Library, London: Bank of British West Africa Ltd. papers (hereafter 'BBWA Papers'), Ms 28623/15 'Kumasi Branch. Annual Report 31st March, 1922' and Ms 28623/19, 'Kumasi Branch. Annual Report 31st March, 1927'.

19. Great Britain (Colonial Office), *Report of the Commission on the Marketing of West African Cocoa* (1938) (hereafter, the 'Nowell Report').

20. AF: interview with Mr. Kojo Asiedu (grandson of Osei Kwami) in Huntado, 11 July 1980. I reported this case earlier, in Austin, 'Capitalists and Chiefs', 68.

21. ARG 9/1/8, esp. 'Inventory of articles seized in the case of A. K. Ofori Vs. Kojo Abebreseh and others of Huntadu', 11 Nov. 1936.

22. AF: 2nd interview with Mr. Asiedu in Huntado, 17 July 1980 (compare the first).

23. ARG 9/6/13, Return of Civil Cases for March, and for April, 1931.

24. Rhodes House Library, Oxford: Papers of John Holt and Company (Liverpool), (hereafter 'Holt Papers'), MSS. Afr. S825/536(ii), 'Memorandum: Justification of a cocoa buying agreement as seen from the Merchants' standpoint' (n.d. but 1937–38; no author named).'.

25. ARG 1/12/1/33, W. R. Danby to Asst CCA, Kumasi, 18 May 1933.

26. Nowell Report, 28, 29, 31, 70 (quotation p. 31).

27. Rhodes House Library, Oxford: Cocoa Marketing Board papers, MSS Afr. s913(2), 'Memorandum for transmission to the Commission of Enquiry', by W. H. Beckett, Senior Agricultural Superintendent [n.d. but early 1938], p. 3.

28. Fortes Papers, 6.45, 'Agricultural indebtedness and the issue of credits to farmers' (incomplete[?] carbon copy of memo by a—de facto—anonymous DC or former DC. No date survives [but apparently c.1945].

29. Fortes Papers, 9.68, 'My experiences in cocoa buying' by B. K. Nsiah [n.d. but 1945–46].

30. Fortes Papers, 6.45, 'Agricultural indebtedness'.

31. *Loc. cit.*

32. Bray, *Cocoa Development in Ahafo*, 46.

33. A rare exception was the case of A. B. Thompson (Alfred Kwaku Duah), mentioned earlier. His debt secured on his cocoa and rubber farm was owed to a European firm, Russell's. Circumstances which may account for this exception to the rule include: Thompson's possession of documentary proof of purchase of the farm; the location of the site on the edge of Kumasi, making it of increasing value for potential urban uses; and Thompson's employment as a broker for the firm (NAGK D1609).

34. West African Lands Committee, Minutes of Evidence, p. 165, Fuller's evidence, 6 Nov. 1912.

35. AF: interview with Nana Osei Kofi, former Amoafohene, and other elders of Amoafo: Amoafo, 6 May 1980.

36. NAGA ADM 50/1/3 Juaso DLB: Gilbert C. Heathcote, DC, to Omanhene of Juaben, Juaso 28 Sept. 1917.

37. The rest of the paragraph is based on NAGA ADM 53/4/7 Obuasi Civil Record Book, 1919–21, Yaw Jumbo v. Kwesi Kwamie, 24 April 1920–1 June 1921; NAGK SCT 204/83 Bekwai Civil Record Book, 1922–25, Yaw Jumbo v. Kweku Gyima and others, 6 April–27 May 1922. In referring to the Dadiase stool he occupied as Akwamuhene I follow informants in Asiwa (AF: various interviews in Asiwa, 1 Sept. 1980).

38. Herskovits Memorial Library, Northwestern University: Polly Hill Papers, 2/4, 'Notes on the MS of the Report of the Committee on Agricultural Indebtedness' (n.d.).

39. *Loc. cit.*

40. Great Britain, *Report of the Commission of Enquiry into Disturbances in the Gold Coast 1948* (Colonial No. 231: hereafter cited as the Watson Report), 53.

41. This is my observation, which probably needs refinement. On the disturbances, the commission and government reactions to the report see Rathbone, 'Introduction', in Rathbone, *Ghana*, Part 1, xliii–xlvii.

42. We will consider the policy debate in Chapter 17.

43. Gold Coast, *Report of the Commission of Enquiry into the Affairs of the Cocoa Purchasing Company Limited* (Accra, 1956: hereafter *Jibowu Report*), 21.

44. Bray, *Cocoa Development in Ahafo*, 46.

45. Speech to the Legislative Assembly, 3 March 1954, quoted in *Jibowu Report*, 26.

46. *Jibowu Report*. For the political controversy see Allman, *Quills of the Porcupine*, *passim*, and also various Colonial Office documents reproduced in Rathbone, *Ghana*, Part 2.

47. Dennis Austin, *Politics in Ghana 1946–1960* (London, 1964), 343–44.

48. Bray, *Cocoa Development in Ahafo*, 46.

49. See Björn Beckman, *Organising the Farmers* (Uppsala, 1976).

50. Ghana, *Survey of Cocoa Producing Families in Ashanti, 1956–57*, Table 52.

51. ARG 9/22/1 Bekwai Civil Record Book 1922–25: Kwami Moshi v. Kwadjoe Nsiah, 11 Sept. 1922.

52. Polly Hill, *The Pledging of Ghana Cocoa Farms*, No. 15 in *Cocoa Research Series* (cyclostyled: University of Ghana, Economics Department: Legon, 1958); Hill, *Development Economics on Trial, passim*.

53. Previously in Kintampo district, as in Map 3, before one of the many boundary reorganizations.

54. It is hard to see it as efficient (for either party) to secure a loan on just a handful of trees within a farm, whereas it could be efficient to sell and buy beans in advance.

55. Computed from ARG 1/12/1/33, enclosures in DC to Asst CCA, Wenchi 7 July 1933.

56. ARG 1/12/1/33, DC to Asst CCA, Kumasi 31 May 1933.

57. See pp. 304–9 below.

58. In one case the only figure is '10' and it appears in the (old) pence column, implying that a farm was mortgaged for £0.04. This is literally incredible. I have assumed that the '10' should have been in the shillings column, i.e. £0.5. All the data above in this paragraph are from ARG 1/12/1/33, enclosures in DC to Asst. CCA, Wenchi 7 July 1933.

59. See table enclosed in NAGK Bekwai File 35, 'Cocoa Crop Report',Walker, Ag DC, to CCA, Bekwai 23 Jan. 1934.

60. NAGK Bekwai File 35, Walker to CCA, Bekwai 23 Jan. 1934.

61. ARG 1/12/1/33, enclosures in DC to Asst CCA, Wenchi 7 July 1933.

62. See table enclosed in NAGK Bekwai File 35: Ag DC to CCA, Bekwai 23 Jan. 1934.

63. As previous note.

64. ARG 1/12/1/33, enclosures in DC to Asst CCA, Wenchi 7 July 1933.

65. NAGK Bekwai File 35, Walker to CCA, 23 Jan. 1934.

66. See pp. 358–59.

67. Tudhope, *Enquiry into the Gold Coast Cocoa Industry, Final Report*, 17.

68. For clarification that the reference was to the war, see Tudhope, *Final Report*, 3.

69. Anonymous, 'Farm debt and mortgages', *The Gold Coast Farmer* (Gold Coast Department of Agriculture), Feb. 1934, 134. The source uses the term 'crop mortgaging' to refer to what is here termed 'farm mortgaging'.

70. ARG 1/12/1/33, Danby to Asst CCA, 18 May 1933; Devin to Asst CCA, 17 May 1933.

71. NAGK D133, Diary—Bekwai District, 12 Feb. 1930.

72. NAGK D133, 24 Feb. 1930; also on farm mortgaging, 11 and 12 March, 12 Aug., 2 and 18 Sept.

73. For evidence of how the survey was conducted see ARG 1/212/1/33, CCA to Ag CCA, Kumasi, 10 May 1933; Walker to Asst CCA, Bekwai, 19 June 1933.

74. Beckett, 'Memorandum for transmission to the Commission of Enquiry'.

75. Calculated using total output given in Bateman, 'Econometric analysis of Ghanaian cocoa supply', 363.

76. ARG 1/212/1/33, Walker to Asst CCA, 19 June 1933.

77. For the figures of 5,838 and 123 see Ghana, *Survey of Cocoa Producing Families in Ashanti, 1956–57*, Tables 51 and 52 respectively. No separate figures were given for charging, the other form of mortgage.

78. Ghana, *Survey of Cocoa Producing Families in Ashanti, 1956–57*, Table 35. Figures rounded to nearest shilling.

79. 'During this enquiry I have travelled over 2,000 miles [3,200 kilometres], all—with the exception of 220 miles by rail and motor car—being by cycle and on foot and for the most part through cocoa farms frequently off the beaten track.' Tudhope, *Final Report*, 3.

80. Beckett, 'Memorandum for transmission to the Commission of Enquiry'. The data are presented and discussed in more detail in Gareth Austin, 'Competition, labour credit and economic rent: the political economy of cocoa advances system in colonial Ghana, 1915–1938', in Endre Stiansen (ed.), *More Than Money Matters: Financial Institutions in Africa's Political Economy* (Nordic Institute of African Studies: Uppsala, forthcoming).

81. Beckett, 'Memorandum for transmission to the Commission of Enquiry', 2.

82. ARG 1/212/1/33, Walker to Asst CCA, 19 June 1933.

83. E.g., in Jan. 1917 the CSPA noted that 'Cocoa advances are now being called in', leading to cases before his court (NAGA ADM 46/5/1, PC's Diary, Obuasi, 22 Jan. 1917).

84. See, e.g., the description by Edward J. Organ, 'The Gold Coast cocoa industry & its recent developments', 5–6 (paper read at the Exhibition of Rubber, Other Tropical Products and Allied Industries, June 1921: copy in Cadbury Papers); Great Britain, *ARAs for 1915* (p. 6), *1916* (p. 8) and *1918* (p. 7).

85. The logic of this will be developed in detail in Ch. 18.

86. For numerous detailed examples of pledging of cocoa farms in the early years after Ghanaian independence see NAGK Juaso DAO File 2681.

87. ARG 1/2/30/1/2, CSDA to CCA, 13 Sept. 1907. Cf. Armitage to Bekwaihene, 22 Dec. 1907, in same file.

88. E.g., this was a sub-heading in A. W. Paterson, 'The co-operative societies movement applied to the problems of the Gold Coast cacao industry', *Tropical Agriculture* 9:9 (1934), 242.

89. NAGK D4, Hunter to Plants and Produce Inspectorate, 24 Dec. 1929; ARG 1/212/1/33, 1933 correspondence between commissioners in Asante, beginning with CCA to Assistant CCA, 10 May.

90. E.g. ARG 1/212/1/33, CCA to Asst. CCA, Kumasi, 10 May 1933; cf. C. Y. Shephard, *Report on the Economics of Peasant Agriculture in the Gold Coast* (Accra, 1936), 41.

91. NAGK Bekwai File 118, Sinclair, Ag DC, to CCA, 7 April 1940.

92. NAGK D133, 24 Feb. 1930.

93. D133, 12 Feb. and 11, 12 March 1930.

94. Bekwai DAO File 35, Ag DC to all Tribunals, Bekwai, 4 July 1933.

95. Fortes Papers, 6.45, 'Agricultural Indebtedness'.

96. NAGK Bekwai File 35, Inspector of Plants and Produce, Bekwai, to DC, 18 May 1933; Shephard, *Report on the Economics of Peasant Agriculture*, 26–27 (cf. D4, Hunter to Superintendent, 24 Dec. 1929); Ghana, *Report of the Committee on Agricultural Indebtedness* (Accra, 1957), 14.

97. Holt Papers: MSS Afr. s825/536(ii), R. Beard to Rawlings, Accra, 7 April 1938.

98. *Annual Report of the Department of Agriculture for 1930–31.*

99. PRAAD Accra ADM 46/5/9, 370.

100. All this is apparent from a useful discussion whose tone is notably sympathetic to the cooperative ideal: J. C. deGraft-Johnson, *African Experiment: Cooperative Agriculture and Banking in British West Africa* (London, 1958), 127–40.

101. NAGA ADM 46/5/9, 370.

102. deGraft-Johnson, *African Experiment*, 139–40.

103. Ibid., 140.

104. Revenue calculated from Bateman, 'Econometric analysis of Ghanaian cocoa supply', 315, 318.

105. *Watson Report*, 53.

Chapter 16

1. Jean Allman, 'Fathering, mothering and making sense of *ntamoba*: reflections on the economy of child-rearing in colonial Asante, 1924–1945', *Africa* 67 (1997), 312.

2. Clark, *Onions Are My Husband*, 316–22; Allman and Tashjian, *'I Will Not Eat Stone'*, 13–16.

3. Cf. p. 109.

4. *ARA for 1920*, 11.

5. Austin, 'Rural Capitalism', esp. 224–314.

6. Ibid., 250–52.

7. Anonymous, 'Oldest cocoa farm in Ashanti', 25.

8. AF: information from Mr. J. W. Owusu, a retired agricultural officer born in 1925, and a relative of Afua Fofie (interviews with Mr. Owusu and Mr. P. Osei, Bekwai, 14 May 1980; interviews with Mr. Owusu, Bekwai, 28 Aug. 1980 and 30 Sept. 1987). The description in the text corrects a statement in my thesis, that the farm 'may well' not have been made until the interwar period. The statement referred to just one of the 1980 interviews (Austin, 'Rural Capitalism', 513): taking both together, the implication is that it was made with the pods she got in Akyem; a conclusion consistent with the 1987 interview.

9. ARG 1/20/34, M. Alexis, Travelling Instructor, Diary of tour in Manso Nkwanta district, May–June 1921.

10. Kyei, *Our Days Dwindle*, 25.

11. Miles, 'Size of cacao farms in Ashanti', 54–56.

12. J. C. Muir, 'Crop surveys, Gold Coast', *Bulletin of the Department of Agriculture, Gold Coast* vol. 20 (1928), 172–80; Muir, 'Survey of cacao areas—Western Province, Ashanti', 57–64.

13. Miles, 'Size of cacao farms in Ashanti', 55; Muir, 'Crop surveys', 173.

14. See Rhodes House Library, Oxford: Arthur Jones Papers, MSS. Afr. s. 979, vol. 3, Cocoa Surveys: Monthly Report, Feb. 1944, by W. H. Beckett, Officer-in-Charge, Division of Statistics and Surveys, Accra.

15. This part of Muir's study seems to have been implemented in 1928. His reports are not entirely clear or consistent about the timing of the two parts of the investigation, but the most plausible interpretation is that the survey itself was carried out in 1928, while checks on the volume of cocoa passing out of the main producing districts extended into 1929 (see

Muir, 'Survey of cacao areas' and 'Crop surveys'). Muir used the term 'farmers' rather than 'cocoa farmowners', but it is clear from context that by the former he meant the latter.

16. As the last note.

17. Use of R assumes that the relationships are linear, which seems to be the case. See the table, and also the representation of the western Asante data in a scatter diagram, Fig. 18.1.

18. Because the number of districts is so small I have not proceeded to calculate the coefficients of determination (R^2), as the results are likely to be misleading. Rather than offering probably spurious figures for the strength of the causal relationships, it is enough to note that the figures reported here suggest the 'tentative conclusion' formulated in the text.

19. Miles actually seemed to think it had, but was evidently comparing the percentage of cocoa farmers among the total population of the Western Province cocoa areas with that amongst the *adult* population of Asante-Akyem (Miles, 'Size of cacao farms in Ashanti', 56). On the determinants of the rate of adoption in particular districts, see [ch. 3] above.

20. ARG 9/3/2, enclosure to item 104, Petition by Kwaku Nsemfoo and 52 others to the governor, dd. Kumasi, 20 Sept. 1944; item 170, Heward Mills, solicitor, to DC, Bekwai, dd. Kumasi, 7 July 1947.

21. ARG 9/3/2, Kofi Kwakey, Gold Coast Regiment, to DC, Bekwai, dd. 13 Jan. 1944.

22. Fortes, Steel and Ady, 'Ashanti survey, 1945–46', 163. Polly Hill was misled by the inconsistency of Fortes's categories into slightly over-stating the female:male ratio among 'cocoa farmers' (Hill, 'West African farming household', 136).

23. N. O. Addo, 'Some employment and labour conditions on Ghana's cocoa farms', in R. A. Kotey, C. Okali and B. E. Rourke (eds), *Economics of Cocoa Production and Marketing* (Legon, 1974), 204–5.

24. Miles, 'Size of cacao farms in Ashanti', 55–56.

25. Ibid, 55.

26. Ibid., 56.

27. AF: interviews with Nana Kweku Agyeamang, former Omanhene, in Esumeja, 5 May 1980; Mr P. Osei and Mr J. W. Owusu in Bekwai, 14 May 1980; Nana Kojo Appiah Darko II, Regent of Manso Nkwanta, Manso Nkwanta, 23 July 1980.

28. AF: interview with Nana Frema II (and Nana Adu Darkoh II) in Jacobu, 2 Sept. 1980.

29. Kyei, *Our Days Dwindle*, 25, 111.

30. As n. 28 above.

31. Bray, *Cocoa Development in Ahafo*, 41.

32. Muir, 'Survey of cacao areas', 61.

33. Fortes Papers, 8.7, 'Notes on Kwotei Village', n.d. but c1945–46.

34. Fortes, Steel and Ady, 'Ashanti survey, 1945–46', 165.

35. Ibid., 165.

36. Fortes Papers, 8.7, 'Notes on Kwotei Village', n.d. but c1945–46.

37. E.g. PRAAD Accra ADM 11/1641, 'The Cocoa Situation': [unofficial] minutes of Meeting of the Ashanti Farmers Association, 23 Nov. 1937.

38. Bray, *Cocoa Development in Ahafo*, 42.

39. Fortes Papers, 9.2, 'Akyinakrom. Donkor. Land' (n.d. but 1945–46).

40. Ibid.

41. Kyei, *Our Days Dwindle*, 28; read in context of ibid., 25–27.

42. AF: interviews with Nana Kweku Agyeamang, former Omanhene, in Esumeja, 5 May 1980; Nana Osei Kofi, former Amoafohene, Amoafo 6 May 1980; Mr K. Addai and others in Asikaso, 26 Aug. 1982; and in Asiwa on 1 Sept. 1982 with (1) a group of elders, then (2) Opanyin Kofi Agyepong and Nana Baffuor Asare Bediako, Akwamuhene of Dadiase.

43. AF: interviews in Esumeja, Amoafo and Asikaso, as in n. 42.

44. 'Oldest cocoa farm in Ashanti'; AF: interviews in Asiwa, cited in n. 42; interview with Mr Kojo Asiedu, in Huntado, 11 July 1980.

45. AF: interview with Mr Peter Osei, Mr J. B. Oppong, Opanyin Kwandaho and others, in Sanfo, 8 May 1980.

46. Bray, *Cocoa Development in Ahafo*, 41.

47. See Christine Okali, *Cocoa and Kinship in Ghana* (London, 1983), 130. Ironically, Okali does not seem to have been aware of Bray's work.

48. Ibid., 132.

49. On the latter see Addo, 'Some employment and labour conditions on Ghana's cocoa farms', 204–18. On real producer prices see Merrill J. Bateman, Alexander Meeraus, David M. Newbery, William Asenso Okyere and Gerald T. O'Mara, *Ghana's Cocoa Pricing Policy* (World Bank: Washington, DC, 1990), p. 2.13.

50. AF: interviews in Asikaso and Sanfo, cited in nn. 42, 45; with Nana Owusu Sekyere, Chief Linguist, and Mr Kwesi Kaabi, in Kokofu, 12 May 1980; with Mr P. Osei and Mr J. W. Owusu, Bekwai, 14 May 1980; and with Mr J. O. Mensah, Bekwai, July 1987.

51. Kyei, *Our Days Dwindle*, 26–27.

52. AF: interview in Sanfo, as n. 45.

53. AF: interview in Jacobu, cited p. 526 n. 28.

54. AF: interview in Asikaso, cited in n. 42.

55. Fortes Papers, 9.2., 'Akyinakrom. Donkor. Land' (n.d. but 1945–6). The greater detail in Kyei's memoirs, together with the positive differences between the two descriptions, enable us to dismiss the possibility that his recollections of childhood had been reshaped by his subsequent work as Fortes's assistant on the Survey.

56. AF: interviews with Mr J. O. Mensah, Bekwai, 1 May and 10 July 1980 and July 1987.

57. *ARA for 1904*, 20.

58. PRAAD Accra ADM 53/1/3 Obuasi DLB 1906, Armitage to Kokofuhene, Obuasi, 24 Feb. 1906.

59. NAGK D1343, 'Draft Rules for Regulation of Cocoa and Rubber Brokers', Dudgeon, 'Fifth Report upon the Agricultural and Forest Products of the Gold Coast and Ashanti', Feb. 1910.

60. ADM 46/5/1 P.C.'s Diary, 26 Nov. 1915; ADM 53/5/1 PC's Diary, 21 Feb. 1919.

61. PRAAD Accra ADM 53/5/1 PC's Diary 1918–22: entries for 15, 25 and 29 April 1919. See also NAGK Obuasi File 147, 'Bekwai Riot'; AF: interview with Nana Akomiah, former Krontihene, Bekwai, 18 August 1982.

62. Kyei, *Our Days Dwindle*, 28, 29.

63. AF: interview in Asikaso, cited in n. 42; interview with Osei and Owusu, Bekwai, cited in n. 50.

64. AF: interview in Esumeja cited in n. 42.

65. AF: interview with Nana Kwaku Gyekyi, Ofoase-Kokoben, 28 July 1980.

66. AF: interviews in Huntado and Sanfo cited in nn. 44, 45.

67. AF: interview in Sanfo, as n. 45.

68. AF: interview in Huntado, cited in n. 44.

69. ARG 1/20/34.

70. *ARA*, 1921, 6: ARG 1/20/34, 'Report on Bekwai & Obuasi District' by T. J. S. Smellie, Assistant Superintendent of Agriculture (n.d.: tour Oct.–Nov. 1921).

71. E.g., European firms were offering 8/6d. per 60 lb. load in Kumasi at the end of 1930 (D4; 'Report on Meetings with Chiefs and Farmers in Kumasi, Ashanti Akim, Mampong and Bekwai Districts', by T. Hunter, Ag Provincial Superintendent of Agriculture [encl. in Hunter to CCA, 30 Dec. 1930]). The average annual price recorded for Kumasi Agricultural station produce had not been below 17/- since 1924, when it was 9/-. The station's cocoa 'always received a small premium' (D2907; 'Average Price of Cacao from 1913 to 1930', Hunter to CCA, 27 Aug. 1930), so 9/- for it probably implied about 8/6d. for the farmer.

72. NAGK D133, 13 Jan. and 19 March 1931; ARG 9/6/13, 'Native Tribunal Ohene of Essumeja', Return of Civil Cases for Feb. 1931, and DC to Esumejahene, 31 March 1931; SCT 204/86, Bekwai Civil Record Book, 630.

73. As was remarked in J. R. Dickinson, 'Report on Labour Conditions in the Gold Coast', July 1938, p. 63, encl. in PRO CO96/760/16.

74. PRAAD Accra ADM 46/4/1, Bekwai Criminal Record Book, 463, 717–22.

75. Bekwai File 26, Kofi Buachie to DC, 1 March 1926, and Ya[a] Aduwa to DC, 15 March 1926.

76. AF: interviews with Mr P. Osei and Mr J. W. Owusu in Bekwai, 14 May 1980; Mr K. Addai and others in Asikaso, 26 Aug. 1982; Nana Kweku Agyeampong and Nana Kofi Edu No. 1, in Esumeja, 5 May 1980.

77. Wage-labourers in this period were identified as northerners, explicitly or implicitly, in the Esumeja and Asikaso interviews cited above, and in interviews with: Peter Osei and others, Sanfo, 8 May 1980; Nana Kojo Appiah Darko II, Manso Nkwanta, 23 July 1980. Mossis and Gyamans were variously specified, while Mr J. Oduro Mensah (interview in Bekwai, 1 May 1980) employed a Mamprussi at Manso-Abiram in the early 1930s.

78. This is the only reference I have come across to a woman farm wage-labourer in this period: whereas such workers are often explicitly or implicitly described as male.

79. Fortes Papers, 8.7, 'Notes on Kwotei Village', n.d. but c1945–46.

80. Ibid.

81. Dickinson, 'Report on Labour Conditions in the Gold Coast', p. 63.

82. AF: interviews in Manso Nkwanta, Esumeja, and Sanfo, cited on p. 526 n. 27 and p. 527 nn. 42, 45; and with Opanyin Kwasi Owusu and Mrs Mary Owusu in Morontuo, 24 July 1980.

83. ARG 9/1/8, 'Osei Kwami—Deceased. Estate of'.

84. Kwame Arhin (ed.), *The Minutes of the Ashanti Farmers Association Limited 1934–36* (Legon 1978), 66.

85. MRO CF89, Labour Officer, Timber & Cocoa Survey to Secretary, Ashanti Confederacy Council, 28 Nov. 1946.

86. MRO CF89, 'Analysis of investigations made during period October 1946–March 1947'.

87. Quoted in NAGA CSO 0001/SF52, Minute by Ag. Commissioner of Labour to CS, Accra, 22 Nov. 1946.

88. Ghana, *Survey of Cocoa Producing Families in Ashanti, 1956–57*. The data discussed in this paragraph come from Table 22.

89. See ibid., 14.

90. See pp. 15–16.

91. As n. 87.

92. The survey specifies that 'caretakers' received 'Share payments'; as distinct from 'Payments to labourers, carriers etc.' which, it implies, were made on non-share terms (Ghana, *Survey of Cocoa Producing Families in Ashanti, 1956–57*, 68). Tom McCaskie informed me, in a personal communication, that 'caretaker' was the usual term by which Twi-speakers referred to it in the village on the outskirts of Kumasi which he studied for his book *Asante Identities*.

93. AF: interviews in Ofoase-Kokoben on 28 and 30 July 1980 with, respectively, Nana Kwaku Gyekyi and Opanyin Kojo Bah.

94. Fortes Papers, 9.18, 'Additional Notes on Land Tenure (Ashanti Cocoa farmers), n.d. and unsigned [but almost certainly 1946 and evidently by Fortes].

95. Ghana, *Survey of Cocoa Producing Families in Ashanti, 1956–57*, 57.

96. UN Report on *The Enlargement of the Exchange Economy in Tropical Africa* (New York, 1954), 31. This has been influential: quoted, for example, by the economist H. Myint in his classic *Economics of the Developing Countries*, 31; and by the substantivist anthropologist George Dalton, who described it as containing 'the best statistical and descriptive information we have on the kinds and extent of commercialization (production for domestic and foreign market sale) in the sub-Saharan Africa of 1950' (Dalton, 'Introduction' to *Research in Economic Anthropology*, 2 [1979], ix). The report was reprinted in the same volume.

97. ADM 53/1/10, p. 240, CSPA to Adansehene, 10 Feb. 1912.

98. Roger G. Thomas, 'Forced labour in British West Africa: the case of the Northern Territories of the Gold Coast 1906–27', *JAH* 14 (1973), 79–103.

99. ADM 53/1/10, CSPA to Adansehene, 10 Feb. 1912.

100. NAGA ADM 46/5/1 PC's Diary, 3 Oct. 1913.

101. Van Hear, 'Northern Labour and the Development of Capitalist Agriculture', 142.

102. J. I. Roper, *Labour Problems in West Africa* (Harmondsworth, 1958), 35–36.

103. Ibid., 14.

Chapter 17

1. See pp. 253–57.

2. Hopkins, *Economic History*, 210–14; Phillips, *Enigma of Colonialism*.

3. Austin, 'Mode of production or mode of cultivation'.

4. NAGK D1877, 'Complaint by Adansihene Preventing His Subjects from Planting more Cocoa' (Ashanti M.P. N13/19): Adansehene to PC, Obuasi, 6 Feb. 1919.

5. D1877: CSPA to CCA: Obuasi, 8 Feb. 1919.

6. There is rich material from and on him in the national archives, esp. in Kumasi. See also Daaku, *Oral Traditions of Adanse*.

7. Matson, *A Digest of the Minutes of the Ashanti Confederacy Council*, 16; NAGK 'Ashanti Confederacy Council Control of Cocoa Farming' (formerly classified as file no. 717 on Shelves 14 and 15) [actual covering dates 31 May 1939 to 18 Jan. 1947].

8. *Annual Report on Soil Erosion in the Gold Coast, 1938* (Gold Coast Government: Accra, 1939), 2.

9. Ibid., 2.

10. NAGK 'Ashanti Confederacy Council Control of Cocoa Farming': Asokorehene to CCA, Asokore 28 June 1939, and Bekwaihene to DC Bekwai, Bekwai, 26 Sept. 1939.

11. *Report on Soil Erosion in the Gold Coast, 1939*, 3.

12. NAGK 'Ashanti Confederacy Council Control of Cocoa Farming', H. W. Chapman(?) to CCA, Bekwai, 9 April 1940: cf. replies in the same file, same month, from the commissioners for Obuasi, Kumasi, and Mampong.

13. NAGK RAO Files formerly classified as on Shelves 12 & 13, no. 2314: Asst DC, Goaso, to DC, Kumasi: Goaso, 19 April 1940. Cf. reply from commissioner in Sunyani, the same month, April 1940, in NAGK 'Ashanti Confederacy Council Control of Cocoa Farming'.

14. MRO SB15 'Cocoa—Control of Planting' (226/35–46/SF1), pp. 7–8.

15. Formally there were to be no prosecutions for planting before Feb. 1946 (ibid., pp. 7–8); and in practice the planting season was unlikely to have started by the time the new order (signed by the Asantehene on 4 March) took effect.

16. Ibid., p. 17, C. K. Opoku, Catholic Mission School to Secretary, Ashanti Confederacy Council, Tepa, 15 July 1947.

17. Ibid., p. 15, Opong Yaw III, Dormaahene, to Secretary, Ashanti Confederacy Council, [Kumasi], 18 Aug. 1947.

18. It is not necessary here to examine how far this relationship was direct, and how far it was mediated by income and savings effects, as argued for Nigerian cocoa farmers by Sara S. Berry, 'Supply response reconsidered: cocoa in Western Nigeria, 1909–44', *Journal of Development Studies* 13:1 (1976), 4–17.

19. See Bateman, 'An econometric analysis of Ghanaian cocoa supply', Table A2.

20. Ibid., 291.

21. See p. 55.

22. The following percentages are calculated from the figures reported in Fortes papers, 9.18, 'Additional Notes on Land Tenure (Ashanti Cocoa farmers)' (annonymous, n.d.: but internal evidence suggests that Fortes himself was the author; almost certainly 1946).

23. See p. 311.

24. ARG 2/3/1/6, Amoafo's 'Economic aspects of land tenure arrangements in Ashanti/Brong Ahafo', 4–5.

25. The chronology is inexact because, in this cyclostyled publication dated Feb. 1959, Bray wrote merely that the evidence had been collected over 'two and a half to three years' (Bray, *Cocoa Development in Ahafo*, i).

26. Ibid., 20.

27. George Benneh, 'Land tenure and farming system in Nkrankwanta: a village in the pioneer-cocoa area of Ghana', *Bulletin of the Ghana Geographical Association* 10: 2 (1965), 11.

28. Amoafo's 'Economic aspects of land tenure arrangements in Ashanti/Brong Ahafo', 3; repeated almost to the word in Division of Agricultural Economics, 'A report on a survey of land tenure systems in Ghana', *Ghanaian Bulletin of Agricultural Economics*, 2:1 (1962), 3.

29. Bray, *Cocoa Development in Ahafo*, 30.

30. Ibid., 20.

31. Ibid., 20.

32. Ibid., 19.

33. See p. 265.

34. Beverly Grier, 'Cocoa marketing in colonial Ghana: capitalist enterprise and the emergence of a rural African bourgeoisie', *Ufahamu* 10:1–2 (1980–81), 102–3. Grier's

formulation emphasizes the role of the Asantehene, as central authority: but he was in exile during the establishment of cocoa-growing in Asante.

35. George Benneh, 'The impact of cocoa cultivation on the traditional land tenure system of the Akan of Ghana', *Ghana Journal of Sociology* 6:1 (1970), 43–61.

36. Wilks, *Asante in the Nineteenth Century*, 51.

37. ARG 2/3/1/11.

38. ARG 1/12/1/21: CWPA to CCA, Sunyani 8 Jan. 1913; minute by Fuller, 15 Jan. 1913.

39. On the issue of efficiency cf. pp. 79–86. The post-colonial measures referred to were the Rents (Cocoa Farms) Regulations 1962 and the Rents Stabilisation (Amendment) Act 1963. See NAGK Juaso DAO File 2681, p. 164, copy of public notice entitled 'Rents (Stabilisation) Act'.

40. D2743, Griffith to CCA, 29 Aug. 1913.

41. ARG 1/12/1/21 'Tribute on Cocoa—Western Province, Ashanti': Fell, CWPA, to CCA, Sunyani 8 Jan. 1913; Fuller, minute to CWPA, 15 Jan. 1913.

42. In 1942, after much debate, the Ashanti Confederacy Council resolved that the tapper should keep two-thirds of the income, the other third to go to the land-owning stool or, if the rubber trees stood on a farm, to be shared equally between the farmowner and the stool. Rhodes House Library, Oxford: Papers of Margery Perham, Mss Perham 391/1, Minutes of the Fifth Session of the Ashanti Confederacy Council, 19–20 October 1942.

43. Quoted above, p. 247.

44. See p. 272–73.

45. Boni, 'Hierarchy in Twentieth-Century Sefwi (Ghana)' (D.Phil., Oxford University, 1999).

46. PRAAD Sunyani RG 2/3/17, p. 11.

47. Belfield, *Report*, 14.

48. D2743, CCA to CS, 6 Oct. 1913, and enclosed minutes of meeting of the Coomassie Council of Chiefs, 2 Oct. 1913.

49. PRO CO96/590, CCA to CS, 23 April 1918 (encl. in Governor to Secretary of State, 31 May 1918).

50. West African Lands Committee, Draft Report, 97.

51. Draft Report, 98.

52. For an overview of the inter-war debate for British West Africa see Phillips, *Enigma of Colonialism*, 118–35.

53. 'Memorandum on the Establishment of a Land Department and the Introduction of Registration of Title' by R. H. Rowe, 28 Sept. 1926, in Gold Coast Government confidential print, *Proposed Reforms in Respect of the Land Legislation of the Gold Coast Primarily in order to Promote Security of Title* (Accra, 1927; copy in PRO CO96/671/6), 76.

54. PRO CO96/663 Memo. on 'Land Tenure in the Gold Coast' by Lt-Col. Rowe, Accra, 18 Feb. 1926; cf. memo. 'The Land Question and Proposed Reforms' by Rowe, same date and file.

55. Rowe's 'On the Establishment of a Land Department' cited above.

56. Rattray's access to the public print was the more important politically because after the resignation in 1923 of the chief commissioner who had appointed him, he lacked influence within the Ashanti administration (see PRO CO996/662, Minute by a Colonial Office official, 21 Feb. 1927, on Rattray's memo. on Anthropology), though, importantly, his memoranda were forwarded to the governor in Accra and the minister in London.

57. Rattray, *Ashanti Law*, quotes from 359 (the first two), 360, 364 respectively.

58. Memo. by R. S. Rattray, 22 Dec. 1927, in Gold Coast Government Confidential Print, *Land Legislation of the Gold Coast*, II (Accra, 1929), cf. Rattray, *Ashanti Law*, 364.

59. Rattray, *Ashanti Law*, 361.

60. Ibid., 365.

61. Memo. by R. S. Rattray, 22 Dec. 1927, cited in n. 58, 5.

62. Rhodes House, MSS. Afr.s.1299, G. W. Stackpoole, Commissioner of Lands, 25 Nov. 1944, memo. on 'registration of title'.

63. ARG 1/3/5/3, Hugh Hurrell, Asst. Commissioner of Lands to CCA, Kumasi, 15 Dec. 1945.

64. Ibid., 'Cocoa Farms—Registration of Title of' (Notes of meeting on 25 Nov. 1945 between Dr. M. Fortes, Mr R. W. Steel and the Asst Commissioner of Lands). Cf. the resource constraints faced earlier by the administration even in demarcating the boundaries of chieftaincies, let alone of individual farms (p. 275 above).

65. Watson Report, 69 (cf. 8).

66. Ibid., 56, 69.

67. See ibid., 69.

68. PRO CO964 Files 16 and 17.

69. Trevor, *Report on Banking Conditions in the Gold Coast and on the Question of Setting up a National Bank* (Gold Coast Government, Accra, 1951), para. 151. Cf. G. D. Paton, *Report on the Development and Control of Banking and Agricultural Credit Facilities in the Gold Coast* (Gold Coast Government: Accra, 1949), 2.

70. Trevor, *Report on Banking Conditions in the Gold Coast*, para. 151.

71. I am grateful to Richard Rathbone for his views of this, based on his unrivalled knowledge of the PRO records on Ghana in the era of decolonization.

72. W. A. Lewis, *Theory of Economic Growth* (London, 1955), 121.

73. Division of Agricultural Economics, 'Report on a survey of land tenure systems in Ghana', 12.

74. Ault and Rutman, 'Development of individual rights to property in tribal Africa'; Bentley and Oberhofer, 'Property rights and economic development'; Gershon Feder and Raymond Noronha, 'Land rights systems and agricultural development in Sub-Saharan Africa', *World Bank Research Observer* 2 (1987), 143–69; Shem Migot-Adholla, Peter Hazell, Benoît Blarel, and Frank Place, 'Indigenous land rights systems in Sub-Saharan Africa: a constraint on productivity?', *World Bank Economic Review* 5 (1991), 155–75; Shem E. Migot-Adholla, George Benneh, Frank Place, and Steven Atsu, 'Land, security of tenure, and productivity in Ghana', in John W. Bruce and Shem E. Migot-Adholla (eds), *Searching for Land Tenure Security in Africa* (Washington DC, 1994), 97–118. All these cite Hill's *Migrant Cocoa-Farmers* with approval in this context (though Bentley and Oberhofer's rendering of Hill is rather muddled: 'Property rights and economic development', 57).

75. Firmin-Sellers, *Transformation of Property Rights in the Gold Coast*.

76. Douglas Rimmer, *Staying Poor: Ghana's Political Economy 1950–1990* (Oxford, 1992), 37–39.

77. See p. 276.

78. Rattray, *Ashanti Law*, 364.

79. A. W. Cardinall, *In Ashanti and Beyond* (New York, 1971: 1st edn Philadelphia, 1927), 278.

80. CO96/700/8 Governor to Thomas, 15 Oct. 1931. Cf. Phillips, *Enigma of Colonialism*, 123–24, 134. It was a similar story in 1927, when the government tried unsuccessfully to introduce in the Gold Coast Colony a statute of limitations ' "to safeguard the title to property and the fruits of individual enterprise from the assaults of those who have unreasonably delayed in asserting their claims" '. The Civil Proceedings Limitation Bill was eventually abandoned. The Supreme Court judges in the Colony argued that setting a time limit by which reversion rights had to be asserted would increase litigation rather than reduce it (Kyerematen, *Inter-Stool Boundary Litigation*, 90–91).

81. See pp. 305–10, 374–78.

82. The classic reference is Ranger, 'The invention of tradition in colonial Africa'. For a revisionist overview see Thomas Spear, 'Neo-traditionalism and the limits of invention in British colonial Africa', *JAH* 44 (2003), 3–27.

83. Rattray, *Ashanti Law*, 366.

84. Cowen and Shenton, 'Bankers, peasants, and land in British West Africa'.

85. Paton, *Report on the Development and Control of Banking and Agricultural Credit Facilities*, 2.

86. G. Hardin, 'The tragedy of the commons', *Science* 162 (1968), 1343–8.

87. See p. 10.

88. Bray, *Cocoa Development in Ahafo*, 17.

89. See above, pp. 327–32.

90. Kojo Sebastian Amanor, *The New Frontier: Farmers' Response to Land Degradation—a West African study* (London, 1994); Mary Tiffen, Michael Mortimore and Francis Gichuki, *More People, Less Erosion: Environmental Recovery in Kenya* (Chichester, 1994); James Fairhead and Melissa Leach, *Misreading the African Landscape: Society and Ecology in a Forest-Savanna Mosaic* (Cambridge, 1996).

91. Coase, 'The problem of social cost' (1966), reprinted in Coase, *The Firm, the Market, and the Law*, 95–156.

92. Hardin, 'The tragedy of the commons'.

93. Ghana, Ministry of Agriculture (Crop Production Division), 'Production Programme 1972: Ashanti Region' (stencilled: Accra, n.d. but presumably 1971).

94. Busia, *Position of the Chief*, 200–205. By the 1980s such claims were much less controversial: for example, in the mid-1980s the *amanhene* of Asumegya and Bekwai both had large private oil palm plantations distinct from the stool farms.

95. NAGK Bekwai File 634: 'Handing-Over Notes' of Captain O. F. Ross, Ag DC Obuasi, 22 Sept. 1924; and of B. D. Austin-Cathie, Asst DC Bekwai, 7 Feb. 1924.

96. NAGK D133, 18 Sept. 1930.

97. ARG 9/3/2, items 111 and 152, and enclosures in items 73 and 170.

98. MRO: Town and Village Affairs, 39, 'Destoolment Charges', 16 May 1938, enclosed in Krontihene and other elders of Denyase to Asantehene, Bekwai, 18 May 1938.

99. NAGK Bekwai File 77, item 39. Cf. for the case of Denyase stool, AF: interview with Mr Kojo Asiedu, Huntado, 11 July 1980.

100. Gold Coast Government, *Report of the Commission of Inquiry (C. R. Havers, K. C.) Into Expenses incurred by Litigants in the Courts of the Gold Coast and Indebtedness Caused Thereby* (Accra, 1945) [hereafter Havers *Report*], 31.

101. NAGK Bekwai 118, Sinclair (Ag DC, Bekwai) to CCA, 7 April 1940.

102. Havers *Report*, 31.

103. On levies in such contexts see ibid., 31, 33. Also, e.g., the Ashanti Farmers' Union in testimony to the Nowell Commission (*African Morning Post*, 11 April 1938: evidence given in Kumasi on 2 April, by James Edusei, AFU Secretary).

104. This paragraph is based on Austin, 'Capitalists and chiefs', 87–88. Some related issues are explored by Sara S. Berry, 'Unsettled accounts: stool debts, chieftaincy disputes and the question of Asante constitutionalism', *JAH* 39 (1988), 39–62 (reprinted in Berry, *Chiefs*).

105. As n. 101 above.

106. Busia, *Position of the Chief*, ch. 6; Austin, 'Rural Capitalism', 518–21: on Christianity, cf. Dunn and Robertson, *Dependence and Opportunity*, 121–37.

107. Robert H. Bates, 'Social dilemmas and rational individuals: an assessment of the new institutionalism', in John Harriss, Janet Hunter and Colin M. Lewis (eds.), *The New Institutional Economics and Third World Development* (London, 1995), 17–26; Firmin-Sellers, *Transformation of Property Rights in the Gold Coast*. On collective action see much of Bates's work on Africa (references in ch. 1) and Olson, *Logic of Collective Action*.

Chapter 18

1. On the former see above, chs 3, 6, 8–10; on the latter see Dumett, 'Rubber trade', 95–96; Arhin, 'Aspects of the Ashanti northern trade', 369, 371–72.

2. Holt Papers, 'Justification'.

3. Bauer, *West African Trade*, 208–9.

4. A convenient brief account is provided by David Fieldhouse, *Merchant Capital and Economic Decolonisation: the United Africa Company 1929–1980* (Oxford, 1994), 119.

5. Discussed by Southall, 'Cadbury on the Gold Coast', 225–28.

6. Cadbury Papers, University of Birmingham Library, 281, 'E. J. Organ's visit to West Africa', report dd. 5 Jan. 1932, pp. 9–11. See also 272, 'William A. Cadbury's report on visit to the Gold Coast', n.d. [1930?], p. 3.

7. *Nowell Report*, 110 (for some specifics, 194).

8. E.g. ibid., 194.

9. PRAAD Accra: ADM 11/1641, Resolution of mass meeting of AFU, Kumasi, 17 Nov. 1937.

10. See quotation and commentary in Austin, 'Capitalists and chiefs', 83.

11. See pp. 413–17; cf. 'Note on Labour in Cocoa Farms of the Eastern Province, Gold Coast', extracted from a memo. by a colonial administrator dd. Koforidua, 25 April 1938, reproduced as an appendix to *Nowell Report*, 193–94.

12. The information for the Eastern Province is that migrant labourers 'always' got credit, 'preferably from the permanent residents of the Zongo' (ibid., 194). The most plausible interpretation is that the migrant labourers, who were mostly from the northern savanna, got credit from fellow northerners who had established themselves as traders in the cocoa belt. This presumably happened in the Zongos in Asante also.

13. This was reflected, e.g., in big corresponding seasonal variation in the amount of currency in circulation. Examples are documented in Cardinall, *The Gold Coast, 1931*, 119–20, though Cardinall misattributed this to Africans not using cheques.

14. Holt Papers, 'Justification'.

15. BBWA Papers, Ms 28623/15 and 23, Bekwai Branch annual reports for 1922 and 1931 respectively.

16. NAGA ADM 46/5/9 Bekwai District RB, I, 1925–33, p. 337.

17. Barclays Bank PLC Group Archives (hereafter Barclays Archives), ACC 11/1027, 'Bank Representation in Bekwai, Ghana': telegram from LHO Lagos to London, 16 Feb. 1956.

18. Cadbury Papers, 'E. J. Organ's visit to West Africa', p. 9. For an example of such 1937–38 testimony see Holt Papers, 'Justification'.

19. BBWA Papers, Ms 28623/19, Kumasi Branch: Annual Report 31st March, 1927.

20. Barclays Archive, ACC 111/044 'Bank Representation in Kumasi, Ghana', 'Extracts from Mr. Cade's Notes on his visit to Kumasi, December, 1955/January, 1956'.

21. E.g. BBWA Papers, Ms 28623/19, Kumasi Branch: Annual Report 31st March, 1927.

22. Cadbury Papers, 'William A. Cadbury's report on visit', 3.

23. UAC was formally created only in 1929, the product of a series of mergers (see Fieldhouse, *Merchant Capital*). But its predecessors had been cooperating in the Ghana market for several years beforehand (Roger J. Southall, 'Polarisation and dependence in the Gold Coast cocoa trade, 1897–1938', *Transactions of the Historical Society of Ghana* 16: 1 [1975], 98–99). On UAC's strategy, alternately competing aggressively for crop share with its rivals and proposing cartels, see ibid., 99–100 and, vividly, Cadbury Papers, 'E. J. Organ's Visit to West Africa', pp. 2–5.

24. *Nowell Report*, 9, 50.

25. The further issue of the 'contestability' of the cocoa-exporting market—implicit competition from potential new entrants, perhaps in the form of an American chocolate manufacturer in a direct-purchase deal with the mobilizers of the hold-up—is considered in Austin, 'Competition, labour credit and economic rent'. This issue arises particularly from important recent work on the 1937 buying agreement. See Jan-Georg Deutsch, *Educating the Middlemen: a Political and Economic History of Statutory Cocoa Marketing in Nigeria, 1936–1947* (Berlin, 1995); Fieldhouse, *Merchant Capital*.

26. *Nowell Report*, 50.

27. Clearly implied, e.g., in Holt Papers, 'Justification'.

28. See p. 44. For the firms' behaviour towards and view of government policy see *Nowell Report*, 75.

29. Ibid., 29.

30. See pp. 358–59.

31. Austin, 'Capitalists and chiefs'.

32. Fortes Papers, 6.1, 'Debtors and Lenders in Agogo'.

33. Ghana, *Survey of Cocoa Producing Families in Ashanti, 1956–57*, Table 27.

34. Holt Papers, 'Justification'.

35. Bauer, *West African Trade*, 208.

36. Holt Papers, 'Justification'.

37. *Nowell Report*, 38.

38. Holt Papers, 'Justification'.

39. Austin, 'Competition, labour credit and economic rent'.

40. Introduced above, p. 296.

41. Beckett, 'Memorandum for transmission to the Commission of Enquiry'.

42. Holt Papers, MSS Afr. s825/536 (ii), statement of evidence by George R. Yebuah, 17 March 1938, encl. in Holt's to Cocoa Commission, Kumasi, 18 March 1938.

43. See Beckett, 'Memorandum for transmission to the Commission of Enquiry', Table 2 (discussed in Austin, 'Competition, labour credit and economic rent'). Beckett's data were for Accra prices, though: Kumasi prices were normally lower than coast prices, as the produce was exported by sea.

44. Shephard, *Report on the Economics of Peasant Agriculture*, 39; Beckett, 'Memorandum for transmission to the Commission of Enquiry', 2; *Nowell Report*, 23–24, 31, 38.

45. E.g., cases brought by Millers against brokers in Bekwai, Asante, 11 April 1922 (ARG 9/22/1 Bekwai Civil RB, 1922–25, p. 9).

46. Holt Papers, Yebuah's statement.

47. Holt Papers, MSS Afr. s825/536 (ii), statement of evidence by Joseph Kenneth Mensah, 18 March 1938, encl. in Holts to Cocoa Commission, Kumasi, 18 March 1938.

48. Ibid., Goddard to Administration Department, Liverpool, Accra, 13 Dec. 1938.

49. Ibid., Goddard to Administration Department, Accra, 17 Feb. 1939.

50. For a specific example see Austin, 'Capitalists and chiefs', 68.

51. P. 285 above.

52. *Nowell Report*, 31.

53. Shephard, *Report on the Economics of Peasant Agriculture*, 39.

54. For Ghana as a whole Nowell estimated that about 1,500 brokers bulked cocoa from (most of) perhaps 37,000 sub-brokers (*Nowell Report*, 29).

55. Cf. ibid., 26–29.

56. Holt Papers, 'Justification'.

57. Holt Papers, 'Justification'.

58. Yebuah's statement.

59. Mensah's statement.

60. See brokers' balance sheet reproduced in Franz Ehrler, *Handelskonflikte zwischen europäischen Firmen und einheimischen Produzenten in Britisch Westafrika: die 'cocoa-hold-ups' in der Zwischenkriegszeit* (Zürich: Atlantis, 1977), 57–58. I thank my departmental colleague Max-Stephan Schulze for help with translation.

61. The average of the mean monthly price for cocoa at the point of shipment in Accra during Nov.–Jan. was 73.6% above that for the preceding July–Sept. (calculated from Beckett, 'Memorandum for transmission to the Commission of Enquiry', Table 2).

62. ARG 1/12/1/33, enclosure in DC to Asst. CCA, Wenchi, 7 July 1933.

63. Ibid., Nana Kwabena Fori, quoted in DC Obuasi to Asst CCA, 30 June 1933.

64. NAGK D1057 'Motion by Kwame Darko re the case Kwame Darko, Pltff-applt. vs. Akosuah Bilaeoe [and] Kojo Ompon, Defts-Respdts, previously tried and determined by the D.C., J'so': Akosua Birago to CCA, Kumawu, 14 Sept. 1936.

65. Ibid.

66. Rhodes House: MSS.Afr.s.1111, Russell papers, 5/3, personal letter by A. J. Loveridge, Chief Regional Officer, to Governor, Kumasi, 27 Sept. 1954.

67. Allman and Tashjian, *'I Will Not Eat Stone'*, 141–43.

68. Besides the claims of wives to shares of cocoa farms they had helped make, it is interesting to note a case in Kumasi in 1919 when a wife inherited her husband's credits. Specifically, she was able to foreclose on a plantation mortgaged to her late husband. It may have made a difference (but exactly what?) that her brother, who acted for her, was one of

the richest and perhaps most powerful men in Kumasi: Chief J. K. Frimpon. See NAGK RAO Files on Shelves 12 & 13, No. 781, 'Rubber and Cocoa Plantation—Mortgage of' (16/1919): Chief Kobina Yebua to CCA, Kumasi 24 March 1919.

69. NAGK D2469: Fuller to Chief Kofi Senchere; Ankasi, 28 Oct. 1916.

70. NAGK Bekwai File 26: Adjuah Aboaku to DC, 17 April 1926.

71. Rattray papers, MS 107:1, 1656.

72. Muir, 'Survey of cacao areas', 62.

73. NAGK Bekwai File 26: Adjuah Aboaku to DC, 17 April 1926.

74. NAGK D133 (EP 9/1929) Diary—Bekwai District, entry for 14 Aug. 1930.

75. Ibid., 16 Sept. 1930.

76. Ibid., 21 July 1930.

77. Ibid., 9 Oct. 1930.

78. Allman and Tashjian, *'I Will Not Eat Stone'*, 143–48 (quotation, 145).

79. Fortes papers, 8.16 'Opinions and experiences of women on marriage matters'.

80. Meyer Fortes, 'The lineage in Ashanti', in his *Kinship and the Social Order: the Legacy of Lewis Henry Morgan* (London, 1970), 170.

81. See pp. 304–9. I have found no evidence of rotating credit societies being used to finance the hire of short-term labour during the colonial period. Karen Legge, in fieldwork in Antoakrom (Amansie), found that '*susu*' groups were 'very common' by 1987. They were composed mainly of women and were used to assemble lump sums for farming as well as for school and hospital fees and clothing (Legge, 'Differentiation in the Rural Economy of Southern Ghana: a Village Case Study' [Ph.D. dissertation, Liverpool University, 1994], 245, 252–3 [quote at 252]). In 1927 a senior colonial agricultural official described '*osusu*' (*sic*) groups as 'common all over the country' (Ghana), but 'not devoted to any productive and profitable purpose' (G. G. Auchinleck, 'Co-Operative Societies in the Gold Coast', *Journal of the Gold Coast Agricultural & Commercial Society* 6:2 [1927], 114). They may have been relatively new in Asante at that time (see pp. 137–38 above).

82. Okali, *Cocoa and Kinship in Ghana*, 103–5, 118–121, 130, 136–39, 144–46.

83. See, e.g., Hill, *Migrant Cocoa-Farmers*; Austin, 'Rural Capitalism', esp. 319, 329–31.

84. See p. 92 above.

85. Busia, *Position of the Chief*, 43.

86. See pp. 280–81.

87. Esumeja Native Court B, Civil RB 1957–59, Kofi Aduh v. Afua Kesewah, 28 April to 9 June 1958 (record book held at the District Magistrate's Court, Bekwai; consulted there in 1987, by permission of the magistrate and registrar).

88. Fortes, 'Ashanti patrilateral kinship and its values', 206.

89. For a still more downbeat assessment of the long-term dynamics of female ownership of cocoa farms, focussed on the Sunyani district to 1981, see Gwendolyn Mikell, 'Filiation, economic crisis, and the status of women in rural Ghana', *Canadian Journal of African Studies* 18: 1 (1984), 195–218.

90. Allman and Tashjian, *'I Will Not Eat Stone'*.

91. Ibid., 105–24.

92. AF: interviews with Mr J. O. Mensah, Bekwai, 10 July 1980; and in Esumeja, Manso Nkwanta and Jacobu, cited above, p. 526 nn. 27, 28.

93. Gordon R. Woodman, 'Ghana reforms the law of intestate succession', *Journal of African Law* 29: 2 (1985), 118–28.

94. Goody, *Production and Reproduction*; cf. Bates, 'Capital, kinship, and conflict: the structuring effect of capital in kinship societies'. See ch. 9.

95. Howard, *Colonialism and Underdevelopment in Ghana*: on usury, 195–97; for context see esp., 195, 214.

96. See p. 27 above.

97. For some empirical insight see Peter C. Garlick, *African Traders and Economic Development in Ghana* (Oxford, 1971), 57–58.

98. Hill, *The Pledging of Ghana Cocoa Farms*, Hill, *Development Economics on Trial*, passim.

99. H. Myint, *Economics of the Developing Countries*, 55, 65.

100. Kaushik Basu, 'Limited liability and the existence of share tenancy', *Journal of Development Economics* 38 (1992), 203–20 (his italics).

101. The seminal paper was by Joseph E. Stiglitz and Andrew Weiss, 'Credit rationing in markets with imperfect information', *American Economic Review* 71 (1981), 393–410.

102. A valuable introduction to the specialist literature is provided by Ray, *Development Economics*.

103. See generally the Shepherd and Nowell reports and sources cited later in this paragraph.

104. Examples are found in the exercise books listing debts in Fortes Papers 6.61, 'Debtors and Lenders in Agogo' [n.d. but 1945–46].

105. Fortes Papers, 6.45, 'Agricultural Indebtedness'.

106. PRAAD Sunyani RG 2/1/2, Bechemhene to DC Sunyani, Bechem 21 Jan. 1935; cf. Kwaku Nsiah to DC Sunyani, Sunyani 22 Dec. 1938.

107. NAGK Bekwai DAO File 35, 'Cocoa Crop Report': item 418, CCA to DC of Bekwai, Kumasi, dd. 23 Aug. 1933. In the letter the CCA quoted his own report. See, further, item 419, DC to amanhene, Bekwai, 30 Aug. 1933.

108. ARG 1/12/1/33, DC Obuasi to Asst CCA, 2 June 1933; J. R. Dickinson, DC Mampon (and ex-DC Obuasi) to Asst CCA, 31 May 1933.

109. Dickinson, as in n. 108.

110. ARG 1/12/1/33, Walker to Asst CCA, 19 June 1933.

111. Fortes Papers, 9.18, 'Additional Notes on Land Tenure (Ashanti Cocoa farmers)'.

112. Kyerematen, *Inter-Stool Boundary Litigation*, 104.

113. Anonymous, 'Farm debt and mortgages', *The Gold Coast Farmer*, Feb. 1934, 134.

114. E.g. R. Galletti, K. D. S. Baldwin and I. O. Dina, *Nigerian Cocoa Farmers* (London, 1956), 597.

115. ARG 1/12/1/33, Ag DC Kumasi to Asst CCA, 26 May 1933.

116. NAGK RAO File on Shelves 12 & 13, No. 1603. See also, for a *fi: fa*: sale in Esumeja, Bekwai File 39, Kobena Kankeri, Esumejahene to DC, 15 Jan. 1930; Kwabena Kramo to DC, 13 Jan. 1930.

117. ARG 1/12/1/33, DC Sunyani to Asst CCA, 18 May 1933.

118. Ibid., DC to Asst. CCA, Wenchi, 7 July 1933 and enclosures.

119. Introduced above pp. 30–31.

120. NAGK D2632, 'Cocoa Purchasing Company'.

121. Bray, *Cocoa Development in Ahafo*, 46.

122. ARG 1/12/1/33, Walker to Asst CCA, 19 June 1933.

123. Fortes Papers, 6.45, 'Agricultural Indebtedness'.

124. NAGK RAO Files on Shelves 12 & 13, No. 781, 'Rubber and Cocoa Plantation—Mortgage of' (16/1919): Chief Kobina Yebua to CCA, Kumasi 24 March 1919.

125. Chief Yebua pleaded that the loans he had received were not quite as large as they appeared because they were subject to 'a custom prevailing among money lenders in Ashanti' under which 5% commission was deducted at the start (ibid.). However, I have not found evidence of this practice in other loans on cocoa farms. It may be that, if genuine, this was practiced by 'specialist' or regular moneylenders rather than by farmers who lent occasionally.

126. McCaskie, *Asante Identities*, 140–41.

127. NAGK Bekwai 35, Walker to CCA, 23 Jan. 1934.

128. Fortes Papers 6.45, 'Agricultural indebtedness'.

129. Ibid., 141.

130. It should be explained that McCaskie's study is explicitly based on papers from the Ashanti Social Survey, but mostly on a different part of them from that which I have used, and cite directly. Like others, I have used the Fortes Papers, held in Cambridge University Library. McCaskie's book primarily used papers given him by Fortes's partner on the Survey, Robert Steel. At the time of writing they are not yet on public deposit, but after cataloguing will be placed in Birmingham University Library (personal communication from Professor McCaskie).

131. McCaskie, *Asante Identities*, 136–38: quotations from 138.

132. Ibid., 139.

133. T. E. Kyei, *Marriage and Divorce Among the Ashanti: A Study Undertaken in the Course of the Ashanti Social Survey (1945)* (Cambridge African Monographs: Cambridge, 1992), 35.

134. ARG 1/12/1/33, Ag DC Kumasi to Asst CCA, 26 May 1933.

135. 1945 testimony, quoted in McCaskie, *Asante Identities*, 142.

136. Fortes Papers 9.2.

137. Hill, *The Gold Coast Cocoa Farmer*, 64–65.

138. Shepherd, *Report*, 44–45; Havers, *Report*, 39.

139. E.g. see pp. 80–81.

140. Quoted in Kyerematen, *Inter-state Boundary Litigation*, 104.

141. Watson Report, 53.

142. Bray, *Cocoa Development in Ahafo*, 50.

143. Ibid., 51.

144. Galletti, Baldwin and Dina, *Nigerian Cocoa Farmers*, 505, 541–42, 599.

145. Interview with Nana Osei Kofi, ex-Amoafohene, and other elders, Amoafo, 6 May 1980.

146. Fortes Papers, 9.18, 'Additional Notes on Land Tenure (Ashanti Cocoa farmers)'.

147. Fortes Papers, 8.32, Yaw Basare of Asokore, [probably] 8 June 1945.

148. Fortes Papers, 9.67, 'Writs of Fi:Fa:'.

149. Fortes Papers, 9.18, 'Additional Notes on Land Tenure (Ashanti Cocoa farmers)'.

150. See p. 319.

151. Cadbury Papers, 289/245, Hunter to J. Cadbury, 29 March 1938. Cf., for the Gold Coast as a whole, Havers, *Report*, 39.

152. Christopher Baker, 'Debt and the depression in Madras', in Clive Dewey and A. G. Hopkins (eds), *The Imperial Impact: Studies in the Economic History of Africa and India* (London, 1978), 237.

Chapter 19

1. For an introduction to the history of hired labour in Africa see Bill Freund, *The African Worker* (Cambridge, 1988).

2. E.g. Samir Amin, introduction to Amin (ed.), *Modern Migrations in Western Africa* (London, 1974), 95.

3. It was then that Native Authorities there were authorized to collect a poll tax.

4. A. I. Asiwaju, 'Migrations as revolt: the example of the Ivory Coast and the Upper Volta before 1945', *JAH* 14 (1976), 577–94; Dennis D. Cordell, Joel W. Gregory and Victor Piché, *Hoe and Wage: a Social History of a Circular Migration System in West Africa* (Boulder, 1996), 77–80, 83–84, 99–100.

5. Takyiwaa Manuh has suggested that a multiplication of the fees paid by men on marriage during 1951–54, compared to their 1940s levels (which she documented for Kona, a village near Kumasi), reflected demand for female labour by men responding to the upsurge in cocoa prices (Manuh, 'Changes in marriage and funeral exchanges among the Asante: a case study from Kona, Afigya-Kwabre', in J. I. Guyer (ed.), *Money Matters: Instability, Values and Social Payments in the Modern History of West African Communities* [Portsmouth NH, 1995], 194). To the extent that this was so, it confirms a relatively low elasticity of supply for wifely labour. On the other hand, increased marriage expenditure may have been a function of the increased consumption power derived from the rising incomes from existing cocoa farms, as well as a function of the desire to establish more of them.

6. Christine Okali, 'The Importance of Non-Economic Variables in the Development of the Ghana Cocoa Industry: A Field Study of Cocoa Farming Among the Akan' (Ph.D. thesis, University of Ghana, 1976), 100, 163, 166, 168; Okali, *Cocoa and Kinship in Ghana*.

7. Kyei, *Our Days Dwindle*, 25.

8. Muir, 'Survey of cacao areas', 61.

9. See p. 309. This pattern continued beyond the colonial period. In the early 1970s, e.g., Okali found in Dominase (Ahafo) that women helped cocoa-farming men primarily on young cocoa farms, because of the food crops, see Okali, 'Importance of Non-Economic Variables in the Development of the Ghana Cocoa Industry', 175, also 170, 172.

10. Asserted by Jonathan H. Frimpong-Ansah, *The Vampire State in Africa: the Political Economy of Decline in Ghana* (London, 1991), 23.

11. Pp. 91–94.

12. AF: interview in Ofoase-Kokoben on 28 July 1980 with Nana Kwaku Gyekyi (the brothers were introduced above, pp. 262, 274, 319).

13. Muir, 'Survey of cacao areas', 61.

14. See pp. 80, 317.

15. See pp. 315–17; cf. Chs 12 and 13.

16. AF: interview with Nana Owusu Sekyere, Chief Linguist, and Mr. Kwesi Kaabi, in Kokofu, 12 May 1980; interviews in Manso Nkwanta, 23 July 1980; and in Asikaso, 26 Aug. 1982; cf. Sanfo interview, 8 May 1980.

17. See p. 310.

18. Gold Coast Department of Agriculture, *Monthly Newsletter*, 38, July 1931.

19. See, e.g., Rhodes House, Holt s825 536(ii), memo.: 'Justification of a Cocoa Buying Agreement as Seen from the Merchants' Standpoint', 1938.

20. Nowell, *Report*, 20.

21. *The African Morning Post* [Accra], 12 April 1938: evidence given to Nowell Commission in Kumasi on 2 April.

22. T. Hunter, 'Cost of establishing cacao by Ashanti farmers', Gold Coast Department of Agriculture *Year Book*, 1930. 'In all three cases the methods of working have to a large extent followed ordinary native practices'. Any deviation from these was in the direction of the agricultural practices advocated by the government (ibid.), which tended to be rather more labour-intensive (Cadbury Papers 289/247, Hunter to Cadbury, 1 April 1938; see Ch. 4). The difference would not have been sufficient to affect the present issue. The farms were, respectively, about 43 kilometres west, 82 kilometres northwest, and 63 kilometres north of Kumasi.

23. Compare Ch. 8.

24. See p. 94 (cf. 91–93).

25. Beckett, *Akokoaso*, 60.

26. Rhodes House Library, Oxford: Papers of John Holt and Company (Liverpool) Limited, MSS Afr. s825/536 (ii), statement of evidence by George R. Yebuah, 17 March 1938, encl. in Holts to Cocoa Commission, Kumasi, 18 March 1938.

27. Bray, *Cocoa Development in Ahafo*, 42.

28. On this case see pp. 264, 274.

29. He recruited two men to work on his farm in Sefwi district in the Gold Coast Colony (NAGK Bekwai File 150, 'Labour Agreement' [31/43]: agreement 7 May 1946 between Kobina Manu of Bekwai, farmer, and Mama Grumah and Ali Grumah).

30. Figures computed from the individual contracts collected in NAGK Bekwai File 150.

31. This follows the discussion above, pp. 110–12, 313–14.

32. E.g. AF: interview with Nana Frema II (and Nana Adu Darkoh II), Jacobu, 2 Sept. 1980.

33. John Tosh, 'The cash-crop revolution in tropical Africa: an agricultural reappraisal', *African Affairs* 79: 314 (1980), 87–88. In southeastern Cameroon in the later twentieth century, Geshiere argues, both pressures were found, and remained in tension, in the working groups which Maka cocoa- and coffee-growers organized amongst themselves (Geschiere, 'Working groups or wage labour?').

34. Kyei, *Our Days Dwindle*, 27; cf. pp. 313–14 above.

35. AF: interviews in Jacobu, Asikaso and Sanfo, cited above, p. 526 n. 28 and p. 527 nn. 42, 45.

36. AF: Sanfo interview 8 May 1980.

37. This had changed by 1995, when over half the *nnɔboa* groups in the southwestern Asante village of Nagore operated on wages rather than reciprocity (Tsutomu Takane, *The Cocoa Farmers of Southern Ghana: Incentives, Institutions, and Change in Rural West Africa* [Chiba, Japan, 2002] 13–14). Land was scarcer by then, especially because of population growth.

38. See p. 317.

39. AF: interview in Kokofu in 1987. The question I had asked was 'What is the difference between *nnɔboa* and *adopaa?*'

40. During fieldwork in 1987 it was mentioned to me—though unfortunately I cannot document this properly—that in one village *nnɔboa* labour had ceased (when, my informant did not say), because people could not rely on each other to reciprocate the help that they had received. This statement was untypical, but confirms that the institution is not proof against free-riding and that particular work groups might have restricted lives.

41. Fortes, in Fortes, Steel and Ady, 'Ashanti survey, 1945–46', 162.

42. Discrepant or paradoxical relationships between social attitudes, even apparently well-internalised ones, and the economic behaviour of individuals were famously noted in the context of entrepreneurship by Alexander Gerschenkron, 'Social attitudes, entrepreneurship, and economic development', in his *Economic Backwardness in Historical Perspective* (Cambridge MA, 1962), 52–71. For a fascinating African example, see Robert Harms, *River of Wealth, River of Sorrow: the Central Zaire Basin in the Era of the Slave and Ivory Trade, 1500–1891* (New Haven, 1981), 197–211. For a brief survey of research on this issue for western Africa see Gareth Austin, 'African business in nineteenth-century West Africa', in Alusine Jalloh and Toyin Falola (eds.), *Black Business and Economic Power* (Rochester NY, 2002), 128–31.

43. Penelope A. Roberts, 'The state and the regulation of marriage: Sefwi Wiawso (Ghana), 1900–40', in Haleh Afshar (ed.), *Women, State and Ideology: Studies from Africa and Asia* (Basingstoke, 1987), 52.

44. PRAAD Kumasi ARG 9/12/1 E. A. Burner, DC for Bekwai and Obuasi, to CCA, Bekwai, 29 June 1938.

45. See pp. 311–12.

46. Calculated from Ghana, *Survey of Cocoa Producing Families in Ashanti, 1956–57*, Tables 2, 3. The figures given in the text are the sums of those given in the source for 'Ashanti', 'Brong', and 'Other Ashanti'.

47. Polly Hill, *The Gold Coast Cocoa Farmer: A Preliminary Survey* (London, 1956), 24.

48. As in Steven N. S. Cheung's argument that the efficient dispersion of risk is the motivation for sharecropping generally, a proposition he supported with Chinese data, 1925–40 (Cheung, *The Theory of Share Tenancy* [Chicago, 1969]).

49. Frimpong-Ansah, *The Vampire State*, 23.

50. Dickinson, 'Report on Labour Conditions', 63.

51. MRO CF89, Labour Officer to Ashanti Confederacy Council, 28 Nov. 1946.

52. AF: interview in Esumeja, 5 May 1980, with Nana Kweku Agyeamang, former Omanhene, with contributions from Nana Kofi Edu No. 1 of Esumeja.

53. AF: interview with Mr Peter Osei, Mr J. B. Oppong, Opanyin Kwandaho and others, in Sanfo, 8 May 1980. In Morontuo on Lake Bosomtwe an old farmer, Opanyin Kwasi Owusu, said that if you got annual labourers, *abusa* was unnecessary (interview, 24 July 1980).

54. MRO CF89, Labour Officer to Ashanti Confederacy Council, 28 Nov. 1946.

55. Quoted in PRAAD Accra CSO 0001/SF52, Minute by Ag Commissioner of Labour to Colonial Secretary, Accra 22 Nov. 1946 (cf. AF: Esumeja interview, cited in n. 52 above).

56. Nicholas Van Hear, 'Northern Labour and the Development of Capitalist Agriculture in Ghana' (Ph.D. thesis, University of Birmingham, 1982), 135–43, 152–54, 156, 161–62.

57. International Labour Office, 'Labour health problems in the Gold Coast', *International Labour Review* 34 (1936), 795.

58. That is, the output of one additional unit of labour.

59. There is a parallel with Michael Lipton's classic demonstration that peasants seeking to optimise in this sense in the face of uncertain harvests (his example concerned the volume of output, but the point applies also to its value in the case of violent price

fluctuations) if 'punished with a poor harvest', could 'expect gambler's ruin', with the prospect of 'a crippling burden of debt': Lipton, 'The theory of the optimising peasant', *Journal of Development Studies* 4:3 (1968), 327–51 (quotations from p. 334).

60. Dickinson, 'Report on Labour Conditions', 63.

61. Van Hear, 'Northern Labour', 156, citing PRAAD Tamale, 6/77.

62. A possible reason for the difference between Asante and the Eastern Province of the Gold Coast Colony is that *appa* terms may have been offered more frequently where local cocoa prices were relatively high, because of being closer to the port.

63. Alfred Marshall, *Principles of Economics: an Introductory Volume* (London, 1916: 1st edn 1890), 643–45.

64. See esp. p. 44.

65. E.g. NAGK Bekwai Files, DC's Diary; cp. Dickinson, Dickinson, 'Report on Labour Conditions', 64–65.

66. ARG 9/12/1, 'Notes taken at a Meeting in the Cadbury Hall', Kumasi, 7 Dec. 1937, speeches of Mamponhene and of Kojo Broni, Head Farmer of Asante. A pioneering account of labourers' struggle with farmowners in Ghanaian cocoa-farming generally, 1930–45, is given by Van Hear, 'Northern Labour', 132–33, 145–46, 152, 160–66.

67. The point was documented for the Gold Coast Colony in an appendix to the Nowell Report, but it also applied to Asante (see generally Van Hear, 'Northern Labour', 145–47).

68. Bray, *Cocoa Development in Ahafo*, 40, 69.

69. Ibid., 43.

70. See, e.g., Josephine F. Milburn, *British Business and Ghanaian Independence* (Hanover NH, 1977), 35.

71. For the latter case see p. 288.

72. See pp. 360–61, 365.

73. Bray, *Cocoa Development in Ahafo*, 41.

74. AF: interview with Mr Musa Moshi, Bekwai, 28 Aug. 1980.

75. Stichter, *Migrant Laborers*, 85–87; Cordell, Gregory and Piché, *Hoe and Wage*, 307.

76. Dickinson, 'Report on Labour Conditions', 72.

77. Ghana, *Cocoa Producing Families in Ashanti, 1956–7*, Table 2. The ratio among labourers whose field of employment was not known, and which therefore may well have included some agricultural labourers, was 1,303 to 145 (ibid.).

78. For an amplification of these remarks see Austin, 'National poverty and the "vampire state"'.

79. Addo, 'Some employment and labour conditions on Ghana's cocoa farms', 204–7.

80. J. Adomako-Sarfoh, 'The effects of the expulsion of migrant workers on Ghana's economy, with particular reference to the cocoa industry', in S. Amin (ed.), *Modern Migrations in West Africa* (London, 1974), 138–52.

81. C. Okali, L. O. Gyekye and S. Y. Mabey, *Report on the Socio-Economic Characteristics of the Ashanti Cocoa Rehabilitation Project Area*, Legon 1974, 49.

82. As was repeatedly made clear to me in fieldwork in Amansie in 1979–80 and 1982. There are strong parallels with what was happening in the Nigerian cocoa belt, though there the bidding of labour away from agriculture was fuelled by the oil boom (Sara S. Berry, *Fathers Work for Their Sons: Accumulation, Mobility and Class Formation in an Extended Yoruba Community* [Berkeley, 1985]).

83. Austin, 'Emergence of capitalist relations', 275. On unemployment see Van Hear, 'Northern Labour', 133, 147, 156–59, 161–62.

84. Quoted in Thomas, 'Forced labour in British West Africa', 93.

85. That was their main or sole occupation, according to an elder of Bekwai who was then a young eyewitness. AF: interview with Nana Akumiah, former Krontiehene of Bekwai, Bekwai, 18 Aug. 1982.

86. NAGA ADM 53/5/1 PC's Diary (Obuasi) 1918–22: entries for 15, 25 and 29 April 1919. See also NAGK Obuasi File 147, 'Bekwai Riot'.

87. AF: interview with Nana Akumiah, Bekwai, 7 Oct. 1987.

88. On the zongo as an institution see, esp. for Kumasi, Enid Schildkrout, *People of the Zongo: the Transformation of Ethnic Identities in Ghana* (Cambridge, 1978).

89. For some valuable insights see Carola Lentz and Veit Erlmann, 'A working class in formation? Economic crisis and strategies of survival among Dagara mine workers in Ghana', *Cahiers d'études africaines* 29: 103 (1989), 69–111.

90. Inez Sutton's valuable survey is not immune: Sutton, 'Labour in commercial agriculture in Ghana in the late nineteenth and early twentieth centuries', *JAH*, 24 (1983), 471–73.

91. Hill, *Migrant Cocoa-Farmers*, 188: compare her *Gold Coast Cocoa Farmer*, 11–12, 15–16. See also Sutton, 'Labour in commercial agriculture', 472–73.

92. Jean-Pierre Chauveau and Jacques Richard, 'Une "périphérie recentrée: à propos d'un système local d'économie de plantation en Côte d'Ivoire', *Cahiers d'Études Africaines* 17: 68 (1977), 485–524; Ezekiel Ayodele Walker, 'The changing patterns of labor relations in the cocoa farming belt of southwestern Nigeria, 1950s to 1990s', *African Economic History* 24 (2000), 123–40.

93. Takane, *Cocoa Farmers of Southern Ghana*, 18–34. Compare the earlier observations, for Akyem Abuakwa and the Volta Region respectively, in Hill, *Gold Coast Cocoa Farmer*, 15–16, and Jean-Denis Garceau, 'L'économie du cacao dans une chefferie Akan (Ghana): appropriation des terres et exploitation d'une main-d'oeuvre étrangère', *Culture* 2:2 (1982), 103–4.

94. Ibid., 33.

95. Vallenga, Dorothy Dee, 'Matriliny, patriliny, and class formation among women cocoa farmers in two rural areas of Ghana', in C. Robertson and I. Berger (eds), *Women and Class in Africa* (New York, 1986), 62–77.

96. See Takane, *Cocoa Farmers*, 31–34.

97. ADM 11/1641: Owusu-Ansah, Proceedings of AFA [sic], 17 Nov. 1937.

98. For this thesis about the unequal 'articulation' of precapitalist and capitalist relations of production, see pp. 24–25.

99. Bray, *Cocoa Development in Ahafo*, 45.

100. ARG 9/7/2, extract from Chief Inspector of Labour on 'wages and costs of living', Labour Department, Kumasi, 1 Oct. 1938.

101. Jean Rouch, 'Migrations au Ghana', *Journal de la Société des Africanistes* 26 (1956), 96.

102. See Hill, *Gold Coast Cocoa Farmer*, 17.

103. AF: interview with Mr Musa Moshi, Bekwai, 28 Aug. 1980.

104. *Loc. cit.*

105. Quoted by Bray (from his field assistant, Agyare?), *Cocoa Development in Ahafo*, 49.

106. Robertson, *Dynamics of Productive Relationships*, 78 and generally.

107. Grier wrote of 'a striking resemblance' between the master-slave relationship before colonial rule and 'the relationship that crystallized between landowners and abusa sharecroppers' in the colonial period (Grier, 'Underdevelopment', 36), and in later work referred to '*abusa* sharecroppers who were descendants of slaves' (Grier, 'Contradiction', 43). As I understand it, Grier's point in the earlier passage was partly to note the alleviative aspects of slave status, rather than to emphasize the hardship of sharecropping. And as we have seen in this book, there were indeed major continuities, above all recruitment of both forms of labour from outside the forest zone. But the discontinuity is also crucial: slaves could bargain, could use market forces to their advantage, in a sense fundamentally denied to slaves.

108. W. A. Lewis, *Report on Industrialisation and the Gold Coast* (Accra, 1953).

109. This observation comes from interviews which Paul Coby and I conducted in villages in the Hohoe area in 1977 as part of the research for our respective BA dissertations at the University of Cambridge. Interviews in Lolobi Kumasi with Messrs Daniel Iddah and Raphael Attah (30 Aug.) and with Mr. Marcelinus Dzomeku (14 Sept.); interview in Lolobi Ashambi with Togbi Nana Dzramoah II and elders (10 Sept.); interviews in New Ayoma with Mr. Anthony Manti and with Mr. Vincent Tomekpe (both 29 Sept.). Messrs Victor Koto-Doh, Patrick Adompreh, Sylvester Iddah, and Rev. Manti, kindly interpreted.

110. Jean-Pierre Chauveau and Eric Léonard, 'Côte d'Ivoire's pioneer fronts: historical and political determinants of the spread of cocoa cultivation', in W. G. Clarence-Smith (ed.), *Cocoa Pioneer Fronts* (London, 1996), 176–94.

111. Bray, *Cocoa Development in Ahafo*. For a pioneering study of the history of poverty in northern Ghana itself see Jérôme Destombes, 'Nutrition and Hunger in Northern Ghana, c.1930–c.2000' (Ph.D. thesis, London School of Economics, 2001).

112. E.g. Amin (ed.), *Modern Migrations in West Africa*, 98ff.

Chapter 20

1. Wilks, 'Aspects of bureaucratization in Ashanti'; *Asante in the Nineteenth Century*; 'What manner of persons were these?'

2. McCaskie, *State and Society*.

3. Allman, 'Rounding up spinsters'.

4. David W. Pearce, 'Economics of the Environment', in David Greenaway, Michael Bleaney and Ian Stewart (eds.), *Companion to Contemporary Economic Thought* (London, 1991), 317.

5. See Ch. 8.

6. Recently it has been argued that, from the start, African slaves were not necessarily cheaper than European slaves would have been, and that the reason why Africans rather than Europeans were enslaved for the Americas was extra-economic (David Eltis, *The Rise of African Slavery in the Americas*, Cambridge, 2000, esp. 14–15, 64–70). If so, this illustrates the point that the Nieboer hypothesis is powerful but never sufficient; enslavement—in general or, as usual in historical practice, of members of particular, defined categories of 'enslaveable' people (like nnɔnkɔfoɔ, for Asante captors) presupposes political will and possession of coercive resources.

7. Leys, 'Rational choice or Hobson's choice?'

8. A point elegantly conceded by Bates, 'Social dilemmas and rational individuals: an assessment of the new institutionalism', Harriss, J., Hunter, J. and Lewis, C. M. (eds.), *The New Institutional Economics and Third World Development* (London, 1995), 41–42.

9. E. P. Thompson went so far as to aver that there are *no* sufficient causes in history: Thompson, *The Poverty of Theory and Other Essays* (London, 1978), 241.

10. Cf. Jonathan DiJohn and James Putzel, 'State capacity building, taxation and resource mobilisation in historical perspective', paper presented at the conference 'New Institutional Economics, Institutional Reform and Poverty Reduction', Development Studies Institute, London School of Economics, September 2000.

11. Unlike for the colonial governments in the later colonial period (Cooper, *Decolonisation and African Society*, 1–4).

12. Kay, 'Introduction' to his *Political Economy of Colonialism in Ghana*: the quotation is at p. 13. On government agricultural extension advice see pp. 79–86 above.

13. Karl Marx, *Capital*, Vol. I (London, 1974: German original, 1867), 668.

14. Cooper, 'Postscript' to 2nd edn of his 'Africa and the world economy', in Cooper and others, *Confronting Historical Paradigms* (Madison, 1993), 192.

LIST OF REFERENCES

Because of space constraints the following sections list only those primary and secondary sources actually cited above. Primary sources are listed below by category rather than individually. References to individual files and interviews are given in the notes. The list is arranged as follows:

A. Archival Sources in Ghana
B. Archival Sources Outside Ghana
C. Oral Sources
D. Official Publications and Confidential Prints
E. Unpublished Dissertations and Conference Papers
F. Non-Government Publications

A. Archival Sources In Ghana

Public Records and Archives Administration Department (PRAAD)

The national archives: the biggest and most important single source. Various series from each of the following, in order of importance:

Ashanti Regional Office, Kumasi. In the notes files for which I know the number in the new classification system (see p. n.[ch.1]are prefaced by 'ARG' (Ashanti Region, Ghana). Other files are distinguished by the preface 'NAGK', referring to the old name of the office (National Archives of Ghana, Kumasi).

Headquarters office, Accra (indicated in the notes by 'PRAAD Accra').

Brong-Ahafo Regional Office, Sunyani ('PRAAD Sunyani').

Asantehene's Record Office, Manhyia, Kumasi (MRO)

Various series.

Magistrate's Court, Bekwai

Esumeja Native Court B, Civil Record Book 1957–9. Consulted there in 1987, by kind permission of the Magistrate and Registrar.

B. Archival Sources Outside Ghana

Place-names are from U.K. except where otherwise stated.

Official British Government Records

Public Record Office, Kew: Colonial Office records.

Private Papers of British Former Colonial Officials and Merchants

Rhodes House Library, University of Oxford: many different sets of papers.

Official Company Records

Ashanti Goldfields Corporation archive, Guildhall Library, London.
Bank of British West Africa archive, Guildhall Library, London.
Barclays Bank PLC Group Archives, Wythenshawe, Manchester.
Cadbury Papers, University of Birmingham Library.
John Holt & Company Papers, Rhodes House Library, Oxford.

Papers of Missionaries and Mission Societies

Basel Mission Ghana Archive, Basel Mission, Basel, Switzerland.
(Note also, in selected libraries: Jenkins, Paul, *Abstracts of the Basel Mission Correspondence* [cyclostyled: Basel, n.d.])
'Journal of the Rev. George Chapman, 1843–57', Rhodes University Library, Grahamstown, South Africa (Cory MS 15).
Methodist Missionary Society Archives, School of Oriental and African Studies, University of London.

Papers Deposited By Ethnographers And Historians

Cambridge University Library: Meyer Fortes Papers from the Ashanti Social Survey.
Melville J. Herskovits Memorial Library, Northwestern University, Evanston, Illinois, USA:
    Polly Hill Papers;
    Ivor Wilks Papers
Manuscript Collection of the Royal Anthropological Institute, housed in the Museum of Mankind, London: R. S. Rattray papers.

(Note also):

'Economic History of the Gold Coast 1874–1914: Select Documents' from the national archives in Accra, originally compiled by H. J. Bevin and extended by R. Addo-Fening, stencilled, Department of History, University of Ghana (Legon, 1981).

(Note also, in the Methodist Missionary Society Archive cited above):

Thomas Birch Freeman papers, manuscript of unpublished book by Freeman entitled 'Reminiscences and Incidents of Travels and Historical and Political Sketches in the Countries Bordering on the Gold and Slave Coasts and in Ashantee, Dahomey, etc.' (n.d. but c.1860).

Gold Coast Newspapers

British Newspaper Library, Collindale, London:
Royal Gold Coast Gazette (Cape Coast), 1822–23.
The Western Echo (Cape Coast), 1885–87.
African Morning Post (Accra) 1938–39.

C. Oral Sources

Collections of Other Researchers' Fieldnotes

K. Y. Daaku (ed.), *Oral Traditions of Adanse* (Institute of African Studies, University of Ghana, Legon, 1969).

Austin Fieldnotes: Own Fieldwork in Asante and Volta Region

I conducted fieldwork, primarily in Amansie district, in 1979–80, 1982, 1985, 1987 and 1992. Full references to those interviews cited in the text are given in the references concerned. For my research assistants, please see the Preface.

Earlier I did interviews, together with Paul Coby, in villages in the Hohoe area of the Volta Region. This was in 1977, for our respective BA History dissertations for the University of Cambridge. Details of the particular interviews cited are given in the note concerned.

D. Official Publications and Confidential Prints

British Parliamentary Papers (London)

C.3386, *Further Correspondence Regarding the Affairs of the Gold Coast* (1882): Lonsdale's report on 1881–82.
Further Correspondence Regarding the Affairs of the Gold Coast (1885): Kirby's report on his mission to Kumasi, Accra, 15 April 1884 C.4477.

Other Great Britain (London)

Cd. 6278, *Report on the Legislation Governing the Alienation of Native Lands in the Gold Coast Colony and Ashanti* (1912): the Belfield report.

Confidential Print, African (West), No. 1047, West African Lands Committee, *Minutes of Evidence, etc* (1916); Draft Report.

Annual Report on Ashanti, various years.

Gold Coast Census of Population: reports for 1901, 1911, 1921, 1931, 1948.

Chipp, T. F., *The Forest Officers' Handbook of the Gold Coast, Ashanti and the Northern Territories* (1922).

Report on the Social and Economic Progress of the People of the Gold Coast: reports for 1935–36, 1936–37, 1937–38.

Report of the Commission on the Marketing of West African Cocoa (1938): the Nowell report.

Report of the Commission of Enquiry into Disturbances in the Gold Coast 1948, Colonial No. 231 (1948): the Watson report.

Greaves, Ida, *Colonial Monetary Conditions* (1953).

Gold Coast Government (Accra)

Tudhope, W. S. D., *Enquiry into the Gold Coast Cocoa Industry: Interim Report* (1919), and *Final Report* (1919).

Proposed Reforms in Respect of the Land Legislation of the Gold Coast primarily in order to promote security of title (Confidential Print, 1927).

Muir, J. C., 'Crop surveys, Gold Coast', *Bulletin of the Department of Agriculture, Gold Coast*, vol. 20 (1928), 172–80.

Miles, A. C., 'The size of cacao farms in Ashanti', *Bulletin of the Department of Agriculture, Gold Coast*, vol. 22, *1929 Year Book* (1929), 54–56.

Muir, J. C., 'Survey of cacao areas—Western Province, Ashanti', *Bulletin of the Department of Agriculture, Gold Coast*, vol. 22 (1929), 57–64.

Muir, J. C., 'The cola industry in the Western Province of Ashanti', *Bulletin of the Department of Agriculture, Gold Coast*, vol. 22, *1929 Year Book* (1929), 218–24.

Miles, A. C., 'Cola survey: eastern Ashanti area, and a general review of the cola industry', *Bulletin of the Department of Agriculture, Gold Coast*, vol. 23, *Year-Book 1930* (1930), 135–43.

Gazette, July–December 1930.

Land Legislation of the Gold Coast, Vol. II (Confidential Print, 1929).

Gold Coast Department of Agriculture, *Monthly Newsletter*, 38, July 1931.

Cardinall, A. W., *The Gold Coast, 1931* (n.d.).

Anonymous, 'Farm debt and mortgages', *The Gold Coast Farmer*, Gold Coast Department of Agriculture, February 1934, 134.

Shephard, C. Y., *Report on the Economics of Peasant Agriculture in the Gold Coast* (1936).

The Laws of the Gold Coast (1936).

Annual Report on Soil Erosion in the Gold Coast: 1937, 1938, 1939.

Report of the Commission of Inquiry (C. R. Havers, K. C.) into Expenses Incurred by Litigants in the Courts of the Gold Coast and Indebtedness Caused Thereby (1945).

Matson, J. M. (Mrs.), 1947, 'Report on Land Disputes in the Adansi Division, Obuasi District, Ashanti', original enclosed in Gold Coast No. 62 of 24 March (copies in Balme Library, University of Ghana).

Anonymous, 'Oldest cocoa farm in Ashanti', Gold Coast Department of Agriculture, *Monthly Newsletter*, I:11, 30 November 1947, 24–26.

Paton, G. D., *Report on the Development and Control of Banking and Agricultural Credit Facilities in the Gold Coast* (1949).

Trevor, Sir Cecil, *Report on Banking Conditions in the Gold Coast and on the Question of Setting up a National Bank* (1951).

W. A. Lewis, *Report on Industrialisation and the Gold Coast* (1953).

The Laws of the Gold Coast (1954).

Report of the Commission of Enquiry into the Affairs of the Cocoa Purchasing Company Limited (1956): the Jibowu report.

Government of Ghana (Accra)

Ghana, *Report of the Committee on Agricultural Indebtedness* (1957).

Survey of Cocoa Producing Families in Ashanti, 1956–57 (Office of the Government Statistician, 1960).

Division of Agricultural Economics, 'A report on a survey of land tenure systems in Ghana', *Ghanaian Bulletin of Agricultural Economics* (published by Division of Agricultural Economics, Ministry of Agriculture) 2:1 (1962), 1–15.

(Unpublished: Ministry of Agriculture [Cocoa Production Division], 'Production Programme 1972: Ashanti Region' [stencilled: Accra, n.d. but presumably 1971]).

International Organizations

International Labour Office, 'Labour health problems in the Gold Coast', *International Labour Review* 34 (1936), 794–49.

United Nations, *The Enlargement of the Exchange Economy in Tropical Africa* (New York, 1954). Reprinted in *Research in Economic Anthropology* 2 (1979), 189–246.

E. Unpublished Dissertations and Conference Papers

Aidoo, Agnes A., 'Political Crisis and Social Change in the Asante Kingdom, 1867–1901', 2 vols (Ph.D., University of California, Los Angeles, 1975).

Austin, Gareth, 'Rural Capitalism and the Growth of Cocoa-Farming in South Ashanti, to 1914' (Ph.D., University of Birmingham, 1984).

———, 'The political economy of small and big farmers in Ghanaian cocoa farming, c.1890–1992', paper for SOAS-LSE international conference on Cocoa Production and Economic Development in the 19th and 20th Centuries, London, September 1993.

———, 'Moneylending and witchcraft: the moral economy of accumulation in colonial Asante', paper presented at the Modern Economic History Seminar, London School of Economics, May 2003.

Ball, Rajiv, 'The State and the Development of Small-Scale Industry in Ghana Since c.1945' (Ph.D., London School of Economics, 1997).

Boni, Stefano, 'Hierarchy in Twentieth-Century Sefwi (Ghana)' (D.Phil., Oxford University, 1999).

Brown, James Wilson, 'Kumasi, 1896–1923: Urban Africa during the Early Colonial Period' (Ph.D., University of Wisconsin, Madison, 1972).

Destombes, Jérôme, 'Nutrition and Hunger in Northern Ghana, c.1930–c.2000' (Ph.D., London School of Economics, 2001).

Dickson, K. B., 'Cocoa in Ghana' (Ph.D., University of London, 1960).

DiJohn, Jonathan, and Putzel, James, 'State capacity building, taxation and resource mobilisation in historical perspective', paper presented at the conference 'New Institutional Economics, Institutional Reform and Poverty Reduction', Development Studies Institute, London School of Economics and Political Science, September 2000.

Getz, Tevor, 'That Most Perfidious Institution: the Slow Death of Slavery in Nineteenth Century Senegal and the Gold Coast' (School of Oriental and African Studies, London, 2000).

Hamilton, Robert Earl, 'Asante, 1895–1900: Prelude to War' (Ph.D., Northwestern University, 1978).

Klein, A. Norman, 'Inequality in Asante: A Study of the Forms and Meanings of Slavery and Social Servitude in Pre- and Early Colonial Akan-Asante Society and Culture' (Ph.D., University of Michigan, 1980).

LaTorre, Joseph Raymond, 'Wealth Surpasses Everything: an Economic History of Asante, 1750–1874' (Ph.D., University of California, Berkeley, 1978).

Legge, Karen, 'Differentiation in the Rural Economy of Southern Ghana: a Village Case Study' (Ph.D., Liverpool University, 1994).

McCaskie, Thomas C., 'The Paramountcy of the Asantehene Kwaku Dua (1834–1867): a Study in Asante Political Culture' (Ph.D., University of Cambridge, 1974).

Okali, Christine, 'The Importance of Non-Economic Variables in the Development of the Ghana Cocoa Industry: A Field Study of Cocoa Farming Among the Akan' (Ph.D., University of Ghana, 1976).

Perbi, Akosua A., 'A History of Indigenous Slavery in Ghana from the 15th to the 19th Centuries' (Ph.D., University of Ghana, 1997).

Tashjian, Victoria Beardslee, '"It's Mine" And "It's Ours" Are Not The Same Thing: a History of Marriage in Rural Asante, 1900–1957' (Ph.D., Northwestern University, 1995).

Teal, Francis J., 'Growth, Comparative Advantage and the Economic Effects of Government: a case study of Ghana' (Ph.D., School of Oriental and African Studies, University of London, 1984).

Tsey, Christian E., 'Gold Coast Railways: the Making of a Colonial Economy, 1879–1929' (Ph.D., University of Glasgow, 1986).

Van Hear, Nicholas, 'Northern Labour and the Development of Capitalist Agriculture in Ghana' (Ph.D., University of Birmingham, 1982).

F. Non-Government Publications

Adams, S. N., 'Soils and manuring', in J. Brian Wills, *Agriculture and Land Use in Ghana* (London, 1962), 266–73.

Addo, N. O., 'Some employment and labour conditions on Ghana's cocoa farms', in R. A. Kotey, C. Okali and B. E. Rourke (eds), *Economics of Cocoa Production and Marketing* (Legon, 1974), 204–18.

Adomako-Sarfoh, J., 'The effects of the expulsion of migrant workers on Ghana's economy, with particular reference to the cocoa industry', in S. Amin (ed.), *Modern Migrations in West Africa* (London, 1974), 138–52.

Akurang-Parry, Kwabena Opare, 'Colonial modes of emancipation and African initiatives', *Ghana Studies* 1 (1998), 11–34.

———, 'Colonial forced labor policies for road-building in southern Ghana and international anti-forced labor pressures, 1900–1940', *African Economic History* 28 (2000), 1–25.

———. (See also under Opare-Akurang).

Akyeampong, Emmanuel, and Obeng, Pashington, 'Spirituality, gender and power in Asante History' *International Journal of African Historical Studies* 28 (1995), 481–508.

Alence, Rod, 'The 1937–38 Gold Coast cocoa crisis: the political economy of commercial stalemate', *African Economic History* 19 (1990–91), 77–104.

———, 'Colonial government, social conflict and state intervention in Africa's open economies: the origins of the Ghana Cocoa Marketing Board, 1939–46', *Journal of African History* 43 (2002), 397–416.

Allan, William, *The African Husbandman* (Edinburgh, 1965).

Allman, Jean Marie, 'The youngmen and the porcupine: class, nationalism and Asante's struggle for self-determination, 1954–57', *Journal of African History*, 31 (1990), 263–79.

———, [reply to Rathbone], in *Journal of African History*, 32 (1991), 333–38.

———, 'Of "spinsters", "concubines" and "wicked women": reflections on gender and social change in colonial Asante', *Gender and History* 3:2 (1991), 176–89.

———, *The Quills of the Porcupine: Asante Nationalism in an Emergent Ghana* (Madison, 1993).

———, 'Rounding up spinsters: gender chaos and unmarried women in colonial Asante', *Journal of African History* 37 (1996), 195–214.

———, 'Adultery and the state in Asante: reflections on gender, class, and power from 1800 to 1950', in John Hunwick and Nancy Lawler (eds), *The Cloth of Many Colored Silks: Papers on History and Society Ghanaian and Islamic in Honor of Ivor Wilks* (Northwestern University Press: Evanston, 1996), 27–65.

———, 'Fathering, mothering and making sense of *ntamoba*: reflections on the economy of child-rearing in colonial Asante, 1924–1945', *Africa* 67 (1997), 296–321.

Allman, Jean and Victoria Tashjian, *'I Will Not Eat Stone': A Women's History of Colonial Asante* (Portsmouth NH, 2000).

Amanor, Kojo Sebastian, *The New Frontier: Farmers' Response to Land Degradation—a West African Study* (London, 1994).

Amin, Samir, (ed.), *Modern Migrations in West Africa* (London, 1974).

———, *Unequal Development: an Essay on the Social Formations of Peripheral Capitalism* (Hassocks, Sussex, England, 1976: French original, 1973).

Amoo, J. W. A., 'The effect of western influence on Akan marriage', *Africa* 14 (1946), 228–37.

Aning, Thomas K., 'Re-opening of the National Archives of Ghana – Ashanti Regional Archives, Kumas', Ghana Studies Council *Newsletter* 11 (Spring/Summer 1998), 8–9.

Anonymous, *The Gold Coast: General & Historical; Timbers; Cultivated Resources* (London, n.d. but c.1937).

Arhin, Kwame, 'Market settlements in Northwestern Ashanti: Kintampo', *Research Review* (Institute of African Studies, University of Ghana), Supplement 1, *Ashanti and the Northwest*, ed. by J. Goody and K. Arhin (1965).

———, 'The structure of Greater Ashanti (1700–1824)', *Journal of African History* 8 (1967).

———, 'Succession and gold mining at Mansu Nkwanta', *Research Review* (Institute of African Studies, University of Ghana) 6:3 (1970), 101–9.

———, 'Aspects of the Ashanti northern trade in the nineteenth century', *Africa* 40:4 (1970), 363–73.

———, 'The Ashanti rubber trade with the Gold Coast in the eighteen-nineties', *Africa* 13:1 (1972), 32–43.

———, 'Some Asante views of colonial rule: as seen in the controversy relating to death duties', *Transactions of the Historical Society of Ghana* 15 (1974), 63–84.

———, 'The pressure of cash and its political consequences in Asante in the colonial period', *Journal of African Studies* 3:4 (1976–77), 453–68.

———, 'Gold-mining and trading among the Ashanti of Ghana', *Journal des Africanistes* 48:1 (1978), 89–100.

———, (ed.), *The Minutes of the Ashanti Farmers' Association Limited 1934* (Legon, 1978).

———, *West African Traders in Ghana in the Nineteenth and Twentieth Centuries* (London, 1979).

———, 'The economic and social significance of rubber production and exchange on the Gold and Ivory Coasts, 1880–1900', *Cahiers d'études africaines* 20:77–78 (1980), 49–62.

———, 'The political economy of the expansionist state', *Revue française d'historie d'Outre-Mer*, 68 (1981), 13–36.

———, 'Peasants in 19th-century Asante', *Current Anthropology* 24:4 (1983), 471–75.

———, 'Trade, accumulation and the state in Asante in the nineteenth century', *Africa* 60 (1990), 524–37.

Armitage, C. H. and Montanaro, A. F., *The Ashanti Campaign of 1900* (London, 1901).

Asiwaju, A. I., 'Migrations as revolt: the example of the Ivory Coast and the Upper Volta before 1945', *Journal of African History* 14 (1976), 577–94.

Auchinleck, G. G., 'Co-operative Societies in the Gold Coast', *Journal of the Gold Coast Agricultural & Commercial Society* 6:2 (1927), 113–19.

Ault, David E., and Rutman, Gilbert L., 'The development of individual rights to property in tribal Africa', *Journal of Law and Economics* 22 (1979), 163–82.

Austen, Ralph A., *African Economic History* (London, 1987).

Austin, Dennis, *Politics in Ghana 1946–1960* (London, 1964).

Austin, Gareth, 'The Kumase branch of the National Archives of Ghana', *History in Africa* 13 (1986), 383–89.

———, 'The emergence of capitalist relations in South Asante cocoa-farming, c.1916–33', *Journal of African History* 28 (1987), 259–79.

Austin, Gareth, 'Capitalists and chiefs in the cocoa hold-ups in South Asante, 1927–1938', *International Journal of African Historical Studies* 21 (1988), 63–95.

———, 'Indigenous credit institutions in West Africa, c.1750–1960', in Austin and Kaoru Sugihara (eds), *Local Suppliers of Credit in the Third World, 1750–1960* (Basingstoke, 1993), 93–159.

———, 'Human pawning in Asante c.1820–c.1950: markets and coercion, gender and cocoa', in T. Falola and P. Lovejoy (eds), *Pawnship in Africa: Debt Bondage in Historical Perspective* (Boulder, 1994), 119–59. Reprinted in Lovejoy and Falola (eds), *Pawnship, Slavery, and Colonialism*.

———, 'Between abolition and *jihad*: the Asante response to the ending of the Atlantic slave trade, 1807–1896', in Robin Law (ed.), *From Slave Trade to 'Legitimate' Commerce: the Commercial Transition in Nineteenth-Century West Africa* (Cambridge, 1995), 93–118.

———, ' "No elders were present": commoners and private ownership in Asante, 1807–96', *Journal of African History* 37 (1996), 1–30.

———, 'Mode of production or mode of cultivation: explaining the failure of European cocoa planters in competition with African farmers in colonial Ghana', in W. G. Clarence-Smith (ed.), *Cocoa Pioneer Fronts Since 1800* (Basingstoke, 1996), 154–75.

———, 'National poverty and the "vampire state" in Ghana: a review article', *Journal of International Development* 8 (1996), 553–73.

———, 'New introduction', 2nd edn of Polly Hill, *The Migrant Cocoa-Farmers of Southern Ghana* (Hamburg and Oxford, 1997), ix–xxviii.

———, 'African business in nineteenth-century West Africa', in Alusine Jalloh and Toyin Falola (eds), *Black Business and Economic Power* (Rochester NY, 2002), 114–44.

———, 'African rural capitalism, cocoa farming and economic growth in colonial Ghana', in Toyin Falola (ed.), *Ghana in Africa and the World: Essays in Honor of Adu Boahen* (Trenton NJ and Asmara, 2003), 437–53.

———, 'Competition, labour credit and economic rent: the political economy of cocoa advances system in colonial Ghana, 1915–1938', in Endre Stiansen (ed.), *More Than Money Matters: Financial Institutions in Africa's Political Economy* (Nordic Institute of African Studies: Uppsala, forthcoming).

Baesjou, René, (ed.), *An Asante Embassy on the Gold Coast: the Mission of Akyempon Yaw to Elmina, 1869–72* (Leiden, 1979).

Baker, Christopher, 'Debt and the depression in Madras', in Dewey, Clive, and Hopkins, A. G. (eds), *The Imperial Impact: Studies in the Economic History of Africa and India* (London, 1978), 233–42.

Bardhan, Pranab K., 'Interlocking factor markets and agrarian development: a review of issues', *Oxford Economic Papers* 32 (1980), 82–98.

———, and Udry, Christopher, *Development Microeconomics* (Oxford, 1999).

Barter, Major C., 'Notes on Ashanti', *The Scottish Geographical Magazine* 12:9 (1896), 441–58.

Basu, Kaushik, *Agrarian Structure and Economic Underdevelopment* (Chur, Switzerland, 1990).

———, 'Limited liability and the existence of share tenancy', *Journal of Development Economics* 38 (1992), 203–20.

Basu, Kaushik, *Analytical Development Economics: the Less Developed Economy Revisited* (Cambridge MA, 1997).

Bateman, Merrill J., 'An econometric analysis of Ghanaian cocoa supply', in R. A. Kotey, C. Okali and B. E. Rourke (eds), *Economics of Cocoa Production and Marketing* (Legon, 1974), 286–326.

———; Meeraus, Alexander; Newbury, David M.; Okyere, William Asenso; and O'Mara, Gerald T., *Ghana's Cocoa Pricing Policy* (World Bank: Washington, DC, 1990).

Bates, Robert H., *Markets and States in Tropical Africa* (Berkeley, 1981).

———, *Essays on the Political Economy of Rural Africa* (Cambridge, 1983).

———, *Beyond the Miracle of the Market: the Political Economy of Agrarian Development in Kenya* (Cambridge, 1989).

———, 'Capital, kinship, and conflict: the structuring influence of capital in kinship societies', *Canadian Journal of African Studies* 24:1 (1990), 145–64.

———, 'Social dilemmas and rational individuals: an assessment of the new institutionalism', in Harriss, J., Hunter, J. and Lewis, C. M. (eds), *The New Institutional Economics and Third World Development* (London, 1995), 17–26.

Bauer, P. T., *West African Trade: A Study of Competition, Oligopoly and Monoply in a Changing Economy* (Cambridge, 1954).

Beckett, W. H., *Akokoaso: a Survey of a Gold Coast Village* (London, 1956: 1st edn, 1944).

Beckman, Björn, *Organising the Farmers* (Uppsala, 1976).

Beinart, William, *The Political Economy of Pondoland 1800–1930* (Cambridge, 1982).

———, 'African history and environmental history', *African Affairs* 99:395 (2000), 269–302.

Belcher, Donald W.; Wurapa, Frederick K.; Ward, William B.; and Lourie, Irvin M., 'Guinea worm in Southern Ghana: its epidemiology and impact on agricultural productivity', *American Journal of Tropical Medicine and Hygiene* 24:2 (1975), 243–49.

Bell, Clive, 'Credit markets and interlinked transactions', in Hollis Chenery and T. N. Srinivasan (eds), *Handbook of Development Economics* (Amsterdam, 1988), Vol. I, 764–830.

Benneh, George, 'Land tenure and farming system in Nkrankwanta: a village in the pioneer-cocoa area of Ghana', *Bulletin of the Ghana Geographical Association* 10:2 (1965), 6–15.

———, 'The impact of cocoa cultivation on the traditional land tenure system of the Akan of Ghana', *Ghana Journal of Sociology*, 6:1 (1970), 43–61.

Bening, R. B., 'Evolution of the administrative boundaries of Ashanti, 1896–1951', *Journal of African Studies* 5 (1978), 123–50.

Bentley, J. Marvin, and Oberhofer, Tom, 'Property rights and economic development', *Review of Social Economy* 39 (1989), 51–65.

Bernstein, Henry, 'Notes on capital and peasantry', *Review of African Political Economy* 10 (1978), 60–73.

Berry, Sara S., 'Supply response reconsidered: cocoa in Western Nigeria, 1909–44', *Journal of Development Studies* 13:1 (1976), 4–17.

———, *No Condition is Permanent: the Social Dynamics of Agrarian Change in Sub-Saharan Africa* (Madison, 1993).

Berry, Sara S., 'Unsettled accounts: stool debts, chieftaincy disputes and the question of Asante constitutionalism', *Journal of African History* 39 (1998), 39–62.

————, *Chiefs Know Their Boundaries: Essays on Property, Power, and the Past in Asante, 1896–1996* (Portsmouth NH, 2001).

Bhadhuri, Amit, *The Economic Structure of Backward Agriculture* (London, 1983).

Binswanger, Hans P., and McIntire, John, 'Behavioral and material determinants of production relations in land-abundant tropical agriculture', *Economic Development and Cultural Change* 36:1 (1987), 73–99.

Boaten, Kwasi, 'Trade among the Asante of Ghana up to the end of [the] 18th century', *Research Review* (Institute of African Studies, University of Ghana) 7:1 (1970), 33–52.

Bohannon, Paul, and Dalton, George, 'Introduction' to their (eds), *Markets in Africa* (Evanston, 1962).

Bohannon, Paul and Bohannon, Laura, *Tiv Economy* (Evanston, 1968).

Bonaparte, E. E. N. A., 'An agronomist's assessment of recent research findings and their implications for cocoa production', in R. A. Kotey, C. Okali and B. E. Rourke (eds), *Economics of Cocoa Production and Marketing* (Legon, 1974), 73–85.

Boni, Stefano, 'Twentieth-century transformations in notions of gender, parenthood, and marriage in Southern Ghana: A critique of the hypothesis of "retrograde steps" for Akan women', *History in Africa* 28 (2001), 15–41.

————, 'A precolonial, political history of the Sefwi Wiawso oman', *Ghana Studies* 4 (2001), 139-68.

Booker, H. S., 'Debt in Africa', *African Affairs* 48, 191 (1949), 141–9.

Bowdich, Thomas E., *A Mission from Cape Coast Castle to Ashantee* (London, 1819: reprint, 1966).

————, 'Remarks on civilisation in Africa', in his *The British and French Expeditions to Teembo with Remarks on Civilisation in Africa* (Paris, 1821).

Brackenbury, H., *The Ashanti War*, 2 vols (Edinburgh, 1874).

Brammer, H., 'Soils', in J. Brian Wills (ed.), *Agriculture and Land Use in Ghana* (London, 1962), 88–102.

Braverman, Avishay, and Stiglitz, Joseph E., 'Sharecropping and the interlinking of agrarian markets', *American Economic Review* 72:4 (1982), 695–715.

Bray, Francesca, *The Rice Economies: Technology and Development in Asian Societies* (Oxford, 1986).

Bray, F. R., *Cocoa Development in Ahafo, West Ashanti* (cyclostyled; Faculty of Agriculture, University of Ghana: Achimota, 1959).

Brenner, Robert, 'Agrarian class structure and economic development in pre-industrial Europe', *Past and Present* 70 (1976), 30–75.

————, 'The origins of capitalist development: a critique of neo-Smithian marxism', *New Left Review* 104 (1977), 25–92.

Brown, James W., 'Increased intercommunication and epidemic disease in early colonial Ashanti', in Gerald W. Hartwig and K. David Patterson (eds), *Disease in African History* (Durham NC: 1978),

Browne, Angela W. 'Rural industry and appropriate technology: the lessons of narrow-loom Ashanti weaving', *African Affairs* 82:326 (1983), 29–41.

Busia, K. A., *The Position of the Chief in the Modern Political System of Ashanti* (London, 1951).

Byfield, Judith A., *The Bluest Hands: A Social and Economic History of Women Dyers in Abeokuta (Nigeria), 1890–1940* (Portsmouth NH, 2002).

Cardinall, A. W., *In Ashanti and Beyond* (New York, 1971: lst edn Philadelphia, 1927).

Chauveau, Jean-Pierre, and Eric Léonard, 'Côte d'Ivoire's pioneer fronts: historical and political determinants of the spread of cocoa cultivation', in W. G. Clarence-Smith (ed.), *Cocoa Pioneer Fronts* (London, 1996), 176–94.

Chauveau, Jean-Pierre, and Richard, Jacques, 'Une "périphérie recentrée: à propos d'un système local d'économie de plantation en Côte d'Ivoire', *Cahiers d'études Africaines* 17:68 (1977), 485–524.

Cheung, Steven N. S., *The Theory of Share Tenancy* (Chicago, 1969).

Christaller, J. G., *A Dictionary of the Asante and Fante Language called Tshi* (Basel Evangelical Missionary Society: Basel, 1881; revised edn, Basel 1933).

Clarence-Smith, Gervase, William Gervase, and Ruf, François, 'Introduction', to Clarence-Smith (ed.), *Cocoa Pioneer Fronts Since 1980* (Basingstoke, 1996).

Clark, Andy, 'Economic reason: the interplay of individual learning and external structure', in Drobak and Nye, *Frontiers of the New Institutional Economics*, 269–89.

Clark, Gracia, *Onions Are My Husband: Survival and Accumulation by West African Market Women* (Chicago, 1994).

Coase, R. H., *The Firm, the Market, and the Law* (Chicago, 1988).

Cohen, Abner, 'Cultural strategies in the organization of trading diasporas', in Claude Meillassoux (ed.), *The Development of Indigenous Trade and Markets in West Africa* (London, 1971), 266–81.

Collins, Edmund, 'The panic element in nineteenth-century British relations with Ashanti', *Transactions of the Historical Society of Ghana* 5:2 (1962), 79–144.

Commander, Simon, Howell, John, and Seini, Wayo, 'Ghana', in Commander (ed.), *Structural Adjustment and Agriculture: Theory and Practice in Africa and Latin America* (London, 1989), 107–26.

Cooper, Frederick, *Plantation Slavery on the East Coast of Africa* (New Haven, 1977).

——, 'The problem of slavery in African studies', *Journal of African History* 20 (1979), 103–25.

——, *From Slaves to Squatters* (New Haven, 1980).

——, 'Africa and the world economy', *African Studies Review*, 24: 2/3 (1981), 1–86; reprinted with postscript in Cooper and others, *Confronting Historical Paradigms: Peasants, Labor, and the Capitalist World System in Africa and Latin America* (Madison, 1993).

——, *On the African Waterfront* (New Haven, 1987).

——, 'Work, class and empire: an African historian's retrospective on E.P. Thompson', *Social History* 20 (1995), 235–41.

——, *Decolonization and African Society: the Labor Question in French and British Africa* (Cambridge, 1996).

Cordell, Dennis D., Gregory, Joel W., and Piché, Victor, *Hoe and Wage: a Social History of a Circular Migration System in West Africa* (Boulder, 1996).

Cowen, M. P., and Shenton, R. W., 'Bankers, peasants, and land in British West Africa 1905–37', *Journal of Peasant Studies* 19:1 (1991), 26–58.

Crisp, Jeff, *The Story of an African Working Class: Ghanaian Miners' Struggles 1870–1980* (London, 1984).

Cruickshank, Brodie, *Eighteen Years on the Gold Coast of Africa*, 2 vols (London, 1853: reprint, 1966).

Curtin, Philip D., 'The lure of Bambuk gold', *Journal of African History* 14 (1973), 623–31.

Dalton, George, 'Introduction' to *Research in Economic Anthropology* 2 (1979).

Danquah, Francis, *Cocoa Diseases and Politics in Ghana, 1909–1966* (New York, 1995).

deGraft-Johnson, J. C., *African Experiment: Cooperative Agriculture and Banking in British West Africa* (London, 1958).

———, 'The population of Ghana 1846–1967', *Transactions of the Historical Society of Ghana* 10 (1969), 1–12.

Demsetz, Harold, 'Toward a theory of property rights', *American Economic Review* 57:2 (1967), 347–59.

Deutsch, Jan-Georg, *Educating the Middlemen: a Political and Economic History of Statutory Cocoa Marketing in Nigeria, 1936–1947* (Berlin, 1995).

Domar, Evsey D., 'The causes of slavery or serfdom: a hypothesis', *Journal of Economic History* 30 (1970), 18–32.

Drescher, Seymour, 'Abolitionist expectations: Britain', in Howard Temperley (ed.), *After Slavery: Emancipation and its Discontents* (London, 2000), 41–66.

Drobak, John N., and Nye, John V. C., (eds), *The Frontiers of the New Institutional Economics* (San Diego, 1997).

Dumett, Raymond E., 'The rubber trade of the Gold Coast and Asante in the nineteenth century', *Journal of African History* 12 (1971), 79–101.

———, 'Pre-colonial gold mining and the state in the Akan region: with a critique of the Terray hypothesis', *Research in Economic Anthropology* 2 (1979), 27–68.

———, 'Traditional slavery in the Akan region in the nineteenth century: sources, issues, and interpretations', in D. Henige and T. C. McCaskie (eds), *West African Economic and Social History: Studies in Memory of Marion Johnson* (Madison, 1990), 7–22.

———, *El Dorado in West Africa: the Gold-Mining Frontier, African Labor, and Colonial Capitalism on the Gold Coast, 1875–1900* (Athens OH, 1998).

Dumett, Raymond, and Johnson, Marion, 'Britain and the suppression of slavery in the Gold Coast colony, Ashanti, and the Northern Territories', in S. Miers and R. Roberts (eds), *The End of Slavery in Africa* (Madison, 1988), 71–116.

Dunn, John, and Robertson, A. F., *Dependence and Opportunity: Political Change in Ahafo* (Cambridge, 1973).

Dupuis, Joseph, *Journal of a Residence in Ashantee* (London, 1824: reprint, 1966).

Ehrler, Franz, *Handelskonflikte zwischen europäischen Firmen und einheimischen Produenten in Britisch Westafrika: die 'cocoa-hold-ups' in der Zwischenkriegszeit* (Zürich, 1977).

Eggertsson, Thráinn, *Economic Behavior and Institutions* (Cambridge, 1990).

Ellis, A. B., *The Tshi-Speaking Peoples of the Gold Coast of West Africa* (London, 1887).

Ellis, Frank, *Peasant Economics: Farm Households and Agrarian Development* (Cambridge, 1988).

Eltis, David, 'The abolitionist perception of society after slavery', in J. Walvin (ed.), *Slavery and British Society, 1776–1846* (London, 1982), 195–213, 255–62.

Eltis, David, *The Rise of African Slavery in the Americas* (Cambridge, 2000).

Engerman, Stanley, 'Some considerations relating to property rights in man', *Journal of Economic History*, 33 (1973), 43–65.

Engerman, Stanley, 'The economics of forced labor', *Itinerario* 17 (1993), 59–77.

Engmann, E. V. T., *Population of Ghana 1850–1960* (Accra, 1986).

Ensminger, Jean, *Making a Market: the Institutional Transformation of an African Society* (Cambridge, 1992).

Evans, E. W., and Richardson, David, 'Hunting for rents: the economics of slaving in pre-colonial Africa', *Economic History Review* 48 (1995), 665–86.

Fairhead, James and Leach, Melissa, *Misreading the African Landscape: Society and Ecology in a Forest-Savanna Mosaic* (Cambridge, 1996).

Falola, Toyin, and Lovejoy, Paul E., 'Pawnship in historical perspective', in Falola and Lovejoy (eds), *Pawnship in Africa: Debt Bondage in Historical Perspective* (Boulder, 1994), 1–26. Reprinted in Lovejoy and Falola (eds), *Pawnship, Slavery, and Colonialism*.

Feder, Gershon and Noronha, Raymond, 'Land rights systems and agricultural development in sub-Saharan Africa', *World Bank Research Observer* 2 (1987), 143–69.

Feeny, David, 'The decline of property rights in man in Thailand, 1800–1913', *Journal of Economic History* 49 (1989), 285–96.

Field, M. J., *Search for Security: an Ethno-Psychiatric Study of Rural Ghana* (London, 1960).

Fieldhouse, David, *Merchant Capital and Economic Decolonisation: the United Africa Company 1929–1980* (Oxford, 1994).

Firmin-Sellers, Kathryn, *The Transformation of Property Rights in the Gold Coast* (Cambridge, 1996).

Foggie, A., 'The role of forestry in the agricultural economy', in J. Brian Wills (ed.), *Agriculture and Land Use in Ghana* (London, 1962), 229–35.

Folbre, Nancy, 'Cleaning house: new perspectives on households and economic development', *Journal of Development Economics* 22 (1986), 5–40.

———, 'Hearts and spades: paradigms of household economics', *World Development* 14:2 (1986), 245–55.

Fortes, M., Steel, R. W., and Ady, P., 'Ashanti survey, 1945–46: an experiment in social research', *Geographical Journal* 110:4–6 (1947), 149–79.

Fortes, Meyer, 'Kinship and marriage among the Ashanti', in A. R. Radcliffe-Brown and Daryll Forde (eds), *African Systems of Kinship and Marriage* (London, 1950), 252–84.

———, 'The social background' in Frank Lorimer et al., *Culture and Human Fertility* (UNESCO: Paris, 1954), 255–95.

———, *Kinship and the Social Order: the Legacy of Lewis Henry Morgan* (London, 1970: 1st edn, USA, 1969), 154–90.

———, 'Ashanti patrilateral kinship and its values', in Fortes, *Kinship and the Social Order*, 192–216.

———, 'The prologue: family studies in Ghana 1920–1970', in C. Oppong (ed.), *Domestic Rights and Duties in Southern Ghana* (Legon, 1974), 1–27.

Fox-Genovese, Elizabeth, and Genovese, Eugene D., *Fruits of Merchant Capital: Slavery and Bourgeois Property in the Rise and Expansion of Capitalism* (New York, 1983).

Freeman, Richard Austin, *Travels and Life in Ashanti and Jaman* (London, 1898).

———, 'The interior of the Gold Coast', *Macmillan's Magazine* LXXX: 476 (1899), 105–13.

Freeman, Thomas Birch, *Journal of Various Visits to Ashanti* (3rd edn, London 1968; 1st edn, 1844).

Frempong, M. P., 'A history of the Presbyterian church at Bompata in Asante-Akyem' (transl. from Twi by E. A. Kyerematen), *Ghana Notes and Queries* (June 1972), 20–23.

Freund, Bill, *The African Worker* (African Society Today series: Cambridge, 1988).

Friedman, Milton, 'The methodology of positive economics', in his *Essays in Positive Economics* (Chicago, 1953), 3–43.

Frimpong-Ansah, Jonathan H., *The Vampire State in Africa: the Political Economy of Decline in Ghana* (London, 1991).

Fuller, Sir Francis, *A Vanished Dynasty: Ashanti* (London, 1921).

Galletti, R.; Baldwin, K. D. S.; and Dina, I. O., *Nigerian Cocoa Farmers* (London, 1956).

Garceau, Jean-Denis, 'L'économie du cacao dans une chefferie Akan (Ghana): appropriation des terres et exploitation d'une main-d'œuvre étrangère'. *Culture* 2:2 (1982), 99–112.

Garlick, Peter C., 'The development of Kwahu business enterprise in Ghana since 1874—an essay in recent oral tradition', *Journal of African History* 8 (1967), 463–80.

——, *African Traders and Economic Development in Ghana* (Oxford, 1971).

Garrard, Timothy F., 'Studies in Akan goldweights (3)', *Transactions of the Historical Society of Ghana* 14:1 (1973), 1–16.

——, *Akan Weights and the Gold Trade* (London, 1980).

Gerschenkron, Alexander, 'Social attitudes, entrepreneurship, and economic development', in his *Economic Backwardness in Historical Perspective* (Cambridge MA, 1962), 52–71.

Geschiere, Peter, 'Working groups or wage labour? Cash-crops, reciprocity and money among the Maka of southeastern Cameroon', *Development and Change* 26 (1995), 503–23.

Getz, Trevor, 'A "somewhat firm policy": the role of the Gold Coast judiciary in implementing slave emancipation, 1874–1900', *Ghana Studies* 2 (1999), 97–117.

Goody, Jack (ed.), *Changing Social Structure in Ghana* (London, 1975).

——, *Production and Reproduction: a Comparative Study of the Domestic Domain* (Cambridge, 1976).

——, 'Slavery in time and space', in James L. Watson (ed.), *Asian and African Systems of Slavery* (Oxford, 1980), 16–42.

Gould, Peter R., *The Development of the Transportation Pattern in Ghana* (Evanston, 1960).

Grace, John, *Domestic Slavery in West Africa with particular reference to the Sierra Leone Protectorate, 1896–1927* (London, 1975).

Granovetter, Mark, 'Economic action and social structure: the problem of embeddedness', *American Journal of Sociology* 91:3 (1985), 481–510.

——, 'The sociological and economic approaches to labor market analysis: a social structural view', in Granovetter and Swedberg, Richard, (eds), *The Sociology of Economic Life* (Boulder, 1992), 233–63.

Green, R. H., and Hymer, S. H., 'Cocoa in the Gold Coast: a study in the relations between African farmers and agricultural experts', *Journal of Economic History* 26 (1966), 299–319.

Grief, Avner, 'Microtheory and recent developments in the study of economic institutions through economic history', in David M. Kreps and Kenneth F. Wallis (eds), *Advances in Economics and Econometrics*, Seventh World Congress, vol. II (Cambridge, 1997), 81–113.

Grier, Beverly, 'Cocoa marketing in colonial Ghana: capitalist enterprise and the emergence of a rural African bourgeoisie', *Ufahamu* 10:1–2 (1980–81), 89–115.

————, 'Underdevelopment, modes of production, and the state in colonial Ghana', *African Studies Review*, 24:1 (1981), 21–47.

————, 'Contradiction, crisis, and class conflict: the state and capitalist development in Ghana prior to 1948' in Irving Leonard Markovitz (ed.), *Studies in Power and Class in Africa* (Oxford, 1987), 27–49, 336–8.

————, 'Pawns, porters, and petty traders: women in the transition to cash crop agriculture in colonial Ghana', *Signs*, 17:2 (1992), 304–28. Reprinted in Toyin Falola and Paul E. Lovejoy (eds), *Pawnship in Africa: Debt Bondage in Historical Perspective* (Boulder, 1994); and in Lovejoy and Falola (eds), *Pawnship, Slavery, and Colonialism*.

Gunnarsson, Christer, *The Gold Coast Cocoa Industry 1900–1939: Production, Prices and Structural Change* (Lund, 1978).

Guyer, Jane (ed.), 'Food, cocoa, and the division of labour by sex in two West African societies', *Comparative Studies in Society and History* 22 (1980), 355–73.

————, 'Wealth in people, wealth in things—introduction', *Journal of African History* 36 (1995), 83–90.

Gyasi, Edwin A., 'The adaptability of African communal land tenure to economic opportunity: the example of land acquisition for oil-palm farming in Ghana', *Africa* 64:3 (1994), 391–405.

Haenger, Peter, *Slaves and Slave Holders on the Gold Coast* (eds. J. J. Shaffer and Paul E. Lovejoy, transl. Christina Handford) (Basel, 2000).

Hall, J. B., and Swaine, M. D., 'Classification and ecology of closed-canopy forest in Ghana', *Journal of Ecology* 64 (1976), 913–51.

Harms, Robert, *River of Wealth, River of Sorrow: the Central Zaire Basin in the Era of the Slave and Ivory Trade, 1500–1891* (New Haven, **0000**).

Hancock, W. K., *Survey of British Commonwealth Affairs*, vol. 2, *Problems of Economic Policy 1918–1939*, Part 2 (London, 1942).

Hardin, G., 'The tragedy of the commons', *Science* 162 (1968), 1343–8.

Harries, Patrick, 'Kinship, ideology and the nature of pre-colonial labour migration', in Shula Marks and Richard Rathbone (eds), *Industrialisation and Social Change in South Africa* (Harlow, 1982), 142–66.

Harrison, C., Ingawa, T. W., and Martin, S. M., 'The establishment of colonial rule in West Africa', in J. F. Ade Ajayi and Michael Crowder (eds), *History of West Africa*, II (2nd ed.: Harlow, 1987), 485–545.

Heap, Simon, 'The development of motor transport in the Gold Coast, 1900–39', *Journal of Transport History* 11:2 (1990), 19–37.

Hill, Polly, *The Gold Coast Cocoa Farmer: a Preliminary Survey* (Oxford, 1956).

————, *The Pledging of Ghana Cocoa Farms*, no. 15 in *Cocoa Research Series* (cyclostyled: University of Ghana, Economics Department: Legon, 1958).

Hill, Polly, *The Migrant Cocoa-Farmers of Southern Ghana* (Cambridge, 1963: 2nd edn, with new introduction by Gareth Austin, LIT and James Currey with International African Institute: Hamburg and Oxford, 1997).

Hill, Polly, *Studies in Rural Capitalism in West Africa* (Cambridge, 1970).

———, 'The West African farming household', in Goody, *Changing Social Structure in Ghana* (1975), 119–36.

———, *Indigenous Trade and Market Places in Ghana 1962–64* (Jos, Nigeria, 1984).

———, *Development Economics on Trial: the Anthropological Case for a Prosecution* (Cambridge, 1986).

Hilton, T. E., *Ghana Population Atlas* (Achimota, Ghana, 1960).

Hodgson, Geoffrey M., *Economics and Institutions* (Cambridge, 1988).

Hoffman, Philip T.; Postel-Vinay, Gilles; and Rosenthal, Jean-Laurent, 'Information and economic history: how the credit market in old regime Paris forces us to rethink the transition to capitalism', *American Historical Review* 104 (1999), 69–94.

Hogendorn, J. S., and Gemery, H. A., 'Continuity in West African monetary history', *African Economic History* 17 (1988), 127–46.

Hogendorn, J. S., and Goldberg, M., 'Origins of the Gold Coast cocoa industry: example of a vent-for-surplus?', *Itinerario* 6:2 (1982), 46–58.

Hogendorn, Jan, and Johnson, Marion, *The Shell Money of the Slave Trade* (Cambridge, 1986).

Hopkins, A. G., *An Economic History of West Africa* (London, 1973).

———, 'Rationality and technology in African history', *Technology and Culture* 16:4 (1975), 462–65.

Howard, Rhoda, *Colonialism and Underdevelopment in Ghana* (London, 1978).

———, 'Formation and stratification of the peasantry in colonial Ghana', *Journal of Peasant Studies* 8 (1980), 61–80.

Hutton, W., *A Voyage to Africa* (London, 1821).

Hymer, Stephen H., 'Economic forms in pre-colonial Ghana', *Journal of Economic History* 31 (1970), 33–50.

Ingham, Barbara, 'Ghana cocoa farmers—income, expenditure relationships', *Journal of Development Studies* 9:3 (1972), 365–72.

———, *Tropical Exports and Economic Development: New Perspectives on Producer Response in Three Low-Income Countries* (London, 1981).

Jenkins, Paul, 'A comment on M. P. Frempong's history of the Presbyterian church at Bompata', *Ghana Notes and Queries*, (June 1972), 23–27.

Jenkins, Ray, 'Confrontations with A. B. Ellis, a participant in the scramble for Gold Coast Africana, 1874–1894', in *European Sources for Sub-Saharan Africa Before 1900: use and abuse*, edited by Beatrix Heintze and Adam Jones, a special issue of *Paideuma: mitteilungen zur kulturekunde*, 33 (1987), 321–33.

Johnson, Marion (ed.), *Salaga Papers* (Legon, 1966), Vol. I.

———, 'The cowrie currencies of West Africa', Part 2, *JAH* 11 (1970), 331–53.

———, 'The population of Asante, 1817–1921: a reconsideration', *Asantesem* 8 (1978), 22–28.

———, 'Elephants for want of towns', in Christopher Fyfe and David MacMaster (eds), *African Historical Demography* II (Edinburgh, 1981), 315–30.

———, 'Ashanti craft organisation', *African Arts* 13:1 (1979), 60–63, 78–82, 97.

Johnson, Marion, 'The slaves of Salaga', *Journal of African History*, 27 (1986), 341–62.

Jones, Christine, Lindauer, David L., and Roemer, Michael, 'Parallel, fragmented, and black: a taxonomy', in Michael Roemer and Christine Jones (eds), *Markets in Developing Countries* (San Francisco, 1991).

Jones, E. L., *Growth Recurring: Economic Change in World History* (Oxford, 1988).

Kay, Geoffrey, *The Political Economy of Colonialism in Ghana: a Collection of Documents and Statistics 1900–1960* (London, 1972).

Kea, Ray A., *Settlements, Trade, and Polities in the Seventeenth-Century Gold Coast* (Baltimore, 1982).

Kimble, David, *A Political History of Ghana 1850–1928* (London, 1963).

Killick, T., 'The economics of cocoa' in W. Birmingham, I. Neustadt and E. N. Omaboe (eds), *A Study of Contemporary Ghana*, vol. 1, *The Economy of Ghana.*

Kirby, Captain Brandon, 'A journey to the interior of Ashanti', *Proceedings of the Royal Geographical Society* 6 (1884), 447–52.

Kirk-Greene, A. H. M., 'The thin white line: the size of the British colonial service in Africa', *African Affairs* 79:314 (1980), 25–44.

Klein, Martin A., *Slavery and Colonial Rule in French West Africa* (Cambridge, 1998).

——— and Richard Roberts, 'The resurgence of pawning in French West Africa during the Depression of the 1930s', *African Economic History* 16 (1987), 23–37 (reprinted in revised form in T. Falola and P. Lovejoy [eds], *Pawnship in Africa: Debt Bondage in Historical Perspective* [Boulder, 1994] and in Lovejoy and Falola [eds], *Pawnship, Slavery, and Colonialism*).

Klein, A. Norman, 'West African unfree labor before and after the rise of the Atlantic slave trade', in L. Foner and E. Genovese (eds), *Slavery in the New World: A Reader in Comparative History* (Englewood Cliffs NJ, 1969), 87–95.

———, 'The two Asantes: competing interpretations of "slavery" in Akan-Asante culture and society', in P. Lovejoy (ed.) *The Ideology of Slavery in Africa* (Beverly Hills, 1981), 149–67.

Konings, Piet, *The State and Rural Class Formation in Ghana* (London, 1986).

Kopytoff, Igor and Miers, Suzanne, 'African "slavery" as an institution of marginality', in S. Miers and I. Kopytoff (eds), *Slavery in Africa: Historical and Anthropological Perspectives* (Madison, 1977).

Kotey, R. A., C. Okali and B. E. Rourke (eds), *Economics of Cocoa Production and Marketing* (Legon, 1974).

Krueger, Anne O., 'The political economy of the rent-seeking society', *American Economic Review* 64 (1974), 291–303.

Kuhn, Thomas S., *The Structure of Scientific Revolutions* (Chicago: 2nd edn, 1970).

Kyei, T. E., *Marriage and Divorce Among the Ashanti: a Study Undertaken in the Course of the Ashanti Social Survey (1945)* (Cambridge, 1992).

———, *Our Days Dwindle: Memoirs of my Childhood Days in Asante*, ed. by Jean Allman (Portsmouth, NH, 2001).

Kyerematen, A. A. Y., *Inter-state Boundary Litigation in Ashanti* (Leiden, n.d. [1971?]).

Lane, D. A., 'The forest vegetation', in J. Brian Wills (ed.), *Agriculture and Land Use in Ghana* (London, 1962), 160–69.

Lass, R. A., 'Labour usage', in G. A. R. Wood and R. A. Lass, *Cocoa*, 234–64.

———, 'Replanting and rehabilitation of old cocoa farms', in G. A. R. Wood and R. A. Lass, *Cocoa*, 210–33.

Latham, A. J., 'Currency, credit and capitalism on the Cross River [Nigeria] in the pre-colonial era', *Journal of African History* 12 (1971), 599–605.

Law, Robin, 'Posthumous questions for Karl Polanyi: price inflation in pre-colonial Dahomey', *Journal of African History* 33 (1992), 387–420.

Law, Robin, (ed.), *From Slave Trade to 'Legitimate' Commerce: the Commercial Transition in Nineteenth-Century West Africa* (Cambridge, 1995).

——, 'Finance and Credit in Pre-Colonial Dahomey', in Endre Stiansen and Jane I. Guyer (eds), *Credit, Currencies and Culture: African Financial Institutions in Historical Perspective* (Uppsala, 1999), 15–37.

Lentz, Carola, and Erlmann, Veit, 'A working class in formation? Economic crisis and strategies of survival among Dagara mine workers in Ghana', *Cahiers d'études africaines* 29:103 (1989), 69–111.

Leston, Dennis, 'The diseconomy of insecticides in cocoa production in Ghana', in R. A. Kotey, C. Okali and B. E. Rourke (eds), *Economics of Cocoa Production and Marketing* (Legon, 1974), 96–104.

Lewin, Thomas J., *Asante Before the British: the Prempean Years, 1875–1900* (Lawrence, KS, 1978).

Lewis, W. A., *Theory of Economic Growth* (London, 1955).

Leys, Colin, 'Confronting the African tragedy', *New Left Review* 204 (1994), 33–47.

Lipton, Michael, 'The theory of the optimising peasant', *Journal of Development Studies* 4:3 (1968), 327–51.

Lovejoy, Paul E., 'Interregional money flows in the precolonial trade of Nigeria', *Journal of African History* 15 (1974), 563–85.

——, *Caravans of Kola: the Hausa Kola Trade 1700–1900* (Zaria, 1980).

——, 'Polanyi's "ports of trade": Salaga and Kano in the nineteenth century', *Canadian Journal of African Studies*, 16:2 (1982), 245–77.

——, 'Fugitive Slaves: resistance to slavery in the Sokoto Caliphate', in Gary Y. Okihiro (ed.), *In Resistance: Studies in African, Caribbean, and Afro-American History* (Amherst, 1986), 71–95.

——, and Hogendorn, Jan S., *Slow Death for Slavery: the Course of Abolition in Northern Nigeria, 1897–1936* (Cambridge, 1993).

——, and Falola, Toyin (eds), *Pawnship, Slavery, and Colonialism in Africa* (Trenton NJ and Asmara, 2003).

Lynn, Martin, *Commerce and Economic Change in West Africa: the Palm Oil Trade in the Nineteenth Century* (Cambridge, 1997).

Maier-Weaver, D. (translator), 'Autobiographical reminiscences of an Asante slave, "Mose"': a translation of an article by Wilhelm Rottmann in the Basel Mission periodical *Der Evangelische Heidenbote* (1892), *Asante Seminar* 3 (Northwestern University: Evanston, 1975), 19–20.

Maier, D. J. E., *Priests and Power: the Case of the Dente Shrine in Nineteenth-Century Ghana* (Bloomington, 1983).

——, 'Military acquisition of slaves in Asante', in D. Henige and T. C. McCaskie (eds), *West African Economic and Social History: Studies in Memory of Marion Johnson* (Madison, 1990), 119–32.

Manning, Patrick, *Slavery and African Life* (Cambridge, 1990).

Manuh, Takyiwaa, 'Changes in marriage and funeral exchanges among the Asante: a case study from Kona, Afigya-Kwabre', in J. I. Guyer (ed.), *Money Matters: Instability, Values and Social Payments in the Modern History of West African Communities* (Portsmouth NH, 1995), 188–201.

Marshall, Alfred, *Principles of Economics: an Introductory Volume* (London, 1916: 1st edn, 1890).

Martin, Claude, *The Rainforests of West Africa* (Basel 1991; transl. L. Tsardakas).

Matson, J. N., *A Digest of the Minutes of the Ashanti Confederacy Council from 1935 to 1949 Inclusive: a Revised Edition of Warrington's Notes on Ashanti Custom Prepared for the Use of District Commissioners* (Cape Coast, 1951).

Maurice, John Frederick (but published anonymously), *The Ashantee War: a Popular Narrative* (London, 1874).

Marx, Karl, *Early Writings* (introduced by L. Colletti, transl. R. Livingstone and G. Benton: London, 1974).

———, *Capital*, Vol. I (London, 1974: German original 1867).

McCaskie, T. C., 'The creation of Ashanti Goldfields Corporation, Ltd., ca.1890–1910', *Asantesεm* 9 (1978), 37–55.

———, 'Office, land and subjects in the history of the Manwere *fekuo* of Kumase', *Journal of African History* 21 (1980), 189–208.

———, 'Time and the calendar in nineteenth-century Asante: an exploratory essay', *History in Africa* 7 (1980), 179–200.

———, 'State and society, marriage and adultery: some considerations towards a social history of pre-colonial Asante', *Journal of African History* 22 (1981), 477–94.

———, 'Rattray and the construction of Asante history: an appraisal', *History in Africa* 10 (1983), 187–206.

———, 'Accumulation, wealth and belief in Asante History: I. To the close of the nineteenth century', *Africa* 53, 1 (1983), 23–43.

———, '*Ahyiamu*—"a place of meeting": an essay on process and event in the history of the Asante state', *Journal of African History* 25 (1984), 169–88.

———, *State and Society in Pre-colonial Asante* (Cambridge, 1995).

———, *Asante Identities: History and Modernity in an African Village 1850–1950* (Edinburgh, 2000).

———, and Wiafe, J. E., 'A contemporary account in Twi of the *Akompi Sa* of 1863: a document with commentary', *Asantesεm* 11 (1979[?]), 72–78.

McCloskey, Donald N., 'The economics of choice', in Thomas G. Rawski (ed.), *Economics and the Historian* (Berkeley, 1996), 122–58.

McLeod, M. D., *The Asante* (London, 1981).

———, 'Gifts and attitudes', in E. Schildkrout (ed.), *The Golden Stool: Studies of the Asante Center and Periphery* (New York, 1987), 184–91.

McPhee, Allan, *The Economic Revolution in British West Africa* (London, 2nd ed., 1971, with an introduction by A. G. Hopkins: 1st edn, 1926).

McSheffrey, Gerald M., 'Slavery, indentured servitude, legitimate trade and the impact of abolition in the Gold Coast, 1874–1901: a reappraisal', *Journal of African History* 24 (1983), 349–68.

Meek, C. K., *Land Law and Custom in the Colonies* (London, 1968 ed.: 1st edn, 1946).

Meillassoux, Claude, 'From reproduction to production: a marxist approach to economic anthropology', *Economy and Society* 1 (1972), 93–105.

———, *The Anthropology of Slavery: The Womb of Iron and Gold* (Chicago, 1991; transl. by A. Dasnois from French original, 1986).

Migot-Adholla, Shem; Hazell, Peter; Blarel, Benoît; and Place, Frank, 'Indigenous land rights systems in Sub-Saharan Africa: a constraint on productivity?', *World Bank Economic Review* 5 (1991), 155–75.

Migot-Adholla, Shem E.; Benneh, George; Place, Frank; and Atsu, Steven, 'Land, security of tenure, and productivity of Ghana', in John W. Bruce and Shem E. Migot-Adholla (eds), *Searching for Land Tenure Security in Africa* (Washington DC, 1994), 97–118.

Mikell, Gwendolyn, 'Filiation, economic crisis, and the status of women in rural Ghana', *Canadian Journal of African Studies* 18:1 (1984), 195–218.

———, *Cocoa and Chaos in Ghana* (New York, 1989).

Milburn, Josephine F., *British Business and Ghanaian Independence* (Hanover NH, 1977).

Murphy, Kevin M., Schleifer, Andrei, and Vishny, Robert W., 'Why is rent-seeking so costly to growth?', *American Economic Association Papers and Proceedings* (1991), 409–14.

Musgrave, George C., *To Kumassi with Scott* (London, 1896).

Myint, Hla, *The Economics of the Developing Countries* (rev. edn, London, 1973).

Nicholson, Sharon E., 'The methodology of historical climate reconstruction and its application to Africa', *Journal of African History* 20 (1979), 31–49.

Nieboer, H. J., *Slavery as an Industrial System* (The Hague, 1900; revd edn, 1910).

Nørregård, Georg, *Danish Settlements in West Africa 1658–1850* (Boston, 1966: Danish original, 1954).

North, Douglass C., and Thomas, Robert Paul, *The Rise of the Western World* (Cambridge, 1973).

North, Douglass C., *Structure and Change in Economic History* (New York, 1981).

———, *Institutions, Institutional Change and Economic Performance* (Cambridge, 1990).

———, 'The New Institutional Economics and Third World development', in Harriss, J., Hunter, J. and Lewis, C. M. (eds), *The New Institutional Economics and Third World Development* (London, 1995), 17–26.

Northrup, David, 'Nineteenth-century patterns of slavery and economic growth in southeastern Nigeria', *International Journal of African Historical Studies* 12 (1979), 1–16.

Nye, P. H., and Stephens, D., 'Soil fertility', in J. Brian Wills (ed.), *Agriculture and Land Use in Ghana* (London, 1962), 127–43.

Nzula, A. T., Potekhin, I. I., and Zusmanovich, A. Z., *Forced Labour in Colonial Africa* (ed. R. Cohen, transl. H. Jenkins) (London, 1979; 1st Russian ed., 1933).

Offer, Avner, 'Between the gift and the market: the economy of regard', *Economic History Review* 50 (1997), 450–76.

Okali, C., Gyekye, L. O., and Mabey, S. Y., *Report on the Socio-Economic Characteristics of the Ashanti Cocoa Rehabilitation Project Area* (Institute of Statistical, Social and Economic Research, University of Ghana: Legon, 1974).

Okali, C., and Kotey, R. A., *Akokoaso: a Resurvey* (Institute of Statistical, Social and Economic Research, University of Ghana: Legon, 1971).

Okali, Christine, *Cocoa and Kinship in Ghana* (London, 1983).

Olson, Mancur, *The Logic of Collective Action* (Cambridge MA, 1965).

Olson, Mancur, *The Rise and Decline of Nations* (New Haven, 1982).

Oni, S. A., and Adubi, J., 'The economics of fertiliser use in cocoa production', in Kotey, Okali and Rourke (eds), *Economics of Cocoa Production and Marketing*, 86–95.

Opare-Akurang, Kwabena, 'The administration of the abolition laws, African responses and post-proclamation slavery in the Gold Coast, 1874–1940', in S. Miers and M. Klein (eds), *Slavery and Colonial Rule in Africa* (London, 1999), 149–66.

———. (See also under Akurang-Parry).

Orde Browne, G. St. J., *The African Labourer* (London, 1967: 1st edn, 1933).

Oroge, E. Adeniyi, '*Iwofa*: an historical survey of the Yoruba institution of indenture', *African Economic History* 14 (1985), 75–106. Reprinted in Lovejoy and Falola, *Pawnship, Slavery, and Colonialism*.

Otsuka, Keijiro; Chuma, Hiroyuki, and Hayami, Yujiro, 'Land and labor contracts in agrarian economies: theories and facts', *Journal of Economic Literature* 30 (1992), 1965–2018.

Paterson, A. W., 'The co-operative societies movement applied to the problems of the Gold Coast cacao industry', *Tropical Agriculture* 9:9 (1934), 240–43.

Patterson, K. David, 'The influenza epidemic of 1918–19 in the Gold Coast', *Journal of African History* 24 (1983), 485–502.

Patterson, Orlando, *Slavery and Social Death: a comparative study* (Cambridge MA., 1982).

Pearce, David W., 'Economics of the environment', in David Greenaway, Michael Bleaney and Ian Stewart (eds), *Companion to Contemporary Economic Thought* (London, 1991), 316–42.

Perbi, Akosua, 'The abolition of domestic slavery by Britain: Asante's dilemma', *Legon Journal of the Humanities* 6 (1992), 1–23.

Perregaux, Edmond, 'Chez les Achanti', *Bulletin de la société neuchateloise de géographie*, 17 (1906), 7–314.

Perrot, Claude-Hélène, *Les Anyi-Ndenye et le pouvoir aux 18e et 19e siècles* (Paris, 1982).

———, and van Dantzig, Albert (eds), *Marie-Joseph Bonnat et les Ashanti: Journal (1869–1874)* (Paris, 1994).

Peters, Pauline E., 'Is "rational choice" the best choice for Robert Bates? An anthropologist's reading of Bates' work', *World Development* 21:6 (1993), 1063–76.

Phillips, Anne, *The Enigma of Colonialism: British policy in West Africa* (London, 1989).

Phillips, J. F. V., *Agriculture and Ecology in Africa* (London, 1959).

Platteau, Jean-Philippe, 'Behind the market stage where real societies exist', *Journal of Development Studies* 30:3 (1994), 533–77 and 30:4 (1994), 753–817.

———, 'The evolutionary theory of land rights as applied to Sub-Saharan Africa: a critical assessment', *Development and Change* 27 (1996), 29–86.

Poku, K., 'Traditional roles and people of slave origin in modern Ashanti—a few impressions', *Ghana Journal of Sociology* 5 (1969), 34–38.

Polanyi, Karl, *Dahomey and the Slave Trade: an Analysis of an Archaic Economy* (Seattle, 1966).

Pomeranz, Kenneth, *The Great Divergence: China, Europe, and the Making of the Modern World Economy* (Princeton, 2000).

Prempeh I, Otumfuo Nana Agyeman, '*The History of Ashanti Kings and the Whole Country Itself' And Other Writings*, ed. A. Adu Boahen, Emmanuel Akyeampong, Nancy Lawler, T. C. McCaskie and Ivor Wilks (Oxford, 2003).

Priestley, Margaret, *West African Trade and Coast Society: a Family Study* (London, 1969).

Quibria, M. G., and Rashid, Salim, 'The puzzle of sharecropping: a survey of theories', *World Development* 12:2 (1984), 103–14.

Ramseyer, Friedrich August, and Kühne, Johannes, *Four Years in Ashantee* (London, 1875).

Ranger, Terence, 'The invention of tradition in colonial Africa', in Eric Hobsbawm and Terence Ranger (eds), *The Invention of Tradition* (Cambridge, 1983), 211–62.

Rathbone, Richard, 'Businessmen and politics: party struggle in Ghana, 1949–1957', *Journal of Development Studies*, 9:3 (1973), 390–401.

———, ' "The youngmen and the porcupine" ', *Journal of African History* 32 (1991), 333–6.

———, *Ghana* (British Documents on the End of Empire. Series B, Vol. I), 2 parts (London, 1995).

Rattray, R. S., *Ashanti Proverbs* (Oxford, 1916).

———, *Ashanti* (Oxford, 1923).

———, *Religion and Art in Ashanti* (Oxford, 1927).

———, *Ashanti Law and Constitution* (Oxford, 1929).

Ray, Debraj, *Development Economics* (Princeton, 1998).

Rimmer, Douglas, *Staying Poor: Ghana's Political Economy 1950–1990* (Oxford, 1992).

Roberts, Penelope A., 'The state and the regulation of marriage: Sefwi Wiawso (Ghana), 1900–40', in Haleh Afshar (ed.), *Women, State and Ideology: Studies from Africa and Asia* (Basingstoke, 1987), 48–69.

Roberts, Richard, and Miers, Suzanne, 'The end of slavery in Africa', in S. Miers and R. Roberts (eds), *The End of Slavery in Africa* (Madison, 1988), 3–68.

Robertson, A. F., '*Abusa*: the structural history of an economic contract', *Journal of Development Studies* 18 (1982), 447–78.

———, *The Dynamics of Productive Relationships: African Share Contracts in Comparative Perspective* (Cambridge, 1987).

Rogowski, Ronald, 'Structure, growth and power: three rationalist accounts', in Robert H. Bates (ed.), *Toward a Political Economy of Development* (Berkeley, 1988), 300–30.

Romer, Paul M., 'The origins of endogenous growth', *Journal of Economic Perspectives* 8:1 (1994), 3–22.

Roper, J. I., *Labour Problems in West Africa* (Harmondsworth, 1958).

Rouch, Jean, 'Migrations au Ghana', *Journal de la Société des Africanistes* 26 (1956), 33–196.

Ruf, François, *Booms et crises du cacao: les vertiges de l'or brun* (Montpellier, 1995).

———, 'From forest rent to tree-capital: basic "laws" of cocoa supply', in Ruf and P. S. Siswoputranto (eds), *Cocoa Cycles: the Economics of Cocoa Supply* (Cambridge, 1995).

Ruttan, Vernon W., and Hayami, Yujiro, 'Toward a theory of induced institutional innovation', *Journal of Development Studies* 20:4 (1984), 201–23.

Sampson, H. C., and Crowther, E. M., 'Report on cocoa production and soil fertility problems', in *The West Africa Commission 1938–1939: Technical Reports* (London: Leverhulme Trust, 1943), 8–58.

Schildkrout, Enid, *People of the Zongo: the Transformation of Ethnic Identities in Ghana* (Cambridge, 1978).

Scott, David, 'An epidemiological note on guinea-worm infection in north-west Ashanti, Ghana', *Annals of Tropical Medicine and Parasitology* 54 (1960), 32–43.

Sender, John and Smith, Sheila, *The Development of Capitalism in Africa* (London, 1986).

Shinnie, Peter, 'Early Asante: is Wilks right?', in J. Hunwick and N. Lawler (eds), *The Cloth of Many Colored Silks: Papers on History Ghanaian and Islamic in Honor of Ivor Wilks* (Evanston, 1996), 195–303.

Skertchly, J. A., 'A visit to the gold-fields of Wassaw, West Africa', *Journal of the Royal Geographical Society* 44 (1878), 274–82.

Southall, Roger J., 'Polarisation and dependence in the Gold Coast cocoa trade, 1897–1938', *Transactions of the Historical Society of Ghana* 16: 1 (1975), 93–115.

Spear, Thomas. 'Neo-traditionalism and the limits of invention in British colonial Africa', *Journal of African History* 44 (2003), 3–27.

Steel, R. W., 'The population of Ashanti: a geographical analysis', *Geographical Journal* 112:1–3 (1949), 64–77.

Stichter, Sharon, *Migrant Laborers* (African Society Today series: Cambridge, 1985).

Stiglitz, Joseph E., 'The new development economics', *World Development* 14:2 (1986), 257–65.

———, and Weiss, Andrew, 'Credit rationing in markets with imperfect information', *American Economic Review* 71 (1981), 393–410.

Stockwell, Sarah, *The Business of Decolonization: British Business Strategies in the Gold Coast* (Oxford, 2000).

Sugihara, Kaoru, 'The East Asian Path of Economic Development: a Long-Term Perspective', *Discussion Papers in Economics and Business*, Graduate School of Economics, Osaka University (Osaka, 2000).

Sutton, Inez, 'Labour in commercial agriculture in Ghana in the late nineteenth and early twentieth centuries', *Journal of African History* 24 (1983), 461–83.

Swindell, Ken, *Farm Labour* (African Society Today series: Cambridge, 1985).

Szereszewski, R., *Structural Changes in the Economy of Ghana, 1891–1911* (London, 1965).

Takane, Tsutomu, *The Cocoa Farmers of Southern Ghana: Incentives, Institutions, and Change in Rural West Africa* (Chiba, Japan, 2002).

Talbot, M. R., and Delibrias, G., 'Holocene variations in the level of Lake Bosumtwi, Ghana', *Nature* 268 (1977), 722–24.

Tashjian, Victoria B., 'The diaries of A.C. Duncan-Johnstone: a preliminary analysis of British involvement in the "native courts" of colonial Asante', *Ghana Studies* 1 (1998), 135–50.

Temperley, Howard, 'The ideology of antislavery', in David Eltis and James Walvin (eds), *The Abolition of the Atlantic Slave Trade* (Madison, 1981), 21–35.

Terray, Emmanuel, 'Long-distance exchange and the formation of the state: the case of the Abron kingdom of Gyaman', *Economy and Society* 3 (1974), 315–45.

———, 'La captivité dans le royaume Abron du Gyaman', in Claude Meillassoux (ed.), *L'Esclavage en Afrique précoloniale* (Paris, 1975), 389–453.

———, 'Contribution à une étude de l'armée asante', *Cahiers d'études africaines* 16: 61–62 (1976), 297–356.

Terray, Emmanuel, 'Réflections sur la formation du prix des esclaves à l'intérieur de l'Afrique de l'Ouest précoloniale', *Journal des Africanistes* 52, 1–2 (1982), 119–44.

———, 'Gold production, slave labor, and state intervention in precolonial Akan societies: a reply to Raymond Dumett', *Research in Economic Anthropology* 5 (1983), 95–129.

———, *Une histoire du royaume abron du Gyaman: des origines à la conquête coloniale* (Paris, 1995).

Thaler, Richard H., 'Doing economics without *homo economicus*', in Steven G. Medema and Warren J. Samuels (eds), *Foundations of Research in Economics: How do Economists do Economics* (Cheltenham, England, 1996), 227–37.

Thomas, Roger G., 'Forced labour in British West Africa: the case of the Northern Territories of the Gold Coast 1906–27', *Journal of African History* 14 (1973), 79–103.

Thompson, E. P., *The Poverty of Theory and Other Essays* (London, 1978).

Thornton, John, *Africa and Africans in the Making of the Atlantic World, 1400–1680* (Cambridge, 1992).

Tiffen, Mary; Mortimore, Michael; and Gichuki, Francis, *More People, Less Erosion: Environmental Recovery in Kenya* (Chichester, 1994).

Tordoff, William, *Ashanti Under the Prempehs, 1888–1935* (London, 1965).

Tosh, John, 'The cash-crop revolution in tropical Africa: an agricultural reappraisal', *African Affairs* 79:314 (1980), 79–94.

Toxopeus, H., 'Planting material', in G. A. R. Wood and R. A. Lass, *Cocoa* (4th ed., Harlow, 1985), 80–92.

Uche, Chibuike Ugochukwu, 'Foreign banks, Africans, and credit in colonial Nigeria, c.1890–1912', *Economic History Review* 52:4 (1999), 669–91.

Vallenga, Dorothy Dee, 'Matriliny, patriliny, and class formation among women cocoa farmers in two rural areas of Ghana', in C. Robertson and I. Berger (eds), *Women and Class in Africa* (New York, 1986), 62–77.

Van Hear, Nick, 'Child labour and the development of capitalist agriculture in Ghana', *Development and Change* 13 (1982), 499–512.

Von Laue, Theodore H., 'Anthropology and power: R. S. Rattray among the Ashanti', *African Affairs* 75:298 (1976), 33–54.

Walker, Ezekiel Ayodele, 'The changing patterns of labor relations in the cocoa farming belt of southwestern Nigeria, 1950s to 1990s', *African Economic History* 24 (2000), 123–40.

Walker, H. O., 'Weather and climate', in Brian Wills (ed.), *Agriculture and Land Use in Ghana* (London, 1962), 7–50.

Warren, Bill, *Imperialism: Pioneer of Capitalism*, ed. John Sender (London, 1980).

Weiskel, Timothy, 'Toward an archaeology of colonialism: elements in the ecological transformation of the Ivory Coast', in D. Worster (ed.), *The Ends of the Earth* (Cambridge, 1988), 141–71.

Wessel, M., 'Shade and nutrition', in G. A. R. Wood and R. A. Lass, *Cocoa* (4th ed., Harlow, 1985), 166–94.

Whitehead, Anne, 'Wives and mothers: female farmers in Africa', in A. Adepoju and C. Oppong (eds), *Gender, Work and Population in Sub-Saharan Africa* (London, 1994), 35–53.

Wilks, Ivor, 'Aspects of bureaucratization in Ashanti in the nineteenth century', *Journal of African History* 7 (1966), 215–32.

Wilks, Ivor, 'Asante policy towards the Hausa trade in the nineteenth century', in C. Meillassoux (ed.), *The Development of Indigenous Trade and Markets in West Africa* (London, 1971), 124–41.

———, *Asante in the Nineteenth Century: the Structure and Evolution of a Political Order* (London, 1975: 2nd edn, with new preamble, Cambridge, 1989).

———, 'Dissidence in Asante Politics: two tracts from the late nineteenth century', in I. Abu-Lughod (ed.), *African Themes* (Evanston, 1975), 47–63 (reprinted with revisions in Wilks, *Forests of Gold*).

———, 'Land, labour, capital and the forest kingdom of Asante: a model of early change', in J. Friedman and M. Rowlands (eds), *The Evolution of Social Systems* (London, 1978), 487–534 (reprinted with revisions in Wilks, *Forests of Gold*).

———, 'The population of Asante, 1817–1921: a rejoinder', *Asantesem* 8 (1978), 28–35.

———, 'The Golden Stool and the elephant tail: an essay on wealth in Asante', *Research in Economic Anthropology* 2 (1979), 1–36 (reprinted with 'minor revisions' in Wilks, *Forests of Gold*).

———, 'Asante: human sacrifice or capital punishment? A rejoinder', *International Journal of African Historical Studies* 21 (1988), 443–52.

———, 'On mentally mapping Greater Asante: a study of time and motion', *Journal of African History* 33 (1992), 175–90 (reprinted in Wilks, *Forests of Gold*, 189–214).

———, *Forests of Gold: Essays on the Akan and the Kingdom of Asante* (Athens OH, 1993).

———, 'Space, time, and "human sacrifice" ', in Wilks, *Forests of Gold*, 215–40.

———, 'What manner of persons were these? Officials of the Kumase administration', in Wilks, *Forests of Gold*, 293–328.

———, 'Asante at the end of the nineteenth century: setting the record straight', *Ghana Studies* 3 (2000), 13–59.

Williams, Clifford, 'Asante: human sacrifice or capital punishment?', *International Journal of African Historical Studies* 21 (1988), 433–41.

Wills, J. Brian (ed.), *Agriculture and Land Use in Ghana* (London, 1962).

Wilson, J. Leighton, *Western Africa: Its History, Condition, And Prospects* (New York, 1856).

Wolpe, Harold, 'Capitalism and cheap labour-power in South Africa: from segregation to apartheid', *Economy and Society* 1 (1972).

Wood, G. A. R., 'Establishment', in G. A. R. Wood and R. A. Lass, *Cocoa* (4th ed, Harlow, 1985), 119–65.

Woodman, Gordon R., 'Developments in pledges of land in Ghanaian customary law', *Journal of African Law* 11 (1967), 8–26.

———, 'Ghana reforms the law of intestate succession', *Journal of African Law* 29:2 (1985), 118–28.

Yarak, Larry W., *Asante and the Dutch 1744–1873* (Oxford, 1990).

———, 'New sources for the study of Akan slavery and slave trade: Dutch military recruitment in Asante and the Gold Coast, 1831–72', in Robin Law (ed.),

Source Material for Studying the Slave Trade and the African Diaspora (Centre of Commonwealth Studies, University of Stirling: Stirling, 1997), 35–60.

Yarak, Larry W., 'Slavery and the state in Asante history', in John Hunwick and Nancy Lawler (eds), *The Cloth of Many Colored Silks: Papers on History and Society Ghanaian and Islamic in Honor of Ivor Wilks* (Evanston, 1996), 223–40.

Zeleza, Paul Tiyambe, *A Modern Economic History of Africa*, I, *The Nineteenth Century* (Dakar, 1993).

INDEX

574

courts: under Asante kingdom, 36;
British courts, 37; chiefs' courts
during colonial period, 37, 376
Cowen, M. P., 27, 125, 381
cowrie shells, as currency in savanna
markets, 129–32
credit and debt: 'timelessness' of debt,
144; 'credit multiplier', 150; credit
rationing and its avoidance, 383–86,
399; 'forced' credit from labourers to
farmers, 360–61, 365, 417; rotating
credit societies, 137–38, 537n81;
varieties of loans in nineteenth
century, 136–38, 140. *See also*
advances; interest; pawns; pledging
Cruickshank, Brodie, 40, 46, 118
'cultural turn' in historiography, 4
currencies, 128–32; gold dust as
pre-colonial Asante currency,
40–42; colonial introduction of
paper currency, 298
Curtin, Philip, 73

Daaku, K. Y., 102
Dadiase, xxiii, 58, 220, 221, 228, 286,
296
Dagaras, 421
Dagarti, Musa, 123, 125, 144, 145,
197, 493n60
Dagomba, xxi, 116
Dahomey, kingdom of, 138
Danby, W. R., 284, 295
Danso, Kwame, 379
Davidson-Houston, Major W. B., 220,
254, 326
death duties, 37
de Graft-Johnson, J. C., 223, 234
Dei, Kwame, 221, 239, 241, 286,
305–6, 312
Denkyira, 243

Denmark, 459n39
Denta, Abena, 375
Denyase, xxiii, 58, 112, 223
Denyasehene Kwesi Aduonin II, 352
dependency theory, 24–25, 27, 248,
424–25, 430, 452–53
Depression, 1930s, 50, 245, 263, 271,
297, 399, 428
Der Sclavenfreund, 216
Destombes, Jérôme, 545n111
Deutsch, Jan-Georg, 535n25
Devin, C. L., 295
Diaba, Kwame, 124
Dickinson, J. R., 276, 318, 412, 414,
416, 426
Djumo, 224
Domar, Evsey, 155–56, 158, 166, 247
Domiabra, xxiii, 229
Domi-Koniago, 426
Dominase (Ahafo), 312–13, 377
Dominase (Amansie), 191, 225–26
Dompoase, xxiii, 90, 268
Donko, Kwadwo, 118, 148, 168–69
Dormaa, 123, 124, 261, 263, 274, 333,
384
Dormaa-Ahenkro, xxi
Dro, Kofi (Bantamahene), 224
Dro, Kwame, 373
Dua, Kwaku (Mamponhene), 233
Dumett, Raymond, 91, 112, 222
Dunkwoh, Kojo, 81, 84
Dupis, Joseph, 61
Dutch, 115–16, 122, 125
Dwaben (Juaben), xxi, xxiii, 35, 58, 64,
227, 229, 258, 282, 327, 384
dwetiri, 135. *See also* capital

economic rent, defined, 10, 458n33
education, 42, 112, 310–12
Efiduase, xxiii, 379